YO-BCK-733

WITHDRAWN

Social Studies in the
Secondary Schools:
A BOOK OF READINGS

Social Studies in the Secondary Schools:

A BOOK OF READINGS

EDITED BY

William E. Gardner
Fred A. Johnson
UNIVERSITY OF MINNESOTA

ALLYN AND BACON, INC.   BOSTON

Contents

Introduction

By all indications social studies education is on the move. In school after school throughout the nation, teachers are examining their social studies programs, introducing new topics and courses, and demanding better equipment and more resources for their classrooms and libraries. On college and university campuses, scholars are studying the processes of learning and teaching; curriculum developers are building innovative materials and designing teaching strategies to raise the level of instruction in social studies. In the midst of this frenetic activity, some people are asking basic philosophical questions about the social studies, its role and potential in general education. Increasingly, all parties to the "revolution" in the social studies are looking for guidelines to what has been written about the field.

The literature to which they turn is especially voluminous. At least a score of methods books are currently in print, written for the most part by social studies specialists, but in a few cases by historians and social scientists. Three professional magazines are concerned exclusively with techniques, methods, and curriculum in social studies, and other national journals frequently publish articles dealing with the fields. Research Bulletin Number 2 of the National Council for the Social Studies lists 566 dissertations related to the field prior to 1964 and indicates that the field has lacked neither empirical nor expository investigations. The current revisionary activity in the field has served to increase the flow of commentary.

One cannot deny that this tremendous bulk of literature is of great value. It contains some magnificent treatments of how and what to teach (as well as some less enlightened illustrations). The research studies, when carefully analyzed, present a wealth of data on classroom activities and strategies that will work and those that will not. Even the much maligned teacher endorsement literature (i.e., "In my classroom, we teach so and so by such and such") has a distinct value for the inexperienced teacher who has not accumulated his own store of techniques.

The sheer quantity of literature about social studies presents certain obvious problems. Libraries frequently possess only one copy of each journal or book in the field. Professional library collections in school districts have been even more limited in the quantity of material available. Thus, a "materials gap" places constraints on the college teacher who seeks to introduce his students to the significant literature in the field, for distributing the library's single copy throughout members of a large class is almost impossible. Similarly, members of a social studies department engaged in curriculum revision, or who want to keep up with the field, have a difficult time with only the resources of their professional library. Another serious problem stems from the fact that the literature is so widely dispersed that students and teachers do not often have the chance to read contrasting statements on an important issue in the field.

Our experience with graduate and undergraduate classes and with in-service teachers has convinced us of the need for a collection of articles and excerpts which would sample the stimulating literature and focus upon a number of carefully delineated areas or issues in social studies education. This book, thus, has two basic purposes: (1) to provide a careful selection of significant commentary regarding problems and issues in the field; and (2) to provide description and discussion of promising techniques and practices in the field.

The book is divided into five parts, each concerned with an important area in the social studies. Part One, "The Social Studies—Its Role in General Education," deals with the issue of broad objectives. The focus is upon basic reasons for instructing the young in social studies rather than upon the lists of generalizations and skills which so often dominate discussions of objectives. Part Two is called "The Changing Social Studies Curriculum." Its theme is that the curriculum is undergoing a basic reorientation, if not a revolution. On the one hand, new techniques are being explored for reducing the massive bulk of social science knowledge to manageable proportions and organizing it for social studies instruction. On the other hand, significant voices are raising the basic issue of whether the social sciences are the best sources of knowledge for the social studies. More information about the "non-American, non-European" areas of the world has already entered the curriculum, and increasing attention will be paid to the behavioral sciences. Articles in Part Two were chosen to illustrate these controversies and changes. Part Three explores the current methods and techniques used to teach the social studies. The failure of our field to adopt an overall teaching theory has long been a matter of concern. Currently, inquiry is the most widely advocated method, but, its need and validity also have been challenged. Although the conflict surrounding "method" is discussed in this section, the major purpose is to provide many specific illustrations of successful teaching techniques. Changes in the media used by teachers is the topic of Part Four. There the major emphases are upon enabling teachers to analyze text material and acquainting them with intriguing and valuable new learning resources. Part Five deals with measurement, curriculum evaluation, and research. Construction of tests to measure student progress toward the goals of instruction is a difficult task but much can be learned from the specific examples provided in this section. Research articles dealing with curriculum evaluation, classroom learning, simulation games, and political socialization are also presented.

Choosing materials to fit these categories required a careful process of selection. Our basic criterion for including an article or book selection was how well it illustrates some aspect of one of the five areas. We paid little attention to whether an author was a well-known figure or which journal published his work. Nor were we overly concerned with any conflict between theory and practice; thus, both background and how-to-do-it articles are included.

Obviously, the content of the book is related to our teaching experience with undergraduate and graduate students in Oregon, Colorado, and Minnesota. Their questions and comments have shaped our thinking about what social studies teachers should know and the controversies they have to engage in. This book of readings is directed toward their needs; if it misses the mark, it is because we have misinterpreted what they have said.

William E. Gardner
Fred A. Johnson

Social Studies in the Secondary Schools:

A BOOK OF READINGS

The Current Scene

William E. Gardner

On October 4, 1957, the Russians sent Sputnik into space, beginning not only the space age, but also creating an important stimulus for the current educational revolution. True, this revolution had its beginnings in earlier events, but Sputnik was the dramatic occasion which pushed into our national consciousness the important question of "quality" in American education. Certainly, the fact that the Russians were the first to orbit a satellite and put man in space was disconcerting and damaging to our national pride. Americans engaged in an orgy of self-examination, and, with some lack of rationality, managed to pin the blame for Russian supremacy on the third-grade teacher who did not know the new mathematics and could not discern a Bunsen burner from a light bulb. So immense have been the effects of Sputnik on American education that one commentator has suggested facetiously that future school children will plant rockets on October 4 as they once planted trees on Arbor Day.

The major early thrust of the educational revolution was in the math and science areas. These school subjects, it seemed, were far more important than the social sciences and humanities (or perhaps, as some have suggested, they were in far worse shape). In any case, social studies teachers watched with awe as their colleagues in mathematics and science went off to NDEA summer institutes or became involved in one of the new "alphabet" curricula (PSSC, BSCS, and so on). They were forced to wend their way to their globeless, equipmentless classrooms past piles of new science equipment purchased on a shared basis with the federal government.

But the voices of reform soon began in social studies education also. One observer, Terry Ferrer, education writer for the *New York Herald Tribune,* made this statement: "Some educators say that social studies is not an academic area but a disaster area."[1] This picture of the social studies as the educational equivalent of a developing nation was galling enough to social studies teachers, but Martin Mayer, a noted free-lance writer, then published a study of social studies education entitled, *Where, When and Why.*[2] This book, although laudatory of some people and some practices, essentially pictured social studies education as the ultimate in futility. To Mayer, the educational world of the social studies was a vast desert which the student entered as a fairly young person and passed through over a period of many years, finding there no intellectual food or water. The historian, Charles Keller, long assoc- iated with the John Hay Fellowship and the Advanced Placement programs in history, added his voice, calling for a revolution in the social studies.[3] Again, the picture of the field was bad. The social studies should, according to Keller, cease to exist, because the area did not produce the kind of learning and the kinds of students needed in twentieth-century America.

The point of view that the field needed rather substantial revision was by no means an exclusive outsiders' perception limited to journalists and histor- ians. From among the large, amorphous group of social studies educators and specialists came demands and plans for changes.[4] The voices from inside the field may have been less raucous and dramatic, but the point was fundamentally the same.

Whatever the source, many classroom teachers were appalled by the criticisms. To them, the picture in social studies was by no means completely dismal. Many schools were teaching an up-to-date and viable program staffed by teachers who were well-trained, interested, and exceptionally well- informed. The case against the social studies was undoubtedly overstated, but most observers would probably agree that it was correct in substance, if not in every detail. Too often, the social studies were as they had been described—weary, dreary hours considered by students to be a complete waste of time.

As the chorus of criticism grew in volume, it became apparent that the comments were centered on one or more of six widespread and serious defici- encies in social studies education:

1. *The social studies are not closely associated with the frontiers of social science scholarship.* The claim was often and early made that social science scholars had abdicated any responsibility for social studies education. As early as 1941, the anthropologist, Robert Redfield, had noted this fact:

A fable, which Aesop somehow neglected to record, tells of a hen who was making an effort to instruct her chicks about their future sources of food supply while she and they were balanced precariously on a chicken coop which was being carried down a river by a flood. It was a long time since the hen had studied the forests on the bank, and the account she was giving her chicks of forests was none too good. So she called to a wise owl on the bank for help. "You know the woods, owl, for you stay in the forest and study it," said the hen. "Will you not tell me what to teach my chicks about life in the forest?" But the owl had overheard what the hen had been telling the chicks about the forest as she came along, and he thought it was scientifically inaccurate and superficial. Besides, he was just then very busy completing a monograph on the incidence of beetle larvae in acorns. So he pretended he had not heard the hen. The hen, turned back upon herself, proceeded as well as she could to prepare and put into effect an instruction unit on the food resources of oak forests, meanwhile struggling to keep the chicks from falling off the chicken coop. The chicks took the instruction very well, and later the chicken coop stopped at a point far downstream, and the chicks all went ashore—to begin their adult lives in a treeless meadow.[5]

The analogy of hens and owls to teachers and scholars may not be completely acceptable to either group, and Redfield certainly overstated the case, since many scholars had been intimately involved with social studies education throughout the twentieth century.[6] But the fundamental fact that social studies education had not been an important province of activity for most social science scholars cannot be ignored, and, as critics pointed out vociferously, the field had drifted from what was considered "good" at the forefront of knowledge. In history, for example, the older interpretations persisted. In the other areas the interpretations and the data used in social studies classes were from a decade or even two or three decades before. The clarion cry went up then for scholars to become involved in the content of social studies education to an unprecedented degree. If social studies was to fulfill its purpose, it must be brought up to date, and the cultural lag which separated the ivory tower and the classroom must be shortened.

2. *Too much material is taught in social studies classrooms which is peripheral or unrelated to the content of history and the social sciences.* The criticisms here fell into three general categories. First, many critics asserted that social studies had become a "dumping ground" for things which may be very important to students and which schools should teach but which were not appropriately a part of the field. Topics such as driver education in the senior high school or telephone usage in a fourth grade class may be considered by some as appropriate topics for a general educational program but not, it was emphasized, in the social studies. Second, the great emphasis in social studies upon contemporary knowledge—the current events syndrome was too pronounced. The claim was made that this type of teaching could produce only superficial analysis and was hardly appropriate for intelligent, mature Americans. Third, the term social studies had negative connotations to other observers who referred to it as a "hash" or the "social slops." Most of these observers claimed that the use of the term indicated that subject matter lines had disappeared completely and that this unfortunate circumstance was one of the great tragedies of American education. Such observers

called for a return to the disciplines and for an expiation of the term social studies from the jargon of American education.

3. *The social studies have emphasized topics and areas which are no longer appropriate.* Some critics noted that the non-Western world (the Soviet Union, Africa, and Asia) was almost completely ignored in the typical social studies course. In world history, for example, one observer noted that the non-West came into the curriculum only on the "decks of a gunboat," meaning, of course, that "world" history had an almost completely ethnocentric emphasis.

Attention was also called to the lack of representation of the new behavioral sciences. Little material in the social studies curriculum, it was claimed, had its source in these dynamic sciences of man; and the material included from the behavioral sciences was inappropriate in the sense that it frequently was more concerned with social *pathology* than social *science.* This assertion emphasized that high school students studying, for example, the problems of a society would be led to conclude that the society was filled with "cancers," or at least "ulcers." (Minority group problems, prostitution, dope-addiction, and the like). They would fail to see that a normal functioning society has many forces which are positive and which serve to hold the society together; the students, it was claimed, would assume that our society was a rapidly disintegrating entity.

4. *Learning in the social studies was pitched at an unusually and unnecessarily low level.* Despite the constant complaints from learning psychologists that low level instruction was neither effective nor long lasting, the social studies seemed oriented toward insignificant facts rather than generalizations. Some observers apparently believed that Teddy Nadler (whose photographic memory enchanted the nation some years before on the "$64,000 Question") had been adopted as the patron saint of the social studies, and that teachers had, by and large, accepted the point of view of the schoolmaster in Dickens' *Hard Times,* who said:

Now, what I want is, Facts. Teach those boys and girls nothing but Facts. Facts alone are wanted in life. Plant nothing else, and root out everything else. You can only form the minds of reasoning animals upon Facts; nothing else will ever be of any service to them. This is the principle on which I bring up my own children, and this is the principle on which I bring up these children. Stick to the Facts, sir! The speaker and the schoolmaster swept with their eyes the inclined plane of little vessels then and there arranged in order, ready to have imperial gallons of facts poured into them until they were full to the brim.

5. *The social studies curriculum has no progression, no logical development, no sequence.* According to Gross and Allen, the social studies program was a "gigantic kettle of bouillabaisse."[7] Students enter a course, study some topics, finish the course. The following year they enter another course, repeat many of the same topics in the same ways, and continue this cycle several times during their educational careers. The question raised was: Can not a social studies program be structured so that a student's competencies can build in some wholesome, identifiable, and consistent manner from early elementary school through high school graduation?

6. *Social studies programs have overemphasized the role of the field in the production of good citizens.* Some critics have asserted that the social studies has no more responsibility to produce good citizens than does any other school area. Furthermore, the social studies should never be used to impose a pattern of behavior upon students, since this amounts to nothing more nor less than the conscious, explicit use of subject matter in a process of propagandizing.

It is perfectly apparent even to the casual observer that all these criticisms were not equally valid. The critics, after all, were as limited by their direct experience as any other mortal, and their experience in no case included a research study worthy of the name. Consequently, no supernatural powers of extraordinary vision can be attributed to the group of critics. Nor do their criticisms form a completely consistent and comprehensive pattern, since several are potentially in conflict. For example, the focus upon crucial and relevant topics, when defined, may be in conflict with the desire to return to the disciplines expressed by other critics. Furthermore, most of the criticisms were stated so broadly and so sweepingly that they could be applied to teaching and teachers at any time and any place.

Despite the limitations and the discordant notes in the chorus of criticism, the body of commentary struck a raw nerve in social studies education. There was obvious, if not universal, truth in what the critics said. There was a huge gap between the potential of the field and practice in it.

The net effect of the criticisms was to set in motion a number of forces which promise to produce a "new" social studies and which quite possibly may constitute a revolution in the field. Basically, three things have happened. First, there has been a growth in general interest and concern over the problem of social studies among professionals generally, but among the lay public as well. This interest is characterized by the involvement of many people in discussions and in the broader movements who have not been previously concerned. Having survived the emotional jag of coming to grips with the new math, the public, along with scholars, has become far more interested in social studies.

Another aspect is the injection of federal aid to social studies teachers through the many faced efforts involving primarily the extension of National Defense Education Act Institute concept to include the field of the social studies, the funding of fellowships for teachers, and other allied activities. Whatever its critics may say about the dangers of centralized control and the general inefficiencies of the operation, the federal government through the United States Office of Education already plays a large role in the social studies revolution, and the role shows no signs of diminishing in the near future.

A third set of events, involving both the federal government and private foundations, was the establishment of what were called "national" curriculum development centers or projects. The centers illustrated a fundamental change in the way curriculum is built and developed. Previously teachers at the local level were under the injunction to build a curriculum appropriate to their school. The theory was that ideas should emerge creatively from individuals and small groups in a local district. A national committee or a state department of education might provide an outline and even a course of study, but typically curriculum patterning was a function of relatively small groups of busy people. This process was perhaps very effective in many instances, but generally it responded lethargically to the much advertised explosion of knowledge. Curriculum development being carried on in the national centers shifted the responsibility to a group of social studies specialists, scholars in the various disciplines, and learning psychologists who form a cooperative team charged with the responsibility of building curriculum and/or materials to illustrate the particular point of view, methodology, or area of concern.

The specific approaches to revision taken by the curriculum development centers varied widely in terms of the content emphasized and the mode of organization, but the efforts seem more generally to have great areas of commonality. At their core the projects were addressed to the major areas of deficiencies in the social studies. While they did not speak in a single voice, the projects in general revealed a concern with the following considerations in social studies education.

1. *The role of the behavioral sciences.* Long neglected by social studies teachers, anthropology, sociology, and economics are moving relentlessly into the limelight. The Anthropology Curriculum Study Project has identified courses and topics in which anthropology could make a contribution to the

general social education of students and to prepare materials toward that end. The Project Social Studies Curriculum Development Center at Georgia is concerned with the preparation of anthropological materials for the elementary school. A more recent entry into the field is the professional group of sociologists, which, under NSF funding, has begun a project called Sociological Resources for the Social Studies. Several projects are investigating the possibilities of teaching concepts from behavioral science through the content of history. Whatever else is true about the new social studies, it seems quite clear that future programs will contain far more emphasis upon the behavioral sciences in some form or another.

2. *A concern over the structure of the disciplines.* The concept of structure attracted great attention when enunciated by Jerome Bruner in his provocative little book, *The Process of Education.* Stated in its most simple form, *structure* is said to be the basic sets of relationships which exist in every discipline and which comprise the essence of that discipline.[8] The concept of structure assumes that each discipline has an internal organization which in some respects defines it as a discipline. Structure may be stated in terms of key concepts in a given field (for example, *power* in political science, *culture* in anthropology and sociology) or in terms of generalizations which are drawn from the knowledge of a single social science or the social sciences collectively.

With several notable exceptions, the projects have attempted to define the structure of a discipline or the disciplines. These attempts do far more than provide interesting intellectual gymnastics for those working on the projects; rather the search for structure has constituted an important first step in the curriculum process since, if found, structure provides a convenient mechanism to select relevant data from the disciplines and should give a substantial answer to the question of what knowledge is of most worth.

Unfortunately, attempts at finding structure have not always been rewarding, and, as yet, agreement does not exist as to what the structure of any social science discipline is. Nonetheless, the attempt continues and will undoubtedly be of great import to social studies education.

3. *A concern for reform in methodology.* Another "Brunerism" has provided the stimulation for a wide group of activities by project people designed to raise the level of learning in the social studies. Bruner claims that the most effective and highest level learning occurs when a student discovers a relationship by himself rather than being given a pat answer to a question.[9] The names given to the new approaches to teaching vary (discovery, induction, inquiry, and so on), but by whatever name, they have one thing in common—

all entail a shift from a teaching strategy of *tell-recite* to one of *excite-discover*.

Such ideas, of course, are not new, as anyone who has read the description of Socrates teaching the Pythagorean theorem to an ignorant slave boy can testify. Possibly the same general class of ideas which characterizes the current emphasis on "discovery" has been present at all days and in all ages when people have considered the question of how children can best learn. What seems to be particularly present in the new social studies is the seemingly larger number of people interested and involved in propagating this method of teaching, and, more important, in providing more concrete hardware for use by the classroom teacher and his students.

4. *A concern over new techniques of instruction.* Textbooks and various fiction and non-fiction materials have long been identified as the basic tools of instruction in social studies. The materials have been supplemented by typical audio-visual aids (films, filmstrips, and so on). Such devices are currently available in greater quantity and better quality than ever before.

While the materials developed by most curriculum projects suggest the use of these typical materials, greater emphasis is devoted to newer materials and techniques. Programmed instruction is achieving some prominence, and programs are now available to teach various skills and principles in geography and government classes. Great attention is also being devoted to the development of case studies, which provide the depth treatment so necessary to student analysis. Several of the development centers (as well as scores of school districts) are experimenting with the concepts of gaming and simulation in the hope of achieving more student involvement and greater learning. While few illustrations of the use of computers in teaching social studies are currently available, the near future will undoubtedly see wider experimentation in this area. Students and teachers may find significant applications for computer technology in doing original research, for instance, or in replicating some of the classic research in the social sciences.

It is possible to overemphasize the potential of the curriculum development projects, and it may be that their products will have the primary function of gathering dust on library shelves. Present indications, however, are that this will not be the result. The four general areas of thrust noted above have become the norms for change in social studies, and the curriculum patterns and materials developed by the projects have become models for work done at the local and state level. Throughout their short history, the projects provided a stimulus to school districts bent on changing their programs and have convinced some reluctant schools that the idea of change should be investigated.

The current developments in social studies, then, appear to contain immense possibilities for improving learning. They do not, however, contain a guarantee that this will happen, for great activity is obviously not the same as progress. To become truly effective, the reforms noted earlier will have to be internalized by and implemented through social studies teachers. Indeed, the ultimate judges and evaluators of what is new in social studies will be the teachers.

The situation in social studies seems to demand that prospective and in-service teachers be well-informed as to what the issues are in the field today. They need to examine the pressures and cross-pressures in the field. They must engage in a constant dialogue with their colleagues, with social scientists, and with social studies specialists over the questions *why* to teach, *what* to teach, and *how* to teach.

References

[1] Terry Ferrer, "Classroom Revolution" (Reprint, *New York Herald Tribune*, n.d.)

[2] Martin Mayer, *Where, When, and Why—Social Studies in American Schools* (New York: Harper and Row, 1962).

[3] Charles R. Keller, "Needed: Revolution in the Social Studies," *The Saturday Review*, September 16, 1961.

[4] See, for example, Maurice P. Hunt and Lawrence E. Metcalf, *Teaching High School Social Studies* (New York: Harper and Brothers, 1955); George L. Fersh, ed., *The Problems Approach and the Social Studies*, Curriculum Series Number Nine of the National Council for the Social Studies (Washington: The Council, 1955). Other publications of NCSS during the immediate pre- and post-Sputnik era anticipated most of the current activities in the field.

[5] Robert Redfield, "Research in the Social Sciences: Its Significance for General Education," *Social Education*, December, 1941, p. 568.

[6] Most notable was the group of scholars assembled by Professor A. C. Krey for the Commission on the Social Studies. The Report of the Commission ran to 16 volumes and included books by Charles A. Beard, George S. Counts, Henry Johnson, and Merle Curti.

[7] Richard E. Gross and Dwight W. Allen, "Stop Playing Blindman's Buff," *Scholastic Teacher*, October 11, 1963.

[8] Jerome S. Bruner, *The Process of Education* (Cambridge: The Harvard University Press, 1961), pp. 6-8, Ch. 2.

[9] Bruner, *op. cit.*, pp. 20-22.

PART ONE

The Social Studies —
Its Role in General Education

William E. Gardner

All societies must establish and maintain a process of preparing children for adult living. This process provides young people with models of appropriate behavior, information, attitudes about the conduct of business and personal affairs, and, most significant in the long run, ideas and beliefs about what is basically "good" and "true." This process, a "humanizing," "socializing" venture, proceeds in many different ways, but in all cases its basic function is to transform a human baby into a participating adult member of a specific cultural group.

In relatively simple societies, the process may be almost totally an unconscious one. Children share completely in community affairs and make a significant contribution to winning the family livelihood. They learn the folkways and the rituals of their society easily and naturally as they observe adults at work and play. In complex industrial societies, the process assumes different proportions. There, certain activities in the socialization processes are carried on within an institutional framework, in schools. Systems of formal education arise basically in response to the vocational needs of a hungry industrial machine, an advanced technology, and the increasing complexity of the resulting culture.

Building a system of schools to perform part of the important socialization process has the effect of raising the process to the conscious level. When school programs are designed, choices must be made among alternatives. The entire culture needs to be examined with the eye to selecting appropriate content to be fed into the system. Decisions must be made as to how this content will be taught to the young. Future needs for workers of various kinds must be assessed and decisions made about the intellectual and manual skills they will need. Furthermore, adults need to decide what should be taught to the child about what the world is really like (or, what adults think it's like), what ideals are significant, and what a person's posture should be toward the broad social environment in which he lives. Essentially, a relationship must be established between the educational system and the controlling political and social ideals which have served to hold a particular culture together. Should the schools reinforce traditional societal values and goals? Should schools attempt to "indoctrinate" those values or allow them to develop as a matter of course? Should a society's basic values be subjected to criticism and analysis by students with the blessing and within the shelter of the school system? What should be the relationship between education and the polity?

What has emerged as the discussion topic here, of course, is the need for and the nature of educational objectives. Teachers ordinarily approach such discussions with as much eagerness as they visit a homebound student suspected of having scarlet fever. And who, in reality, can blame them? Educational policy-making in a modern society is a complex undertaking. At the highest level—the establishment of major purposes for carrying on an education program at all—it involves making choices from among a number of appealing alternatives. Simply understanding the alternatives demands a comprehensive knowledge of society, learning theory, child and adolescent development, and applied anthropology; making sound choices requires even more—the wisdom of the most intellectual and best informed people in our society.

Unfortunately, the difficult problem of objectives does not disappear when ignored; it is one which demands decisions. True, no purpose is served by constant haggling over fundamental purposes, but those concerned with the educational enterprise need to give careful attention to the selection of the policies which will guide their efforts.

Our purpose in this section is to examine some of the points of view concerning the broad overarching objectives which can give the social studies field meaning and a reason for being as a part of the general education of all American youth. Clear specification of broad goals and dominating purposes seems to us to be a high priority question. The social studies, a curious amalgam of subjects, topics, and values drawn from many different disciplines, is far more conducive to aimless wanderings by teachers and students than are most other subject areas. The math teacher, for example, may have some doubts about what from math is important for all students, but the range of potential data is not terribly wide and he knows that certain arithmetic processes are significant and should be taught. In short, some of his objectives are relatively clear. In the social studies, the legitimate topics range from anthropology through geography to political science and sociology, from the slums of Chicago to the culture of the Manus, from the valley of the Tigris and Euphrates to the first space ship on the moon. And no one is completely certain as to what students need to know. Clearly, making sense out of the bewildering array of possibilities requires some goal-setting in the broad sense.

Traditionally, the major goal of social studies teaching has been associated with what political scientists have termed the political socialization of children and adolescents, or, in the common vernacular, the development of citizenship. Whether the subject matter of a social studies course is American history or economics, sociology or government, the assumption most often underlying its teaching is that future citizens "need" it for their personal development and/or that it will help create the citizens a society needs. While statements of citizenship goals have often been indefinite and citizenship education programs have sometimes been educational monstrosities, the attempt to relate citizenship to social studies is fundamentally an effort to link education to an important societal function.

Stating the goal of the social studies as citizenship education merely scratches the surface of the issue, however, for several basic and very complex questions still demand attention. What is a "good" citizen? Do we define him by the way in which he behaves, by the degree and extent of commitment to certain American ideals, or by his ability to function as a decision-maker, an analyzer, and a critic of the society in which he lives? What, if any, are the unique responsibilities of schools in a society like ours which claims to be open and democratic? In view of the fact that other agencies and institutions of society play important parts in the socializing process, what is the role of the school? What types of programs would be most effective to achieve citizenship goals?

While the majority opinion among social studies educators has held that social studies should be taught with citizenship in mind, a minority view holds that the whole concept of attempting to educate "good" citizens is in reality a negation of education. Those holding this view maintain that citizenship education leads inevitably to indoctrination, the imposition of a certain value system, a blind obedience to things "patriotic" and a distortion of the parent social science disciplines. Those points of view raise the legitimate questions of whether schools are justified in attempting to change the values of students in any direction at all and, more specifically, whether there is a *single set* of values which students should be encouraged (or taught) to adopt.

It is easy, of course, to mock the "party-line," indoctrination type teaching which at times has gone on under the label of citizenship; but in a strict sense, to argue that social studies instruction should proceed without concern for identifying its relationship to the broader society misses the point. An adolescent's experiences in a social studies class are part of the relentless process of political socialization *inevitably,* whether citizenship is a stated goal or not. Consequently, the question is not truly *whether* but rather *how* the social studies will be related to the polity.

It is unlikely that any single, completely final solution will ever be possible. The pluralistic nature of American society is bound to be reflected in the ways people perceive school objectives, and hoping for unanimity of opinion is wishful thinking. Undoubtedly, people will tend to cluster around various opinions, all of which may change over time. The most important thing, though, is that the issue is open for informed dialogue and discussion.

We feel that discussion of these broad questions of purpose should take place among lay people and professional alike, but the brunt of the decision-making most certainly belongs with the teachers of social studies. Not only do they have the right to engage in the dialogue, but it is also a fundamental obligation of their role as teachers. Administrators, boards of education, and lay groups of various kinds are less qualified to consider the issues and, moreover, are at least once removed from the instructional process. Even if social studies teachers could be pressured into adopting a particular point of view, there is grave doubt whether they would continue to be willing once the door of the classroom is closed. Thus, from both theoretical and practical standpoints, the question of "why teach the social studies" must be answered ultimately by those most closely connected with students.

This is not to suggest that decisions in this area should be made unilaterally by groups of teachers. Such an eventuality would be unwise. Our point is merely that teachers need to engage in the dialogue on issues in a fundamental way, since implicitly or explicitly they are the ones who will ultimately make the decisions.

The articles in Part One have been carefully selected to reveal the various dimensions of the issue. Of the eight reprints, three are concerned with definitions of the concept "citizenship," and five deal with the broad question of how to educate responsible members of a society.

In Section A, "What is Citizenship?", Roselle takes what could be termed a conventional or traditional view of citizenship goals in the social studies. His list of 12 goals basically describes a set of behaviors or points of view which are thought to be necessary for the preservation of a democratic society. In the other two articles in this section, Newmann and Almond and Verba analyze the concept "citizenship" empirically and take issue with the typical definition. All three excerpts should be of value to teachers in sharpening their perceptions of what citizenship entails.

Section B is introduced by Shirley Engle's argument that knowledge of facts and principles from the social sciences is insufficient for the development of future citizens. Rather, he claims, the emphasis should be upon the process of making "quality-decisions" regarding social issues. Engle's view is representative of an influential group of social studies educators who advocate teaching students to deal with value conflicts in societal issues. In the two articles which follow, Frogge and Miller argue that explicit attention must be paid to the teaching of values or social studies will contain little significance for students. A somewhat different position is taken by Sykes who maintains that citizenship education goals essentially involve indoctrination, and, hence, make it impossible to teach the social sciences in a scholarly fashion. Finally, in an extremely thoughtful essay, Charles Frankel reviews the entire issue, centering his discussion on the central questions: "Does not a school system have an obligation to transmit certain attitudes to the young. . . ? Do the social studies insofar as they are scholarly disciplines and not exercises in piety, shake such attitudes?"

The literature of the social studies is filled with provocative pieces on the issue "Why teach the social studies," and Part One of this book does no more than open the topic for discussion. Readers are encouraged to explore the rich resources available to them in their search for a raison d'être for the social studies.

CITIZENSHIP GOALS FOR A NEW AGE

Daniel Roselle
Formerly, State University of New York
Editor, Social Education

Each generation of Americans must redefine the meaning of the term "good citizen" for itself, drawing on the past for wisdom, on the present for challenge, and on the future for promise. It may be true that a good citizen—like a good poem—"should not *mean* but *be*"; yet meaning can lead to being in the crucible of time.

In 1965 the Civic Education Project,[1] sponsored by the National Council for the Social Studies and financed by the Danforth Foundation, was asked to visit public, private, and parochial secondary schools throughout the nation to identify "the most promising practices in the making of citizens." A major part of its report (to be published by the NCSS in the latter part of this year) is structured on the Project team's response to the key question: "What is a good citizen?" Here, in modified form, is the team's position on the nature of good citizenship and citizenship goals for a new age.

WHAT IS A GOOD CITIZEN?

Goal 1. A citizen who believes in BOTH liberty of the individual and equality of rights for all, as provided by the Constitution of the United States. It may have seemed logical for John Randolph of Roanoke to exclaim in his day: "I love liberty, and I hate equality." Today this schism in the democratic ideal is archaic. In the new social mathematics of our times, the simple division between liberty and equality has been replaced by the more advanced equation: "Democracy = Liberty X Equality."[2]

Goal 2. A citizen who recognizes that we live in an "open-end" world, and is receptive to new facts, new ideas, and new processes of living. It is difficult

Reprinted with permission of the author and the National Council for the Social Studies, from *Social Education,* 30 (October, 1966): 415-419.

for men to forgo what Crane Brinton[3] has called "the delights of certitude"; yet our age demands flexibility. Jacques Barzun puts the matter this way:

> . . . no one idea, no one explanation, is omnicompetent. Contradiction, or at least nonuniformity, is a fact of experience. Even in the world of matter, physicists have found it expedient to regard light now as waves, now as corpuscles, for it acts by turns as if it were each of these things. Men in society act in more diverse ways than matter, and the arts are pragmatic techniques for recording these diversities.[4]

The good citizen may believe that "nothing is very new that is not at the same time very old,"[5] but he does not permit the past to blind him to the present. On the contrary, he is always open to the endless currents and crosscurrents of new ideas. Even his priceless possession of democracy he views as still in the *process of becoming,* rather than as rigidly fixed for all time. "Democracy is not an abstract concept of the kind that can be set forth mathematically in terms of pure ratiocination," writes Pierre Teilhard de Chardin. "Like so many of the notions on which modern ideologies are based . . . it was originally, and to a great extent still is, no more than the approximate expression of a profound but confused aspiration *striving to take place.*"[6] The good American citizen, living in an "open-end" world, would agree.

Goal 3. A citizen who makes value judgments that enable him to function constructively in a changing world. Values, as Robin M. Williams, Jr. makes clear, "are not the concrete goals of action, but rather the criteria by which goals are chosen."[7] A major dilemma of Americans is how to construct values in an age when new explosions of knowledge disrupt—or overwhelm—the foundations of their society. At a time when astronaut John Glenn's space capsule is already considered dated enough to be placed in the Smithsonian Institution, the mere memorization of a body of facts is no longer a guarantee of an "informed citizenry possessing sound values."

Thus an American educator declares:

> Change in our own time has had a profound effect on the social character of people. This effect has been widely noted and studied, but its implications for responsible citizenship in a free society have not been appraised adequately or taken into sufficient account in making policy for our schools. Change, among other effects, has made it increasingly difficult for the individual to gain an adequate inner sense of *self.* Some of the most evident social facts of our time are impermanence, diversity, and movement. In consequence, stable values and a sense that one's life is coherent and meaningful are harder to come by than they were even a generation ago.

The search for self is a central task of adolescence. The questions of adolescence are those of identity: "Who am I? Where am I heading? What do I believe in?" To the degree that firm personal values and agreement between one's values and actions are not achieved, the search for self fails. The result is a modern phenomenon: the adult adolescent—thé chronically uncertain, restless, and often irresponsible adult.[8]

Recognizing the seriousness of the problem, a good citizen does not settle for philosophic nihilism. Instead, he conscientiously develops "a spirit of critical inquiry"[9] in a persistent effort to form sound value judgments. Such citizens ask themselves: "What *quality* of life [do] we want, both public and private, as citizens of this great republic?"[10] And they make full use of their critical intelligence in their search for answers.

Goal 4. A citizen who accepts the responsibility to participate in decision making by informing his representatives, experts, and specialists of his reactions to alternative public policies. No American citizen is expected to be an automated cornucopia of facts and figures on every matter handled by society. As Evron and Jeane Kirkpatrick point out: "Fortunately, democracy does not require that all men be equally expert in their knowledge of politics or public policy. Fortunately—because if democracy required every citizen, or every voting citizen, or even most voting citizens to understand and judge the myriad of complex issues which confront the nation in this age of technical specialization, international involvement, and interdependence, democracy would be impossible."[11] Further, "It is important to recognize our dependence on experts, and to disabuse ourselves and our students of the notion that good citizenship requires omnicompetence concerning public policy and the institutions by which it is made."[12]

What *is* required of the good citizen is that in major issues of public policy—where alternative plans of action are proposed to the American electorate—he make every effort to participate in the process of inquiry, discussion, and debate leading to a decision. Thus, E.E. Schattschneider, who believes that the power of the people in a democracy depends on the *importance* of the decisions made by the electorate, not on the *number* of decisions they make, defines democracy in this way:

> Democracy is a competitive political system in which competing leaders and organizations define the alternatives of public policy in such a way that the public can participate in the decision-making process.[13]

Such participation is a basic responsibility of a good American citizen. Rousseau's statement, "'As soon as any man says of the affairs of the State,

'What does it matter to me?' the State may be given up for lost,"[14] seems unnecessarily dramatic in today's Age of the Expert. But the implication behind his remark still holds.

Goal 5. A citizen who develops skills and acquires knowledge to assist in the solution of political, economic, social, and cultural problems of his time. Critical thinking skills are among the most important for the American citizen to develop. These have been described in this way: The citizen

> ... (a) locates and evaluates evidence relevant to the issues at hand, (b) analyzes the elements of a controversial issue and weighs the motives of interested parties, (c) understands the methods and devices of the propagandist, (d) reserves his reasoned decision until considerable evidence has been weighed, then takes a working hypothesis which he acts upon if action is necessary, (e) subjects this working hypothesis to future modification if new evidence warrants it.[15]

Related skills invaluable to the American citizen in decision making are "those of *gathering information* through reading and listening; of *interpreting information* by organizing logically and evaluating accurately; and of *communicating information* through speaking effectively and writing lucidly."[16]

A third group of skills involves the effective use of *techniques of group participation*. The importance of these skills was stressed by Hubert H. Humphrey in a letter written in 1958: "... Luckily, in the last few years, a number of fine books have been written by people with experience in government at many levels. The great improvement, in my mind, has been that they deal with government as a *process* rather than merely as a *structure*. Students now are able to get a much more realistic view of government and an appreciation of its dynamic, human component. Specifically, some of the concepts that are now put across are the tremendous role of *group action* in politics, without the connotation that somehow such activity is evil. . . ."[17]

Goal 6. A citizen who takes pride in the achievements of the United States, and at the same time appreciates the contributions to civilization of other peoples throughout the world. A citizen does not idolize every aspect of the American past, but he is proud that he is unalterably linked to it. He can visualize himself in the current of time, and find identification and purpose in this statement by John F. Kennedy: ". . . The torch has been passed to a new generation of Americans—born in this century, tempered by war, disciplined by a hard and bitter peace, proud of our ancient heritage—and unwilling to witness or permit the slow undoing of those human rights to which the nation has always been committed. . . ."[18] A citizen demonstrates his pride in his American heritage by gladly meeting his responsibilities: he votes, obeys the laws; educates his children to understand his country's traditions; and, in time of peril, defends his nation.

At the same time, a good citizen makes a conscientious effort to understand how *other* human beings in *other* lands view the world and its development. He recognizes and appreciates the contributions to civilization of other peoples. As early as 1916, the famous *Report* of the Committee on the Social Studies urged "the cultivation of a sympathetic understanding of . . . [other] nations and their peoples, of an intelligent appreciation of their contributions to civilization, and of a just attitude toward them. . . ."[19] Such an attitude on the part of the American citizen has never been more important than it is today.

Goal 7. A citizen who remains constantly aware of the tremendous effects of scientific discoveries on American and world civilizations, and works for their use in the quest for improved living for all mankind. Ours is an age in which modern scientists investigate the number of atoms (not angels) that can dance on the point of a needle, and other more complicated problems.[20] As each discovery is disclosed, it may bring with it new and profound political, economic, social, or cultural problems for society to solve.

Thus, in the early 1960's, molecular biologists reported that they were on the verge of discovering the specific relationship between the geometric shape of the molecules present in the cell chromosomes and the specific genetic characteristics of a living organism. Such knowledge would make it possible for the organic chemist to modify, in a predetermined way, the shape of certain chromosome molecules. This step in turn would modify the basic hereditary characteristics of the organism—human or otherwise—developed from these cells. According to scientist Oscar E. Lanford:

> This discovery, which in the scientific circles is known as "breaking the genetic code," will mean that man is close to the point at which he can by laboratory procedures vary, in a predetermined way, the hereditary characteristics of his offspring.[21]

A good citizen recognizes the vital moral problem that arises from this discovery: *Does man dare to alter the pattern of human life itself?* The importance of being aware of this and other problems created by major scientific breakthroughs can no longer be minimized by stating that "the chief duty of the American citizen is to vote." Vote he must for *national* survival—but for *human* survival, he must come to terms with science.

Goal 8. A citizen who realizes the importance of economic security and economic opportunity in the lives of all men, and concerns himself with strengthening both. The sum total of human knowledge has increased tremendously in the last two decades. This development has confronted the American citizen with economic problems of great complexity. New knowledge about production is a case in point. Hubert H. Humphrey reports:

> Between 1960 and 1970, estimates are that 22 million jobs will be eliminated [in the United States] by automation and more efficient production techniques. At the same time an additional twelve-and-a-half million new persons will have moved out of classrooms and into the labor force for the first time. We shall have to provide close to 300,000 jobs per month just to keep up with the current effects of automation and new labor force alone.
>
> Three hundred thousand jobs a month, just to stay even, is equivalent to a whole new industry the size of the entire meat-processing industry or all of the General Motors production complex per month. Put another way this means we shall have to find new jobs every single month for a group of workers the size of the population of Miami or Akron or Omaha.[22]

In 1964 President Lyndon Johnson summed up the situation when he said: "In this political democracy, what you have and what you own and what you hope to acquire is not secure when there are men that are idle in their homes and there are young people adrift in the streets, and when there are thousands that are out of school and millions that are out of work, and the aged lying embittered in their beds."[23]

A good citizen faces up to this fact. He realizes that economic security and economic opportunity—like political and social democracy—are vital factors in the health of his country.

Goal 9. A citizen who uses the creative arts to sensitize himself to human experience and to develop the uniqueness of his personality. "America may end in spontaneous combustion, but never in apathy, inertia, or uninventiveness," wrote Alistair Cooke in 1952.[24] The good citizen contributes to the spontaneity, energy, and creativeness of American society by developing his individual potentialities fully.

In his search for what John W. Gardner called "perpetual self-discovery, perpetual reshaping to realize one's best self, to be the person one could be,"[25] the good citizen turns to the creative arts—music, art, literature, and related fields. These multicolored fountainheads of thought and feeling enable him to develop the uniqueness of his personality by *sensitizing* him to a variety of human experience. Harold Taylor describes the importance of this function in these words:

> Until the individual becomes sensitive to experience and to ideas, until they mean something to him personally, or, to put it differently, until he

becomes conscious of the world around him and wishes to understand it, he is not able to think creatively either about himself or about his world. His sensibility, his values, his attitudes are the key to his intellect. It is for this reason that the arts, *since they have most directly to do with the development of sensibility,* are an essential component of all learning, including scientific learning.[26]

The good citizen views mankind in the mirror of the arts, and in the process discovers the unique features of his own image.

Goal 10. A citizen who has compassion for other human beings, and is sensitive to their needs, feelings, and aspirations. As the philosopher Martin Buber points out, each person has a responsibility to treat every other person as a "Thou," not as an "It"—that is, as a fellow human being, not as an object of political, economic, or social exploitation. [27] In an age of increasing "depersonalization," compassion for and sensitivity to others are essential.

In Asia the average life expectancy is only 45 years; in Africa nine out of ten Africans are illiterate; in the Middle East thousands of children waste away from brutal diseases; and in the rich and powerful United States over 35 million persons live in poverty. A good American citizen does not ignore these and similar facts, nor does he assume that intellect without compassion can solve the world's problems. He realizes that sensitivity to the conditions of others is a necessary first step leading to intelligent civic behavior.

Lyndon B. Johnson identifies the humanistic task of the American citizens in these words: "The task before us is truly for the educated mind because the educated mind sees things not only clearly but *compassionately.* Otherwise, that mind is merely trained. We are dealing with humanity and if we do not treat people as human beings the educated mind is a sham and a fraud."[28]

Goal 11. A citizen who understands that the continuation of human existence depends upon the reduction of national rivalries, and works for international cooperation and order. . . .

The good citizen is deeply disturbed by the magnitude of such destruction, and equally concerned by the useless death of even one human being. He realizes that man *can* alter archaic ideas from the past; and that if he remains a prisoner of a war mentality, he is his own jailer. Recognizing that human existence depends upon peaceful relations among men, the citizen strives to reduce national hatreds and to strengthen international cooperation and order.

"It is painfully and incontrovertibly clear," writes Henry Cabot Lodge, Jr., "that without world order our ultimate destruction is only a matter of time.

When we face this alternative, we know that we can, will and must create world order."[29] The good citizen agrees. He does not demand that all people fit into a single mold of life, but welcomes them with the words: Give me your difference."[30] The good citizen works with his fellow men everywhere to build a world of law and order.

Goal 12. A citizen who develops a set of principles consistent with his democratic heritage, and applies them conscientiously in his daily life. The citizen sets up principles not as inflexible censors of his conduct, but as intelligent guides to democratic behavior. In the words of Francis Biddle, the citizen-philosopher has a responsibility "not so much to formulate a rationalized and comprehensive system as to develop what Jacques Maritain calls 'an adequate ideological formulation,' expressing the American view of civilization in new symbols and fresh language."[31]

It is of prime importance that the citizen translate his principles into action. "What Americans have done," writes historian Henry Steele Commager, ". . . is to realize, to institutionalize, to actualize, the principles and doctrines and values inherited from older civilizations, to translate them, that is, out of the realm of theory and doctrine and into the realm of practice, *to transform them from bodies of cherished opinion to bodies of felt activity and practice.*"[32]

The good citizen will continue to test his principles on the basic issues of his own times—and to strengthen his *sense of purpose* in an ever changing world. . . .

References

[1] Members of the Civic Education Project team are: Dr. Donald Robinson, *Chairman*, Associate Editor *Phi Delta Kappan;* Dr. Elmer Pflieger, Director of Social Studies, Detroit Public Schools; Dr. Harold Oyer, Assistant Superintendent of Schools, Elkhart, Indiana; and Dr. Daniel Roselle, State University of New York at Fredonia.

[2] Leslie Lipson. *The Democratic Civilization.* New York: Oxford University Press, 1964. p. 543.

[3] Crane Brinton. *Ideas and Men.* Englewood Cliffs, N.J.: Prentice-Hall, 1950. p. 423.

[4] Jacques Barzun. *Of Human Freedom.* Philadelphia, Pa.: J.B. Lippincott. 1964. p. 183.

[5] Lin Yutang. *The Secret Name.* New York: Farrar, Straus, 1958.

[6] Pierre Teilhard de Chardin. *The Future of Man.* New York: Harper and Row, 1964. p. 238. (italics mine)

[7] Robin M. Williams, Jr. *American Society, a Sociological Interpretation.* New York: Alfred A. Knopf, 1960. p. 400.

[8] Franklin Patterson. *High Schools for a Free Society.* New York: The Free Press of Glencoe, 1960. p. 66.

[9] *The Statement on Academic Freedom,* jointly sponsored by the American Historical Association and the National Council for the Social Studies, takes the position that "the

development in students of a scientific temper in history and the related social studies, of a spirit of critical inquiry accompanied by a necessity of confronting unpleasant facts, are far more important objectives than the teaching of special interpretations of particular events."

[10]Question posed by Adlai Stevenson in *Life,* May 30, 1960. p. 99.

[11]Evron M. Kirkpatrick and Jeane J. Kirkpatrick, "Political Science," in Erling M. Hunt, Meyer F. Nimkoff, *et al. High School Social Studies Perspectives.* Boston: Houghton Mifflin Company, 1962. p. 101.

[12]*Ibid.,* p. 102.

[13]E. E. Schattschneider. *The Semisovereign People.* New York: Holt, Rinehart and Winston, 1960. p. 141.

[14]*The Social Contract.* Book III. Chapter 15.

[15]Ryland W. Crary, editor. *Education for Democratic Citizenship.* Twenty-Second Yearbook. Washington, D.C.: National Council for the Social Studies, 1951. p. 157.

[16]Helen McCracken Carpenter, "Skills for Democratic Citizenship in the 1960's," in Helen McCracken Carpenter, editor. *Skill Development in Social Studies.* Thirty-Third Yearbook. Washington, D.C.: National Council for the Social Studies, 1963. p. 15. (italics mine)

[17]Letter from then Senator Hubert H. Humphrey to Daniel Roselle, dated May 23, 1958. (final italics mine)

[18]Extract from Inaugural Address, January 20, 1961.

[19]Cited in Henry Johnson. *Teaching of History.* New York: The Macmillan Company, 1940. p. 113-114.

[20]In June 1962 a microscope that can show the number of atoms dancing on the point of a needle was installed in the Henry Krumb School of Mines at Columbia University.

[21]Extracted from an address by Dr. O. E. Lanford delivered at his installation as President of State University of New York College at Fredonia, May 1963.

[22]Hubert H. Humphrey. *War on Poverty.* New York: McGraw-Hill Book Company, 1964. p. 152.

[23]Cited in *ibid.,* p. 31.

[24]Quoted in John W. Gardner. *Excellence.* New York: Harper and Brothers, 1961. p. 17.

[25]*Ibid.,* p. 136.

[26]Harold Taylor. *Art and the Intellect—Moral Values and the Experience of Art.* New York: Museum of Modern Art, 1960. p. 13. (italics mine)

[27]Martin Buber. *I and Thou.* New York: Charles Scribner's Sons, 1958.

[28]Lyndon B. Johnson. "The Century of the Educated Man," in *Vital Speeches of the Day,* August 15, 1963. p. 654-655. (italics mine)

[29]Quoted in *Pathway to Peace.* (Minneapolis, Minn.: T.S. Denison & Co., 1957) p. 89.

[30]Words of Dr. Everett Clinchy, former president of the National Conference of Christians and Jews. Quoted in *ibid.,* p. 30.

[31]Francis Biddle. "Freedom and the Preservation of Human Values" in *Preserving Human Values in an Age of Technology,* and the Franklin Memorial Lectures, Vol. 9, edited by Edgar G. Johnston. (Detroit, Mich.: Wayne State University Press) p. 68.

[32]Henry Steele Commager. "Human Values in the American Tradition." *Ibid.,* pp. 29-30.

CONSENT OF THE GOVERNED AND CITIZENSHIP EDUCATION IN MODERN AMERICA

Fred M. Newmann
University of Wisconsin

THE TRADITIONAL IDEAL OF CONSENT

One may collect specific statements from standard high-school textbooks on American government,[1] from professional organizations like the American Association of School Administrators[2] or the National Council for Social Studies,[3] from sociologists,[4] or from foreign observers,[5] and though stated from different frames of reference, these statements would all reflect a common objective of citizenship education in the United States: belief in the consent of the governed. The belief seems to be advanced by teachers, textbooks, and other educative influences on both the normative and empirical level. That is, we teach that consent of the governed is an ideal, a positive "good," to strive for, and that our social system is superior in part because we do in fact enjoy consent of the governed.

The concept is often communicated through a combination of Lockian, Jeffersonian, and Jacksonian notions of popular sovereignty.[6] Liberal theory, having received its most articulate statement during the Enlightenment, is conveniently explained in terms of late eighteenth- or early nineteenth-century America. Conditions of that environment support the image of people gathered in small rural communities, electing their leaders, discussing and voting on public issues, abiding by majority decisions. The consent process can be easily taught in terms of the former environment where most social problems were resolved on a local level, where much of the citizenry had personal interests in community affairs, where government of, by, and for the people could be directly observed and experienced. But as the population has expanded, as the society has changed from a localistic pattern of agrarian communities to a complex of massive urban centers, governed by powers both distant and diffuse, the original construct of consent of the governed has become more difficult to apply and explain.

Since the construct originated in the existential context of an earlier period, this is the context in which it is taught and generally accepted. I

Reprinted with permission of the author and the publisher, from *School Review,* 71, No. 4 (Winter, 1963): 404-409, 415-421.

suggest, however, that several environmental phenomena or conditions in modern America seriously threaten the traditional view of the consent process. This hypothesis evokes several questions: Do the alleged conditions exist? If so, do they challenge the empirical operation of consent of the governed? If they do exist and do present a challenge, how should curriculum designed for citizenship education deal with them? These are the issues explored below.

EMPIRICAL ASSAULTS ON THE TRADITIONAL IDEAL

The social sciences, within the last twenty years, have produced a variety of findings which tend to attack the traditional consent sterotype. We apparently lack the ideal democratic citizen: the citizen who views the affairs of the community as his own, who demonstrates active interest and participation in the policy-making of the groups to which he belongs, and who adopts an informed, critical, open-minded approach to the resolution of social issues.

CITIZEN BEHAVIOR

Major studies on voting behavior, [7,8,9,10] on the authoritarian personality,[11] and on the formation of American foreign policy[12,13,14] confirm the hypothesis that most citizens are not interested in, do not participate in, and have virtually no knowledge of community affairs; that, moreover, they behave non-rationally and uncritically in situations requiring consent of the governed.

Studies on political ignorance report that about 40 per cent of the public is totally uninformed on public issues,[7] and even in election years not more than a third of the voters accurately perceive the candidates' stand on various issues.[8] Almond reports that no more than 25 per cent of the citizenry shows any meaningful knowledge of foreign affairs.[14] In addition, we have estimates on various types of interest and participation in public affairs,[7,13,15,16] and generalizing over all these studies, one might conclude that less than 20 per cent of the adult population actively takes part in their government "by the people."

On the other hand, those who do show interest and participation are less likely to remain open-minded or to stray from their homogeneous groups— family or political party, for example—that merely reinforce their original views.[7,8] The more interested voters seem to be the more rigid and more biased.[13] In Burdick's opinion the voter "quite obviously is incapable of the kind of rationality which Locke expected of him, to say nothing of his ability to make the kind of intricate 'felicific calculus' which Bentham required of his citizen."[10]

The charge of apathy is common in the United States and is often attributed to a general feeling of political helplessness. Campbell and others, through their test of political efficacy, investigated this attitude during the 1952 national elections, and found that only about 25 per cent of the population showed a "high degree" of political efficacy.[9] In a more local study, Gamson reports data that portray about 55 per cent of the subjects as feeling politically helpless.[17] Keniston seems to attend to such findings in his observations on youth:

> Today the feeling of powerlessness extends even beyond matters of political and social interest; many young people see themselves as unable to influence any but the most personal spheres of their lives. . . . They are pessimistic about their own chances of affecting or altering the great corporations, bureaucracies, and academics for which most of them will work.[18]

A by-product of this feeling, called "privatism" by some, directs the attention of youth only to personal, not social, matters. Keniston continues: "The experience sought is private, even solipsistic; it involves an indifference to the beckonings of the wider society."[18] Adorno and others reach similar conclusions in explaining the political apathy and ignorance of high scorers on the authoritarian personality inventory.[11] This evidence on feelings of political detachment or powerlessness and the reasonable interpretations thereof certainly contradict the image of the citizen who is able to shape his own destiny through an active and effective consent process.[19]

Elections and Majority Rule

In replying to the studies on voter behavior, one might retort, "Regardless of their knowledge, interest, participation, or rationality, the voters still exert their consent through majority rule." However, voting statistics[20] show that:

1. In three presidential elections the winning candidate did not even acquire a plurality (much less a majority) of the popular votes cast. One of these minority presidents was Abraham Lincoln in 1860.
2. In nine other presidential elections the winning candidate did not receive a majority of the popular votes cast.
3. In spite of necessary qualifications,[21] never in the history of the United

States has a president been elected by a popular majority of the eligible voters.

Clearly liberal political doctrine prescribes necessary limitations on majority rule—the Electoral College, equal representation in the Senate, the Supreme Court—but whatever the limitations, if they deny popular majority choice in the election of the national leader, majority rule (as one dimension of the consent image) is modified practically into nonsense.

The arithmetic explanation of the lack of majority rule lies in the small per cent of eligible voters who vote in presidential elections, at the most about 60 per cent. To argue that the will of the non-voters is probably reflected in the will of the voters, and so a majority of the votes cast essentially equals the true majority will, is to speculate without evidence and to ignore the scant evidence available on this question.[9] Some would cite the decision not to vote, to let others perform the elective act, as merely one avenue or way in which to use one's consent power. In this line of argument consent of the governed need not be construed in terms of an active process of self-government, but only as the opportunity to vote or not to vote. Consent in this style would depend only on maintaining the opportunity for majority rule through elections, not on the actual achievement of it. Yet even this transfiguration must be qualified. It is convincingly shown that voters who select a particular candidate entertain different and occasionally opposite notions of the specific policies the candidate supports.[23] A candidate with a majority mandate from the populace (though never attained in United States history) may be evidence of majority rule, but not of majority will on policy matters.

The recent exposure of unequal apportionment in state legislatures offers further support for the contention that the United States lacks the kind of majority rule requisite to the traditional consent paradigm. It is generally estimated that urban areas account for more than 70 per cent of the population, supply more than 90 per cent of the internal revenue, yet can elect only about 20 per cent of the representatives in state legislatures.[24] In more than half the states, majorities in a state's senate and lower house can be won by less than 35 per cent of the voters.[25] Since in most of the states the power of apportionment and the introduction of constitutional change require legislative approval, the correction of unequal apportionment rests on the willingness of representatives to vote themselves out of office. If the objection is raised that the majority have so chosen to perpetuate their lack of representation, examination of the facts presented here demonstrates that this has never been a majority decision.

Demographic factors alone signify the demise of effective popular representation. With a population of 180 million, each representative in the House theoretically speaks for more than four hundred thousand citizens. As these conditions accelerate, so does the impossibility of representatives to identify (much less follow) the will of their constituents, and the political detachment between them causes "consent" to evolve into the delegation of increasing power. . . .

THE IDEAL RECONSTRUCTED

Alternative Approaches

If most citizens do not participate in public affairs; if none of our national elections evidence majority rule; if the elected representatives do not represent the majority; if the administrative policy-makers are appointed instead of elected; if much of our government is bureaucratically, not democratically, organized; if machines create the answers to public questions; if a corporate oligarchy exercises vast social control; and if we are incapable of dealing with several major issues, what then does consent of the governed mean in modern America? How should citizenship education deal with the facts presented herein?

A meaning different from the traditional consent image will be developed in the course of evaluating alternative approaches that curriculum-planners might consider. Four main routes are available: first, continue to teach the traditional ideal, sheltered from the assault of reality; second, abandon the teaching of the ideal in the light of overwhelming evidence that destroys its empirical validity; third, advocate vigorous social reform to reinstate the paradigm of consent that is vital to democracy, but seems to be decaying; or fourth, teach the ideal as modified by an analytic consideration of the empirical threats.

The first alternative rests on two bases: *(a)* The traditional ideal should be taught as always, because there is no environmental threat to its operation. *(b)* Although modern conditions do impose a challenge, this should not be made apparent to sensitive youngsters. If the children have developed an emotive and/or normative attachment to the consent ideal as the foundation of democratic government, presentation of hostile facts might inflict confusion and bombard the child's basic value structure. This could have serious consequences for both his individual personality and the society at large. Perhaps this would produce a lack of commitment and create cynical attitudes toward our heritage and political system.

In answer to *(a)*, the evidence provided in most of this paper supports the assertion that a number of environmental and behavioral findings challenge the existence of the consent process as historically understood. But we should acknowledge arguments contrary to the evidence reported. Does not public opinion exert more influence than I have been willing to grant? Do elected representatives not try to please their constituencies by "giving the people what they want"? Has not technological revolution made consent *more* effective by providing greater communication between the leaders and the electorate? Even writers who support elitist theory do not contend that oligarchs can utterly ignore or violate public sentiment. Nor would I argue that the process of consent has vanished from the repertoire of human behavior. One might list several "pockets" of experience in which the classical image survives in fact; for example, in private associations like the home or church. These points are persuasive, but in the context of public experience, unconvincing. We lack evidence on the extent to which public opinion is effective in policy-making and the extent to which "opinion" itself is manufactured by the ruling groups. The evidence mustered against various dimensions of the consent concept seems to outweigh tenuous speculations on the influence of private groups and public opinion.

Argument *(b)* is appropriately cognizant of general psychological findings that stress the role of affective and cognitive consistency in personality,[28,29] but it implies a research finding yet to be confirmed. This author is aware of no systematic attempts to investigate the reactions of pupils to instruction in what has been called "empirical assaults upon the consent process." Nor would he ever advocate the teaching of these facts in any form that might foster cynicism, neuroticism (personal or social), or lack of patriotism. Besides, is it not highly probable that any reactions depend upon the nature of the instruction—teacher technique, attitude, and other variables in addition to content that influence pupil behavior? My position is that the concept of consent can be redefined in a "healthy" way; that a realistic understanding of one's culture, along with commitment to basic values, breeds more steadfast and energetic devotion than curriculum designed to obscure from the pupil the disturbing empirical inconsistencies that he may discover later on his own. Hopefully the student, having emerged from the school, will appreciate the fact that the school has helped him *solve* dilemmas between democratic ideals and social reality, rather than resent the school for having disguised them from him.

The second alternative implies that evidence against the operation of consent is so insurmountable that the claim of any widespread, meaningful consent process is farcical at most, and that the school cannot evade its obligation to intellectual honesty. It should, therefore, surrender the consent process to societies, halt the perpetuation of a mythical belief, and teach pupils the "truth," however unpleasant.

While in sympathy with a concern for intellectual honesty, realistic evaluation of evidence, and the changing of educational curricula with the times, this alternative lacks understanding of the essence of liberal thought. From Locke to Lincoln to Lippmann, one component basic to liberalism has been consent of the governed. Although the concept bears a variety of interpretations within a variety of contexts, all of them insist on consent as one pillar of democratic government. The abandonment of consent as an ideal would corrode a *sine qua non* of our political philosophy and aid the forces of tyranny and totalitarianism that the American school is committed to combat. Concern for the truth need not obliterate from the curriculum an ideal deemed vital to the functioning of a free society, which can be rescued from the onslaught of the foregoing evidence.

The third alternative, which regards the teacher as a social reformer, is, to this writer, unrealistic. The historical developments noted in my discussion of assaults on the traditional ideal cannot be reversed even by dedicated and intelligent social studies teachers. Vigilance in those areas where consent is still cherished and operative—the home, personal relationships, local clubs—may help to forestall invasion of these areas by more distant forces, but to assert that teachers alone can change society is to endow them with a power that I would prefer be reserved for no one group. Moreover, our argument for the fourth alternative will attempt to show that the historical trends have not diminished, but magnified, the significance of consent; that what is needed is not radical reformers in the classroom, but those able to redefine consent, making it applicable and vital to the present.

The decision to teach the ideal of consent as modified by an analytic consideration of the empirical threats stems from two assumptions: education should encourage rigorous intellectual inquiry; and traditional "fictions" can be exposed in an instructive way without destroying their useful social functions (that is, serving as models, objects of identification, or devices by which to maintain social cohesion).

Consent Redefined

If one views consent of the governed in terms of the era in which the concept was born, he does little more than engage in therapeutic nostalgia.

This is not to suggest, however, that the process of consent ever operated in its idealized form. One could argue that the idealized notion has never achieved empirical validity. The early years of the American republic, while providing environmental conditions fertile to the development of the process (e.g., town meetings, small communities, minimal influence from distant state or federal government), bore many "anti-consent" characteristics: suffrage limited to the propertied minority, state legislators casting all votes for national offices, slaves composing one-fifth of the population. But this study assumes that pupils are taught (and they learn) that the consent sterotype both describes our actual social system and accounts for its superiority when compared with others. Since careful inquiry refutes the first premise, it unfolds corresponding implications on the second.

To avoid discarding a concept which has been dearly valued, one must modify it to conform to contemporary conditions. Yet one must take care that the modification does not render the concept meaningless. In accepting the evidence presented thus far, one might argue that we still have consent but that in these times it means that the masses agree to be governed by corporate giants, by machines, by specialized, appointed administrators, and by those who choose to participate in public affairs. In this sense, one, by his own consent, delegates much of the consent process to persons and techniques considered to be more able and/or more interested than he. This position is supported by Schumpeter[27] and Schattschneider,[30] although they work from drastically different political theories. They define the political system of the United States as one in which interested men gain the right to rule by competitively seeking the people's vote, a system in which the only meaningful popular voice or mass participation rests in the periodic electoral power. Benn and Peters[6] and Hook[31] also define consent strictly in terms of the electoral right to choose one's masters.

I agree, but would first offer two qualifications. Consent, if conceived as majority rule, has not heretofore prevailed in this country. Even if the majority had rules by way of electoral process, this might be interpreted only as an illusion of choice in the selection of one's masters. That is, the remoteness and technicality of public issues, the opportunities for manipulation of public opinion, and the length of time between elections all tend to modify the significance of the consent process if conceived merely in terms of majority electoral power. To conclude that such factors "modify" the significance of consent is not to imply that they deflate its significance. On the contrary, all the evidence gathered can be shown to enhance and enlarge the importance of the concept.

As discussed earlier, consent of the governed has been historically conceived in terms of majority rule and the image of an interested, active citizenry that controls its own destiny through a process of rational self-government. If the consent concept is bound to these particular ideas, it has only mythical value, because the fulfilment of these dimensions has yet to be observed. However, if consent is separated and isolated from its traditional conceptual appendages, then its existence is real and its significance continually magnified. *Let us define "consent" as the opportunity of people to select the men to whom they delegate the power of government.* In this form, the consent process exists whenever and wherever the stated opportunity exists, and fortunately it exists at present in the United States (although some states still deny certain people the electoral power).

With increasing complexity of public issues, a population too large for mass participation in the formation of policy, and a period of time between elections that gives leaders and representatives substantial leeway, the power that one delegates by voting has reached enormous proportions. As the operations of government exert potentially more control over individual behavior, so increases the amount of power that one delegates when choosing the leaders that guide such control. *By consenting to delegate magnified power, one magnifies the influence of the consent process itself.* If approached from this angle, teaching of the consent concept need not rest on illusory foundations. Its validity does not depend on its traditional linkage with other ideals that are shown here to be mythical. If differentiated from these peripheral images and interpreted in terms of the facts of political life, consent of the governed can serve constructively as a concept that unites free men.

References

[1]F. A. Magruder, *American Government.* Boston: Allyn and Bacon, 1958 (revised edition).

[2]*Educating for American Citizenship.* Thirty-second Yearbook of the American Association of School Administrators. Washington: American Association of School Administrators, 1954.

[3]R. Crary (editor). *Educating for Democratic Citizenship.* Twenty-second Yearbook of the National Council for the Social Studies. Baltimore: Baltimore Press, 1951.

[4]See W. M. McCord in *Citizenship in a Free Society: Education for the Future,* p. 187; Thirtieth Yearbook of the National Council for the Social Studies, edited by F. Patterson (Washington: National Council for the Social Studies, 1960).

[5]Gunnar Myrdal. *An American Dilemma: The Negro Problem in Modern Democracy.* New York: Harper and Brothers, 1941.

[6]S. I. Benn and R. S. Peters. *Social Principles and the Democratic State.* London: George Allen and Unwin, 1961. For analysis of consent theories of the liberal thinkers see their pp. 318-31.

[7]Bernard Berelson. "Democratic Theory and Public Opinion," *Public Opinion Quarterly,* XVI, No. 3 (1952), 313-80.

[8]Bernard Berelson, P. F. Lazarsfeld, and W. N. McPhee, *Voting: A Study of Opinion Formulation in a Presidential Campaign.* Chicago: University of Chicago Press, 1954.

[9]Angus Campbell, Gerald Gurin, and W. E. Miller. *The Voter Decides.* Evanston, Illinois: Row, Peterson and Company, 1954.

[10]E. Burdick and A. J. Brodbeck (editors). *American Voting Behavior.* Glencoe, Illinois: Free Press, 1959.

[11]T. W. Adorno, E. Frenkel-Brunswik, J. Levinson, and R. N. Sanford. *The Authoritarian Personality.* New York: Harper and Brothers, 1950.

[12]T. A. Bailey. *The Man in the Street: The Impact of American Public Opinion on Foreign Policy.* New York: Macmillan Company, 1948.

[13]A. O. Hero. *Americans in World Affairs: Studies in Citizen Participation in International Relations,* Vol. I. Boston: World Peace Foundation, 1959.

[14]Gabriel A. Almond. *The American People and Foreign Policy.* New York: Frederick A. Praeger, 1960.

[15]C. R. Pace, "What Kind of Citizens Do Our College Graduates Become?" *Journal of General Education,* III (April, 1949), 197-202.

[16]S. E. Dimond. "Citizenship Education," *Encyclopedia of Educational Research.* Edited by C. W. Harris. New York: Macmillan Company, 1960.

[17]William A. Gamson. "The Flouridation Dialogue," *Public Opinion Quarterly,* XXV (Winter, 1969), 526-37.

[18]Kenneth Keniston. "Social Change and Youth in America," *Daedalus,* Winter, 1962, 145-71.

[19]For a fascinating explanation of the lack of dedicated public servants in this country, see H.S. Commager, "Urgent Query: Why Do We Lack Statesmen?" *New York Times Magazine,* January 17, 1960.

[20]S. E. Morison and H. S. Commager. *The Growth of the American Republic,* Vol. II. New York: Oxford University Press, 1951.

[21]S. Rokkan and A. Campbell. "Norway and the United States, Citizenship Participation in Political Life," *International Social Science Journal,* XII, No. 1 (1960), 69-99.

[22]For a relevant analysis of non-respondents in social surveys, see C.A. Moser, *Survey Methods in Social Investigation* (London: distributed in the United States by Macmillan Company, 1959).

[23]Robert A. Dahl. *A Preface to Democratic Theory.* Chicago: University of Chicago Press, 1956.

[24]M. Lerner. *America as a Civilization: Life and Thought in the United States Today.* New York: Simon and Schuster, 1957.

[25]"Decision on Reapportionment Points Up Urban-Rural Struggle," *New York Times,* April 1, 1962.

[26]A. J. Lukas. "Barnyard Government in Maryland," *Reporter,* April 12, 1962, pp. 31-43.

[27]Joseph A. Schumpeter, *Capitalism, Socialism, and Democracy.* New York: Harper and Brothers, 1947.

[28]L. A. Festinger. *A Theory of Cognitive Dissonance.* Evanston, Illinois: Row, Peterson and Company, 1957.

[29]Robert B. Zajone. "The Concepts of Balance, Congruity, and Dissonance," *Public Opinion Quarterly*, XXIV (Summer, 1960), 280-96.
[30]E. E. Schattschneider. *The Semi-Sovereign People: A Realist's View of Democracy in. America*. New York: Holt, Rinehart and Winston, 1960.
[31]S. Hook. *Reason, Social Myths, and Democracy*. New York: Humanities Press, 1940.

CITIZENSHIP—AN EMPIRICAL DEFINITION

Gabriel A. Almond and Sidney Verba
Stanford University and University of Chicago

In 1963, Gabriel A. Almond and Sidney Verba published the results of a study into the relationship between political attitudes and democracy in five nations. Their book, *The Civic Culture*, contains a wealth of data which is provocative for the social studies teacher. Among the significant ideas to emerge from their work is a concept of how the democratic citizen behaves. According to Almond and Verba, he plays three roles. He is a *citizen* interested in affecting and influencing the political system. Typically, he also plays the role of *subject* in which his orientation is toward the outcomes of the system (i.e., "how does a new law affect me") and a *parochial* role, in which his interests are apolitical.

The selection reprinted below presents the theory that all three roles are significant in a democratic society (an idea which has been virtually ignored in discussions of social studies programs) and discusses the sensitive balance of relationships that exists in stable democracies.

Civics texts would have us believe that the problem facing the citizen in a democracy is to quote the title of a recent book in the field, *How to Be an Active Citizen*.[1] According to this rationality-activist view, a successful democracy requires that citizens be involved and active in politics, informed about politics, and influential. Furthermore, when they make decisions, particularly the important decision of how to cast their vote, they must make them on the basis of careful evaluation of evidence and careful weighing of alternatives. The passive citizen, the nonvoter, the poorly informed or apathetic

Reprinted with permission of the authors and the publisher, from "The Civic Culture and Democratic Stability," *The Civic Culture*, Chap. 13 (Princeton: Princeton University Press, 1963), pp. 473-489.

citizen—all indicate a weak democracy. This view of democratic citizenship stresses activity, involvement, rationality. To use the terminology we have developed, it stresses the role of the participant and says little about the role of the subject or parochial.

Recent studies of political behavior call the rationality-activist model into question, for it is becoming clear that citizens in democracies rarely live up to this model. They are not well informed, not deeply involved, not particularly active; and the process by which they come to their voting decision is anything but a process of rational calculation.[2] Nor does this model accurately represent the civic culture we have found in Britain and the United States. It is true—and this point is both substantively important as well as indicative of the usefulness of comparative data—that the informed, involved, rational, and active citizen is more frequently found in the successful than in the unsuccessful democracies. The characteristics of the rationality-activist model of democratic citizenship are indeed components of the civic culture; but the point to be stressed here is that they are only *part* of that culture.

The civic culture is a mixed political culture. In it many individuals are active in politics, but there are also many who take the more passive role of subject. More important, even among those performing the active political role of the citizen, the roles of subject and parochial have not been displaced. The participant role has been added to the subject and parochial roles. This means that the active citizen maintains his traditional, nonpolitical ties, as well as his more passive political role as a subject. It is true that the rationality-activist model of the citizen does not imply that participant orientations replace subject and parochial ones; but by not mentioning the latter two roles explicitly, it does imply that they are irrelevant to the democratic political culture.

Actually, these two orientations do more than persist: they play an important part in the civic culture. In the first place, the parochial and subject orientations modify the intensity of the individual's political involvement and activity. Political activity is but one part of the citizen's concerns, and usually not a very important part at that. The maintenance of other orientations limits the extent of his commitment to political activity and keeps politics, as it were, in its place. Furthermore, not only do the parochial and subject orientations persist side by side with the participant orientations, but they penetrate and modify the participant orientations. Primary affiliations, for instance, are important in the patterns of citizen influence. In addition, a diffuse set of social attitudes and interpersonal attitudes tends to affect the content of the political attitudes—to make them less intense and divisive. Penetrated by primary group orientations and by general social and interpersonal attitudes, political attitudes are not solely the results of articulated principle and rational calculation.

How can we explain the discrepancy between the ideals of the rationality-activist model and the patterns of political attitudes we actually find, even in the more stable and successful democracies? One possible explanation, and the one most often found in the literature on civic education, is that this discrepancy is evidence for the malfunctioning of democracy. Insofar as people do not live up to the ideal of the active citizen, democracy is a failure. If one believes that the realities of political life should be molded to fit one's theories of politics, such an explanation is satisfactory. But if one holds to the view that theories of politics should be drawn from the realities of political life—a somewhat easier and probably more useful task—then this explanation of the gap between the rationality-activist model and democratic realities is less acceptable. From the latter point of view, one would probably argue that the gap exists because the standards have been set unreasonably high. Given the complexity of political affairs, given the other demands made upon an individual's time, and given the difficulty of obtaining information necessary for making rational political decisions, it is no wonder that the ordinary citizen is not the ideal citizen. In the light of an individual's nonpolitical interests, it might be quite irrational to invest in political activity the time and effort needed to live up to the rationality-activist model. It may just not be worth it to be that good a citizen.

But though a completely activist political culture may be a utopian ideal, there may be other, more significant reasons why an intricately mixed civic culture is found in the more successful democracies. The civic culture, which sometimes contains apparently contradictory political attitudes, seems to be particularly appropriate for democratic political systems, for they, too, are mixtures of contradictions. Harry Eckstein has suggested that a democratic political system requires a blending of apparent contradictions—he calls them "balanced disparities" —if it is to function effectively. On the one hand, a democratic government must govern; it must have power and leadership and make decisions. On the other hand, it must be responsible to its citizens. For if democracy means anything, it means that in some way governmental elites must respond to the desires and demands of citizens. The need to maintain this sort of balance between governmental power and governmental responsiveness, as well as the need to maintain other balances that derive from the power/responsiveness balance—balances between consensus and cleavage, between affectivity and affective neutrality—helps explain the way in which the more mixed patterns of political attitudes associated with the civic culture are appropriate to a democratic political system.[3]

POWER AND RESPONSIVENESS

The maintenance of a proper balance between governmental power and governmental responsiveness represents one of the most important and difficult tasks of a democracy. Unless there is some control of governmental elites by nonelites, it is hard to consider a political system democratic. On the other hand, nonelites cannot themselves rule. If a political system is to be effective—if it is to be able to initiate and carry out policies, adjust to new situations, meet internal and external challenges—there must be mechanisms whereby governmental officials are endowed with the power to make authoritative decisions. The tensions produced by the need to pursue the opposing goals of governmental power and governmental responsiveness become most apparent in times of crisis. Wars, for instance (hot or cold) have often shifted the balance so far in the direction of governmental power and authority as to cause concern about the preservation of democratic responsiveness. Yet if the balance is not so shifted, it is argued that democratic governments may succumb to external challenges.

Crises bring to the fore the problem of maintaining an adequate balance, but the problem exists in the day-to-day running of a democracy. How can a governmental system be constructed so that a balance is maintained between power and responsiveness? As E. E. Schattschneider has put it, "The problem is not how 180 million Aristotles can run a democracy, but how we can organize a community of 180 million ordinary people so that it remains sensitive to their needs. This is a problem of *leadership, organization, alternatives, and systems of responsibility and confidence.*"[4] In trying to resolve this problem, political scientists have usually spoken in terms of the structure of electoral conflict. An electoral system, designed to turn power over to a particular elite for a limited period of time, can achieve a balance between power and responsiveness: the elites obtain power, yet this power is limited by the periodic elections themselves, by the concern for future elections during the interelection period, and by a variety of other formal and informal checks. For a system of this sort to work, there must obviously be more than one party (or at least some competing elite group with the potentiality of gaining power) to make the choice among elites meaningful; and at the same time there must be some mechanism whereby an elite group can exercise effective power—perhaps by the giving of all power to the victorious party in a two-party system, or by the formation of workable coalitions among a group of parties. Most of the debate on the most appropriate electoral system for a democracy (proportional representation, single member districts, or some mixed form) has resolved around two questions: how to maximize the competing goals of power and responsiveness, and how to decide which goal deserves greater stress.[5] There has also been much concern over the proper organization of political parties to maximize both of these goals. This concern clearly motivated the members of the American Political Science Association's Committee on Political Parties, when, in their report, they called for a political party system that is ". . . democratic, responsible, and effective—a system that is accountable to the public, respects and expresses differences of opinion, and is able to cope with the great problems of modern government."[6]

The tension between power and responsiveness can be managed to some extent by the structure of partisan conflict. But our main interest is in the relationship between this tension and political culture, particularly the civic culture. Can the set of attitudes held by citizens help to maintain the delicate balance between the contradictory demands placed on a democratic system? This concentration upon the political attitudes of ordinary citizens does not imply a rejection of the important role of political structures or of elite attitudes and behavior. These are important as well, and we shall return to them below when we consider the way in which the attitudes of ordinary citizens and of elites interact.

The tension between governmental power and responsiveness has a parallel in the conflicting demands made upon the citizens of a democratic system. Certain things are demanded of the ordinary citizen if elites are to be responsive to him: the ordinary citizen must express his point of view so that elites can know what he wants; he must be involved in politics so that he will know and care whether or not elites are being responsive, and he must be influential so as to enforce responsive behavior by the elites. In other words, elite responsiveness requires that the ordinary citizen act according to the rationality-activist model of citizenship. But if the alternate pole of elite power is to be achieved, quite contradictory attitudes and behavior are to be expected of the ordinary man. If elites are to be powerful and make authoritative decisions, then the involvement, activity, and influence of the ordinary man must be limited. The ordinary citizen must turn power over to elites and let them rule. The need for elite power requires that the ordinary citizen be relatively passive, uninvolved, and deferential to elites. Thus the democratic citizen is called on to pursue contradictory goals; he must be active, yet passive; involved, yet not too involved; influential, yet deferential.[7]

Within the civic culture, then, the individual is not necessarily the rational, active citizen. His pattern of activity is more mixed and tempered. In this way he can combine some measure of competence, involvement, and activity with passivity and noninvolvement. Furthermore, his relationship with the government is not a purely rational one, for it includes adherence—his and the decision maker's—to what we have called the democratic myth of citizen competence. And this myth has significant consequences. For one thing, it is not pure myth: the belief in the influence potential of the average man has some truth to it and does indicate real behavioral potential. And whether true or not, the myth is believed.

THE MANAGEMENT OF AFFECT

We have discussed the way in which the civic culture balances involvement and activity with indifference and passivity. But the balance achieved by the civic culture goes further. Not only must involvement and activity be balanced by a measure of their opposites, but the *type* of political involvement and activity must itself be balanced. In particular, there appears to be a need for a balanced affective orientation to politics; or rather, there must be a balance between instrumental and affective orientations to politics. Politics must not be so instrumental and pragmatic that participants lose all emotional involvement in it. On the other hand, the level of affective orientation to politics ought not to become too intense.

There are several reasons why this balance, rather than a maximization of either pragmatism or passion, is needed in an effective democracy. In the first place, political commitment, if it is to be dependable, cannot be completely unemotional. Loyalty to a political system, if it is based on purely pragmatic considerations of the effectiveness of that system, represents, as Lipset has suggested, a rather unstable basis of loyalty, for it is too closely dependent upon system performance.[18] If it is to remain stable in the long run, the system requires a form of political commitment based upon more general attachment to the political system—a commitment we have called "system affect." Furthermore, as Eckstein suggests, a purely pragmatic and unemotional political involvement implies a politics of opportunism; a politics that will probably lead to cynicism.[19] On the other hand, if an affective commitment to politics or to a particular political group is too intense, this can have unfortunate consequences for a democracy. In the first place, an intense emotional involvement in politics endangers the balance between activity and passivity, for that balance depends on the low salience of politics. Second, such intense involvement tends to "raise the stakes" of politics; to foster the sort of mass, messianic movements that lead to democratic instability.[20] Furthermore, the consequences can be harmful whether the commitment is to the system as a whole and the incumbent elites or only to particular subgroups in society. It is clear that intense commitment to particular political parties or groups can produce an unstabilizing level of fragmentation in the system. But even an intense commitment to the political system and to the incumbent elites is likely to have harmful effects. If citizens are to maintain some control over political elites, their loyalty to the system and to the elites must not be complete and unquestioning. Furthermore, the civic culture implies the maintenance of the more traditional parochial roles along with the role of citizen. The preservation of a sphere of activity that is outside of politics is important if one is to have the balanced participation of the civic culture.[21]

References

[1] Paul Douglass and Alice McMahon, *How to Be an Active Citizen*, Gainesville, Fla., 1960.

[2] See, for instance, Berelson et al., *Voting*, chap. XIV; Campbell et al., *The American Voter*, chap. X; and Julian L. Woodward and Elmo Roper, "Political Activity of American Citizens," *American Political Science Review*, XLIV (1950), pp. 872-85.

[3] The contradictory demands placed upon democratic political systems have been stressed in some as yet unpublished lectures by Professor Harry Eckstein, upon which this chapter draws. The authors are grateful for the opportunity to see his notes on this subject. That democratic systems are called upon to pursue apparently opposing goals is also stressed in Berelson et al., *op. cit.*, Chapter XIV, and in Parsons, "Voting and the Equilibruim of the American Political System," in Burdick and Brodbeck (ed.), *American Voting Behavior*, Glencoe, Ill., 1959.

[4] E. E. Schattschneider, *The Semi-Sovereign People*, New York, 1960, p. 138. Italics in original.

[5] On this continuing debate, too, among others, Enid Lakeman and James D. Lambert, *Voting in Democracies*, London, 1955; F. A. Hermens, *Democracy or Anarchy*, South Bend, Ind., 1941; and M. Duverger, *Political Parties*, London, 1954.

[6] "Toward a More Responsible Two Party System," a report of the Committee on Political Parties, of the American Science Association, *American Political Science Review*, XLIV (1950), Special Supplement, p. 17.

[7] It should be clear that the tension described here is not the same as that between the obligations of the citizen and the obligations of the subject, as discussed in Chapter I. There we dealt with the fact that the democratic citizen has a set of role expectations within the input structure of the political system. He is expected to participate in some ways in decisions. At the same time he has "subject" obligations toward the output aspects of the political system. He is expected to abide by decisions once they are made.

This mixture, too, is part of the civic culture. But the tension described in this section is not between an individual's role in relation to the output structure (i.e., as subject)—a tension that at least in theory appears fairly easy to resolve. Rather, the tension described here is between two modes of relating to the input structures. The citizen has both to be influential and to affect the course of policy; at the same time he must be noninfluential and allow political elites to make decisions independently. Thus the tension we are describing lies within the role of citizen.

[18] Lipset, *Political Man*, pp. 77-83.

[19] Eckstein uses as an example of this the politics of *Trasformismo* of pre-World War I Italy. See his *Theory of Stable Democracy*, p. 33.

[20] William Kornhauser, *The Politics of Mass Society*, Glencoe, Illinois, 1959.

[21] This helps explain the way in which nonissue crises—that is, political events which, though considered important and salient by the population, do not involve citizen demands for influence over governmental decisions—may destroy the balance of the civic culture. It was suggested in note 11 that they destroy the balance by increasing demands for leadership and therefore shifting balance away from elite responsiveness. Crises of this sort may upset the balance of civic culture in another way: by increasing the amount of loyalty to the system to such a high level that it is considered "unpatriotic" to question the actions of elites. When this state is reached, democracy is obviously in danger. Furthermore, a crisis such as a war may destroy the balance within the civic culture between the parochial and the citizen roles. Too much of life—including the non-political sphere or relations—may become political.

Toward Responsible
Citizenship Education

DECISION MAKING: THE HEART OF
SOCIAL STUDIES INSTRUCTION

Shirley H. Engle
Indiana University

My theme is a very simple one. It is that, in teaching the social studies, we should emphasize decision making as against mere remembering. We should emphasize decision making at two levels, at the level of deciding what a group of descriptive data means, how these data may be summarized or generalized, what principles they suggest; and also decision making at the level of policy determination, which requires a synthesis of facts, principles, and values usually not all found on one side of any question.

In order to make my case, it is useful to draw certain distinctions between the social sciences and the social studies. The social sciences include all of the scholarly, investigative work of historians, political scientists, economists, anthropologists, psychologists, and sociologists, together with such parts of the work of biologists and geographers as relate primarily to human behavior. Closely related fields include philosophy, literature, linguistics, logistics, and statistics. The social studies, including the content of the textbooks, courses of study, and whatever passes in the school for instruction in civic and social affairs, are based on the social sciences but they clearly involve always a selection of and distillation from the social sciences—they encompass only a minor portion of the social sciences.

Selectivity, therefore, is one of the features which distinguishes the social sciences from the social studies. To social science, knowledge is useful for its own sake; all knowledge is of equal worth; there is no concern for immediate usefulness. To the social studies, a central consideration must always be that of determining what knowledge is of most worth. If all of the knowledge of a

Reprinted with permission of the author and the National Council for the Social Studies, from *Social Education,* 24 (November, 1960): 301-304, 306.

field of study is to be boiled down into one textbook, what is to be emphasized? If all of the knowledge of the area is to be boiled down into one course of study, what is most important?

There is a more basic distinction to be drawn between the social sciences and the social studies than merely that of selectivity. The impelling purpose of the two is quite different. The orientation of the social scientist is that of research. The more scientific the social scientist, the more specialized becomes his interest, the more consuming becomes his desire to know more and more about less and less, the less concern he shows for broad social problems. He is far more inclined to analyze, dissect, and proliferate than to unite, synthesize, and apply. His absorbing interest is to push back the frontier of dependable knowledge in some limited sector of the social scene.

In marked contrast to the meticulous research orientation of the social sciences, the social studies are centrally concerned with the education of citizens. The mark of the good citizen is the quality of decisions which he reaches on public and private matters of social concern. The social sciences contribute to the process of decision making by supplying reliable facts and principles upon which to base decisions—they do not supply the decisions ready-made. The facts are there for all to see but they do not tell us what to do. Decision making requires more than mere knowledge of facts and principles; it requires a weighing in the balance, a synthesizing of all available information and values. The problems about which citizens must reach decisions are never confronted piecemeal, the facts are seldom clearly all on one side, and values, too, must be taken into consideration. A social problem requires that the citizen put together, from many sources, information and values which the social sciences treat in relative isolation. Thus in the social studies the prevailing motive is synthesis rather than analysis. The social studies begin where the social sciences end. Facts and principles which are the ends in view in the social sciences are merely a means to a further end in the social studies. The goal of the social studies lies not merely in information but in the character of people. The goal is the good citizen.

A good citizen has many facts at his command, but more, he has arrived at some tenable conclusions about public and social affairs. He has achieved a store of sound and socially responsible beliefs and convictions. His beliefs and convictions are sound and responsible because he has had the opportunity to test them against facts and values. In the process of testing his ideas he has greatly increased his fund of factual information and he has become increasingly skillful at intelligent decision making. The development in the mind of students of such a synthesis of facts and values, together with the development of skill in making decisions in the light of numerous and sometimes contrary facts and values, is the special forte of the social studies.

If the purpose of the social studies is to be education for citizenship, if its primary concern is to be the quality of the beliefs and convictions which students come to hold on public questions, and if we are to be concerned with the development of skill at decision making, then there are some things which it becomes imperative that we do in teaching the social studies. I would like to develop briefly some of these imperatives.

We must abandon our use of what I shall call the ground-covering technique, and with it the wholly mistaken notion that to commit information to memory is the same as to gain knowledge. By ground covering I mean the all too familiar technique of learning and holding in memory, enforced by drill, large amounts of more or less isolated descriptive material without pausing in any way, at any time, to speculate as to the meaning or significance of the material, or to consider its relevance and bearing to any general idea, or to consider its applicability to any problem or issue past or present. Even when such material is interesting, and it sometimes is, merely to cover it in this uncritical, matter-of-fact fashion robs the material of its potential for accurate concept formation or generalization which will be useful to students in understanding events and conditions in other times and places in which like data appear. Simply reading and remembering the stories about Indians in our history, no matter how many times repeated, has never insured the development of accurate concepts about Indians or correct generalizations about the relationships between people of divergent cultures and histories. Or, if in our haste to cover ground, we refuse to deal contemplatively and critically with the material we are covering, the student may generalize haphazardly and may, without our help, arrive at totally erroneous conclusions. Thus, it may be said with good reason that the study of Indians frequently does more harm than good, teaching more untruth than truth.

The ground-covering fetish is based on the false notion that remembering is all there is to knowing or the equally false notion that one must be well drilled in the facts before he can begin to think. M. I. Finley, noted British historian, says about ground-covering that "a mere telling of individual events in sequence, no matter how accurately done, is just that and nothing else. Such knowledge is meaningless, its mere accumulation a waste of time. Instead, knowledge must lead to understanding. In the field of history this means trying to grasp general ideas about human events. The problem is to move from particular events to the universal; from the concrete events to the underlying patterns and generalities."

Equally fallacious is the background theory of learning, or the notion that we must hold the facts in memory before we are ready to draw conclusions from them or to think about their meaning. This theory is at considerable variance with recognized scientific method and the ways in which careful thinkers approach an intellectual problem. The thinker or scientist frequently engages in speculation or theorizing about possible relationships, from which he deduces tests or possible facts which, if observable, verify his theory. (Some of the great break-throughs in knowledge have come about in this way.) To say that a thinker must know all that he needs to know, let alone hold all this in memory, before engaging in thought is to completely hog-tie his intellectual development. And there is no valid reason in this respect for differentiating between a student trying to understand Indians and Einstein speculating about the meaning of space.

What happens in our classrooms from too strict an adherence to ground covering is that the number of facts committed to memory is reduced to a relatively small number. These are the so-called basic facts which we learn, and just as promptly forget, over and over again. Thus ground covering actually works to reduce and restrict the quantity of factual information treated in our classes. What is needed instead is a vast multiplication of the quantity of factual material with which students are asked to deal in the context of reaching a reasoned conclusion about some intellectual problem. Such an enrichment of factual background will come about when we turn from our preoccupation with remembering to a more fruitful concern for drawing conclusion from facts or for testing our speculations and ideas about human events with all of the relevant data we are able to collect.

For ground covering, or remembering, we should substitute decision making, which is reflective, speculative, thought provoking, and oriented to the process of reaching conclusions. My thesis is simply this, decision making should afford the structure around which social studies instruction should be organized. The central importance of decision making in the social studies has been cited earlier. The point here is that students are not likely to learn to reach better decisions, that is, grounded and reasoned decisions, except as they receive guided and critically oriented exercise in the decision-making process.

Decision-making opportunities in the social studies classroom may run the entire gamut of difficulty, from very simple situations which take the form merely of posing questions for class consideration which require some thought and a synthesis of information supplied in a single descriptive paragraph to very complex social problems involving questions of public policy or individual behavior. Thus, in studying the Plains Indians in the post-Civil-war period a low level decision could be required by asking which of the following sentences accurately, or most accurately, summarizes the difficulty continually experienced in Indian affairs: (1) The Indians were treated by the settlers as trespassers on land which they (the Indians) had inhabited and claimed as their own for centuries: (2) The Plains Indians were wanderers who knew no fixed abodes and recognized no exclusive right of anyone to own the land; (3) Renegade Indians and white outlaws were at the seat of Indian trouble (this is the Hollywood version of Indian affairs); (4) The handling of Indian affairs by the United States government was characterized by wanton disregard of Indian rights, by treachery, and by broken promises; or (5) The different manner of using the land by the Indians and the whites made agreement between the two impossible. At a higher level of difficulty a decision would be required if one asked, "Do you think General George Crook dealt fairly with the Shoshone chief, Washakie, during the military campaigns to pacify the Plains Indians? What are your grounds? Or at a still higher level of complexity, there is the question of what should be the policy of the United States toward Indians who contest the sovereignity of the United States.

Some decisions involve essentially matters of fact. For example, suppose we are reading about the building of the transcontinental railroads in the 1870's, and 1890's and how the government gave large grants of land and money to the railroad companies to encourage them to build the railroads. We read further that subsequently the railroads, or most of them, went into bankruptcy but also that following their construction the country experienced a great expansion of agricultural and industrial wealth whereby our exports of wheat and corn multiplied in 20 years and in the same period the value of our manufacturers' products increased 200 percent, 180 new factories were being built in Philadelphia alone. We have these and many other facts. But the decision rests in concluding what these facts mean. What do they all add up to? Which of the following generalizations accurately summarize these facts? Government subsidization of key industries brings a vast multiplication of other industries under private ownership; private investors will not take the extraordinary risk necessary to start a really new industrial development; one industrial development inevitably leads to other industrial developments; industry in which the government interferes is always inefficient and will fail in the end; private industry can never be expected to provide the transportation facilities needed for an expanding economy; government participation in industry tends to dry up the growth of private industry; industry resulting from government spending is uneconomical and is doomed to fail in the end; if the government had foregone the tax money used to aid the railroads, private individuals would have had money which they would have invested in the railroads. Clearly, the making of decisions among the alternatives listed above is essentially a matter of sorting out and applying facts until a conclusion is reached which honestly and accurately summarizes all facts that are relevant to the problem.

Other decisions, perhaps we should say most decisions, involve values as well as facts. Thus, in dealing with the issue of which of two proposed solutions to the problems of farm surpluses is best, one may conclude, factually, that government support of farm prices lead inevitably to inefficiency in agriculture and to unnecessarily high cost for food and fibre which the farm produces. This much is a factual conclusion. But this does not necessarily get us out of the woods, for one might still prefer government-supported agriculture to an unregulated agriculture because he feared the control of large agricultural corporations (which will almost inevitably follow the removal of governmental restrictions—another factual generalization) more than he fears governmental controls. The latter decision is a value judgment, though one fraught, as are all value decisions, with still further implications which would be grounded factually. For instance, in a hierarchy of values, the greatest degree of individual freedom may be the value sought or agreed upon by all involved in the decision. From this premise a factual investigation could be conducted of the relationship between government regulation and individual freedom on the one hand and between corporate control and individual freedom on the other. Thus, though the decision as to value is not in this way resolved, the exact issue over value is clarified by such a factual investigation of the alternatives.

If decision making is to be the focus of social studies instruction, we will need to introduce vastly larger quantities of factual information into our classrooms. Drill to the point of memory on a few basic facts will never suffice. The superficial coverage of one textbook will never be enough. The very moment that a conclusion, such as any of those suggested above, is reached tentatively, the natural demand is for more facts with which to test the conclusion. This means almost surely the introduction of large quantities of supplementary materials, with far too much content to be committed to memory. It means a reversal in the usual attitude on reading habits whereby students will be expected to read larger quantities of materials, to read them more rapidly, and to read them for purposes of getting general ideas or of locating relevant information rather than to read small quantities of material, slowly and laboriously, a few pages each day, for purposes of committing the material to memory. It may mean in the end the abandonment of textbooks and the substitution of numerous, more substantive, more informative, and more exciting books and other materials.

If the quality of decision making is to be the primary concern of social studies instruction, we must take steps to up-grade the quality of intellectual activity in the social studies classroom. Research is demonstrating the disquieting prevalence in many social studies classrooms of what is generally labelled shoddy thinking procedures. In fact, social studies classrooms seem to exhibit a quality of logic far below that exhibited in classrooms in which science, mathematics, or even English is being taught. Admitting the greater difficulty of our content, this is still something about which we cannot be complacent. Among the common errors in logic easily observed in social studies instruction is the acceptance of an assertion as if it were a fact, the confusing of fact with opinion, the validation of the truth of something on authority, the acceptance of a merely plausible explanation for a sufficient explanation, the failure to agree on the meaning of key words (frequently value laden) before engaging in an argument in which the meaning of the word is essential as, for instance, to argue over whether the first Roosevelt was a good or a strong President without first agreeing on a common meaning for "good" and for "strong" and the confusing of questions which must be referred to facts for an answer and those which defer to values for an answer. The persistent practice in our classrooms of errors in logic of the kind mentioned can lead only to intellectual confusion and irresponsibility. If we are really concerned with effective citizenship, we must not only provide the opportunity for decision making but we must see to it that decisions are made in keeping with well known rules of science and logic and that students get practice in making such decisions.

Lastly, if responsible decision making is the end of social studies instruction, we must recognize values formation as a central concern of social studies instruction. Real life decisions are ultimately value decisions. To leave a student unaware of the value assumptions in his decision or to leave him untrained in dealing with value questions is literally to lead an innocent lamb to the slaughter. Such a student could, and he frequently does, return to our fold and say, "But you didn't tell me it was this way." Or he may quickly sink into cynicism or misbelief. The question of what values he should hold probably cannot be settled in the classroom, but values can be dealt with intelligently in the classroom. The nature of the values which people hold can be made explicit, the issues over values can be clarified, and the ends to which holding to a particular value will lead can be established factually to some extent. For instance, it is possible to predict with some accuracy the factual results of valuing segregation over integration in the United States with respect to such matters as economic productivity of the American people, the respect with which America is held abroad, the effect on the efficiency of our educational system, the genetic mixing of the races, etc. Thus, it becomes possible to engage in some appraisal of the value in terms of other values held, as, for instance, world peace, Christian brotherhood, economic security and well being, national unity, the right to choose one's own friends, etc. We can compare and appraise value, to some extent, in an extended hierarchy of values from lower value, such as a preference for having one's hair cut in a segregated barber shop, to high values, such as the belief that all men should be treated with equal respect.

To duck the question of values is to cut the heart out of decision making. The basic social problem of America today is a problem of value. In simple terms the problem may be stated as to whether we value more the survival of a free America which will require sacrifice for education, for materials of defense, etc., or whether we value more our right as individuals to spend our resources on extra fins for our cars and for all the other gadgets of conspicuous consumption. It is not impossible to predict the outcome of hewing to either choice. It is not at all certain that our students are being prepared to make the right decision and to make it in time.

My thesis has been a very simple one. It is that quality decision making should be the central concern of social studies instruction. I could cite many renowned people as having essentially supported the position I have here tried to state. Among the ancients these would include Socrates, Plato, and Thucydides, the father of objective history. These would include the great modern philosopher Alfred North Whitehead and such modern critics as the economist Peter Drucker and President Robert F. Goheen of Princeton. But to quote these would continue the discussion overlong, as I suspect I may have done already. So may I quote instead a simple statement from the noted modern scientist Hans Selye, who has said that "facts from which no conclusions can be drawn are hardly worth knowing."

THE MYTH MUST DIE

Robert M. Frogge
Late, University of Wisconsin, Milwaukee

Myths are not without utility. They may function as a vehicle of insight into the human predicament or reveal the nature of man's deeply subconscious fears and yearnings. On another level, myths provide easy answers to uncomfortable questions and conveniently simple descriptions of complex processes. Myths on the former level, obviously, have considerable legitimacy; as a substitute for thinking, however, they represent a hazard to progress.

In social studies education, for example, the development of responsible democratic citizens has been so universally accepted as the central aim of this area of secondary education that it no longer is the subject of much disputation. Surprising agreement exists, furthermore, that the essential characteristic of the democratic citizen consists of a rational empiricism tempered by compassion.

It is at this point that we encounter as persistent a myth as one is likely to meet. The myth, stated in non-mythological terms, is that the full development of the responsible citizen is effected by the mastery of appropriate skills and information. Bernard Berelson termed differences of opinion on the aims of education as "spurious" and proceeded to observe that everyone could subscribe to an inculcation of ". . . the best available knowledge from the social science disciplines *as a means to the end* [sic] of producing responsible citizens."[1]

Nor is Berelson's view unique. The April 1963 issue of *Social Education* contained a number of authoritative statements indicating that responsible citizenship would be a natural, if not inevitable, result of whatever specific manipulation of content or sequence was being advocated. Even the Council for Basic Education has pronounced itself on this subject, declaring the characteristics of responsible citizenship, ". . . are not directly teachable matters but are the by-products of ordered knowledge."[2] A recent progress report concerning the work being done at the various centers involved in Project Social Studies implied rather general acceptance of this assumption.[3]

This, then, is the myth. A student needs only to master the magic words and the magic ritual; he is thereby transformed into a responsible citizen. The

Reprinted with permission of the author and the National Council for the Social Studies, from *Social Education,* 31 (February, 1967): 114-116.

high priests may differ in minor ways as to which words or which ritual has the most power, but they are in agreement concerning the general cabalistic process.

While this description is neither particularly precise nor very just, it points up the highly questionable assumption which continues to resist exorcism. The belief that knowledge of history or political science, logic or the scientific method, or the like, automatically causes one to think and act in ways consistent with the democratic ideal is, at best, a gross oversimplification. Such a model appears to assume that behavior emanates from something other than beliefs and values. It disregards the fact that an ability to recite the fundamental principles of the democratic society in no way insures a propensity to act on the basis of them.

Although we all know the folly of equating knowledge with wisdom, our myth does just that. We insist on believing (or acting as if we believed) that knowledgeable people are wise, virtuous, and compassionate just because they are knowledgeable. But we know this is not true. Experience with our fellow man has informed us otherwise. Our own introspection has informed us otherwise.

A number of writers, from a variety of fields, have recognized that the character of man's behavior is not determined by how much he "knows." John K. Galbraith described for us so lucidly in his *The Affluent Society* the phenomena of "conventional wisdom." We have all seen this kind of thing in action: the system of values and beliefs at any given time to which everyone is expected to subscribe but which is carefully and purposely protected from contamination by critical analysis. David Reisman provided a name for that inhabitant of our modern industrial society we have all known more or less intimately, "the other-directed man," whose behavior, rather than being governed by empiricism and compassion, is dictated by what he believes others expect him to think or do. Most of us remember the Jacob study which indicated that a college education may well have little, if any, impact on an individual's value system.

These men, with the exception of Jacob, do not speak directly to our point, perhaps, but they do provide some foundation for suspicions. We can, furthermore, easily find more authoritative evidence indicating that the knowledgeable are not necessarily the wise and that what an individual has acquired in the way of information may have little to do with how he behaves or what he believes. After indicating that the members of fanatic mass movements can be recruited from the ranks of a number of different kinds of groups (intelligent and dense, educated and naive, rich and poor), Eric Hoffer speaks of the reasons for the effectiveness of these people. "It is the true believer's ability," Hoffer decided,

> . . . to "shut his eyes and stop his ears" to facts that do not deserve to be either seen or heard which is the source of his unequaled fortitude and constancy. He cannot be frightened by danger nor disheartened by obstacle nor baffled by contradictions because he denies their existence. Strength of faith, as Bergson pointed out, manifests itself not in moving mountains but in not seeing mountains to move. And it is the certitude of his infallible doctrine that renders the true believer impervious to the uncertainties, surprises, and the unpleasant realities of the world around him.[4]

Mr. Hoffer is dealing, of course, with the extreme case. To assume, however, that this tendency is present only in a particular or rare type of personality seems unwarranted. It would seem more logical that individuals differ in regard to this trait only in degree—we all may be potential "true believers."

Fifteen years ago and more, T. W. Adorno and his associates published *The Authoritarian Personality.*

"The central theme of the work . . . ." was, according to the authors,

> a relatively new concept—the rise of an "anthropological" species we call the authoritarian type of man. In contrast to the bigot of the older style, he seems to combine the ideas and skills which are typical of a highly industrialized society with irrational or anti-rational beliefs. He is at the same time enlightened and superstitious, proud to be an individualist and in constant fear of not being liked by all others, jealous of his independence and inclined to submit blindly to power and authority.[5]

As a result of their investigations, the authors concluded that an individual's political and social orientations are heavily influenced by family relations in early childhood. Again, it would seem risky to assume that such functioning is restricted solely to an "authoritarian" type. All of us confront the difficulty of having our perceptions colored by the anti-rational in human relations.

Further discussion of a suspected personality trait or state will shed additional light. Psychologists have recognized for some time a human propensity toward what Ortega called "arteriosclerosis of belief." Everyone, it appears, tends to retain old patterns of behavior, even when such behavior becomes inappropriate or self-defeating.[6] This is not the place to summarize the experimental evidence supporting the existence of this functional rigidity; the point is that it is possible that the human personality carries with it (in varying degrees) a compulsion to preserve old attitudes and behavior patterns and to resist new ones for reasons unrelated to their apparent or actual utility.

In his studies of belief and disbelief systems, Milton Rokeach has come to a number of conclusions not dissimilar to those regarding rigidity. The implications of his findings include the suggestion that ". . . important aspects of mental functioning are attributable to personality rather than to intellectual ability as such."[7] He indicates further:

> . . . the findings suggest that a person's belief system has pervasive effects on different spheres of activity—ideological, conceptual, perceptual, and esthetic. What these different spheres of activity seem to have in common is something structural. On the surface they are indeed different kinds of behavior; but beneath the surface . . . they are seen to have something in common. This accounts for the generality of man's behavior in spheres of activity that are apparently different. Seen in this way we can perhaps better grasp why it is that a person's score on a personality test enables us to predict such diverse things as how he will behave on a perceptual task, whether he will enjoy a problem put to him, whether he will solve it, and remember it, whether he will enjoy a musical composition, and so on.

All of this discussion serves only to suggest that attitudes and values, including those comprising the democratic personality, do not result primarily from the acquisition of knowledge, that the values we seek to instill are not wholly the "by-products of ordered knowledge." The pertinence of a conclusion of Berelson and Steiner warrants a final, extended quotation. The individual, according to these scholars,

> . . . adjusts his social perception to fit not only the objective reality but also what suits his wishes and his needs; he tends to remember what fits his needs and expectations, or what he thinks others will want to hear; . . . his need for psychological protection is so great that he has become expert in the "defense mechanisms;" in the massmedia he tends to hear and see not simply what is there but what he prefers to be told, and he will misinterpret rather than face up to an opposing set of facts or point of view; he avoids conflicts of issues and ideas whenever he can by changing the people around him rather than his own mind, and when he cannot, private fantasies can lighten the load and carry him through. . . .
> For the truth is, apparently, that no matter how successful man becomes in dealing with his problems, he still finds it hard to live in the real world undiluted; to see what one really is, to hear what others really think of one, to face the conflicts and threats really present, or for that matter, the bare human feelings.[8]

It should be obvious from this discussion that those of us wishing to encourage the development of democratic personalities face a greater obstacle than ignorance. A student once graced my classroom who had more insight than she knew when she announced that she did not care what science proved; she would not believe it if she did not want to. This young lady had an unknown brother, half a world away, in a Polynesian lad described to me. This boy could tell a school visitor that the world was round and could offer good, rational support for his belief. When asked, however, how he would convince the people of his village that the world was indeed round, he replied, "When I return to my village, the world will be flat."

To repeat, all of this only emphasizes what we all know: Knowledge alone is not an omnipotent factor in the development of the democratic personality. It is an important one, to be sure, but not the sole factor.

I have sought to underline two pleas. First, in reference to curriculum planning, it is imperative that we learn much more than we now know regarding how to teach the values and attitudes that mark the democratic personality. I am well aware that the phrase, "how to teach," is not considered to be a subject meriting serious thought. It strikes me, nonetheless, that the absence of serious thought in this area has been in large part responsible for the absence of conspicuous success. It should be clear to all of us that human beings tend to harbor personality traits which are inimical to those of the democratic personality and which are not subject to modification through the acquisition of information and scholarly skills. Only by accident could any new curriculum which ignores this assessment be more successful than its predecessors.

My second plea follows from the first; it has to do with teacher selection and training. We do know some things about the teaching of values, and one of these is that the example of the teacher is important. A rigid, authoritarian personality is not likely to foster a democratic one. A fearful, closed and anxious personality will not produce its opposite. A bigot cannot teach tolerance. If we have experienced difficulty producing competent democratic citizens, it may be because, in part at least, students have never been exposed to one for emulation.

The implications of the significance of teacher-example for teacher education are not altogether clear. It may be that a personality evaluation of some kind is necessary for all prospective teachers. But personality evaluation is a tricky business at best. There may be further implications for the teachers college, but one thing is clear: Unless the teacher demonstrates the qualities he would like to have his students acquire, he is likely to be less successful.

And this fact the teacher training institutions must consider in the selection and training of teachers.

If our profession, and particularly those of us in social studies education, continue to accept citizenship as the most important objective of our instruction, it is necessary, first, to reject once and for all the myth that acquired knowledge, alone, does the job. It is also necessary to discover what kinds of experiences and what kinds of teachers could meet with more success. The final task, and certainly no simple one, is to persuade curriculum planners and teacher training institutions to be influenced by these discoveries.

References

[1]The American Council of Learned Societies and the National Council for the Social Studies. *The Social Studies and the Social Sciences.* New York: Harcourt, Brace and World, 1962 p. 6-7.

[2]*CBE Bulletin* 8:3; October 1963.

[3]*Social Education* 29:206 ff; April 1965.

[4]Eric Hoffer. *The True Believer.* New York: The New American Library, 1958. p. 76.

[5]T. W. Adorno, et al. *The Authoritarian Personality.* New York: Harper and Brothers, 1950. p. ix.

[6]An excellent introduction to the subject of rigidity may be found in Abraham and Edith Luchins. *Rigidity of Behavior.* Eugene, Oregon: University of Oregon Books, 1959.

[7]Milton Rokeach. *The Open and Closed Mind.* New York: Basic Books, 1960. p. 288.

[8]Bernard Berelson and Gary Steiner. *Human Behavior: An Inventory of Scientific Findings.* New York: Harcourt, Brace and World, 1964. p. 664.

THE QUEST FOR VALUES IN A CHANGING WORLD

Bernard S. Miller
Hunter College, New York City

John Patrick's play, *The Teahouse of the August Moon,* deals with the fortunes and misfortunes of two U.S. Army of Occupation officers, Colonel Purdy III and Captain Fisby, as they try to build a school house in Okinawa. Captain Fisby, an associate professor of humanities, has failed miserably in

Reprinted by permission of the author and the National Council for the Social Studies, from *Social Education,* 29 (February, 1965): 69-73.

every position he has held while in the military service. When Fisby complains that perhaps he was not cut out to be a soldier, Colonel Purdy explodes:

> *Purdy:* Captain—none of us was cut out to be a soldier. But we do the job. We adjust. We adapt. We roll with the punch and bring victory home in our teeth. Do you know what I was before the war?
> *Fisby:* (hesitates unhappily)—A football coach?
> *Purdy:* I was the Purdy Paper Box Company of Pottawatomic. What did I know about foreigners? But my job is to teach these natives the meaning of Democracy if I have to shoot every one of them.

We can be amused and reject this simple-minded, military method of establishing democratic values, but when values are considered in our schools, too often the teaching is based on compulsion rather than commitment. Because we are older, and stronger, and society has decreed that education is compulsory, our students come to school, they listen, they learn, they regurgitate the facts we have made them memorize for our examinations, and they leave.

Far too many of our captive students pass courses and pass through courses without becoming involved in the meaning of the subject. We place so much stress on what students have to learn that they have too little time to discover what they themselves want, believe, and value. George Santayana commented years ago that never before have men known so many facts and been master of so few principles.

The problem is not new. Early in the seventeenth century Comenius protested against the way in which teachers try to impose values by preaching:

> Most teachers are at pains to place in the earth plants instead of seeds, and trees instead of shoots, since, instead of starting with the fundamental principles, they place before their pupils a chaos of diverse conclusions. . . . [The schools] have taken no trouble to open the fountain of knowledge that is hidden in the scholars but instead have watered them with water from other sources.

How can we "open the fountain of knowledge" and have students recognize that values which have stood the test of time have meaning for their own generation? Does it make sense to believe that in a rapidly changing world, some values should not be changed? What kinds of learning experience will encourage young people to act as though human beings are closer to the angels than to the animals?

I believe with those who say that values are not taught, they are caught; I subscribe to the proposition that if we wish to develop character in our students, we should have a large supply of it ourselves.

Virtually every school system is prepared to present a list of goals, a statement of beliefs and values, whenever the question is raised. Values we have aplenty. Lists of school goals and values will be found in the teacher and student handbooks and often inside an impressive frame in the main school corridor. What are these values? Generally in first place are the skill values of reading, writing, and arithmetic. Such values as a belief in the United States of America, a faith in democracy, respect for property and human rights, tolerance, good health, and character development are also to be found in most school philosophies.

Our school systems can make a tolerable case for our success in developing skill values, but the headlines in newspapers each day provide painful testimony that both north and south of the Mason-Dixon Line, the commitment to ethical values is, at best, inconsistent.

Both the Declaration of Independence and the Constitution of the United States stress the sacredness of life and liberty as hallmarks of humanity. One would suppose that after so many years these values would be as much a part of every American as breathing out and breathing in. Laws are a legitimate way to express the moral conscience of a community. But to write our beliefs into laws, or to inscribe them on the facades of public buildings is not enough. I quote from the trial proceedings in Jackson, Mississippi, as jurors were selected to determine whether Byron De La Beckwith, a fervid segregationist, murdered Medgar Evers, Mississippi field secretary for the N.A.A.C.P.

"Do you think," asked the prosecutor, "it is a crime for a white man to kill a nigger in Mississippi?" The prospective juror was silent. "What was his answer?" asked the judge. "nothing, Judge," said the prosecutor. "He's thinking it over."

Emerson has observed that "a man is what he thinks about all day long." The values we acquire come not from memorization of words or events; they come from living and identifying with people around us. Young people in particular, who seem to be attracted to the latest thing, need models of greatness, models of what man at his best can be. Too many girls consider it a sign of womanhood when they dye their eyelids green, their nails red, and their hair yellow. Too many boys think they are men when they drive too fast, drink too much, and need a shave. We may bemoan such surface values, but for some girls and boys, these are the adult cultural images with which they identify.

Nor will young people pay more than lip service to a value system that permits no questions to be raised, that insists that the only purpose in study is to learn and to obey. The truth may set us free, but what is truth for one generation may be old-fashioned nonsense for another. Values to be viable can not be embalmed and set apart for reverent worship. When a new generation in a changing world is unable to have a choice in determining values, the values lose their vitality. Young people will not readily accept a life of death.

Last year a group of distinguished professors assembled at Boston University for a symposium on values. On and on, and round and round went the talks. Seeking to bring the discussion down to earth, the chairman asked: "Is it possible to say, 'These are the values that we should be reaching for in schools'? And, if so, how do we know we are working on first rather than secondary priority values?" Professor Theodore Brameld, assessing the temper of his colleagues and the times in which we live, replied, "That is an exceedingly embarrassing question, and I suspect that we will do everything we can to avoid answering it."

Finding general agreement on what values to stress and what to subordinate is an endless task. Indeed, some will even object to so-called non-controversial values like good health. The story is told of a teacher who got downwind in a rural Kentucky schoolhouse, took a short whiff, and promptly sent Farmer Brown's two children home for a bath. Back came the children with a note from their Pa. "I send my kids to school to be taught. Your job is to teach them, not to smell them."

I intend neither to teach nor to smell values with you. Instead, I propose to give examples of classes in which students seem to have gained a sense of understanding about themselves, their past, and their present. In diverse but meaningful ways the important questions posed by Dr. Charles R. Keller, the director of the John Hay Fellows Program, were being asked: "Who am I? What is the meaning of life? Where have I come from? Where am I going? In what do I believe? Why?" Teachers in these classes were more interested in involving than impressing the students, and in the process the students discovered values for themselves.

We go first to a new high school in the San Francisco Bay Area. In this school, teachers and students in English and history have been scheduled back-to-back so that, when appropriate, the English and history teachers can work together for a double period with the same students, or they can divide the class and the lessons into other combinations. The nature of the work determines the organizational pattern from day to day, not the other way round.

On the day of my visit, the two teachers and 30 eager students were having a grand time discussing symbolism in Hawthorne's *The Scarlet Letter.* "Why," asked the English teacher, "did Hawthrone choose the name of Pearl for Hester's illegitimate daughter?" Answers ranged from a detailed explanation of how oysters create pearls as a result of an irritation, to the comment that Hawthorne wanted Pearl's children to have a mother-of-pearl.

When the dialogue moved from symbolism to Calvinism, the history teacher related the concept of justice in *The Scarlet Letter* to the stern Puritan ethic of the Massachusetts Bay Colony. Not one student could find any kind words for the strict, predeterministic, Calvinist philosophy. After the members of the class had finished congratulating themselves for living in our more enlightened twentieth century, the students heard the following:

> Perhaps you are right when you all insist that the Puritan ethic, with its alternatives of Hell or Heaven, with its demotion of man's will to a subordinate role, with an eternity hanging upon each act, with no possibility of salvation after sin, did present a truly tragic way of life. You say that today we are better adjusted, broad minded, relativistic. But our lives lack the greatness of a tragic dimension. Today an analyst can explain the behavior of Hester, and Dimmesdale, and they can be exonerated from blame for their actions, but somehow, the world seems a little stale, flat, and unprofitable, a world in which actions, instead of having eternity hinge upon them, have no consequences.

The silence in the room could be felt as the teacher continued:

> If Puritan beliefs make for repressed and frustrated human beings, I invite you to formulate an ethical system which would be an improvement. In an essay you will be writing on this theme, be certain to explain why our modern world, so air-conditioned, neon-lit, and superhygienic, has led to so much frustration, repression, and violence.

Then from the English teacher, "Would you want to spend some time on ways in which to approach a problem in writing an essay of this kind?" Thirty voices chorused "yes," and the class moved enthusiastically into composition work. In this class the teachers were succeeding in opening the eyes and minds of students, not just in loosening their tongues.

We move from the West Coast to an up-state New York high school English class where the students were required to read and report on four novels from the Victorian period. Some students, of course, consider any reading contrary to the child labor laws. One student handed in a report which showed that she had gained more than knowledge. Here, in part, is what she wrote:

These novels have shown different people in different situations. They have explored the cruelty of children, the ignorance of so-called intelligent adults, the love between two young people, the distrust and dislike between brothers and sisters, and the disgust that certain types of people inspire. . . . These novels have been helpful to me; they have shown me how not to raise a child and how to understand and tolerate younger children. Possibly more important, however, is the idea that is produced in these novels; the idea that I may be very much like these adults.

And then the teen-ager made an observation that illustrates how the arts can give us maturity beyond our years. She wrote:

The most important aspect of these novels is self knowledge. In the difficult process of growing up, getting to know oneself is the hardest, most frightening, and saddest experience in life. These novels have helped me to see myself and have shown me some of the possible things I can do with my life.

We shift from high school to elementary school students and to a seven-year-old reading *The Wizard of Oz*. Suddenly the child exlaims, "Golly, I think the Scarecrow does have a brain. He's the one who thinks of all the ideas." The teacher replied that this was an interesting thought and then asked what she thought of the tin woodsman's search for a heart. The child looked for a moment and then, you could see the flash, it was so plain, "I think he already has a heart," she said. "He feels sorry for the animals, and cries." And then the girl went on, exploring the idea further in relation to the Lion, and the whole group combined. "Dorothy's friends," concluded the girl, "are like some of my own friends who are always complaining about not having things that they really have." Observed the teacher: "If a seven-year-old can discover, explore things, and make value judgments in this fashion, how absurd we are as teachers to interpret the reading for them."

In contrast, I recall visiting a first-grade class and listening attentively as the boys and girls had a wonderful time identifying the hours, half-hours, and 15-minute periods on a large cardboard clock. When the students wished to go on to identify individual minutes and seconds, the teacher brought the lesson to a halt. "You learn about minutes and seconds in the second grade," she said.

We are now in Rochester, New York, where students are discussing Sir Francis Bacon's essay on revenge. The teacher quotes Bacon, "Revenge is a kind of wild justice," "Perhaps," suggests the teacher, "justice is a kind of deliberate or rational or conscious revenge. Perhaps justice, or at any rate punishment, cannot be justified at all with complete certainty." The students talked about utilitarian and retributionist theories of punishment, the efficacy of punishment, and when they were mad enough either at the teacher or at one another, they were told to start writing."When the papers were returned the next day," the teacher has written, "they were not superb, but they did show a genuine effort to think through a knotty, philosophical problem."

In Garfield High School, Seattle, Washington, the concepts of justice, loyalty, and human values are approached by comparative studies of how other civilizations and cultures dealt with these issues. To illustrate that what seems to be justice is not always justice, the students are shown the films, *Les Miserables* and *The Ox-Bow Incident.* Then they read what Plato, John Milton, John Marshall, and Judge Learned Hand had to say about justice. After their smug preconceptions have been thoroughly upset, the students write a paper on their concept of justice.

On March 13, 1964, *Life* magazine ran a feature article entitled "The Rewards Of A Great Teacher." The great teacher cited was Mrs. Henrietta Miller, chairman of the history department in Chicago's Senn High School, and (of course) a John Hay Fellow. Here are quotations from two of the 150 students she greets each day in her five classes:

> I hate this class, I positively hate it; its's too interesting—it makes me work.
> She's always asking "Why? Why?" That makes you do the same thing to your fellow students.

Reports the education editor of *Life;*

> Mrs. Miller refuses to go over the factual "story," as she calls it. "Why should I spend my time giving students what they can get in books?" she asks. "I always take the position that we are learning together and I must never slip into the role they expect me to play—the superhuman being who can meet all their questions with the truth." Instead, Mrs. Miller fires back her own questions.

Three teachers in different school systems in the West Cleveland area noticed that high school students in their respective schools were brought together only for athletic events. "Why not for academic events as well?" they asked. And then they acted. Two hundred eleventh-grade students from five high schools—Bay Village, Berea, Fairview, Midpark, and Rocky River— were invited to attend an afternoon and evening series of Humanities Seminars. The first session was on Thomas Jefferson. Prior to the meeting the students read suggested material by and about Jefferson. At the seminar the students heard a Jeffersonian scholar lecture on Jefferson, and then they divided into groups of ten for dinner and discussion. The second Humanities Seminar was on "Thoreau," the third on "The Role of the American Artist."

So enthusiastic were these juniors about the Humanities Seminars, that this year, as seniors, when they heard that the new Humanities Seminars would be limited to juniors, the students insisted on starting a Humanities Seminar for seniors. When I attended the first Humanities Seminar for seniors in October, I heard a philosopher, Professor Alburey Castell, talk on "The Humanities Give You The Modern World." The students had read C. P. Snow's *Two Cultures,* and the discussion on the conflict between science and humanism, and between man as a maker or a product of destiny, was both spirited and worthwhile.

"Not to know the principles and presuppositions on which we act," said Professor Castell, "is to be naive." I am happy to report that many of the seniors cited examples to show that human beings were not ruled entirely by outside forces and pressures. They were inclined to say about man, not with Pavlov, "How like a dog," but with Hamlet, "How like a God."

You may comment that these examples involved students from relatively secure communities where the desire to learn, to think, to succeed in school by really trying, is self evident. How about students who come to school with no love for learning, who are our "sit-ins" and at an early date become our "drop-outs"?

I take you to such a school and to a classroom filled with so-called slow learners. The teacher was unaware of my pending visit until the principal brought me to her classroom door. I asked if I could observe her class. She was less than overjoyed. "This is a very slow class," she protested. "We are not doing anything you would find of interest." But my foot was in the door and I would not be moved. Reluctantly, she allowed me to enter.

More than 30 students were in the room. And what students! One glance and I knew that here were boys and girls not fated for intellectual greatness. What were they doing? Reading *Huckleberry Finn.* The teacher asked why Huck's father smashed the furniture in the room and tore to shreds the clean clothing given to him by the kindly judge. Several hands went up. One burly youngster indicated that the old man was drunk and didn't know what he was doing. "Why would Mark Twain put such an episode in the story?" asked the teacher. Again hands went up. "He just wanted to show that getting nice stuff ain't enough. You have to learn to appreciate good things or you'll go right back to being a bum." The boy who gave that answer will not go to college—

he may not even graduate from high school—but I like to believe that reading and discussing *Huckleberry Finn* in this class has helped him understand himself and his own world a little better; he has become a better human being.

In a letter we later received from this teacher she told more about her program:

> We use no grammar text, realizing that the teaching of formal grammar to slow students is frustrating to both them and the teacher. Their retention is limited and their grasp of the material practically nil. Instead we give them many short writing assignments and concentrate on correct spelling, complete sentences, and interesting presentation. Both good and poor papers are duplicated for class discussion, and the emphasis is put on finding something to praise. Some reading is done in class. As you know, if the teacher can be excited by a book, she can pass this excitement along to the pupil and make him eager to read ahead.

Here is a teacher who exposes a student's intelligence rather than his ignorance. She knows with E. E. Cummings that one times one is still one and she makes certain her students will come in contact with ideas and values that will help them grow.

We are now in an overcrowded classroom on Long Island. Most of the boys are majors in auto mechanics, the girls in office practice and beauty culture. They are reading an abridged version of John Steinbeck's *The Pearl.* In answer to the teacher's question, "What does *The Pearl* mean to you?" one student replies: "All of us wish for a pearl. But I think he's trying to show that you don't get all you want even if you have a pearl." And from another student this summary: "Some things are more important than making money."

In an industrial community in central Ohio, a history teacher helped eighth-grade students as they read haltingly, almost painfully, from Plato's *The Apology.* The way some of the words were pronounced would make Socrates wish to die again. "Was Socrates a nut to prefer death to freedom?" the teacher asked. One student observed that Socrates would rather die than switch. Most of the answers indicated that the students understood why, at times, a human being may set greater value on law than on life.

In the Fall 1964 issue of *The English Leaflet* is an article by two teachers describing their humanities program for non-college-bound sophomores. Here is not the usual watered-down curriculum; instead, we find the emphasis is on challenging intellectual assignments, on substance rather than survey, as the means of affecting the student's self-image. The teachers have written:

How do we know what the students learn from the course? Term tests and final exams . . . tell us whether the pupil has anything to say, whether his imagination and intellect have in any way been aroused. . . . Most important are the questions a student begins to ask us. . . . If he sees that the ideas we discuss are interesting enough, relevant to him, thought provoking, and worth asking questions about, we think he is moving toward our goal. For his questions show when his attitude toward school, education, and himself are changing. We hope the course opens new possibilities for the pupil as an individual, that it begins to affect his aspirations, taste, attitude, and self-awareness so that eventually he may acquire satisfaction in his work and in his leisure. We are hoping for much but we have no right to strive for less if we really believe what we teach: that for better or worse, man is a creature with potential.

Certainly the humanities—history, literature, music, art, philosophy—can expose students to the whole spectrum of values and help them see for themselves the relationships between past, present, and future. Edmund Burke believed that "the individual is bound to his past and committed to the future by ties which though light as air, are as strong as links of iron." And it is to the humanities we must turn to understand why Walter Lippmann has written that "young men die in battle for their country's sake and. . . old men plant trees they will never sit under."

Humanities courses are important, but like a civilization, a school is more than a sum of its courses. It is an atmosphere, a mode of conduct, a spirit that can add powerful elements to the values derived from an education. A school system needs teachers and administrators who will provide the mood for learning as well as the tools for learning.

Harold Howe, writing on the topic "Schools and Character Development," has observed that "the school's contribution to character growth is determined first by who teaches, secondly by how he teaches, and only thirdly by what is taught." Humanities courses in and of themselves offer no panacea for strengthening ethical values in a society. I emphasize this point because too often in our country we are offered a simple solution for all our ills—pass a law or add a course.

Nor can we rely entirely on divine faith to preserve and enhance values. You know the story of the parishioner who came running to his religious leader in a state of great excitement. "Something most unusual has just happened" he exclaimed. "A man on crutches walked into the Temple, went to the altar, said a prayer, and then threw one of his crutches away. He said a second prayer, and he threw his other crutch away." "A miracle right in our

Temple!" rejoiced the religious leader. "Where is this person? I want to meet him." Replied the parishioner, "He's still there in front of the altar—flat on his face."

In the final analysis then, the quest for values begins and ends with the teacher. Not too many miles from here a teacher was asked to appear before the Board of Education and justify why she assigned and discussed in class Harper Lee's *To Kill A Mockingbird*. The teacher gave the following reply to the question, "Why do you choose to teach *To Kill A Mockingbird?*"

> When I teach this book, I look at my students and hope that they and I will learn to be like Atticus Finch, to meet ignorance, hatred, prejudice, not with more ignorance, hatred, prejudice, but with understanding, goodness, love. . . .
>
> Students respect Atticus because he is an adult who practices what he preaches. More than ever today young people are questioning us as adults when our lives do not measure up to our words. . . .
>
> I have spent over half my life working with young people in school and in church and working with language, the miracle that makes us human. It is through language that we think, communicate, express our ideas, and transmit them down the years. Why study literature? Because it is one of the humanities—one of the ways by which man expresses his beliefs, his hopes, his understandings. The study of literature helps us to develop an understanding of ourselves and others without having to experience directly every aspect of life. . . . It helps us to develop values, ideals, a sense of purpose, an understanding of what life is all about. I consider this book a superior resource for such development because the basic idea of the book is that prejudice poisons the mind, and that the only cure is understanding. . . .

The school board voted unanimously to continue using the book. No students had to be shot to understand why some values that have stood the test of time made sense for their present and their future.

SOCIOLOGY

Gresham M. Sykes
Dartmouth College

I. INTRODUCTION

Many professional sociologists have watched the rapid growth of sociology over the last several decades with unquestioning approval. After all, an intellectual specialty demonstrates its health in the expansion of research, school enrollments, and the scope of application in every-day concerns.

However, such growth has created a number of problems for sociology— and this has happened in other disciplines as well, I suspect. Recruitment of competent personnel has become more difficult; speculative assertions of the classroom have sometimes been translated into policy too quickly in some areas; and it seems that a passion for growth for the sake of growth has sometimes taken the place of a desire for more solid advances. I suppose all this is familiar enough since many bodies of knowledge recurrently suffer from the pains of irregular development. But I think the problems of expansion are particularly marked in relatively new academic disciplines such as sociology; and among their various manifestations these growing pains are apt to show up as a lag between the presentation of sociology in the college or university and the presentation of sociology in the high school. There is a serious danger that the current substance of a rapidly developing field such as sociology will be reflected imperfectly in current teaching in the secondary schools.

It is true, of course, that few high schools have programs in sociology as a separate subject, but many courses in social studies do embrace important sociological issues. Since a variety of sociological topics appear under the name of social studies and since these topics are supposedly viewed from a sociological perspective, the question of whether sociology should be taught in the high schools and preparatory schools as an independent course can be put to one side for the moment. The difficulty is that many teachers of sociology in colleges and universities doubt, at the present time, that their discipline is adequately represented in the high school, regardless of whether

Gresham M. Sykes, "Sociology" in *The Social Studies and the Social Sciences,* pp. 156-160, © 1962 by Harcourt, Brace & World, Inc. and reprinted with their permission.

it is called social studies or something else—and regardless of whether the work in the high school is a preparation for more advanced training or the end of academic schooling.

II. THE STUDY OF SOCIETY: MEANS AND ENDS

What does the teacher of sociology in the college expect of the high school? There's no easy answer to the question, of course, since as one writer has said, "The social sciences are too fluid and too varied to warrant neat generalizations about their nature and their methods.... Social scientists, moreover, even within their respective disciplines, have varied approaches."[1] And finding a worthwhile answer to the question may be made still more difficult because the question is often fobbed off, in effect, with a too easy statement about the purpose of teaching sociological topics under the heading of social studies. "Educating citizens for democratic intergroup relationships," "educating citizens for responsible individualism," "educating citizens for world responsibilities"—all are praiseworthy ends, but they come dangerously close to what Professor Hager once called an "apostolic laying-on of words."[2]

Now I have no desire at this point to resurrect old debates about teaching values in the secondary schools, subject teaching versus a concern with overall growth, and so on. But the plain fact is that many college and university teachers of sociology are not primarily interested in "educating citizens" and many believe that the high school can perform a disservice by placing too heavy an emphasis on the utilitarian aspects of social studies. For the professional sociologist, his discipline is—or at least is in the process of becoming—a science of human behavior.* I am sure that the professional sociologist is happy if a student becomes a better citizen or acquires responsible individualism by learning something about society. But the professional sociologist is also convinced that if his discipline is treated mainly as a means to an end (no matter how lofty that end may be), his discipline will eventually be weakened and the student will be shortchanged. The spirit of free inquiry and objectivity is the foundation of sociology, just as it is the foundation of all other liberal arts and sciences; and it cannot help but be undermined if the study of society is curbed and channeled by the demands of an ideology, even a democratic one.

---

*The problem posed by the fact that sociology is a science in the making will be touched on below. For the moment, I think it is enough to point out that if sociology is not fully mature as a science, the problem is ill met by falling away from the standards of science. Poor science is made better by better science, not worse.

The reluctance of the college teacher to convert sociology into a tool for the production of good citizens is coupled with qualms about stressing the immediate, material benefits of social studies for the individual. If an examination of the community's occupational structure becomes a form of instruction for the techniques of job seeking, if an analysis of the family is transformed into a course on better family living, or if the study of the American economy is seen as a sort of consumer's guide, the professional sociologist is apt to feel that his field is being subverted. Again, I should stress the fact that the professional sociologist may think these are worthwhile aims; his quarrel is not with vocational guidance, aid in personal adjustment, and so on. Rather, his argument is that nothing but confusion can result from equating the objective study of society with a means for securing the good life. A knowledge of society may prove useful to the student. But this is not necessarily the result, and an excessive concern with this result carries the danger that the content of sociology will be distorted.

In short, I think there is apt to be an important disagreement between the college and the high school about the purpose of teaching about society. It is a disagreement best brought out into the open. The study of society at the college or university level, from the viewpoint of the professional sociologist, is primarily a matter of transmitting a systematic knowledge of a scientific discipline. The study of society in the high school, it seems to me, is likely to put its heaviest emphasis on instilling pieces of knowledge and attitudes that will adapt the student to the society in which he will live.

I realize that the contrast may be overdrawn. I realize that the college teacher of sociology will also resort to an "apostolic laying-on of words," if driven, and will justify his work not as an end in itself but as a means of elevating the human mind and spirit. And I realize that the high school does not claim to provide a comprehensive view of sociology. But differences do exist between colleges and high schools in their treatment of sociological topics. As one college teacher has said, "The notion that a college or university is designed to equip and train its graduates for fruitful occupational and societal equilibrium is a demeaning one."[3] I doubt that the majority of social studies teachers in the secondary schools would agree with this statement as far as their own work is concerned and it seems to me a great mistake to ignore this fact or disguise it.

References

[1]Pendleton Herring, "Toward an Understanding of Man," in *New Viewpoints in the Social Sciences,* ed. by Roy A. Price, Twenty-Eighth Yearbook, National Council for the Social Studies, 1958, p. 1.

[2]Don J. Hager, "Some Observations on the Relationship between Social Science and Intergroup Education," *The Journal of Educational Sociology,* Vol. 23, No. 5, Jan. 1950, pp. 278-90.

[3]Charles A. Fenton, "The Sweet, Sad Song of the Devoted College Teacher," *AAUP Bulletin,* Vol. 46, No. 4, Dec. 1960, p. 362.

NEEDED RESEARCH ON SOCIAL ATTITUDES, BELIEFS, AND VALUES IN THE TEACHING OF SOCIAL STUDIES

Charles Frankel
Columbia University

My discussion will fall into three parts. In the last part, I shall make some specific suggestions concerning areas where, I think, additional research into social attitudes, beliefs, and values might contribute to the improvement of the teaching of the social studies. But in the first two parts, I want to do something else which, I think, is a necessary preliminary.

In the first part of my remarks, I want to put a rather large bundle of questions before you. They are not questions that are normally asked, or, at any rate, asked out loud, but I think they enter the minds of most of us who have anything to do with the social studies. They have to do with certain ambiguities in our attitudes, and certain intellectual and moral hesitations— ambiguities and hesitations about the character of the social studies and their function in the education of the young. These questions are in essence philosophical and moral. They require us, as citizens, as teachers, and as students of society, to be clearer than we now are about our own attitudes, beliefs, and values with regard to the social studies. To deal with these questions successfully, we have to pin down our fundamental principles and make certain basic moral decisions. I believe that the airing of these questions is an indispensable preliminary to any rationally devised program of research aimed at the improvement of teaching in the social studies. To my mind, the greatest weaknesses in the teaching of the social studies in the United States today are due to indifference to these issues or to fear of them, and to a willingness to give fuzzy and compromised answers to them.

Reprinted with permission of the author and the publisher, from Roy A. Price, ed., *Needed Research in the Teaching of Social Studies,* Research Bulletin 1 (Washington: the National Council for the Social Studies, 1964), pp. 27-41.

In the second part of my remarks, therefore, I should like to indicate two or three of the basic intellectual issues which, to my mind, are buried in these questions. In the very limited time available to me, I shall not have a chance to do more than sketch my own approach to these issues, and to mention briefly my principal reasons for adopting this approach. But I shall feel that I have done my job if the significance and the interest of these issues has been made clearer. The word "research," like most other sacred words, has come to be used to cover an extraordinary range of ill-assorted activities these days. I do not wish to add to the confusion by suggesting that the word "research" be applied to the more careful exploration and analysis of the issues of which I shall speak. The activity that is involved is not empirical inquiry, but self-interrogation, a disciplined dialogue with oneself and others, an effort to find out, by following an argument, just what the principles are to which we are willing to commit ourselves. I am not sure that we shall all come to the same answers, but I am persuaded that the teaching of the social studies will be much improved if teachers and scholars have the habit of such inquiry, and are more steadily aware, in consequence, of some of the intellectual and moral perils and possibilities of their trade.

Let us start out, then, by looking at some of the embarrassing questions which we normally prefer to answer, as it were, by innuendo. Consider the question that has been put before us as the first theme of this conference. It is that of determining what research it would be useful to conduct into social attitudes, beliefs, and values so that the schools of the United States could do a better job in teaching the social studies. The moment this question is stated, I suggest, it becomes plain that it contains a hornet's nest of ambiguities, and that it is not one question but two dozen questions.

What is the purpose, for example, of conducting new research into social attitudes, beliefs, and values? Let us assume that we want this information in order to incorporate it into the courses we offer. But what sort of information is it, then, that we want? Do we simply wish information about the attitudes which people, say in Boston or Birmingham, happen to hold? Or do we wish to inquire as well into the causes and consequences of their holding these attitudes? And since we have begun to raise such sticky questions, do we also wish to know—and to report to our students—whether the beliefs on which these attitudes rely are true or false?

Moreover, what people say is one thing, what they actually do is another. Research into social attitudes, beliefs, and values is naive and incomplete unless the attention that is paid to verbal responses and official utterances is supplemented by the investigation of actual institutions and habits of behavior. Do we wish the kind of research, then, which invites attention to the contrast between the principles that men profess and the principles or unprinciples that are operative in their conduct? Should research and teaching in the social sciences stress such contrasts or avoid them? And what attitude should be taken toward them? Are we quite sure that we should invariably condemn a social practice when it violates a professed principle? May not the practice sometimes be preferable to the principle?

Indeed, as these questions suggest, is it our purpose in speaking of "needed research," simply to discover what beliefs, attitudes, and values people actually hold, or do we not also have an obligation to make inquiries about the beliefs, attitudes, and values they *ought* to hold? But where a subject of this sort is concerned, how does one do "research" or come to an impartial answer? Is it the kind of question with respect to which the social studies have anything conclusive—or even relevant—to say? Or shall we take it that the answer to the question concerning the beliefs and values that people ought to hold is already foreclosed? Do teachers and students of society simply have the obligation to propagate the values of their society? Unfortunately, even this morally convenient solution has its practical difficulties. Quite apart from the question as to why we should take the reigning conventions to be sacrosanct, how do we find out, in the absence of a Big Brother who lays down the law, just what *the* values of our diversified and kaleidoscopically changing society are?

There are still other ambiguities in the phrase "research into social attitudes, beliefs, and values." Is it possible to understand any given set of social attitudes without also looking at alternatives, real or imagined, to them? However jaundiced one's view of the actual accomplishments of the social studies may be, no one will deny, I presume, that they aim to increase the student's understanding of his own and other societies. Normally speaking, however, the first step in coming to understand a subject *is* to recognize that there is something there to be understood, some puzzle to be unlocked, some oddity to be explained. In the case of understanding one's own society, this is particularly difficult. The student can normally be brought to this recognition only if his emotions can be disengaged from what is familiar to him, and his mind brought to dwell on the shocking fact that there are alternatives—quite viable and plausible alternatives—to the arrangements under which he lives. Otherwise, he is likely to go through life, as most of us do, in the innocent and happy condition of the lady who brushed her teeth in champagne every morning, and, when asked why she did so, replied, "Doesn't everybody?"

But particularly when we are talking about the education of the young and of early adolescents, how far do we really wish to go in studying social beliefs and attitudes in a context of alternatives to them? If we are going to mention the value which most Americans place on private property, ought we at the same time to discuss—dispassionately—the opinions that members of the Chinese Communist Party hold on this subject? If we are going to discuss sexual attitudes, how much attention should we give to attitudes that prevail in Latin countries, or among adolescents themselves? And what shall we say about the relation between inherited moral beliefs about extra-marital sexual relations and the new conditions, that will in all probability exist very soon, when a cheap oral contraceptive will have been created? Should the schools dodge this subject? If they should, what happens to the claim that the schools must prepare young people for effective lives in their community? Or is this sort of talk, which is the commonplace of every educational meeting, mere fakery, and do we in fact prefer to feed our students on pablum?

Nor should it be imagined, while we are dealing with these embarrassing subjects, that conservatives will simply take one point of view and liberals another. I do not, for example, think it is possible to engage in a genuinely serious discussion of racial attitudes in the United States without making it plain to students that very large numbers of white people in other countries look upon the attitudes of even moderate Americans toward intermarriage between the races with disbelief and dismay, and that they feel the same amusement and contempt toward us that we Americans might feel if we met a large group of educated and prosperous people who solemnly informed us that tomatoes were poisonous. But I think that in a serious discussion it also should be said that these quite different attitudes toward race relations belong to people who do not inhabit a biracial society; and it has to be pointed out, too, that the United States is the only instance of a society in which an attempt at forming a single national community of citizens is being made while still hopefully maintaining the notion that two different and distinguishable races will continue to exist. All these bits of information are necessary, it seems to me, to gain perspective on the problem of race relations in the United States. None of them are facts which it is easy to state without making subsequent discussion emotionally difficult. Are we prepared to accept sweetly diluted discussions of difficult social problems in grade schools and high schools, or are we going to insist, in sublime indifference to all the frailities of human flesh, our own included, that the truth, the whole truth, and nothing but the truth is going to be told our children, and in the classrooms of our public schools? Is this an unfair statement of the alternatives? If it is not, why should we not admit when we are licked, and not teach the social studies at all?

I raise these questions to make more than the obvious point that it takes courage to teach the social studies honestly. I raise them to suggest to you that there is also an intellectual problem, a genuine set of dilemmas, concerning what it is intelligent and morally right to teach our children in the name of the social studies. For there may be an antagonism between the goals of the social studies and other quite legitimate goals of a school system. One of these goals, for instance, is the formation of a single national community in which people have learned tolerance, mutual respect, and fidelity to the democratic etiquette. And as an everyday matter, it is at least possible that the democratic etiquette—and perhaps any workable etiquette—depends upon the ability not to say all that one knows, or, at any rate, to say what one knows unclearly and tactfully. The subjects which polite people avoid discussing in public, as we know, are those subjects where the truth is likely to sound impolite.

This is a problem which I do not think can be easily avoided in most classrooms in elementary or secondary schools. There is a commonplace assumption that students need only to be exposed to the social facts, to the truth, to the spirit of tolerance, and intolerance disappears and love triumphs. This seems to me a dangerous illusion. Yet the effort to sustain that illusion is often behind the choices that are made concerning the attitudes, beliefs and values we wish to study or present to our students. In looking at the attitudes of people in Boston or Birmingham, for example, we plainly have to decide whether we mean Boston Brahmins or Boston Irish or both, or Birmingham whites or Birmingham Negroes or both, and whether we want their opinions about sin, about the post office, about the Catholic Church, or about the desegregation of the school in their immediate neighborhood. Honest inquiry and honest teaching are likely to reveal that there are some important differences of opinion between these different groups; and it is also likely to indicate that these differences cannot be resolved simply by saying that everybody is equally right, or even that everybody is entitled to his opinion. The more vigorous the social studies are, the more likely they are to deal with divisive subjects of this sort. Are we prepared to say that this raises no question except the question whether we have the courage of our convictions? Do not schools also have the quite legitimate mission of promoting a sense of common citizenship among their students?

Nor are these the only questions which lie in our path like scorpions waiting to sting. In teaching the social studies we are teaching human beings about themselves, and the secret has long since leaked out that there are all sorts of obstacles which human beings themselves set up in order to prevent themselves from making any progress in this field. These obstacles are both institutional and psychological, and they are formidable, particularly because they do more than simply prevent the acquisition and dissemination of objective knowledge. They also subtly penetrate the process of inquiry itself, dictating the questions that are asked, the answers that are accepted as satisfactory, and the very notion of what it means to be objective in the discussion of human affairs. Accordingly, when we speak of "needed research on social attitudes, beliefs and values," do we mean only research whose results will eventually be included in the courses offered in schools, or do we mean research into attitudes, beliefs, and values that prevent the social studies from being taught as effectively as we should hope?

And, finally, how effectively *should* we hope that these studies be taught? Must we not at least face this question, which is normally raised only by people we prefer to dismiss as "reactionaries," and then only when their guard is down? Does not a school system have an obligation to transmit certain attitudes to the young, including, not least, a belief in the strength and rightness of the society to which they belong? Do the social studies, insofar as they are scholarly disciplines and not exercises in piety, shake such attitudes? For they must at least raise the suspicion that all may not be well and that, even in this best of all possible worlds, a great many things are not what they are cracked up to be. Socrates, it is worth recalling, never quite answered the charge that he taught impiety to the young. He said that that was not his intention, which is rather different.

Nor is there too much help, I think, in taking refuge in the much worked-over distinction between education (usually prefaced by the word "genuine") and indoctrination. There is, of course, an obvious difference between telling a student what is so and inviting him to discover what is so by a free examination of evidence; and there is also an obvious difference in atmosphere between schools in which it is permissible to say that the teacher is wrong—or, at any rate, unconvincing—and schools in which this is not considered proper. But while these distinctions are important, they hold only up to a point; we are talking about differences in degree. The teacher, whatever methods he employs, remains a representative and symbol of social authority; he carries the social system on his back, so far as the student is concerned. If he tells the student to decide things for himself, the student has implicitly been told—and he may not like it—what his duty is. Permissiveness is a way of exercising authority, and in some people's hands it is authoritarian. It is not a way of eliminating authority. So, in the end, there is a certain pressure upon the student, even in democratic schools, to think that some things are so and that some aren't. I shall be convinced that students have been "educated" rather than "indoctrinated" in their social opinions—which means, I presume, that they have come to their opinions purely by examining the evidence in the cool light of reason—when I discover more teachers who have come to their opinions in this way.

Now all these questions seem to me to suggest certain philosophical and moral dilemmas. The first of these is the relation of the social studies to value questions. If the social studies are not value-free, then what claim do they have to be neutral or objective? If, on the other hand, they are value-free, are they not also irresponsible?

As you know, this is a much debated question, and a voluminous literature dealing with it exists. Most discussions swing between two positions. The first is that the social studies, since they are studies of human beings by human beings, must inevitably be shot through with value-commitments which make them simply the servants of some political or social outlook. Now I would myself agree that the social studies do very often simply reflect reigning values—or fashions—among social scientists; and these values or fashions often reflect attitudes, values, and conventions of the larger community. Still, even granting this point, I do not see that this makes it impossible for the social studies to be objective. Whatever the values may be that happen to motivate an inquiry, it is still the case that the answers the inquiry obtains, if properly formulated, are capable of being called "true" or "false" on impersonal grounds. It is or is not the case that, in a given society, pure scientific work commands lower monetary rewards than applied science; it is or is not the case that the number of years spent in school is directly correlated to the intensity of participation in politics.

As must be plain, I do not have the space here to discuss all the aspects of this question. It has been discussed by a great many people, living and dead. I sometimes doubt that anything new can be said on the subject, but I have no doubt whatsoever that disagreements will continue.[1] But if I may cut a long story short, at the price of some dogmatism, I would say that the fundamental fallacy in the position that the social sciences are inevitably committed to some value position is that this assumes that such a position is itself not subject to correction and criticism in the course of carrying on an inquiry. Let us grant that every inquiry rests on certain assumptions; and let us grant, too, that some of these "assumptions" are value-judgments. Still and all, it is a commonplace of responsible inquiry that the assumptions with which an inquiry begins are often revised and corrected in the light of the problems that turn up.

In this respect, the view that the social studies are and must be the servants of values that we fix in advance seems to me to be the cousin of the view that the social studies are and must be indifferent to questions of value. Both reduce the social studies to the position of mere instruments in the attainment of goals which have themselves been selected without the discipline of rational inquiry. It seems to me correct to say that facts are facts whether or not we like them; that it is possible to state the facts so that all competent observers can judge the truth of such statements, regardless of the values of these observers; and that it is the purpose of the social studies to conduct inquiries in precisely this spirit. But this does not mean that the social studies cannot or should not make inquiries about values too. The social studies do not become irresponsible when they avoid complex and controverted questions about values because they fear being forced to take sides. Taking sides is one of the things that the truth sometimes does.

In sum, it seems to me that one major task of the social studies is the examination and appraisal of the actual causes and consequences of given value-systems, so that the price of maintaining these value-systems can be responsibly assessed. And this, it seems to me, may help us to see in somewhat clearer perspective another of the major issues implicit in the questions I have raised. This is the question concerning the role of the social studies with regard to the transmission of the values of the surrounding society, and in the education of the young. Here, it seems to me, we face a paradox to which I have already alluded. First, we are simply not teaching the social studies as a discipline, or as an intellectual value in themselves, unless the attitudes, beliefs, and values of the surrounding community, including the attitudes, beliefs, and values of the teachers and students, are also held up to critical examination. For students have not been initiated into the concept of social study unless they grasp the idea that nothing is sacred, not even their own ideas. That's one part of the dilemma. The other part of the dilemma is that the school system is, of course, committed to the transmission to the young of desirable attitudes, and, in dealing with very young students particularly, this means a whole variety of psychological and social problems, not to mention the psychological and social problems presented by the young students' parents. Is there any way of solving this problem?

The suggestion I would make, for the purposes of our discussion this morning, has three parts. First, it is important to remember that moral and social attitudes are in general transmitted by the entire atmosphere of the school. No particular course of studies has the sole responsibility for transmitting a set of attitudes or values. This applies to higher education too, where I think it is a mistake to imagine that you learn ethics in philosophy or civics or the social sciences, but of course not possibly in chemistry. There is, I think, an unfortunate confusion in the public mind between courses in the social studies and courses in civics, and there is some encouragement of this confusion by many educators. Good citizenship is surely one of the things that one would hope students would learn in school. They might learn it in some other places too, but certainly one would hope that the schools would contribute; and I would agree that the social studies have an obligation in this respect, which is to convey to students necessary information for the informed and effective practice of citizenship. But the social studies cannot be viewed as the sole, or even the principal, transmitters of the values of the community.

The second part of my suggestion is this—to recognize that the social studies do, after all, incorporate certain special values of their own. These are intellectual values. The social studies embody, in very difficult and trouble-some areas of inquiry, the attempt to be objective; to look at oneself or one's own group dispassionately; to recognize how stubborn the diversities between different individuals and between different groups are; to distrust simple formulas and simple solutions in the government of human affairs. These are intellectual values; they are basically coherent with democratic values. They are not, indeed, only intellectual values. They are at the same time moral values. Such values can be taught in social studies courses; I'm not sure they can be taught, in the sense that they can be put into a doctrine, and that a student who has learned this doctrine will auto-matically be more virtuous.

However, a problem still remains. It is a fact that the social studies, par-ticularly at the more advanced levels, will encourage some degree of doubt, some degree of skepticism, about sacred or quasi-sacred aspects of the status quo. With respect to this issue, a third point seems to me to be relevant. This is that the social studies by no means have a monopoly as factors making for skepticism. The conservative celebration of fixed and eternal truths can also produce skepticism. It can produce skepticism because it invites the students' attention to the extraordinary contrast between high-sounding abstractions and the facts which ordinary, intelligent students see around them. It is not the case that repetition of statements such as that the United States is a land of opportunity for all is a necessarily efficacious way to promote patriotism. Among the intelligent, it very frequently promotes the opposite. Even more to the point, however, is a fundamental moral question: What kind of democracy do we want? Democracy, to my mind, is not necessarily congruent with the ideal of liberal civilization. It is not necessarily incongruent with this ideal, despite what opponents of democracy through the ages have said, but it is by no means an invariable prelude to liberal achievement. It was a democracy that condemned Socrates. It was a democracy in New England that was responsible for witch-hunting. The question is whether we are committed to the ideal of liberal civilization—to the ideal of training our children to take a dispassionate and self-critical attitude toward themselves and their society, to the ideal of looking upon our society, for a moment at least, as we would look upon it if it were not our society. If we believe in this ideal, if it is a primary moral commitment, then the role of the social studies in the education of our children is a commanding one, and it can only be fulfilled if they are themselves exemplars of free and honest inquiry.

Once this broad ideal is stated, we have still to face the question regarding another important function of the school, particularly in the United States. This is to help form integrated democratic communities. The social studies are likely to cause a little trouble here. I have in mind, of course, the touchiness of students, teachers, and parents with regard to many of the most important questions covered by the social studies. Two considerations seem to me to be relevant with regard to this issue. I shall state the first dogmatically, although it is only an hypothesis. It is that the discussion of controverted social issues at the sixth grade level lies beyond the intellectual reach as well as the capacity for balanced emotional response of most children at that age. Certain intellectual materials—mathematics, some aspects of the history of the past, certain types of literature and music—can be put before children in simple form without the simplifications adding up to falsehoods. I do not think this is the case where discussions, say, of communism, or of American racial problems, are concerned. At any rate, the suitability of such subjects as a regular part of the curriculum, for example, in the sixth grade, seems to me as questionable as the reading of, say, Stendhal's *The Red and the Black* or Pasternak's *Doctor Zhivago* in the sixth grade. It is sometimes necessary, of course, to discuss communism or the race problem in the early grades simply because the children raise the question, or because the relations among the children in the classroom require the airing of the issue. But then the issue should be faced in this practical and therapeutic context. It should not be introduced as a regular part of a social studies curriculum whose object is to indoctrinate students in the discipline and spirit of dispassionate social inquiry.

I recognize, to repeat, that I say this dogmatically. But I should like to see whether materials accurately and adequately presenting the issues of, say, the Communist movement in the U.S.A. and elsewhere can be prepared for the sixth grade, and used successfully there. That is the test. I am not myself optimistic about the outcome. And the problem is all the more serious because our presumed commitment to a democratic as against an authoritarian approach in the classroom will here be tested as perhaps nowhere else. Social circumstance, the weight of the mass media, and the facts and fantasies of everyday life all conspire to give premature discussion of so-called "controversial" issues an authoritarian character. The most careful and sensitively designed precautions have to be taken if this is not to be so. Moreover it is always tempting, when discussing certain kinds of controversial issue, to leave much unsaid, or to retreat into higher generalities and platitudes, which are either internally inconsistent, or else reduce to the edifying thought, "Wouldn't it be loverly if . . .?" We can thus encourage students, at a tender age, in the thought that the exchange of goodhearted platitudes is serious social inquiry. This is to do serious damage, I think, to the child's further intellectual development, and if that is the cost of the early discussion of controverted social issues in the classroom, it seems to me a heavy price, and perhaps a forbidding price to pay.

What, then, is the kind of thing that can be done, say, in the sixth grade? I speak with diffidence, but I would suggest another direction for curriculum-building, another goal or purpose for education in the social studies in the elementary grades. What could be done, I suggest, is to start to prepare students for the *idea* of the social studies, for the social studies as dissolvents of fixed attitudes. I believe that this involves giving students a background in the recognized disciplines, such as history, geography, or economics. But it also involves the selection of materials within these disciplines with a special end in view—the steady, cumulative habituation and preparation of the child, emotionally and intellectually for the intelligent and self-controlled discussion, in the final years of high school, of current and controverted social questions. As an example of what I have in mind, there are portions of Thucydides in which the conflict between rich and poor is treated with extreme force and lucidity, and where the idea of social class can begin to be grasped. Discussions, even in the early years of school, can be meaningful, I think, when pinned down to a text of this sort. And if children are equipped with such central concepts, if they have learned to use them in talking and thinking about other cultures and other times, they will be in a better position, I believe, to approach their own society, when the time is ripe, with that special attitude of combined curiosity, concern, and detachment that marks the social studies when they are properly conducted. I should like to see a program of this sort tried; I don't know what the results would be, but I think we would learn a great deal from the effort.

This brings me to the third part of my remarks. I have promised, and I must now diffidently fulfill the promise, to suggest where research would be useful in the improvement of education in the social studies.

My first suggestion will surprise no one. For a number of years now, some first-rate work has been going on in the United States in the empirical study of existing social attitudes and beliefs. This work is valuable in itself, and it also provides invaluable object-lessons in the difference between genuine knowledge and mere opinion about the social facts. Yet I do not believe that our social studies curricula have been systematically reviewed to see whether this valuable work can be reflected in what is taught to our secondary school students.

My second suggestion is to investigate the possibilities of new curricula built around and stressing the concepts of constitutional government and the American Bill of Rights. I take it that it is not controversial to say that the first ten Amendments to the Constitution exist, and that young citizens of the United States should have this information; it should also be plain that the rights incorporated in these amendments cannot be understood simply by reading the language of these amendments. There is a body of judicial decision, there is a history of controversy and struggle, there are everyday dilemmas in democratic life, which democratic citizens have to be acquainted with if they are to conduct democratic government successfully. Yet we know that ignorance about the American Bill of Rights, and naiveté as to the problems that are bound to exist in any democracy—and that do a democracy credit—are very widespread in the United States. They exist, indeed, among teachers of the social studies.

I would urge that considerable attention be given to this matter. It is, I believe, a job inviting cooperative work by law schools, political scientists, perhaps some philosophers, and by teachers in the secondary schools. And I would stress that this program has important intellectual advantages, quite apart from its direct relevance to the problems of a democratic society. It would encourage students at an early age to deal with ideas, with basic arguments over principles, with considerations of the relations between abstract rules and concrete situations. This discipline, to my mind, is indispensable to the development of minds capable of objective reflection on social issues.

As a brief footnote to this last remark, I would add that it might be worthwhile to encourage some of the members of my own guild—the professors of philosophy—to look into the suitability of classic materials in philosophy, particularly in political and social philosophy, for courses in the high schools. Many of the problems confronted in the study of politics or anthropology, for example, are explored in classic dialectical form by traditional philosophers; and some of the debates in the Platonic dialogues seem to me, in their elevation, freedom, and quality of imagination, to be particularly suited to students of fifteen or sixteen.

Finally, I come to a large set of problems—the problems that are raised when one asks the following question: What can be taught in the elementary grades so as to prepare students for the objective examination of attitudes, beliefs and values in the later grades? What subjects are most conducive to promoting the attitudes that we want in students, attitudes that will permit them to study the social sciences, that will permit the raising of explosive issues in class without causing either explosions or the enunciation of polite platitudes?

My hunch is that the social studies will be best taught if we can find some way to make them sequential courses. In mathematics, a student cannot go on to the next stage unless he has mastered the preliminary stage. I do not think this has been the case in the social studies, and it is not mainly the fault of the teachers. The social studies themselves have not developed the refined theoretic structure which permits their clear sequential organization. Nevertheless, it seems to me at least possible that there are certain key concepts in the social studies which tie large bodies of material together. Can these be presented to students in an intelligible and arresting way, so that as they move from one concept to another they will get the sense of cumulative progress and mastery? Perhaps there is mileage, for example, in the idea of social class, or the idea of political power. The question to ask, I suggest, in the making of curricula is just this: What can be done in the earlier years to prepare students to deal effectively with concepts like money or power in the later years?

As an illustration, there is the story of Cortez's invasion of Mexico, as told by one of the soldiers in his army, Bernal Diaz. Along with everyone else on the expedition, Diaz was revolted by the Aztec practice of human sacrifice.

But he reports that the Aztecs suspected that the Conquistadores also had a religion based on human sacrifice, and in evidence pointed to the image of the Crucifix, which the Spanish carried into battle. Again, it is of particular interest that when the Aztecs fought a battle, they fought it, won it or lost it, and apparently thought that that was that. They did not get the idea, until very late, that a battle, for the Conquistadores, was not a discrete event, like a game, but a step in a campaign, and that the Conquistadores were there to destroy them and their war-making power. Now, in this latter case, there is a radical difference in the entire idea of war between the Aztecs and the Europeans. And in the former case, there is a religious difference, but there is also a similarity. And what seems to me to be useful about stories of this sort is that they may engage the child, and help him to begin to absorb the fact—the impossible fact—that the world is immensely varied, and that his own ways are as odd to others as their ways are to him. This is a first step in the education of children's attitudes for the effective study of the social sciences.

For some time, the basic approach to early instruction in the social sciences has been, I think, to tie the materials taught to the homely experience of the child in his familiar environment—the post office, the neighborhood construction project, and the like. But we might think it a function of the social studies, even and especially in the early grades, to present students with thoughts they never would have had before, to tell them fairy tales, as it were, and then to make it plain that these fairy tales are true. I do not think that this runs against the psychological grain of the young. The young love games, they love fairy tales: and there happen to be a lot of fairy tales that are true. The history of the Roman emperors, for example, is a fairy tale, an implausible one, and a true story. Until the child learns that what is extraordinary to him is ordinary someplace else, until he not merely learns that fact but lives easily with it, until it is an invitation to him to enjoy the difference, to explore it, and to find out *how come,* he has not caught the attitudes, the values, that make progress in the social studies likely. A fundamental area for investigation, it seems to me, lies in finding out what we can do to promote this attitude. Indeed, I am convinced that training in the social studies, whether in the first grade, high school, or college, always has as its main function the encouragement of this attitude. It is the attitude that marks the liberally educated man. We hold it, even the best of us, very precariously; we need all the education we can get—and education as subtly devised as possible—to have any assurance that we can keep this attitude going in the world, and transmit it to our children.

References

[1] My own views have been stated, in briefest form, in "Philosophy and the Social Sciences," reprinted in Charles E. Boewe and Roy F. Nichols (eds.), *Both Human and Humane* (Philadelphia: University of Pennsylvania Press, 1960).

PART TWO

The Changing
Social Studies Curriculum

William E. Gardner

In *High School Students Speak Out,* David Mallory relates the comment of a young student which may well reflect the point of view held by a majority of secondary school pupils. When asked why he and his friends infrequently mention the curriculum in their discussion of school, he replied:

> Well, curriculum is curriculum. We have it for twelve years. We haven't mentioned it to you because we wanted to tell you first about the things that really matter.[1]

The young man appears to realize something about schools which teachers, principals, parents, and other adults too often ignore—that the school is a social system into which a student is placed for a long period of time so that he may receive an introduction to the culture, but that the things he learns most well are not necessarily those that adults think he is learning. He may learn, for instance, to get along with his peers and with adults, to compare his performance with others in a number of important activities, and, in short, to adapt to a system very similar to the one in which he will spend the rest of his life. The knowledge that is acquired may be less important to the student than his total performance and the sum of his experiences in school. Thus, the school has a definite relevance to the life of the student, but the things that really "matter" are often the opportunities he has to "test" himself and to "find" himself, rather than the chance to become acquainted with the important scholarly disciplines.

The comment quoted above apparently condemns all areas of the school curriculum equally, but it is especially appropriate to a discussion of social studies. Research has indicated repeatedly that the content and mode of presentation in social studies courses do little to "turn on" the typical adolescent. With math and English, social studies share the ignominy of especially low student esteem. Charges of "dullness" and "uselessness" are often the most polite indictments brought against the field.

Yet it should be emphasized that what serious students complain about is not the irrelevance of social study *per se,* but the crowding of the typical curriculum with out-moded data. That is, students are concerned with significant interpersonal and societal issues and topics, but the social studies curriculum seldom presents the opportunity for students to become actively engaged with problems that concern them and society as a whole. Nor does the curriculum invite them to apply what they have learned to the analysis of such problems. Part (but not all) of the problem is the seemingly inevitable cultural gap that separates curriculum from the realities of life. As Alfred North Whitehead once put it, formal curricula quickly tend to become burdened with "inert ideas. . .that are merely received into the mind without being utilized, or tested, or thrown into fresh combinations.[2]

While most teachers and curriculum developers readily agree that schools teach many things outside of the classroom, they do not feel that schools are merely mechanisms in which students adapt and adjust to one another and to adults. They continue to hope that the formal curriculum could be made more significant to students than it appears to be and that the cultural lag is not inevitable. The watchword in social studies curriculum today is change, and most of those involved in developing new programs and testing new ideas agree that social studies courses can contain significant ideas which should be used in fresh combinations by secondary school students.

The problem, then, becomes one of finding ideas wherever they may be and building teaching materials which challenge students. This process involves consideration of two fundamental questions: How shall material be selected for inclusion in the social studies? How shall this material be organized for instructional purposes?

Viewed superficially, these are simple questions. Even after a decade of revisionary efforts in social studies, perhaps the most common response to both questions is that the answers are self-evident. The traditional view of the social studies, the model on which the curriculum has been based, is that the field consists of a group of subjects which correspond to the social science disciplines and that the curriculum is a set of courses to teach the simpler aspects of history and geography primarily, but also some sociology, economics, and political science. Using this model, selecting content is virtually automatic (that which is most amenable for secondary school classes) and organization is implicit (courses in the several social sciences).

Such a model has the virtue of simplicity but is so superficial that it begs more questions than it answers. In the first place, the model implies that the social sciences should be an important part of general education, but there is no indication of why this is true. Secondly, the model implies that the social sciences are static entities with fixed content and that the student's job is to learn the data which have been produced through the arduous efforts of the scholars. Social science knowledge is thus awarded a status it probably does not deserve, since within the disciplines old knowledge is constantly being challenged and the situation, to say the least, is in flux. Most important the model establishes no true criteria for screening the mass of information generated in the social sciences or elsewhere. The "simplicity" criterion does not seem to provide the kind of selecting device which would tend to produce a live and vibrant curriculum.

A major feature of the current revision of the social studies is the attempt to build alternative models for selection and organization. As we shall see, curriculum theorists differ sharply in their views on these questions, but there is wide consensus in at least three matters. The first is that it makes little sense to continue wasting pupils' time on the trivia that too often dominates social studies classes. If the field is to be taught at all, its content should be the major ideas, principles, generalizations, or problems which have claim to significance in the total scheme of things. The low-level data of this field have importance, but *only* as they are related to or illustrate higher level propositions. Another area of agreement is that the content of social studies, however selected, should be approached as dynamic rather than static. If, for example, the social sciences are to be sources of content, the principles and concepts drawn from these disciplines should not be taught as absolute truth; they must instead be approached as material to be tested to see how powerful the content is in explaining the phenomenon of the social world. Finally, there is agreement on the proposition that social studies content in various grade levels should be related so that growth in ability and understanding is maximized.

Despite these agreements, there are deep divisions among the revisionists on what the sources of content should be and how material should be organized so it can be learned. Current effort at establishing criteria for selecting content has been directed toward identifying the "structure" of the disciplines or the major generalizations generated by social science. Each of the disciplines, it is assumed has a number of interrelated concepts or ideas which are its most fundamental elements. Such structural elements, when transferred to the social studies, will provide students with the power to understand the social world in which they live. Because the structure of the disciplines by definition consists of its most powerful insights, a social studies curriculum built on the structure of the disciplines will insure that inert ideas will be screened out and more vital ones allowed in.

Proponents of using structure as a way of selecting content from the social sciences constitute a large proportion of curriculum developers, but there are some vociferous critics of the structural approach as well. One of their criticisms is that the concept of structure in social sciences is an elusive one. An examination of the social disciplines reveals that the interlocking concepts are tenuous and that there is not sufficient agreement on what constitutes the structure of any discipline. Consequently, it makes little sense to use structure as a basis for selection. Another criticism involves the relevance of the structure of social science knowledge to the lives of students (assuming structure can be found). As Hunt and Metcalf maintain, "One of the unexamined assumptions (of current developments in social studies) is the idea that knowledge of the structure of disciplines is an essential part of a general education."[3] The net effect of the arguments is the point of view that the major concepts of an academic discipline do not provide an adequate framework for a social studies course precisely because the disciplines are not directly focused on the "world of affairs." Hence, the social studies curriculum should be structured around major issues of society and content selected from the social sciences or from other sources as it is related to those issues.

There are also differences of opinion on the question of the best way to organize the social studies for instruction. One division here is between those who prefer organizing along discipline lines and those who opt for some interdisciplinary or combined approaches. The first group assumes that each discipline is in a sense a system of concepts, ideas, and principles which is best understood if taught systematically as a discipline. The second group claims either that the social sciences are irrelevant to the needs of a general education program and, hence, courses should not be organized along those lines, or, that concepts and generalizations from several disciplines can be combined and taught under a problems, thematic, or value-conflict organization. Even some of those who wish to teach the structures of the various disciplines are in favor of interdisciplinary organization because of the lack of time in the school schedule for separate, year-long courses in each discipline.

While the issues surrounding selection and organization are perhaps the most volatile, they are by no means the only ones nor necessarily the most baffling. Consider several other significant curriculum problems: Assuming that content from scholarly disciplines is important, how shall the social studies program be balanced between the behavioral sciences and the more traditional subjects of history and geography? Between courses which emphasize national concerns and those emphasizing international relations? Between the cultures of the East and those of the West? What provisions need to be made to keep the social studies up-to-date?

Each of these questions constitutes an area of controversy, and serious debates are being conducted in the hope that the issues can be resolved. The articles in this section have been selected to illustrate aspects of the current discussion. The sheer bulk of the literature pertinent to social studies curriculum makes an adequate sampling virtually impossible and mandates that whole areas of controversy be ignored completely. For example, this section contains none of the provocative literature dealing with the structure of the various disciplines. Nor does it deal with the placement of social studies skills, the problem of the overall scope of the curriculum, and the related problem of how information should be sequenced to encourage learning at an optimal level. Rather, articles in this section deal only with the basic issues of selection of content from the social sciences or other sources and its organization as "social studies" material.

Becker's introductory article analyzes the nature of curriculum developments and suggests ways by which change can be encouraged. The next two articles in Section A discuss the pros and cons of using structure to select content; Bellack analyzes current efforts in that direction and Newmann criticizes these efforts as unprofitable. Patterson argues for the inclusion of more behavioral science in the curriculum while Ward claims that the orientation of history courses should change.

The articles in Section B contain a cross-section of promising new practices. Several writers deal with more dynamic ideas for organizing history and geography classes, while other authors describe approaches to teaching behavioral science in the social studies.

Authors of the articles in Part Two obviously disagree on the answers to many of the important curriculum questions, but, in sharp contrast to the student quoted earlier, they all believe that the content of social studies can and should be significant. They further believe that careful attention must be paid to the *quality* of curriculum content and that knowledge from the social sciences, however vague and tentative it may appear at times, is not barren of import and meaning for modern man.

References

[1]David Mallory, *High School Students Speak Out* (New York: Harper and Row, 1962), p. 17.
[2]Alfred North Whitehead, *The Aims of Education* (New York: New American Library Edition, 1961), p. 13.
[3]Maurice P. Hunt and Lawrence E. Metcalf, *Teaching High School Social Studies,* Second Edition (New York: Harper and Row, 1968), p. 280.

PROSPECT FOR CHANGE IN THE SOCIAL STUDIES

James M. Becker
School Services Director
Foreign Policy Association

In attempting a discussion of the problems and possibilities of curriculum change in the social sciences, one is immediately confronted with a paradox: Never before in our history has there been such general agreement about the need for change in the high school social studies curriculum; never before in our history has there been less general agreement about precisely what needs changing and how the changes should be made. This combination of a widely recognized and urgently felt need on the one hand, and, on the other hand, nearly total confusion concerning ways of defining and meeting that need, underlies the predicament of curriculum reform in this vital segment of secondary education. A brief examination of this paradox will be useful to us in understanding the problems and in assessing the possibilities.

On the first side of the paradox, the proposition that the teaching of social studies in American high schools urgently needs improvement no longer requires much defense. The social studies have been surveyed, inventoried, studied, analyzed, criticized, and reported on enough, and from enough different points of view, that it seems safe to say that no new views of their present state are likely to be forthcoming. The general consensus seems to focus on two main elements in explaining why change is so urgently demanded. The first is the explosive increase in content; the second, which in part arises from the first, is a breakdown in method.

The explosion of content refers to the pressure exerted on the social studies curriculum by a steadily mounting volume of material to be taught. A half a century ago, when the world was a simpler place (or at least most people *thought* it was a simple place, which amounts to the same thing in respect to what is taught in the schools), it was relatively easy to list the main

Reprinted with permission of the author and the National Council for the Social Studies, from *Social Education,* 29 (January, 1965): 20-22, 31.

content objectives for a good high school course in what has since come to be called the social sciences. In those days they were usually just called history and geography. In both, it was generally assumed by course designers (we didn't even have curriculum supervisors then) that the *facts were known.* And the facts were what counted. World history could be adequately surveyed in one year with the main outline of the development of Western civilization sketched in. (The term "world" in the course title was seldom construed as meaning anything other than Western world.) Crucial dates, eras, and historical figures could be "covered." The history of man and the geography of the world were *known quantities.* The pedagogical problem was simply how to transfer this knowledge from the book to the students.

Today the emergent disciplines of economics, sociology, social psychology, anthropology, archaeology, and political science all bring powerful insights to bear on the study of man and his career on this earth. The very nature of history itself has been subjected in recent years to the most searching examination. Greatly improved techniques both of gathering facts and of analyzing them have made their results felt. And the role of the United States in the world has undergone in less than one lifetime such a profound and pervasive change that the basic stance from which we as a people, and therefore our children as students, view the world about us is almost totally different from our grandfathers. Not only have our position and our attitudes changed. They have brought with them a vast increase in the number and kinds of things we need to know and to understand. Today we feel that students must know something about the Federation of the Congo as well as the Federation of the Thirteen Colonies; about the civil war in China as well as about our own; about the drive for modernization in the Middle East as well as in nineteenth-century America; about how new nations emerge in the midst of modern tensions and pressures as well as how they once developed in the slow processes of maturing civilizations. Whereas once we could (or at least we *did*) regard large areas of the planet and many of its peoples as "unimportant" to an understanding of our own lives and times, who now will risk such a description of any spot on the face of the earth.

This enormous increase in both the number of facts about mankind and the ways of dealing with these facts has not been accompanied by any corresponding increase in the number of hours in the school day or the number of courses in the curriculum available to the social studies departments. So one source of the urgent pressure for change is just this: We must teach more—much more—and more difficult materials to the same kinds of students in the same time. Stated that way, the situation sounds impossible, and leaves no wonder that it has been accompanied by what is increasingly recognized as a breakdown in pedagogical method. This is not to say that first-rate teaching is not going on in many social studies classrooms across the nation. Nor do I mean to imply that there is anything wrong with teaching students known facts about the history and geography of the world. The problem of teaching method is not that we can't teach facts well, but rather that we have more facts to teach than can be taught well. The alternatives which face a conscientious teacher include: a resort to more and more superficial survey courses; the arbitrary elimination of large areas in an attempt to do a good job on something rather than a hasty job on everything; a search for some substitute for factual knowledge which will enable students to understand history without really knowing any—or giving the whole thing up and going into guidance. Recent attempts to streamline courses and rely on gimmicks and machines have manifestly failed to meet the challenge. The hard fact is that the social studies have become pedagogically unmanageable. Change—some change big enough to meet the needs—is urgently required.

The other side of the paradox—the confusion about what the goals of the social studies should be and how they should be met—is summed up by the recent comment of an eminent social scientist that "the social sciences are in such intellectual disarray that it would be impossible to get agreement among them on any one thing we would want a high school student to know." This statement is quoted not in criticism of the incalculable contributions which the social sciences have made and are making to American society, but rather in sober recognition of a basic fact underlying curriculum reform in this vital area; namely, that the social sciences *per se* are too young and too yeasty a field to be able to provide us in the schools with a neatly packaged set of goals and objectives. They can help us, as I have suggested, with methods, understanding and insights, and as I shall propose, with creative energy and concern, but they are unable to tell us what to teach, or how to teach it.

There is another reason, or perhaps set of reasons, for this confusion of goals. The social sciences, unlike the physical and natural sciences, deal directly with the stuff of human society. And it is here, close to where we live, that controversy is most likely to occur and emotions become involved.

It is one thing for a group of distinguished physicists to get together and debate whether or not quantum theory should be included in the high school curriculum. It is quite another thing for a group of distinguished economists to try to hammer out a common view of how the American economic system shall be understood and taught in the schools. And even that example doesn't really describe the case, for often the parties to the debate about social studies curriculum are far from being distinguished economists or even very well informed citizens. We are all too familiar with the efforts of various pressure groups, special interests, and representatives of the lunatic fringe to influence what shall be and what shall not be taught in the schools. And from one point of view, who has a better right? They are talking about what is taught to their own children, they cherish strong convictions about what's right and what's wrong, and they pay taxes. The irate father in the principal's office protesting that his son is being brainwashed into a socialist (or a reactionary, or an organization man, or whatever) may be wrong and irrational, but he is responding to the quite accurate perception that the social studies curriculum does *matter*—that what kids learn in school about the subjects of social science inquiry directly affects, for good or ill, the kind of people they will be.

Incidentally, it seems to me that a real irony exists here. The natural and physical sciences, whose model of large scale curriculum reform and improvement in the last decade is such a challenge to us, these very disciplines which were once sometimes called "the precise sciences" have long since found that they can get along very well without certainty, and have invented a whole theory of probability to help them do it. Yet we in the social sciences, who deal with the obscurity and elusiveness of human nature and human relationships, seem to be reluctant to commit ourselves to any curriculum change unless certainty is guaranteed in advance. Two conflicting and mutually contradictory theories about the nature of light have been abroad in the scientific world for years. Their very existence has made the study of physics more challenging to students, and helped new generations of scientists to sharpen their minds and direct their curiosity. And nobody has marched on the school board about it.

This was not always the case. One need only remember the precautions of Galileo or Copernicus, or in modern times the famous Scopes trial in twentieth-century America, to recognize that dispassionate dedication to the truth has been a hard-won prize of the natural sciences. Perhaps it is a sign of scientific maturity, which the social sciences may reasonably anticipate in time. But I suspect that the social sciences will always find themselves in the position of denying the "common sense" notions of many people, and of undermining the usually oversimplified views of man and society which are often the "sacred" dogmas of some organized group. The social sciences may, hopefully, find better ways to live with this source of conflict, and increasingly be able to play the role of constructive and insightful analyst in the processes of social change.

Meanwhile, we must take the social sciences as they are, and somehow bridge the gap between them and the social studies in the classroom. Not to do so, to try instead to ignore the scholarly ferment with all its riches, would be, I think, an ignoble retreat and a betrayal of our calling. How to do so, how to undertake the vast revitalizing and reforming of the social studies curriculum, is the task toward which I would like to make a tentative suggestion here.

But before venturing even a modest proposal for an approach to change in the social studies, let us first look briefly at educational change in a broader context. For while, as I have indicated, the social studies have some important problems which are unique to them, at the same time they share with the educational enterprise in general a number of characteristics which help to explain why needed changes come with such agonizing slowness.

Our society might have been designed deliberately to insure that the will of the people shall be expressed—*but not too fast*. Right from the Constitution on down through all the informal structures of society is found this emphasis upon pluralism, upon a dispersion of power and control upon the guarantee that all voices shall be heard but none shall dominate, so that when society moves and changes, it always does so slowly and on the base of a general consensus. This has always been irritating to reformers. It is frustrating to those blessed with a clear vision of how things ought to be that the rest of the country doesn't listen to them breathlessly, ready at a moment's notice to alter its values and attitudes and revise its organizational structures. But it is, of course, this same pluralism, this same openness and lack of centralized control, that permits the apostles of change, reform, and progress to function at all, that guarantees them a platform and a hearing. And, more often than not, the reformers' proposals will be given a try, although not as quickly or as wholeheartedly as they would like. Our pattern, then, is one of continuous but seldom radical change and progress.

Our educational organization has followed this pattern very closely. Widely dispersed power, lack of strong central authority, responsiveness to variations in ideological, social, and political outlook—our schools are the mirror of our society in these respects, at least. As Dr. James Conant says, "The schools are the object of a power struggle among groups advocating competing views of the good society. Much of the history of American education is a record of this struggle."[1]

But precisely because the society itself is diffuse and decentralized, and the schools are too, this struggle usually lacks decisive battles and clear-cut issues. As in the society as a whole, change does take place, but the thrust of particular efforts by specific groups is blunted, and a balance of forces, always shifting but always present, is uneasily maintained.

The particular forms and mechanism through which this process of educational change seeks expression are familiar. There are the forces of tradition such as the conservative schools of education, voluntary associations, and textbook publishers, striving by maintaining the status quo to protect their interests as they see them; and the school boards seeking to keep everybody happy at once. But there are also voices of reform—the special interest groups pressuring for this or that revision; and, more recently, the university scholars and foundation-backed projects subsidizing intensive research and development in their pet areas. As an only slightly exaggerated account of this process, let me quote the following:

> Consider the way by which a new study is introduced into the curriculum. Someone feels that the school system of his (or quite frequently nowadays *her*) town if falling behind the times. There are rumors of great progress in education being made elsewhere. Something new and important has been introduced; education is being revolutionized by it; the superintendent and board become somewhat uneasy; the matter is taken up by individuals and clubs; pressure is brought to bear on the school system; letters are written to the newspapers . . . editorials appear; finally the school board ordains that on and after a certain date the particular new branch . . . shall be taught in the public schools. The victory is won, and everybody—unless it be some already over-burdened and distracted teacher—congratulates everybody else that such advanced steps are taken.

That was from a speech by John Dewey to the National Education Association in 1901.[2] It serves to remind us of another and important ingredient in the process of educational change—the teacher. Some of the most interesting and brilliant innovations in education have come to nothing because their originators overlooked the fact that teachers must learn, too. The level and the content of teacher education is one of the strongest brakes upon radical and sweeping reform in curriculum. Even if the teacher-training institutions went at it with a will, the problem of major change in teacher education is a very large one. For those who have already finished their education and entered the profession, the problem of retraining looms even larger. How many summer institutes can one person attend?

So the record would seem to indicate that educational change does take place, but that it seldom moves far ahead of public attitudes and that teacher competence and availability of materials are further inhibiting factors.

In the light of this rather gloomy picture of educational change in general and the conditions in the social studies in particular, what can be done? The key to a hopeful approach to this problem is to be found, I believe, in the very pluralism and openness which is also one of its causes. For if this freedom and diversity make it harder to get big changes, they also make it easier to get small ones. If it prevents us from agreeing on nation-wide goals for the social studies, it also permits us to adopt whatever goals we believe in in our own department, school, or district. If it hampers large scale national programs supported by millions of foundation dollars, it also creates the climate in which we, with our American commitment to freedom and the right to disagree, can try our own experiments on a small scale.

What I want to propose is that curriculum developers and school administrators quit expecting some *one* right way to revise the high school social studies to come out of the blue, and get underway with whatever modest experimental projects they are able to devise. My guess is that it's an unusual high school without at least one teacher on its staff who would welcome a chance to work out a new unit, a new approach, or a new course. Naturally, not many of them have the competence to do this alone. But again, its my guess that it's a rare college or university without a competent historian, geographer, or other social scientist who could be interested in the high school's problem if approached. If, instead of assembling bodies of scholars and teachers to argue about goals, we put together small working teams of teachers and social scientists, aided by educators and psychologists where necessary, to work closely together on developing new materials and methods, we would accomplish two crucial steps. First, we would produce some actual new material for use in classrooms; and second, we would gain some invaluable experience in the over-all problem of the best way to handle the social sciences in the schools. A few months of close association with a university scholar will result in real learning by the social science teacher, and a few months of struggling along with competent teachers, to translate the social sciences into high school classrooms will be most instructive for the scholars. Of course, this costs money, even on a small scale. The time of university scholars can't be had for nothing, and Mr. Dewey's over-burdened teacher is still very much with us. I believe that in the future, our school systems must recognize research and development as a vital part of their operation, just as successful scientific and business enterprises do, and be willing to invest a reasonable percentage of their budgets in it. I would like to see a school board plan to set aside the salaries of several teachers every year to free part of their time for just such projects as I have suggested. And I would like to see colleges and universities accept *their* responsibility to make the training and expertise of their faculties available to the schools. Until this time comes (and, incidentally, it will come sooner if school administrators argue for it) we must look to the foundations, public and private. The North Central Association has advanced a proposal for the support of just such projects as these, in which working teams of teachers and scholars would be compensated for their time, and provided with administrative and logistical support. We hope it will be funded, and that the Association will be in a position to assist school people who are willing to take action.

To summarize, the problems posed for educational change, and especially reform in the social studies, arise largely from the decentralized educational organization in a pluralistic society where responsibility for decisions is broadly dispersed. This very source can also be our greatest advantage if, instead of bogging down in the futile attempt to agree on over-all goals and philosophies, we put together small working projects composed of teachers and scholars who use their freedom to create new approaches and materials to fulfill *their* goals. From this effort, in time will come the consensus needed for long-range general change.

This approach would embody the values of American education at their best—experimental, flexible, and responsive to local control. Above all, it would enable us to get started.

References

[1] James B. Conant. *The Education of American Teachers.* New York: McGraw-Hill Book Company, 1963.
[2] N.E.A. *Proceedings,* 1901, p. 334-35.

STRUCTURE IN THE SOCIAL SCIENCES AND IMPLICATIONS FOR THE SOCIAL STUDIES PROGRAM

Arno Bellack
Teachers College, Columbia

During the current period of educational reform, most of the debate hinges upon two old and familiar problems: What is knowledge? How should it be studied and taught?

At different times in the history of our schools, widely different answers have been given to these questions. The traditionalists, for example, taught the time-honored subjects as anthologies of separate topics, with the hope that the bits and pieces of information would somehow or other turn out to be useful. History became a recital of "one damned thing after another" (the phrase is Toynbee's); civics turned out to be a collection of miscellaneous information about government; and geography was nothing more than a catalogue of facts about places scattered over the globe.

Convinced that this kind of teaching would not prepare students to face the increasingly complex problems of their society, the progressive reformers of the 1930's and 1940's proposed a new curriculum, one centered on the personal and social problems of youth and drawing on the academic disciplines as they became relevant to the problems under study. The disciplines were viewed as reservoirs from which facts and ideas could be drawn as needed; emphasis was on the *practical* ordering of knowledge with reference to problems to be solved.

A widely held contemporary approach to curriculum-building places emphasis on the *logical* order inherent in knowledge itself, on the structures of concepts and principles that characterize the various disciplines. An articulate spokesman for this point of view is Professor Jerome Bruner of Harvard, who is largely responsible for introducing the concept of structure into educational discourse. "Knowledge," he writes, "is a model we construct to give meaning and structure to regularities in experience. The organizing ideas of any body of knowledge are inventions for rendering experience economical and connected. We invent concepts such as force in physics, the bond in chemistry, motives in psychology, style in literature as means to the

Reprinted with permission of the author and the publisher, from G. Wesley Sewards, ed., *The Social Studies: Curriculum Proposals for the Future* (Chicago: Scott, Foresman and Company, 1963), pp. 95-118.

end of comprehension. . . . The power of great organizing concepts is in large part that they permit us to understand and sometimes to predict or change the world in which we live. But their power lies also in the fact that ideas provide instruments for experience." Therefore, he contends, "the structure to knowledge—its connectedness and its derivations that make one idea follow another—is the proper emphasis in education. For it is structure, the great conceptual inventions that bring order to the congeries of disconnected observations, that gives meaning to what we may learn and makes possible the opening up of new realms of experience."[1]

Bruner proposes that the structure of ideas and generalizations of the various disciplines serve as the basis for instruction at all levels of schooling beginning with the elementary grades. The hypothesis is that "any subject can be taught effectively in some intellectually honest form to any child at any stage of development."[2] Evidence for this hypothesis is to be found in the research of Piaget and other psychologists on the intellectual development of children. The results of this research suggest that "at each stage of development the child has a characteristic way of viewing the world and explaining it to himself. The task of teaching a subject to a child at any particular age is one of representing the structure of that subject in terms of the child's way of viewing things."[3]

Within the past few years this approach to curriculum building has captured the imagination of both educators and laymen. Although this view has found application principally in the teaching of mathematics and science, projects are under way in other fields, including the social studies. My purpose is to discuss those developments in social studies programs for elementary and secondary schools which place special emphasis on the structure of the social sciences. The discussion will be in three parts: first, an analysis of the concept of structure as it applies to the social sciences; second, a description of contrasting curriculum proposals based on the structure of the social sciences; third, a discussion of certain issues and problems related to these proposals.

THE STRUCTURE OF THE SOCIAL SCIENCES

The objective of the social sciences is to describe and explain the social and cultural behavior of man, just as the aim of the natural sciences is to describe and explain physical and biological phenomena. We shall consider the structural characteristics of the natural and social sciences, and then distinctive features of the social sciences.

The Structure of the Natural and Social Sciences

Dr. James B. Conant, who is uncommonly articulate in portraying the nature of science in terms that even laymen can comprehend, characterizes science as "a process of fabricating a web of inter-related concepts and conceptual schemes arising from experiments and observations and fruitful of further experiments and observations."[4] Scientists have developed concepts such as power in political science, energy in physics, homeostasis in biology, scarcity in economics, and social class in sociology; and in terms of these concepts they frame their questions, their hypotheses, and their conclusions. Each of these concepts takes its meaning and significance in large measure from its relationships to other concepts. In economics, for example, the concept of price gains greater meaning when seen in relation to the concept of the market. In all the sciences there is a continuing attempt to establish significant patterns and relationships among the concepts in their respective fields. The organization of a science can thus be viewed as a system of related concepts and conceptual schemes, ranging from the vaguely connected to the highly systematized, that are used by researchers to guide and control inquiry.

Within such a system there is a hierarchy of ideas, some more fundamental than others. The more fundamental ideas are those that have greater explanatory power; that is, they are distinguished by their power to explain a number of more particular ideas. Anyone who has studied high-school science knows, for example, that the molecular theory of matter is more fundamental in this sense than Boyle's law, inasmuch as the molecular theory provides an explanation for Boyle's law. In all the sciences there are similar key ideas and theories that characterize a field and are fundamental to its understanding. Because these ideas are fundamental, they serve as an effective means for introducing students to the various fields of knowledge.[5]

Curriculum planning must take into account the fact that conceptual schemes do not remain stable over time, but are modified as they are tested in the course of inquiry. Frequently they are replaced by more fruitful concepts and concepts of greater scope. This process accounts for the rapid change in knowledge in many fields; extensive reorganization of a given body of scientific knowledge can be expected not once in the coming century but several times, at intervals of five to fifteen years.[6]

A second component of the structure of a scientific field is represented by its procedures and methods—the way it goes about using its conceptions to attain its goals. Probably the most significant aspect of a discipline's methodology is the logical process employed in evaluating the outcomes of inquiry, that is, the way in which a field certifies the truth of its findings. Methods of verification vary from field to field: a valid reason for believing that two lines perpendicular to the same line are parallel to each other is logically different from a valid reason for believing that litmus paper turning blue in an aqueous solution is an indication of alkalinity. The first involves abstract geometrical relationships; the second, interpretation of an empirical experiment. If, as Professor Joseph Schwab suggested at the Disciplines Seminar convened by the National Education Association's Project on Instruction, the results of inquiry "should be taught and learned not as a rhetoric of conclusions but according to the extent and the sense in which they are true,"[7] then students will have to come to understand the logical processes by which the results of inquiry are verified.

This brief survey reveals that the structure of scientific field includes two dimensions—the *conceptual* and the *methodological*—and both must obviously be taken into account in curriculum planning.

One additional comment before we move on to discuss distinctive characteristics of the social sciences: most disciplines have several structures, not one. Continuing discussion concerning fundamental concepts and methods in most fields is evidence of a plurality of structures. This is particularly true of the social sciences, as we shall see shortly. Many of these variations arise because researchers in these fields have conceived of many different questions to ask of their subject matter and each question gives rise to different patterns of experiment, different data, and different ways of interpreting data. This suggests that in most disciplines it is possible to structure the curriculum in more than one way. The Biological Sciences Curriculum Study, for example, organized three approaches to teaching biology, in each of which the biological world is examined from a different vantage point.

Distinctive Features of Social Sciences

What has been said thus far about the structure of the sciences applies in general to the social sciences as well as the natural sciences. There are, however, certain distinctive features of the social sciences that deserve attention, for they have a bearing on curriculum planning and organization.

The social sciences today are characterized by a plurality of methods and conceptual schemes developed by sociologists, anthropologists, historians, social psychologists, political scientists, geographers, and economists to deal with problems within their individual spheres. Instead of a unity of method or a single universe of discourse, we are confronted with a vast confederation of separate areas of study. Modes of thinking and analysis differ from field to field and even from problem to problem within the same field. In time, a Bacon of the sciences that bear on social and cultural behavior may emerge, but that time is not yet.

To be sure, the social disciplines are all seeking explanations of the same phenomenon—man's social life; that is what makes it reasonable to group them together as the *social* sciences. All of them have grown out of man's attempt to interpret, understand, and control the social environment. But each field formulates its own questions about this subject matter and develops its own system of concepts to guide its research. Each science is abstract, dealing with the only certain facets of actual social relationships and institutions.

Man's social life as it is actually lived is, therefore, far more complex than the limited image of it reflected in the generalizations of any one of the social disciplines. It follows then, as Professor Kingsley Davis has suggested, that "in so far as the prediction of actual events is concerned, the various social sciences are mutually interdependent, because only by combining their various points of view can anything approaching a complete anticipation of future occurrences be achieved."[8] Policies that are proposed and actions that are taken to deal with problems in social affairs are of necessity interdisciplinary, for concrete social reality is not mirrored in the findings of any one discipline.

Now this is a matter of central importance to those whose job it is to plan and organize the social studies curriculum. To focus exclusive attention on one or two aspects of the social world as seen through the eyes of one or two of the social sciences is to give students a myopic vision of man's social behavior and his institutions. For anything approaching a comprehensive view of man's functioning in society, the specialized perspectives of all the social sciences are needed. Curriculum builders in the social studies have the enormously difficult job of providing a place in their programs for all the social sciences, each of which contributes its distinctive perspective on human institutions and human behavior.

When one examines the individual social disciplines, one finds great internal diversity. Increasing specialization during recent years has resulted in restructuring the boundaries of the various fields. Anthropology, for example, was at one time regarded as *the* science of man. It has since subdivided into several specialties: physical anthropology, social and cultural anthropology, archaeology and linguistics; and within each of these in turn even more specialized areas of inquiry have evolved. Or consider the situation in political science. Dr. Evron Kirpatrick,[9] executive director of the American Political Science Association, has identified five major specialities, in addition to political philosophy, in which political scientists work: comparative government, constitutional law, international politics, American government, and public administration. Approaches and methods appear to be equally diverse, for he lists five major methods followed by political scientists: historical, analytical, prescriptive, descriptive, and a relatively recently developed method, the "political behavior approach," which draws heavily on sociology and social psychology. And when it comes to the field of history, it is impossible in anything less than an essay of substantial length to identify the variety of viewpoints held by historians and philosophers of history regarding the nature of historical studies.

As a further complication, the various social sciences, in spite of increasing specialization and internal differentiation, borrow rather handily from one another when it comes to both concepts and methods. Historians, for example, make use of concepts from all the other social sciences. Political scientists interested in political socialization get their methods from behavioral scientists and seem in many respects more closely related to sociologists and social psychologists than to fellow political scientists. Certain anthropologists have utilized the Freudian view of human development in analyzing patterns of various cultures. Geographers make extensive use of the perspectives of history and concepts developed by the behavioral sciences.

Furthermore, we find not only interchange of concepts and methods but growing collaboration among specialists. For example, studies of the nature and function of *authority* are now undertaken jointly by political scientists and sociologists, and there have been recent studies conducted by economists in collaboration with anthropologists to determine whether certain economic theories hold for different types of economic systems. The convergence of social scientists upon the same problems has given rise to what Professor Robert Merton calls "interdisciplines,"[10] such as social biology, political sociology, and sociological history.

The picture that emerges from this cursory review of the current state of affairs in the social sciences is one of great diversity. Given this mosaic of disciplines and interdisciplines, each characterized by multiple conceptual schemes and methods, how shall the curriculum builder approach the problem of developing structures for teaching that avoid undue fragmentation of knowledge and that match growing complexity of ideas with growing intellectual powers of students? To this question we now turn.

CURRICULUM PROPOSALS

The basic curriculum problem is twofold: first, what concepts and methods in the social sciences are so important that they should be included in the curriculum for all students? What ideas will help them to create meaning and order out of the complex world in which they find themselves? Second, how can these ideas be organized into a program of instruction so that at successive levels students will be provided with repeated opportunities to deal with them, each time at a higher level of understanding?

We have observed that contemporary psychology makes much of the fact that ideas can be learned at all stages of mental growth, provided they are translated into form and language appropriate for the student at his level of mental maturity. How to match the intellectual level of students with the growing complexity of ideas is a problem that cannot be solved in the abstract; it is rather an empirical question and one of the central problems for curriculum research and experimentation.

But before experimentation can get under way, a decision must be made regarding the ideas that are to be taught. Currently, this problem is approached in two ways by those who are committed to the structural approach to teaching the social studies. The first approach organizes the program around broad conceptions and generalizations representing a synthesis of ideas from the various social sciences; the second approach organizes the program around the conceptual schemes of the individual social disciplines. Specific examples of these two viewpoints will reveal their similarities and differences.

Unified Social Science Approach

The first approach is illustrated by a curriculum project carried on under the auspices of the American Council of Learned Societies and Educational Services Incorporated.[11] The purpose of this project is to develop a design for teaching the social studies in elementary and secondary schools. The group is headed by Dr. Elting Morison, professor of history at M.I.T., and includes Professor Jerome Bruner, the Harvard psychologist; Professor George Homans, the Harvard sociologist; Professor Franklin Patterson of Tufts; Professor Edwin Fenton of Carnegie Tech.; as well as several other educators and social scientists.

This group's basic concern is "to have students begin to learn a science," and since the heart of a science is its structure of generalizations, the first step in developing their proposal was to build a structure of ideas drawn from the social sciences. The value of such a structure, they contend, is that "it simplifies a welter of facts by showing how a variety of different facts can be explained by a limited number of generalizations, and how the latter can generate predictions of new facts." They justify teaching the social sciences as a single subject on these grounds: "History, sociology, anthropology, economics, and political science may for convenience be separated as academic disciplines but they all deal with a single thing: the behavior of men in society. Accordingly we propose to teach them jointly, not separately."

The following two examples give some notion of the nature of the twenty-four generalizations included in the structure the group has developed:

1. The members of a society develop rules (institutions) by conforming to which they collaborate to obtain rewards, both instinctual rewards, like sex, and those they have acquired by conditioning. The whole, made up by these rules, is called a culture.
2. All societies have developed in different degrees of elaboration special institutions for ensuring conformity to other institutions (law) or for changing institutions. These we shall broadly call political institutions. All ultimately use the threat of force to try to ensure that conformity to institutions shall be rewarding.

These generalizations are to be taught not in the abstract but through the study of concrete subject matter, organized in several ways. What the group proposes is a developmental sequence of topics from the elementary grades through the junior high school, historically ordered in that they will follow a sequence of social development.

Separate Disciplines Approach

The second approach is illustrated by the program under way in the Elkhart, Indiana, public-school system, directed by Professor Lawrence Senesh of Purdue University.[12] This twelve-year experimental program, now in its fourth year, is designed to teach economics at all grade levels, from the first to the twelfth grade. "The experiment," according to Professor Senesh, "rests on the hypothesis that children on every grade level, with proper motivation, can become excited about the abstract ideas underlying their experiences, and that these ideas can be presented in such a way as to reflect the basic structure of the body of economic knowledge."

Professor Senesh has outlined what he calls "the basic contours of the economics world" to serve as a framework within the program as planned at all grade levels:

1. All people and all nations are confronted with the conflict between their unlimited wants and limited resources. The degree of the conflict may vary, but the conflict is always present.
2. From the beginning, men have tried new ways and means to lessen the gap between unlimited wants and limited resources. Their efforts to invent new machines and improve production processes are evidence of the desire to produce more, better, and faster.
3. In all countries the basic questions to be answered are: What goods and services will be produced; how much of these will be produced; how will they be produced—that is, with more men or more machines or more raw materials; and who will receive the goods and services?
4. In the United States what and how much will be produced, how it will be produced, and for whom are largely determined by the free choices of the American people, either as consumers or participants in the production process.
5. Through their political process the American people sometimes limit their individual choices in order to increase the general welfare.

The basic network of ideas on which economics as a discipline rests is incorporated in the social studies curriculum at all grade levels within this framework, beginning with the first grade. As the students move from grade to grade, they will encounter the same ideas again and again, but will always relate them to their more mature experiences, thus adding depth and complexity to the basic relationships. In the elementary grades students may discover these relationships when studying units on "My Home," "My Neighborhood," or "My School"; in high school, when studying courses in problems of democracy, history or economics.

ANALYSIS OF CURRICULUM PROPOSALS

Let us now consider three issues related to these contrasting approaches to structuring the social studies curriculum.

Social Sciences in Elementary Grades

The first issue grows out of the view shared by proponents of both approaches, that the structure of the social sciences should serve as the basis of instruction from the first grade in the elementary school through the high-school years. This is in harmony with one of the cardinal tenets of the contemporary approach to curriculum building, namely, that any subject *can* be taught effectively in some intellectually honest form to students at all stages of development. For some, however, it is difficult to accept the suggestion that the basic ideas of the social sciences *should* be taught beginning in the earliest grades. Is the elementary school child ready for these ideas? Shouldn't the study of sociology, political science, and economics be postponed until students are more mature?

The fact of the matter is that children of elementary school age *are* forming ideas about social institutions and human behavior as it is molded by these institutions. Call to mind Celia Stendler's study, *Children of Brasstown*,[13] in which she studied children's awareness of symbols of social class at different grade levels in elementary school. She found that although first-graders showed no awareness of symbols of social class, by the fourth grade students recognized some of the symbols of social class, particularly the ones with which they had first-hand experience. By the sixth grade the children she studied revealed their awareness of social class symbols in many ways; for example, they rated the class position of their schoolmates on the basis of home and family, occupation of father, clothes, and manners.

Or consider the studies of political socialization by Professors Easton and Hess[14] of the University of Chicago. They report that children begin to learn about government and politics even before they enter school. The formative years in political understanding appear to be the years between the ages of three and thirteen, and by the time children leave the eighth grade, their political attitudes and values are fairly well established.

We need to know a good deal more than we now know about children's conceptions of the social, economic, and political aspects of their world. Only when we are equipped with such knowledge will we be in a position to know how the child will translate into his own patterns of thought what we present to him at various stages in the school program. But what evidence there is from studies such as those just cited suggests that already in the elementary grades students, on their own, begin to develop ideas and attitudes about social and cultural affairs.

The objective of teaching the social sciences in all the grades is to expose the folk wisdom and common sense that students absorb, through participation in the culture, to the light of analysis and empirical inquiry, always at *their* level of mental development and in terms of *their* way of viewing the world. How to match the intellectual level of students with growing complexity of ideas is, as has already been suggested, one of the central problems for curriculum research and experimentation.

Balance in the Program

The second problem has to do with ways of achieving balance in the social studies curriculum. As noted earlier, man's social life is always more complex than the limited model of it reflected in the findings of any one of the social sciences. If students are to achieve a balanced view of human affairs, the program will have to be organized in such fashion that all the social sciences can contribute their distinctive perspectives.

The unified approach attempts to do this by organizing a structure of related concepts and generalizations synthesized from all, or a number, of the social sciences. This is not a startling innovation in curriculum development; many and varied have been the plans proposed in the past for a unified approach to the teaching of the social studies. Even though it is not a new idea, the proposal of the group sponsored by the American Council of Learned Societies and Educational Services Incorporated strikes me as a breath of fresh air in the stifling climate that has developed recently in some educational circles in which any curricular organization other than that provided by the individual discipline is rejected out of hand. My purpose here is not to urge this approach as the solution to the problem of building a structure of ideas for the social studies curriculum, but rather to suggest that it does represent one way of approaching the problem. I know of no established pedagogical principle that would lead one to reject this approach as one way of organizing ideas for teaching. Only systematic evaluation of the outcomes of programs based on this approach can provide evidence on the basis of which to make a judgment of its worth.

It would seem important to keep two things in mind when attempting to develop a synthesis of ideas from several fields. First, the job should be undertaken only by competent scholars representing the various disciplines involved, for integrating different disciplines is itself a disciplined activity. Second, it is essential that ideas included in a structure that is based on more than one field be related logically to each other to form a system of ideas and not merely a listing of concepts or generalizations, for relationships among ideas is at the heart of the notion of structure. Ideas in a structure based on several fields logically related, not in the sense that they form a theoretical framework for social science research, but rather in the more informal sense that they form a system of ideas coherently and consistently organized for social studies teaching.

Proponents of the approach that focuses attention on the individual disciplines assume that students will be able to achieve a balanced view of man's cultural and social life through the study of the separate fields. Task forces of economists, geographers, sociologists, and anthropologists have already made proposals, or are in the process of doing so, for teaching the structure of their individual disciplines. Work on these projects has proceeded with little or no relationship to each other and, to my knowledge, no one has come forward with even a tentative curriculum design within which the individual fields might find their place. To be sure, economists suggest ways in which economic ideas can be taught in history; and anthropologists show how some of their generalizations can be woven into courses in geography. This is all to the good; it even seems to suggest that integration of a limited variety might be appropriate for teaching purposes.

One might argue that it is premature to attempt the development of a framework for the social studies program at this time. Given the diversity within each discipline, there are those who contend that a necessary first step is to have each of the fields integrate its constituent subspecialities into a structure or alternative structures for teaching, and only after this has been done should the problem of building an overall design be tackled. It might be that alternative designs will emerge as experimentation proceeds in the individual fields. Indeed, this seems to be what is happening in the Elkhart project headed by Professor Senesh, for plans now call for the inclusion of sociology and political science.

In addition to collaborative efforts that develop as work proceeds in the individual fields, it might be helpful if direct attention were given to some of the problems of curriculum organization inherent in the individual disciplines approach: Which of the social sciences should be included in the program for all students— all of the basic fields (economics, geography, sociology, history, social psychology, anthropology, and political science)? If not all of them, then which ones, and on what basis should they be selected? Furthermore, since whatever disciplines included in the program obviously cannot be taught every semester or at the same time during the semester, in what cyclical pattern should they be introduced into the curriculum?

Another group of questions has to do with the relationships of social sciences to one another and to problems in the world of human affairs. These problems do not come neatly labeled "historical," "economic," or "political"; they come as decisions to be made and force us to call upon all we know and make us wish we knew more. How can students be helped to see the limitations as well as the uses of a single discipline in interpreting events as they actually occur? How can the perspectives of all relevant fields be brought to bear in dealing with problems that cross the boundaries of individual disciplines? Consideration of questions such as these will bring to light problems that can be adequately dealt with only within the framework of the social studies program as a whole, and not within the context of a single discipline.

Criteria are not at hand to permit unequivocal judgment regarding the relative merits of the two approaches in providing a balanced program. Indeed, they might very well be viewed as complementary; for certain facets of the program and for certain levels of schooling, one or the other might be more suitable. My own inclination is to stress the importance of having young children achieve some intuitive sense of the wholeness of social living out of which will grow the more specialized conceptions of the separate disciplines. This would suggest organizing the program in the early grades around broad conceptions developed through a synthesis of ideas from a variety of fields and in the later grades around the conceptual schemes of the disciplines. Dewey's notion of "progressive organization of subject matter,"[15] long ignored by most of his interpreters, might well serve as a guiding hypothesis in building such a program.

The Role of Values in Social Studies Teaching

The approaches under discussion emphasize the importance of introducing students to the ways of thinking represented by the disciplines in such a way that they in fact become economists, historians, and political scientists. Since economists as economists and sociologists as sociologists are concerned with the description and explanation of events and not with the evaluation of them, do values have no place in the social studies classroom?

Both of the proposals answer this question in the negative. The committee sponsored by Educational Services Incorporated recognizes the necessity for nonevaluation in scientific inquiry. However they also point out that teachers and students, as citizens, are committed to certain ideas about what is good and share certain convictions about the type of society in which these values may be realized. Similarly, Professor Senesh holds that economic education need not exclude values from the classroom, since the success of our economic system is measured by the extent to which it fulfills our social values.

It is clear that social scientists as social scientists are in no position to prescribe courses of action regarding the host of policy issues we face in public affairs. But each of the social disciplines does provide us with a body of theory that is essential in examining the probable consequences of alternative public policies, and a good many of these analytical tools ought to become part of the intellectual equipment of all students.

Economists, for example, are able to tell us what the probable consequences will be if the supply of money is increased or if the interest rates are
lowered, though they cannot as economists tell us whether or not we ought
to take either of these two courses of action. Decision regarding these
alternative courses of action involves technical economic analysis *and* weighing of values. It is therefore clear that both values and economic analysis
come into play in deciding courses of action in economic affairs, and both
should find their place in social studies teaching. Whereas technical economic
analysis involves the empirical mode of thinking (that is, it is concerned with
matters of fact and theory), considering alternative values involves the evaluative mode of thinking (that is, it is concerned with criteria of what is desirable
or undesirable). The teacher's job is to help students learn to make these
necessary distinctions, so that they recognize when questions of fact and
analysis are under consideration and when questions of value are at stake.

This distinction between social analysis and valuing obviously holds for
instruction in fields other than economics, which I have used here for purposes of illustration. If we wish to give the social sciences a vital place in the
school curriculum, the indispensable condition is to make this distinction
between fact and value.

The difficulties in developing a social studies program for the schools, let it
be recognized, are overwhelming. The greatest difficulty is that the job
involves the collaboration of specialists—specialists in the social sciences, in
psychology, and in teaching. One characteristic shared by all specialists is the
tendency to view their individual bailiwicks as the center of the universe.
Only as specialists from these three camps develop commitment to a new
center of professional interest—the curriculum of the school—will the social
studies curriculum reflect the best in scholarship, in learning, and in teaching.

References

[1] Jerome Bruner, *On Knowing* (Cambridge: Harvard University Press, 1962), p. 120.

[2] Jerome Bruner, *The Process of Education* (Cambridge: Harvard University Press, 1960),
p. 33.

[3] *Ibid.*, p. 33.

[4] James B. Conant, *Modern Science and Modern Man* (Garden City, New York:
Doubleday Anchor Books, 1953), pp. 106-107. See also Ernest Nagel, *The Structure of
Science* (New York: Harcourt, Brace & World, Inc., 1961).

[5] Philip Phenix, "Key Concepts and the Crisis in Learning," *Teachers College Record*,
Vol. 58, No. 3, December 1956, pp. 137-143.

[6] Joseph Schwab, "The Concept of the Structure of a Discipline," *Educational Record*,
Vol. 43, No. 3, July 1962, p. 200.

[7]Joseph Schwab, *The Scholars Look at the Schools* (Washington, D.C.: National Education Association, 1962), p. 4.

[8]Kingsley Davis, *Human Society* (New York: The Macmillan Co., 1948), p. 8.

[9]Evron Kirpatrick and Jeane J. Kirpatrick, "Political Science," in *High School Social Studies Perspectives* (Boston: Houghton Mifflin Co., 1962).

[10]Robert K. Merton, "The Mosaic of the Behavioral Sciences," in *The Behavioral Sciences Today,* ed. Bernard Berelsen (New York: Basic Books, Inc., 1963), p. 253.

[11]Information and quotations of this section are from "A Preliminary and Tentative Outline of a Program of Curriculum Development in the Social Studies and Humanities," by The American Council of Learned Societies and Educational Services, Incorporated, February 15, 1963. Unpublished. Quoted by permission.

[12]Information and quotations in this section are from Lawrence Senesh, "The Organic Curriculum: A New Experiment in Economic Education," *The Councilor,* Vol. 21, No. 1, March 1960, pp. 43-56.

[13]Celia Stendler, *Children of Brasstown* (Urbana, Ill.: Bureau of Research and Service of the College of Education, University of Illinois, 1949).

[14]David Easton and Robert Hess, "The Child's Political World," *Midwest Journal of Political Science,* Vol. 6, No. 3 (August, 1963), pp. 229-246.

[15]John Dewey, *Experience and Education* (New York: The Macmillan Co., 1938), Chapter VII, "Progressive Organization of Subject-Matter,"

QUESTIONING THE PLACE OF
SOCIAL SCIENCE DISCIPLINES IN EDUCATION

Fred M. Newmann
University of Wisconsin

Implicit in recent social studies curriculum efforts is the mandate or recommendation: "Social studies instruction should be based on the structure of academic disciplines as the social (behavioral) sciences." Such a mandate raises serious problems in at least three areas: A) *Definition*—It is difficult to define "disciplined" thought in a way that clearly sets it apart from nondisciplined or other forms of inquiry. B) *Selection*—Assuming that one might adequately define the concept of disciplined inquiry, it is doubtful whether

Reprinted with permission of the publisher, from *Teachers College Record,* 69, no. 1 (October, 1967): 69-74. Presented to National Council of Social Studies Convention, November, 1966.

scholars can in fact reach consensus on the nature of the particular "structures" of social science disciplines. The resulting plurality of possible structures creates a problem of selection, but the general mandate above provides no criteria or guidance concerning which structures would be educationally most appropriate. C) *Justification*—Assuming that one could adequately define social science inquiry, identify alternative structures, and also establish criteria for the selection of particular structures, we are still left with the question: "Why teach the social sciences at all?" The goals or values that social science instruction is presumed to advance have not been adequately explicated, scrutinized or justified by educational planners. As we deal with each of these general problems, it should become clear that much of the present critique is not necessarily generic to social sciences but applies to other disciplines as well.

PROBLEMS OF DEFINITION

If we are to teach the structure of a discipline, we must know what we mean by "structure" and "discipline." Schwab[1] distinguishes between substantive structure (findings, conclusions, confirmed knowledge that a discipline provides) and syntactical structure (methodological procedures for investigation and testing of hypotheses, conventions that define what the discipline considers as "evidence".) Bruner[2] finds structure in *relationships* among "fundamental ideas" within a discipline (including presumably both substantive and syntatic ideas). The question arises, "What must be shown to hold true about a discipline before it is recognized as having a structure?" Must all of its findings be consistent? Must the key concepts relate to each other hierarchically from the most simple to the most complex, and must they be interdependent in a coherent logical system? Must investigators agree on the primary questions that the discipline seeks to investigate? To what extent must inquiry be pursued according to a standard methodology? Although structure may be more easily "visible" in natural sciences and mathematics, the search within social sciences resembles a quest for transcendental intellectual natural law: "Although we have not precisely defined the concept of structure, and although social scientists have not yet articulated the content of structures in their disciplines, nevertheless, disciplined inquiry is governed by structures that do exist in the abstract, awaiting our discovery."

If we are to teach disciplined thought, we must be able to discriminate between disciplined and non-disciplined thought. Phenix[3] proposes three general criteria for disciplined knowledge: analytic simplification (using key concepts that organize large amounts of seemingly random data), synthetic coordination (establishing patterns and relationships among variables), and dynamism (methods and attitudes that stimulate further inquiry and new questions). We might agree that disciplined social science consists of empirical inquiry aimed toward the making of more accurate predictions about human behavior. This involves creating concepts that help to simplify the perceptions of experience, observation procedures that guarantee objectivity, measurement and evaluation techniques that allow for quantitative statements, etc. Participants in the discipline share a common language; they constitute a social institution with agreed upon goals, positions of differing authority and status, procedures for training newcomers into the craft or profession. One way to challenge this apparently reasonable definition is to imagine a football team viewing films of themselves and of future opponents. The team attempts to map strategies for next week's contest. The coach and players analyze human behavior, trying to make predictions about it; they test hypotheses through empirical observation; they use a common language, have status differentials, a system for training novices to become experts. Although one intuitively feels that the football skull session should not be equated with a social science seminar, it is difficult to distinguish between them on the basis of the above defining criteria. What differentiates the thought process of the players from an economist making predictions about tax policy?

The definitional problem is further complicated when we notice several levels of "disciplined thinking": a) the scholar "doing the discipline," engaged in research, writing monographs, arguing with colleagues about findings and theories; b) the teacher of the discipline whose primary objective is to train novices to perform like the scholars; c) the student who confines himself to the kind of thinking that will help him learn to behave like the "doer" or "teacher" eventually. Are all of these people engaged in similar forms of disciplined thinking? Finally, we find d) the maverick of a discipline—the individual who concludes that his discipline is essentially asking the wrong questions. He, therefore, attempts to revise or even destroy the discipline as an intellectual institution. We have in mind here "seminal" or creative thinkers who cross discipline lines: Marx, Freud, Erikson, Tocqueville, Lippman, or McLuhan. To what extent does the creative interpretive leap, that escapes the confines of an established discipline, constitute "disciplined" thought? In making decisions about the structure of a discipline, it may be necessary to take into account various levels of thinking within the discipline and to clarify the level for which instruction is designed. One might argue, for example, that we should concentrate on training for the breakaway seminal thinker, rather than the meticulous plodding monograph researcher. If so, perhaps the most relevant discipline is synectics.[4]

PROBLEMS OF SELECTION

For the moment, let us assume that in spite of the issues raised above we can reach consensus on the meaning of structure and disciplined thought for social sciences. The next step is for scholars in each of the disciplines to articulate structures that guide their inquiry. This work has been pursued in several social studies curriculum projects, especially the Midwest Social Science Education Consortium, where scholars produce papers outlining structures for separate disciplines. Other projects, rather than focusing on individual disciplines, have tried to discover integrated general structures with elements common to most of the social sciences (e.g., Social Studies Curriculum Center at Syracuse). The most striking result of most of this work is the diversity of structures that emerge. As a simplified illustration, consider the field of political science yielding perhaps one structure primarily concerned with political philosophy, one with comparative legal-political systems; and one with behavioral analysis of voters and politicians. Controversy between the approaches of Leo Strauss and those of Harold Lasswell are instructive here. In the field of psychology, we find alternative structures in the psychoanalytic versus stimulus-response orientations. History has its Collingwoods and its Toynbees.

It seems that in the social sciences a given discipline reveals not one, but many structures. Moreover, the boundaries and structures of disciplines seem to be rapidly changing (witness "new" academic labels such as urban studies, linguistics, international relations). We must assume that it is physically impossible to teach all of the available social science structures. We must, therefore, choose to include some and reject others. What principles or values shall we use to make these decisions? Should disciplines be taught discretely or should they be integrated into an "interdisciplinary" structure for general education? The educator must make a choice between an interdisciplinary or a separate discipline approach, he must decide which disciplines, and finally, within a discipline, he must choose among alternative structures. Unfortunately, the simple mandate to use social science structure as the basis of curriculum brings us no guidance or direction as to *which* structures are appropriate, and which should be discarded. If the search for structure produces dozens of alternative "courses" in each of the social sciences, so much the better, for then teachers and students will have options. We must realize however, that principles for the selection of structures must be sought in the realm of educational philosophy, not in the impulse to teach science.

PROBLEMS OF JUSTIFICATION

Finally, we must ask: Why teach social sciences at all (assuming of course that we could define what they are and that we could find principles to select some structures over others)? Those who emphasize social science in formal education may justify their programs either a) on the ground that such instruction leads to socially desirable results or b) that regardless of the results, such inquiry is an important aspect of human nature. Consider each of these points.

A) The type of thinking characteristic of social science inquiry results in socially desirable consequences: for example, economic development, mental health, political stability, aesthetic enjoyment. The crux of this argument (sometimes described as "utilitarian") is that "disciplined" (social science) thought has given man greater control over his destiny, having uplifted the human condition from past stages of development considered lower or less desirable. There are several problems with this argument. First, it is difficult to identify the intellectual determinants of social "progress". To what extent is Western economic development the result of disciplined social science thought? It could be construed as end product of the dogged pursuit of self-interest by greedy entrepreneurs, untrained in disciplined thinking as we know it. Political achievements of Lyndon Johnson cannot be traced to his abilities in the discipline of political science. While some people can attain mental health only through treatment by those trained in psychology, millions of parents, through "common sense", raise children to have peace of mind. Second, even if we could show a connection between social science thought and environmental change, we must entertain the possibility that some of the changes are undesirable and destructive, rather than beneficial. Social psychology can be invoked to inspire riots, mass movements, deception in advertising; economics can be used to exploit; political science for domination, rather than self-government; the natural sciences produce hydrogen bombs as well as penicillin; history can perpetuate myths that becloud and distort rather than clarify the present. With "negative" results so conspicuous, one would be hard pressed to demonstrate that the net effect of disciplined social science has aided man's quest for the good life.

Third, and perhaps most perplexing for the utilitarian argument is the problem of defining what constitutes the good life, progress or social improvement. Utilitarians have not been able to recommend acceptable procedures or formulas for the assessment of pleasure and pain. The position of cultural relativism brazenly challenges most attempts to evaluate merits of different cultures, styles of life, levels of technological development. Whether the life of the noble savage was better or worse than the life of the organization man is a value question that doesn't necessarily have to be answered, *except* by those who make the claim that disciplined thought has brought us ways of life preferable to those in days of yore.[5] Having raised certain difficulties within the utilitarian argument, let us proceed to a somewhat different point.

B) Disciplined inquiry should be valued and taught, not for its positive or negative effects on civilization (which are difficult to establish), but because it is most uniquely human. This argument holds that man's intellectual attempts to comprehend himself and his environment in effect separate man from other animals. Man inevitably seeks intellectual understanding, and disciplined inquiry represents his most sophisticated efforts in this quest. This argument is weakened by two general objections. First let us accept the claim that disciplined thought represents a distinctive feature of human nature. In what way does that claim alone justify attempts to further cultivate and develop the trait? One might argue that intra-species aggression[6] is also distinctively human. Should we accentuate this characteristic or suppress it? Perhaps it is possible to *change* human nature, to make man more of an unquestioning robot, or even more the servant of irrational impulse. If such changes are possible, why work toward the development of some traits (disciplined thought) rather than others (aggression)? The argument that one should follow the dictates of human nature does not resolve the problem of justifying why some characteristics should be nourished and others ignored or extinguished.

Second, social science inquiry represents a relatively limited slice of human experience. As we deliberate on the problem: "Why should children be taught to ask and answer the kinds of questions that interest historians, political scientists, economists, psychologists, etc.?" We begin to sense that social training offers no more than vocational training for success in college or the academic professions. Basing one's curriculum on social science disciplines is an unnecessarily restrictive approach to education in two senses: a) the type of inquiry engaged in is largely *descriptive* (as opposed to prescriptive), b) it ignores the educational value of "non-disciplined" experience. We shall deal with each type of narrowness.

The major orientation of social science inquiry is to provide descriptions of reality that allow us to make factually accurate statements about the way the world is, was or will be. Whether we are concerned with the causes of revolution, the effects of capital investment, the operation of political process, or the identification of systems of status and privilege, the essential task is to describe real human phenomena. Social science inquiry is only minimally concerned with prescriptive questions: When is it right to tell a lie? Should a few lives be sacrificed to save the majority? Should a businessman be able to charge "all the traffic will bear?" When is it right to use violence to overthrow a government? Should the state regulate human procreation? These are questions of value and policy which may be asked in school by many teachers, but they are not major foci for the inquiries of social scientists. Perhaps they are relegated to the fields of ethics, philosophy, religion or "personal opinion," but they are not systematically pursued in the realm of social science research. Disciplined inquiry into these prescriptive, value issues is a vital and legitimate educational activity that is obscured by the predominant social science emphasis on problems of description.

The monopoly of academic disciplines presently embedded in school curriculum (natural sciences included) also tends to preclude from formal education a large number of exciting, though non-disciplined experiences. Many of us believe that there are "ways of knowing" not customarily pursued in the academic tradition: non-rational thought such as fantasy, "day dreaming" that stimulates imagination; deep emotional experiences (love, hate, humor) that communicate meaning on a non-intellectual level; non-verbal skills (craftsmanship, athletics, music) that develop a sense of competence; mystic or religious experience that helps to clarify ultimate meanings; even nonsensical play may have educational value. But the model of the scholar pursuing truth in his study or his laboratory obscures these dimensions of education. This is *not* to suggest that it is the responsibility of social scientists to broaden their interests to include all of these activities. The criticism is offered only to call attention to the relatively limited range of concerns embraced by social science disciplines.

CONCLUSION

This paper has not presented an acceptable alternative to the social sciences as a basis for curriculum, and it should not be construed as an endorsement for "history" in place of social science, or as support for the status quo in social studies instruction. It has attempted to raise, without resolving, several important questions that seem to have been neglected in frantic efforts to produce new social studies curriculum. As scholars from universities try to inject more of their "structures" into the schools, it behooves educators to face such issues as 1) How can we differentiate between disciplined and non-disciplined thinking and what proportion of the resources in formal schooling should be devoted to disciplined versus non-disciplined experience? 2) For what reasons and purposes is disciplined social science thinking a legitimate educational objective? 3) What criteria or principles of selection should be used in choosing among alternative courses and structures? Perhaps it is unreasonable to expect a social scientist committed to spreading his gospel to deal with these issues seriously. The social studies curriculum planner, however, should not avoid them.

References

[1] Joseph J. Schwab, "Problems, Topics, and Issues," in Stanley Elam (Ed.), *Education and the Structure of Knowledge*. Chicago: Rand McNally, 1964.

[2] Jerome S. Bruner, *The Process of Education*. Cambridge: Harvard University Press, 1960.

[3] Philip H. Phenix, "The Use of the Disciplines as Curriculum Content," in A. Harry Passow (Ed.), *Curriculum Crossroads*. New York: Teachers College, 1962.

[4] See William J. J. Gordon, *Synectics: The Development of Creative Capacity*. New York: Harper and Row, 1961.

[5] Regardless of problems in determining the net harm or good contributed by social science, we can predict that in fact scientists are or will be making decisions of great influence on our lives—through public opinion analysis, urban planning, control of the economy, psychological counseling, etc. It is argued that, therefore, the citizen should understand the uses and possible abuses of "science" by the intellectual elite. The person who understands intellectual processes of those who influence him may have greater control over his destiny, but not necessarily. Negroes may understand how whites think; university intellectuals may understand how Congressmen think, consumers may understand how businessmen think, yet these understandings alone do not endow such groups with the power to influence policy.

[6] Konrad Lorenz, *On Aggression*. New York: Harcourt, Brace and World, 1966.

SOCIAL SCIENCE AND THE NEW CURRICULUM

Franklin Patterson
Hampshire College
Amherst, Massachusetts

AN IRONY AND A NEED

It is a curious irony that the curriculum of American schools has remained so little touched by the social sciences in an age when the chief remaining enemy of man is man himself. This irony is compounded by the growth of the social sciences and by their great impact on aspects of our society other than the formal program of the schools.

The impact of the behavioral sciences is certainly widespread, as a report prepared for the President's Science Advisory Committee recently noted.[1] Among other effects, these sciences are changing our society's fundamental ideas about human desires and possibilities. Through the filter of popularization, the social sciences in the past few generations have altered the beliefs that many people have about intelligence, child rearing, sex, public opinion, organizational management, and other matters. It is not uncommon even for unproved behavioral hypotheses to find widespread, casual acceptance, a fact which underlines the need for better education about what the social sciences are and are not.[2]

The society's need for what these sciences may be able to offer, however, goes far beyond the question of accurate translation. It includes a need for policy scientists to give leadership, as de Grazia has put it, in "the posing and staffing of solutions to the great problems ... that remain with modern man."[3] But since we are concerned, despite nearly overwhelming social change, to reconcile social order with individual freedom and initiative and keep the immediate power of those who rule subject to the ultimate power of the ruled, our need is even broader, involving the competence of the general citizenry. The social studies are needed to impart a body of factual knowledge with theoretical apparatus for supplying this knowledge with order and significance, a methodology of inquiry and verification, and an appreciation of the range of values reflected in the study of man. Long has commented that this mixed enterprise needs to be concerned on one hand with the pursuit of scientific knowledge and on the other with the "humanistic and

"Social Science and the New Curriculum" by Franklin Patterson is reprinted from the *American Behavioral Scientist,* Volume VI, Number 3 (November, 1962), pp. 28-32, by permission of the Publisher, Sage Publications, Inc.

philosophical task of entering the student into an informed and critically intelligent appreciation of his cultural inheritance and even of the broader milieu in which the educated and responsible citizen of today must function."[4] It is in the arena of competing social values, conflicting policy choices, and difficult decisions that people generally must be prepared to operate, today and for the indefinite tomorrow.

One would not suspect the dimensions of this need from what is currently offered in the way of social studies in American schools. For the most part, the present social studies curriculum is simply obsolescent. It has remained essentially unchanged for forty years or more. Immense changes in human society and knowledge, in the nature of social responsibility and character, have occurred without compensatory development in the social studies curriculum. The most recent significant change in the social studies offering came as a result of a national commission statement in 1917 and 1918. Since then little new of value has been added and little old dropped. The social studies in elementary and secondary schools, as a result, are not geared to the swiftly changing social, economic, and political world in which we and our children live. The curriculum in most schools still disregards the non-Western world. Areas of public policy that are difficult and controversial are principally avoided. The social sciences other than history (and government, presented as a mechanical system) are largely ignored. As far as the majority of our schools are concerned, it is as though the tremendous development of the sciences of man in the past half century has not occurred. Economics gets short shrift—and mainly as mythology. The findings of anthropology, sociology, social psychology and related field gets little attention. The subject matter that comprises today's social studies in the schools is presented in highly-sanitized mass production textbooks intended to offend no conceivable interest group, and is dealt with chiefly in a read-recite-quiz manner which would seem almost calculated to reinforce both its inanity and its short-term retention. It is hardly remarkable that students characteristically regard social studies as a crashing bore. The irony of all this is that the need for a wide and deep literacy in the studies of man is so critically urgent.

WHY SOCIAL SCIENCE LAGS

The backwardness of social studies in our schools is partially a function of the state of the social sciences themselves. Not only are these fields "new" as disciplines and therefore late-comers to the academic table, but they suffer other disabilities. Their growth in this century has proceeded at a constantly accelerating rate, in a kind of metastatic way. Today, the social sciences seen from the middle distance seem extraordinarily diverse, sprawling, complex, and often either portentously tentative about the obvious or given, as Ann Roe once said, to better and better research designs about matters of less and less importance. As an influence upon the schools, they are handicapped by their lack of anything resembling a unified body of social science theory. Despite the efforts of a few men like Tyler to reflect multi-disciplinary generalizations to the schools, there has been little substantial or coordinated endeavor in this direction, and the school social studies curriculum shows it.[5]

Another, perhaps more serious, obstacle to the modernization of the social studies curriculum arises out of the forbidding nature of the problems that social science may deal with. As Havighurst has pointed out, the chief limitations that the schools have as agents of social change are in the realms of social taboo and controversial social values.[6] In these realms, where social science is accustomed to move with relative freedom, school curriculum is most unresponsive or hostile to change. Here are what Hunt and Metcalf call "areas of belief and behavior characterized by a relatively large amount of irrationality, prejudice, inconsistency, confusion, and taboo."[7] And these areas (e.g., economics, race relations, social class, sex, religion, nationalism, and patriotism) tend to be "closed," in the sense that investigation of materials and reflective treatment of problems are largely inhibited or excluded in contemporary schools.

The dominant role that one discipline, history, plays in the existing social studies curriculum makes the lag in developing a broader base in the new social sciences even more understandable. Feldmesser, in his recent paper for the American Sociological Association, has summed up ably the static reliance of schools on standardized course work in history.[8] His grievance is not only that such offerings are limited and out of date but that, as taught, they are bad social science for the most part. In a 1962 summer conference, Feldmesser was even more direct, saying ". . . in the strongest possible terms: we shall make no progress in transforming the social studies into social science until we slaughter the sacred cow of history."[9] Be this as it may, the cow is tough as well as venerable and may take more than a sociologists's words to slay. Whatever else school history instruction today is, it is *safe*, tiresome, mechanical, and shallow, perhaps, but wonderfully inoffensive, except to social scientists and a few other students of society.

Other factors in lag may be added. At least one has been dealt with by de Grazia, "the hatred of new social science." Distrust, if not hatred, is easy to find. Auden's commandment

> Thou shalt not sit with statisticians
> Or Commit a social science

is repeated in less interesting language and at more length by a wide range of scholars and laymen, not all of whom are poets or classicists. At its best, outside skepticism about social science can be as helpful as it is keen, deflating the turgidity with which we sometimes describe self-evident discoveries. The humanist Fiedler's penetrating critique of voting studies in particular and political sociology in general is a case in point.[10] But the scepticism of the informed and sympathetic critic is less common than the blank hostility of the proudly ignorant. The latter include at least some academics and laymen whose personal anxieties are heightened by the thought that social science deals with phenomena that should not be looked into, at least not with an objective eye.

Another very real reason why the new social science has not been taken up in a new social studies curriculum lies in the teaching manpower available. With notable exceptions that prove the rule, school teachers in the social studies are not characteristically well-prepared even in history or the older social sciences (e.g., economics, geography), to say nothing of the newer fields. Nor do the extreme pressures of day-to-day teaching allow them time in which to read or study to raise their level of scholarly competence, assuming that motivation to do so might be present. By their lack of broad or special preparation in the disciplines and their demolishing schedules, social studies teachers are driven to the easy way out: reliance on a standardized text in history or civics for most of what they try to teach. To expect such hard-pressed people to innovate, especially in a curriculum area as sensitive and inchoate as "the new social studies," would be naive.

SIGNS OF CHANGE

At present and in the recent past, signs have appeared that may signal substantial moves to modernize the social studies. Many of these signs have been raised by leaders in the social disciplines and associations, but there has been complementary activity by certain individuals, groups, and agencies speaking for the school social studies.

In 1958 a special commission of the National Council for the Social Studies, headed by Howard E. Wilson, called for new educational programs responsive to social change and the funded insights of the social and behavioral sciences.[11] This report was followed by the establishment of a joint *ad hoc* committee by the Council and the American Council of Learned Societies, seeking a vehicle for school teachers and social scientists to join forces for curriculum reform. In 1960, the NCSS-ACLS group commissioned a series of papers in which scholars were asked to present the social science concepts and generalizations that high school students should be expected to have learned by the time of graduation. These papers were presented to the annual meeting of the NCSS in November, 1961; their publication is scheduled for the current academic year.

In December, 1961, the School and University Program for Research and Development (SUPRAD) of the Harvard Graduate School of Education conducted a two-day conference, chaired; by Feldmesser, on the Behavioral Sciences in the Secondary School. Some thirty-five sociologists, anthropologists, psychologists, and education specialists took part, concluding (a) that more behavioral science should be taught in secondary schools; (b) that teaching methods and the variability of cultures were important considerations; and (c) that a variety of curriculum innovations should be tried and evaluated.[12]

In the same period at the end of the 1950's, scholarly associations were moving hopefully towards the provision of curriculum leadership for the schools. Thus today all of the social science professional societies have established committees to forward the cause of their several disciplines in the schools of America. All well-intentioned, these committees vary greatly in their sophistication about the conditions and needs of American schools, teachers, and children. The best-known of efforts by these committees has been the work of the Task Force in Economic Education, which produced a report and recommendations in 1961 reflecting the joint conclusions of professional economists, teachers, and the Committee on Economic Development.

In addition, certain school systems (e.g., Newton, Massachusetts, and others) have undertaken social studies curriculum revision on their own. In these efforts, history has tended to be the dominant orientation, with the new social science getting little play. Here and there, individual social scientists have experimented with the teaching of their disciplines at the high school level, but these are isolated undertakings.

Easily the most comprehensive and potentially the most influential current development in school social studies curriculum reform is a proposal of the American Council of Learned Societies and Educational Services, Incorporated. This proposal grew out of a two-week conference in June, 1962, held at Endicott House, the MIT facility at Dedham, Massachusetts. The conference dealt with the relationship of the social sciences *and* the humanities to the school curriculum from kindergarten through secondary school. Some forty scholars from various universities, and school people from several parts of the nation participated. Frederick L. Burkhardt, President of ACLS, and Jerrold R. Zacharias of MIT were co-chairmen of the conference, and the principal general model of curriculum revision considered was the massive program of the Physical Science Study Committee (PSSC) in which Zacharias has been the moving force.

The Endicott House conference relied heavily for its instructional orientation on Jerome S. Bruner, and the non-didactic, inductive approach which characterizes the PSSC program and much of the new teaching in mathematics. For some specialists, e.g., those in anthropology and political science, this orientation was easier to accommodate to and use in thinking about curriculum design than it was for others, notably in economics. The conference group rejected the idea of reproducing in small at the school level separate courses in the several disciplines, except as electives. Instead, the Endicott group saw the long-run task as one of creating *integrated social science* sequences for the lower and secondary schools, related to comparable sequences in the humanities, and geared to varieties of individual development, intellectual growth, and responsible citizenship.

Two forms of follow-up have resulted from the conference. One is experimentation with integrated social science sequences, including the development of a framework of concepts, new materials, and instructional techniques. Douglas Oliver of Harvard is working in this regard with a small group of scholars who are concerned with kindergarten through sixth grade. Richard Douglas of MIT is doing the same thing with another team interested in the senior high school years, and I am working with a group on the junior high school social studies curriculum. The second form of follow-up is the projection of a major effort to program the new social studies in relation to the new social science on a comprehensive scale over a period of time. This large-scale undertaking is in a formative stage, but envisions a modernization comparable to that provided by PSSC, with various new units, courses of study, films, artifacts and other materials, texts, teachers, guides, and the like. The designation of this project at present is the Curriculum Development Program in the Humanities and Social Sciences, and its joint sponsors are the ACLS and Educational Services, Inc. (which now handles the PSSC program).

REQUIREMENTS AND OUTLOOK

Recent and current activity should not be mistaken for solid achievement. Whether papers, pronouncements, and projects are the prelude to genuine modernization of the social studies in a significant way will turn on a number of factors.

One of these is money. To get some idea of how much would be needed in social science-social studies curriculum revision from kindergarten through high school, consider the fact that the successful PSSC program has required approximately a million dollars a year for the past six years to upgrade one course in high school physics alone. Thus far no foundation, agency or group has shown either the wit or courage to venture the level of support that a major across-the-board reorganization of social education would require. Instead, monumental caution and lack of imagination have been displayed by the National Science Foundation and other potential sources of leverage. The NSF, for example, appears committed only to exceedingly modest, tentative, and piecemeal support of "course-improvement" in such areas as the intro-duction of anthropology at the high school level. One is reminded of Gardner's comment that "our thinking about the aims of education has too often been shallow, constricted, and lacking in reach or perspective."[13] Or his suggestion that in American education all along we have had the blue-prints for a cathedral, but that we have insisted on referring to it as a tool-shed. Whether a cathedral or toolshed approach is taken to the building of a new social studies program remains to be seen.

Much depends, too, on the degree to which scholars who are accustomed to working only in their special fields can learn their way into the situation and needs of our vast school enterprise and contrive to see its social studies problem as a whole. Disciplinary parochialism, piecemeal tinkering, or en-thusiastic spinning of wheels in isolated special projects are not apt to do the curriculum much good.

At present, there is a crucial, basic need for elucidating an intellectually viable structure for unified social studies as a school field of learning. What exists currently in our schools is a *mélange* which is mostly dysfunctional in terms of process, substance, and the needs and capabilities of individual learners. Achieving a functional structure of knowledge for the schools, given the diffuse state of the contemporary social sciences, will not be easy; it will involve hard choices and risk, but it is essential. Only scholars in the social disciplines can meet this need. The schools cannot do it alone.

Certain conceptions of the task may assist in developing structure for a new unified social studies approach in the schools. One of these is to conceive social education as being concerned essentially with studying causation and valuation in human experience. Another is to conceive social studies in American schools as contributing to the education of individuals who will be competent citizens in a constitutional democracy faced with rapid change, who will make informed choices among alternatives, basing their choices on values that are critically examined rather than accepted haphazardly and unconsciously. An additional conception is that social studies should contribute to the continuous reorganization of perception, the enhancement of communication, the understanding of group relationships, the capacity for problem-solving, and the development of self and social identity. Closely related is the conception of social studies as operationally introducing students to the methods of the social sciences, their strategies of inquiry.

The new social studies hopefully will be designed for individuals who are seen as *both* learners and citizens. Thus there will be a need to involve students in efforts to deal rationally with fundamental social issues: opening "closed areas," using problem-solving procedures in case materials, gaming, simulation, and other ways.[14] There will be a need, too, as Rokeach, Kemp, and others made clear, to see learning and critical thinking in the social studies as including questions of emotion and personality in addition to the problems presented by an intellectualized body of subject matter.[15] And university scholars will need to remember that every child is not a graduate student, that each goes through developmental stages about which we are only learning, that all come from socio-cultural situations that condition their behavior, that they have widely varying natural endowments, and that while less than half of them will go beyond high school all of them will be potential voters.

The outlook, then, may be determined less by money-support than by the intellectual breadth, social vision, and creative educational inventiveness of those who are willing to set their hands seriously to constructing a new social studies based in the social sciences and closely related to the humanities.

References

[1]*Strengthening the Behavioral Sciences,* Statement by the Behavioral Sciences Subpanel, The Life Sciences Panel, President's Science Advisory Committee, The White House, Washington, D.C., April 20, 1962 (Washington, D.C.: U.S. Government Printing Office, 1962), 19 pp.

[2]*Ibid.,* p. 2.

[3]Alfred de Grazia, "The Hatred of New Social Science," *The American Behavioral Scientist,* Vol. V. No. 2. October, 1961, p. 13.

[4]Norton E. Long, "Political Science in the Schools," mimeographed working paper prepared for the American Council of Learned Societies, 1962, p. 2.

[5]Ralph W. Tyler, "Human Behavior: What Are the Implications for Education?" *The National Education Association Journal,* October, 1955, pp. 426-429.

[6]Robert J. Havighurst, "How Education Changes Society," *Confluence: An International Forum,* No. 1, Spring, 1957, pp. 85-96.

[7]Maurice P. Hunt and Lawrence E. Metcalf, *Teaching High School Social Studies: Problems in Reflective Thinking and Social Understanding.* New York: Harper Brothers, 1955, p. 230.

[8]Robert A. Feldmesser, "Sociology and the Social-Studies Curriculum of the American High School." Duplicated paper prepared for delivery at the meeting of the American Sociological Association, Washington, D.C., August 31, 1962.

[9]*Report,* Conference of the Social Studies and Humanities Curriculum Program, at Endicott House of the Massachusetts Institute of Technology, Dedham, Massachusetts, June 9-23, 1962. Mimeographed, p. 4.

[10]Leslie A. Fiedler, "Voting and Voting Studies," Chap. 9 in *American Voting Behavior,* Eugene Burdick and Arthur J. Brodbeck, editors. Glencoe, Illinois: The Free Press, 1959, pp. 184-196.

[11]"Curriculum Planning in American Schools: The Social Studies." A Draft Report of the Commission on the Social Studies of the National Council for the Social Studies. Washington, D.C.: The Council, November, 1958. Mimeographed, 26 pp.

[12]Feldmesser, *op. cit.,* p. 11.

[13]John W. Gardner, "The Servant of All Our Purposes." Reprinted from the 1958 *Annual Report,* Carnegie Corporation of New York. White Plains, New York: Fund for Adult Education, 1958, p. 1.

[14]CF., for example, Franklin Patterson, *Public Affairs and the High School: A Summer Pilot Program.* Medford, Massachusetts: The Lincoln Filene Center, Tufts University, 1962, 43 pp.

[15]CF., C. Gratton Kemp, "Critical Thinking: Open and Closed Minds", *The American Behavioral Scientist,* Vol. V, No. 5, January, 1962, pp. 10-15.

SHOULD HISTORY BE CHERISHED?
SOME DOUBTS AND AFFIRMATIONS

Paul L. Ward
American Historical Association

Should history be cherished in our schools? I want to voice some serious doubts. They will be historical doubts because I am a historian. But they will be serious. I have not used "historic doubts" in the title of my remarks tonight because that might provoke suspicion in a few of your minds—those of you who are especially well read—that the doubts I am about to express are ironic and not serious. *Historic Doubts Relative to Napoleon Bonaparte* was the title of an essay written about 150 years ago questioning the very existence of Napoleon, who had actually just been defeated and sent to spend

Reprinted with permission of the author, from *Social Education,* 31 (March, 1967): 188-192.

his last days on an island in the South Atlantic. The essay was written by an Oxford logician, who went on to be an economics professor and then an unpopular archbishop, and it was a brilliant bit of writing, arguing against Napoleon's existence in imitation of questions that had been raised about miracles in the New Testament. It was these skeptical questions about miracles which the author was trying to ridicule. His historic doubts, that is, were not seriously meant.

Mine are. One reason is that in our century there has been wholesale questioning of the value of history on grounds that must be respected. The part of mankind that has most exhaustively cultivated history, Western Europe, has turned out to be the source of imperialism and world wars, of communism and fascism and nazism. All these seemed to draw their strength from the accumulation of historical loyalties and indoctrination, the sort of history that was concerned with nation-building, with government and its relation to popular support in peace and war. Now developing countries in other parts of the world are looking to us for means of social betterment. Should we visit on them our accumulation of self-admiring history? Shall we visit this accumulation of cherished facts about past politics upon our own next generation?

These, I take it, are the doubts that are widespread today, as to the value of cherishing history in education. They are not unhistoric, for they spring from recent history. But I take even more seriously doubts which, for me, spring out of the history of history.

England has relatively many more historians of ancient Greek and Roman history than we have, but one of the leaders among them is an American, M.I. Finley, from New York City, who for the past dozen years has been at the University of Cambridge. Among other things, he is particularly interested in better understanding the way the Greeks dealt with history; and a year ago he published in the periodical, *History and Theory,* an important article entitled "Myth, Memory, and History." This article argues firmly that the ancient world of the Greeks and Romans was not historically minded, so that history as a way of thinking, which they invented almost by accident, had a difficult time among them.

The distinctions in that title of his—"Myth, Memory, and History"—may apply to later times and to our own time also. Myth, says Mr. Finley, was the Greeks' great teacher in matters of the spirit. The great myths expressed in the words of Homer and the later poets and dramatists conveyed vividly to the Greeks all that was important in their past. It taught them the virtues important in war and peace, the meaning of their annual rituals. Our analogies might be, might they not, the stories of the Pilgrims for Thanksgiving time, the tale of Washington and Valley Forge, the story of Lincoln?

Under the next heading, "Memory," Mr. Finley grouped not only the spontaneous memories that ran back at most two or three generations, but, more importantly, the oral or written traditions. These traditions were memories preserved for very practical reasons by specific groups: noble families, or priests at Delphi, or whoever. They were explanations and justifications of continuing institutions, and of cherished privileges, and so they naturally were revised whenever the role of these things changed. Inescapably, we have this sort of thing also, do we not? The origin of our national flag and our national anthem at Baltimore is an institutional memory we must cherish. Various espisodes of our domestic war between North and South, and of the Reconstruction that followed, are traditional memories—in Mr. Finley's sense—for different groups within our land.

Mr. Finley's point is that history took its hesitant beginnings with Herodotus as something quite different from both myth and memory; that is, as a skeptical rational inquiry, one which gained realism by centering on politics, the power struggle between men. History meant "inquiry." Unlike myth, which was timeless, and institutionalized memories, for which time was not important, history gained its cutting edge by working toward a systematic account of the past, using dates and asking, "What was the situation then?" and "What preceded it, and what followed?" Herodotus added a great deal else that simply had human interest, and Thucydides was so preoccupied with communicating to the reader his sense of political science that his historical narrative turned out to be less impressive than the speeches he composed to make his "analytical" points. Neither of these men was looking back into the panorama of the past. Both were responding to what they felt to be momentous in current events, so that they wrote essentially no more than contemporary history. But they demonstrated the value of critical inquiry using the tool of chronology; that is, the value of history as an intellectual enterprise.

Since their day, of course, history has come to range back over the past, including in its sweep all our national and group myths, and our explanatory and institutional memories. Western European civilization is shaped by the historical sense. From the Old Testament the Christians inherited the notion that a continuous narrative down through time was the most important way to look at the past, and so in the form of early medieval chronicles history began to take over for Europeans the functions of both myth and memory. The Renaissance revitalized the critical spirit in history at the same time that it gave to Western Europeans a rich store of civilized data which they used as myths and memories of their own down to the time of our Founding Fathers—our Capitol in Washington in both in name and in architecture a testimony of these. Next after the Renaissance, the religious wars in France and the Civil War in England called history into action as critical inquiry in the service of political parties, so that in fact it greatly revised and deepened national myths and memories. In the process, history became a craft by discovering step by step what made its inquiries more successful; and its successes further contributed to the accumulation we now have of valued myths and memories.

So by now the word "history" covers, as you and I know, very much more than "inquiry" which—let me repeat—was its meaning when Herodotus first invented it for us. The word "history" has itself been so commonly used that out of it long ago came the colloquial word "story," and this in my child-hood, when an adult was talking to me sternly, could often mean simply a "lie."

The accumulation of important stories and facts about the past, whether or not touched and improved by critical inquiry, tend to have a sentimental hold on us. We instinctively, many of us, want the younger generation to learn them all—well, most of them. Facts that are the lifeless results of past exciting inquiries, and of past arguments, serve for us the purposes of myths and memory. So we ask youngsters to memorize them and repeat them back on examination.

This is the commonest way in which history is cherished today in our schools and colleges. An eloquent and witty protest against it was the little volume, *1066 And All That,* published in 1931. As you may remember, its title described itself as "A Memorable History of England: Comprising, All the Parts You Can Remember Including One Hundred and Three Good Things, Five Bad Kings, and Two Genuine Dates." Here were the myths and memories of the English schoolboys' history books, Ethelred the Unready and William the Conqueror and Magna Carta all garbled and jumbled up to show how much schoolboys saw them as simply facts to be memorized. One example will recall the flavor to you:

> The greatest of these discoverers, however, was St. Christophus Columba, the utterly memorable American, who, with the assistance of the intrepid adventurers John and Sebastian Robot, discovered how to make an egg stand on the wrong end. (Modern history is generally dated from this event.)

The last chapter of *1066 And All That* reveals, poignantly, the deeper reason for the disgust with history that underlies the joking and fooling in its preceding chapters. This last chapter follows a summary of President Wilson's Peace of Versailles and is only one sentence long. Americans do not read it correctly. In American English a dot at the end of a sentence is a "period," whereas in English English it is a "full stop." So this last chapter, titled "A Bad Thing," reads "America was thus clearly top nation, and history came to a. [full stop] "

In other words history, the history this little book was summarizing at the same time it made fun of it, was history that had been serving the purposes of patriotic myths for the English, very like Homer's tales for the Greeks. Its heroes and events defined for the English their qualities of greatness and power: King Alfred and the spider, the defeat of the Armada. With a wry twist, this last chapter says that England's being suddenly reduced to the level of a second-class nation put the ax to that particular accumulation of history —made it just so much lifeless data.

Humor is often an aid to honesty, and in this honest though bitter comment of 1931 on history in English schools we can see something important for ourselves now. A new generation is coming into our schools, one for which the wars with Germany, and even the threat of communism, are not as real as they were for us. The facts that we find it easiest to put before them are facts that embody *our* myths and memories, the heroic poses that *we* took as our inward models, the explanations that answered the questions of 20 years or more ago. Should these be cherished in today's schools?

Unlike many people I respect, I cannot simply say no. My reaction is one of doubts, not denials. In 1931 the accumulation of historical facts for English schools may have seemed worthy only of the rubbish can. When *1066 And All That* was published, the great depression was deepening. But only ten years later Winston Churchill, by his use of words and his very bearing drew upon the same fund of heroic myths, and the English performed heroically, fully up to that measure. There is power in the past for us to call upon when we can with honesty and with right timing. We must not reject it out of hand.

But our choice is not between accepting or rejecting. Even the first critical history by Herodotus and Thucydides was useful patriotic explanation at the same time that it was enlightening inquiry. I have serious doubts that we do right to cherish indiscriminately, in our schools, the accumulation of historical knowledge at our disposal. What I want to put before you as personal affirmation is the importance of restoring to it, as vigorously as we can, the spirit of inquiry.

I see three strong reasons. One I have already indicated. If I read its own history correctly, history begins as inquiry and its importance in our life is due to the successes of inquiry in the past, which has produced the present rich accumulation of historical knowledge. The tendency in schools over the past few generations to treat history as simply a body of facts, to be learned and repeated by students, is due only partly to the tendency of hard-pressed teachers to do what is easiest. It is also due to the disposition of historians at the beginning of this century to think of their study as a science centering on facts that they were establishing. The American Historical Association's first *Guide to Historical Literature* in 1931 had only a very thin section, something like 60 titles, of books on the nature of history, its interpretation, and its method. The new edition of the same book in 1961 had nearly eight times as many titles in its section focused on the nature of history as inquiry, and the section's preface includes the remark that the revival of these theoretical interests has invigorated historical study.

In other words, the inquiry or inductive or discovery approach, so much talked about nowadays, is essential to the value of history. It was wholly appropriate that, as Jerome Bruner has reported in his *Process of Education,* two historians were present and "contributed mightily" at the Woods Hole conference of 1959. What causes trouble is simply that "inquiry" in history is significantly different from the inductive or discovery or inquiry approach in other social science fields—as indeed they themselves differ from each other. The character of historical "inquiry," if I may risk oversimplifying, comes largely from its having to combine, at all times, the effort at truth with the effort at human encounter. (By "human encounter" I mean the equivalent of an enlightening human interchange between equals.) But this is not a subject for me to pursue here.

My second contention is that, at the most practical level, students remember pieces of historical evidence more easily and correctly if these are introduced from the first as items that matter for meaningful inquiry. This is particularly worth recognizing as true of the facts that function as our national myths and memories in Mr. Finley's sense. If a student picks up a historical datum out of our nation's past in the course of his pursuing an honest question, he is far less likely to relapse into thinking of it as a "true fact," and more likely to understand that it is a "finding" of past investigation that may be helpful to him in his inquiry and also in future ones. Historians today are learning to be uncomfortable over talk about the "facts of history"—they prefer to talk about the "evidence," the "findings," the "conclusions," the "interpretations." This is not because we are less certain than we used to be, or less concerned for truth; it is because we know better than we did previously that to refer to conclusions as if they were isolated items of hard truth invites the sort of teaching and the sort of learning that makes nonsense out of attempts at historical understanding.

But my key point here is implied in my references to "honest" and "meaningful" questions. The historical findings now at our disposal are, very many of them, the result of lively inquiries in the past directed by underlying questions to do with nation-building. Questions of this sort, about the successes and failures of past governments in their efforts at popular support, produced the sort of history caricatured in *1066 And All That.* These are the questions that seemed overwhelmingly important to the German historians whose skills were so much admired, for example, by the founders of the American Historical Association in the last years of the nineteenth century. These background or motivating questions are not necessarily relevant to the younger generation today, or even fully relevant to ourselves unless we re-think them in today's terms.

Curriculum makers and teachers of history today may, therefore, have to put new efforts into recognizing and thinking out the underlying questions for historical inquiry, which then can guide their selection and organization of study materials. Two sorts of questions have to be distinguished, of course. One sort of questions are for explicit classroom work or homework, and these must do their jobs as historical questions; that is, yield satisfying answers built out of historical evidence of dates or words actually used. This means, incidentally, that they should be questions which, when followed out, illuminate how historians proceed most effectively.

The other sort of questions are the underlying or background questions which these should reflect and suggest. These second questions are the ones that, I am suggesting, should no longer be so exclusively concerned with nation-building. They need to be questions carrying the same sense of fresh realism that questions about politics did for Greeks who had been brought up on myths. They can be questions about man and society in our land that are already in students' minds. They can be questions that adolescents naturally have about the myths and memories which adults consider important. Even more deeply, they can hook up to the inarticulate questions young people have about their own personal inadequacies and possibilities. Historical inquiry is likely to be only play-acting in the classroom unless it strikes home at the level of questions of this depth of meaning.

Does this seem an impossible recommendation for most teachers hard pressed by large classes of poorly motivated students, and forced to be content with poor textbooks? Ideally, I have been implying, no teacher of history should ask students to focus upon more than the pieces of information and evidence that have a point—that the student can feel to be findings likely to be helpful in his present inquiries or in future ones. The new textbooks, the paperbacks, and the new curriculum efforts are perhaps making possible today what has not been possible in past years. But to rethink coverage and emphasis, so as to make sure that every study task reflects or raises some underlying question or questions recognizable by one's students, is a burdensome job. History teachers in our schools need every conceivable help in doing just this. Nothing less than this strenuous remedy can make the teaching of history in our schools more what it deserves to be, and must be; that is, the accurate learning of information that will be helpful in the students' own present and later understandings and inquiries.

Thirdly, I would affirm the positive value of seeing to it that historical study is always more than simply a mastering of topics that have recognized importance, whether these are the myths and memories of which we have been speaking or the concepts we know to be useful for understanding men and society. Historical inquiry, examining a piece of the past systematically in hopes of getting an answer to questions which honestly matter to us, is crippled unless it is prepared to accept unexpected answers.

For answers to be valid and enlightening, the explicit questions must be workmanlike; that is, framed as effective historical questions. Then, at the least, there is a chance that the answer will carry with it a sense that we are encountering in the lives or deeds of men long dead a bit of convincing human experience, something that stretches our knowledge of what man is like. It may be an eye-opening experience for a student, for example, suddenly to grasp the intensity of Thoreau's feelings against the hanging of John Brown, and this is clearly the kind of discovery to which the classic historian Von Ranke was referring when he spoke of the effort to see "how it really was." His "really" means "actually, in contrast to what it might look like on the surface." The very human dimension of inner conflicts and of mixed loyalties is, I am suggesting, one of the most important parts of what he was referring to. In the history books caricatured in *1066 And All That* this dimension was painfully lacking. The patriotic figures such as King Alfred too often had no more depth than pasteboard.

To sum up, history, if it is "inquiry" in Herodotus' sense, especially when it is directed to the area of our myths and memories, means bringing to bear honest questions in a way that will yield for students in return a gain both in rational understanding and an expansion of human sympathy.

This is a set of standards, of course, that even the exceptional teacher, even with the best of the new materials from the Curriculum Centers, will rarely meet fully. What is so remarkable about teaching, however, is that the teacher has to succeed in the deeper sense only once in a while for the students sooner or later to get the idea, so that thereafter they contribute actively in the same sense to turn their own study and their own classroom initiatives into more honest learning than they have previously seemed capable of. Each of us, probably, can think back to years when from September to June nothing seemed to get across with a particular class. But few of us have not had the experience of a class' suddenly getting the idea, and thereafter operating at a gratifyingly higher level. My affirmations rest on the belief that this becomes more possible if we try to restore to history in the schools more of the quality of honest inquiry.

I need add only two final qualifications. History's method of inquiry requires something of a continuum of knowledge, so that each new question will be seen in proper context and each new datum in its connections. The students will always face the prospect of some examination or testing on their coverage of historical data, even if most teachers come to agree on the "new social studies." After all, ability at remembering data and relationships will always be one of the clearest evidences of a student's having focused well and profitably on a subject. Admissions officers, and teachers of freshman college courses, will always, many of them, take the easy way out and not trouble to see whether a student knows how to think historically. But none of this justifies choosing to lay out the facts in a way that chokes off the life blood of history, which is question-asking.

It is especially tragic, I must add, when for extraneous reasons students do feel such interest in the data of history that they seem to respond perfectly to textbooks or lectures that have no inner argument whatever and reflect no questions that strike home. For them their experience is a shallow one, one which almost certainly they will soon either quietly forget or indignantly reject. I, for one, feel that the indignant rejections are a healthier influence on us who are history teachers.

My last qualification is that a stronger emphasis on history as inquiry needs to be handled so as to make for better communication between history teachers and teachers of other social sciences. There are real differences among the intellectual approaches of all these fields, and these real differences have been the source of vitality in good education, running back to deep similar differences at the very beginning of good education in our Western world. Each academic field would, of course, like to treat the findings of adjacent fields as dead facts to be fitted into its own inquiries, on its own terms. But this is to kill fruitful interchange and so, in the end, to kill education. Historians should know this as much as any specialists.

Emphasis on inquiry can be a positive help to consultations by historians with persons in other social sciences on questions of common interest. Consultations of this sort are now becoming more interesting and lively, partly because history has been recovering its own sense of its identity as a form of inquiry. The statement that marked the turning point in this recovery was an article published 18 years ago by Dr. Roy Nichols, who, as you no doubt know, is this year President of the American Historical Association. Back then in 1948, surveying the postwar position of historical thinking, he called on historians to be more positive in acknowledging the independence and distinctiveness of history, at the same time that he urged them to concentrate less on the "great American experiment" in government and more on the history of ordinary affairs, where other social scientists were focusing attention. Our *American Historical Review* in its latest issue has published an article surveying the history of the unfortunate split over the past 50 years between the humanities and the social sciences, and this concludes with the statement that "the intellectual commerce we perhaps need most today spans the divide we have created between humanities and social sciences."

Historians have indeed had a significant share in creating this divide. One reason may have been our often uncritical acceptance of the function of cherishing our society's myths and memories. Mr. Finley's article is a timely reminder. To restore to history teaching more of the sense of urgent inquiry, with all this entails of selection and relevance and imagination, will surely help. All of us will then be better able than we are now to judge what in history is worth cherishing.

GEOGRAPHY AND HISTORY
AS INTEGRATING DISCIPLINES

Ridgway F. Shinn, Jr.
Rhode Island State College

There are, as I fully realize, many critical issues about particular aspects of social studies instruction: appropriate methods for dealing with American history or world history or seventh-grade geography or whatever; the type of environment which is conducive to good social studies instruction; the requisite pattern of preparation for teaching social studies; or the serious, and almost staggering, job of selecting content for use in social studies classes. Each of these is a significant task!

Yet, I believe that the central problem and issue before us is this: How should the curriculum for social studies, from kindergarten through twelfth grade, be organized in view of the aims stated[1] and in view of the mass of new knowledge? This is a question which is posed directly about the *structure* of the curriculum. I propose to answer the question by arguing that the best possible way to organize the social studies curriculum is to utilize geography and history as integrating disciplines.

BACKGROUND

I think we need to start by reviewing together three different sets of developments. One deals with the social studies curriculum since 1916; another concerns the programs undertaken in recent years by the national scholarly societies; and the third refers to activities of the Rhode Island Social Studies Association, especially since 1961.

Now to be certain that we are all talking the same language, may I make it clear that I propose to follow substantially the helpful distinction that Edgar

Reprinted with permission of the author and the National Council for the Social Studies, from *Social Education,* 28 (November, 1964): 395-400.

Wesley made some years ago between the social sciences and the social studies. The social sciences are those bodies of knowledge, organized into disciplines with method and vocabulary, taught and studied primarily at the collegiate level; that is, anthropology, economics, geography, history, political science, sociology, and, sometimes, social psychology. Social studies, by contrast, refers to the content which is selected from the social sciences to be taught at the elementary and secondary levels of schools.[2] Thus, there must be a close relationship between the scholarly disciplines, the social sciences, and the content of social studies programs.

You are all familiar with the pattern laid down about 1916 by the National Education Association's Committee on the Social Studies, which tended to cement ancient history, European history, and American history together with English history as the "standard" offerings at the secondary school level.[3] Over the years various modifications of this have taken place, chiefly the decline of English history and the introduction of some study in geography and a rather amorphous, but often exciting, senior course called issues or problems of American democracy. At the elementary level, varied patterns emerged with the first three grades being built around an "expanding horizons" approach of home, school, and community, followed in the intermediate grades with geography and history, at some points distinctly separated and at other points fused, but with American history appearing most frequently in the fifth grade. In junior high school, a wide variety of patterns developed with the only certain feature being American history in the eighth grade.

Since I am sketching rather rapidly the situation that emerged and exists, I would add some observations about this curricular structure.

First, it was built upon a cyclical assumption. It was intended that we repeat certain material at a more complex level as youngsters become older. And this, certainly, still has validity. Yet I am troubled by what I call the "oral tradition" in history. I believe that, because of this cyclical view, we have not paid sufficient attention to the *initial* contact youngsters have with concepts and we still, I gather, introduce Columbus as the *only man* thinking the earth was round because this is the "line" teachers of primary grades have been using, apparently, since that misty October morn late in the fifteenth century—and this still continues in spite of Morison's superb biography of Columbus.[4]

Second, this curriculum was based upon an unconscious assumption that the tide of world events was sweeping all things towards the American model. E. P. Cheyney, in his presidential address to the American Historical Association in 1923, laid down as one of the "laws of history" the principle that all peoples were moving toward democracy.[5] There was a bit of American optimism about all this! And so we have a high degree of ethnocentrism about this curriculum; it tended, and still tends, to center attention on the American achievement primarily for the sale of the American achievement.

Third, this curriculum was designed for a society in which it was common for youngsters to leave school before the eighth grade. Thus, it did seem important that material about American heroes, history, and government be presented before youngsters left school, if they were to function in a democratic society. But, as I understand the present, we now have a society which, because of compulsory attendance laws, finds youngsters most commonly in school until the middle of the eleventh grade with an increasing number remaining all throughout high school.[6]

Fourth, this curriculum provided for social studies instruction through the elementary grades and through junior high school for all students. Only one year of instruction was, and in most places still is, provided for *all* at the senior high school level and that is the year of American history.

Fifth, this curriculum during much of the twentieth century developed apart from close contact with the social sciences. Part of the explanation for this is the fact that some of the disciplines have only evolved during this century, notably anthropology and sociology. Part of the explanation lies, however, in the degree of detachment that college and university people manifested for what was going on in the schools. I suspect that many college and university people had only one clear notion about the schools: Whatever was going on certainly was not adequate "if my freshmen are any sample."

Perhaps the most dramatic change in the last ten years has been the shift in the attitude of scholars in the social science disciplines towards the collegiate preparation of students in social studies. And this brings us to the second set of developments that we need to consider. For the learned societies in each of the disciplines have undertaken curriculum development projects. Let me just sketch the direction of these projects, some of which have been financed with federal money, some with foundation money, and some with money from the business world.[7]

For instance, the American Anthropological Association has a curriculum study project specifically pointed at the development of anthropological materials for high school use. Anthropologists believe that these materials will provide the resources for "correcting perspective and for supplying techniques of learning."[8] The American Political Science Association has, I believe, revived its committee on government in the high schools. The Association of American Geographers and the National Council on Geographic Education have been involved in a high school geography project to develop materials—study guides, selected readings, and tapes. The American Economic Association together with the Joint Council on Economic Education and the Committee for Economic Development have undertaken studies to make analyses of present economics content with a view to preparing a sequence of work in economics. The American Historical Association has devoted its energies in the area of curriculum to the development of an excellent series of pamphlets issued through the Service Center for Teachers of History. And, finally, the American Sociological Association has undertaken a project to see about course content improvement with respect to sociology. Thus, we have the learned societies concerned about, specifically, programs in the social studies in high school. And, as you would guess, each survey finds the social studies program lacking!

While all this activity has been in progress, the Rhode Island Social Studies Association has attempted to give some leadership in the development of social studies curricular changes. We have planned our programs for the last three years to deal with specific steps in curriculum development. We have heard from leading persons involved in social studies work and in the social science disciplines at the national level, in the universities, and in some of the states. We have adopted a statement of aims which has now been filtered through many of the school systems of the state and, I am told, has been most helpful and widely accepted. We have conducted two June conferences, one to deal with a tentative structure to implement the stated aims, and the second to wrestle with concepts out of the social sciences and their possible placement in the proposed structure.[9]

Our situation, then, is one of considerable activity within the social sciences and within our own association to the end of improving social studies instruction. This, together with the excellent work of the National Council for the Social Studies, especially in the Yearbooks, is, I believe, about to result in an abundance of first-rate material!

BASIC ASSUMPTIONS AND QUESTIONS

This is an appropriate time to emphasize one of the assumptions we have made all along; namely, that it will take a program that runs for 12 or 13 years, from kindergarten through grade 12, for *all students* to do the job of effectively fulfilling the aims we have accepted. Or to put it more boldly: We believe that students at their most mature years must have instruction in social studies!

There is a second assumption implicit in the proposals of the association and in my own thinking: This is that all students should participate in the same social studies program, regardless of whether or not students are college-bound. This rejects the notion of "tracks" in determining the structure of the social studies curriculum. I see considerable variation possible within the same curricular structure, but such variation will essentially come within the classroom as good teachers provide for different abilities and experiences that their students possess.

If we are to make these assumptions, and I believe them essential, then we need to be much clearer about how we will organize our curriculum.

I indicated earlier that I saw our central problem right now as one of structure, for I believe we would all reject the proposition that we ought to organize our instructional time into six vertical segments, one for each of the social science disciplines! I think we would also reject the notion that we ought to organize our curriculum into two six-layer cakes, to start with anthropology in the first grade and end with sociology in the sixth grade, and to repeat the process between the seventh and twelfth grades! Yet, if each of the learned societies should develop a proposal for kindergarten through grade 12, then we would be confronted with such possibilities, together with the resultant competition for time and space. And while I am rejecting alternatives, may I make it clear that I reject the proposition that a goal of social studies instruction is to turn out economists or anthropologists or geographers or historians.

How, then, shall we organize these 12 or 13 years of social studies? We should use geography and history as integrating disciplines. On page 5 of the *Report from the Conference on Social Studies* of June, 1962, is this statement:

> All of the social sciences are concerned with man and his various relationships with man and with environment; but both geography and history seek to see man whole: Geography focuses on place and history focuses on time.

It is at this point that I wonder whether Dr. Samuel McCutchen may not have been right when in his presidential address to the National Council for the Social Studies in November, 1962, he called for "A Discipline for the Social Studies."[10] I am fearful that, when I talk about geography and history as integrating disciplines, some of my listeners may simply conclude that these are both old wineskins and we had best discard them as being unable to contain new wine! I still find them useful and I do believe they can hold much content without any danger!

I think that now I must answer three questions: What is an integrating discipline? What is geography; why and how is it useful as an integrating discipline? What is history; why and how is it useful as an integrating discipline?

What is an integrating discipline? I have taken the word "discipline" to mean, in this sense, an area of knowledge with concepts, methods, and vocabulary. "Integrating" refers to the ability and the necessity for this "discipline" to draw upon concepts, method, and vocabulary from other and, usually, closely allied fields. For social studies, then, an "integrating discipline" is one which has generalizations which can, and indeed, must rest upon concepts, method, and vocabulary from all the social sciences. As Dr. Eschenbacher so aptly put it in the Rhode Island Social Studies Association's *Newsletter* (Fall, 1963), the integrating discipline becomes *"a vehicle of expression,* a setting to accommodate concepts from the other social sciences."

Let me use an illustration to see if I can make clearer the nature of an integrating discipline. Take the problem of poverty to which President Johnson has so emphatically called our attention. This is an issue both in its domestic and in its world setting which can be studied in a variety of ways. The anthropologist would wish to know something about the cultural adaptation that a particular group of persons has made in the face of poverty and might wish to compare this adaptation with similar ones elsewhere. The sociologist would wish to see what happened to the group involved in this condition, what were the relationships that exist between persons, between employers, between the state and persons and employers. The economist would wish to uncover those elements dealing with employment patterns as these are related to the kinds of production normally taking place in a given area and then relate this to the entire notion of purchasing power within the setting of national income. The political scientist would wish to make an analysis to find out the ways in which the state was responding to this situation and the ways in which this condition was or was not related to the probable patterns of voting and of political power. The geographer would wish to pin-point the places where poverty existed, and to find out the degree to which it did or did not stem from resource allocation and utilization. The historian would wish to know about the longer view of the problem. It exists now, but was it always there? What were the conditions that caused it initially?

Now, for social studies instruction, that is, instruction at the elementary or secondary level, we need an approach that will draw on the preceding analysis. Clearly, these concepts stemming from analysis could be related around the notion of region or around the notion of time. An understanding of this problem rests upon the correlation of all the separate studies in an attempt to see the problem whole, that is, to the level of development of the youngsters who are engaged in this study. Each of the six social science disciplines must contribute to analysis of this problem, but social studies instruction could, I believe, best be focused upon region, in this illustration. If you took the notion of region, you would have a "vehicle of expression" in which to place the content that the social science disciplines have to offer. This is what I mean by an integrating discipline.

INTEGRATING GEOGRAPHY AND HISTORY

Let us turn, then, to the question of geography and history as they may be utilized in this manner.

What is geography; why and how is it useful as an integrating discipline? I am always hesitant to attempt to define the nature of either geography or of history, for each of these, as a scholarly discipline, performs implicitly an integrating function. And I think this helps as we try to understand how they may be useful for social studies. So that we may discuss their particular use, I must attempt definition.

Let me state two excellent definitions for geography. The first is from the *American College Dictionary:*

The study of areal differentiation of the earth surface, as shown in the character, arrangement, and interrelations over the earth of elements such as climate, relief, soil, vegetation, population, land use, industries, or states, and of the unit areas formed by the complex of these individual elements.

The second was presented at the conference last June by Dr. Lewis Alexander:

Geography may be defined as the study of the location and interaction of phenomena on the earth's surface. The term "phenomena" implies both physical and cultural types, that is, those which would exist independent of man's occupance of earth (climate, landforms, water features, etc.) and those which are the result of man's activities (cities, highways, farms, political boundaries).[11]

In a sense, geography deals with the problem of areal differentiation, then, and is dealing with the problem unfolded in the story of the farmer being visited by his preacher. The farmer was out in the field at work when the preacher came and leaned across the fence—to interrupt work. The preacher's greeting was, "My, what a fine field you and God have here." The farmer's rejoinder, and he must have been a laconic New Englander: "Yup! But you ought to seen it when God had it alone!"

Now, it seems to me that the notion of land and man's activities upon it provides a most useful framework for social studies instruction. To understand land and man's activities upon it, a person would need concepts and content out of all the social sciences and, indeed, this frame helps to bridge the gap as well to the physical and biological sciences. It seems to me immensely fruitful to use geography as an integrating discipline in the elementary grades, as a structure within which we can place concepts and develop these within a sequence between kindergarten and grade 7. It also has great potentialities, I believe, for horizontal articulation with the sciences and with a reading program.

Perhaps I can make myself clearer if I take one grade level and consider how geography might function as an integrating discipline? Let's take grade 6, which we have suggested might take as its focus Latin America and Africa.

If we use geography as the setting for social studies instruction, we are not interested in turning out expert geographers stuffed full of "facts" or statistical models. Rather we are concerned to further our aims—specifically, the development of critical thinking, the acquisition of functional information, and "the awareness of and sensitivity to the iterations and contributions of seemingly alien cultures."[1 2] As we approach the study of these areas, questions such as the following spring to mind: Where are these areas? What is the difference between Latin America and South America? What sorts of regions exist? What is the slope of the land in these regions? How many people? Where? How do they earn their living? What languages? What forms of political or social organization? When and under what circumstances did these areas come into contact with expanding Western civilization? Were there civilizations or cultures which existed prior to the impact of Western civilization? If so, what happened to them? What kinds of human, raw material, and industrial resources exist? What types of government? What were the models for government? What art forms are characteristic? What sort of literature? Who are the heroes? How many independent political units exist in these areas? Are they within the United Nations? Are they within any other international organizations? Why are there problems in Panama or in Zanzibar in today's headlines? And you can spin out many, many more questions.

Our problem in the social studies is not that we lack relevant questions or information to answer the questions. The problem is, rather, the matter of structure: What is the best framework within which a class can carry out its investigations so that the students will gain insights rather than a mere accumulation of knowledge?

I can see developing a sixth-grade program around a geographic frame. If you start answering these questions by laying down some concept of region and the varieties of regions, I think you will have a meaningful base for an exciting year's study. Let me be more direct. I think that such a sixth-grade social studies program would have to draw upon content out of all the social science disciplines (including history), but it could be most effectively organized around a geographic "vehicle of expression." Latin America, incidentally, is a term which geographers use, and it reflects the impact of an anthropological concept, culture, upon geographers. You will note that at the June, 1963, conference, participants made an excellent start in suggesting the placement of concepts from geography, economics, sociology, and anthropology within this geographic frame for grade 6.[13]

Now to turn our attention to history and consider its possibilities as an integrating discipline for social studies instruction, especially at the secondary-school level.

What is history: why and how is it useful as an integrating discipline? Henry Johnson, in his classic, *Teaching of History,* starts his book right off with a no-nonsense definition of history: "History, in its broadest sense, is everything that ever happened."[14] This is certainly comprehensive and would suggest that if one were to understand everything that ever happened, someone would need to invent a framework within which such understanding could occur. And, in a very real sense, this is what history is. I see it as "that area of disciplined knowledge which deals with the problems of man and his varied relationships in the perspective of time; this knowledge may be transmitted from one generation to the next."[15]

In this connection, I have always found the task of the historian helpfully stated by Shepard Clough and Charles Cole in the introduction of their *Economic History of Europe:*

> Before any considerable portion of the past can be comprehensible to the people of the present, someone must study the records, select, classify, and interpret them. The person who does this work is the historian. His task is extremely difficult.[16]

History, like geography then, sees Man's activities on the land as an important point of study and adds to this the essential dimension of time. I would argue that a sense of time is of critical importance for any perspective on the present. We have constantly to remember that youngsters now in school have a vivid, visual image of the Berlin Wall, while the "rude bridge at Concord" is shrouded in dense and, sometimes it seems, impenetrable fog!

I see history as a vehicle for social studies instruction functioning as an integrator and helpfully related to the achievement of our aims. To understand man's activities on the land within the perspective of time, one must draw upon content and concepts out of all the social sciences.

Again, I may be able to make my point clearer if I take a particular level of our curricular proposals and indicate the ways in which history might function as the frame. Let's take the eighth-grade proposal which we labeled "Early Civilizations through the Eighteenth Century." At first reading, it may appear that the intent of this year's social studies program is to deal chronologically with material from Adam and Eve to Adam Smith and the *Wealth of Nations!* And this would be, I suppose, the "orthodox" way in which an historian would organize the year's study. But I believe that the purpose here is to fulfill the aims we have stated and it is not to prepare professional historians, even at a junior grade, who will be full of "facts"!

I would use the concept of a civilization in time as the moving idea in organizing this year's instruction.[17] And the concept of civilization is intelligible only when one draws upon content out of all the social sciences, the sciences, and the humanities. Yet we do need a particular point of reference. Thus, I would attempt first to identify one civilization and attempt to see it whole. When did it exist? Where was it? How did people earn their living? What kind of resources? How were they utilized? How many people were there? Why don't we know? Where did people live? How were they governed? What significant contributions did they make in art, literature, architecture, or whatever? What were the central problems of the civilization? How were they resolved or not resolved? How long did it last? What central ideas, especially ethical ideas, were transmitted from one generation to another? How were they transmitted—formally or informally? What difference, in the long run, did the existence of this civilization make? Again, you can go on and on to raise further questions. The answers to the questions will come from the work of social scientists who have the method of analysis. Yet the results of this analysis, translated into concepts, can, and indeed must, be related to the instructional process if students are to see this civilization whole and be able to compare it to other civilizations.

Here, then, history is used as a vehicle of expression to permit drawing together of content and concepts around the perspective of time.

I do believe that we are on the verge of some exciting changes in social studies curriculum and instruction. I believe that the use of geography and history as integrating disciplines makes great good sense. I believe that with careful research, evaluation, and planning, together with full cooperation from scholars in the social sciences, we can evolve a vital, effective social studies program for all youngsters that will, in fact, fulfill our aims and will develop the sort of behavior and attitudes appropriate for Americans set in the midst of a rapidly changing world in mid-twentieth century!

References

[1]*Report from Conference on Social Studies, June, 1962.* Providence, R.I.: Rhode Island College, October 1962. p. 2. Mimeographed report available by writing to Rhode Island Social Studies Association, Rhode Island College, Providence, Rhode Island.

[2]Edgar Bruce Wesley. *Teaching the Social Studies.* New York: D.C. Heath and Company, 1937. p. 4-6.

[3]See the essay, "Changing Perspectives in the Social Studies," by Erling M. Hunt, in Erling M. Hunt, and others, *High School Social Studies Perspectives.* Boston: Houghton, Mifflin, 1962. p. 3ff.

[4]Samuel Eliot Morison. *Admiral of the Ocean Sea.* Boston: Little, Brown and Company, 1942. 2 volumes.

[5]Edward P. Cheyney. "Law in History." *American Historical Review* 29:231-248; January 1924.

[6]Percentage of Population of Given Age in School. Adapted from Table 147 in U.S. Bureau of the Census, *Statistical Abstract of the United States: 1963.* Eighty-fourth edition. Washington, D.C.: U.S. Government Printing Office, 1963. p. 117.

Age	1920	1930	1940	1950	1960
12 years	93.2	97.1	95.5	95.9	97.5
13 years	92.5	96.5	94.8	95.9	96.9
14 years	86.3	92.9	92.5	94.8	95.3
15 years	72.9	84.7	87.6	91.4	92.9
16 years	50.8	66.3	76.2	80.9	86.3
17 years	34.6	47.9	60.9	68.2	75.6
18 years	21.7	30.7	36.4	39.8	50.6

[7]See the following places for recent statements of projects. *The Professional Geographer* (November 1963); *Journal of Geography* (November 1961); *High Schools Geography Project Newsletter* (April 1963); *American Sociological Review* (December 1963); *American Economic Review* (May 1962); *Economics in the Schools,* Supplement to the *American Economic Review* (March 1963). Also, see *The Social Studies and the Social Sciences,* sponsored by The American Council of Learned Societies and the National Council for the Social Studies. New York: Harcourt, Brace and World, 1962.

[8]American Anthropological Association, *Fellow Newsletter.* November 1962. p. 678.

[9]*Report from Conference on Social Studies, June, 1962* (see footnote 1); and *A Report on the Workshop in the Social Studies Curriculum, June 24-28, 1963.* Kingston, R.I.: Department of Education, University of Rhode Island, November 1963. Copies of this report are available by writing to Rhode Island Social Studies Association, Rhode Island College, Providence, Rhode Island. Both conferences were sponsored by the Rhode Island Social Studies Association, together with Rhode Island College, the University of Rhode Island, and several public school systems.

[10]Samuel P. McCutchen. "A Discipline for the Social Studies." *Social Education* 27:61-65; February 1963.

[11]*A Report on the Workshop in the Social Studies Curriculum, June 24-28, 1963.* p. 10.

[12]*Report from Conference on Social Studies, June, 1962.* p. 2.

[13]*A Report on the Workshop in the Social Studies Curriculum, June 24-28, 1963.* p. 19.

[14]Henry Johnson. *Teaching of History.* Revised edition. New York: Macmillan, 1940. p. 1.

[15]Ridgeway F. Shinn, Jr. "History–For What?" *New England Social Studies Bulletin.* October 1963. p. 16.

[16]Shepard B. Clough and Charles W. Cole. *Economic History of Europe.* Revised edition. Boston: D.C. Heath, 1946. p. xv.

[17]See Arnold Toynbee. *A Study of History.* London: Oxford University Press, 1934. Volume I, Chapters 1 and 2.

THE COMPARATIVE STUDY OF POLITICAL SYSTEMS

Alfred Diamant
University of Indiana

The teaching of the social sciences, regardless of the shape and form of the curriculum, has always presented certain difficulties not shared by the sciences and mathematics. Most obviously, the social sciences deal with controversial issues which in the high school are more directly under the close scrutiny of the community than they are in the college or university.

DIFFICULTIES

Though biology still raises such questions of community sensitivity in certain parts of the United States even today, on the whole sciences and mathematics are free from the sort of community scrutiny to which the social sciences are still subject. As one political scientist has pointed out, "Accurate political analysis touches too close to real political power. And political power always resists its own reformation.... The political scientist has one problem in addition to that of the scientist-engineer. His field of expertise is precisely the political system whose leaders employ him. The conditions of

Reprinted with permission of the author and the National Council for the Social Studies, from *Social Education,* 28 (November, 1964): 407-412, 440.

his employment relationship veto the development of his science when that science touches (as it always must) the mainsprings of power."[1]

A second difficulty of the social sciences in the high school is the need for a variety of separate disciplines to get together for a more or less integrated effort. While the various science disciplines are able to develop their own separate courses, following the general science work in the elementary and junior high schools, no single social science discipline, with the possible exception of history, is free to organize part of the high school curriculum. This means that teachers and scholars from a variety of specialties must sit down together in order to come to some understanding about their common purpose. Though the orientation of most social sciences toward a behavioral core will bring about a greater harmony among the various fields, the difficulties will continue to be great. As Bernard Berelson has suggested, making the social science curriculum continues to be a sort of "League of Nations effort."[2]

Finally, there is the question of student readiness for an increasingly sophisticated and rigorous approach to the social sciences. This question has been causing increasing tension in colleges and universities where freshmen seem to be able to begin work in the sciences and mathematics reserved to juniors only a few years ago, while no comparable upgrading seems to have taken place in the social sciences and humanities. There is much talk about the need for the greater maturity of the student required for the mastery of social science concepts or philosophical ideas, but little concrete evidence about this differential is available. Some social scientists are skeptical about it and have suggested that "the problem of readiness is more serious among untrained instructors than immature youth."[3]

Of these, and possibly other, problems facing the social science curriculum, only the question of community sensitivity continues to present serious difficulties. At the risk of sounding overly dramatic it must be said that in this respect, as in any other sensitive area, eternal vigilance is the price of freedom. The work now being done in the area of education on the Bill of Rights may well bear fruit, and where possible the academic community through the A.A.U.P. or other organizations must stand by the public school and its teachers when such issues arise.

At the same time there is no escaping the dilemma the social sciences face in the question of "civic indoctrination." Once we agree that one of the principal purposes of public education, or even its one principal purpose, is the development of "desirable socio-civic behavior," then we must make a distinction between social sciences as a branch of more or less exact knowledge and the teaching of social sciences in the schools.[4]

The question then becomes who is to determine what is "desirable behavior"? The school board the state legislature, the U.S. Congress? Can there be an orthodoxy in the sort of pluralistic society we have in the United States? As is so often the case, there is no clear-cut answer as far as the schools are concerned. One cannot close one's eyes to the fact that the schools in any society are one of the principal agents of the socialization of the child and the young adolescent; but at the same time the social sciences that do nothing but serve the prevailing mystique will not be worth pursuing, as their fate in modern totalitarian regimes has fully demonstrated. Yet the situation is not hopeless, for there is a conception of citizenship education that the social scientist can accept and which he can implement. It can be the role of the social sciences to help educate the young not as future specialists, but as future voters and citizens, giving them not a set of values or beliefs, but a set of tools which will enable them to act intelligently as citizens in a pluralistic society:

> We can scarcely expect to motivate the young to any lasting and strong desire to effectively participate in the community's politics with the milk-and-water moralism of the average civics text, nor is the bland emptiness of a junior chamber of commerce get-out-the-vote campaign such that it inspires a ritual of even ceremonial significance. Political competence can stem from a hard material purpose that schools itself to a realistic study of the facts. . . . What is especially needed in the schools is the development of a sense for a great tradition to which the youth can adhere not in a spirit of uncritical acceptance but as a matter of free and intelligent allegiance.[5]

It would seem to me that there is no better way to develop such a critical understanding of one's own values and social institution than disciplined comparative study. Is it too much to hope that units on comparative politics and comparative economic systems, once they have been introduced into the curriculum, can eventually be developed in such a way that they will meet the real needs of a modern social science curriculum?

GOALS

What is it, then, that the social sciences hope to accomplish in the high schools? I would like to identify three tasks.

First, they should sensitize the student to the tremendous cultural diversity which exists in the world today and which has always been characteristic of human experience.

Secondly, the social sciences, if properly handled, should enable the student to look at man and his world not only through the eyes of his own national culture or even that of the Western point of view, but provide him with what one might call a clinical perspective on values and institutions. This second task is, of course, closely related to the first.

Finally, the social sciences in the high schools can begin to introduce the student to the new research methods and research tools of the social sciences. It is a pleasure to be able to report that many students coming to college now have been required to make use of some of the standard research tools and methods in the high school. Though this has been largely in the general area of history (past as well as current), there is increasing need to acquaint the students with the new non-historical techniques of the social and behavioral sciences. I can well imagine that community surveys, the study of the local political and social power structure, the analysis of the voting record of local, state, or federal representatives would present grave difficulties to the social science teacher who would want to initiate such projects. Nevertheless, I believe that a beginning can be made in the high schools, especially in the pre-college tracks of the comprehensive high school.

In a recent analysis of the place of political science in the high school social science curriculum, Norton Long unerringly put his finger on the core of the problem: "There is at present no adequately developed body of theory that can be taught the student independently of the study of particular institutions. . . . Yet clearly the best way to understand and evaluate is to compare."[6] This statement contains the elements of all the major aspects of political science as an intellectual discipline.

First, though political science has long been engaged in the study and analysis of the political ideas and theories of the past usually beginning with Plato's *Republic,* we do not have a coherent statement of the nature of the political system which rests on a base of empirically verifiable observations.

Second, to the extent that we have any empirically based generalizations about politics at all, we cannot manage to teach about them except through the study of particular institutions. For there is a danger that the student when presented with a body of generalizations about political behavior—either individual or collective behavior—has difficulty gaining a realistic understanding of the workings of these generalized concepts unless he is shown how men act out their demands in the framework of particular political institutions.

Third, the comparative method is likely to be the most successful in communicating to the student an understanding of the values and institutions of his own political system, as well as alerting him to the profound difference that does exist among political systems, both now and in the past. What has been said earlier about the tasks of the social sciences applies particularly to political science. An exploration of diverse political cultures, a supplementing of the "common sense" and "intuition" of the community about how his own and other political systems work with some hard and sophisticated empirically-based knowledge, and an introduction to the methods of the new behavioral science of politics, all these can best be accomplished by the comparative method. By exposing the student to a variety of political systems and types of political behavior not just in isolation or seriatim, but by a continuous juxtaposition of values, institutions, behavior, and institutional performance, we will be able to achieve some of the goals which have been set for the social science curriculum in the last 50 years.

I believe that I have arrived at a position not very different from that of the authors of the 1962 report, "The Role of the Social Studies," of the National Council for the Social Studies.[7] In this report the three key terms were *values, knowledge, and skills.* Like most generalized goals, it would indeed be difficult to question them or take issue with them. But if I understand the report correctly, I feel that the content I would give these terms would approximate that of the NCSS report. However, I would like to carry that argument one step further and suggest that the most effective way to communicate about values, knowledge, and skills, is through the comparative method.

ASSUMPTIONS

The present proposal for the incorporation of the comparative study of political systems in the social science curriculum of the high school rests on a number of assumptions and conditions which should be made more explicit at this time.

First, the present approach resembles closely that of the National Task Force on Economic Education developed three years ago.[8] It seems to me that it would be unthinkable merely to push some of the largely obsolete college courses down into the high school, and to expect the high school to "cover" a certain amount of cut-and-dried material. Instead the student should be exposed to the intellectual structure of political science, to the best disciplined approaches available, and the principal emphasis should be on concepts and not on facts and/or current events. The stress must be on concepts which can apply to and be made operational for as many political systems as possible, and which will facilitate comparison and contrast between Western and non-Western political systems, between liberal-democratic, Socialist, Communist, and other types of value configurations. To be sure, there will be no attempt to create a straitjacket into which data about all countries can be fitted in an exactly uniform manner, but the way in which the student will confront the material will make it possible for him to face continuously the question: How do these systems differ, how are they alike?

Secondly, though there will be considerable pressure both from authorities on the high school and the college level to remain on the safe ground of the study of formal institutions and thus only foster continued indoctrination and the presentation of the human experience in "good-guys-bad-guys" terms, every effort should be made to avoid such stultification. We should begin to press ever more insistently for a realistic and behavioral approach to political science, for a study of political behavior and political institutions which will excite and fascinate the student because he gets a picture of how things are, how they came to be the way they are, and perhaps even of how things might work out.

The third point is closely related to what has just been said. Comparative government as conventionally established in colleges and universities has become too specialized to be directly relevant to the needs of the high school. As now constituted, comparative government is concerned with the government and politics of foreign countries; it usually excludes consideration of foreign policy and international affairs; and very often has little to say about the substantive policies and activities of these foreign countries. Because the program here proposed would include consideration of American government and politics, of international relations and international politics, and of the specific programs and policies pursued by a variety of countries, the academic discipline called comparative government or comparative politics can provide only part of the material we need.

Fourth, it will be apparent quickly to anybody familiar with the condition of political science that the discipline has become increasingly sophisticated in its ability to answer questions about the "how" of politics. We are able not only to describe, but also to show how certain parts of the political system are related to each other. We are able to answer questions about possible correlations between certain social facts like age, sex, income, residence, family background, and certain political facts like voting or political opinion—and it should not be overlooked that an opinion is a "fact" just as much as the act of casting a ballot. But at present, at least, political scientists have only very few answers to the questions about the "why" of political events. With the sort of tools and methods suggested below it will be possible to state how political institutions differ from one society to another, or how one society meets certain functional requisites in a manner quite different from another society or how value configurations vary from society to society. Only rarely will we be able to say *why* they differ—at least the answers will be highly tentative. It seems to me important to state this limitation of political science as clearly as possible.

Finally, I do not consider myself competent at this time to suggest where the comparative study of political systems would best fit into the high school social studies curriculum, exactly how many weeks should be assigned for it, etc. But I hope that a Political Science Task Force will be created soon which, unlike the Economics Task Force, will not be limited to making a statement of goals, but will proceed to implement them in close collaboration with the responsible authorities from the high schools.[9]

A PROPOSAL

The proposed unit on comparative politics is divided into five sections: (1) the nature of the social system (society); (2) the nature of the political system; (3) a section in which a number of political systems will be examined following a prescribed common format; (4) the nature of inter-system political relations; and (5) a section in which the systems will be directly compared according to certain major categories.

The central concept of the first section is identification of the social system, the society, as the unit of which the political system, as defined below, is a sub-system. It will be necessary here to establish—or to assume that the task has been accomplished in some other unit of the social science curriculum—the general nature of a social system and of its major aspects and sub-systems. Any given society can be studied in at least two ways, the two being complementary and not exclusive.

One aspect of a social system is its history, and thus it can be studied historically and it can be learned how it developed, what were the major stages of its development, and what particular features of the past remain relevant for the present.

But a social system can also be examined in a number of ways that make the historical aspect only ancillary. Perhaps the most important of these is structural functional analysis: "It views all . . . systems both in terms of common functions which must be performed . . . and in terms of certain structures or institutions which perform them. In different . . . systems a given function may be associated with quite different structures and institutions."[10] In this method attempts are made to identify the functions which must be performed in all social systems, or at least to pinpoint those common to many systems. In turn, institutions and structures established to carry out these functions are described. As indicated above, the student will find a wide variety of institutions fulfilling some of the basic functions of the social system. At the same time, he will also encounter situations where one society has developed a functional equivalent for a function which appears in radically different form in another social system.

A particularly important concept in modern social systems is that of "development." Traditional or primitive societies were characterized by functional diffusion; that is to say, the same institution carried out a wide variety of functions. An example would be the extended family (clan) which was a social, a political, an economic, and a military structure. The very concept of development from traditional to modern societies implies an increasing specialization of functions and division of labor. Functions have become assigned to a variety of institutions which are thus functionally specific for that particular single purpose. This latter is the picture we get from an advanced or modern society in the Western world. No society existing today is actually a fully traditional one; most societies in the so-called rapidly developing part of the world—Asia, Africa—are what one might call transitional societies in which some specialization and differentiation of functions and institutions has taken place but where traditional ways of doing things are still prevalent. The tensions, unrest, and difficulties we usually identify with these societies is chiefly the result of the pains of transition from traditional to a modern system. In the study of political systems since the end of World War II, the concept of "development" has become ever more important, and it is imperative that the student gain some understanding of this basic sociological concept for his work in comparative politics.

The second section is devoted to a definition and analysis of the concept "political system." Because one finds very little agreement among political scientists about this basic concept I can only suggest here one possible interpretation; I hope that it will produce only a minimum of argument and will prove useful for our purpose. I consider the political system to be that part (or aspect) of the social system that makes decisions and allocates values, material rewards, etc., for the entire society and whose decisions are binding on the entire society. It is, in short, what has been called the "legitimate, order-maintaining or transforming system in the society."[11] Working with a concept like "political system" has the advantage of not being narrowly limited to either "government" or to other formal institutional authority. To be sure, what is conventionally called government, especially in highly developed societies, will usually turn out to be the principal order-maintaining instrumentality, but the allocation of values and the making of decisions binding for the entire society also takes place in many other segments of the social system. These should be identified as ranging all the way from such formally recognized elements of the political as political parties to informal and often formally illegal entities such as the Mafia. It is most important to sensitize the student to a conception of politics as an aspect of society that is not coterminous with government. Politics as a system of action—using Talcott Parsons' central notion—is represented principally, but not exclusively, by formal governmental institutions.

In any comprehensive study of the political system it will soon become apparent that in some social systems most of the legitimizing and decision-making functions are concentrated in "government" while in others these functions are more nearly distributed among other aspects of the social system—kinship groups, religious bodies, etc. You will recognize that I have identified here another aspect of development or specialization of functions, this time what one might call "political development." The comparative study of political systems which now covers highly developed as well as transitional and traditional types needs an ordering concept like "political development" to make possible a classification or typology of systems according to their degree of "development."

Another way in which the student can be given an understanding of the general concept of a political system is by acquainting him with several possible alternative functional or decisional categories which could be used to study a variety of systems in a comparative manner. One of these, by Gabriel Almond, is based on a set of functional categories. Borrowing the basic notions of input from economics, Almond specifies a series of input and output functions of the political system. The former are the sort of functions which feed demands into the political system, the latter are categories of the outputs of the system in the form of legislation, administrative orders, court actions, services, etc.[12]

It will be obvious that a good part of the "output" of a political system will become in turn an "input" for further processing by the system. This has suggested to some political scientists that it might be fruitful to consider the political system as resembling a feedback or self-steering mechanism.[13] In today's world of thermostats, automatic elevators, automated Times Square shuttles, and guided missiles, it should not be impossible to use a concept like feedback to enable students to grasp some of the complexities of the political system.

A second possible set of functional categories has been suggested by Harold Lasswell.[14] Looking at the political system as chiefly a decision-making system, he proposes to replace such oversimplified categorizations as "legislative-executive-judicial" with a more complex, but also more realistic set of decision-making steps:

Intelligence: Information, prediction, planning
Recommendation: Promotion of policy alternative
Prescription: The enactment of general rules
Invocation: Provisional characterization of conduct according to prescription, including demand for application
Application: The final characterization of conduct according to prescription
Appraisal: Assessment of the success or failure of policy
Termination: Ending of prescription and of arrangements made within their framework

One should not be put off by these attempts to be overly specific and to create what might seem a special vocabulary. Many of the categories developed by men like Almond and Lasswell can easily be given simpler terms and can be identified with some of the more traditional categories. What matters, however, is to get the student to take a fresh look at the political process without being hampered by legal or traditional categorizations which only conceal the realities of that process. Both Almond's and Lasswell's categories have the added advantage that they can be applied to categories of domestic as well as foreign policies and political action, and thus might help in bridging the chasm between these two branches of more traditional political science.

Also part of the general treatment of the concept of "political system" should be an attempt to define, or at least identify, some of the key variables the student will encounter in the systematic study of politics. The ones requiring particular attention would be the following: (1) power—which probably should be defined chiefly in relational terms, not as some sort of measurable substance; (2) values—statements about what the "good" society should be, who should rule, etc.: (3) group and interest—the notion that individuals in a society act mostly as members of groups and their interests are often defined in group terms; (4) organization—renewed attention has been given to the rules governing the functioning of men joined together in complex enterprises; (5) decision-making (the use of categories like Lasswell's is one possible approach); (6) social determinants of individual political behavior (there is an increasingly sophisticated body of data about the sort of social characteristics that influence political behavior). All I can do at this time is suggest some of the principal concepts which should be clearly specified; I do not claim that this is an exhaustive list. But I should emphasize that such clarification of basic terms is essential for the remainder of the enterprise.

Finally, in this general treatment of the political system an attempt must be made to select certain political systems for examination and to specify the basis for selection. To give only one example: In a recent two-volume set of texts for the introductory course in comparative politics, Britain, France, Germany, and the U.S.S.R. were included in one volume, while the second, dealing with Asia, included sections on China, Japan, India, Southeast Asia, and Southwest Asia (more commonly called the Middle East).[15] It would be more useful, however, to specify criteria of political systems such as democratic-totalitarian, multi-party-single-party, traditional-transitional-modern, etc. I should warn that on this issue, too, political scientists speak with many tongues and that whatever selection one makes and whatever set of criteria one specifies, some will take issue with the selection.[16]

The third section will probably be the longest, for it will contain the materials on several political systems. Let me emphasize again, however, that we should not aim at encyclopedic coverage but on concepts and on developing a typology of political systems which can help the student identify key concepts and will sensitize him sufficiently so that the working of other political systems, not specifically "covered" in the course, will make sense to him.

The study of a single political system should start with a consideration of the wider context of which the political system is a part. Here should be included: (1) material elements such as geography, basic economic characteristics; (2) the major historical determinants; (3) the major social determinants; and (4) the principal values, beliefs, and ideologies relevant for the political system. What is to be included here will vary widely from country to country, and it might well happen that as outsiders we will miss some significant element of the social context. This should be followed by a treatment of the "dynamics of politics," that is to say, the interaction of these contextual elements with the political system. Here we will have to deal with (1) parties and social movements, their organization, composition, and operation; (2) the functioning and structure of other groups relevant for the political process; and (3) election or other processes by which leaders are chosen and policies determined in the society.

Next should come a segment which might be called "institutions of government" where we can deal, if possible in a given system, with the basic framework (the Constitution), legislative bodies, executives, bureaucracies, the process of adjudication, etc. It should be noted that the bureaucracy might well turn up earlier as one of the groups relevant for the political process—and in some political systems the bureaucracy is the chief group in the political process. But it will also need to be considered in its other aspects as part of the governmental institutions.

Finally, there will be a section identified as "the performance of government." After outlining the scope of government activity and after considering the issues raised by possible disagreements in the system over the scope of these activities, this section will describe and analyze the content and nature of domestic and international government activity.

Because of the lack of a truly unified general theory of politics, a separate section on international politics is necessary at this time, though every effort should be made to integrate this section as closely as possible with the preceding three. The pattern of inter-system actions might be analyzed under the following four headings: (1) The ways in which inter-system and intra-system factors are related should be specified. That is to say, the international politics of a nation must be related to its material situation, its values, its internal dynamics of politics, etc. Part of this will have already been done in the final segment of the preceding section. (2) The concept of power in international politics must be clarified. (3) Power and ideology must be related to each other. (4) The structure of the inter-system pattern of action must be examined, with special attention on recent efforts at restructuring the system, such as regionalism, the common market, etc.

In the final section of the comparative politics unit we will be ready to draw together in a series of comparative observations the data we have gathered and organized in the preceding ones. The principal categories for comparison should be the following: (1) contrast and conflict of value systems; (2) functional variations and similarities among political systems; (3) structural variations and similarities among political systems; (4) the variety of patterns of performance characteristics of political systems; and (5) the pattern of inter-system actions and the relationship between intra-system and inter-system factors.

CONCLUSION

There is no conclusion to this essay in the conventional sense. I have been asked to assess the place of the comparative study of political systems in the high school curriculum and to suggest a possible way for organizing a unit on comparative politics; this I have done. There are many other possible ways of organizing the material which might have been proposed by other political scientists.[17] There exists at the present time a considerable body of concepts and data which can be utilized in the high school social science curriculum, but it is not sufficient for the political scientists in colleges and universities to issue "calls to action." We must establish permanent and close working relationships between the universities and the secondary schools, for only in this way will the needed reform of the social sciences come about.

References

[1] Harvey Wheeler. "The Short and Happy Life of a Research Consultantship." *Western Political Quarterly* 13:852-857; 1960. Reprinted in Nelson W. Polsby, Robert A. Dentler, and Paul A. Smith, editors. *Politics and Social Life: An Introduction to Political Behavior.* Boston: Houghton Mifflin Company, 1963. p. 801-802.

[2] Bernard Berelson. "Introduction." *The Social Studies and the Social Sciences.* (Sponsored by the American Council of Learned Societies and the National Council for the Social Studies.) New York: Harcourt, Brace and World, 1962. p. 13.

[3] Bernard Berelson, *op. cit.,* p. 11. See also in the same volume essays by W. J. McKeachie ("Psychology," p. 171-190) and Michael B. Petrovich ("Teaching about Russia and Eastern Europe," p. 241-281).

[4] Lewis Paul Todd. "Afterword: Revising the Social Studies." *The Social Studies and the Social Sciences.* p. 290.

[5] Norton E. Long. "Political Sciences." *The Social Studies and the Social Sciences.* p. 97,98.

[6] Norton E. Long, *op. cit.,* p. 95.

[7] See the discussion of the report in Lewis Paul Todd, *op. cit., passim.*

[8] *Economic Education in the Schools.* New York: Committee for Economic Development, 1961.

[9] Fred M. Hechinger. "Tired Task Force: Science Reforms Lesson Called Key to Better Economics Teaching." *The New York Times.* August 18, 1963. Section 4.

[10] Roy C. Macridis and Robert E. Ward. "Introduction." In Marcridis and Ward, editors. *Modern Political Systems: Europe.* Englewood Cliffs, N.J.: Prentice-Hall, 1963. p. 7. I have quoted this simple and straightforward definition from the introduction of a new college text to indicate to what extent the tools and methods suggested here have indeed entered the mainstream of the teaching of comparative politics.

[11] Gabriel Almond. "A Functional Approach to Comparative Politics." In Gabriel Almond and James Coleman, editors. *The Politics of Developing Areas.* Princeton, N.J.: Princeton University Press, 1960. p. 7.

[12] Gabriel Almond, *op. cit.,* p. 17.

[13] See the recent and most exciting attempt at constructing a feedback model of government by Karl W. Deutsch. *The Nerves of Government: Models of Political Communication and Control.* New York: The Free Press of Glencoe, 1963.

[14] Harold D. Lasswell. "The Decision Process; Seven Categories of Functional Analysis. Nelson W. Polsby, *op. cit.,* p. 93.

[15] Of these two volumes the first has been cited in footnote 12. The second, also edited by Macridis and Ward, is *Political Systems: Asia.* Englewood Cliffs, N.J.: Prentice-Hall, 1963.

[16]The following constitute efforts to develop typologies of political systems: Seymour M. Lipset, "Some Social Requisites of Democracy: Economic Development and Political Legitimacy," *American Political Science Review* 53:69-105; 1959. James Coleman, "Conclusion: The Political System of the Developing Areas," in Gabriel Almond and James Coleman, editors, *op. cit.,* p. 532-576, especially the tables on p. 534, 541, and 542. John H. Kautsky, "An Essay in the Politics of Development," in Kautsky, editor, *Political Change in Underdeveloped Countries: Nationalism and Communism,* New York: John Wiley and Sons, 1962, p. 13-30, 90-119. For a simple but effective threefold classification of political systems, see Gwendolyn M. Carter and John Herz, "Conclusion," in Carter and Herz, editors, *Major Foreign Powers,* Fourth edition, New York, Harcourt, Brace and World, 1962, p. 610-627. And for a rather simple democracy v. totalitarianism categorization, see Dennis W. Brogan and Douglas H. Verney, *Political Patterns in Today's World,* New York, Harcourt, Brace and World, 1963.

[17]For a brief survey of the available literature, see Heinz Eulau, "Political Science," in Bert F. Hoselitz, editor. *A Reader's Guide to the Social Sciences.* Glencoe, The Free Press, 1959. p. 89-127.

THE INTERDISCIPLINARY APPROACH
TO TEACHING SOCIAL STUDIES

Stuart C. Miller
San Francisco State College

The central position of history in the high school social studies curriculum is now being seriously challenged by the historian's academic cousins in the social sciences. Their silence, or relative silence, until recently has been due, in part, to the theory that history offered the best synthesis for all of the social sciences. The very nature of history makes it easier to fuse useful concepts and theories from many fields as the story of the development of man and society is unfolded. Since all of the social sciences could not be taught in the high school, this seemed to be the best compromise. Today, few social scientists believe that any real fusion takes place in the geography and history courses which make up the bulk of the curriculum. Unlike many of the popular critics of this curriculum, they refuse to take the title of a course at face value. They know that upon closer examination a course entitled "Understanding Current Problems in Our Country" is apt to be a standard

Reprinted with the permission of the author and the National Council for the Social Studies, from *Social Education,* 28 (April, 1964): 195-198.

course in American history. My own experience indicates that Arthur Bestor's "social stew" exists more often in curriculum theory than in the classroom.

But the rebellion has gone far beyond this. These social scientists no longer want any fusion, but separate courses in their own disciplines. Too often the fusion of economics, the economist argues, is at best superficial, and taught by someone illiterate in this discipline. More often than not it is economic history and not economics. Inflation, for example, may be dutifully mentioned at the appropriate time in the history of the Western world, but rarely is any attempt made to conceptualize it from the point of view of the economist, illustrating the relationship between the economic variables involved. Is it no wonder that "inflation" has been used so effectively to frighten voters into supporting a program that virtually starves the public sector. Generations of Americans have been taught that inflation is an unmitigated evil instead of understanding that a certain amount of it is probably a necessary evil in an expanding economy. There are many such examples in economics. The Federal Reserve System is taught frequently by having the students memorize districts and how many directors there are for each Federal Reserve Bank, etc., without once mentioning its relationship to the need for an elastic supply of money. When the latter is pointed out, too often the mechanics of controlling bank credit and the amount of money in circulation is erroneously presented, attributing control to its discount rate rather than its open market operations. Budgets may be mentioned when the history teacher gets to the New Deal, or in discussing current events, but rarely is fiscal policy discussed as a possible stimulant for economic growth. As a result, the economist is demanding, and getting, a separate share in the training of high school teachers.

The behaviorists, anthropologists, sociologists, and social psychologists have even gone beyond simply a demand for a separate course. They often argue that history is not a social science at all and does not offer the best possible synthesis for these disciplines. Professor Chilcott has put in a bid for anthropology, and Professor Donald Oliver for social psychology to displace history in this role. Their disciplines, it is argued, would not ignore history but would focus on contemporary society, and more efficiently achieve that often stated goal in teaching social studies: to develop an understanding of the political, economic, and social world in which we live.[1]

The fears and complaints of these social scientists are not without justification. The teacher of social studies receives the bulk of his training from historians who frequently manifest a kind of siege mentality in rejecting any kind of influence from the behavioral sciences. Thus it is not simply ignorance of these disciplines when a teacher refuses the aid of any of their analytical tools, but a strong bias against such "sociological jargon." If the curriculum for training teachers requires some exposure to them, the historian tells the student to equate it with their education courses as utter nonsense, and certainly to leave it outside of their history classrooms. Perhaps, some of the very exciting history being written using behavioral concepts by such traditionally trained historians as David Potter and Lee Benson will alter this in the future.

The teacher of social studies should take a second look at the possibilities of an interdisciplinary approach to history. Actually he fuses concepts given to him by the geographer and political scientist all the time. He would consider this a legitimate part of history. But it might be that the behavioral sciences can offer him concepts and theories which will enable him to organize and explain historical data more efficiently. History courses in grades 10 and 11 already encompass more material than can possibly be covered with any meaning in a single year. The teacher frequently presents huge doses of factual and descriptive material, more closely resembling antiquarianism than history, simply because he does not know how to conceptualize the material. A model like W. W. Rostow's stages of economic growth could provide him with a useful conceptual scheme upon which to hang his facts and show important relationships between political, economic, and social variables. Or the theory of "status politics" may be worth the time needed to develop it in class if it affords a clearer explanation of the behavior of the abolitionists, progressives, and McCarthyites. Historians such as David Donald and Richard Hofstadter have, in fact, used this last concept to interpret these movements.

In teaching a high school history course it behooves the teacher to examine the different ways in which anthropologists and sociologists have conceptualized social change. As an example, let us look at one possibility. We often hear of the dichotomy between "heroes" and "social forces" in explaining change. But these social forces are rarely spelled out in the classroom. They remain vague and almost mystic to the student. Max Rafferty's recent lamentation over the disappearance of the hero from the classroom has little relationship to reality.[2] True, Nathan Hale and John Paul Jones may be missing, but that is only because we have so much more history to cover; and other types of heroes—industrial, technical, and political ones—are deemed more important. It is not unusual for even bright students to arrive at college under the impression that Andrew Jackson brought about mass democracy, T. R. broke the trusts, and F.D.R. was the cause of the New Deal.

How can the behaviorists help us to get across a more realistic view of social change? For one thing, they are more interested in social forces than individuals and spell out the important sources of change. Generally they are divided into six categories: Technological change, population change (size, migration, and distribution), changes in natural resources, changes in neighboring communities, natural occurrences, and lastly, ideas. The last category is seriously debated by some who view ideas more as a rationale for change already occurring than as a source of change. These forces first affect our value system which leads to institutional change, the behaviorist contends. The teacher might justifiably ask which of the myriad definitions of social values and social institutions he should use. Certainly a study of these definitions leads to a good deal of semantic confusion. My advice would be to use the one best understood by himself, and best suited for classroom use. I would define social values as an emotionally charged preferential list of cultural products, standards or ideas which the people of a society prize not only for themselves, but for the group and the descendants of that group. These products and patterns of behavior and belief have importance in themselves over and beyond their practical utility; e.g., Christianity, individualism, democracy, Shakespeare, the automobile. Social institutions I would define as formal groups engaged in behavior directed at meeting the basic needs of man or society. Putting across these concepts requires illustration by the teacher, but their utility in a history course may be worth the time invested.

Armed with such a conceptual model of social change, the teacher can efficiently explain a good deal about both the past and the present. It can be introduced at almost any point and used again in later units. The two broad areas through which it cuts most efficiently in American history are Westward expansion and industrialization. The student can more readily visualize how values would undergo change as a result of migration, rapidly expanding economic opportunity, and adaptation to new conditions. For example, the values associated with egalitarianism, individualism, mass democracy and social mobility can be explained in terms of people migrating ahead of many of their social institutions. The lack of occupational specialization, one of the key determinants of social stratification, made equality a reality to begin with along the frontier. Since these pioneers had to serve as lawyers, judges, doctors, and preachers at one time or another, they were less in awe of the authentic professional with traditional training once he did arrive. The potential abundance and wealth of the West enhanced the value placed upon the self-made man and again lessened the esteem of those upper classes of inherited wealth. There is no end to the available travel books and diaries to illustrate this in the classroom. Reverend Bayard Rush Hall, a Union and Princeton graduate who went out to the Iowa territory, quoted one Westerner who paused outside of his house to exclaim to a friend: "Well thats whar thet grammur man lives that larns 'em latin and grandlike things. Allow we'll oust him yet." Hall also quoted a circuit rider's sermon to illustrate his resentment of the presence of a formally trained minister in the territory:

> Yes, bless the Lord, I am a poor humble man—and I don't know a single letter in the ABC's, and couldn't read a chapter in the Bible no how you could fix it, bless the Lord! I jest preach like old Peter and Pall by the Speret. Yes, we don't ax pay in cash nor trade neither for the Gospel, and aren't no hirelins like them high-flowered college larned sheepskins.

De Tocqueville said a good deal about the American's predilection for equality, even at the expense of freedom if necessary.[3] This insight can help to explain both the populists and the McCarthyites. What better way to explain the Wisconsin Senator's reckless attacks upon the very pillars of our society, such symbols of authority and inequality as *The New York Times,* Harvard, Yale, and Princeton, the National Council of Churches, and the State Department, or his preoccupation with traitors who were born with a silver spoon in their mouths?[4] There was more to McCarthyism than this, to be sure. "Status politics," ethnic considerations (German and Irish) and isolationism all help to explain this phenomenon, but the strong egalitarian motive in our society can also help to account for it.

What institutional change resulted from this alteration in values associated with the frontier? Well, the more democratic manner in which presidential candidates were nominated and elected, the spoils system and log cabin campaigns all reflect these new values. Rather than the popular conception of Jackson bringing this about, it was due to social forces of which Jackson took advantage. He was a back-country aristocrat, a "nabob" in Tennessee who fought the democratic forces of Grundy and Carroll, and a Mason as was Van Buren, who originally opposed the nominating conventions initiated by the Anti-Masonic party, the real party of egalitarianism. No period in our history, perhaps, better illustrates that the "hero" cannot alter these forces, but only use them more efficiently than can others.

There were other important institutional changes: land grant colleges with an emphasis upon practical subjects; frontier revivalism and the creation of new sects around personalities such as William Miller and John Smith; the breakdown of the authoritarian structure of the family. Perhaps the most important result was our inability to nominate and elect a really strong

President after Jackson until the twentieth century with the lone exception of Lincoln, who could be considered almost an accident.

One important result of such an approach is that it breaks down the dichotomy between Western migration and industrialization. The values of the frontiersman were remarkably similar to those of the early industrialist. The former we forget bought land for speculation, too, and behaved as a good capitalist. In fact, one could view the industrialist as simply another type of pioneer, and industrialization as an economic frontier. If we view both as a social process, we can salvage some of the Turner thesis.[5] Of course, the student has to understand that the results are only intelligible if he keeps in mind the values brought to the frontier: the democratic beliefs of the radicals in the Revolution which, in turn, can be traced to seventeenth-century England, the Puritan emphasis upon an emotional experience of conversion, and the "Protestant ethic."

This conceptualization of change can constantly be referred to in later units. The student should be asked to analyze later changes in terms of these traditional sources of change. In looking at the New Deal, he should be able to see its relationship to technological changes known as the industrial revolution and accompanying migration to urban centers, and to visualize how these social forces would alter values and lead to institutionalized change. The less obvious and less concrete changes brought about by industrialization are too often overlooked in the classroom. The student should be made aware of what migration into the city meant in terms of total dependency upon wages; lack of personal satisfaction and identification working on an assembly line; effect of premium placed upon physical space; the transition of the family from a producing unit to a consuming one. I have witnessed lessons in high school classrooms on the standardization of goods without a single mention of the concomitant standardization of life itself, or on increased economic specialization without the direction of the students' attention to the fact that this increases the dependency of members of society on each other to satisfy their wants. The booms, crashes, panics and depressions are recorded in the classroom in good chronological order without any consideration of how it must have increased the feeling of insecurity as men faced more abstract, complex economic forces over which they had less control. Taught correctly, the student quickly sees how technological and ecological changes can greatly alter values. The response was a collectivistic one on all levels. That is, the industrialist formed pools and then trusts to mitigate the effect of competition and business cycles. The distributors formed associations and were perhaps, more instrumental than any other group in bringing about railroad regulation and the Interstate Commerce Act. The workers formed unions and the farmers cooperatives. All of these organizations sought government aid, both state and federal, at one time or another. The very density of population in cities would necessitate greater group cooperation in areas such as crime prevention and fire and health controls. All this would have to affect values associated with rugged individualism. With such an understanding, it would be difficult for the student to view the New Deal as a betrayal of Jeffersonian liberalism, or a left wing plot hatched in the economics department at Harvard.

Current events can be analyzed with the same conceptual model. For example, the student could be asked to analyze today's increased Negro militancy in terms of these traditional sources of change. It would be difficult for him to view it as the result of a Yankee or Communist plot. A more fruitful approach would be apparent in the migration of Negroes into cities during the two world wars. In the cities the Negro is less dependent upon the white man than he was as a sharecropper, and even has greater economic power as a consumer due to his higher wages. All this will alter his values. He no longer accepts Uncle-Tomism or displaced aggression against his own, or humor as the only responses to Jim Crow. He is now in a position to demand more, and the timing of this demand at the very moment when we are competing with Soviet Russia for the allegiance of the underdeveloped world inhabited largely by non-Whites sensitive to the racial issue, has put the whites in a position which makes it difficult to refuse him his demands. Lastly, ideas associated with Christianity and democracy have afforded him powerful arguments with which to irritate the conscience of the white man. In other words, traditional sources of change, i.e., migration, effect of neighboring states, and ideas, have altered to a degree the values of both the Negroes and the whites on this issue. With this understanding, the debate, fostered largely by the White Citizens Council, over whether or not Martin Luther King is a card-carrying Communist becomes totally irrelevant.

Medicare may well be "creeping socialism," but the student is made aware that changing values are behind it and not a left wing plot pulling the wool over our eyes. Since 1880 the percentage of people over 65 in our population has increased from 3.4 to 8.1 in 1950.[6] This means that more families support people over 65 whose social security checks hardly begin to cover their medical bills. A few heavy bills from a nursing home will quickly alter their attitudes toward a collective plan which will offer them relief. Increased medical costs are in turn partially due to technological changes in the field of medicine.[7] If they continue to increase at the same rate, it is not inconceivable that our values will change enough to permit some sort of health plan similar to the one in the United Kingdom. If it comes, it cannot be attributed simply to the administration that initiates it, but to social forces now in operation.

This is, of course, only one of the many possibilities in utilizing the approach of the anthropologist and sociologist to social and cultural change. It can provide the teacher with a valuable pedagogical tool permitting him more efficiently to organize a mass of material. It also is a better approach to the period discussed than the usual broad coverage that includes "locofocos," "barnburners," "hunkers," and such, in that it more clearly illustrates cause and effect relationships. Moreover, such a conceptualization avoids the liberal or conservative indoctrination that often takes place in the social studies classroom. The teacher does not have to assign moral values to these events but simply stick to the cause-and-effect relationships, much the same way a teacher of physics would do. It is immaterial whether the teacher approves or disapproves of the current Negro militancy. Given the social forces that have brought it about, there is little we can do beyond slowing down or speeding up the social process by which Negroes are achieving equal status. One can discuss plans to make this transition more orderly and less costly for all concerned,[8] but we cannot prevent it. Lastly, this conceptual model not only provides the student with too much sophistication to swallow a silly conspiracy theory of history and social change,[9] but it also equips him to anticipate change. In other words, such a model may help him to see what Robert Heilbroner calls "the forward edge of history."[10]

References

[1]J. H. Chilcott. "A Proposal for the Unification of Secondary School Courses Through Anthropology." *Clearing House* 36:391; 1962; Donald Oliver, "The Selection of Content in the Social Studies." *Harvard Educational Review* 27:294-301; 1957.

[2]Max Rafferty. "What's Happened to Patriotism?" *Readers Digest.* October 1961.

[3]Alexis de Tocqueville. *Democracy in America.* Vol. II. New York: Vintage Press, 1954. p. 99-103.

[4]Martin Trow. "Small Businessmen, Political Tolerance and Support for McCarthy." *American Journal of Sociology* 64:279-80; 1958. See also S. M. Lipset. "The Sources of the 'Radical Right,'" in Daniel Bell, editor. *The New American Right.* New York: Criterion Books, 1955. p. 166-219.

[5]See George Wilson Pierson. "The Frontier and American Institutions." *New England Quarterly* 15:224-255; 1942. For an excellent criticism of the Turner thesis and an attempt to salvage it as a migration thesis. See also David Potter. *People of Plenty.* Chicago: University of Chicago Press. Chapter VII.

[6]Warren Thompson. *Population Problems.* New York: McGraw-Hill Book Company, 1953. p. 95.

[7]See *The New Republic*. November 9, 1963. p. 9-12. Almost this entire issue was allocated to an excellent discussion of the problems facing both the doctors and the patients (p. 5-43).

[8]For example, see Morton Grodzins. "The Metropolitan Area as a Racial Problem." In *American Race Relations Today*. Edited by Earl Raab. New York: Doubleday and Company, 1962. p. 85-123. See also Ingle Dederer Gibel. "How Not to Integrate the Schools." *Harper's*. November 1963.

[9]This is not to imply, of course, that the teacher using a strictly disciplinarian approach inculcates such interpretation. But it does suggest that the usual, bland description of the past with little real analysis leaves the student more vulnerable to the plot thesis of either right or left wing variety, depending upon his own political predilections.

[10]Robert Heilbroner. *The Future as History*. New York: Harper and Brothers, 1959. p. 13-58.

SOCIOLOGY IN THE JUNIOR HIGH SCHOOL

William E. Gardner
University of Minnesota

Since its inception in 1963, the Project Social Studies Curriculum Development Center at the University of Minnesota has been developing a new sequential curriculum. Thirteen courses have been developed covering all grades from kindergarten through grade twelve and are currently being used by cooperating teachers in public schools. . . . a special feature of the curriculum pattern is the amount of material drawn from anthropology, sociology, and economics.

The seventh grade course in this curriculum draws material primarily from the discipline of sociology but includes data from history and anthropology as well. The course is made up of five units: The Physical Basis of Man's Behavior; The Social Basis of Man's Behavior; the Family (Illustration of a Social Institution); The School (Illustration of a Bureaucratic Institution); and Minority Group Relations.

This sociology course has several characteristics not readily apparent from this brief description.

1. The course consists basically of resource units, now in their third revision, books of readings, skills exercises, and additional supplementary

Reprinted with permission of the author and the publisher, from *Men and Societies* (London: Heinemann Educational Books Ltd, 1968) pp. 38-44.

materials. No attempt has been made to prepare textbooks in the typical sense of the word.

2. The course is "concept based" in the sense that it seeks to make relevant to students a number of significant concepts from sociology and to give students the ability to analyze social situations through the use of these concepts. The concepts stressed are those identified by the staff sociologist as comprising, in part, the "structure" of sociology, but a determined effort is made to avoid teaching the concepts as ends in themselves. The emphases are definitely upon the functional character of the concepts and upon student use of the concepts in simulated or real situations.

3. Since there were neither text nor non-text materials specifically designed to teach sociology to seventh graders, the course developers made use of a wide variety of learning and teaching materials in constructing the course. A particularly heavy stress was placed upon the use of adolescent literature. For example, Conrad Richter's novel *Light in the Forest* is used early in the course to show in part how human beings acquire a particular type of culture, and Esther Forbes' *Johnny Tremain* is used later in the course to indicate some of the contrasts and similarities between the social structures of colonial times and the present day. The use of such literature proved to be a rich resource for teaching and illustrating the desired concepts.

4. While not all of the teaching techniques could be described as "discovery," "induction," or "inquiry," the basic methodology used could be so classified. As often as seems feasible, teachers are asked to lead their students to follow a procedure which involved analyzing specific illustrations of social phenomena, making a general statement or conclusion which is illustrated by the phenomena being analyzed, and then applying and testing the general statement in new situations.

One of the obvious problems in teaching such a course is the difficulty of making concepts from sociology coherent to relatively young students. In fact, this difficulty has been used as an excuse by many who would reserve the teaching of sophisticated social science data for the late years of high school or until students enter college. This point of view holds that social science knowledge is far too complex for young minds to grapple with and that it is a waste of time for them to try.

Granted that the teaching of social science to young students may present unique problems, the Center staff and the cooperating public school teachers believe strongly that such teaching can be successful. Our experience indicates that the key to solving the problem lies in a venerable teaching technique—finding ways of getting the students involved with the content.

Not surprisingly, concepts from sociology can be used to analyze literally thousands of social situations which are readily recognized by students and in which they are interested. Each student, we find, comes to the course having already adopted a kind of "sociological" framework; that is, he has developed a way or ways of interpreting and understanding the behavior of people based upon his past experience. He may, for instance, believe that delinquent behavior is inherited or that certain racial and ethnic groups are inferior mentally to others. Even if his perceptions of the social world are more sophisticated than this, he is unable to explain the anomalies and contradictions in social situations. By presenting the basic concepts of sociology in the context of real social situations, teachers of this sociology course attempt to give their students the power needed to develop a better, more scientific understanding of the social world.

Two illustrations drawn from actual classroom experience will serve to illustrate the basic teaching technique used in the course. In one seventh grade class, the teacher is introducing the concept *socialization* in the second unit of the course. Since this concept is highly abstract and difficult to present through a typical mode of defining and explaining, the teacher attempts to get her students to analyze social situations with which they are familiar. This is an edited version of a transcription of the classroom dialogue.

Teacher: Suppose we set up a situation and I ask you what will happen in this situation. Let's take two boys (call them Tom and John) at a school party which is chaperoned by Mr. Jones, the physical education teacher. Tom just happens to spill a bottle of Coke on John, and the two boys begin to argue and then fight. John gives Tom a left to the eye; Tom responds with a right to the jaw. Then Mr. Jones enters the room. Your problem is to tell me what Mr. Jones does.
Student: He stops the boys from fighting.
Teacher: Anything else?
Student: He gives them a lecture.
Student: Since their behavior is so bad he sends them to the principal. He may also notify their parents that they have been behaving badly at the school dance. . . .
Teacher: So you think that Mr. Jones will tell them in one way or another that their behavior is not what it should be and they will be punished. Fine; I think that's what would happen, too.
   Suppose we shift now to the morning following the fight. The boys are now in Physical Education class and Mr. Jones is their teacher. In the center of the gym is a boxing ring, and by luck of the draw, Tom and John are chosen to put on the gloves. We might think that this is just what the two boys wanted but for some reason (perhaps they are too tired) they don't do any more than move slowly around the ring. Not a blow is struck.

Enter Mr. Jones again, now what does he do?
Student: He probably tells the boys to mix it up, to start to box.
Teacher: I agree, but the night before he told them *not* to do that. Why
would he change his mind? Or did he change his mind? What do you
think?
Student: It's not so strange; adults always act like that.
Student: The boys weren't doing what they were supposed to do in both
cases. On the one hand, they were supposed to fight but at the dance they
weren't.

The teacher goes on to present other situations where the social context
determines how people should behave. (1. How do you dress to go to a
dance? To a religious service? Why do you dress differently? 2. How do you
address your best friend when you meet him at school? How do you greet a
strange person you've never met before? Suppose you were to meet the
President of the United States, how would you greet him? How do you know
you should address these people in different ways? 3. Suppose you were
going to spend a year in another country. Would you eat the same foods?
Would your table manners be the same? Why?)

Slowly and without naming the process of socialization the class becomes
aware of apparent inconsistencies in social behavior which indicate that
people learn what are to them appropriate and inappropriate ways of behaving in certain social situations. The class then reads descriptions of lost or
abandoned children (including a fascinating account of "wolf children") and
people who move from one culture to another, experiencing difficulty in
many of the common everyday activities. The stage is set for a further discussion of how people acquire values and norms in a society and what
importance this has for the individual.

The beginning of the concept "socialization" acquired by the students
through the analysis of social situations is used repeatedly later in the course.
In the family unit, the students see the significant impact of this primary
group on the socialization process. In their study of the school, the students
note the continuing influences of social institutions on the behavior of
people.

As the following illustration shows, the concept "socialization" appears in
classroom discussion even when the teacher does not directly elicit it. This
classroom episode, again an edited version of a transcript of classroom dialogue, took place in the unit on minority groups. The class is in the process of
studying the life of American Negroes under slavery and has read excerpts
from the contemporary commentary on this institution.

Teacher: We have now looked at some descriptions of what slavery was like. At least, what certain people thought it was like. We've read some comments by slaves, by slave-owners, and by foreign observers. Do you have any questions or comments about these readings?

Student: Well, I guess I'm a little confused. I always thought that all slaves hated it under slavery, but some of them said it was better than life after the war when they were free.

Student: Sure, they got food and clothes and everything when they were slaves. They just naturally liked that better.

Student: You're just saying that the Negro is naturally more dependent than the whites were—and I think that's wrong. Because, I guess, under slavery they—some of them anyway—just *learned* to expect that they would get food and all. When they were free, they had to learn how to plan for a rainy day and to budget their money. It was bound to be a little confusing. Anyway, not all of the slaves liked it—Frederick Douglass didn't.

[Other students agree, the class concludes that most slaves probably did not really like life under slavery.]

Student: What I can't see is why more of them didn't rebel. Sure, some of them liked slavery but most must have hated it. I guess I'd rather be dead than be a slave.

Student: They did revolt. I read a book that told about all the slave rebellions in the South. There must have been 50 revolts.

Student: But that means that only a few revolted, and I know a lot ran away. But most of them didn't. Why didn't more revolt?

Student: I keep telling you; they "learned" to act as slaves. As the one guy said, when the slave talked to a white man he hung his head and mumbled and shuffled away. He wasn't born that way—he learned it.

Teacher: When you say he learned it, what really do you mean?

Student: I mean he was socialized in the same way we are. We learn to talk to our teachers in a certain way. Slaves learned a whole bunch of things in the same way. It's easy for us to say we'd rebel if we were slaves; but the reason slavery lasted so long was that the slaves were taught to be slaves and we weren't.

These illustrations deal with only one of the ten or so major concepts dealt with in the course. While variations appear in the method and techniques used by the cooperating teachers, most often each concept is approached by placing the students on the "horns of a dilemma" and getting them to see that their previous interpretations of social phenomena were inadequate to the task.

Because this course attempts to teach unusual content to young students, it has been the object of fairly intensive research and study to gauge its effectiveness. The data accumulated in this process are of several types: (1)

Cooperating teachers returned reaction forms each week on which they noted their comments on the work covered. Staff writers used these forms in revising the materials for the next year; (2) Teachers were also brought together for group meetings during which they gave additional criticisms of the course, made suggestions for improvement, and presented subjective evidence of the ways in which students used basic ideas from the course in new situations; (3) Objective and subjective tests were administered which were designed to assess student achievement in the course.

A complete discussion of the results of the evaluation is impossible here, but the three major conclusions may be stated:

1. On the basis of the test results, we are convinced that students learn and use the concepts from sociology taught in this course. Moreover, the learning is not the mere attachment of verbal labels to social phenomenon, but, with most students tested, the ability to understand the multitude of social situations with which an individual must constantly deal.

2. The reaction of cooperating teachers (although highly critical of parts of the initial version of the course) has been overwhelmingly favorable. They report that teaching has taken on new meaning for them and possesses an excitement which was formerly lacking. They also report some amazement at the readiness, skill, and eagerness with which students approach the sociology content.

3. The reaction of students also has been positive. While no formal attempt was made to assess student attitudes, teachers have documented hundreds of instances which reveal high student interest and the lasting quality of the learning.

Despite these positive results, the Center staff realizes that all the evidence is not yet in. We have only a beginning knowledge of how well students understand the concepts and whether they will use them to understand new situations in society. We know little or nothing about the effects of sociological knowledge on students who are very much in the formative years. The question is: Will knowledge about the socialization process when acquired by young students hinder or enhance the development of strong, stable personalities? Furthermore, no amount of research can deal with the philosophical issue of whether sociology *should* be taught to seventh grade students.

Nevertheless, if behavioral science has any place in the social studies curriculum, it seems apparent that such content cannot be postponed until relatively late in the school program. Our experience indicates that a sociology course can be taught successfully in public schools and that both teachers and students receive it enthusiastically. This conclusion stands in opposition to the claim that such "difficult" learning must await greater maturity, a claim that may ultimately prove to be another of education's shibboleths.

THE JUNIOR HIGH SCHOOL DEVELOPS ECONOMIC UNDERSTANDING

John F. Soboslay
Pittsburgh Public Schools

The teaching of economics which so long appeared to be a dismal and esoteric undertaking, has experienced an uprising against the status quo, an uprising led by social scientists determined to put a generous portion of sparkle and bounce into economics without doing any violence to the basic principles of the science.

This revolt by a new wave of economic educators has come none too soon if we are to maintain any hope of developing appreciable economic understanding among a group long in rebellion against boring texts, teachers, and trivia; namely, junior high school students who refuse to be bored. Those who wish to develop economic understanding in the junior high school must, to use an old army saying, "shape up or ship out."

In a splendid example of cooperation between members of the Pittsburgh public schools and professional economists from the local college and business communities, a major three-year effort is now under way to improve economic understanding, not only among students, but also among teachers and community leaders of the Pittsburgh area.

In our first year of operation we have developed supplementary student materials in the field of economics for the eighth-grade United States history course and the ninth-grade social science (civics) course.

We have not simply drawn up another outline of *what* economics should be taught. (Heaven knows the land abounds with the withered bones of abandoned scope and sequence charts!) Specific student readings have been listed, audio-visual aids have been developed, and a teacher's manual with a detailed lesson plan to accompany each lesson has been completed.

Reprinted with permission of the author and the National Council for the Social Studies, from *Social Education,* 30 (April, 1966): 259-260, 273.

Each lesson plan includes a particular economic understanding objective, a skill objective, detailed procedural methods of teaching the lesson, and key questions to be asked in order to stimulate class discussion. The lesson plans are designed in such a way that an average social studies teacher, unsophisticated in economics, can lead a class through each lesson with the reasonable hope that the students will carry away with them each day the feeling and the certainty that a few more pieces of the economics jig-saw puzzle have fallen into place.

An imaginative teacher can feel free to add to or subtract from the suggested lesson plan, for ours is not an inflexible method which would frustrate any enterprising teacher. Our lesson plans were written mainly to help teachers who have been struggling to carry out their assigned responsibility to teach economic content. The lessons were not written to represent the last word, but rather, they were written to supply the often needed first word.

Wherever it is possible to do so, the lessons encourage the inductive method of reasoning to be used by the student. The lesson structure is so devised that he sharpens his ability to use problem-solving techniques in analyzing the material presented.

The experience of discovery for the junior high school student cannot be overestimated. Being at an age where all people insist in telling him what is correct, he is thrilled to be able to conclude for himself what is so, and what is not so.

For all who construct a junior high school curriculum it is wise not to attempt to do too much, but rather to give the necessary time to doing things well. It is better for a young student to develop an understanding of a few basic economic concepts. Because he is not ready at the age of 12 or 13 to master advanced work in economics, it is important that a lesson not be overloaded with too many or too complicated ideas. As John Locke once noted, "The great art of learning is to understand a little at a time."

If university people act as curriculum consultants, it is important that they make a number of visits to a public school classroom before they begin intensive and detailed work. Such visits give them an opportunity to see the real world for which they will be helping to prepare materials. Many university economists have never taught below the college level and often do not have a true picture of junior high school classroom situations.

In Pittsburgh, our eighth-grade efforts concentrate on one major continuing theme throughout the school year, that theme being economic growth—its measurement and explanation. We frequently had to remind ourselves as we went about our work that the eighth-grade course is primarily one in United

States history, and not an economics course; therefore, we had to develop supplementary economics material which would do a better job of presenting certain economic aspects of our history, not handled well by the classroom history text.

Our eighth-grade United States history teacher covers the period from the fifteenth-century voyages of discovery to the twentieth-century voyages in the new ocean of outer space; therefore, demands made upon him to handle supplementary economics material must be reasonable in light of his over-all responsibility. Even though at times we recommend the classroom omission of certain chapters of the history text, which do a very poor job with economic content, we are still a bit hesitant about imposing upon the teacher the 30 lessons of our own creation. Field-testing, now underway, will tell us if our new classroom demands are reasonable or out of touch with the reality imposed by calendar and clock.

In our material for the eighth-grader, we have composed a reading dealing with Pilgrims which incorporates the economic idea of scarcity and how this requires making choices as to how limited resources should be employed. All this is focused upon in the reading by describing how, once settled in Plymouth, the Pilgrims were desperately afraid of Indian attacks, yet they dared not take the time and materials necessary to build a fort. It was December; their need for immediate shelter from cold, rain, and snow was too urgent to permit them the luxury of securing themselves against possible future Indian attacks. When spring came, their most pressing need was to plant corn so food could be available for the next winter. There was also game in the forest which could give the settlers meat, but men who went hunting weren't available for planting and hoeing corn.

There is also a lesson in the same unit on the Puritans who came after the Pilgrims, and seemed to adjust readily to their new environment, perhaps because of better education and organizational ability. Another lesson provides a description of Boston in 1742 as seen through the eyes of a young boy helping his father operate a lumber business. Things had changed greatly in New England since the coming of the Pilgrims a century earlier, for the activity of this growing city since then had developed around shops and shipbuilding. From the reading it is hoped that the students see that developing technology and greatly increased specialization were important aspects of New England's early economic growth.

Included also in the unit is an excerpt from the diary of a true-to-life Frenchman who visited Pittsburgh in 1834. (It was spelled "Pittsburg" without the "h" at that time.) He commented on how industrious the people of the city seemed to be and how little they were given to pleasure. The Frenchman thought the area would prosper, but conditions such as the limited nightlife made it a dull place to live, according to his thinking.

Another lesson which has been developed as a result of our program, points out the economic significance of certain clauses in our Constitution. The students are asked to judge whether Adam Smith, whose philosophy they review, would have favored or disapproved of various powers given to the government by these clauses.

Toward the end of the eighth-grade year, a unit is introduced entitled *Prosperity and Depression—the 1920's and 1930's.* In the first lesson, the two decades are compared by referring to certain literary descriptions of each period. The prosperity of the 1920's is described to the students by a passage from F. Scott Fitzgerald's *The Great Gatsby,* in which a lavish party at the Gatsby estate is depicted. Next, the students are introduced to the problems of the 1930's through an excerpt from John Steinbeck's unforgetable tale of the wandering Oakies in *The Grapes of Wrath.*

Another part of the same unit makes effective use of audio-visual materials. While a tape recording of period musical selections plays in the background, a series of slides showing flappers, "wets and drys," breadlines and oppressive poverty, flash upon the classroom screen. Students are asked briefly to jot down their reactions as the slides are shown.

The concluding lesson turns to a section from Edward R. Murrow's classic recording, "I Can Hear It Now" for examples of the voices and the vocabulary that dominated the 1920's and 1930's. Students are then asked to recall factors affecting economic growth that were mentioned in the Murrow presentation.

In our ninth-grade material for the social science course, 40 basic economics lessons for 14-year-olds were prepared for use over a 12-week period.

The problem of scarcity and real cost is the main theme of one lesson which sets up a situation in which student planners are asked to choose between using existing space around a school either for a parking lot or for a playground.

Another unit focuses on a description of three economic systems (tradition, command, and market) which is then followed by six brief, readable—though fictional—cases, each of which the students are asked to identify properly as an example of one of the economic systems. In one of the stories, the traditional system is described to the students through the President of Moritanzia who still proudly displays Air Force planes built from blueprints 60 years old because they have always been a symbol of his nation which gained its independence 60 years ago. In another case, illustrating the market system, is the story of Robert Travis, an excellent science teacher who leaves the classroom to become a space technician because he can obtain a 100 percent salary increase by doing so.

In an attempt to help the students comprehend the complexity of planning in a command economy, a lesson is introduced in which a comparatively simple input-output table is used which, of course, is not easy going even in its most simple form.

One of our most interesting ninth-grade units deals with the problem of poverty. Is it possible to define poverty? What is to become of the people rejected by the market system, such as the businessman who fails or the person who can't find a job? What is the influence of poverty on consumer demand, and on the community supply of labor? Can the pent-up frustration and anger of poverty have an economic effect on the community? How does a community go about upgrading the ambition of the deprived? Is self-interest necessarily bad? Is lack of community conflict necessarily good?

This article contains a description of what has been accomplished in Pittsburgh over the last year in trying to develop economic understanding in the existing junior high school curriculum. Valuable guidance in various stages of preparing our material was given by many busy and talented people, such as Doctors Bach, Coleman, and Saunders of Carnegie Institute of Technology, without whose help we would have repeated many of the errors of the past in the selection of economic content. If the Pittsburgh economics material is judged to be successful, it will be largely due to the extraordinary abilities of our chief lesson-maker and resident economist, Mrs. Mindella Schultz. In addition, the Joint Council on Economic Education is continuing its efforts to help our school system take another step towards the goal of quality education.

The economics project for junior high schools in Pittsburgh hasn't conquered the world in one year. Yet it is wonderful to see a new, positive attitude about economics developing among the many and varied people touched by such efforts.

PART THREE

Methods and Techniques
of Instruction

Fred A. Johnson

The creditability gap is not new to the social studies. Critics of the field have long recognized a dichotomy between its theory and practice. Though lists of objectives, educators' statements, and teacher comments pay lip service to the goals of making students critical thinkers, equipping them with broad principles about man in society, and enabling them to live productively, classroom instruction most often has been limited to the rote transmission of knowledge. Meaningful change in the social studies demands the narrowing of this credibility gap.

It is rather bromidic to say that the transformation of the social studies curriculum will have little meaning if not accompanied by qualitative changes in instruction, but it is true. This is not to say that curriculum change, the introduction of new content, and the development of new materials are not important. It is self-evident that these changes are vital. Neither is it our purpose to revive fruitless polemics concerning the relative importance of content and method. It merely is to recognize that instruction must be the focal point of all meaningful change in the social studies.

Social studies teachers should have no guilt feelings about the credibility gap. Relating instruction to social studies goals is a difficult task. What learning experiences contribute to the development of critical thought processes? How can students be challenged to examine their values and beliefs and those of others so that they may construct a viable value system? How can students be induced to see the relevance of the past and helped to discover the structure of the present? How may instruction be differentiated to meet individual and cultural differences without creating or reinforcing undesirable attitudes? These are but a few of the puzzling questions which must be answered if progress toward the abstract and complex goals of the social studies is to be realized.

Instruction is a profound undertaking, but it may be defined simply as the process by which teachers seek to change learner behavior. While at the present time we have relatively less scientific knowledge about instruction than about learning, the tempo of research is increasing. Educators who have studied instruction have approached it from a variety of directions. Dewey advocated that problem-solving be studied, described and applied to the class-room. This has never been done on a large scale. Other researchers have tried to determine the influence of interpersonal teacher-student relations and other affective components of classroom interaction upon learning. Their research identified two basic classroom "Atmospheres"—the democratic or learner-centered classroom opposed to the authoritarian or teacher-centered one. Though these studies do not demonstrate decisively the effect of the emotional climate on learning, the findings are of obvious import to the teacher interested in the development of democratic citizens.[1]

Another approach to the study of instruction has been to compare the relative effectiveness of various "methods." For example, research has attempted to establish the superiority of the discussion method versus the lecture method. Although a recent review of a few carefully selected method studies has yielded noteworthy insights,[2] collectively the results of this type of research are so inconclusive and contradictory that it is difficult to know what has been established.[3] Many social studies educators believe that some of the confusion is due at least in part to the failure of researchers to dis-tinguish adequately the experimental variable. It is now widely held that what these studies compared were instructional techniques, not method.

Perhaps it is useful to recognize the distinction between these concepts at this time. Method describes the overall approach that the teacher has to instruction. If instruction is conceptualized as a social system, method becomes the set of laws which the teacher attempts to follow in order to influence the output of the system. The teaching method defines the roles of the participants in the learning process and determines the legitimacy of instructional activities. Using this conception of methods, two basic methods may be distinguished in the current educational literature. In the first of these, which may be called the expository method, the major instructional goal is the transmission of knowledge. The teacher plays a very dominant role. He selects, organizes, and presents most of the material learned to his students. The role of the student is to accept the information, assimilate it, and give evidence upon request in recitation or examination of having re-ceived it.

The second basic method, the one which most educators believe to be the more realistic and superior one, has several labels.[4] The name given the method is not important, but the attitude which the teacher has toward knowledge, his students, the learning process, and the goals of instruction all are important. Though there are distinctions made, most educators would agree that the teacher who uses this method must view instruction as a process for critically examining knowledge, beliefs, and values. Generalizations from the social sciences are regarded as tentative hypotheses, which may be rejected after critical examination or further research. Students are expected to be active participants in a search for answers to meaningful questions. The teacher in this methodological construct initiates and guides instruction. He does not regard himself as the ultimate source of knowledge, but as a coordinator of the search for meaning.

Instructional techniques, as defined here, refer to the specific practices and procedures used by the teacher. Lecture or class discussion, though referred to elsewhere as methods, are in this construct, techniques. Other examples of techniques include the use of case studies, programmed learning, simulation games, writing activities, and oral reports. Simply stated, techniques are the specific procedures used to influence student behavior. Techniques are an integral part of, but subordinate, to method. Method is the overall teaching strategy, technique the specific classroom tactic. All classroom procedures should be used in a manner consistent with the method employed. This simply means that techniques, such as films, case studies, and games may be used in diverse ways and for different purposes. For example, a film, depending on content and instructional goals, may be used to transmit knowledge, stimulate discussion, or to provide an opportunity for emotional identification.

If the technique is selected and used in a manner consistent with the method employed, there is general agreement among social studies educators that instruction should be characterized by the use of a variety of materials and procedures. Several arguments support this position. First, there is no definitive body of research establishing the relative effectiveness of the various instructional techniques. Second, citizenship education demands that instruction deal effectively with concepts, skills, and values. Some procedures are clearly more appropriate to one type of specific objective than others. The learning of map-reading skills requires, among other procedures, explanation and practice with map-reading problems, whereas, acquiring an understanding of labor's basic point of view may be efficiently accomplished by the use of certain types of case studies and socio-drama techniques. Individual differences in learning styles also seem to justify the use of a variety of techniques.[5] For example, it seems some individuals learn more effectively from audio-visual experiences than from reading; some learn effectively by lecture, others do not. Finally, the psychological law of diminishing returns tends to support the use of a number of techniques. Social scientists have noted that even the most intense and dramatic events lose their effectiveness when the audiences' perception system has become adjusted to their impact. Applying this principle to the classroom, it seems reasonable to suppose that even such a novel technique as a game may lose its effectiveness if continually repeated.

Recent study of classroom interaction has focused on beliefs, logical tasks, and linguistics. Kemp, using Rokeach's basic construct of open and closed belief systems, has found learning is adversely affected by dogmatic and rigid beliefs.[6] Smith and Meux have begun a long term effort to describe and analyze the logical relevant tasks of teachers.[7] Arno Bellack and his associates at Columbia recently completed a study which describes the linguistic behaviors of students and teachers.[8] These studies collectively give great promise that we shall soon have a descriptive model of instruction. The task of implementing a proscriptive model, however, remains a puzzling problem.[9]

In sum, research has not established the superiority of any method or technique. Since the goals of social studies instruction are quite diverse, we urge that the expository and inquiry methods and a variety of instructional techniques be examined and tried by teachers.

The readings in this Part are organized into three sections, problems, methods, and techniques of teaching. Relating to students is a major problem for many teachers. Our first reading, James Michener's provocative short story, "Who is Virgil T. Fry," describes a teacher who established almost a chemical relationship with his students. Understanding human relationships is a fundamental goal of social studies instruction. Two articles in this section discuss this basic problem of teaching. Ernest Horn in "The Problem of Meaning" explains how the nature of the problem, the instructional media, and the characteristics all influence understanding. Then, Seymour H. Fersh illustrates how semantics may distort meaning in the study of other cultures.

The readings in Section B deal with "method." First, Jerome Bruner's highly instructive article, "The Act of Discovery," raises several fundamental questions about purpose, reward, and learning. The second reading by Byron C. Massialas and C. Benjamin Cox provides a model for the reflective method. The last reading in this section, Kenneth Henderson's "Anent the Discovery Method," critically examines the assumptions and learning outcomes of the inductive method which is so widely advocated at the present time. Although focused upon the teaching of mathematics, this article has many implications for social studies teachers.

The eleven readings in the "techniques" section offer specific illustrations of student activities and classroom procedures. Three articles deal with the teaching of geography. How "set theory" may be used to modify the influence of geographic determinism is the subject of the first reading. Next, Leonard M. Lansky and Howard Stafford describe some of the goals and procedures of the "Manufacturing Unit of the High School Project." The last reading, dealing with the teaching of geography, presents several means of "Using Maps and Diagrams More Effectively."

The next four articles are concerned with the teaching of history. Mitchell P. Lichtenberg and Edwin Fenton of Carnegie Tech's Social Studies Curriculum Development Center explain how A—V materials may be used inductively. Teaching history to culturally different students presents special problems. Robert W. Edgar, Director of the Bridge Project, reports a successful bridging of the cultural gap in the next reading entitled, "History, Reading and Human Relations." John Georgeoff, the author of the third article in this series, explains how the writing of historical fiction may be used to increase student achievement. The last article in this group, "Making History Inevitable," by Arnold Rothstein, offers teachers a technique for avoiding the danger of teaching history from the vantage point of hindsight.

The last four articles in this section focus on the teaching of critical thinking and values. Wayne Mahood describes how reflective thinking may be used to discuss the controversial or closed areas of economics. The meaningful study of current events and civil liberties demands the focusing on values, according to the next two readings by Parker and Econopouly and Lieberman and Simon, respectively. The last reading in this section, Samuel Polatnick's "A Vote for Citizenship" cogently describes New York City's program to increase intelligent voting and other forms of civic participation.

References

[1] Richard C. Anderson, "Learning in Discussions: A Résumé of Authoritarian-Democratic Studies," *Harvard Educational Review,* (29) Summer, 1959, p. 209.

[2] Lawrence E. Metcalf, "Research on Teaching the Social Studies," in N.L. Gage, ed., *Handbook on Research on Teaching* (Chicago, Rand McNally & Company, 1963), pp. 929-965.

[3] Richard E. Gross and William V. Badger, "Social Studies," *Encyclopedia of Educational Research* (New York: The Macmillan Company, 1960), p. 1305-1308.

[4] To some it is the method of reflective thought; others call it the discovery method; still others refer to it as inquiry.

[5]T. A. Ryan, "Selecting and Using Varied Instructional Approaches to Increase Learning Outcomes," *Phi Delta Kappan* (46), 1965, pp. 534-36.

[6]C. Gratton Kemp, "Critical Thinking: Open and Closed Minds," *The American Behavioral Scientist* (5), January 1962, pp. 10-15; Milton Rokeach, *The Open and Closed Mind* (New York: Basic Books, 1960.)

[7]B. Othanel Smith and Milton O. Meux, *A Study of the Logic of Teaching* (Urbana: Bureau of Educational Research, University of Illinois, 1962.)

[8]Arno A. Bellack, Herbert Klubard, Ronald T. Hyman, and Frank L. Smith, *The Language of the Classroom* (Teachers College, Columbia University: New York Teachers College Press, 1966.)

[9]Donald W. Oliver and James B. Shaver, *Teaching Public Issues in High School* (Boston: Houghton Mifflin Company, 1966). pp. 286-324.

WHO IS VIRGIL T. FRY?

The remarkable facts about a man who
is either a master teacher or a big fraud

James A. Michener

I have never known a man more fascinating than Mr. Virgil T. Fry. His fascination grows daily because I have never met him.

Mr. Fry, you see, was my predecessor in a small Indiana high school. He was a teacher of the social studies, and he was fired for incompetency. I was brought in to take his place.

Dr. Kelwell, the superintendent of schools in Akara, first told me about Virgil T. Fry. "Fry," he said, "was a most impossible man to work with. I hope you will not be like him."

"What was his trouble?" I asked.

"Never anything in on time. Very hard man to work with. Never took advice," was the reply. Dr. Kelwell paused and leaned back in his chair. He shook his head violently: "Very poor professional spirit." He nodded as if to agree with himself, then repeated, "I hope you won't be like him."

The principal, Mr. Hasbolt, was considerably more blunt.

"You have a great chance here," he said. "Mr. Fry, your predecessor, was a very poor teacher. He antagonized everyone. Constant source of friction. I don't recall when we ever had a teacher here who created more dissension among our faculty. Not only his own department, either. Everyone in this building hated that man, I really do believe. I certainly hope you won't make the same mistakes." He wrung my hand vigorously as if to welcome me as a real relief from a most pressing and unpleasant problem.

The head of the social-studies department in which I worked was more like Dr. Kelwell than like Mr. Hasbolt. He merely hinted at Mr. Fry's discrepan-

Reprinted with permission of the publisher, from *The Clearing House*, 26 (October, 1941): 67-70.

cies. "Very inadequate scholar. Very unsound. Apt to go off half-cocked," he mused.

"In what way?" I asked.

"Oh—lots of ways. You know. Crack-pot ideas. Poor tact in expressing them. You have a real opportunity here to do a good job. I certainly hope you won't make Fry's mistakes."

But if the head of my department was indirect, the head of the English department wasn't. "That man!" she sniffed. "He really was a terrible person. I'm not an old maid, and I'm not prudish, but Virgil T. Fry was a most intolerable person. He not only thought he could teach social studies and made a mess of it, but he also tried to tell me how to teach English. In fact, he tried to tell everyone how to do everything."

Miss Kennedy was neither an old maid nor prudish, and she was correct when she intimated that the rest of the staff felt as she did. Mr. Fry had insulted the music department, the science department, and above all the physical-education department.

Tiff Small was head of athletics. He was a fine man with whom I subsequently played a great deal of golf and some tennis. He wouldn't discuss Fry. "That pansy!" and he would sniff his big nose into a wrinkle. "Pretty poor stuff."

Mr. Virgil T. Fry's landlady ultimately became my landlady, too, and she bore out everything the faculty had said about her former boarder: "Never cleaned his room up. Smoked cigarettes and dropped the ashes. I hope you don't smoke. You don't? Well, I'm certainly glad. But this Mr. Fry, my he was a hard man to keep house for. I pity the poor girl that gets him."

Remembering Tiff Small's insinuation, I asked my landlady if Fry ever went with girls. "Him? He courted like it was his sole occupation. Finally married a girl from Akara. She was a typist downtown. Had been to the University of Chicago. Very stuck-up girl, but not any better than she had to be, if you want my opinion. Quite a girl, and quite good enough for Virgil T. Fry."

As the year went on I learned more about Fry. He must have been a most objectionable person, indeed, for the opinion concerning him was unanimous. In a way I was glad, for I profited from his previous sins. Everyone was glad to welcome me into the school system and into the town, for, to put it badly, I was a most happy relief from Virgil T. Fry.

Apart from his personality he was also a pretty poor teacher. I found one of his roll books once and just for fun distributed his grades along the normal curve. What a mess they were! He had 18% A's where he should have had no more than 8%! His B's were the same. And when I reached the F's, he was following no system at all. One person with a total score of 183 was flunked. The next, with a total score of 179, had received a C! And in the back of his desk I found 247 term papers he had never even opened! I laughed and congratulated myself on being at least more honest than my predecessor, even if I excelled him in no other way.

I was in this frame of mind when Doris Kelley, the sixteen-year-old daughter of a local doctor, came into my room one evening after school. "May I ask you a question?" she said.

"Of course."

"Maybe you won't like it," she replied, hesitating a moment.

I laughed. "Certainly I will. What is it?"

"Why don't you teach the way Mr. Fry did?"

I was taken aback. "How did he teach?" I asked.

"Oh," was the answer, "he made everything so interesting!"

I swallowed and asked her to elaborate.

"Well, Mr. Fry always taught as if everything he talked about was of utmost importance. You got to love America when you got through a course with Mr. Fry. He always had a joke. He wasn't afraid to skip chapters now and then.

"He could certainly teach you how to write a sentence and a term paper. Much better than the English teachers, only they didn't like it very much. And did you *read books* when Mr. Fry taught you! Ten, maybe, a year, and all in the very kinds of things you liked best. Hitler, strikes, the Constitution, and all about crime. Just anything you wanted to read.

"And class was always so interesting. Not boring." She stopped and looked at me across the desk with a bit of Irish defiance in her eye.

She was a somewhat mature girl and I concluded that she had had a crush on this remarkable Mr. Virgil T. Fry. "Did all the pupils feel that way?" I asked her.

"I know what you're thinking," she said, smiling. "But you're wrong. Everyone liked him. Almost every one of them did. And the reason I came in to see you this evening is that none of us like the way you teach. It's all so very dull!"

I blushed. Everyone had been telling me what a fine job I was doing. I stammered a bit, "Well, Mr. Fry and I teach two different ways."

"Oh, no," she insisted, "It's not that. Mr. Fry really taught. He taught us something every day. I'll bet if you ask all the pupils they'll all say the same thing. He was about the only real teacher we had."

I became somewhat provoked and said a very stupid thing. "Then why was he fired?"

No answer.

"You did know he was fired, didn't you?"

Doris nodded.

"Why?" I repeated.

Doris laughed. "Don't you know? All the kids do." And she stood in the door, smiling. "Jealousy," she said.

I was alarmed. I wondered if the pupils really did dislike my teaching as much as Doris had implied. The next day in a class of which Doris was not a member I tried an experiment.

"Well," I said, "We've now reached the end of the first unit. I wonder if it wouldn't be a good idea to go back to a discussion of the big ideas of this unit?"

I paused.

Not much response, so I added: "The way Mr. Fry used to do?"

Immediately all the pupils sat up and started to pay attention. Most of them smiled. Two of the girls giggled and some of the boys squirmed. They obviously wanted to accept my suggestion. "Tom," I asked, "will you take over?" for I had no idea what Mr. Fry's method was.

Tom nodded vigorously and came to the front of the room.

"All right," he rasped, "who will dare?"

"I will," said a girl. "I believe that Columbus came to the New World more for religious reasons than for commercial reasons."

"Oh!" groaned a group of pupils, snapping their fingers for attention. Tom called on one.

"I think that's very stupid reasoning, Lucille. Spain was only using religion as a mask for imperialism."

Lucille turned in her seat and shot back, "You wouldn't think so if you knew anything about Philip the Second."

And the debate continued until Tom issued his next dare. A pupil accepted and defiantly announced: "I think all that section about Spain's being so poor at colonizing is the malarkey. Everything south of Texas except Brazil is now Spanish. That looks pretty good to me."

I winced at the word "malarkey" and the pupils winced at the idea. The tigers of Anglo-Saxony rose to the defense of the text and the challenging pupil did his best to stand them off.

A few nights later I drove some other pupils to a basketball game in a nearby city. One of the boys observed, as we were coming home: "Class has been much better lately. I sort of like history now."

"How do you mean, better?" I asked.

"Oh, more the way Mr. Fry used to teach."

"Was Mr. Fry such a good teacher?" I asked.

"Oh, boy!" chortled the crowd, all at once. And one continued, "Was he? Boy, he could really teach you. I learned more from him than my big brother did at the university, in the same course. That's a fact! I had to read more, too, but I certainly like it."

"I always thought he was rather—well, sissy?" I observed.

"Fry? Oh, no!" the boys replied. "It's true he didn't like the athletic department and used to make some pretty mean cracks about athletes, but we all liked it a lot. No, Mr. Fry was a very good tennis player and could swim like a fish."

The question of reading bothered me. I had always aspired to have my pupils read a great deal, and here they were all telling me that last year they had read and this year they hadn't. I went to see Miss Fisher, the librarian, about it.

"No," she said, "the books aren't going out the way they did last year."

"Could it be that maybe Mr. Fry knew how to use the library better?" I asked.

"Oh, no!" was the laughing reply. "You're twice the teacher Mr. Fry was. All the staff thinks so. He was a terrible person around a library!"

This depressed me, and I sought for an answer outside the school. I went around that night to visit Dr. Kelley, Doris' father.

"The fact is," he said, "You're in a tough spot. Virgil T. Fry was a truly great teacher. You're filling the shoes of a master. I hear the children talking at table and about the house. Fry seems to have been the only teacher who ever really got under their skins and taught them anything."

He paused, then added, "As a matter of fact, the pupils find your teaching rather empty, but I'm glad to say they think it's been picking up recently." He knocked out his pipe and smiled at me.

"Then why was Fry fired?" I asked.

"Difference of opinion, I guess," the doctor replied. "Fry thought education consisted of stirring up and creating. He made himself very unpopular. You see, education is really a complete social venture. I see that from being on the school board. Fry was excellent with pupils but he made a terrible mess of his adult relationships."

"You're also a father," I said. "Don't you think your daughter deserves to have good teachers?"

He lit his pipe again. "Of course, if you want the truth, I'd rather have Doris study under Fry than under you. In the long run she'd learn more." He smiled wryly. "At the same time, what she learns from you may be better for her in the long run than what she would have learned from Fry."

"May I ask you one question, Doctor?" I inquired. He assented. "Did you concur in Fry's dismissal?"

Dr. Kelley looked at me a long time and drew on his pipe. Then he laughed quietly. "I cut board meeting that night. I knew the problem was coming up."

"How would you have voted?" I persisted.

"I think I would always cut board meeting," he answered. "Fry was a disruptive force. He was also a very great teacher. I think the two aspects balanced precisely. I would neither hire him nor fire him. I wouldn't fight to keep him in a school and I wouldn't raise a finger to get him out of one."

I frowned.

He continued: "The fine aspect of the whole thing is that you, a beginning teacher, don't have to be all Fry or all yourself. You can be both a great teacher and a fine, social individual. It's possible."

Dr. Kelley laughed again as he showed me to the door. "Don't worry about it. And you may be interested to know that your superintendent, Dr. Kelwell, feels just as I do about the whole problem. He stood out till the last minute to keep Fry. Very reluctant to have him go."

I went home badly confused, and I have remained so ever since.

As I said before, I have never known a man so fascinating as Mr. Virgil T. Fry. Not a member of his faculty has a good word to say for him and not a pupil in any of his classes has an unkind word to say against him.

THE PROBLEM OF MEANING IN THE SOCIAL STUDIES

Ernest Horn
Late Professor of Education
University of Iowa

THE FUNDAMENTAL IMPORTANCE OF UNDERSTANDING

Intelligent understanding of social conditions, processes, and problems ranks high in frequency of mention and in emphasis among the objectives that are stated to guide instruction. And this is as it should be, for not only is intelligent understanding good in its own right; it is also intimately bound up with the accomplishment of all of the other major purposes of social education, whether stated in terms of thinking, attitudes, ideals, or conduct. Thus thinking is dependent upon the ideas that one possesses; conduct should be guided by the dictates of insight and understanding; ideals and attitudes should be permeated with intelligence. . . .

It is to be regretted that so many of the basic problems pertaining to meaning and understanding are matters of controversy. Different schools of psychology, for example, approach these problems with very diverse hypotheses and investigate them with very different techniques. Philosophers and logicians are not less at odds. It is impossible here to discuss or even to list the controversies that rage around the theories of meaning and understanding, but attention is called to the fact that these issues, far from being resolved, are more numerous and more complicated than ever before. Yet these issues are by no means academic, for every teacher is influenced by assumptions that relate to logic, philosophy, and psychology, no matter how naive or lacking in systematic formulation these assumptions may be. Whatever troubles the logician, the epistemologist, or the psychologist in his study of the problems of meaning and understanding is likely also to harass those who are concerned with these problems in relation to teaching the social studies. The loose and faulty way in which such terms as meaning, understanding, insight, imagination, and reality are used in current pedagogical literature suggests that writers in the fields of curriculum and methods might well acquaint themselves with a few of the penetrating books and articles that treat these topics.[1] Although the psychological, logical, or epistemological problems related to meaning and understanding are not here discussed directly, an attempt is made, in this and the following chapters, to point out their most significant implications for teachers of social studies.

UNDERSTANDING AS AN ACTIVE PROCESS

Understanding is an active process. No matter how docilely receptive the student may be, he cannot be given ideas ready-made and, as one writer has expressed it, "under seal"; he must build them out of the materials of his experience. The teacher can only stimulate and guide his efforts. The term "construct," which is sometimes used to describe either the process or its result, places a useful emphasis on the active way in which ideas are formed. But while there is no such thing as purely passive reception of meaning, the student's activity may be so slight, his attention so fickle, and his will to understand so weak that the ideas he forms, if he forms any, are too vague and too lacking in dynamic quality to be of much use to him. The emphasis upon active learning under the guidance of purpose in contrast with pedantic instruction under teacher domination has long been prominent in the writings of educational reformers and notably, in recent times, in the writings of John Dewey. It is in harmony with the theory and evidence on learning and is revolutionary, in so far as it is understood and applied, in transforming instruction in the social studies. Teachers become educators in the vital and generic sense of the term; pupils share in setting up problems and assume a large part of the responsibility for their solution. Ideas become growing rather than static things. The whole atmosphere of the school is changed.

This active process of understanding is, moreover, exceedingly complicated, even in the case of relatively simple matters.[2] It involves selective attention, inference, evaluation, and organization. The affective and volitional aspects, as well as the reflective, have been increasingly emphasized, both in theoretical discussions and in the interpretation of experimental results. The more urgent and complex the problem, the more significant these aspects become. The full import of this dynamic view of understanding becomes increasingly apparent upon more detailed analysis of the elements that determine the adequacy or inadequacy of ideas.

FACTORS WHICH INFLUENCE UNDERSTANDING

The meaning that a student gets in the study of any problem in the social studies is dependent upon three factors: *first, the inherent nature of the problem; second, the nature of the instructional media through which he comes to grips with the problem; and third, the student himself—his experience, interest, and ability.* These three factors are so interrelated in their operation that it is impossible to isolate one completely from the other. Yet, for purposes of discussion, it is useful to focus attention upon each in turn.

THE NATURE OF THE PROBLEMS IN SOCIAL STUDIES

The social sciences, as Dewey points out, are concerned with "the largest, most inclusive and most complex of all the phenomena with which the mind has to deal."[3] Yet the inherent difficulty, complexity, and remoteness of the problems that are found in typical curricula in the social studies appear to be greatly underestimated in discussions of learning. Indeed, there is little in pedagogical literature to show that these important factors have even been seriously considered. For how, except by assuming some such neglect or underestimation, could one explain the vast number of complicated problems that are crowded into the course of study?

Forget, for the moment, the immaturity, the poverty of experience, and the limited ability of the average student. Forget the meagerness of the facilities available in most schools. Assume a mature and gifted individual. Assume also every requisite facility for study in the way of libraries, travel, and scholarly guidance. Even to this person, working under these favorable conditions, such topics as the following, from a representative course of study, must appear complicated, extended, and difficult: prehistoric man, Greek civilization, feudalism, the Renaissance, the French Revolution, the Industrial Revolution, the formation of the Constitution of the United States, the growth of nationalism, and the geography of world trade. These are but a small fraction of the topics included in the typical course of study, and such individual units, difficult as they are, are not meant to be learned in a piecemeal fashion, but are to be fitted into larger patterns, the most common of which are such organized bodies of knowledge as history, geography, economics, sociology, political science, ethics, and the great variety of courses designated as "social studies."

THE MEDIA THROUGH WHICH SOCIAL REALITIES ARE APPROACHED

An examination of courses of study shows that the bulk of instruction in the social studies is concerned with problems or topics outside the limits of the community that the child knows at first hand. Except in rare instances, the student does not deal directly with the realities of the world but with more or less adequate symbols of them; language, pictures, models, maps, charts, statistical tables, and the like. All of these symbols must be evaluated from two points of view: first, according to their adequacy as representations of the realities for which they purport to stand, and second, according to the degree that they are intelligible to the students who are to use them. Johnson has pointed out the sharp limits of our ability to reproduce historical phenomena in the classroom.[4] Practical difficulties of the same kind are found in dealing with the phenomena in other fields of the social studies. The ideas that an individual forms of his social environment are refracted in many ways, as Lippmann has shown:[5] by the limitations of language, which in the school is the chief approach to social knowledge; by the limitations of even such relatively effective symbols as maps, photographs, and models; and by the student's interests, feelings, and the patterns of his thought. As a result, the ideas obtained are in a real sense unique, partial, and distorted versions of reality.[6]

Surveys of actual classroom instruction show that language, spoken or written, is the chief medium of teaching and learning, for although such aids as pictures, models, and maps find a place in school, a relatively small part of what is taught can be represented by such means. Most of the child's ideas of other times, of other places, and of other conditions must be built chiefly out of what he reads or hears.

Language is not, however, a mere pedagogical tool. Those who criticize its predominance in instruction ignore the fact that, quite apart from its uses in the school, language is not only the chief instrument of thought but also the principal means of communication. "It is therefore indispensable for any high development of thought," says Dewey, "that there exist intentional signs. Language supplies the requirement."[7] It not only identifies individual meanings; it makes possible their organization into the most complicated patterns. A satisfactory understanding of even a contemporary problem in one's immediate community is impossible without the use of language. Although he is one of the most relentless enemies of verbalism in teaching, Dewey warns,

"Taken literally, the maxim, 'Teach things, not words,' or 'Teach things before words,' would be the negation of education; it would reduce mental life to mere physical and sensible adjustments. Learning, in the proper sense, is not learning things, but the *meanings* of things, and this process involves the use of signs, or language in its generic sense. In like fashion, the warfare of some educational reformers against symbols, if pushed to extremes, involves the destruction of intellectual life, since this lives, moves, and has its being in those processes of definition, abstraction, generalization, and classification that are made possible by symbols alone. Nevertheless, these contentions of educational reformers have been needed. The liability of a thing to abuse is in proportion to the value of its right use."[8]

It is evident that criticism should be directed not to the employment of language but to its limitations and abuses. Books are not used too extensively in teaching the social studies; they are used improperly. There is not too much talk in school, but the wrong kind of talk.

Even at its best, however, language gives an inadequate portrayal of the social realities that it attempts to represent.[9] This is true even when the reality to be symbolized is of the simpler sort, as in the case of an object or a concrete act. Thus, what is said about the first printing press is very much less than the press itself. Nor are the shortcomings of language less marked in the representation of movements, influences, aspirations, or the intellectual climate of any place or period.

The limitations of language are strikingly exhibited in the books used in elementary and secondary schools. In many schools the textbook is the only book to be found, and even when other books are available, it is predominant in the instruction of most classrooms. The textbook treats so much in so small a space that the language is inevitably vague and abstract, and as a result, it is difficult, if not impossible, for one who does not know the field with which it deals to read it with understanding. Even in most schools where collateral readings are provided, this problem is still serious, for the additional books are often little less general than the texts. Consequently, the reading of the students results either in mere verbalisms or in concepts which are foggy, partial, or definitely erroneous.

It is not, however, the limitations of language in *embodying* thought so much as in *conveying* thought that constitute the most serious problems in teaching. The term "convey" is actually a little misleading, for language stimulates and guides the formation of ideas rather than imparts them. And language performs this limited function only to the degree that it is related to the student's experience.

LIMITATIONS INHERENT IN THE STUDENT

The full significance of the difficulty of concepts in the social studies and the inadequacy of the media through which the student comes to grips with them are seen when these factors are viewed in relation to the limitations and potentialities of the students themselves. As has been earlier shown, we do not give the student meanings; we merely stimulate him, usually through language, to construct them for himself. The adequacy of the mental constructs that a student makes as the result of the stimulation of what he hears or reads is dependent on many factors, the most important of which are his experience, interest, intelligence, command of language skills, and his methods of work, including capacity for persistent effort. These same factors, not even excluding language, also influence the constructs made under the stimulation of pictures, maps, models, and of the concrete experiences in actual life situations. They would have to be taken into account if learning were regarded only as a matter of passive impression and memorization, but they are doubly significant when learning is understood to be an active, creative process.

Influence of experience

Ideas must be built by the student out of the materials of his experience. This fact was pointed out years ago by the exponents of apperception. Yet many of the data of history, geography, and other social studies are far removed from the experience of the students at the grade levels where these data are presented. Indeed, the gap between the experience of the child and the realities that he is expected to understand is so wide that it can be bridged only with great difficulty. What meanings, for example, can an elementary school student who has lived only on the treeless plains obtain from the following statement? "On the seaward side of the mountains of Australia are dense hardwood forests. Among the most valuable trees are the eucalyptus, sometimes known as gum trees." What sort of mental constructs can be made of *the seaward side of mountains;* of *dense forests;* of *hardwood;* of *eucalyptus;* of *gum trees?* What significance will he attach to the statement as a whole? The books and references that are placed in the hands of students should abound in concepts much farther removed from their experience than this one and much more complicated and difficult to comprehend.[10]

On the other hand, the failure to utilize the available resources of the local community may make the life of other times and places seem more foreign to the student's interest and experience than it really is. A survey of the way in which fundamental needs are met shows unmistakably how dependent any community is upon the people of other localities. The past, as well as the present, moreover, impinges upon each community in a number of ways. This is evident in such material things as implements, bridges, and architecture, and it is still more evident in ideas, tastes, and value systems. To neglect these relationships is to squander educational capital. The pervading influence of these historical and geographical factors on the life of the local community constitutes one of the chief reasons for teaching history and geography.

The mere accumulation of casual contacts secured by the individual both in and out of school is not, however, an adequate experiental basis for thinking about the problems that confront him. The satisfactory apprehension of new ideas depends upon the clearness, accuracy, and organization of the ideas that the student already possesses. Unfortunately, much of what he knows is hazy, inaccurate, and haphazard. Its immediate value as well as its probable future usefulness in the solution of any problem demands, therefore, that it be clarified, supplemented, and organized. This is one of the distinctive functions of instruction in the school.

Learning should be a very much more orderly enterprise, then, than the casual, desultory thing into which it so often degenerates. It demands the acquisition and use of the organized bodies of fundamental knowledge. Beard, in one of the volumes of this Commission, has attempted to sketch, in rough outline, the backgrounds of knowledge that are essential to thought in the social studies.[11] The concepts and principles in this or any ordered series cannot, however, be imparted ready made. Nor does the student get them all at once. They are to be conceived rather as a guide to growth, a growth facilitated from the outset to the degree that accuracy, thoughtfulness, and system are maintained.

The antagonism of certain curriculum theorists toward all organized social disciplines cannot be viewed, therefore, with unconcern, and especially since these theorists do not offer, as a substitute, arrangements of knowledge that are deemed satisfactory by any competent group of social scientists. On the contrary, the individual units that they suggest are for the most part shallow in quality and lacking in either logical or psychological sequence. As a result, the student is not only deprived of the background of systematic knowledge that makes possible growth and effective thinking but is also habituated to superficial methods of work.

Interest Related To Experience

When the problem to be attacked is too far removed from the student's experience, there is lacking not merely the raw material out of which the solution of the problem may be developed but also the will to work. Interest and purpose inhere in experience as much as does cognition. Indeed, under-standing and interest are reciprocal in their influence. Interest and purpose afford the basis for the organization of meanings or constructs, and are pro-gressively increased as understanding is deepened. For a topic to be uninter-esting, therefore, is a serious matter. Yet a great many of the topics, problems, or units of the social studies curriculum have little, if any, relation-ship to the present needs and interests of the student so far as he can see. In fact, it is difficult to demonstrate that some of these problems are funda-mentally pertinent even to the needs of the great majority of adults.

As remoteness from the student's life increases, motivation decreases, and, with the exception of the few individuals who read history or other social sciences as forms of vicarious experience, recourse must be taken to such extrinsic motivation as school marks and other devices. These devices are poor substitutes for the interests that grow out of pertinence to social pur-pose, being inferior not only in the degree to which they energize the making of constructs but also in their usefulness as norms for guiding the selection and evaluation of data and their organization into usable form.

The tendency for the social studies to be dissociated from the needs of life is caused in great part by selecting and organizing the curriculum in history or in other fields according to traditionally academic patterns. It would be much less marked if curricula were constructed to deal primarily with the problems, processes, and norms that most deeply concern the common man.[12] Such content would not only have greater initial appeal and greater possibility of accomplishment; it would lead also to the development of interests of more abiding value. It is no narrow or rule-of-thumb immediacy that is meant, however, but the broadest and richest background of knowledge and insight pertinent to the goals of instruction.[13]

In stressing the importance of interest, one should avoid two fallacious theories. The first views interest as the product of the methods and devices of the immediate classroom situation; the second assumes that instruction should be based upon whatever interests students manifest at the moment. Both of these fallacies originate in the same source—the failure to recognize that interests arise out of values; that is, out of a sense of pertinence to fundamental needs. It is not the purpose of the school to interest the child in the sense of entertaining him, but to utilize and develop interests in those things that are most universally significant in life outside the school. Students in schools where this more fundamental view is taken not only show greater interest day by day than do those in schools dominated by either of the two fallacious theories given above, but they also develop a more critical sense of values and a superior power to evaluate. Their interests become intelligent.

The Effect Of Intelligence

Any mental construct, whether simple or elaborate, is *prima facie* evidence of the operation of intelligence. It is to be expected, therefore, that psychologists should stress the significance of the limitations of intelligence for understanding and thinking in the social studies. After discussing various types of intelligence, Gates suggests that our best-known tests, such as the Stanford-Binet Scale, presumably measure the kind of intelligence needed in dealing with abstract subject matter, such as that ordinarily included in the courses of study in history, geography, and civics. . . . After estimating that nearly two-thirds of the population have an I.Q. of less than 105, he gives examples of the probable limits of the comprehension of individuals at these levels. The meaning of the paragraphs that he cites as beyond their reasonable understanding are certainly easier to grasp than many that are found in junior high school textbooks in the social studies. He concludes: "It is therefore possible that the intellectual grasp of abstract ideas of half of our population is less than sufficient to provide the basis for thorough and comprehensive reasoning concerning many of our complex social, political, and economic issues."[14]

Scores on intelligence tests, however, must be interpreted very cautiously. As pointed out in the discussion of the classification of pupils, the correlations between these scores and achievement in the social studies, while positive, are not high, and there is great probability that many types of intelligence required for the understanding of social problems are not adequately measured by present intelligence tests. There is also considerable evidence indicating that other factors, such as interest, industry, experience, and systematic training count far more heavily, as compared with intelligence, than has been generally assumed.[15] Both evidence and common sense indicate, however, that intelligence, whether regarded as unitary or manifold and although not yet adequately measured, must always be an important factor in achieving social understanding.

Attention has already been called to the inherent difficulty of many topics in typical courses of study. To think effectively about such topics or to achieve an understanding that is sufficiently valid and comprehensive to serve any useful purpose would seem to demand intelligence of a relatively high order. In the light of our present knowledge of intelligence and its operation in learning, it would be rash to estimate the limits of intellectual capacity below which understanding is frustrated. Both understanding and thinking are matters of degree, and every one achieves at least a modicum of social knowledge and insight. There is substantial evidence, however, to show that, with most of the instructional methods commonly employed, students at the lower levels of intelligence develop very little comprehension of any of the larger problems now confronting them in typical curricula.

Perhaps we attempt the impossible. The statements of chimerical objectives, the range and complexity of curricula, the concern with the specialized paraphernalia of research—all these seem to imply unlimited talent, native and acquired, on the part of the mass of students in our schools. But the existing evidence on the range of intellectual capacity, on the ability of students to read with understanding, and on the knowledge and insight possessed by students who have completed our courses of instruction is very sobering. The ambitious goals that are set up in the typical course of study are probably attained by only a scattered few among our school population and by these few only to a modest degree, through long and arduous effort. Nevertheless, it is sound policy to encourage all students to think as hard as they can and to understand as much as they can. It is better to see through a glass darkly than not to see at all. Nor should there be any thought of deciding beforehand which students can attain adequate understanding and social inventiveness. The opportunity should be open to all.

The unquestionable evidence of marked differences in the ability to learn, whatever the causes may be, must be faced squarely by those responsible for instruction in the social studies. In fact, these differences have far-reaching implications for social policy, as well as for education. Gates points out, for example, "The vote of the moron, of the average man, and of the genius count equally."[16] Ignorance, apathy, or wrong attitudes toward social problems must be combated wherever found, in the genius as well as in the dullard. A romantic disregard for limitations of ability and their implications leads to futile attempts to accomplish the impossible, causing both students and teachers to seek "escapes," of which verbalism, symbolism, fantasy, and make-believe are common types. Tough-mindedness in facing squarely the extent and significance of these limitations need not lead to a defeatist or pessimistic view of the limits of social educability but to the establishment of fundamental and attainable goals and to the devising of more effective means for their accomplishment. It is not uncommon to find instances in which the best fourth of the students in one school accomplish no more than the poorest fourth of the students in a school of like population. Experiments in other fields suggest that, with patient and skillful teaching, students of below-average ability achieve very much more satisfactory results than has heretofore been thought possible. Indeed the evidence indicates that the limits of social education at any level of ability have not yet been closely approached.

Command Of Language Skills

Since language is essential to thought, and since the data for building most of the student's ideas in the social studies are obtained from what he reads or hears, the command of language is indispensable. So fundamental, indeed, is the part played by language that the entire instructional program should be organized so as to promote its effective use. Every influence that encourages verbalism should be combated. From the earliest days at school students should be accustomed to regard words as signs only and to seek the meanings for which the signs stand. They should develop those habits of critical reflection that safeguard their efforts to comprehend. They should be led to see that carelessness and inaccuracy in their own language, as well as in their interpretations of the language of others, make clear thinking impossible.[17]

Methods Of Work

Valid ideas are obtained only through critical thinking. The differences between critical and superficial thinking are due in part to the richness and orderliness of the student's background of ideas and in part to his methods of work. Dewey points out that the ". . . control of observation and memory so as to select and give proper weight to data as evidence depends upon the possession of . . . standardized meanings, or conceptions."[18] Failure to provide the student with sound and organized knowledge is almost certain to be associated with improper methods of work. The superficiality of the product is evidence of the superficiality of the process. As a matter of fact, all ideas, attitudes, and skills reflect the methods by which they are attained, for the experiences associated with their attainment cannot be dissociated from the results. The quality of the learning process determines how dynamic and usable the resulting concept, attitude, or skill will be. Viewed in this light, methods of work become a basically important matter.

There are no ways of arriving at an adequate understanding of any social problem except those used by the social scientists themselves. If, for example, a student is to learn to think historically, he must use the methods that the best historians use. While the student does not have the time, the resources, or the ability to reproduce all the minutiae of research pertaining to each unit in the course of study, the fundamental requirements of the methods in the various fields must be met and rigorous exercises in methodology must occasionally be given. "It is quite possible," Johnson points out, "to leave the pupil at the end of his high school course with fairly definite impressions of history both as a process of establishing and organizing truth and as a body of organized truth."[19] This relationship of method to organized knowledge holds also for geography and other social studies. The recognition of the importance of methods of thinking in the attainment of ideas is not meant to disparage the importance of a scholarly grasp of detail. Far from being incompatible, knowledge and thinking are interdependent.[20]

Much more time than that usually provided is necessary for a satisfactory understanding of even the simpler concepts in the social studies. In the days of Herbartianism one of the favored topics for demonstration teaching in arithmetic was the rule for finding the area of the rectangle. The skill with which this rule was developed was a source of great envy and admiration on the part of the students who observed the work. Several lessons were needed in order to develop the concept adequately, and additional lessons were required to perfect the application of the formula to the practical circumstances of life.

There are few topics in the social studies whose essential meanings are so easily constructed in the mind of the student as is this one. Yet the student is frequently expected to make adequate constructs of a number of difficult topics in one class period. At the conclusion of the study of the Civil War, for example, a single day's assignment included, in one instance, all of the following topics: the cost of the war in money, the cost of the war in lives, the effect of the war on business, the influence of the war on immigration, the effect of the war on women, permanent benefits from the war. Any one of these topics is more complicated than the problem of how the area of a rectangle is found. The data requisite for understanding are less available, the remoteness from the student's experience is more marked, and the time needed to master the fundamental meanings is much longer. What happens under these conditions, of course, is that no student achieves the essential meanings, and some students do not acquire even verbal memory of any important statement in the text. . . .

Persistent effort, as well as time, is required to make an adequate mental construct of any important idea. As has been pointed out, problems in the social studies are the most difficult and complex of all those with which the student has to deal. The requisite data must be found, critically interpreted, and organized into an idea that is self-consistent and in harmony with other ideas. The ability to work unremittingly is one of the most important factors in determining the adequacy of the ideas that are obtained. There is no escape from arduous work, even by the most brilliant student.

The foregoing review of the factors and conditions that influence understanding in the social studies is purposely brief, since it is expanded in other chapters.[21] It is necessary, however, to consider the effect of these factors upon understanding.

THE EFFECT UPON UNDERSTANDING

When the concept to be formed is excessively difficult, when the instructional media are inadequate, when the student's experience, interest, ability, and training are limited, or when the time for learning is short, the constructs that the student makes will necessarily be unsatisfactory. Under extremely unfavorable conditions he may not attempt to make any construct at all, or, if he does make an attempt, may fail. The conscientious student, actuated by pride, marks, or the desire for approval, may memorize or paraphrase the words of the text or lecture even though little understanding attend his efforts. This is verbalism. It centers chiefly upon words rather than upon the ordering and authenticating of meanings, and either fails completely to give the student ideas of any sort or leads to ideas that are not sufficiently accurate or complete to be of use. Verbalism is not a thing of the remote past, when, indeed, it did sometimes flourish in an exceedingly extreme form; it is still widespread at every level from kindergarten to the graduate school, as well as in society at large. It is a form of refuge for the individual who is unable to solve the problems that confront him or who, although potentially capable, is unwilling to put forth the necessary effort. Yet the distinction between verbalism and understanding is not clear-cut except in extreme instances. Pure verbal memory, completely divorced from understanding, is probably rare, even under the most formal memoriter methods. Concepts are not so often *un-understood,* to borrow a word from Shotwell, as *misunderstood,* or vaguely comprehended. Some meaning is obtained, some constructs are made, but the result is vague, partial, distorted, or wholly erroneous. Vagueness, which Dewey refers to as "the aboriginal logical sin—the source from which flow most bad intellectual consequences,"[22] is probably more frequent than actual misconceptions, and the difficulty of combating it is certainly much greater. "Totally to eliminate indefiniteness," says Dewey, "is impossible; to reduce it in extent and in force requires sincerity and vigor."[23]

Any teacher who has had much experience in reading student examination papers can recall amusing instances of "boners" or "howlers." Thus a student is reported to have written, "The French Revolution wrote insulting letters to the American Revolution." She justified this, when questioned about it, as a paraphrase of the statement made by the instructor himself. Her notes, confirmed by the instructor, showed the statement to be: "The French Revolution corresponded in a rough way with the American Revolution." In a recent investigation by Newburn, one student wrote, "All conservatives are radicals and should be jailed."[24] Scott and Myers report that some members of a class of rural teachers "were thinking of the United States foreign minister to Japan as a Presbyterian clergyman, some as a Methodist, some as a Catholic priest, and so on. . . ."[25] Student errors are not always so amusing as these, but they frequently depart as far from adequate understanding. . . .

The attainment of adequate understanding is a difficult process even with good teaching, with ample instructional equipment, and with the support of intelligent public opinion. These favorable conditions do not always exist, however. False ideas are frequently inculcated by the deliberate intention of those who control the sources of information. Evidence of such machinations is discouragingly abundant, both at home and abroad—in the narrow and perverted nationalism of many allegedly patriotic societies, in the subversive propaganda of special-interest groups, in the misleading slogans of political parties, and in the distorted reports of a partisan press. Bias, intentional or unconscious, is manifested by teachers and textbooks in the schools themselves. Students can hardly be expected to search impartially for the truth when all these influences are moving in the opposite direction. It is because of the difficulties that have just been enumerated that training in dependable methods of thought and inquiry is of crucial importance.

Much as we wish it to be otherwise, it is clear that at the end of the period of schooling, even upon graduation from college, few students have either an understanding of our social problems or the background of accurate knowledge and disciplined thought by which understanding can be achieved. Nor are these shortcomings limited to students in the schools. Most adults are either uninformed or misinformed about much that goes on about them, and have many ideas that are wholly fictional. Certain it is that nations, as well as individuals, have been and are devoted to many ideas and ideals that will not check with reality. Cynical writers sometimes argue that the great mass of people are happier in clinging to fictions than in facing the facts. But whatever policy other nations may adopt, American schools are committed to the ideal, although at times with lip service only, that the truth should be taught. The intelligent rather than the servile or "conditioned" citizen is their goal.

There are practical limits, however, as to the amount and degree of knowledge that students can be expected to secure. They cannot know everything about the many topics now included in the course of study. They cannot attain even a respectable minimum grasp of them. And although, as has been suggested, the time allotment in social studies may be increased, the superficial system of cycles abandoned, and the number of topics reduced, there will still remain the problem of deciding how much to teach about any topic.

In order to solve this practical problem, it is necessary to posit some theories regarding the nature and function of ideas, as well as the manner in which they are formed. The position here taken is that purpose not only guides their construction but holds them together. The function that an idea is to have in the intellectual life of the student determines the appraisal, selection, and organization of the data of which it is built. Meaning, import, significance, and value all imply the question, "For what?" In order to determine what and how much to teach about any topic, therefore, it is necessary to decide what uses are to be made of the ideas involved in it. These uses should be in the minds of the teachers, and, as rapidly as possible, they should be evolved also in the minds of the students. For it is use in thought and in action that motivates and guides the construction of ideas, gives them dynamic quality, and measures their attainment. . . .

References

[1] A standard reference is Ogden, C. K., and Richards, I. A., *The Meaning of Meaning.* Harcourt, Brace & Company, Inc., New York, 1923. For a simpler introduction to this problem see, Langer, Susanne K., *The Practice of Philosophy.* Henry Holt and Company, New York, 1930.

A penetrating analysis of the higher thought processes in relation to education is given in Dewey, John, *How We Think* (new edition). D. C. Heath and Company, Boston, 1933. A brief description of the various schools of psychology in relation to teaching the social studies is given in "The Social Studies Curriculum," *Fourteenth Yearbook,* Department of Superintendence, Washington, D.C., 1936, Chap. III.

[2] Thorndike, Edward I., *Human Learning.* The Century Co., New York., 1931, Lecture 9.

[3] Dewey, John, "Philosophy," in Gee, Wilson (ed.), *Research in the Social Sciences.* The Macmillan Company, New York, 1929, p. 261.

[4] Johnson, Henry, *Teaching of History in Elementary and Secondary Schools.* The Macmillan Company, New York, 1928, Chaps. VIII-X.

[5] Lippmann, Walter, *Public Opinion.* Harcourt, Brace & Company, New York 1922, p. 76.

[6] Dewey, John, "Context and Thought," *University of California Publications in Philosophy* XII, 1931, pp. 203-224.

[7] Dewey, *How We Think* (new edition), p. 232.

[8] *Ibid.,* p. 236.

[9] *Cf.* Ballard, Philip Boswood, *Thought and Language.* University of London Press, Ltd., London, 1934.

[10] Suggestions for meeting this difficulty are given in Chaps. VI to XI.

[11] Beard, Charles A., *The Nature of the Social Sciences.* Charles Scribner's Sons, New York, 1934.

[12] See, for example, Robinson, James Harvey, *The Humanizing of Knowledge.* George H. Doran Company, New York, 1924; and Robinson, James Harvey, *The New History.* The

Macmillan Company, New York, 1918, especially Chap V, "History for the Common Man."

For descriptions of the efforts of curriculum makers in this respect, see the *Twenty-second Yearbook,* Part II, National Society for the Study of Education. Public School Publishing Company, Bloomington, Illinois, 1923; and *Fourteenth Yearbook,* Department of Superintendence, Chap. VII.

[13] See *Conclusions and Recommendations of the Commission.* Charles Scribner's Sons, New York, 1934, Chaps. I-IV; see also Beard, Charles A., *A Charter for the Social Sciences in the Schools.* Charles Scribner's Sons, New York, 1932.

[14] Gates, Arthur I., "Psychology," in Dawson, Edgar (ed.), *Teaching the Social Studies.* The Macmillan Company, New York, 1927, pp. 106-12.

[15] See Turney, Austin H., "Intelligence, Motivation, and Achievement," *The Journal of Educational Psychology* XXII (September, 1931), pp. 426-34.

[16] Gates, "Psychology," in Dawson, *Teaching the Social Studies,* p. 109.

[17] The significance of language abilities, as illustrated in reading, is developed in detail in Chap. V.

[18] Dewey, *How We Think* (new edition), p. 179.

[19] Johnson, *Teaching of History,* p. 387. Chapter XIV, from which this quotation is taken, is an excellent discussion of "School History and the Historical Method."

[20] For a discussion of the relationship between knowledge and thinking, see Chap. III.

[21] See especially Chaps. IV and VI.

[22] Dewey, *How We Think* (new edition), p. 160.

[23] *Ibid.,* p. 160.

[24] Newburn, Harry K., "The Relative Effect of Two Methods of Vocabulary Drill on Achievement in American History," University of Iowa *Studies in Education* IX, No. 3, State University of Iowa, Iowa City, 1934, p. 25.

[25] Scott, Flora, and Myers, Garry C., "Children's Empty and Erroneous Concepts of the Commonplace," *Journal of Educational Research* VIII (November, 1923), p. 327.

SEMANTICS AND THE STUDY OF CULTURE

Seymour H. Fersh
Education Director of the Asia Society

Why do men make mistakes?" asks Walter Lippmann, and answers: "Because an important part of human behavior is reaction to the pictures in their heads. Human behavior takes place in relation to a pseudo-environment—a

Reprinted with the permission of the author and the National Council for the Social Studies, from *Social Education,* 27 (May, 1963): 259-261.

representation, which is not quite the same for any two individuals. What they suppose to be—not what *is*—the reality of things. This man-made, this cultural environment, which has its being in the minds of men, is interposed between man as a biological organism and the external reality."

The problem is one of bringing "pictures in the mind" and "external reality" into truer alignment. The best way—though certainly not infallible—is through first-hand experiences, followed by audio-visual representations, and lastly by words. It is through words, however, that most of our "education" takes place and much is inevitably lost in the telling as word descriptions are substituted for their real-life counterparts. Consider words such as poverty, underdeveloped, hot, cold, democratic, progressive, backward, and the like. Dictionaries carry definitions but people carry connotations—and it is connotations which rule thinking and influence behavior.

Throughout history many writers in many cultures have called attention to the fact that words misinform as well as inform, but it was not until 1897 that a Frenchman, Michel Breal, gave it the name *semantique,* or the science of meaning. More recently, in the 1920's in the United States, a movement called General Semantics, often referred to as G.S., was pioneered by Alfred Korzybski and subsequently popularized by researchers and writers, including Stuart Chase, Wendell Johnson, S.I. Hayakawa, and Irving Lee.

From these and other writers on the subject, we have drawn a number of examples to illustrate the contribution General Semantics can make to the study of other peoples and ways of living different from our own. Although these particular examples refer to India, it is obvious that they are equally applicable to other cultures. We do not claim that greater attention to these and other G.S. assumptions and techniques will in itself eliminate all problems of *"meaning,"* but it should be incontestable that descriptions of "things out there" can and must be conveyed more precisely and with more accurate interpretation.

SOME APPLICATIONS

No two things are identical, and no one thing remains the same.

For example: $Indian_1$ is not $Indian_2$ is not $Indian_3$ is not $Indian_4$.... In other words Indian (Nehru) is not Indian (Krishna Menon) is not Indian (farmer in a rural village). ... Although by convention we refer to the 450 million people who live in an area called India as "Indians," the truth is that no two Indians are identical. Statements which purport to talk about "the Indians" as if they were one entity must be carefully qualified. Questions like

"What do Indians think about Americans?" become clearly unanswerable. Answerable questions—those which have some likelihood of being verified—are less dramatic and perhaps less satisfying, but that is the nature of the problem. It is only by taking liberties with language that we appear to be better informed than the data permits. Similarly, it may readily be seen that terms such as "Asian," "Moslem," "Oriental," and the like conceal differences as well as reveal group affinities.

India$_{1857}$ is not India$_{1947}$ is not India$_{1962}$ is not India$_{1970}$ ·····
Change is certain. One who forgets this is destined to be shocked when confronted with the discrepancy between what he thinks is true and what is so.

The same word may be used to connote different "realities," while similar events or experiences are sometimes called by different names.

For example, a term like "socialism" is used by many to describe economic systems like those of the Soviet Union, Great Britain, and India—systems which first-hand examination reveals as quite dissimilar. Consider, for instance, that in "capitalist" United States $_{1962}$ the part of the Gross National Product represented by federal, state, and local governmental expenditures was well over twice the percent purchased by similar governmental bodies in "socialist" India $_{1962}$. Words whose meanings have become meaningless from being used to carry too heavy and too diversified loads of information should be set apart by enclosing them with quotation marks (" ") to alert the reader. Korzybski used to wiggle two fingers of each hand to achieve the same effect when speaking.

Statements of opinion are often confused with statements of fact. For example, verb forms of "to be" often cloud the relationship between subject and predicate, as when someone says, "It *is* hot." The "hotness" is more a description of the speaker's state of mind than it is of the temperature reading, since what constitutes "hot" is a matter of opinion. "Cold wave" could mean anything from 20 or 30 degrees below zero (F) in the Himalayas to 40 degrees above in New Delhi where, incidentally, a continuous string of days in the 90's in May would scarcely qualify as a "heat wave." Very often, the addition by the speaker of the words "to me" and the addition by the listener of the words "to you" helps to identify so-called statements of fact as bogus.

It is not possible to tell all about anything.

No matter how complete a listing or how comprehensive an explanation, the possibility always remains open that something more might be said about the matter under consideration. All descriptions are "open-ended" with the last word unsaid. Completeness may be a goal, but like infinity it eludes mortal grasp. Thus, for example, an examination of Hinduism might include reference to reincarnation, caste, Karma, and so on, but no matter how extensive the treatise a mental "etc." should be added to the last punctuation point. The practical effect of this orientation is to leave the door open, albeit a crack, for additional information which may be forthcoming.

SOME SUGGESTIONS

The list of "devices" for applying G.S. can be extended almost indefinitely. Here are a few more cautions to consider:
—Try to use descriptive terms rather than those expressing approval or disapproval. For example, the words "clean" and "unclean" are relative. The comment that cow dung is used for fuel in many Indian villages often provokes reactions of disgust from many urban dwellers in the United States$_{1962}$. It may be instructive on this point to quote from a Kansas editor, writing in 1879 at a time when buffalo and cow dung (he calls them "chips") were commonly used for fuel: "It was comical to see how gingerly our wives handled these chips at first. They commenced by picking them up between two sticks, or with a poker. Soon they used a rag, and then a corner of their apron. Finally, growing hardened, a washing after handling them was sufficient. And now? Now it is out of the bread, into the chips and back again—and not even a dust of the hands."
—Try to use phrases which indicate certain conditions which should be considered with a statement. For example, awareness may be increased by using such phrases as "in our culture," "from our point of view," "at that time," and the like.

An article by David Mace "Marriage by Arrangement" (*McCall's,* August 1959) illustrates the miscalculations which result from assuming that other cultures hold the same values as one's own. The author writes about an experience he had in India when discussing Western "romance marriages" which he assumed would be the envy of those who were "doomed" to marriages which were arranged by the parents:

"Wouldn't you like to be free to choose your own marriage partner?" I asked. "Oh no!" several voices replied in chorus. I was taken aback. "Why not?" I asked.
"Doesn't it put the girl in a very humiliating position?" one girl said. . . . "Doesn't she have to try to look pretty, and call attention to herself, and attract a boy, to be sure she'll get married? . . . And if she

doesn't want to do that or if she feels it's undignified, wouldn't that mean she mightn't get a husband? . . . Well, surely that's humiliating. It makes getting married a competition, in which the girls fight each other for the boys. And it encourages a girl to pretend she's better than she really is. She has to make a good impression to get a boy, and then she has to go on making a good impression to get him to marry her. . . . In our system, we girls don't have to worry at all. We *know* we'll get married. When we are old enough, our parents find a suitable boy, and everything is arranged. . . . How could we judge the character of a boy we met? We are young and inexperienced. Our parents are older and wiser, and they aren't as easily deceived as we would be. I'd far rather have my parents choose for me. It's important that the man I marry is the right one. I could easily make a mistake if I had to select him myself."

—Try to move in the direction of substituting more precise words for vague ones. For example, it is often said that "heavy rains" fall on India during the monsoon season. The statement would carry more meaning if it were pointed out, for example, that Allahabad, a city in the Ganges Valley, and New York City both receive on the average 40 inches of rain annually *with* the significant difference that New York City gets from two to four inches monthly whereas Allahabad is hit by some 37 inches from June to October.

—Become more alert to the ways in which cultural conditioning shapes one's value judgments. An exercise in seeing one's own culture as it might be seen by a stranger is a useful start. Consider, for example, the following excerpt from Horace Miner's article, "Magical Practices Among the Nacirema" (*American Anthropologist* 55:3; 1956).

The focal point of the shrine is a box or chest which is built into the wall. In this chest are kept the many charms and magical potions without which no native believes he could live. . . . The charm is not disposed of after it has served its purpose, but is placed in the charm-box of the household shrine. As these magical materials are specific for certain ills, and the real or imagined maladies of the people are many, the charm-box is usually full to overflowing. The magical packets are so numerous that people forget what their purposes were and fear to use them again. While the natives are very vague on this point, we can only assume that the idea in retaining all the old magical materials is that their presence in the charm-box, before which the body rituals are conducted, will in some way protect the worshipper.

Of course, here Miner has been discussing the medicine cabinet in American culture!

—Become more suspicious of one's own "wisdom." Anatole France once said of a man, "He flattered himself on being a man without prejudices; and this pretention itself is a very great prejudice." In *The Devil's Advocate: A Plea for Superstition,* written in 1909, Sir James G. Frazer argued that so-called superstitions more often than not embody a realistic distillation of experience whereby the uninitiated and unwary may receive tested guidance. Behind many "myths" are "truths" which have helped people to rationalize and maintain social order and organization. Thus, for example, the "superstition" held widely in many Asian countries that the left hand is "evil" or in some ways inferior to the right hand becomes more acceptable to the Western-minded when he becomes familiar with the functions for which the left hand is reserved exclusively—functions which he would readily agree were "unclean" and worthy of giving the left hand its "bad reputation."

SOME IMPLICATIONS

Of course, much of what has been pointed out will not come as a startling revelation. None of the ideas are new and, under different names, many of the G.S. techniques have been used by intelligent people who have never heard of the word "semantics," let alone been exposed to the writings of Korzybski and others. So much the better! Our concern is not so much with *how* people distinguish between a "map" and the physical territory that it describes, but that they *do* distinguish. George Orwell writes, "What is above all needed is to let the meaning choose the word, and not the other way about. . . . Probably it is better to put off using words as long as possible and get one's meaning as clear as one can through pictures and sensations."

No one is suggesting that all abstractions be distrusted. "In demanding that people cease reacting to abstract names as if they were realities-in-themselves," says S. I. Hayakawa, "we are merely saying in another way, 'Stop acting like suckers.' " And until we do give more disciplined attention to words, we will continue to stockpile symbols and labels while the "precious commodities" which are being symbolized and labeled escape our detection and comprehension. The argument-ending gambit, "It is *only* a matter of semantics," must give way to the more sophisticated recognition that the "real" search for "meaning" may very well start where words leave off.

References

Especially for newcomers to General Semantics
Wendell Johnson. *People in Quandaries.* New York: Harper and Brothers, 1946. The semantics of personal adjustment.

Catherine Minteer. *Words and What they Do to You.* Elmsford, New York: Row, Peterson and Company, 1953. Beginning lessons in General Semantics for Junior and Senior high school.

Other sources to be read and consulted

Stuart Chase. *The Tyranny of Words.* New York: Harcourt, Brace and Company, 1938.

S. I. Hayakawa. *Language in Thought and Action.* New York: Harcourt, Brace and Company, 1949.

Alfred Korzybski. *Science and Sanity.* Lancaster, Pennsylvania: Science Press Printing Company, 1933.

THE ACT OF DISCOVERY

Jerome S. Bruner
Harvard University

Maimonides, in his *Guide for the Perplexed*,[1] speaks of four forms of perfection that men might seek. The first and lowest form is perfection in the acquisition of worldly goods. The great philosopher dismisses such perfection on the ground that the possessions one acquires bear no meaningful relation to the possessor: "A great king may one morning find that there is no difference between him and the lowest person." A second perfection is of the body, its conformation and skills. Its failing is that it does not reflect on what is uniquely human about man: "he could [in any case] not be as strong as a mule." Moral perfection is the third, "the highest degree of excellency in man's character." Of this perfection Maimonides says: "Imagine a person being alone, and have no connection whatever with any other person? all his good moral principles are at rest, they are not required and give man no perfection whatever. These principles are only necessary and useful when man comes in contact with others." "The fourth kind of perfection is the true perfection of man; the possession of the highest intellectual faculties. . . ." In justification of his assertion, this extraordinary Spanish-Judaic philosopher urges: "Examine the first three kinds of perfection; you will find that if you possess them, they are not your property, but the property of others. . . . But the last kind of perfection is exclusively yours; no one else owns any part of it."

It is a conjecture much like that of Maimonides that leads me to examine the act of discovery in man's intellectual life. For if man's intellectual excellence is the most his own among his perfections, it is also the case that the most uniquely personal of all that he knows is that which he has discovered for himself. What difference does it make, then, that we encourage discovery in the learning of the young? Does it, as Maimonides would say, create a

Bruner, Jerome S., "The Act of Discovery," *Harvard Educational Review* 31, no. 1 (Winter 1961): 21-32. Copyright ©1961 President and Fellows of Harvard College.

special and unique relation between knowledge possessed and the possessor? And what may such a unique relation do for a man—or for a child, if you will, for our concern is with the education of the young?

The immediate occasion for my concern with discovery—and I do not restrict discovery to the act of finding out something that before was unknown to mankind, but rather include all forms of obtaining knowledge for oneself by the use of one's own mind—the immediate occasion is the work of the various new curriculum projects that have grown up in America during the last six or seven years. For whether one speaks to mathematicians or physicists or historians, one encounters repeatedly an expression of faith in the powerful effects that come from permitting the student to put things together for himself, to be his own discoverer.

First, let it be clear what the act of discovery entails. It is rarely, on the frontier of knowledge or elsewhere, that new facts are "discovered" in the sense of being encountered as Newton suggested in the form of islands of truth in an uncharted sea of ignorance. Or if they appear to be discovered in this way, it is almost always thanks to some happy hypotheses about where to navigate. Discovery, like surprise, favors the well prepared mind. In playing bridge, one is surprised by a hand with no honors in it at all and also by hands that are all in one suit. Yet all hands in bridge are equiprobable: one must know to be surprised. So too in discovery. The history of science is studded with examples of men "finding out" something and not knowing it. I shall operate on the assumption that discovery, whether by a schoolboy going it on his own or by a scientist cultivating the growing edge of his field, is in its essence a matter of rearranging or transforming evidence in such a way that one is enabled to go beyond the evidence so reassembled to additional new insights. It may well be that an additional fact or shred of evidence makes this larger transformation of evidence possible. But it is often not even dependent on new information.

It goes without saying that, left to himself, the child will go about discovering things for himself within limits. It also goes without saying that there are certain forms of child rearing, certain home atmospheres that lead some children to be their own discoverers more than other children. These are both topics of great interest, but I shall not be discussing them. Rather, I should like to confine myself to the consideration of discovery and "finding-out-for-oneself" within an educational setting—specifically the school. Our aim as teachers is to give our student as firm a grasp of a subject as we can, and to make him as autonomous and self-propelled a thinker as we can—one who will go along on his own after formal schooling has ended. I shall return in the end to the question of the kind of classroom and the style of teaching that encourages an attitude of wanting to discover. For purposes of orienting the discussion, however, I would like to make an overly simplified distinction between teaching that takes place in the *expository mode* and teaching that utilizes the *hypothetical mode*. In the former, the decisions concerning the mode and pace and style of exposition are principally determined by the teacher as expositor; the student is the listener. If I can put the matter in terms of structural linguistics, the speaker has a quite different set of decisions to make than the listener: the former has a wide choice of alternatives for structuring, he is anticipating paragraph content while the listener is still intent on the words, he is manipulating the content of the material by various transformations, while the listener is quite unaware of these internal manipulations. In the hypothetical mode, the teacher and the student are in a more cooperative position with respect to what in linguistics would be called "speaker's decisions." The student is not a bench-bound listener, but is taking a part in the formulation and at times may play the principal role in it. He will be aware of alternatives and may even have an "as if" attitude toward these and, as he receives information he may evaluate it as it comes. One cannot describe the process in either mode with great precision as to detail, but I think the foregoing may serve to illustrate what is meant.

Consider now what benefit might be derived from the experience of learning through discoveries that one makes for oneself. I should like to discuss these under four headings: (1) The increase in intellectual potency, (2) the shift from extrinsic to intrinsic rewards, (3) learning the heuristics of discovering, and (4) the aid to memory processing.

1. *Intellectual potency.* If you will permit me, I would like to consider the difference between subjects in a highly constrained psychological experiment involving a two-choice apparatus. In order to win chips, they must depress a key either on the right or the left side of the machine. A pattern of payoff is designed such that, say, they will be paid off on the right side 70 percent of the time, on the left 30 percent, although this detail is not important. What is important is that the payoff sequence is arranged at random, and there is no pattern. I should like to contrast the behavior of subjects who think that there *is* some pattern to be found in the sequence—who think that regularities are discoverable—in contrast to subjects who think that things are happening quite by *chance*. The former group adopts what is called an "event-matching" strategy in which the number of responses given to each side is roughly equal to the proportion of times it pays off: in the present case R70; L30. The group that believes there is no pattern very soon reverts to a much more

primitive strategy wherein *all* responses are allocated to the side that has the greater payoff. A little arithmetic will show you that the lazy all-and-none strategy pays off more if indeed the environment is random: namely, they win seventy percent of the time. The event-matching subjects win about 70% on the 70% payoff side (or 49% of the time there) and 30% of the time on the side that pays off 30% of the time (another 9% for a total take-home wage of 58% in return for their labors of decision). But the world is not always or not even frequently random, and if one analyzes carefully what the event-matches are doing, it turns out that they are trying out hypotheses one after the other, all of them containing a term such that they distribute bets on the two sides with a frequency to match the actual occurrence of events. If it should turn out that there is a pattern to be discovered, their payoff would become 100%. The other group would go on at the middling rate of 70%.

What has this to do with the subject at hand? For the person to search out and find regularities and relationships in his environment, he must be armed with an expectancy that there will be something to find and, once aroused by expectancy, he must devise ways of searching and finding. One of the chief enemies of such expectancy is the assumption that there is nothing one can find in the environment by way of regularity or relationship. In the experiment just cited, subjects often fall into a habitual attitude that there is either nothing to be found or that they can find a pattern by looking. There is an important sequel in behavior to the two attitudes, and to this I should like to turn now.

We have been conducting a series of experimental studies on a group of some seventy school children over the last four years. The studies have led us to distinguish an interesting dimension of cognitive activity that can be described as ranging from *episodic empiricism* at one end to *cumulative constructionism* at the other. The two attitudes in the choice experiments just cited are illustrative of the extremes of the dimension. I might mention some other illustrations. One of the experiments employs the game of Twenty Questions. A child—in this case he is between 10 and 12—is told that a car has gone off the road and hit a tree. He is to ask questions that can be answered by "yes" or "no" to discover the cause of the accident. After completing the problem, the same task is given him again, though he is told that the accident had a different cause this time. In all, the procedure is repeated four times. Children enjoy playing the game. They also differ quite markedly in the approach or strategy they bring to the task. There are various elements in the strategies employed. In the first place, one may distinguish clearly between two types of questions asked: the one is designed for locating constraints in the problem, constraints that will eventually give shape to an hypothesis; the other is the hypothesis as question. It is the difference between, "Was there anything wrong with the driver?" and "Was the driver rushing to the doctor's office for an appointment and the car got out of control?" There are children who precede hypotheses with efforts to locate constraint and there are those who, to use our local slang, are "pot-shotters," who string out hypotheses non-cumulatively one after the other. A second element of strategy is its connectivity of information gathering: the extent to which questions asked utilize or ignore or violate information previously obtained. The questions asked by children tend to be organized in cycles, each cycle of questions usually being given over to the pursuit of some particular notion. Both within cycles and between cycles one can discern a marked difference on the connectivity of the child's performance. Needless to say, children who employ constraint location as a technique preliminary to the formulation of hypotheses tend to be far more connected in their harvesting of information. Persistence is another feature of strategy, a characteristic compounded of what appear to be two components: a sheer doggedness component, and a persistence that stems from the sequential organization that a child brings to the task. Doggedness is probably just animal spirits or the need for achievement—what has come to be called *n-ach*. Organized persistence is a maneuver for protecting our fragile cognitive apparatus from overload. The child who has flooded himself with disorganized information from unconnected hypotheses will become discouraged and confused sooner than the child who has shown a certain cunning in his strategy of getting information—a cunning whose principal component is the recognition that the value of information is not simply in getting it but in being able to carry it. The persistence of the organized child stems from his knowledge of how to organize questions in cycles, how to summarize things to himself, and the like.

Episodic empiricism is illustrated by information gathering that is unbound by prior constraints, that lacks connectivity, and that is deficient in organizational persistence. The opposite extreme is illustrated by an approach that is characterized by constraint sensitivity, by connective maneuvers, and by organized persistence. Brute persistence seems to be one of those gifts from the gods that make people more exaggeratedly what they are.[2]

Before returning to the issue of discovery and its role in the development of thinking, let me say a word more about the ways in which information may get transformed when the problem solver has actively processed it. There is first of all a pragmatic question: what does it take to get information processed into a form best designed to fit some future use? Take an experiment by Zajonc[3] as a case in point. He gives groups of subjects information of a controlled kind, some groups being told that their task is to transmit the information to others, others that it is merely to be kept in mind. In general, he finds more differentiation and organization of the information received with the intention of being transmitted than there is for information received passively. An active set leads to a transformation related to a task to be performed. The risk, to be sure, is in possible overspecialization of information processing that may lead to such a high degree of specific organization that information is lost for general use.

I would urge now in the spirit of an hypothesis that emphasis upon discovery in learning has precisely the effect upon the learner of leading him to be a constructionist, to organize what he is encountering in a manner not only designed to discover regularity and relatedness, but also to avoid the kind of information drift that fails to keep account of the uses to which information might have to be put. It is, if you will, a necessary condition for learning the variety of techniques of problem solving, of transforming information for better use, indeed for learning how to go about the very task of learning. Practice in discovering for oneself teaches one to acquire information in a way that makes that information more readily viable in problem solving. So goes the hypothesis. It is still in need of testing. But it is an hypothesis of such important human implications that we cannot afford not to test it—and testing will have to be in the schools.

2. *Intrinsic and extrinsic motives.* Much of the problem in leading a child to effective cognitive activity is to free him from the immediate control of environmental rewards and punishments. That is to say, learning that starts in response to the rewards of parental or teacher approval of the avoidance of failure can too readily develop a pattern in which the child is seeking cues as to how to conform to what is expected of him. We know from studies of children who tend to be early over-achievers in school that they are likely to be seekers after the "right way to do it" and that their capacity for transforming their learning into viable thought structures tends to be lower than children merely achieving at levels predicted by intelligence tests. Our tests on such children show them to be lower in analytic ability than those who are not conspicuous in overachievement.[4] As we shall see later, they develop rote abilities and depend upon being able to "give back" what is expected rather than to make it into something that relates to the rest of their cognitive life. As Maimonides would say, their learning is not their own.

The hypothesis that I would propose here is that to the degree that one is able to approach learning as a task of discovering something rather than "learning about" it, to that degree will there be a tendency for the child to carry out his learning activities with the autonomy of self-reward or, more properly by reward that is discovery itself.

To those of you familiar with the battles of the last half-century in the field of motivation, the above hypothesis will be recognized as controversial. For the classic view of motivation in learning has been, until very recently, couched in terms of a theory of drives and reinforcement: that learning occurred by virtue of the fact that a response produced by a stimulus was followed by the reduction in a primary drive state. The doctrine is greatly extended by the idea of secondary reinforcement: any state associated even remotely with the reduction of a primary drive could also have the effect of producing learning. There has recently appeared a most searching and important criticism of this position, written by Professor Robert White,[5] reviewing the evidence of recently published animal studies, of work in the field of psychoanalysis, and of research on the development of cognitive processes in children. Professor White comes to the conclusion, quite rightly I think, that the drive-reduction model of learning runs counter to too many important phenomena of learning and development to be either regarded as general in its applicability or even correct in its general approach. Let me summarize some of his principal conclusions and explore their applicability to the hypothesis stated above.

I now propose that we gather the various kinds of behavior just mentioned, all of which have to do with effective interaction with the environment, under the general heading of competence. According to Webster, competence means fitness or ability, and the suggested synonyms include capability, capacity, efficiency, proficiency, and skill. It is therefore a suitable word to describe such things as grasping and exploring, crawling and walking, attention and perception, language and thinking, manipulating and changing the surroundings, all of which promote an effective—a competent—interaction with the environment. It is true of course, that maturation plays a part in all these developments, but this part is heavily overshadowed by learning in all the more complex accomplishments like speech or skilled manipulation. I shall argue that it is necessary to make competence a motivational concept; there is *competence motivation* as well as competence in its more familiar sense of achieved capacity. The behavior that leads to the building up of effective grasping, handling, and letting go of objects, to take one example, is not random behavior that is produced by an overflow of energy. It is directed, selective, and persistent, and it continues not because it serves primary drives, which indeed it cannot serve until it is almost perfected, but because it satisfies an intrinsic need to deal with the environment.[6]

I am suggesting that there are forms of activity that serve to enlist and develop the competence motive, that serve to make it the driving force behind behavior. I should like to add to White's general premise that the *exercise* of competence motives has the effect of strengthening the degree to which they gain control over behavior and thereby reduce the effects of extrinsic rewards or drive gratification.

The brilliant Russian psychologist Vigotsky[7] characterizes the growth of thought processes as starting with a dialogue of speech and gesture between child and parent; autonomous thinking begins at the stage when the child is first able to internalize these conversations and "run them off" himself. This is a typical sequence in the development of competence. So too in instruction. The narrative of teaching is of the order of the conversation. The next move in the development of competence is the internalization of the narrative and its "rules of generation" so that the child is now capable of running off the narrative on his own. The hypothetical mode in teaching by encouraging the child to participate in "speaker's decisions" speeds this process along. Once internalization has occurred, the child is in a vastly improved position from several obvious points of view—notably that he is able to go beyond the information he has been given to generate additional ideas that can either be checked immediately from experience or can, at least, be used as a basis for formulating reasonable hypotheses. But over and beyond that, the child is now in a position to experience success and failure not as reward and punishment, but as information. For when the task is his own rather than a matter of matching environmental demands, he becomes his own paymaster in a certain measure. Seeking to gain control over his environment, he can now treat success as indicating that he is on the right track, failure as indicating he is on the wrong one.

In the end, this development has the effect of freeing learning from immediate stimulus control. When learning in the short run leads only to pellets of this or that rather than to mastery in the long run, then behavior can be readily "shaped" by extrinsic rewards. When behavior becomes more long-range and competence-oriented, it comes under the control of more complex cognitive structures, plans and the like, and operates more from the inside out. It is interesting that even Pavlov, whose early account of the learning process was based entirely on a notion of stimulus control of behavior through the conditioning mechanism in which, through contiguity a new conditioned stimulus was substituted for an old unconditioned stimulus by the mechanism of stimulus substitution, that even Pavlov recognized his account as insufficient to deal with higher forms of learning. To supplement the account, he introduced the idea of the "second signalling system," with central importance placed on symbolic systems such as language in mediating and giving shape to mental life. Or as Luria[8] has put it, "the first signal system [is] concerned with directly perceived stimuli, the second with systems of verbal elaboration." Luria, commenting on the importance of the transition from first to second signal system, says: "It would be mistaken to suppose that verbal intercourse with adults merely changes the contents of the child's conscious activity without changing its form. . . . The word has a basic function not only because it indicates a corresponding object in the external world, but also because it abstracts, isolates the necessary signal, generalizes perceived signals and relates them to certain categories; it is this systematization of direct experience that makes the role of the word in the formation of mental processes so exceptionally important."[9,10]

It is interesting that the final rejection of the universality of the doctrine of reinforcement in direct conditioning came from some of Pavlov's own students. Ivanov-Smolensky[11] and Krasnogorsky[12] published papers showing the manner in which symbolized linguistic messages could take over the place of the unconditioned stimulus and of the unconditioned response (gratification of hunger) in children. In all instances, they speak of these as *replacements* of lower, first-system mental or neural processes by higher order or second-system controls. A strange irony, then, that Russian psychology that gave us the notion of the conditioned response and the assumption that higher order activities are built up out of colligations or structurings of such primitive units, rejected this notion while much of American learning psychology has stayed until quite recently within the early Pavlovian fold (see, for example, a recent article by Spence[13] in the *Harvard Educational Review* or Skinner's treatment of language[14] and the attacks that have been made upon it by linguists such as Chomsky[15] who have become concerned with the relation of language and cognitive activity). What is the more interesting is that Russian pedagogical theory has become deeply influenced by this new trend and is now placing much stress upon the importance of building up a more active symbolical approach to problem solving among children.

To sum up the matter of the control of learning, then, I am proposing that the degree to which competence or mastery motives come to control behavior, to that degree the role of reinforcement or "extrinsic pleasure" wanes in shaping behavior. The child comes to manipulate his environment more actively and achieves his gratification from coping with problems. Symbolic modes of representing and transforming the environment arise and the importance of stimulus-response-reward sequences declines. To use the metaphor that David Riesman developed in a quite different context, mental life moves from a state of outer-directedness in which the fortuity of stimuli and reinforcement are crucial to a state of inner-directedness in which the growth and maintenance of mastery become central and dominant.

3. *Learning the heuristics of discovery.* Lincoln Steffens,[16] reflecting in his *Autobiography* on his under graduate education at Berkeley, comments that his schooling was over specialized on learning about the known and that too little attention was given to the task of finding out about what was not known. But how does one train a student in the techniques of discovery? Again I would like to offer some hypotheses. There are many ways of coming to the arts of inquiry. One of them is by careful study of its formalization in logic, statistics, mathematics, and the like. If a person is going to pursue inquiry as a way of life, particularly in the sciences, certainly such study is essential. Yet, whoever has taught kindergarten and the early primary grades or has had graduate students working with him on their theses—I choose the two extremes for they are both periods of intense inquiry—knows that an understanding of the formal aspect of inquiry is not sufficient. There appear to be, rather, a series of activities and attitudes, some directly related to a particular subject and some of them fairly generalized, that go with inquiry and research. These have to do with the *process* of trying to find out something and while they provide no guarantee that the *product* will be any *great* discovery, their absence is likely to lead to awkwardness or aridity or confusion. How difficult it is to describe these matters—the heuristics of inquiry. There is one set of attitudes or ways of doing that has to do with sensing the relevance of variables—how to avoid getting stuck with edge effects and getting instead to the big sources of variance. Partly this gift comes from intuitive familiarity with a range of phenomena, sheer "knowing the stuff." But it also comes out of a sense of what things among an ensemble of things "smell right" in the sense of being of the right order of magnitude or scope or severity.

The English philosopher Weldon describes problem solving in an interesting and picturesque way. He distinguishes between difficulties, puzzles, and problems. We solve a problem or make a discovery when we impose a puzzle form on to a difficulty that converts it into a problem that can be solved in such a way that it gets us where we want to be. That is to say, we recast the difficulty into a form that we know how to work with, then work it. Much of what we speak of as discovery consists of knowing how to impose what kind of form on various kinds of difficulties. A small part but a crucial part of discovery of the highest order is to invent and develop models or "puzzle forms" that can be imposed on difficulties with good effect. It is in this area that the truly powerful mind shines. But it is interesting to what degree perfectly ordinary people can, given the benefit of instruction, construct quite interesting and what, a century ago, would have been considered greatly original models.

Now to the hypothesis. It is my hunch that it is only through the exercise of problem solving and the effort of discovery that one learns the working heuristic of discovery, and the more one has practice, the more likely is one to generalize what one has learned into a style of problem solving or inquiry that serves for any kind of task one may encounter—or almost any kind of task. I think the matter is self-evident, but what is unclear is what kinds of training and teaching produce the best effects. How do we teach a child to, say, cut his losses but at the same time be persistent in trying out an idea; to risk forming an early hunch without at the same time formulating one *so* early and with so little evidence as to be stuck with it waiting for appropriate evidence to materialize; to pose good testable guesses that are neither too brittle nor too sinuously incorrigible; etc., etc. Practice in inquiry, in trying to figure out things for oneself is indeed what is needed, but in what form? Of only one thing I am convinced. I have never seen anybody improve in the art and technique of inquiry by any means other than engaging in inquiry.

4. *Conservation of memory.* I should like to take what some psychologists might consider a rather drastic view of the memory process. It is a view that in large measure derives from the work of my colleague, Professor George Miller.[17] Its first premise is that the principal problem of human memory is not storage, but retrieval. In spite of the biological unlikeliness of it, we seem to be able to store a huge quantity of information—perhaps not a full tape recording, though at times it seems we even do that, but a great sufficiency of impressions. We may infer this from the fact that recognition (i.e., recall with the aid of maximum prompts) is so extraordinarily good in human beings— particularly in comparison with spontaneous recall where, so to speak, we must get out stored information without external aids or prompts. The key to retrieval is organization or, in even simpler terms, knowing where to find information and how to get there.

Let me illustrate the point with a simple experiment. We present pairs of words to twelve-year-old children. One group is simply told to remember the pairs, that they will be asked to repeat them later. Another is told to remember them by producing a word or idea that will tie the pair together in a way that will make sense to them. A third group is given the mediators used by the second group when presented with the pairs to aid them in tying the pairs into working units. The word pairs include such juxtapositions as "chair-forest," "sidewalk-square," and the like. One can distinguish three styles of mediators and children can be scaled in terms of their relative preference for each: *generic mediation* in which a pair is tied together by a superordinate idea: "chair and forest are both made of wood"; *thematic mediation* in which the two terms are imbedded in a theme or little story: "the lost child sat on a chair in the middle of the forest"; and *part-whole mediation* where "chairs are made from trees in the forest" is typical. Now, the chief result, as you would all predict, is that children who provide their own mediators do best—indeed, one time through a set of thirty pairs, they recover up to 95% of the second words when presented with the first ones of the pairs, whereas the uninstructed children reach a maximum of less than 50% recovered. Interestingly enough, children do best in recovering materials tied together by the form of mediator they most often use.

One can cite a myriad of findings to indicate that any organization of information that reduces the aggregate complexity of material by imbedding it into a cognitive structure a person has constructed will make that material more accessible for retrieval. In short, we may say that the process of memory, looked at from the retrieval side, is also a process of problem solving: how can material be "placed" in memory so that it can be got on demand?

We can take as a point of departure the example of the children who developed their own technique for relating the members of each word pair. You will recall that they did better than the children who were given by exposition the mediators they had developed. Let me suggest that in general, material that is organized in terms of a person's own interests and cognitive structures is material that has the best chance of being accessible in memory. That is to say, it is more likely to be placed along routes that are connected to one's own ways of intellectual travel.

In sum, the very attitudes and activities that characterize "figuring out" or "discovering" things for oneself also seems to have the effect of making material more readily accessible in memory.

References

[1] Maimonides, *Guide for the Perplexed* (New York: Dover Publications, 1956).

[2] I should also remark in passing that the two extremes also characterize concept attainment strategies as reported in *A Study of Thinking* by J. S. Bruner *et al.* (New York:

J. Wiley, 1956). Successive scanning illustrates well what is meant here by episodic empiricism; conservative focussing is an example of cumulative constructionism.

[3] R. B. Zajonc (Personal communication, 1957).

[4] J. S. Bruner and A. J. Caron, "Cognition, Anxiety, and Achievement in the Pre-adolescent," *Journal of Educational Psychology* (in press).

[5] R. W. White, "Motivation Reconsidered: The Concept of Competence," *Psychological Review,* LXVI (1959), 297-333.

[6] *Ibid.,* pp. 317-18.

[7] L. S. Vigotsky, *Thinking and Speech* (Moscow, 1934).

[8] A. L. Luria, "The Directive Function of Speech in Development and Dissolution," *Word,* XV (1959), 341-464.

[9] *Ibid.,* p. 12.

[10] For an elaboration of the view expressed by Luria, the reader is referred to the forthcoming translation of L. S. Vigotsky's 1934 book being published by John Wiley and Sons and the Technology Press.

[11] A. G. Ivanov-Smolensky, "Concerning the Study of the Joint Activity of the First and Second Signal Systems," *Journal of Higher Nervous Activity,* I (1951), 1.

[12] N. D. Krasnogorsky, *Studies of Higher Nervous Activity in Animals and in Man,* Vol. I (Moscow, 1954).

[13] K. W. Spence, "The Relation of Learning Theory to the Technique of Education," *Harvard Educational Review,* XXIX (1959), 84-95.

[14] B. F. Skinner, *Verbal Behavior* (New York: Appleton-Century-Crofts, 1957).

[15] N. Chomsky, *Syntactic Structure* (The Hague, The Netherlands: Mouton & Co., 1957).

[16] L. Steffens. *Autobiography of Lincoln Steffens* (New York: Harcourt, Brace, 1931).

[17] G. A. Miller, "The Magical Number Seven, Plus or Minus Two," *Psychological Review,* LXIII (1956), 81-97.

THE REFLECTIVE MODEL

Bryon C. Massialas   and   C. Benjamin Cox
University of Michigan   *University of Illinois*

The reflective method is here conceived as comprised of six phases, each one of which is characterized by certain kinds of skills and activities. In some respects, as shall be demonstrated later, these phases comprise a model of critical thinking in its application inasmuch as they describe a sequential

Reprinted in an abridged version with permission of the authors and the publisher, from Bryon G. Massialas and C. Benjamin Cox, *Inquiry in Social Studies* (New York: McGraw-Hill Book Company, 1966), pp. 115-119.

pattern of behavior which moves the student from problem to solution. As shown below, the phases include orientation, hypothesis, definition, exploration, evidencing, and generalization.

The inception, continuation, and direction of intellectual forces employed in moving any discussion from its problem orientation to the culminating generalized solution may be represented by the following figurative model.

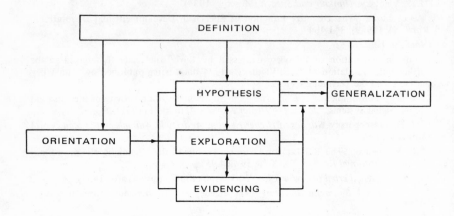

We shall now define and amplify each of these phases and illustrate them with a hypothetical case going from orientation to generalization.

ORIENTATION

In this phase of the procedure students and teacher alike become sensitive to an existing problem situation. An awareness of the problem may arise from a textbook passage, or springboard, which students read in the course of their preparation. Or the problem may be expressly prepared by the teacher and assigned as a question. An orientation may be gained by means of isolated facts, summaries, ideas, or generalizations. At some point, whatever its course, this phase comes to focus on a question which calls for an explanation, relationship, solution, or policy. . . .

HYPOTHESIS

This is the primary, declarative, general statement of explanation or solution; it expresses as clearly as possible the antecedent and consequent relationship, explanation, description, or policy which would apply to the social phenomenon under consideration. The hypothesis or hypotheses—alternative solutions are often hypothesized—represent search models which subsequently guide the students and teacher toward relevant evidence. The hypothesis escapes the particular by restating the elements and relationships in general terms.

From the summary statement in our example it is hypothesized that "Contact with different cultures results in changed values and desires." This hypothesis is now tested by the teacher and class in terms of (1) its validity as an explanation of the springboard episode, (2) its compatibility with previously devised generalizations and the experiences of the pupils and teacher, and (3) the existence of other historical facts and evidence which are relevant to its proof or disproof.

Prior to this testing process an attempt is made by the teacher and his students to clarify and define all terms of the hypothesis in order to avoid ambiguity and provide a common ground for the discussion. Verifiability of a hypothesis depends upon both content and communicability of meaning.

DEFINITION

The task of defining is really not to be isolated in the process inasmuch as meaning and definition are constant elements in all phases of reflective inquiry. Agreement on the meaning of terms is a requirement of the dialogue of inquiry. This task frequently demands the construction of operational definitions when authoritative meanings do not fit the case. While definition is emphasized in the orientation and hypothesizing phases, the entire reflective enterprise is characterized by the question, "What do you mean by_____?"

For example, with reference to our illustration it may have been hypothesized to begin with that "contact with different cultures results in progress." Here an ambiguous term, *progress,* requires either clarification and definition or substitution by another term or terms, the meaning of which has more specific connotations to the teacher and class.

As a further procedure in the testing of the hypothesis, logically deduced implications are formulated in the exploration stage.

EXPLORATION

Whereas orientation and hypothesizing tend to be inductive in nature, this phase tends to be deductive. The hypothesis is more carefully explicated in terms of logical deductions and implications, and assumptions and premises. Qualifying and delimiting factors are more exactly spelled out. The finding of logically untenable grounds may cause a major reconstruction of the hypothesis at this time.

In our example a logical implication could be stated as follows: "If contact with different cultures results in changed values and desires, then people involved in trade outside their own territory are more likely to undergo cultural change." Or, to state another possible implication, "If a given people live in isolation, then their culture will remain relatively static." The statement of implications leads directly to the searching for evidence to support the original hypothesis.

EVIDENCING

The process of making reference to empirical data for support and proof of the hypothesis is conjunctive with exploration. That is, the search-model character of the hypothesis and its implications indicates the kind of facts and evidence needed to support the hypothesis.

In pursuing the implications made in our illustrative case, questions like the following are asked: "Do you know of people who trade(d) extensively and who in the process of exchanging goods also trade(d) ideas and cultural patterns?" Or, with reference to the second implication, "Do you know of any such isolated people; and is it true that their culture has (did) not change(d) over a long period of time?"

As evidence relevant to these deductions the early feudal experience of Europe presents a clear case of isolation whereas the Crusades and the Renaissance in Europe are examples and results of intercultural exchange. The transformation that took place in Japan following its opening to Western trade in the mid-nineteenth century offers additional evidence applicable to both deductions. Other historical, anthropological, sociological, and social science data relevant to these and other deductions are brought to bear on the hypothesis to prove or refute its validity in all times and places. In many cases, of course, insufficient data preclude any pursuit of the inquiry beyond this phase. In such an instance students and teachers should recognize that further examination without available evidence is not warranted. In any case, the end result of reflective analysis is the reaching of a conclusion or tested generalization warranted by available evidence.

GENERALIZATION

The conclusion of the process is the expression of an explanatory, casual, correlative or practical generalization. This statement represents the most tenable solution to the problem based on all available evidence. The generalization, however, is never taken to represent a final truth. Its tentative nature is recognized.

If we assume that in the example sufficient evidence for its support, and no evidence leading to its refutation or major reconstruction is found, the warrantable conclusion to be drawn from the reflective procedure may be stated as follows: "If a people of one culture contact a people of a different culture, then a culture different from either of these but characterized by identifiable elements of each emerges."

If in the discussion episodes, phenomena, situations, or facts are discovered which show that the original hypothesis is true only under certain conditions or that it needs to be qualified in some way, then it is reconstructed so that the conclusion reflects these qualifications. Quite naturally the generalization undergoes some syntactical and grammatical change simply on the basis of the greater clarity and understanding growing out of the discussion.

It must be borne in mind that the final conclusion does not constitute an absolute—even though all possible data have been brought to bear on its proof—but is always considered as tentative. . . .

ANENT THE DISCOVERY METHOD

Kenneth B. Henderson
University of Illinois, Urbana

For some time now the discovery method has been receiving attention from theorists in mathematics education. The method goes by various names, for example, the laboratory method, the developmental method or the inductive method. As described by some of these theorists, the method appears to be a

Reprinted with the permission of the author and the publisher, from *The Mathematics Teacher* (April, 1957), pp. 287-291.

formalized procedure not unlike Herbart's formal steps. As the first step, the teacher has in mind a generalization he wants his students to learn. The generalization is usually either a categorical proposition, such as the sum of the angles of a triangle is 180º, or a hypothetical proposition, such as if a decimal is multiplied by ten, the decimal point is moved one place to the right. In either case, it is a statement about a relationship between two or more classes. We may regard this generalization as of the form where every case of p is also a case of q.

As the second step, the teacher selects, or has the students select, instances of the generalization for study. In the case of the generalization that the sum of the angles of a triangle is 180º, the teacher encourages the students to select different kinds of triangles, varying the shape, size, and orientation of the triangle on the blackboard or paper.

Next, the teacher directs the students' thinking relative to the instances selected by means of prescriptions and questions. He may say, "Measure each of the angles in each of the five triangles and record your measurements in the table," "Find the sum of the three angles in each triangle," or "Compare the sums of the angles in each of the five triangles." Or he may ask, "Do you think the size of the triangle has anything to do with the sum of its angles? How can we find out?" or "Looking at all the sums of the angles of a triangle, what value seems to occur most frequently?" The purpose both of the prescriptions and the questions is to focus the students' attention on the common relationship amidst all the irrelevant details.

The fourth step grows out of the preceding one. It is to educe if possible the statement of the generalization from the students. Whether the teacher seeks to have the students immediately state precisely the generalization or not depends on their facility with language. The more facile they are, the sooner the verbalization of the generalization can be attempted. But even though the verbalization may be postponed, ultimately the teacher encourages the students to state their discovery as a generalization. If the students have difficulty in formulating the generalization, the teacher often repeats steps two and three, going more slowly and leading their thinking more carefully by means of questions.

Teachers usually follow the fourth step with one which makes the students apply the generalization they have just acquired in new situations or problems. This has the effect of extending the generalization.

Let us now look at the logic of the discovery method. The logic is that of the logic of a probable inference, for when a student predicates to the entire class that relationship he has identified as true of the sample with which he has been working, he makes a probable inference.

As was pointed out above, the generalization may be regarded as being of this form: Every case of p is also a case of q regardless of other contingencies. The following may be regarded as a paradigm of the argument for the material truth of a generalization expressed in this form.

Let us represent "being a triangle" by "p," "having 180° as the sum of the interior angles of the triangle" as "q," "being an acute triangle" as "r," "being a scalene triangle" as "s," "being so oriented on paper that the longest side is toward the bottom of the paper" as "t," and so on—identifying all the factors we think might be relevant.

1. Each instance (measurement or comparison) which confirms the generalization is essentially a report that in addition to p and q, other factors such as r, s, and t, occur or fail to occur.
2. Both p and q, but no other factor, occur in all instances.
3. No instances are found in which p occurs but no corresponding q, that is, no contrary evidence turns up.
4. Therefore ("therefore" is used in the sense of "it probably follows" and not in the sense of "it necessarily follows") every case of p is also a case of q regardless of other contingencies.

This is the familiar method of agreement. (The method of difference can be used in employing the discovery method or the joint method of agreement and difference, depending on the nature of the generalization to be "discovered.") The persuasiveness of the paradigm may be attributed to two factors: (1) its application affords an accumulation of confirmatory instances, and (2) factors r, s, t, et al. are shown not to be relevant.

In the empirical sciences, correct use of the method of agreement depends on the investigator's ability to identify all possible relevant factors. In a body of analytic truth like mathematics, this is no problem for the teacher. He knows for certain the factors and only those factors which are relevant. The students who are in the role of investigators do not have this knowledge, hence the teacher may help them by such leading questions, as "Do you think the shape or size of the triangle has anything to do with the sum of the angles? How can we find out?"

The generalization limited to the sample of instances is an enumerative generalization. The criterion for its verification is clear. It is true for the sample if and only if it is true for every member of the sample. But if the generalization is limited to the sample, it has little power. It needs to be extended to the class from which the sample was drawn. But as Hempel[1] has pointed out, there are no criteria to establish the confirmation of an empirical generalization about a population (class) which is larger than the class for which the generalization has been verified. To apply this to the example we have been using, when the teacher limits his teaching to the discovery method, there is no way of verifying the generalization which the student is supposed to reach. The teacher does not even know how many triangles he should have the students measure to confirm the generalization. Acceptance of the generalization is based on a psychological rather than a logical criterion.

Let us now look at the psychology of the discovery method from the point of view of the student. If the student is told by the teacher what the objective of the study is, namely, to develop a generalization from the comparisons or measurements he makes, his thinking is structured to some extent. In analyzing his thinking, three concepts are useful. The first of these is that of logical form. One kind of logical form is a relationship, expressible in language, between two or more classes of elements. Such a logical form is an intellectual construct or abstraction which characterizes the instances of it.

The second concept is that of content. The content is the medium in which a logical form is expressed. To turn to the example we have been using, the content is the class of triangles of different sizes, shapes, and orientations which the student studies. But all have the common logical form or property that the sum of the interior angles is 180⁰. The same form is expressed in different content. As we have seen, it is this logical form that the teacher wants to teach. He varies the content in which this form appears so the students can see the common logical form in differing content.

The third concept is that of analogy. Analogy is the recognition of a common form in different content. An analogy is an inference. When the student sees the correct analogy, he makes the discovery, or, as we sometimes say, has the insight. His ability to see the analogy is determined to some extent by his native ability and to some extent by whatever previous training he has had designed to help him understand the process he is going through. He proceeds by formulating verbally or non-verbally hypotheses (inferences) which he tests. He tests these by means of various data which are either relevant to the logic of the process or are extraneous to the logic. Examples of the former are the comparisons or measurements he has made or makes anew. Examples of the latter are the cues he gets from the teacher's facial expressions, tone of voice, or verbal responses. As a result of the testing, he either accepts or rejects the hypothesis. If it is the latter, he searches for a new hypothesis and the whole procedure is re-enacted. Once he accepts the hypothesis, he has made the discovery. If he has studied several members of the class and if he does not understand the logic of the method of induction, he readily makes the some-to-all extension and predicates to the entire class that relationship which he has found true of the sample with which he worked.

A strong case can be made for the discovery method at least pragmatically. Teachers who have tried it testify to the great interest the students maintain. They also feel that the quality of the students' thinking is higher than in the telling method. A third advantage is that in using the discovery method, it is hard to go too fast for students. The teacher usually is aware whether the students have made the discovery. A smile or an "I see" are often cues which the teacher can use to detect the insight. If the insight has not been manifested, the teacher retraces his steps, reducing the diversity of the content and guiding the students more carefully by leading questions. These cues are not so readily available in the telling method, hence it is easy to go too fast for the students. Finally, it is felt by some theorists that when the student makes the discovery for himself, the generalization is more meaningful and better understood.

So often the discovery method is made to glitter by comparing it with the drab kind of teaching that sometimes is done when the telling method is used. I have never felt that such a loaded comparison is quite fair, for so often a description of an ineffective use of the telling method is given. The teacher using this method is portrayed as presenting a straight lecture without setting the stage for learning by showing how what the students are to learn is related to what they already know, without checking to see if the students understand the terms that are used in the presentation, and without giving them a chance to apply the generalization they have learned.

Using an unfair comparison, one could just as easily make the user of the discovery method look bad. He could be portrayed as not leading the students' thinking effectively, as forcing them to generalize from two or three instances, as allowing the bright students to state the generalization as soon as they conceive it, thereby immediately destroying the motivation of the other students, or as furnishing extraneous cues by facial expression or tone of voice which enable the students to test their hypotheses. Let us realize that the discovery method can be abused just as the telling or deductive method can be abused. And in my opinion it would be abused if students subtly were taught to generalize from a few instances or if they were just as subtly taught to pay attention to the teacher's reactions rather than to the data which become relevant once the hypothesis is formulated. After observing the teaching of some teachers who say they use this method, I fear that some of their students may be acquiring these undesirable learnings.

One further point about the discovery method is bothersome. Suppose suddenly all mathematics teachers were to shift from the telling or deductive method to the discovery method. Would not the students come to think that mathematics is like science in that we arrive at generalizations in both subjects by using the same method? Might they not come to think that mathematics, like science, is a body of synthetic or contingent truth? Of course, mathematics is not this kind of truth. It is not so bad if students in the elementary school and junior high school acquire some generalizations by the discovery method and never verify them deductively. But sometime in high school they should learn the distinctive nature of mathematics as a system of postulational thinking. They should learn the different logic of the methods of induction and deduction and when each method is appropriate. Conventionally this is done, if it is done at all, in demonstrative geometry. But it does not necessarily have to be learned in this subject alone. It can be learned initially in ninth-grade algebra and re-enforced in succeeding courses. It would seem that the farther the student goes in high school mathematics, the more the deductive method should be used. The discovery method can be used to identify hypotheses, but these in most cases should then be proved or disproved deductively.

It would seem that the relative advantages of different methods of teaching should be appraised largely on the depth of understanding their use affords. It helps to identify six levels of understanding. Let us for simplicity's sake assume that we are interested in teaching a generalization. The first level is represented by a student who can give a verbatim statement of the generalization which he has memorized from the textbook or from the statement the teacher has written on the blackboard. He does not know what all the words in the generalization mean, and he cannot give an instance of it. This certainly is a low level of understanding. Some people may even not want to call this behavior understanding at all, since there seems to be no meaning for the student. But such a student probably could recognize some permutations of the words in the generalization as nonsense. For example, such a student who could repeat "the sum of the angles of a triangle is 180º" without knowing what an angle or a degree is, might say the progression of words, "the is of the 180º triangle angles sum" is nonsense. Were he to say this, I would be willing to say the generalization had some sort of syntatic meaning for him, meager though it is.

The second level is represented by a student who can give a correct statement of the generalization in his own words. He cannot give an instance of the generalization or apply it, but his ability to paraphrase it correctly seems to indicate that it has a syntactic meaning for him which goes beyond the meager syntatic meaning of the first level.

The third level is represented by a student who, in addition to being able to perform at the second level, can give instances of the generalization, instances which are not those that the teacher or the textbook has given. We might say that the generalization has a semantic meaning for this student.

The fourth level is represented by a student who goes beyond the third level by being able to apply the generalization in problems for which he knows the generalization is relevant. Perhaps the teacher or the textbook has stated, "Find the third angle in a triangle, two of whose angles are 90 degrees and 50 degrees" directly after teaching the generalization about the sum of the angles of a triangle. In this case the student would have to be quite incapable not to guess that the generalization he had just learned had something to do with the problem.

The fifth level is represented by a student who, besides being able to operate at the fourth level, can apply the generalization in problems where there is no second party to give him a cue that the generalization is relevant. For example, such a student should be able to solve the problem, "One angle of a triangle is twice the second angle and three times the third angle. Find the size of each angle of the triangle."

The sixth and final level is manifested by a student who not only can operate at the fifth level, but also can explain or prove the generalization in the sense of showing that it is necessarily implied by certain other propositions.

Although I have no conclusive evidence, I would hazard a guess that the discovery method enables a student to move readily to what I have arbitrarily designated as the fourth level of understanding. Perhaps it will do this even better than the telling method, but I am not sure. But if the teacher limits his teaching to the discovery method, I doubt that his students ever will reach the sixth level, the stage of understanding at which they can give reasons why the generalization is true for all the instances for which they apply it. When I say this, I am not implying that I believe the sixth level should be aimed at for every generalization. I doubt that it should. I am simply indicating what I believe is an inherent weakness of the discovery method as far as mathematics teaching is concerned.

I would like to close with a reaffirmation of my belief in the efficacy of the discovery method. I have voiced some reservations about the method because of the great attention the method receives in professional journals, if not in the classroom. I fear that teachers who are looking for a panacea to solve their problems of methodology might uncritically climb on the bandwagon. What the classroom teacher needs is an understanding of and an ability to use several different methods, for to date there is no royal road to teaching and learning.

References

[1]Carl G. Hempel, "Studies in the Logic of Confirmation," *Mind,* LIV (1954), 1-26; 97-121.

SECTION C   Techniques of Teaching

AN ATTEMPT TO MODIFY THE INFLUENCE OF GEOGRAPHIC DETERMINISM IN TEACHING THE MAN-AND-PLACE RELATIONSHIP

Muriel Moulton
Francis W. Parker School, Chicago

Teachers generally agree that the concept of geographic determinism fails to provide an accurate understanding of the relationship between "man" and "place." Yet, in dealing with high school freshmen, it is most tempting for the teacher to allow the students, however subtly, to retreat into a deterministic interpretation.

Children at that level of uncertain maturity are most at ease with one-dimensional questions and absolute or unqualified answers. For example: having learned that some Eskimoes build snow houses, some thirteen-year-olds are distressed to learn that the Chuckchee and the Koryak, having a physical environment essentially identical to that of the Eskimo, do not build snow houses, but persist in building clumsy, burdensome tents of hides.

Compared with the direct simplicity of a deterministic approach, one can readily appreciate the uneasiness and resistance which may arise when presenting to students the principle that while the physical environment *sets limits* of probable practices upon cultural development, the physical environment is not in itself ultimately *decisive,* and that there may be *different cultural reactions* to *similar physical environments.*

Children, wanting to cling to a simpler explanation of the bewildering world, receive this more complicated relationship—however well illustrated by movies, photographs, and text materials—with only a superficial degree of understanding. The connection, for example, between the presence of wood in a physical environment and the utilization of wood as a resource remains to them inexorable.

Reprinted with permission of the publisher, from *The Journal of Geography,* 61 (December, 1962): 400-403.

POSSIBLE METHODS

One possible solution might be an investigation of several lines of cultural development. To have significant effect, however, this approach usually requires a great deal of time—more than there is available in a first-year geography or social studies course.

A second possible solution presents itself: If the students struggle actively in the development of a basic premise, they will be more realistically receptive to its implications. That is, instead of allowing the students simply to receive these statements and their illustrations passively, the teacher can, to better advantage, put the student into an active role in the development of the desired principle. He can, for example, throw out guide points from which students may both articulate questions and then formulate answers to their own questions. This is not an easy teaching procedure. It requires facility in managing a class without the traditional controls of either strict discipline or highly structured ends. The author was considerably aided in her presentation by being able to present the new concept partly in the terms of a concept already familiar to the students—a simple application of the theory of sets which they had studied extensively in their mathematics classes.

Using this approach to the man-and-place relationship, the author found that the students' responses were at first hesitant. However, when the students found themselves, roughly speaking, carving out an important idea with their bare hands, enthusiasm began to develop and spread through the class. In addition, the writer feels that her explicit refusal to convince them overtly of anything, and the fact that resistance was met with interest instead of disapproval, contributed to the end result of more realistic understanding.

PROCEDURE

The writer began with a brief introductory session in which the students learned the meaning of a few basic terms such as "physical environment," "culture" and "decisive." Then they were asked where they would find a physical environment. They answered, "in a Place." The best students were suspicious of the simplicity of the answer; others were not yet interested enough to respond in any fashion.

The next question was, "How would you represent a Place on the blackboard?" They suggested a square, a circle or a similar figure. A square was drawn on the blackboard and labeled "A Place," another square was labeled "A Place," and still another and another; then the writer waited. Finally someone called out, "Well, are they all the same place?"

"If they are not all the same place, what will be different about them?" they were asked.

Several students this time resignedly, but with good humor, declared that there was no point waiting "for her" to tell them the answer and began to try to find it themselves. Their suggestions came haltingly; at first they seemed very uncertain. They suggested that if the squares represented different places, probably the things that would be different about them would be climate, vegetation, buildings, soil, etc. "Say all that in just a couple of words," they were told, "and leave out the things that man would have done."

"Physical environment," shouted several students.

"Then what do the lines of one of these squares represent?" they were then asked.

The more perceptive students took only a few moments to declare that the lines of the square represented the limits of the physical environment of the Place. Almost immediately some of the other students wanted to know: "What do you mean by limits?" and "What kind of limits?"

This time the quicker students didn't wait for an answer to be supplied, instead, in several forms, with varying degrees of conviction, declared that: "The lines indicate the limits of what can be done in a Place."

Now they were getting closer to the distinction between the physical environment as *setting limits* of practicability and culture as being *decisive* in development. At this point the students were reminded of a simple definition of culture that had been agreed upon earlier (culture is a way of living), and they were asked to compile quickly a list of things which might be done in a Place as an expression of culture. The list included such cultural behaviors as "growing edible plants," "building shelters" and "organizing governments." Nearly everybody contributed to the list. The writer, attempting to bring the newcomers along a step farther, asked: "If it is possible to perform these kinds of behaviors in a Place represented on the blackboard, how might one group or *set* of such behaviors be represented in that Place?"

The question brought forth grins and protests. They complained that this was a Social Studies class and that they'd had enough of set theory in their mathematics classes. A student known to be successful in mathematics when asked to give a simple definition of a set, said that a group of things which all have something in common could be called a set.

Then the original question was repeated and the answer came easily: "Any series of similar marks, such as x's can be used to represent any particular group or set of behaviors." It was interesting to note that at this point the student's language seemed to become more precise than it ordinarily was in a

Social Studies class. It would seem this reflected the stricter and more limited vocabulary of their mathematics classes.

Turning to one of the squares on the blackboard, the writer asked how one ought to indicate a set of behaviors in that Place. The figure on the blackboard which was drawn according to their directions, was a simple oblong with the lines of the oblong representing the physical limits of the Place and the series of x's representing the set of all *possible* combinations of edible plants which *could* be grown in that Place (Fig. 1A).

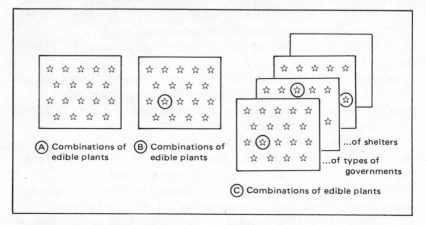

Fig. 1. Each square represents the set of all possible combinations of a particular cultural behavior. The circled stars represent the chosen sub-set of each set.

DEVELOPMENT OF A CONCEPT

At this point some of the characteristically apathetic students began to ask a few questions. Partly, they were trying to bait their teacher and their more articulate classmates. However, baiting a trap can be dangerous. Typically, they wanted to know if all possible combinations are grown in any one physical environment. The trap snapped, and under the questions of other students, the baiters found themselves trying to answer their own question. The followers were drawn more and more into the development of the concept. A steadier stream of questions was being supplied by the students. Answers were tried out with many rejections, again by the students.

Some of the students still wanted to know "how it is decided" which sub-set of the set of all possible combinations of edible plants will actually be grown in a Place, or more simply, "which x is chosen?" They were answered with the guiding question: "Since any one of all the sub-sets is *possible,* is there anything in the physical environment which would *decide* which sub-set would be selected?" In other words, they were asked if there was a purely physical factor which would be decisive in selecting which one of all the possible combinations would be chosen. The students who thought there were such decisive physical factors, made suggestions, and the ones who thought there were not such physical factors replied.

Physical factors which might be decisive were finally listed on the blackboard and the list was analyzed item by item. Physical factors such as climate and soil were among those suggested as possibly being decisive. It was pointed out that these factors would allow for several possible combinations of plants to be grown. A choice would still have to be made: which x would be chosen? The writer felt that it was important that students be given enough time to satisfy themselves that they could not find a decisive physical factor. The writer preferred to have some chronic doubters rather than mere acquiescence.

When it seemed as though all those students who were going to be satisfied on this point were satisfied, the class moved ahead. Some of the students did continue to grope for a decisive physical factor while the rest of the group went on. Several of the doubters dropped in after school to pursue the point.

To turn their attention from trying to find a decisive physical factor, the students were asked what else might be decisive.

"Man," they asserted. It was tried out. Reasons were listed which might determine man's selection of one possible combination over another possible combination in a Place. An x was selected and circled in the figure on the blackboard (Fig. 1B). This the class labeled the sub-set of the set of all edible plants which man, through his *reaction to his physical environment,* has selected to use in a Place. Some of the reasons helping to influence man's selection which were suggested by students were "custom," "tradition," "chance," "religion" and "attempts to gain power."

The attention of the students was then directed to the list of cultural behaviors they had made earlier. It was pointed out that for each behavior (building shelters, organizing governments, etc.) one could construct another figure such as the one the class had constructed on the blackboard. They were reminded that the figure they had constructed represented only one element of a very long list of cultural behaviors which are present in most societies.

Instead of drawing all these figures on the board, this writer felt that it was more effective at this point to ask the students to imagine the figure on the board as being one of a long line of similar figures, lined up neatly, one in front of another. Then, if one could step back, and, imagining the figures transparent, except for the circled x's, he could see the outline of a physical environment filled with the series of *selected* x's, each of them the chosen sub-set of a set of a particular cultural behavior (Fig. 1C).

SUMMARY

In employing this method, the main point of emphasis must be handled most carefully. Students, having constructed the figure and filled it with sub-sets of a set of possible combinations of a behavior, may be expected to resist the decisive role of culture in development. Time and patience are essential. It is most important that students be satisfied that they have really exhausted every possibility of proving decisiveness of the physical environment except as it sets the practical limits. It is the fact that the students have participated in the *process* of building the more complicated theory that forestalls their acceptance of the deterministic explanation.

MANUFACTURING UNIT OF THE HIGH SCHOOL PROJECT

Leonard M. Lansky and Howard A. Stafford
University of Cincinnati

What is manufacturing? What do the terms input, processing, and output mean? How is manufacturing distributed in the United States and the rest of the world? Why is it distributed in that way and not in some other? What is the significance of manufacturing as an urban activity? How are location decisions made by manufacturers? What computations must a person make in order to decide about a location? How is this done?

The answers to these and a number of other questions, make up the factual and conceptual objectives of the manufacturing unit of the High School Geography Project. There were also some attitudinal goals. One was to arouse students' enthusiasm about geography as a scientific subject; another

Reprinted with permission of the author and the publisher, from *The Journal of Geography*, 66 (April, 1967): 175-182. An earlier version of this paper was presented at a symposium on the High School Geography Project at the 62nd annual meetings of the AAG, Toronto, Ontario, August, 1966.

was to impart the scientific attitudes of respect for objective evidence, tentativeness in drawing conclusions and accepting theories, and skepticism about one's pet developments and ideas.

This listing of objectives is deceptively simple. The geographer in this effort (HAS) developed it after considerable struggle, argument, hard work, and badgering from the psychologist (LML), the consultants, and data from school children and teachers. The most common question the geographer had to answer was: "What do you want them to learn?" Another was "How does the activity relate to your learning goals?" Yet another version of these questions was "Why are they spending so much time on that? Is that what you are after?" In a sense, the (psychological) consultant's role is an easy one. He only has to *ask* the embarrassing questions.

PSYCHOLOGICAL ASSUMPTIONS

The psychological consultant can also offer some hunches about children, learning, and schools which the unit designer may find helpful in his planning. At some level of awareness—hindsight is 20-20—the psychologist had the following facts and theories, some old, some new, some seemingly new but merely old wine in new bottles:

1. People are always learning. This idea is new; indeed for years we have been assuming that we have to make people learn. Not so. We know now that we really must worry about *what* they learn, *where, how,* what learnings are used *where,* etc. This idea can be expressed another way. New learning fits into what is already known so that everyday events merely add to the old. For example, children learn again and again that school is boring, that grades are important, that no one really pays much attention to the plight of the student, teacher, school building, and the like. Granted that these learnings are changing because of Sputnik, our ex-school teacher in the White House, and other factors, the changes are still coming slowly and are fighting a population which still feels quite negative—a learned reaction—about education.

2. People seek tension and this motivating force may be more important than the classic equilibrium-seeking which we have all been taught. The ideal state for the human is not the baby asleep after being fed at the breast. Rather man's ideal state may be exemplified more accurately by the alert astronaut trying to dock his vehicle, by the Western poker player trying to figure out the gambler's hand, by the scientist sweating out the results in the laboratory or frustratingly trying to figure out what the data mean. This view

is new in academic psychology, old in philosophy, and still in considerable disrepute in education even though it was one postulate of Dewey's recommendations.

3. Emotions and feelings are part of the reality of any situation even though much of our philosophy of work and education relegates feelings to the unreal—to interference with the job and learning. Today industry and government know very well that the emotional components of work are ignored to our peril. The idea is not as accepted in education. Even where the idea is accepted, we do not yet know how to translate the growing awareness of the importance of emotions into effective classroom practice. One important feeling which affects learning is that of commitment and/or of caring. When we want to learn or are involved in the task, the learning proceeds more easily. We recall better, we see connections better, we stay at difficult tasks longer.

4. Learning does not proceed without feedback—without knowledge of results. Here again, the truth is not new but is honored more in the breach than in the observance. The student sitting in a class of thirty to forty students gets too few rewards for what the teacher might want him to learn— the teacher cannot manage to provide them. Insofar as our schools are organized as custodial institutions—similar to hospitals, mental institutions, and prisons in that they have worker to manager ratios of 30 to one and up—they are forced to limit what they can teach and how they parcel out rewards for certain kinds of learning. None of us can name working groups in industry, government, the military, or science which operate with working teams of more than seven or eight underlings to a supervisor—the usual ratios are smaller. The extreme case of altering this situation is the one-to-one ratio provided by such self-instructional devices as the teaching machine. Of course, the teaching machine is not a person. But that is another story.

5. This item is closely related to the last two—emotions are related to learning and rewards related to learning. This refers to social structure, group size, and similar variables. From research on brainwashing, studies of group problem-solving, and the like, we have learned that social structures and the physical situation affect what is learned, how rapidly, and what is transferred. For example, if chairs and desks are fixed in rows facing the front of the classroom, the situation almost "demands" a teacher-centered lecture or question-answer session. If the teacher is the major source of knowledge for each student, the teacher-learning ratio is one to the number of students in the class. Other physical and social arrangements are possible. However, they are rarely used.

Let me restate these five points: (1) people are always learning, (2) people seek tension, (3) emotions are part of any situation, (4) learning depends upon feedback, and (5) social structures affect learning. These items have several implications for designing curriculum materials. Let us list a few which affected the planning of the manufacturing unit. One is that small groups can cover more ground more rapidly on specific materials than large groups. Furthermore, in small groups, more different kinds of learning can be experienced, rewarded, channeled because more communication among members is possible. Another implication is that teaching a small group can enhance learning. The difficulties in clarifying concepts are a challenge; the feedback from a small group leads to corrective action about the meanings of the concepts.

These ideas and two others were the psychologists's assumptions in working on the unit. The two additional notions were: (1) teachers, other things being equal, have been and are poorly educated. They know little about the subject matters they are supposed to teach, less about children and their feelings and motives, and even less about how to promote the learning they, the teachers, often say they are interested in. In addition, as we have mentioned, the organization of the school and classroom militate against the teachers using whatever skills they do possess. (2) Experts in all fields— sciences, arts, humanities—are being asked to identify central concepts in their fields and to develop new methods for helping teachers and students learn these concepts. One strong emphasis in these new efforts is the rediscovery of the joy of discovery. This idea draws, of course, on the notions that tension-seeking is a motive in people and that people are learning organisms.

METHODS USED

Given the knowledge of the psychologist about learning, motivation, groups, et al., and the wishes of the geographer to impart attitudes, facts, and some sophisticated ideas about the difficulty of making location decisions, we used a variety of methods for the unit. To start off, we asked ourselves "Where are the students? What do they know about manufacturing?" We found out by talking to a group of tenth-grade students. We learned that youngsters of this age know several fundamental concepts which are needed for this unit. We also assumed that they would learn other concepts from units which precede this one.

The manufacturing unit starts as we did. The teacher finds out where the class is by helping the class, as a whole, to work toward a definition of manufacturing by giving examples from their city, country, and region. The teacher's role is to ask questions and list answers. The class does the work. Two additional devices are available to the teacher. One is to ask the class to consider the school as a manufacturing enterprise. The analogy to a factory is not foreign to many American tenth-graders. And some central ideas hold. Schools are settlement-making activities, they provide products for other schools, some concepts of input-output economics seem to fit the choice of locations, etc.

The second device which the teacher may use at this point is to invite a community manufacturer to talk to the class about his firm, its problems and its role in the community. This item is also left as a teacher option.

After manufacturing has been defined, discussed, and read about, the emphasis shifts to a decision-making problem. The goals here are to teach about the multiple factors—input data, production data, output data, and the relationships among these—which go into a location decision. In order to reach these goals, the teacher outlines the general problem and divides the class into five-man teams. Each team consists of the management group of a company—the President, the Treasurer, the Purchasing and Production Officer, the Personnel Manager, and the Sales Manager.* The firm Metfab Incorporated, a newly formed metal fabricating firm, is faced with a problem: where shall we locate our plant? Real-life complexity is built into the roles by giving each team member some information which he holds in common with the other members of his team, and some information which he alone possesses and must, therefore, transmit to his colleagues. Theoretical considerations are included, without even referring specifically to location theory, by leading some team members toward "least-cost" types of solutions, and others toward "maximum demand" types of solutions. Resolution of the resulting conflicts between team members is a major learning device of this role-playing game.

As soon as the teams are formed, each man on each team goes off to a convention of his peers in order to learn about his job. At these conventions, which would each have 7 persons in a 35 student classroom, the students work on the data provided for their roles. The teacher is only the consultant to each convention; the students are responsible for teaching one another the material in their roles. For example, all the Purchasing and Production Officers have to work together on tables describing steel production and costs in the United States, costs of transportation, and labor markets. All computations can be checked by the teacher's manual. (The correct answers were added to the teacher's manual after some difficulties with pilot groups.) Each student then begins to see where he might want to locate Metfab.

When the data are learned, the conventions end. Each role-player returns to his own Metfab team. At the meeting of each management team, the President presents the location problem. The first order of business is for each member of the team to educate the others in his specialty—input, production problems, sales figures, banking needs, etc. Here again, the teacher serves as a consultant who is available to help any team which needs it. When all the data are reported, the President leads the team in making a decision. The President's role tells him to get a unanimous decision. Thus the team has to resolve conflicting views.

Then the class as a whole hears each team's decision, discusses the rationales, differences, similarities, and the like, among the choices, and looks at its experience in relation to the concepts which had been discussed earlier. They learn—we hope—that each team member could not share all his knowledge with the others (a fact of everyday life), that each team was influenced more by some members than others, and the applicability of the concepts. Lastly, the teacher and class review the ideas of the unit and apply the generalizations to manufacturing in other countries.

How has the unit worked out? So far as we can tell from the first trials, the concepts are being learned and the teachers and students enjoy the unit. The complaints and difficulties seem to be correctible without hurting the curriculum or the general plan. To date, the case has served its purposes. Because of the data selected by the geographer and because each team must come to a unanimous decision, the teams have consistently selected an appropriate *region* for Metfab's new plant. However, within the region, the location criteria have led to several meaningful possibilities, a clear, but unidentified, application of the concept of geographical optima and limits. In other words, the role-playing case gets across the ideas about manufacturing and attitudes toward current theory (and lack of theory) which were intended.

This last point brings us back to the psychologist. His facts and theories have been helpful in planning the manufacturing unit. But he must remain tentative and skeptical. The unit is only a small step in exploiting psychological knowledge. For example, we have focused very little attention on the emotional factors which affect each team's decision. On the average, students and teachers are not prepared to discuss this material. Yet, as we noted above, the emotional factors are there; they do affect learning; they do affect decisions in real life. We just are not using them.

We have also only scratched the surface in designing participative techniques, techniques which help children and teachers discover the joys and
struggles of teaching and learning.

References

*At the suggestion of Dr. E. J. Taafe, a sixth role may be added, a representative of
government, in order to broaden the case. The new role would provide information
about labor surpluses, incentives for supporting the economy in depressed areas, and the
like. These variables are, of course, very relevant for location decisions.

USING MAPS AND DIAGRAMS MORE EFFECTIVELY

Leslie P. Cummings
University of Guyana
Guyana, South America

Despite the attention which has been given to map reading and map-making
skills by professional geographers, curriculum study groups, textbook writers,
and others, maps and graphs are often inadequately used in the teaching of
geography. As Kohn[1] has reported, ". . . tests given to freshmen entering our
colleges and universities demonstrate over and over that map making and
map-reading skills are not being well developed in most elementary and
secondary schools."

One of the reasons for the inadequate grounding in mapwork is the lack of
interest-creating factors in many geography classes. There are at least two
possible ways to improve this situation:

1. Prepare more lessons in which the mapping of spatial distributions is a
   central part of the classwork.
2. Introduce some of the ideas now used only at the college level.

To illustrate, two recent articles on population pyramids[2] discuss pyramids as
graphic methods useful in portraying population structure. Such diagrams
might be introduced in a lesson dealing with the development of generalizations relating to the age structure of a country's population. Similar graphs

Reprinted with permission of the author and the National Council for the Social
Studies, from *Social Education,* 30 (December, 1966): 623-626.

can be used to depict employment structure, as well as age-sex relationship, as in Figure 1.

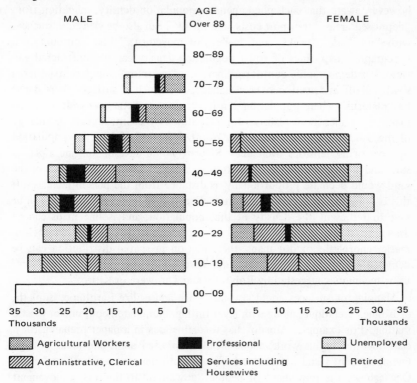

Figure 1. Hypothetical Data

At the junior high school level pyramids similar to these might be constructed on graph paper by different members of the class, then colored and displayed on a wall map of the world so that differences and similarities in the population structure of the world's political units might be visualized more readily. Data for the construction of these diagrams are readily available in the *United Nations Demographic Yearbook.*

PORTRAYING SURFACES ON MAPS

Ninth and tenth graders can be introduced to many of the more abstract concepts underlying spatial distributions. One of these concepts is that of "surface." Most high school students are familiar with the notion of viewing land areas as surfaces, with their hills, valley, rivers, or plateaus. They are not, however, aware that such phenomena as population density, migration from "depressed areas," transport costs, and the like, can also be viewed as surfaces with "pits" and "peaks" and "valleys of movement." Like contours on a topographic map, lines of equal population density can be constructed and viewed as demographic contours. Where the "contours" are close together, a sharp fall-off in density may be visualized; or on such a "surface" there might be "plateaus" where population density varies very little over wide areas. To make these lines more realistic, John Q. Stewart[3] has introduced the analogy of the Sand Pile Citizen, quoted by Warntz.[4] Instead of depicting population by dots or as densities over areas, Stewart would have us imagine a person surrounded by a sandpile built up to some arbitrary height. The heights of the sand would decrease proportionally as distance from the person increases. If this is done for each person, the three-dimensional model so obtained can be said to represent the density of that population, and isoline maps can be drawn to show "terrain." Instead of representing densities by chorochromatic, chorpleth, or dot maps, the variation in spatial distribution can be depicted graphically by isolines, and these isolines converted to "surfaces" using techniques suggested by Robinson and Thrower[5] or Kitiro.[6]

Mapping of surfaces could also introduce and utilize isarithmic, isopleth, or isoline[7] techniques along with layer tinting, illuminated contours or plastic shading. For example, Amedo[8] has used this idea in a paper prepared for a class lecture. In his work, economically depressed areas and areas of high unemployment stand out as "peaks," while prosperous areas become "pits." One can see the movement of people "down-hill" to the pits, a movement which one can equate with the down-slope movement of water. In addition, the intensity of movement bears a visual relationship to the degree of steepness of the "slopes." The idea here is to translate data into some visual form which will convey to the class much more quickly the relevant relationships.

Since the effectiveness of the portrayal of equal intensity areas by isolines depends very much on the frequency and/or density of observation, one should always choose those distributions for which numerical observations exist at a large number of points. For example, records at climatic stations could serve as the basis of a class exercise geared to the construction of a "surface" of rainfall or temperature distribution. Even here, however, the fit of the isolines is partly a matter of judgment, as Blumenstock[9] has pointed out. In portions of a map where control points are sparse, isolines must be subjectively drawn. When introducing isoline maps, a teacher should choose an area of the country for which sufficient information is available, and use this knowledge in making decisions about the location and trends of isolines. For example, because of the probability of greater rainfall on the windward slopes of a mountain, one would place the isolines closer together than one would if he were drawing a rainfall map for a lowland area.

Adequate information concerning the making and reading of isoline maps is found in Robinson[10] while the notion of "surfaces" and suggestions for its classroom use will be discussed in a forthcoming publication.[11]

SAMPLING PROCEDURES IN MAP MAKING AND MAP READING

The need for sampling in map making arises from the impossibility of obtaining observations for every conceivable location on the "surface" of a distribution. Some points have to be selected in a random manner (the sample), and inferences made about the total study area (the "population," statistically speaking) from the sample values. Before using any of the usual sampling plans (random, systematic, stratified, and cluster sampling),[12] the teacher must stress:

1. The need for sampling in geography.
2. The necessity for random selection.
3. The procedures for making random samples.

Mundane examples of sampling can be used:

A. A doctor makes inferences about a patient's blood stream by examining a single drop.
B. One soil sample tells us something about a large area.
C. Public opinion polls, election predictions, and TV ratings are based on samples.
D. Examining a few rats may disclose facts about the unexamined millions.

In the classroom many devices can be used to make a random selection:

1. Shuffled deck of cards.
2. Numbers from a hat.
3. Numbered balls as in bingo.
4. Random number tables.[13]

The use of Random Number Tables is again a relevant interest-creating device, especially for the upper grades of the high school. Certain elementary computations (mean, standard deviation of the sample values)[14] can accompany the lessons on sampling. If the teacher selects the sample size carefully and sees that no two students use the Random Number Tables the same way, much interest can be generated when they see how small the difference is for the class as a whole. Sampling can be introduced for example, when studying the average size of farms in an area, or the dominant types of slopes on a topographic map, and so on. The procedure is relatively simple. First, the study area should be gridded; then numbers assigned to the small squares; and finally, the sample should be drawn randomly by any of the methods mentioned above (See Figure 2).

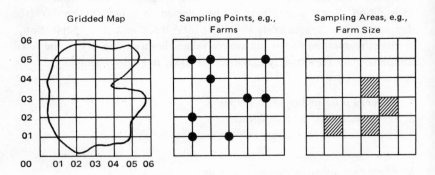

Figure 2

COMPARING MAPPED RELATIONSHIPS

In a classroom situation the teacher has to use visual methods when comparing pyramids, surfaces, and the like. The shortcomings of this method have been investigated by McCarty and Salisbury.[15] After tests on selected groups, they concluded that "only in cases in which the degree of association is very high does the process (visual comparison) produce results which approach the standards of accuracy generally demanded in present day research and teaching."[16] The teacher might circumvent this difficulty by choosing data in which the range is sufficiently large to bring out contrasts. Colors can also be utilized. For example, a rainfall "surface" can be drawn on transparent paper and shaded yellow, while the crop distribution for the same area can be colored blue. Superimposition of the maps will show the area of correspondence as green.

Map making and map reading are important interest-creating factors. The high school teacher should not only plan his lessons so that they will culminate in some map exercises, but should try to introduce some ideas not yet included in geography texts. A well-prepared series of exercises will repay the effort in the great amount of class interest generated.

References

[1] C. F. Kohn, in James D. Koerner, editor. *Case for Basic Education* Boston: Atlantic-Little, Brown, 1959, p. 67.

[2] Frank Seawell and Jerome Clemens. "A Population Profile." *The Professional Geographer* 16:20; March 1964; L. D. B. Heenan. "The Population Pyramid: A Versatile Research Technique." *The Professional Geographer* 17:18-21; March 1965.

[3] John Q. Stewart, *Coasts, Waves and Weather for Navigators."* Boston: Ginn and Company, 1945, p. 164-65.

[4] William Warntz. "A New Map of the Surface of Population Potentials for The United States, 1960. *Geographical Review* 54:170-184; April 1964.

[5] Arthur H. Robinson and N. J. W. Thrower. "A New Method of Terrain Representation." *Geographical Review* 47:507-520; October 1957.

[6] Tanaka Kitiro. "The Relief Contour Method of Representing Topography on Maps." *Geographical Review* 40:444-456; July 1950.

[7] There has been no agreement on the use of these terms. See E. Raisz. *General Cartography*. New York: McGraw-Hill, 1948, p. 246-249; J. K. Wright. "The Terminology of Certain Map Symbols." *Geographical Review* 24:653-654; 1944; E. A. Robinson. *Elements of Cartography*. John Wiley and Sons, 1953.

[8] D. Amedeo. "Potential Migration." Unpublished paper. Department of Geography, The University of Iowa, 1965.

[9] D. Blumenstock. "The Reliability Factor in the Drawing of Isarithms." *Annals of the Association of American Geographers* 43:289-304; 1953.

[10] E. A. Robinson., *op. cit.,* p. 178-194.

[11] K. W. Rumage and L. P. Cummings. "Introduction to Geography—A Conceptual Approach." Intended as a one-semester course outline for the A.A.G. Commission on College Geography.

[12] H. M. Blalock. *Social Statistics.* New York: McGraw-Hill, 1960. Explains also the use of the Random Numbers Table.

[13] H. M. Blalock, *op. cit.,* p. 437-449, can be put on the over-head projector for use by the class.

[14] H. E. Yuker. *A Guide to Statistical Calculations.* New York: G. P. Putnam's Sons, 1958. An excellent step-by-step method for computation is given.

[15] H. H. McCarty and Neil Salisbury. *Visual Comparison of Isopleth Maps as a Means of Determining Correlations Between Spatially Distributed Phenomena.* Department of Geography, University of Iowa, 1961.

[16] H. H. McCarty and Neil Salisbury, *op. cit.,* p. 78.

USING AV MATERIALS INDUCTIVELY
IN THE SOCIAL STUDIES

Mitchell P. Lichtenberg and Edwin Fenton
Carnegie-Mellon University, Pittsburgh

"I would like to begin today's class by showing you two paintings. The first comes from the medieval period in European history. Michelangelo painted the second during the Renaissance. As you look at each of the two paintings, write down adjectives which describe them."

These directions introduce one day's lesson in a European history course developed at Carnegie Tech's Social Studies Curriculum Development Center. As students compile a list of adjectives for the chalkboard, they notice a number of differences between the paintings. The Renaissance painting contains background, depicts anatomy accurately, and emphasizes the beauty of the human body. In contrast, the medieval painting seems flat, is not modeled from life, and fails to emphasize the human qualities of the figures represented.

With the two pictures still in view, we ask a question: "What do these paintings suggest about changes in values which may have taken place between the Middle Ages and the Renaissance?" The students usually hypothesize that the Renaissance focused on man's secular life rather than on his sacred concerns, the focus of the medieval period. During the following three days, students bring data from their reading to bear on this hypothesis. The entire procedure demonstrates an inductive use of visual material as part of a systems approach to learning.

This brief description of teaching with visual material is incomplete. It does not mention whether slides, a filmstrip, or actual paintings were used. It does not say if the pictures were in color or in black and white. It does not discuss seating arrangements for viewing, light level, or any of the other topics which we might associate with writing about audiovisual instruction. Instead the description emphasizes a teaching strategy, a method of dealing with data presented visually. The description underlines our major contention: each piece of audiovisual material should be developed to achieve a particular teaching objective through a consciously selected teaching strategy. This contention, although it may seem obvious, lies at the roots of a major audio-

Reprinted with the permission of the publisher, from *Audiovisual Instruction,* 11 (May, 1966): 330-332.

visual problem in the social studies: the development of new instructional materials based on new principles for the new social studies curricula.

Within the past five years, more than 50 major curriculum projects have grown up in the social studies field. Operating at all grade levels and financed generously by the government, private foundations, and school systems, these projects promise to revolutionize social studies instruction in the schools. They stress a range of objectives, employ new teaching strategies, develop a host of new materials, utilize a number of ways to deploy students, and measure progress through new evaluating instruments. This reform movement has a number of implications for the development and utilization of audiovisual materials.

In the past, social studies teachers have been largely satisfied to teach for knowledge of content using expository teaching strategies and materials. Like textbooks, audiovisual materials conformed to this pattern of instruction. Although skills of critical thinking and the formation of attitudes and values were acknowledged in the pious lists of general objectives found in typical courses of study, few teachers paid attention to them in class. These practices are now changing; the changes imply new opportunities to develop imaginative audiovisual materials.

Most of the directors of the social studies curriculum projects would be willing to cluster objectives under three general headings: knowledge of content, the use of inquiry skills, and the development of attitudes and values (affective objectives). They would also agree that each group of objectives implies an optimal teaching technique. Facts and generalizations can be taught efficiently by expository techniques. But the ability to use the mode of inquiry of historians and social scientists, that is, the ability to develop and test hypotheses, can only be acquired through repeated practice gained in discussion and independent study. Teaching by exposition does not permit each student to practice the use of the mode of inquiry. Nor does it help him attain many affective objectives, such as willingness to contribute to class discussion. Emphasizing inquiry skills and affective objectives implies the utilization of a wider range of teaching strategies than many teachers have employed in the past. It also implies the development of new materials specifically designed for these strategies.

The beginning point for the development of audiovisual materials should always be a statement of objectives: What behaviors should a student exhibit as a result of using particular materials? If the sole objective is the mastery of a preselected body of facts and generalizations, then a film or a sound filmstrip designed for expository teaching may be appropriate. If a teacher wishes to stress the use of a mode of inquiry, a single-concept slide show, a tape or a record, a silent film, or a set of transparencies designed for inductive teaching may be more useful. If a teacher has affective objectives in mind, the entire battery of AV materials is at his command; the appropriate one will be determined by which attitude or value he wishes to attack. Willingness to listen often comes as a by-product of seeing an excellent expository film. But willingness to respond and to participate in class discussion involving inquiry skills requires materials and teaching strategies which engage students actively. Objectives determine both teaching strategy and choice of materials.

Not that material is either inductive or expository; it is neutral. The way in which instructional materials are used to attain particular objectives determines whether they are "inductive" or "expository." A film becomes an inductive device if a teacher asks his students to determine the frame of reference of the producer from the way in which he chose and presented his content. Although the producer may have intended to teach facts and generalizations, the teacher is using his work to get at an aspect of the mode of inquiry through an inductive process. Hence, the teacher's objectives and his choice of a teaching strategy determine whether the film will be used in an expository or an inductive manner.

Resourceful teachers have long used audiovisual materials designed for content objectives and expository teaching techniques for other purposes. They have frequently turned the sound track off, blocked captions out of filmstrips, or used only part of a slide set in order to work toward inquiry skills or affective objectives through inductive techniques. The results have often been unsatisfactory. Optimal use of audiovisual devices requires the development of specific bodies of material directed toward specific objectives. For the past year, the staff of Carnegie Tech's Social Studies Curriculum Development Center has been developing AV materials as part of a systems approach to social studies instruction. Our experiences suggested a number of tentative ground rules for the development of audiovisual materials for inductive teaching.

The particular audiovisual medium chosen should be a function of the objectives. Three examples may make this point clear. In a course in political science, we wanted students to distinguish the types of appeals made by political leaders in speeches. Some appeals were directed to a particular interest group; others emphasized American folkways and mores in a manner designed to enlist the support of typical citizens from all interest groups. We recorded a number of political speeches on a tape, mixing these two types of appeals indiscriminately. Students listened to the tape just as if they were hearing political speeches, discussed the nature of the appeals being used, and classified the speeches into the categories they had devised.

In a European history course, we wanted students to contrast war during the seventeenth century with modern war at the same time that they practiced other cognitive skills. They had previously studied seventeenth-century warfare and could be directed to review their notes. To dramatize the nature of modern war, we made some 20 slides from pictures of England and France during World War I. They showed masses of people involved in the war effort on the front, in factories, and in the fields; mass destruction of both military and civilian property; the total involvement of the entire society with the war effort; and several other aspects of modern conflict. We flashed each picture on the screen for a few seconds, asking students when we were finished to write a paragraph about the nature of modern war. Then, without examining these paragraphs, we showed each slide again, asking the students to discuss the meaning of each picture and devise a scheme to classify the data drawn from the pictures. Near the end of the class period, students were asked to write a second paragraph about the nature of modern war. The entire procedure was designed to teach content as well as the cognitive skills of analysis and synthesis.

The transparency units produced by Encyclopaedia Britannica Films under the general title *The Fenton-Wallbank World History Program for the Overhead Projector* illustrate these same principles. In one of the units, we wanted students to develop knowledge of the cause of the population explosion and skill in the use of charts and graphs. The unit employs eight transparencies. The first introduces the topic, using three quotations from authorities. The students are asked to read the three quotations and to write a preliminary definition of the population problem. The next seven transparencies present charts, tables, or maps which add detailed data about population growth. After the class has discussed each transparency, we ask students to restate their understanding of the population problem in the light of the additional knowledge they have learned. Transparencies present data like this appropriately because they show charts well, they encourage overlaying one chart with another, and they can be marked with a grease pencil.

Audiovisual materials should be designed as part of a systems approach to learning. Many excellent audiovisual lessons are not self-contained. Sometimes they supplement readings; in other cases, they can be used effectively to introduce a subject to be assigned later as homework or to provide a contrasting point of view to something which students have already read. But to be used in this manner, AV materials must be designed for a specific role in a specific lesson. If pictures or recordings form the basis for the development of a hypothesis, the written word may provide the evidence to test it. We have found virtually no AV materials produced commercially for the general market which were maximally useful for the specific purposes of our curriculum. The implications of this general conclusion for the entire profession need no emphasis.

The class time devoted to the use of AV materials can vary widely. On the whole, using AV materials inductively consumes more time than the expository mode. If only raw data is presented, students must be given time to discuss it and to draw conclusions. Some of our most successful presentations, such as the one about the nature of modern war, consume an entire class period. But we have also found a number of ways to employ AV materials inductively for only a few minutes. Sample ballots from the United States and the Soviet Union made into transparencies for the overhead projector can draw from students in 10 minutes some of the basic differences between the organization of election procedures in democratic and totalitarian societies. The exercise with the two paintings described at the beginning of this article takes only a few minutes. But on the whole, inductive use of any material consumes class time voraciously. For this reason, curriculum workers who design it should be sure that the objectives for which they are striving are worth the cost in time consumed.

Inductive audiovisual materials should not give away the answers. The two illustrations which follow demonstrate expository and inductive presentations of the same material. The first tells all the answers and calls on the students

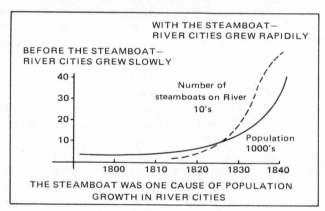

Figure 1

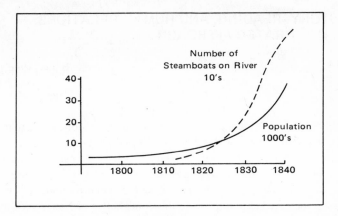

Figure 2

to memorize responses. The second presents data and calls on students to analyze its meaning, develop a hypothesis, and think about additional data to confirm or change the hypothesis. The first was designed for content objectives alone; the second combined content objectives with the use of inquiry skills and, in addition, has significant implications for the development of attitudes.

Most commercially prepared AV materials give away the answers and call upon students only to memorize. Films have a sound track; slides, filmstrips, and transparencies have captions; explanations precede speeches on tapes or records. All of these products can be used to teach inquiry skills only with great difficulty. If audiovisual materials are to reach their full potential as an integral part of a systems approach to learning content, inquiry skills, and attitudes and values in the social studies, we must learn not to give away all the answers.

Teachers need lesson plans to accompany inductive AV materials. The structure of inductive AV materials is implicit rather than explicit. Its role in a systems approach often seems obscure to a busy teacher preparing a lesson late at night. Moreover, many teachers have not yet become accustomed to self-conscious attention to inquiry skills and specific affective objectives. For all these reasons, inductive AV materials require an elaborate system of teachers' aids which explain what the materials are intended to do (objectives) and outline ways of doing it (teaching strategies). Without such assistance, teachers are likely either to employ the materials for objectives for which they are not suitable or to leave them unused in the AV room.

HISTORY, READING, AND HUMAN RELATIONS:
AN INTEGRATED APPROACH

Robert W. Edgar
Queens College
Flushing, New York

The work that I am about to describe is an outgrowth of an effort to study the problems of beginning teachers in difficult schools with the ultimate intention of devising an improved program of teacher preparation. Since 1961 a group of us at Queens College have been concerned with bridging the gap which exists between middle-class oriented college students and the youngsters they are likely to teach in the slum ghettos of New York City. The title of our Project, BRIDGE,[1] has been a symbol of our intentions.

The total Project has had three aspects: (1) a small-school-within-a-school organized to facilitate the study of the problems of beginning teachers; (2) a program of participation of undergraduates in after-school centers; and (3) the involvement of college staff members in research and curriculum development related to educationally handicapped children. I shall describe very briefly only one, the first, of these aspects.

In this aspect we set up a center for the study of the problems of the educationally disadvantaged in an all-Negro junior high school in Queens, one of the five boroughs of New York City. Two hypotheses were used as guidelines in the organization of the center: (1) that the children in this junior high school would learn more if they remained with the same teachers in four academic subjects, including social studies, for the seventh, eighth, and ninth grades, and (2) that inexperienced teachers would have a better chance for success if they had the services of a full-time supervisor. In the three years from 1961 to June 1964, this plan was implemented. Eighty-five children were organized in three classes. Fifty-seven of them stayed in the school and in the program for the three years. The withdrawees were replaced by new entrants into the school. In a careful comparison of the intellectual growth of the children in the Project with a control group in the same class in the same school, the Project children gained on the average of five points in IQ scores as measured on the Wechsler Intelligence Scale for Children in two-and-one-half years as contrasted with the control group which gained less than two points. We who participated in the Project are convinced that this form

Reprinted with permission of the author and the National Council for the Social Studies, from *Social Education*, 29 (March, 1965): 155-158.

of organization of the junior high schools in depressed areas merits further trial on an expanded scale.

However, I am not going to continue with an extended description of that Project. Instead, I propose to discuss a development that emerged from our initial program.

At one point in the BRIDGE Project we made a search for social studies materials to which our pupils would respond. Since they happened to be studying American history at the time, we decided to try out some simple biographical materials with them. The rather remarkable success of that initial tryout has led me to a more formal effort.

Perhaps before I begin my exposition it might be well for me to describe briefly some of the major academic characteristics of culturally deprived children as we got to know them. Our group in 1961 had a mean intelligence of 88 as measured on an individually administered intelligence test. This statistic means that at least half of the children fell below average as compared to a standard group. They ranged from 115 to 65. In reading and social studies information and skills, as they entered the seventh grade, they averaged about the middle of the fifth grade. A substantial number of them read at third and fourth grade levels. It is this lower half of the group that most of us have in mind when we speak of the culturally deprived. They represent an exceedingly difficult problem of adjustment for the teacher prepared to teach academic subjects in secondary schools.

Secondary school social studies is not often successfully taught to these children. Its teachers, untrained in the technicalities of reading instruction for example, are often unskilled in making social studies content comprehensible to such children. They forget that to understand history one must have a highly complex cognitive structure related to the who, when, and where of past events. We have only to recall our own confusions over the names of the leaders in South Viet Nam, Cambodia, or the Soviet Union to remind ourselves that we, too, can be confused over who, when, and where. These children react this way to such names as John C. Calhoun, James Oglethorpe, John Winthrop, Peter Stuyvesant, and to such places as New Orleans, Kansas, West Virginia, and Idaho. A brief but critical examination of the average social studies book reveals the density of its vocabulary especially when proper nouns are seen as vocabulary. The rapid shifts in time, place, and person, typical of social studies, are bewildering to a child who has not yet developed a cognitive system which provides meaningful categories in which new data can be classified.

Too often a vocabulary learning in the social studies is treated as a problem in simple repetition. Teachers forget that our functioning vocabulary is a product of meaningful repetition in an endless variety of new situations. How can James Oglethorpe be the name of a full-bodied person when one's complete exposure is a sentence or two stating that he was the proprietor and founder of Georgia and interested in the victims of an oppressive prison system in England? One of my favorite illustrations of a much more meaningful appreciation of what is involved in understanding a word is drawn from Ruth Kraus's *A Hole Is to Dig.*[2] In this brief book for pre-school children she uses the word "hole" in eight delightful situations. First there is the title which is repeated in the body of the book and then: "Maybe you could hide things in a *hole,*" "A *hole* is to sit in," "A *hole* is to plant a flower," "A floor is so you don't fall in the *hole* your house is in," "A *hole* is for a mouse to live in," "A *hole* is to look through," "A *hole* is when you step on it you go down." All accompanied with delightful illustrations! Even with all this I suppose we would conclude that a child's meaning for the word "hole" is based on substantial firsthand experience. In many misguided efforts to reduce the vocabulary load of social studies material, the need for extensive repetition in a variety of meaningful situations is forgotten. Mere reduction of vocabulary is considered sufficient. However, the reader with a small vocabulary needs not just content with fewer new words, but longer, not shorter, accounts with repeated use of new terms in interesting contexts.

I should like now, to turn briefly to the academic characteristics of the children. It is a cliché in educational circles to say that the study of a subject is only effective insofar as it produces student interest. Cliché or not, it is true. We as teachers have come to understand that the responses of children are valid clues to whether or not we are meeting their needs. If they respond positively to what we put in front of them, their needs are being met, even if we are not exactly sure just what those needs are and how this specific material meets them. My own contact with culturally deprived children has led me to expect them to respond when the following conditions are met.

1. They will respond when lessons are clearly and simply organized. They want to know what a teacher is trying to teach and how she proposes to teach it. In addition, her purposes must make sense to them. Such objectives as developing democratic attitudes, recognizing the rights of others, and exercising independent critical judgment, through giving larger meaning to the day-to-day efforts of the teacher, are too vague for culturally disadvantaged children to comprehend and act on. They expect to learn information and to develop skills. They recognize and approve efforts directed toward these ends. In spite of the inadequacy of these goals in the eyes of the teacher, she must at least take account of the pupils' expectations.

2. They understand social, political, and economic ideas or events when human beings are vividly involved in these ideas or events. An extremely interesting characteristic of culturally deprived children is their unusually well-developed insight into the unspoken and often unconscious anxieties, motivations, and feelings of others, especially teachers. Though not academically apt, they are "hep" (or is it "hip"?). They know the score and have many acute perceptions into the significance of the behavior of their elders as well as their peers. This heightened sensitivity can be used to develop their interests in people distant in time and place.

3. They respond to assurance of success. Reacting to a school system which has constantly emphasized their weaknesses, they protect themselves from failure in whatever manner is individually possible and effective. They often refuse to perform, cheat, are insubordinate, or withdraw when faced with exposure of ignorance. Close analysis of these behaviors will reveal that they have a positive, rather than a negative function. A youngster who can sustain any one of these responses avoids failure and preserves his self-respect even though he incurs the teacher's displeasure. During our Project we discovered that the very tests which we used to evaluate the growth of the children such as the Metropolitan Achievement Tests, were viewed by many of the pupils simply as efforts on our part to demonstrate once again how stupid they were. Consequently they resisted taking them.

More of their responses could and should be described, but I think that these three are the most relevant to what I have to say. If you agree with me thus far, our problem of teaching these children has become clearer. We must develop approaches to teaching the basic concepts of social studies which are consonant with the characteristics of culturally deprived children, methods which will reconcile the limitations of their responses with the demands of the subject itself.

In an effort to contribute to the understanding of this problem, Professor Carl Auria of the Queens College Department of Education and I embarked on a cooperative venture with five teachers in three New York City depressed-area schools. These teachers teach American history to eighth graders. In two of the schools all of the children are Negroes; in the other, about two-thirds are Negro and the remainder mostly Puerto Rican.

We have set out to test two hypotheses: (1) that the children in these classes will learn more, retain the learning longer, and be more interested in their studies when material on the Negro is included in their studies than they will using the customary text, and (2) that the children will learn more, retain the learning longer, and be more interested in their studies when their reading on the Negro is in fictional and biographical form rather than in a text. Each teacher is teaching American history to three classes of eighth-grade pupils. In one he is using the customary text; in a second he is using his text plus the text-like supplement that has been prepared by the Detroit Public Schools entitled *The Struggle for Freedom and Rights;* and in the third, eliminating the text entirely, he is using three biographies and two historical novels as the basis for pupil reading.

We are assuming (1) that the emphasis on Negroes will make it more possible for these predominantly Negro children to identify with the people involved in the events of American history, and (2) that reading materials combining a substantial decrease in the conceptual density with an *increase* in the amount will be more effective in developing historical knowledge, reading skill, and an understanding of human relations in these children than will a text.

This endeavor is only in an exploratory stage. We and the five teachers have had to get to know each other, to develop some security within the group, and to adjust to each others' strengths and weaknesses. In view of our limitations at this stage, we decided to confine our efforts to one historical period, selecting the period 1820 to 1880. It is a period of critical importance to the understanding of the Negro American. It also happens to be a period for which there are rich and varied materials about the Negro.

Our first cooperative task was to make our goals explicit. Since we planned to use different materials to develop an understanding of a given historical period, we had to decide just what aspect of that period we wanted the pupils to learn. We listed all the concepts which seemed relevant to the period, rated them according to their importance, and grouped them into categories: concepts of time, of place, and of people; critical vocabulary; basic social, economic, military, and political concepts; and finally, the Negro as slave and freeman. Though our categories are not of the same order and sometimes overlap, they do provide us with a framework within which we can work.

Having this framework, Professor Auria and I now proceeded to construct an instrument by which we proposed to measure the growth of the pupils. We constructed a test which we hoped would make diagnosis as well as gross measurement possible. We carried over our conceptual categories into the structure of the test. Each conceptual category is approached from several points of view. For example, we want to know how these children view time: (1) Do they think of time from a personal view, that is in relation to themselves, to their own birthdate, or to their age, or to their parents, grandparents, or other personally known figures? (2) Do they think of time in terms of familiar historical figures such as Washington, Lincoln, F.D.R., etc.? (3) Is their concept of time based on the evolutionary development of common objects such as the means of transportation, (stagecoach, locomotive, automobile, airplane), of communication, of household appliances, and of dress? (4) Is their concept of time based on the classifications of history—eighteenth, nineteenth, and twentieth centuries, Civil War, Reconstruction Period, 1820, 1861, etc.? Our intention is to discover some of the ways they try to build an understanding of chronology as well as to determine their levels of comprehension. The approach to place and people is similar.

This conceptual analysis also became the framework for our lesson planning. Since our five teachers were all experienced in teaching eighth-grade American history, we had little difficulty in relating the concepts to their customary text-based lessons. The teachers quickly absorbed them into the developmental unit which is their customary organization. The Detroit pamphlet was also easily integrated into their customary lesson planning. The transfer to the biography and fiction was not so easily made. Many of the concepts were not directly related to the lives and events of our books. Consequently most of our workshop time was devoted to the elaboration of our methods in using the biography and fiction.

It is now time to describe to you the biographical and fictional material which we used. I have been examining material on the Negro for several years and have occasionally experimented with various books in different junior high schools. Though the idea is not original with me, my approach relies on a classroom library designed to teach a single unit. This somewhat parallels the classroom library based on themes being exploited by Scholastic, among others. The classroom library we are using has *Frederick Douglass*[3] by Arna Vontemps as the basic book. This book is written for the fifth- or sixth-grade reading level, the level of many of the youngsters in eighth grade with whom I have been working. However, its general appearance does not make this fact too apparent to the young reader. The two other biographies are Dorothy Sterling's *Freedom Train; The Story of Harriet Tubman*,[4] and the same author's *Captain of the Planter: The Story of Robert Smalls.*[5] The selections are not capricious for they have been chosen to satisfy certain classroom needs. *Freedom Train* covers the same period at the same reading level. It is, however, about a woman, an illiterate in contrast to Douglass, who risks her life repeatedly to help others escape, another contrast with Douglass. It provides a new view of the same subject. *Captain of the Planter,* on the other hand, is somewhat more difficult and concentrates on the Civil War and the

Reconstruction Period. It is suitable for those who are either somewhat advanced or for those who have become ready for more difficult reading as a result of their work in the other books. The fiction, Meadowcroft's *By Secret Railway*[6] and Sterne's *The Long Black Schooner,*[7] add blood and thunder and excitement to the other accounts of the period. They are set in different locales and describe different but related events. The complete library consists of 30 copies of the *Douglass,* ten of the *Tubman,* 15 of the *Smalls,* ten of the *Schooner,* and five of the *Railway*—a total of 70 books.

At long last we have come to the title of this article, *History, Reading, and Human Relations: An Integrated Approach.* With this library and these books we hope to teach the basic concepts of a given historical period, a few selected reading skills, and some elementary human relation insights. I shall omit further discussion of the basic history goals, assuming that my prior discussion of the conceptual framework of the period gives you some idea of our method of achieving them. I turn briefly to the others.

The three reading skills we chose were: simple recall of factual information, the making of simple inferences, and vocabulary with political, economic, or social significance. To assist us in this endeavor, we developed a homemade workbook. As the pupils read *Frederick Douglass,* they had dittoed workbooks containing five reading exercises, each covering four chapters of the book. An exercise consisted of ten multiple-choice items and a list of ten words drawn from the relevant chapters. The first five multiple-choice questions were simple recall. For example, "What did Mrs. Auld begin to teach Fred?" The correct answer, among a choice of four, was "To read." The next five items demanded simple inferences, that is, the answer was implicit, not explicit, in the book's content. For example, "What effect do you think reading the book *The Columbian Orator* had on Fred?" Answer, "Made him determined to be free some day." The vocabulary for the same exercise included "molasses," "law," "progress," "entitled," and "estimate."

This workbook served both pupil and teacher. For the pupil it met his need for structure and for success. The task was clear. He knew what to do and was able to do it. It was usually easy. Most pupils answered most items correctly. It also individualized instruction. The pupils were able to progress at the speeds adapted to their ways of working. At one point we debated whether or not the exercises would discourage them from reading the book, breaking their rhythm and their interest. Our misgivings were unnecessary. The clear structure and the constant success developed strong motivation.

These exercises also made it possible, in fact demanded, that each teacher follow the progress of each youngster. We in the workshop agreed that teacher correction of the exercises was necessary, desirable, and not onerous. As our study continued we planned to discuss the progress of individual children in our workshops. We tried to keep our attention on the child as well as on our materials and the teacher. In addition, the child's workbook contained a record of his progress with the other books. His homework consisted of extensive reading in three related books, with *The Planter* serving the function of the *Frederick Douglass* in the latter half of the unit.

Our third goal was the development of insight into human relations. We tried to achieve this goal by helping teachers to identify, create, and capitalize on opportunities to use our materials for enlarging understandings of why people think and behave as they do. We were concerned with opportunities to discuss feelings, needs, values, and moral judgments as they affected human behavior. Using a biography, the *Frederick Douglass* for example, we tried to develop the habit of asking:

How did Fred *feel* when he arrived in Baltimore alone, without a relative or friend, to live as a slave in a strange house?

How would *you feel?* Have you ever slept overnight in a strange place away from your family? How did you *feel?*

Why did Fred work so hard to learn to read? When his lessons were forbidden, *why* didn't he just give up?

Why did Harriet Tubman, with great danger to herself, go back south to help others escape? *Why* didn't she just try to be safe herself?

Why didn't Frederick Douglass do the same as Harriet Tubman? What would you have done? Why?

What was Fred's owner's *view of Fred?* Where did he get such ideas? Was he a *wicked* man? Did all white people agree with him? *Why* did some differ?

What *kind of man* is a slave driver? *Why* do some people beat other people? What does it mean to try to break someone's spirit? When should one *obey?* When should he *disobey?*

In addition we tried to change the image of the Negro American as it is often developed from accounts of his role in history. Instead of presenting him simply as a slave, ignorant, docile, and childlike, we studied those leaders who displayed intelligence, skill, resourcefulness and courage. We portrayed Negroes as participating in the determination of their fate as well as having it determined for them. Negroes were seen as skilled workers, daring rebels, eloquent speakers, brave pilots, and responsible legislators and officeholders.

We also sought to examine the impact of status on the lives of people in the past and the present. We attempted to get at the feelings and reactions of the rejected and lowly person in any society.

What is the effect of being poor, not just on one's food, clothing, housing, but on one's spirit?

What is the effect of being enslaved? Of being excluded? Of being ridiculed?

What price does society pay for these actions?

As we tried to think through the classroom possibilities in this area, we were sometimes blind, insensitive or overly sensitive, fearful, and distrustful of our judgments. As white teachers working with Negro youth we were sometimes afraid that we would enlarge the gap between them and us. But we were committed to an open confrontation of the problem in the faith that rational examination and study lead to better interracial understanding.

Perhaps I can summarize best for you by reiterating a few statements about the culturally deprived that were the basis of our work:

1. Culturally deprived children need a program of studies which satisfies their need for security through clear goals and simple methodology.
2. Culturally deprived children need the reassurance of repeated success experiences. The materials that are read must be well within their grasp and must be more rather than less extensive than customary text materials.
3. Culturally deprived children are person-oriented, not abstraction-oriented. They need materials which place people, not generalizations, in the center of the stage.
4. Culturally deprived children are often acutely aware of the feelings, motivations, and values of people in their environments. This sensitivity can be used in the illumination of the problems of human relations in our past and in the present.

Teachers of the culturally deprived need to develop all the skills that the above four propositions suggest: skill in analyzing their subject to identify its basic concepts, skill in the selection of materials which meet the needs of their pupils at their levels, skill in individualizing instruction in order to diagnose and meet individual pupil needs, and finally, skill in illuminating the problems of human relations. These skills are not beyond the ability of current classroom teachers and they can be learned. Let's hope that social studies teachers will set out to learn them.

References

[1] The research was performed pursuant to a contract with the U.S. Office of Education, Department of Health, Education, and Welfare, Project Number 935.

[2] New York: Harper and Row, 1952.

[3]New York: Alfred A. Knopf, 1957.
[4]Garden City, N.Y.: Doubleday and Company, 1954.
[5]Garden City, N.Y.: Doubleday and Company, 1958.
[6]New York: Thomas Y. Crowell Company, 1958.
[7]New York: Scholastic Book Services, 1961.

THE WRITING OF HISTORICAL FICTION:
A Technique for Teaching History

John Georgeoff
Purdue University

The writing of historical fiction has seldom been viewed as an appropriate activity for students in history classes, whether at the secondary or the elementary school level. Nevertheless, historical fiction-writing can be a very valuable supplementary technique in history instruction.

For a student to do writing of this type accurately, he needs to grasp certain basic historical concepts. He needs, for instance, to understand the period in which his story is placed, the technical developments of the time, economic, social, and political problems, the chronological order of events, and the geographic setting. He needs also to command a vocabulary of terms that are rather specific to the period: terms such as long-horn, jerked buffalo meat, Mountain Men, etc.

A student whose writing is devoid of imagination, or whose accounts lack interesting details, or whose descriptive statements are so general that they could fit many historical epochs, has probably acquired only a vague understanding of his subject. He cannot reconstruct and apply in another context the material which seemingly he has learned: it still is not vivid enough to him that he can express it in a somewhat different way from the one in which he has studied it. This is almost certainly the case if he possesses adequate skill in story-writing. Such an individual is only slightly superior to the student whose paper contains anachronisms, erroneous concepts, incorrect factual information, reversals or omissions of significant events, and similar inaccuracies.

Reprinted with permission of the publisher, from *The Social Studies,* 56 (October, 1965): 182-187.

The large number of approaches possible in the writing of historical fiction offers the teacher many varied opportunities for using the technique in his daily program. Instead of the usual research type of report, which some students copy practically verbatim from the encyclopedia or textbook, the class members can write fictional accounts centering around the topics being studied. In this way, the students are provided with a basic purpose for studying the material.

A teacher can also use historical fiction-writing for evaluation. As a culminating activity to a unit or a topic, the technique can help the teacher appraise development of the fundamental concepts and understandings. Though not as precise as an objective test, it can nevertheless be of significant value to a perceptive teacher. It can provide information regarding pupil progress which would be very difficult, if not totally impossible, to obtain through the more widely used evaluational devices.

The technique has still other advantages to the teacher. It helps to integrate at least two subjects, English and history, by providing more meaningful learning experiences to the students and simultaneously achieving a more effective use of the available time in school. For teachers of self-contained classrooms, this means that less time need be spent on the correcting of papers. One set of papers needs to be read instead of two. Even in departmentalized situations, provided the teachers of history and English have adequate backgrounds in each others' subjects, some arrangement can be worked out between them so that the responsibility for assigning and correcting the work is shared. The technique has a still further advantage in that it can be adapted to almost any grade or achievement level.

As an introduction to the writing of historical fiction, students may be given open-ended statements or paragraphs to complete. The following examples from American history, in which both time and place are delineated, have been used successfully in the intermediate grades and junior high school. Similar opening statements readily can be written to fit the needs of senior high school students. The illustrations which are presented here suggest ways in which a teacher can employ historical fiction-writing to meet the particular requirements of her classes.

I. Providing endings to imaginary stories:

    A. Pierre Rocque was a French trapper and one of the Mountain Men following the North Fork of the Platte River in search of beaver. As he was rounding a bend in the river, he . . . .

B. Paul was a young boy in Puritan New England. Paul lived in a small log cabin at the edge of a great forest. He had a father, mother, and a little baby sister. One day Paul was alone in the cabin with his baby sister. Paul's father was hunting game in the woods. His mother had gone to see Mrs. Smith, a sick neighbor who lived a mile away. Suddenly Paul saw at the window a . . . .

C. The enemy had dug in on top of "Old Baldy." They had the United Nations Forces pinned down under deadly machine gun fire. To attempt to advance would mean certain suicide for the United Nations Troops. Sergeant Cole appraised the situation. He had an idea. He . . . .

II. Complete stories which are based upon actual events:

A. For many years peg-legged Peter Stuyvesant had been governor of the Dutch colony of New Netherlands. He was a stern governor. His word was law. Few of the jolly Dutch settlers liked him. Sometimes he would hobble up and down the streets of the colony giving orders to this person and that person.

One day four English ships sailed into the harbor of the city. They demanded that New Netherlands surrender to them. Peter Stuyvesant shouted, "Never!" He stamped hard on the cobblestones with his wooden leg. Then he rushed . . . .

B. William Penn was a rich English gentleman. He was also a Quaker. The Quakers were not popular in England because of their beliefs. Often they were punished and put in prison. William Penn felt very sorry for them.

The king owed Penn a very large sum of money. He had owed it for a long time and could not pay it back. One day Penn thought of a plan. He would ask the king to pay up the debt by giving him land in North America. There the Quakers could live in peace.

William Penn went to the king with his plan. "Your Majesty," he said . . . .

D. It was the year 1831. A tall, gangling youth has just arrived at the little town of New Salem. In order to test the strength and courage of Abe Lincoln, the newcomer, Jack Armstrong, one of the community's toughest men, challenged him to a wrestling match. All the town turned out to see the fun. The two men began to fight. They circled each other warily; they grappled; they twisted. Suddenly . . . .

E. When Andrew Jackson was ten years old the Revolutionary War broke out. Although he was still only a boy, he helped fight against the British and was captured. When he refused to black the boots of a British officer, the officer struck young Andrew with his sword and then put him in prison.

While he was in prison . . . .

III. Complete the endings of stories which may or may not be understood as having a historical basis.

Little Sarah was crying as she ran along the street in Washington, D.C. She had just learned that her brother who was fighting for the Union had been wounded in the Battle of Bull Run. She was now hurrying to see him at the military hospital. Suddenly, she bumped into a tall, thin man wearing a stovepipe hat. She . . . .

IV. Use a "You Are There" approach.

A. Writing news bulletins.
Imagine that you are an American war correspondent. You witness the famous battle between the *Serapis* and *Bonhomme Richard*. Write a news bulletin describing the battle.

B. Writing news accounts.
When Jackson was a general in the War of 1812, he fought many battles with the Indians, especially the Creeks. Pretend that you are a newspaper reporter with his army. Write a news account describing one of these battles.

C. Reporting an interview.
You are a newspaper reporter. The editor has ordered you to interview Lieutenant Andrew Rowan who has just returned from Cuba. The Lieutenant has successfully completed a very dangerous mission. He delivered a letter from President McKinley to Garcia, the Cuban rebel leader. Follow this procedure:
(1) Make an outline of the questions you would ask Lieutenant Rowan.
(2) Write replies to the questions as you think the lieutenant would have given them to you.
(3) Finally, write out the interview as it would appear in the paper.

D. Writing letters.
You are a pioneer who has found himself (or herself) at the Siege of Boonesborough. The siege has just been lifted. For the first time in days you can think about your relatives back in Virginia. You sit down and write them a letter. In it you tell about your experiences during the siege. Write a letter that you think such a person might have written.

E. Keep a diary.
You are a pioneer traveling west in a covered wagon. You have just left Westport for Fort Laramie. You are keeping a daily diary of your trip. Write an account of each day for this portion of your trip.

V. Make inferences and draw conclusions.

A. After Andrew Jackson had finished his two terms as President, he returned to his estate, called the Hermitage, near Nashville, Tennessee. Here he spent the last years of his life.
Describe a typical day in the life of Jackson as a landowner and master of the Hermitage.

The forms above illustrate only a few of the approaches possible for the use of fictional writing in the teaching of history. Once the students have become acquainted with these forms, open-ended sentences and paragraphs need no longer be employed. The students can be assigned only the historical situation and the compositional approach they are to use; and at a still later stage, each student can be permitted to determine both of these elements for himself.

As a supplementary teaching method, then, the writing of historical fiction helps to make the subject of history more interesting and purposeful to students. It is an effective means through which a better instructional and evaluational program can be achieved. Furthermore, it serves to integrate history and composition in a way which is both meaningful and challenging.

MAKING HISTORY INEVITABLE

Arnold M. Rothstein
Hofstra College
Hempstead, New York

"Hindsight is better than foresight"—so runs the saying. Hardly anywhere is this more true than when one looks back into history. Yet, there is a danger in teaching history from the vantage point of hindsight. If it is safe to assume that there is within us a natural tendency to accept the status quo, then that which *is* normal and right! To a certain extent this is as it should be, psychologically speaking, for nature seems to build in a safeguard against excess. But what happens when cumulatively we have taught that the status quo should be accepted because it all had to happen that way? Somewhere there is an invisible Hand guiding the destiny of our Republic. Somewhere there is a working out of the Absolute Idea. Now most of our social studies teachers would protest that they are teaching uncritical acceptance of the status quo. Nevertheless, there is a subtle process at work from the time the child enters school in grade one till the time he leaves school at the end of grade twelve

Reprinted with permission of the publisher, from *The Social Studies,* 55 (November, 1964): 206-210.

that cements and confirms the notion that that which *is* is somehow right because that is the way it had to happen. Let us look to a few illustrations.

Frequently, the period when the States were confederated under the Articles is taught as a trying one, a *Critical period*—but as one that somehow was all prelude and overture to the main event. Often there is a chapter heading in a textbook entitled: "The Confederation was a Failure." Then the battery of facts is presented: the states were disunited, there was no uniform currency, trade was at a standstill, there was little respect for the central government at home or abroad, the Articles themselves were weak, and so forth. Frequently, this is followed by a chart or diagram which compares the Federal Government to the government of the Confederacy. Very often the comparison is full of value statements to the effect that the one solved the "problem" while the other did not. Is not one justified in asking what problem? Now there is something terribly wrong when teachers mouth or permit students to mouth shopworn clichés. To be sure it is the textbook which contains the clichés, but it is the teacher's responsibility to prevent the textbook view from dominating his thinking with regard to the period 1781-89. Some powerful assumptions are being made tacitly and these should be explicated. To say that in the period 1781-89 the government was weak implies the judgment that things should be strong (as they are now?). To say that the states were disunited implies that they should have been united. A very fruitful lesson might be had if one were to look for the assumptions behind our judgments. The writer did just that when he taught eleventh grade American History several years ago.

The class was given the problem of examining the historical judgment: The Confederation was a failure. They were asked to abstract the assumptions upon which the conclusion rested. (It should be noted here that the process is certainly more significant than the product.) The following were identified:

1. The Confederation did not accomplish its purposes.
2. The states had to unite into a political union.

Obviously these were the assumptions underlying the judgment, *the Confederation was a failure,* since the lack of unity among the states is the chief reason given for the failure of the Confederation. In the course of our deliberations, the class raised some pertinent questions:

1. What was the initial purpose of the Confederation? (Obviously a confederacy means a loose union of sovereign independent states, so is there not a contradiction to expect it to be strong?)

2. Is somebody "looking back" into history?

Several students pointed out that the United States could very well have remained disunited, i.e., thirteen separate nations could have grown up on the continent. Had the states been more widely dispersed geographically and separated perhaps by more formidable mountain ranges, as in the case of the South American republics which did not form a single political union, for example, the ensuing Federal Union might not have been a reality. Some students pointed to the disunited German and Italian states as illustrations of how political union was not inevitable simply because common culture was involved.

The class as a whole was quick to see that the Confederation actually did accomplish its main purpose, for this was *not* to weld the separate states into a cohesive whole at all. Rather it was intended to be a weak union which would permit the states to remain supreme and autonomous. The situation is not unlike today where many of our UN critics say that the UN has failed to achieve its purposes. Of course, the failure is judged by the purposes usually within the heads of the critics themselves or more accurately perhaps, within their viscera. One of these notions holds that the UN should exercise supranational powers (over *other* nations). But this is not the purpose of the organization at all. It is as strong as the member nations want it to be and there was no intention that it should have supra-national powers. Hence, one can only judge failure in terms of purposes set from *within,* not from without. Similarly, the Confederation of 1777 from our twentieth-century perch seems to be all wrong, but from the standpoint of achieving *its* purpose (not ours), the Confederation was a success!

Now in the illustration cited, it should be evident that students not only demonstrated the skills of pulling out assumptions upon which conclusions rest (for which they were obviously being trained throughout the year), but they were also able to observe that much of what passes for historical fact is indeed personal hindsight which attempts to make past happenings predictable.

Another illustration of making history inevitable via the hindsight lens is here presented. The writer once asked his class in American History: "If we could remake history, in your judgment would it have been wiser to have held open sessions at the Constitutional Convention?" The following answers from the students' homework papers were duplicated and presented back to the class for analysis:

1. People would have found fault with it. [the Constitution]
2. The Constitution might never have been written.

3. There would have been disturbances.
4. Our present day government would not be as strong.
5. It would just make *things* [italics added for emphasis] more confusing and nothing would be accomplished by the interference.
6. No, the people wouldn't want the new idea.
7. The Constitution would never have been passed.
8. The Federal government wouldn't have had a chance.
9. Nothing would have gotten done.

As a class exercise, the students were asked to list the assumptions upon which these (their) statements rested. It soon became apparent to them that that which happened is readily accepted almost as it had to be. "Nothing would have gotton done"—i.e., there would have been no constitution like we have now. (And that would never do! We have to have what we have now!)

As a follow-up exercise, students were asked to draw some inferences from their statements (examples above). They pointed out the obvious one that the Constitution was by no means a popular document in its day. Some found it difficult to justify closed door sessions with the ideal of self-determination. Others said that they now could justify the statement that "the Constitution was an act of revolution" if called upon to do so. Certainly it may be seen that ideas and relationships were here being illumined. Listed below are some of the inferences that the students drew on the basis of the answers to the assignment and the ensuing discussion thereon. Attention is called to the sardonic nature, particularly of numbers four and five, and the rather mature perception which is revealed throughout:

1. Changes in the past are o.k.
2. We have to defend what *is*.
3. The way history developed is the right way.
4. The Confederation had to give way or else it would have remained.
5. Feudalism had to give way or else feudalism would have remained.

Particularly gratifying in these answers is the apparent recognition of the fallacy that history is a necessary sequence of orderly steps. It would seem that we can not attribute such examples of weak thinking (as in the nine items above) simply to maturational factors or to what Piaget calls juxtaposition and syncretism alone. There are many adults who retain childish notions of the meaning and interpretation of history—interpretive notions which reveal all the pathology of "what we have now is the way things had to be"—simply because few opportunities to examine such notions were provided. It would seem that teachers must create opportunities for student judging and student interpreting and for student analysis of such judgments and interpretations. The difference in skillful use of mental processes in the five items above as compared to the nine preceding should be obvious and also indicative of the effects of practice.

To sum up: History teaching is fraught with the pitfall and danger of subtly instilling into the young the notion that the way history happened was inevitable. This demands the corollary that the way it happened is the "right way." As teachers we have to be particularly careful of using hindsight ourselves. When we say something is good or bad we should be prepared to analyze the grounds on which such judgments are made. This is obvious. Not so obvious are the effects of historical judgments which have become commonplace. It is precisely these commonplace judgments which must ruthlessly be laid on the dissecting table.

For example, one often finds the statement that the Magna Carta is the basis of Anglo-American democracy because there was limitation of a king's power. Indeed, sometimes a chart of documents, beginning with Magna Carta and ending with the Constitution, is presented in such a way that students come away with the notion that democracy is nothing more than a series of documents—all safe under the lock and key of the curator. One could argue that feudalism is the basis of democracy since under feudalism the king's power was exceedingly weak and certainly the "democratic" feature of decentralized authority was omnipresent. Pulling out the one item of similarity is fallacious to be sure, but do we make students aware of the fallacy? It is not here important which of the two statements above is more correct. It is important that students be led to compare and examine such statements.

One further illustration. Let us take the word *renaissance* which is an historical interpretation frequently taught as an historical datum. The word itself seems to imply a rebirth of culture in the world. Some would say that it is a birth (not a rebirth) of culture in the west since culture had persisted in the Far and Middle East. Frank Lloyd Wright talks of "the setting sun which Europe mistook for the dawn." When the writer studied about the so-called Renaissance period in history, implicit was the notion of linear progress. Now, it is not my purpose to quibble over interpretations of the word renaissance. It is my purpose to argue that such concepts be taught as interpretations that are subject to analysis not only of the facts which purportedly support them but of the assumptions implicit in the use of the word itself. This, I believe, is calling for history teaching that is a little different than mere instruction in chronicle.

Some ways for teachers to prevent the growth of that phantasm known as the inevitability of historical events might be: when talking of slogans such as critical period, era of good feeling, tragic era, modern era, age of invention, age of discovery, the industrial age and other such encapsulated interpretations, care should be exercised that students do not get the notion that you are teaching them fact. Show students that there is an art to interpretation as represented by common historical phraseology. Indeed, students might be encouraged to try some interpreting themselves. One can provide many exercises which will encourage students to distinguish between fact and interpretation. (The results might be revealing.) Other exercises may be constructed which will permit students to unearth the assumptions underlying a given interpretation. One might present many interpretations of history, not just the one melange that is usually found in the typical textbook. If many interpretations were presented—theological, military, economic, great men, the absolute idea—there would be little opportunity for fanciful legend to ensconce itself as the proper interpretation. The writer offers the illustration used in this article as an example of how to proceed. Given the hypothetical situation regarding the Constitution, students were asked to:

1. Project backward;
2. Take a position and justify it;
3. Analyze their own answers;
4. Interpret their own answers;
5. Resolve apparent conflicts;
6. Engage in self-criticism.

Bertrand Russell once remarked that, "the words, William the Conqueror, 1066, become a verbal habit during early years at school; a significant number of such habits will make you a learned historian." Russell does more than joke and besides there is more truth than just plain sarcasm in that remark. If it is not true of our historians, there is much truth in the remark in terms of our history teaching practices. Let us stop teaching interpretations as facts. Instead, let us spend more time in analyzing interpretations. Furthermore, let us cease to cultivate habits of cant and phrase mongering. As a consequence, we might not produce citizens whose thinking is so pathologically immature as to believe that that which happened, happened because it had to be.

OPENING UP THE CLOSED AREAS OF ECONOMICS

Wayne Mahood
York Community High School
Elmhurst, Illinois

ECONOMICS AS A CLOSED AREA

It seems almost axiomatic that a mature reflective citizenry can produce a society able to resolve conflicts. Unfortunately, at critical junctures the United States has not demonstrated the maturity which would be helpful for resolution of its conflicts which emanate largely from within the individual. This paper looks toward resolution of these intrapersonal conflicts.

Economics serves as an example of an area within which there is lack of reflective thinking and is labeled a "closed area" by one text, i.e., an area "of belief and behavior which [is] largely closed to rational thought."[1] It is an area wherein social pressures obscure the real issues and obviate rational solutions. This inability to resolve conflicts weakens a democratically oriented society, which presents sufficient reason for exploring certain aspects of economics.

Particularly, this paper will explore the difficulties blocking reflective thinking in the concepts of government debt and economic stability. The purpose is to prepare students to resolve their intrapersonal conflicts democratically and cooperatively where resolution vitally affects their lives. If the assumption that teachers are as unable to rationally resolve conflicts as students is accepted as highly probable, it is imperative that these closed areas, such as economics, be opened to rational thinking by first concentrating on the teachers. They must be made aware of the dominant beliefs and contradictions in this area of economics and must first be prepared to reflect before encountering the students. Thus, it would seem worthwhile to try to recognize what some of these beliefs and contradictions are.

DOMINANT BELIEFS AND CONTRADICTIONS

1. *Spending and Business Cycles.* It is believed that the federal debt should be reduced through less government spending; but it is also believed that the government should moderate economic fluctuations, which may entail spending.

Reprinted with permission of the publisher, from *The Social Studies,* 57 (March, 1966): 110-116.

To most Americans debt is a subject of enormous confusion, for there is the belief that it means simply owing money, and the larger the obligation to repay, the nearer the borrower is to bankruptcy. If this debt is owed by the federal government, so much the worse for the people, for the collapse of the government is an inherent threat. This reasoning concludes that the only sane economic policy is one that demands reduction, culminating in complete removal of the debt.

Reduction or removal of the debt necessitates a policy of increased taxes or decreased spending. The first alternative is usually dismissed with little consideration, because any increase in taxes reduces the spending and investing power of individuals who are taxed. In fact when George Gallup asked, "Do you consider the amount of federal income tax which you have to pay as too high, about right, or too low?", forty-seven percent of the people asked said too high. (It is unlikely even with the recent tax cut that the response would be very different today.) Nonetheless, taxation at the present level is still preferred to debt by seventy-two percent of the population. (*St. Louis Post Dispatch,* August 2, 1962, Part 2, p. 1.) Decreased government spending is more appealing, for it demands sacrifices from an impersonal government, which needs to pare down expenses anyway.

Conflicting with this belief is that based on experience with the 1933-1939 depression, post-war inflation, and less severe recessions since World War II. These economic fluctuations have amply demonstrated the need for some moderation by an agency with a power commensurate with the responsibility. The federal government is the only agency which answers this description. It is to provide a steady and stable growth through spending and jobs, and if borrowing is required, so be it.

The resolution of such a commonplace, but nonetheless disturbing, conflict is imperative if there is to be the desired functioning of a government based on the rational will of the people. Any resolution must come from reflection, which most profitably can be cultivated in the classroom. Such a classroom approach will be discussed later in this paper.

2. *Balanced Budget and Government Activities.* It is believed that the federal government should balance spending with income and prevent increased federal debt; but it is also believed that there should be increased government activities to meet an expanding and changing population.

With regard to debt much the same argument is made here as in the first discussion. "The ancient test of fiscal sanity . . . was the balanced budget . . . It is the symbol of all that is sane, sound, and respectable."[2] It consists of keeping expenditures equal to income, which, according to this belief, means less spending, not an increase in taxes or any other method of "gouging" the poor taxpayer.

Clearly contradictory to this belief is that which may demand from the government any or all of the following: care for the aged, unemployment relief, aids to agriculture, regulation of monopolies, larger and better equipped state colleges and universities, better highways, ad infinitum. The government is in an advantageous (and sometimes the only) position to provide these activities. Present income is usually inadequate to meet these immediate needs, so the government must borrow. Again the conflict must be resolved reflectively.

3. *Debt and Growth.* It is believed that growth is good for the country, but it is also believed that growth entails borrowing to provide for immediate needs which will be countered by increased production.

There is no need to reiterate the argument against debt at this point. Let it suffice to say that debt is an evil which must be rooted out. Or as Walter Trohan in the July 27, 1962, *Chicago Tribune* has suggested, we should chant, "A Debt Is A Debt Is A Debt," so the public will not be confused by euphemisms hiding the truth about debt.

On the other hand, "Growth is fast becoming a hallowed word alongside Democracy and Motherhood."[3] Growth means expansion in employment, productivity, and capital, which requires money outlay not always available from private sources. It might mean engaging in unproductive enterprises, where private capital is unwilling to assume the risk. In either case only the federal government may be in a position to act decisively. This conflict is quite disturbing in light of the international crises, which demand that the United States not only keep pace with the Russians, but surpass them in all aspects of the economy. Hence, the emphasis today is on growth, without even an attempt at a clear understanding of the concept.

4. *Price Stability and Defense.* It is believed that the average price level should change slowly or not at all, but it is also believed that the defense program should be enlarged.

The argument here is that a price stabilization program would have to control consumer saving, taxation, and price and wage ceilings, but permit continuation of private enterprise in production and distribution. Whatever steps are taken must prevent rising prices which may lead to labor strikes, hoarding of goods, and uncertainty. Often this is the result of an enlarged defense spending program.

The defense of the United States in the Cold War period has taken on supreme importance in the thinking of many Americans, and there is little disagreement over the need for defense. Identified with this need, however, is the growing drain of men and materials from the civilian economy into military production. As mentioned before, in the past the result has been increased purchasing of scarce goods, forcing prices up and leading to the need for compensatory changes in wages, rents, etc.

It is these types of beliefs and contradictions which create the conflicts within the individual and subsequently express themselves in the society. To resolve these conflicts is to pave the way for greater understanding of society. This understanding may permit the consensus so essential to a democratic society.

MATERIALS ILLUSTRATING DOMINANT BELIEFS AND CONTRADICTIONS

Any listing of materials to indicate the sources of these beliefs would not only be cumbersome, but inadequate. Fruitful discussions of dominant beliefs and contradictions are in such texts as: Paul A. Samuelson, *Economics—An Introductory Analysis* (New York, 1958); Marshall A. Robinson, Herbert C. Morton, James D. Calderwood, *An Introduction to Economic Reasoning* (Washington, 1962); William Van Til, *Economic Roads for American Democracy* (New York, 1947); various books by Stuart Chase, including *Idle Money Idle Men* (New York, 1940); Kennard E. Goodman, C. Lowell Harriss, *Economics* (New York, 1963). They are particularly helpful, for they offer instructive analyses of these conflicts with a view toward resolution.

On a more popular level are the books by Vance Packard, including *The Waste Makers* (New York, 1960), John K. Galbraith, *The Affluent Society* (Boston, 1958) and *Economics and the Art of Controversy* (New Brunswick, New Jersey, 1955). The first two, however, are intended to be more revelatory than analytic.

Periodicals are a constant source of contradictions and biases. The slicks such as *Time* and *Newsweek* are supplemented by newspapers like the *Chicago Tribune* and the Hearst chain. These are countered by the more analytic *Business Week* and such papers as the *New York Times* and *Christian Science Monitor*.

It might be suggested that commonly the source of many conflicts is the head of the household, whose views stem largely from limited time and outlook. This is not an unqualified evil, for it does provide the familiarity which students may use as a tool for opening up the closed areas.

OPENING UP THE CLOSED AREAS

Closed areas by definition present innumerable difficulties for the classroom teacher, for discussion of them requires self-appraisal, student awareness, and administrative and community cooperation. Failure to surmount any one of these obstacles may prevent reflective thinking, which, it is argued, will open up the closed areas. The teacher's most immediate task is, not unlike the approach herein taken, that of recognizing some of the dominant beliefs and contradictions and sources thereof. His recognition may then enable him to be persuasive toward others who are similarly confronted by these conflicts. His persuasion must be complemented by a method whereby these conflicts can be broken down preparatory to investigation and testing. Perhaps this complementation may be viewed as a process rather than as a clearly defined method. The suggestion is that this opening up of the closed areas will be possible through the reflective method; "the complete act of thought . . . with certain safeguards attached."[4]

THE REFLECTIVE METHOD

The reflective method entails casting doubt on a dominant belief; using hypotheses which can be tested by all the pertinent evidence available, which is observable, conducive to experimentation, and publicly verifiable. These are the "rules of the game," but they throw only a little light on the problem which actually faces the teacher confronted by a classroom of many and varied conflicts. Required here is the transition from theory to practice. It means that these conclusions must be concrete. There must be a real harmony of outlook necessary to enable reflective thinking to make the transition from the classroom to the real world; the latter used in a derogatory, but all too often prevalent, sense.

THE REFLECTIVE METHOD IN THE CLASSROOM

Since no student comes into the classroom without any background, the first step the teacher must take is to elicit from the students the preconceptions formed from their backgrounds. The ways this may be done are innumerable: the introduction of generalizations in texts, materials consumed outside of class, statements or questions by the teacher, remarks by the students themselves, and a variety of situations which inevitably are presented simply by daily occurrences at school. Generally the elicitation of preconceptions is the least difficult step in the reflective method; it is an almost natural consequence of dealing with social studies subject matter. Economics, in the sense of satisfaction of the material needs of the people, pervades much of the thinking of students, even though it is not always verbalized.

Budget and government activities are popular topics with conflicts aplenty. It remains for the teacher to insure that these dominant beliefs and contradictions are brought out and recognized as such. If there is no provision for a separate economics course, a problems course or a course in United States history may provide as suitable a setting as any for discussion of these beliefs. For example, it is not difficult to encounter the statement that the "federal budget should be balanced" and in the next moment, "but it is imperative that we have better highways to serve our commuter needs" or "we need larger and better equipped colleges and universities." These generalizations almost beg for analysis.

Dana Kurfman in "Concept Development in the Social Studies" has said,

> It is the fact that many of our concepts have not been made explicit by analysis that makes it possible, and even likely, that we should hold incompatible concepts without being aware of their inconsistency.

Perhaps here lies not only the reason for closed areas, but the key to opening them. Analysis of the concept of budget could be approached first by eliciting responses from students' own backgrounds and putting them into syllogistic form:

Generalization: A balanced budget requires either increased revenues or decreased government activities.

Major Premise: An expanding and changing population demands increased government activities.

Minor Premise: But the population demands tax reduction.

Conclusion: The population demands a deficit (debt).

Using this syllogism which negatively represents the generalization of the contradiction expressed by the previous statements, it might be possible then to direct certain questions at either an individual student or the class as a whole. The purpose is to analyze the concepts of budget, debt, taxes, and government activities in this generalization by defining and testing it. Some sample questions with regard to budget are:

1. Do your parents budget?
2. What are the elements of their budget?, i.e., what is a budget in the sense that they use the term? or what does it purport to measure?
3. What have they done to "balance" their budget?
4. Does your parents' budget have anything in common with the federal budget?

Many standard economics texts would be helpful in illustrating the federal budget, budget procedures, and problems of balancing, including some fairly established definitions and useful diagrams of budgets. The particular application of these texts will depend on the classroom situation.

The next questions might ask:

1. Why is the budget not always balanced, i.e., what would cause an imbalance?
2. What expenditures do your parents have and how do these differ from federal expenditures?
3. Is one set of expenditures (parents' or federal) more important to the individual than another?
4. Are more demands made on the government than on your parents?
5. What demands are made on the government and are they desirable?
   a. Construction of highways?
   b. Maintenance of a court system?
   c. Construction of dams and power projects?
   d. Larger and better equipped state colleges and universities?
   e. Provision of unemployment relief, ADC, care for the aged (medical or social security)?
   f. "Make work" for the unemployed?

A warning is called for with regard to the term "desirable," since this may cause the discussion to degenerate into a show of preferences, which are not conducive to scientific investigation. They may be valuable to illustrate more about the students' backgrounds than about the consequences of government activities. It is important to work toward agreement as to the meaning of desirable in terms of certain qualities which are measurable; that is, some definition which will serve to prove or disprove the statement that the governmental activities are or are not desirable.

Arguments for and against such activities can be found in any of the texts mentioned previously, and can be compared with another argument by John

Stuart Mill based on expedience in Samuelson, *et al., Readings in Economics* (New York, 1958), p. 94.

The succeeding step is obvious. Payment of these expenditures, if the necessity for them can be established, will require investigation, for payment may run counter to beliefs about a balanced budget. Some possible inquiries might be:

1. What form should payment of these activities take?
   a. Taxes? are they a burden? upon whom? who should pay, i.e., according to what principle? ability to pay, benefits?
   b. Borrowing? from whom? who will hold the debt? do they have a stake in the outcome of the government? are they deriving special benefits from the loan to the government? could they use the money in a way that would avoid borrowing by the government, but provide the same activities?
   c. A charge for these activities by the government? payment for use of the national parks, or as benefits are derived, as in federal multipurpose projects?
   d. Printing more money, like greenbacks?
2. Would any of these methods make a difference to the economy?
   a. More or less growth?
   b. Curtailment of individual spending?
   c. Throwing a burden on other sectors of the economy?
3. Will the choice of method be determined by a belief that debt is "immoral?"
4. Is the federal government in a better position to adopt one of these methods than your parents? and do the effects differ whether the government or your parents adopts one of these methods?

To check on some of the results of the answers to these questions another reference to some materials on economics, particularly debt, might be in order. Samuelson, Robinson, *et al.,* and Galbraith, mentioned earlier, provide helpful materials. Arguments for limited debt are to be found in such sources as Robert H. Johnson, "The National Debt as a 'Burden,'" and Wallace E. Ogg, "The Role of Debt in Our Economy," both of which are found in *Farm Policy Forum* (Ames, Iowa, April, 1953). An additional source providing greater depth coverage is "Debt: Public and Private," a Report of the Committee on Economic Policy, Chamber of Commerce (Washington, 1951).

Relevant here also is the pamphlet "Facts and Figures on Government Finance," The Tax Foundation, 30 Rockefeller Plaza (New York, 1959).

The conclusions which can be reached by these arguments and questions will again entail some value judgments, but much evidence can be relied upon, nonetheless. It should be clear that certain government activities are vital to the operation of a government responsible to the needs of the people. Transportation and educational facilities will probably answer the needs of much of the population, as will employment and social security, to provide for economic growth and a degree of prosperity. To maintain such activities, borrowing may well be the most efficient means for paying for them, for it can be shown that borrowing is a contractual obligation unlimited to any particular scheme of payment. It will mean benefiting some who will be vitally interested in the continuance of the government, without placing a burden on any particular group. It may represent an economic relationship between those who wish to spend more than their incomes and those who wish to spend less. It may foster the growth of spending and markets, production, and employment. Debt may enable adjustment of timing of spending and consumption, bridge the gaps between savers and those who need capital, and provide a money supply.

The payment of the debt strengthens a belief in the government's stability to meet obligations, as well as to control harmful fluctuations in economic activity. This can be compared with the risks the private borrower takes. The family which budgets does not possess the same monetary powers as the government, and impending default and bankruptcy are serious threats.

Borrowing then will be a real alternative to taxing, which creates a greater burden on one group than another or greater at one time than another. It may also possess the advantage over any pay-as-you-go plan by enabling the user of the activities to enjoy them without having to meet a payment at the time of enjoyment. Waiting for enjoyment could forestall it and limit growth in certain sectors of the economy at the same time. Certainly it will be more appealing to some than the printing of more money, which has in the past inflated the currency, causing hardships on lenders or those whose incomes rise less rapidly than the general cost of living, such as teachers, retired persons, and civil service employees.

If these conclusions are not warranted, they at least provide alternative ways of resolving conflicts in constructive ways. This method should have demonstrated the incompatibility between the beliefs about balanced budget, tax reduction, and government activities, thus posing a threat to these beliefs. However, this should not have been a personal threat, which might inhibit constructive reflection. The students should have been protected from any loss of status while they have been guided to the development of skills to work with threatening conflicts.

This approach requires the teacher to rely on students' own experiences in a democratically controlled discussion where generalizations can be developed and tested. It is vital, however, to have insured throughout that the whole group has felt the challenge to their beliefs. If the teacher has stuck to the subject, clarified, carefully used resource materials, and avoided over-generalizations and rationalization, he may feel assured that these beliefs have been tested by relevant data. To the students the data will not be "facts," which are memorized, regurgitated, and promptly forgotten, but discoveries of concepts which they feel are observable from their own experiences; real, usable, and verifiable.

Particularly important is the point of making the tests publicly verifiable. There should be no abracadabra or mystic rites attached to the testing of hypotheses, but the constant use of familiar sources with an awareness that testing is simply the "process of reconstruction in light of a particular body of evidence at a given time."[5] There must be the realization that this is the extension of common sense; the control of meaning and the questioning of tentative findings. The students are made aware that thinking is a continuous process unrestricted to a rigid framework, and an unscheduled, ongoing process.

Again, assuming the teacher has been responsible in his approach to reflective thinking, the reconstruction of the individual can be complete. It is a personal affair where the student has challenged a belief, utilized experience, tested his hypotheses, and has selected certain data from his reflection. He has not concluded this process with a right or wrong answer, but has chosen one course of action which seems supported by all the relevant findings. While he may have no absolutes, he is certain that his discovery has been tested in light of all the evidence he presently has. These conclusions represent the resolution of a conflict intelligently without resort to rationalization, repression, withdrawal, or any other unconstructive behavior; there is a whole reconstruction.

RESULTS OF THE REFLECTIVE METHOD

If the teacher has been true to his goals, his students and society should reap the benefits. Hullfish sums up what should be the consequences:

... A properly conceived classroom can facilitate the development of conceptual behavior. A continuing emphasis upon meaning, rather than upon mere fact; a concern for the relatedness of fact, event, and meaning, in opposition to the dreary pursuit of isolated items of information; the attempt to move students to levels of imaginative projection where consequences of alternative answers may be considered before an answer is proposed, instead of demanding immediate reactions that but repeat the answers of others; an unrelenting effort to help students gain a feel for language in its capacity as a tool for advancing the effectiveness of thought, as against the tendency to think of it as an obstacle that fussy people place before them—these represent ways in which teachers may progressively enrich the conceptual responses of students. Each achievement in these terms will represent a contribution to the creation of sensitized, reflective individuals.[6]

This is a big order, and not every teacher, student, school, or community will be ready to fulfill such an order without an awareness of the benefits of such a pursuit.

It calls for a vigilant body of representatives of the school to demonstrate the values of such an approach in their own lives as well as in the classroom. But, this is not really so much to ask. It means quite practically the realization of the democratic society, which was proclaimed with such optimism. Democracy is based on the belief in the dignity and worth of the individual; that he is rational and of good will. If we are to enjoy any of these lofty sentiments, it must come through "sensitized, reflective individuals" working toward cooperative solutions to problems. Lewis Paul Todd has said that "man is the custodian of civilization." If man is to carry out his responsibility, he must resolve his personal conflicts not only in economics, even though this area constitutes one of the real battlegrounds of international disorder, but also in all the areas of social studies. He must not shirk his responsibility for the "critical transmission of his cultural heritage," regardless of the odds. If the cultural heritage is worth having, it is worth working for.

References

[1] Maurice P. Hunt and Lawrence E. Metcalf, *Teaching High School Social Studies* (New York, 1955), p. 7.

[2] John K. Galbraith, *Economics and the Art of Controversy* (New Brunswick, New Jersey, 1955), pp. 64, 65.

[3] Vance Packard, *The Waste Makers* (New York, 1961), p. 21.

[4] Hunt and Metcalf, *op. cit.*, p. 60.

[5] H. Gordon Hullfish and Philip G. Smith, *Reflective Thinking: The Method of Education* (New York, 1961), p. 66.

[6] *Ibid.*, p. 168.

TEACHING CIVIL LIBERTIES BY THE CASE METHOD

Donald Parker
North Shore High School,
Glen Head, New York

Nicholas Econopouly
Coordinator, Social Sciences Research,
American Community School of Athens, Greece

It would be difficult to imagine a secondary school curriculum guide which does not include as a stated goal, "an understanding and appreciation of democratic values." One might ask: Are we achieving this goal? Do our students have an understanding of democratic values? Surveys made by the Division of Educational Reference of Purdue University, and involving a cross section of ten thousand high school students, indicate some rather startling responses.[1]

Thirty-seven percent of our high school students would not object to third-degree police methods.

Forty-three percent favored or were undecided about curbs on public speech.

Thirty-four percent of our youth would abolish the right to circulate petitions.

Thirty-four percent opposed school integration.

Dr. Martin Hamburger of New York University, who coordinated this study of the survey, suggested that civil liberties and equality are not cherished "to anywhere near the degree many parents and educators have assumed."[2]

What meaning does this have for the social studies teacher? This question might be answered in terms of his willingness to accept two responsibilities: (1) Evaluating his present methods for teaching democratic values; (2) Devising techniques which will offer prospects for successfully communicating these values to the students.

Although study of the Constitution and its amendments is an indispensable part of the process of teaching an understanding of civil liberties, this in itself is not enough.

It does not take too many days of teaching to become aware of the gap which can exist between "school knowledge" and the students' personal

Reprinted with permission of the author and the National Council for the Social Studies, from *Social Education,* 25 (October, 1961): 283-285.

world: the tendency to place in separate compartments that which is learned in the classroom and that which is learned to be used outside the classroom. It is unfortunately true that many students can express admiration for the Bill of Rights on one level—and express personal views directly contrary to these principles on another.

Plainly, then, a study of documents *in itself* is not enough. Students are not always helped in relating ideas to their own personal experiences after studying the framework of our federal government. The range of such experiences is often limited and frequently narrow, filled with the kinds of emotions and prejudices that work against effective learning. The inexperienced teacher can vividly attest to the hostilities which can be generated among students in that kind of setting.

Since the leap from the Bill of Rights to the local community may be too great, too real, too filled with personal feelings, an intermediate step is needed. What is demanded is a real-life situation which is only casually personal to the student. A more personal application comes as the student is ready for it; immediately for some, later for others.

The use of fictional case histories can be a valuable aid in this intermediate stage. For several years we have experimented with this technique. It can be extremely effective. Used with sensitivity to the pupils' needs and capacities, it can have a profound positive influence on many students. It has proved valuable enough to convince us that a collection of such fictional case histories should be developed, each focusing on a different type of situation involving civil liberties. As a result, we have compiled approximately 30 of these case histories; some of them quite brief, others extensive, some including follow-up activities, others without the follow-up.

Following are a few of these fictional case histories. Questions included with the study may be used to guide students' explorations. In Case No. 1, the students are prepared by objective study of a hypothetical situation. From here, the possibilities for moving into real situations are apparent.

Case No. 1: Frank Fulton applied to the City of Detroit to hold a public political meeting. The request was granted. During the course of the meeting, Fulton aroused enthusiastic backing from the crowd when he stated that the President of the United States was a deceitful, corrupt person who should be impeached and thrown out of office. The Detroit police who were assigned to the area closed the meeting in order to "protect the city from a possible riot." Fulton filed a legal protest on the basis that his constitutional rights were violated.

Questions
1. What constitutional rights would Fulton be concerned about?
2. Are there or should there be any limits to the extent that Fulton can go in criticizing the President of the United States or other officials of the United States government?
3. Were the Detroit police officials negligent in handling their responsibilities at this public political meeting?
4. The comment has been made that the Bill of Rights has been designed "to protect the unpopular views of the minority; the majority can take care of itself." Do you agree?

The second case focuses attention on the use and misuse of search warrants. Rather than students concentrating on the black-and-white nature of the issues involved, they can begin to develop an appreciation of more complex gray tones.

Case No. 2: The local police have tracked a supply of heroin to a particular neighborhood. If they move quickly, they will be able to seize millions of dollars worth of drugs and to save untold misery of potential addicts. In a lightning move, they search the neighborhood house by house. A resident objects but he is told: "It's okay this time—special emergency!" The dope is found.

Double jeopardy is the theme of the next case history. The teacher can readily guide the study to more complex areas once the elementary problem has been defined.

Case No. 3: You return to your automobile and find there are two parking tickets on your car: one on your steering wheel, another on the windshield wiper. Each ticket refers to the same violation, but the time of issuance on each differs. What do you do?

Some of the case histories introduce a number of problems and issues. In the case which follows, characters have been given personalities which may influence the students' conclusions, and emphasis is placed upon some of the socio-economic factors involved in civil liberties.

Case No. 4: Jack Phillips grew up in a wealthy section of Chicago. Even though his parents provided him with toys and games during his childhood, he began to steal comic books and candy from the local stores. As soon as he reached the age of 16, with his parents' reluctant consent he quit school and began to work as a stock boy in a local sporting goods store. In addition to his earnings from this job, his parents gave him an allowance. This enabled him to flaunt his wealth and as a result he had few if any friends.

During the first few months on his job he found it was quite easy to steal sports equipment and sell it for his own personal profit. However, his boss began to notice that certain items were missing from stock and notified the police. After watching Phillips for a number of days, the police entered his home, searched it, and after finding some sports equipment there, arrested him. He was sent to jail to await trial.

Jack's family spared no expense for they immediately contacted a prominent lawyer who agreed to defend their son. After examining his client's case, the lawyer claimed that several of Jack's constitutional rights were violated and he should be released from jail.

Questions
1. From the description of this case, what rights do you feel might have been violated?
2. The events described all occurred before Jack Phillips appeared before a jury for trial. Do you feel that the case should come to trial?
3. In view of the wealth of the Phillips family and the fact that they spent money on their son, how might you explain Jack's desire to steal?
4. Do you feel Jack's family has any *legal* responsibility for his actions?

The technique and materials, of course, have their limitations. The demands made on the teacher—who must be receptive to the approach in the first place—are considerable: He must be far more sensitive to the students' needs and the climate of the community than would be the case in simply studying the Bill of Rights without special concern for its contemporary applications. Furthermore, the classroom setting must be a flexible one with the teacher prepared to move occasionally into unfamiliar areas which students' inquisitiveness will invariably introduce. In other words, the need is for a certain kind of teacher working in a certain kind of setting—these may not always be conditions which can be met.

Finally, we are discussing how to influence the attitudes and behavior of students, and we are insisting that this should be the basic concern in the study of civil liberties. It is precisely here that the most uncertainty about results exists, perhaps, because we cannot be sure we are dealing directly with basic causes. But there is ample indication that the material is at least helpful in many cases. Students *are* interested, do dig deeply into the many problems and issues raised, and generally appear to take a fair-minded approach in their conclusions.

What course will students follow when facing civil liberty issues in real-life situations? We do not know—but we are hopeful.

A statement by one bright—and puzzled—student emphasizes both the influence and limitations of the technique: "A lot of my 'thinking' about civil liberties wasn't thinking at all—it was a collection of prejudices and impulses.

I think I'm changing. The trouble is that changing is very hard for me, even though I'm trying."

References

[1] The Division of Educational Reference at Purdue University has conducted a number of opinion polls among high school students designed to determine their attitudes regarding civil liberties. Two of these surveys are *Does Youth Believe in the Bill of Rights?* (November 1951), and *Science, Education, and Civil Liberties* (March 1958).
[2] *The New York Times.* February 16, 1960.

CURRENT EVENTS AND VALUES

Phyllis Lieberman
Junior High School Social Studies Teacher
Sidney B. Simon
University of Massachusetts

As consistently as failing marks are recorded in red ink, Friday in American schools is current events day. With Friday comes the ubiquitous oral reports, the dutifully written summaries, the occasional cartoon-holding-up periods and, perhaps, the faithful going over of one of the weekly magazines written expressly, and neutrally, for school children.

It seems terribly tame to carry on such weekly current events lessons in the face of a world which is shot through with rampant doubt, confusion, and contradictions; a world in which we talk of peace, but in which the arms race continues; a world in which Americans fight and die, but we are not at war. We listen to current events reports about the civil rights struggle in classrooms which are often part of blatantly *de facto* segregated schools. These are the problems we need to deal with if we are to help our students make some sense out of a world which strikes most of them as being just this side of overwhelming. If we want our students to grow to adulthood with the skills and the drive to take on some share of the responsibility for what goes on in this world, to make their voices heard on the issues of the day, something more is needed than current events Friday.

Reprinted with permission of the author and the National Council for the Social Studies, from *Social Education,* 29 (December, 1965): 532-533.

We advocate an approach to current events which puts the focus upon value-clarification. The theoretical framework for this method can be found in *Values and Teaching: Working With Values in the Classroom.*[1] This value-clarification approach puts emphasis upon the process, upon the search for an individualized value system that will help students find meaning and structure in their lives, lives which so often now merely reflect apathy, drift, conformity, or blind rebellion. Perhaps a clearer understanding of the type of approach we are recommending can be gained by examining the following three examples of current events lessons.[2]

Let us first look at an article from the *American Civil Liberties Union Newsletter.*

SPEAK UP

In Germany they first came for the Communists, and I didn't speak up because I wasn't a Communist. Then they came for the Jews, and I didn't speak up because I wasn't a Jew. Then they came for the trade unionists, and I didn't speak up because I wasn't a trade unionist. Then they came for the Catholics, and I didn't speak up because I was a Protestant. Then they came for me—and by that time no one was left to speak up.—Pastor Martin Niemoller.

To think on and to write on:
1. In a few words, what is the gist of this statement?
2. What is the Pastor *for* and what is he *against?*
3. Which category are *you*? When would they have come for you?
4. Do you know of any people either personally or in current affairs who were not afraid to take a stand? Tell us about them.
5. What are some things going on in our world right now about which you might need to speak up? List them here.
6. Is there something in your school, some "injustice," about which you could well speak up?
7. How do you think one goes about speaking up? What are the ways?
8. Could you pick something you listed in questions 5 or 6 and work out a strategy by which you could, indeed, speak up?
9. If you are not to speak up, who should do it?
10. We need to *value* what we do and to *do* something about what we value. Do you agree? If so, when was the last time you did?

This lesson helps to clarify the idea that we have a responsibility to speak up about the things we are for or against. Of prime importance are the questions that ask the student to describe in concrete terms how he would change or control the course of one human event.

The following article by Charles A. Wells from *Between the Lines News-letter* was dittoed and distributed to each class member.

THE PRICE OF PEACE

Questions That Scientists Have Been Asking

Why is the total 78-national budget for the International Atomic Energy Agency, which is responsible for the Atoms For Peace program, less than the cost of one single moon shot?

Why are there only eight engineers backing our multi-billion-dollar Agency for International Development against more than 10,000 engineers in our space agency?

Why do we spend more to produce one nuclear submarine than our total annual budget for agricultural research—in a world of hunger?

Of the more than $17 billion a year spent in the United States on research and development, why is only $4 billion spent by American industry for non-military, non-space work?

To think on and to write on:
1. Do you have an answer to these questions?
2. Which point, if any, bothers you the most? Explain.
3. Comment on: "So what? Let the scientists worry about it."
4. What questions have *you* been asking lately? (Write on some things about which you are more concerned.)

The above questions help the student to realize that the choices we make, as a nation and individually, reflect what we value. The student is asked if his values and those expressed in the article coincide, and if not, what he can do about this.

Our last example of what we consider a meaningful current events lesson was taken from the September-October 1964 issue of the *Core-lator*.

LONG ISLAND PICKETS

Long Island CORE won a precedent-setting agreement with Vigilant Associates, one of the largest real estate brokers in the area, despite counter-picketing by pro-Goldwater youths carrying placards such as: "Keep Niggers Out," "Support Your Local KKK," and "I Like Niggers—I Think Everyone Should Own One."

This group counter-picketed during the entire week of picketing by CORE. The picketing started after a CORE test proved discrimination on the part of the realtor. As many as 900 white spectators, most of them supporting the counter-pickets, were drawn to the scene where there was a heavy concentration of police. However, up to 20 white residents of Hicksville had the courage to join the CORE picket line.

To think on and to write on:
1. Do you agree with what CORE did here? Have you disagreed with anything else they have done? Explain.
2. Are you a member of CORE? Have you ever sent them any money? Have you ever attended any of their meetings? Why? Why not?
3. Would you have done what the pro-Goldwater counter-pickets did? Why? Why not?
4. Comment on what the 20 white residents of Hicksville did. What meaning did that have? Would you have done it? Why? Why not?
5. Is there anything else you want to say here?

The students are asked to examine the different viewpoints expressed in the article in an attempt to clarify their own thinking on the subject. In addition, they are confronted with an example of those that were courageous enough to act on their beliefs and are asked if they would do the same.

Such is the values approach to current events. We feel it offers the change that is so drastically needed in current events day. It is our conviction that out of such teaching will come students who are deeply disturbed about the mindlessness, the anxiety, the dangers of our world. It is our belief that these individuals will possess the determination, the knowledge, the courage to fight for the things they value, to change the things they are against. It is our hope that through the search for values we can begin to build a society where diversity is nourished, life itself is valued, and men and women live not in quiet desperation, but in full anticipation of the adventure of life. We invite you to join us in this work.

A VOTE FOR CITIZENSHIP

Samuel Polatnick
*Principal, Springfield Gardens High School,
Springfield Gardens, New York*

Recent articles in *Social Education* and other professional journals have attested to a ferment in the social studies. Postholing; making room for sociology, social psychology, and anthropology in courses of study; team

Reprinted with permission of the author and the National Council for the Social Studies, from *Social Education,* 28 (October, 1964): 343-345.

teaching; and other suggestions for curriculum revision and methodological change have attracted widespread attention. Yet, as we look to the new in social studies, there is a danger that we may neglect or slight a fundamental objective: the cultivation of intelligent, civic-minded behavior in our young people.

The dazzling advances in science, mathematics, and technology have distracted many people from an essential recognition of the need for citizenship and political intelligence of the highest order at this time. The solution of such problems as formulating correct nuclear policy, developing effective leadership, and expanding democratic values throughout the world—to name but a few—call for the fullest mobilization of our nation's wisdom, and the practice of devoted public service by all of us.

Yet it is shocking to learn from surveys that many people, particularly in the lowest eligible age brackets, do not even vote. Surely the intelligent exercise of the franchise is an essential first step in any practice of citizenship. While the exercise of the suffrage and the practice of good citizenship are functions of many institutions and factors such as the home, the church, the community, and the schools, the schools have always accepted a major share of the responsibility for preparing youth to transmit the city a little better than they found it.

As a matter of fact, our schools have developed many useful practices and procedures for developing good citizenship. Perhaps what is needed is a more systematic application of what our schools have learned of such preparation, and a careful evaluation and testing of procedures to determine which might be most effective in developing young people of different ages, backgrounds, and experiences. A survey of curricular, extracurricular, and school-community citizenship-training procedures in the high schools of New York City, conducted under the auspices of the Standing Committee in Social Studies (officers of supervisors' and teachers' professional organizations) and Acting Associate Superintendent Maurice D. Hopkins, Head of the High School Division, revealed a wide variety of valuable practices for the development of intelligent civic-minded voting and other civic behavior.

In the hope that some of the New York City experiences may be valuable to social studies teachers in other communities and that they may serve to stimulate additional thought in the area of citizenship training, we offer the following summary of practices. No one school can hope to do all these things, but surely every school can find time to carry out a few of the suggestions.

ANNUAL EFFORTS DIRECTLY RELATED TO NOVEMBER ELECTIONS

1. Development of a series of lessons on the elections prepared by the social studies departments for social studies classes. These lessons cover such aspects of the elections as issues, candidates, the importance of voting, and the significance of the elections.
2. In some schools teachers prepare special election information sheets containing registration information, election district maps, lists of candidates, brief descriptions of election issues, sample ballots, and a few key questions such as, "In choosing your U.S. Congressman and Senator, have you determined his position on foreign aid, medical care for the aged, civil rights for minorities, aid to public and parochial schools, plans to reduce unemployment, the "Cold War," the uses of atomic energy, and atomic testing?" These materials are designed to stimulate thought and discussion about the particular election.
3. Distribution to students of election materials prepared by non-partisan civic organizations such as the League of Women Voters, American Heritage Foundation, etc.
4. Presentation in class of "socio-dramas" on the problems of votes in which students sign in registration books, inquire about particulars of the election, establish sources of information, and vote.
5. Students organize a special Student Elections Council to develop appropriate election-centered projects in which the school will participate. Some students, for example, act as baby-sitters on election day to release parents for voting.
6. Conducting of school-wide straw votes on local, state, and national elections.
7. Visits to, observation of, and participation in the activities of local political clubs.
8. Use of town meetings and panel discussions in social studies classes on issues and candidates in elections. Special attention is given to the significance of every vote by including analyses of previous close votes.
9. Judicious use of tape recordings of speeches by leading candidates to define issues and evaluate debate.
10. Arrangement for election assemblies involving the candidates for public office, and/or student speakers. Some schools center such assemblies around dramatizations of elections, election procedures, or the significance of elections.
11. Problems of Democracy classes may arrange three- to five-day conventions involving nominations, development of platforms, and straw votes.
12. As a procedure for making elections an opportunity for joint family consideration, Parent-Teachers Associations sponsor community

election meetings which are attended by parents, students, teachers, and candidates.

13. Students interview local candidates for public office.
14. Social studies clubs or discussion clubs hold meetings with local candidates present to debate election issues.
15. Provision for comprehensive bulletin board displays in classrooms and special school areas on such aspects of the elections as registration information, candidates, issues, and results.
16. Printing of features such as interviews with local candidates, and of pro and con treatment of major public issues in the school newspaper.
17. Arrangement on a broad basis—borough or city—of a student nominating convention in which students nominate candidates, debate their qualifications, formulate platforms, evaluate planks of the party platforms, and vote.
18. Demonstration of the operation of voting machines.
19. Students write letters to parents urging them to register and vote. In some schools students have prepared bilingual appeals to parents regarding elections.
20. Post-mortem analyses are made of election results in social studies classes pointing up for students how additional voting might have affected these results, the significance of outcomes for public policy, etc.

LONG-RANGE PREPARATION FOR INTELLIGENT AND CIVIC-MINDED VOTING

1. Consistent efforts are made to relate ongoing instruction in the social studies to meaningful contemporary problems. This is directed to setting issues of the day in historical perspective so that youngsters may be aided in developing intelligent positions on public issues.
2. Provision of thorough instruction on the structure and operation of national, state, and local government.
3. Careful and thorough comparisons between the practices of Communist and other totalitarian societies and the practices of democratic society with specific reference to voting, the role of political parties, and opportunities to influence public policy. The preparation and distribution of mimeographed cartoons, excerpts from public statements, and quotations from reliable secondary sources make for valuable aids in such comparison and instruction.
4. Regular and systematic instruction in current events including current events quizzes and special assemblies. Attention is given to using tools of propaganda analysis in the examination of sources of information on current issues.
5. Provision of a problems-of-democracy course or the use of a problems-of-democracy approach which stresses voter education by

affording experiences in the identification of significant and controversial problems, student research in relevant information, evaluation of sources of information, discussion of issues, and efforts to find reasonable, tentative conclusions about such problems.

6. Operation of an effective program for student participation in school government. This involves developing a statement of areas appropriate for student participation, arranging effective educational procedures for the nomination of student officers, conducting election campaigns on meaningful school issues, organizing opportunities for students to discuss the selection of leaders offering and able to carry out intelligent platforms, establishing a wide extracurricular program, providing for a regular student-developed budget and financing program for student activities, thinking through a program for encouraging good school citizenship, encouraging student-community programs, and making provision for leadership training. Essential here is the creation of an atmosphere in which student suggestions in areas appropriate to their participation are welcomed, and where feasible, put into effect.

7. Organization of a leadership class for training student leaders in problem analysis, research, and formulation of school programs.

8. Analysis of books dealing with political leaders, the operations of government, and influences upon the electorate. Thus, books such as Theodore White's *The Making of the President, 1960,* and James MacGregor Burns' *Roosevelt: The Lion and the Fox* may provide the basis for valuable discussion.

9. Organization of social studies clubs and journals to provide for discussion and research related to significant social studies problems. Such activities may include a Social Studies Forum, a Model Legislature, a Luncheon Seminar, and a Social Studies Journal.

10. Conducting of regional (borough- and city-wide) discussion conferences in which specially trained student leaders conduct afternoon or day-long student discussions of significant public issues.

11. Participation of students under local college or civic organization sponsorship in sessions of a Model Congress or a Model Legislature in which legislation is proposed and drafted under procedures similar to those followed in the Congress of the United States.

12. Stimulation of correspondence between students and legislative representatives on public issues.

13. Encouragement of projects in which students, particularly seniors, participate in political club activities.

14. Visits to legislatures and courts.

15. Preparation by teachers or students of pro and con material on current public issues which is mimeographed and distributed as a basis for class discussion. Special background fact sheets on such issues as urban representation in state legislatures may similarly be prepared.

16. Periodic polls may be conducted to sample student attitudes on current issues.
17. Students' committees prepare a weekly program guide to TV and radio programs dealing with significant issues.
18. The school and civic organizations may jointly sponsor forums on significant contemporary issues.
19. Students keep a record of votes of their legislative representatives.

EFFORTS RELATED TO DEVELOPMENT OF
GOOD CITIZENSHIP BEYOND VOTING

1. Regular involvement of students in community service projects such as work with the aged and the handicapped, entertainment of hospitalized veterans, service in hospitals, construction of toys for needy children, conduct of classes in community houses, and collections for charities. Some schools have organized youth panels to speak before community groups and furnish representation on community advisory councils.
2. Preparation and discussion of case studies in problems of citizenship at a level meaningful to youngsters, e.g., whether to report a friend who has been bribed to throw a basketball game.
3. Awards to students and citizens for outstanding citizenship. This involves the development of criteria for nomination, distribution of summaries of achievements of nominees and discussion of these accomplishments, school-wide vote, and a ceremonial assembly to honor the winner.
4. Awards of certificates of citizenship and character to one student in each social studies class, unrelated to scholastic achievement. Awards for co-operation in government are made at graduation for outstanding leadership and service in student activities.
5. Provision of extensive and varied opportunities for student service to the school on squads, in offices, and for individual teachers.
6. Instructional emphasis on biographies of outstanding civic-minded men and women stressing qualities of character and citizenship.
7. Organization of special assemblies to commemorate patriotic holidays and to support American ideals such as brotherhood.
8. Organization of special historic and patriotic shrines such as Independence Hall and Washington, D.C.
9. Displays of documents and other appropriate materials for illustrating the American heritage.
10. Development of programs such as Big Brother assignments, orientation assemblies and booklets, and visits to home rooms by student officers to orient newcomers to citizenship opportunities in a school.
11. Encouragement of teacher participation in community affairs.
12. Development of codes for school behavior.
13. The school sponsors an annual luncheon involving student officers

and members of the community's civic organizations to discuss achievements, problems, and proposals for further school-community cooperation.

PROPOSALS FOR CITIZENSHIP-TRAINING ACTIVITIES POSSIBLY NOT YET IN WIDESPREAD OR REGULAR USE

1. Creation of a regular, annual well-rounded program to give every Election Day, not only those of presidential election years, the ceremony, dignity, and respect befitting the occasion upon which the citizens of a democracy exercise their precious opportunity to affect public policy and public officialdom. This should involve the whole panoply of distinguished speakers, displays, information, and votes.
2. Expansion of contacts of the school with the political life of the community by establishing regular opportunities for students to serve as witnesses at polls and political headquarters on election evenings, etc.
3. Encouragement of programs for having foreign students visit or live with American students. This affords opportunities for young people to compare American conditions with those of other countries, and to develop a deeper appreciation of the American way of life.
4. Greater use of voting machines for teaching purposes.
5. Greater involvement of public figures in class and school-wide activities.
6. Development or restoration of courses in civics or government: local, state, and national as near to the last year of high school education as possible. "American Constitutional Problems" could be stressed with brighter students, the "Role of the Citizen" with slower children. Regular courses in the social studies should include more material on government.
7. Raising licensing requirements for teachers to require more work in local, state, and national government.
8. Greater availability of appropriate instructional materials on elections and other issues.
9. Arrangements for meetings of social studies teachers to consider voting and other citizenship matters and to develop appropriate instructional procedures and materials.
10. Greater involvement of P.T.A.'s in developing programs for student participation in school-community service and civic projects.
11. Organization of Students' Voter Leagues to undertake regular responsibility for school and community election programs.
12. Teams of students might conduct occasional pools of community attitudes on public issues.
13. Educational television stations could be of service to schools by presenting a series of programs on issues of elections and other relevant educational emphases.

14. Provision could be made for a teacher-coordinator or group of students to maintain a file of community service opportunities for young people, and to oversee such activity.

The interest of the teachers and supervisors of social studies in the high schools of New York City in developing good citizenship has resulted in the preparation of a number of curriculum bulletins. *Developing Student Participation in School Government* (Curriculum Bulletin No. 12, 1960-61 Series) and *Problems of Democracy* (Curriculum Bulletin No. 9, 1960-61 Series) are both available from the Board of Education, New York City, and both are valuable for deeper treatment of some of the suggestions described in this article.

Certainly a further exchange of professional wisdom and experience in citizenship training accumulated in our schools will help us all to provide even more effectively for the development of our young people and for their contribution to our society. As one school reported, "The evidence of the experience here at Morris [Morris High School, Bronx, New York] is that high school youth are more ready to accept responsibility for adult-like tasks than there are opportunities for such experiences."

PART FOUR

Improvements and Innovations in Social Studies Materials

William E. Gardner

The process of teaching is essentially one of communication, and the teacher's major role is to establish a system of interaction with his students. He presents information to them; provides them with skills for the analysis of information, and engages them in discussion of important issues or problems. Much of the quality of this interaction depends upon the way the teacher relates to his class or the degree to which his personality "meshes" or "jells" with those of his students.

But the media used by teachers are also important in establishing communication with students. At some dim point in our educational past, the media were absolutely uncomplicated. Literacy was not common; books were hand-copied and expensive. It is true that Socrates drew sketches in the sand (thereby giving "audio-visual education" its first boost), but, for the most part, the basic medium was the spoken word.

Gutenberg changed all that, of course. Printed matter enabled the teacher to broaden and extend his means of communication with students, and books became the primary aid to teaching. Recently, our rampaging jet-age technology has introduced totally new types of media in the form of television and computers. A study of these new devices has led Marshall McLuhan to suggest that the media is something more than the vehicle along which messages pass. In his view, the form of the media has a substance all its own, because it shapes the way the world is viewed. Books, for example, encourage students to see the world in a sequential, linear fashion; the form of the medium mandates the way in which thought proceeds. Television, on the other hand, operates in a non-linear fashion; it is essentially an extension of the total nervous system of man and enables him to view the world in a different nonlinear fashion.[1]

As yet, the social studies have not been greatly affected by this "media revolution." The typical social studies teacher still considers the text as his only supplement to the spoken word. Too often, in fact, the text is the course, supplemented only slightly by teacher explanation and elaboration. The great energies poured out by teachers in examination of "basal" texts as members of textbook evaluation teams bear witness to the strength of this medium in the social studies.

While the media revolution has not as yet generated fundamental changes in the ways social studies are taught, there are signs that changes are in the offing. Specifically, three things are happening:

(1) *Textbooks are improving.* Quite possibly, the textbook has always been the object of some critical comments, but recent years have seen a definite increase. Depending upon who was doing the criticizing, texts have been labeled too liberal or too conservative, pro-labor or pro-business, too ethnocentric or too internationalistic. Obviously, some of the criticisms have been unfounded because the person criticizing has had an axe to grind or because texts have been expected to do things that the form of the medium make very difficult. Despite a steady stream of unjust and even irrational criticism, there is no doubt that texts have serious deficiencies in scholarship and point of view. Also, it is evident that publishers and authors are trying hard to improve the quality of their efforts.

(2) *Traditional "supplementary" materials are increasing in quantity and quality.* Good social studies teachers have always known that a course cannot be encapsulated between the covers of a single book and that other learning resources must be an integral part of social studies learning. Yet there were certain inherent problems in using written materials other than texts—library books were expensive and obtaining more than one copy was virtually impossible; school boards and officials were often quite unwilling to grant that materials other than texts were needed.

All this is quite obviously changing. Additional materials and library resources are now purchased with money from the federal government. Paperbacks have moved *en masse* from the drug store counters to the social studies classrooms. Not only are single titles available inexpensively and in large quantities, but publishers are now producing series of paperbacks dealing with special topics in various fields. So great has been the outpouring of paperbacks in recent years that one recent article lists more than 50 series dealing solely with the teaching of world affairs.[2]

Audio-visual aids for teaching social studies have greatly improved as well. Dreary educational films and filmstrips have been transformed into bright, cogent learning resources. The variety of commercial maps and globes has increased greatly, accompanied by an improvement in quality.

(3) *Newer types of media are becoming more widely used.* Increasingly, social studies teachers are experimenting with unfamiliar types of materials.

The case study is a superb tool for putting students in a position where they must analyze a situation and resolve it in their own terms, rather than merely accumulate information about the event. The case study also is an excellent way to provide the depth of knowledge so lacking in text material. Gaming and simulation devices are also entering social studies classrooms. Far from being revolutionary as many teachers assume, games actually bear a gross similarity to the role playing techniques used by so many good teachers. For example, the question, "John, suppose you were King George III. What would you do in these circumstances?" is definitely related to the techniques used in gaming. The differences between such techniques and classroom games are essentially the difference between informality and formality, simplicity and complexity. Another materials innovation, programmed instruction, has not had the impact on social studies that it has had on other areas of the curriculum, but, as more and better programs are prepared, the use of such material will undoubtedly increase.

The selections in Part Four have been chosen as they bear on the three areas above. It is obvious that the potential field of commentary about social studies materials has not been adequately sampled. Bibliographies of materials become out-dated quickly, and only one is included in this part, chosen because it suggests books for an area of the curriculum ignored by other compilers. No article on using maps and globes or other audio-visual materials has been included, but, since several general works and most methods books treat the use of such materials, selections were chosen which deal with less well-known areas. Consequently, Part Four presents articles selected (1) to help in-service and prospective teachers to become analytical about the reading material they have at their disposal; and (2) to inform them about the rationale and potential use of important innovations in the field.

The first seven articles (Section A) are concerned with textbook analysis and constitute a solid introduction into present-day criticism and commentary. In the first selection, Palmer sets up several criteria for the selection of materials; his basic point is that materials must be chosen only after consideration of the aims of the course, students to be taught, and methods employed. The next two articles (by Sady and Shaver) examine texts in world history and American government. Their articles deal respectively with the quality of anthropological knowledge and the provision for analysis of value conflicts in American society.

Perhaps the most damning general criticism of American texts is that the role of the Negro is largely ignored. The slave has been pictured in the "Sambo" tradition as simple, happy, and accepting of his servitude. After the Civil War, the Negro goes "underground" in many texts and does not reappear until 1954. The concern here is only partly for historical accuracy; also at stake is the psychological damage done to Negro youth who find no source of pride or identification in the prevalent, distorted view of our past. The articles by Millard and Davis deal with aspects of this problem.

Section B contains five articles about learning resources other than texts. In the lead article, Larkin suggests uses for paperbacks in the "vitalization" of social studies. The various styles of case studies and their uses are discussed by Oliver and Newmann; they conclude that case studies are especially valuable in teaching students to generalize. The next article, by Majak, discusses and analyzes the use of a gaming device in social studies. In the final selection, Newmann discusses the potentialities for programmed instruction in social studies.

References

[1] Marshall McLuhan, *Understanding Media: The Extensions of Man* (New York: McGraw-Hill Book Co., 1964); and *The Medium is the Message: An Inventory of Effects* (New York: Random House, 1967).

[2] H. Thomas Collins, "Paperback Series on World Affairs," *Bulletin of the National Association of Secondary School Principals,* January, 1967.

ESTABLISHING ADEQUATE CRITERIA FOR
SELECTING SOCIAL STUDIES MATERIALS

John R. Palmer
University of Wisconsin, Madison

The selection of social studies materials can be lifted above the level of mere chance or exercise of fancy only when the interplay among objectives, methods, materials, and the students to be taught is clearly understood.[1] Certain criteria are obvious and beyond dispute—with very few exceptions the materials must be accurate and reflect contemporary scholarship and the level of difficulty and the emotional and social maturity required must be appropriate for the students. While such criteria are not always simple to carry out, they are reasonably clear cut. But the primary decisions that must be made in selecting materials are those of establishing aims and translating them into behavioral terms, selecting methods, and determining what types of instructional materials will accomplish the designated aims and be compatible with the methods. There is no defensible procedure for choosing materials that does not involve making such decisions. This is the crux of the matter. If the objective is to change a certain attitude or value, how, in fact, can this be accomplished? Are film strips effective, and, if so, what type of film? Do facts influence attitudes, and, if so, how can they best be presented? What classroom method is most appropriate to the objective and the materials chosen? It is only to the extent that questions of this sort are dealt with that one can claim to be selecting materials on defensible and adequate grounds. The purpose of the discussion which follows is to explore each of the major factors pertinent to the selection process and offer some guidelines to direct that process.

Reprinted by permission of the publisher, from *High School Journal,* 49 (October, 1965) (Chapel Hill: University of North Carolina Press): 6-12.

ESTABLISHING OBJECTIVES

The criticism of social studies materials has been undertaken by liberals, conservatives, social studies teachers, professors, journalists, and other assorted individuals. The criticisms themselves are as diverse as their sources: the materials are too difficult; the materials are too simple; inaccuracies, half-truths, and poor scholarship are much in evidence; the message conveyed to the student is too nationalistic and chauvinistic; the materials are un-American; the writing is sterile and dull; too much space is given over to illustrative devices; the authors have been unselective and encyclopedic; very significant material has been slighted; and so on. The nature of these criticisms suggests certain problems of significance for selecting materials in the social studies.

Why, for instance, are the complaints so inconsistent and contradictory? Why haven't the materials been changed and the attackers silenced? While almost certainly a complex of factors is involved, many of the weaknesses individuals claim they find in social studies materials stem from disagreements about the aims of social studies instruction. Any book or film which does not appear to enhance the purposes accepted by the critic is immediately suspect. Not only are there many conceptions of the purpose of the social studies, but few people seem fully aware of the meaning and import of what they profess to believe in this regard.

Arthur Bolster has concluded, for example, that three of the major reasons historians use to justify the teaching of history are: (1) only historical studies permit the individual to examine social issues in the perspective of time; (2) historical method requires exercise of critical judgment which is necessary for democratic citizenship; and (3) commitment to democratic ideals is enhanced by the study of western civilization. After examining each of these in terms of educational practice and the difficulties involved in carrying them out, Bolster concludes that none of them is being realized. The task proposed by the first objective is simply impossible to carry out, the teaching methods used to develop the second are inconsistent with the objective itself, and the third is functionally inconsistent with the second.[2] The implication is clear that either the historians in question do not understand their professed purposes in teaching history or they do not really mean them. Were they to select materials consistent with their objectives, these would be less than satisfactory because the objectives are not being carried out. It is more likely that the materials being used are selected on some other basis than the professed objectives. In either case the relationship between materials and objectives is rather muddled.

In a more comprehensive analysis, Shirley Engle brought together statements of social studies objectives gleaned from the writings of prominent persons in the field and national committees.[3] He concluded that the aims are so diverse that they do not form a single continuum but must be grouped in dichotomous fashion into process objectives and content objectives. Within each of these the range is very broad. Many lists mix the two types of objectives and are so comprehensive that it is very doubtful if they give any direction to the curriculum. At best, a teacher can select out those that appeal to his biases and ignore the rest. At worst, he may actually attempt to incorporate all the objectives into his teaching and as a consequence present a buzzing confusion to the students. Virtually any piece of social studies material would be acceptable in terms of such sweeping claims. It is difficult if not impossible to discriminate between appropriate and inappropriate materials if the objectives sought are vague, inconsistent, or too comprehensive.

In contrast to current practice, objectives selected to guide the social studies curriculum should be few in number, clearly understood, and arranged in order of importance. It should also be noted that the problem of formulating aims is partly philosophical in character. It involves taking a position with respect to the purpose and function of the school in our society, the nature of the learning process, and the nature of the social sciences themselves. It requires an understanding of the kinds of knowledge contained in social studies materials and the relationship of that knowledge to behavior.

While there are obviously serious problems of consistency and comprehensiveness in many statements of aims, Engle's concluding remark suggests the further problem of translating any aim of whatever sort into practice. "Future studies should focus on operationalizing the objectives of social studies instruction by relating goals to curricula, to methods of instruction, and to more specific student behavioral outcomes."[4] Unfortunately aims such as "To assume social and civic responsibility" or "to teach critical thinking" are meaningless clichés for many. Little progress has been made in defining precisely what these objectives mean in terms of student behaviors and teaching method. The few individuals who have seriously attempted to negotiate the gap between professed aims and classroom practices only serve to bring the less desirable but more common practice of "just doing something and hoping" into sharper focus.

Even the most cherished social studies objective, education for citizenship, is not free from serious attack. Two political scientists, Evron and Jeane Kirkpatrick, have challenged the traditional role of the social studies in developing good citizens "first, because it is based on a distorted conception of how citizens are made; second, because it is based on a distorted conception of democracy; and, third, because it is based on a misconception of political science."[5] As they indicate, if their position is correct, those who set out to produce good citizens in social studies courses are "foredoomed to failure." A number of recent studies in political socialization indirectly challenge the validity of using formal schooling for citizenship education and raise serious doubts about the conventional meaning of this almost universally accepted objective.

It appears that educators are very unsophisticated with respect to what can be accomplished by direct teaching in the way of developing habits, values, and dispositions among the young. While there is much yet to be learned about the role of formal education in the acculturation process, there is now enough research evidence to raise serious questions about those social studies objectives related to acculturation as well as the methods being used to accomplish them. It is not quite correct, either, to plead that we have been trapped by the recent research. At least thirty years ago George Counts asserted that the essence of democracy is a sentiment with respect to the moral equality of the individual. It is the sentiment that is required of every citizen of a democracy rather than the knowledge of particular political practices and institutions. The extent to which democratic sentiment can be developed through formal instruction is probably slight, or at least there is little clear proof of it.

ANALYZING THE MATERIALS

The use of audio-visual materials illustrates well the difficulties of moving from aims to developing a course which will realize those aims. Research clearly supports the principle that motion pictures, television, and many other visual media teach information of "facts" as effectively as the reading of printed material followed by discussion. Retention is also very good. However, the moment one shifts to the teaching of values, attitudes, and dispositions, the situation becomes very uncertain. In selecting teaching materials for inclusion in a unit on "The Progressive Era," for example, one asks, "Will films or filmstrips assist in realizing the objectives of the unit?" If the students are to learn items of information as arbitrary associations, the answer is "Yes," but it is difficult to know how to respond if the outcomes are in the affective domain. There is too little research evidence to enable one to make sure judgments, but what is known should make the teacher very cautious about expecting audio-visual materials to change student values and attitudes.

Experiments which attempted, by using motion pictures, to change certain attitudes of automobile drivers which would in turn influence their driving behavior produced discouraging results. Although conditions were more carefully controlled and the films more thoroughly analyzed than is feasible in most classroom situations, the effect on the subjects was negligible.[6] The armed forces have also demonstrated on a number of occasions that motion pictures made for the purpose of influencing attitudes have little or no effect on behavior.

Too little attention has been given to the peculiar characteristics of the various learning materials that might be used in the social studies. Textbooks are still central in most social studies classes, and, like all printed material, they may be used to communicate narration and description, prescriptions and directives, generalizations, and theories. Each of these types of verbal communication has a particular function and is necessary for the realization of certain learning objectives.[7]

Narration and description, for example, are frequently used as artistic tools in order that the reader may share in the experience of others. The great historical writer has the ability, through his handling of these tools, to give the reader the feeling that he is taking part in the storming of the Bastille or sharing the loneliness of the pioneer housewife living in a sod house on the Nebraska prairie. The teaching power of narration is not limited to relating cognitive elements but is particularly useful for developing emotionalized meanings. While this is very desirable in some instances, it also involves the danger that the teacher may not be fully aware of the values being communicated by the materials.

Prescriptions and directives, on the other hand, provide direct suggestions for action. While this type of material may be required in teaching skills, it is doubtful that much is accomplished when a student reads, "A good citizen should always vote." Social behavior is too variable and subject to changing situations for such directives to be suitable in most instances. Prescriptive teaching is appropriate when the task can be carried out immediately, or when it is very clear that the situation to which it is to be applied is fixed and determined. Few social behaviors dealt with in the social studies satisfy these criteria.

The primary purpose of learning generalizations appears to be in order to use them to direct behavior, but the mere knowledge of a given generalization does not insure that it will influence the behavior of the learner. The effectiveness of material which intends to convey generalizations is improved if the writer establishes a challenge situation which arouses the curiosity of the reader and then suggests a generalization in order to clarify the matter. The generalization then has the function in the text of explaining or bringing order. A text which consistently introduces generalizations to the reader in this manner presumably is quite effective in teaching generalizations.

While there is much more that could be said about each of the types of material found in textbooks, perhaps this brief mention of a few key points is sufficient to establish the importance of looking into the matter further. Anyone who selects text materials should understand clearly the kind of behavior he is trying to produce in the learner, and in light of this consider carefully which type or types of material are appropriate to produce the desired responses.

SELECTING THE METHODS

Strong supporters of a particular teaching method will argue very force-fully that the dimension of teaching procedure must also be considered when selecting classroom materials. Even if aims are clearly defined in behavioral terms, the way in which the teacher brings student and materials together to accomplish the aims is as significant as any other element in the situation. Recently, such techniques as the case study, reflective method and the utilization of certain logical operations have been added to the more tra-ditional emphases on recitation, lecture, and discussion. It is obvious that certain of these are relatively untested with respect to how well they assist in realizing particular aims, although it should be acknowledged that some bear close resemblance to teaching procedures dating at least as far back as the Greek schoolmasters, Socrates and Isocrates.

To a considerable extent classroom method is dictated by objectives. While no teacher uses one method exclusively, it usually is possible to characterize a teacher's method as primarily recitation or focused on reflective thinking or what have you. It also seems reasonably certain that the lecture-dominated classroom, to take one example, is not most conducive to the development of critical thinking, although in the hands of some teachers a lecture does stimulate critical thought on the part of students. Through the ages every distinctive method has suffered at the hands of devoted followers, and the present day is no exception. Few practitioners interpret and apply a tech-nique in precisely the way the originator intended and teachers generally employ one method or another in the most haphazard way. Educational outcomes would be improved if methods were carefully selected in con-junction with aims and materials and if teachers clearly understood and were proficient in the execution of the methods selected.

SUMMARY

While it is possible to describe what is involved in establishing adequate criteria for selecting social studies materials, it is not now possible to carry through the procedure in an entirely satisfactory manner. As has been indicated, our knowledge of the cause-effect relationships that obtain among the factors of aims, methods, materials, and students existing in a particular social context is simply not fully adequate to the task. But the procedure must go on and decisions must be made. I have tried to indicate that there is a good deal of reliable information now available that can be used to improve the decisions being made. Even more fundamental, however, is an understanding of the significant factors involved in selecting materials so that what is relevant will be taken into account.

References

[1] It might well be argued that the most significant factor, the personality and peculiar psychological make-up of the teacher, has been excluded from consideration. My only defense is the difficulty of saying anything sensible about this very elusive factor and the belief that it is intimately involved in the method used. Some attention is given the matter in Seymour B. Sarason, Kenneth Davidson, and Burton Blatt, *The Preparation of Teachers.* (New York: John Wiley and Sons, 1962).

[2] A. S. Bolster, Jr., "History, Historians, and the Secondary School Curriculum," *Harvard Educational Review,* Winter, 1962, pp. 39-65.

[3] Shirley H. Engle, "Objectives of the Social Studies," in *New Challenge in the Social Studies,* Byron G. Massialas and Frederick R. Smith, eds. (Belmont, California: Wadsworth Publishing Company, 1965), pp. 1-19.

[4] *Ibid.,* p. 17.

[5] Evron M. Kirkpatrick and Jeane J. Kirkpatrick, "Political Science," in *High School Social Studies Perspectives,* Erling M. Hunt, *et. al.,* (Boston: Houghton Mifflin Company, 1962), pp. 99-125.

[6] H. H. McAshan, "An Experimental Study of Traffic Safety Films," *Journal of Experimental Education,* XXXI, No. 1 (1962), 43-53; Irving R. Merrill, "Attitude Films and Attitude Change," *Audio-Visual Communication Review,* X, No. 1 (1962), 3-13; and Loran C. Twyford, *et al.,* "Behavioral and Factual Analysis," *Audio-Visual Communication Review,* VII, No. 3 (1959), 182-193.

[7] Lee J. Cronbach, ed., *Text Materials in Modern Education.* (Urbana: University of Illinois Press, 1955), pp. 28-58.

ANTHROPOLOGY AND WORLD HISTORY TEXTS

Rachel Reese Sady
Anthropology Curriculum Study Project

Anthropologists and educators are increasingly concerned with how anthropology can best contribute to the teaching of secondary school social studies courses. One part of this concern is with world history textbooks, both because anthropology and history share the same subject matter and because texts are so influential in molding courses.

The feeling is widespread that anthropology can help improve these texts, but the question is, how? Ordinarily, anthropology enters world history courses at the same point that Neanderthal man rears his heavy-browed head, and leaves it not far from his heels. The recent emphasis on non-Western cultures has led some course designers to turn for particular data to anthropologists who are area specialists. But anthropologists feel that their discipline has a greater potential, a potential that can be proven in the explanation, exploration, and illustration of concepts that students can apply throughout their social studies. To clarify the nature of this potential, five world history textbooks, widely used in secondary schools, were examined from an anthropological point of view, and eight other texts were skimmed.[1]

The five texts analyzed are good books. They are well-organized, well-written, and packed with information and interpretation. The task of synthesis and selection of facts involved in writing a secondary school world history is not an easy one, however, and looked at from the particular point of view of anthropology, each text has certain deficiencies. The texts were examined in regard to their scope—that is, "whose world" they consider, their use of anthropological concepts, and their use of anthropological data.

WHOSE WORLD?

The majority of the texts look at the world narrowly, blocking off as insignificant those areas and those times that seem unconnected with the main line of development of Western civilization. These books do not ignore Asia and Africa; neither has Western civilization ignored them. A typical

Reprinted with permission of the author and the publisher, from *Phi Delta Kappan*, 45 (February, 1964): 247-251.

world history starts off with the birth of the earth, skips quickly through the beginnings of life, and then goes on to discuss early man and the development of early civilizations (always in Egypt and Mesopotamia, often in the Indus and Hwang Ho valleys, and more rarely in the American Indian centers). Once Greece is reached, the chapters march on with Western civilization, and the rest of the world is held in abeyance until "discovered," by Europeans, of course. In brief, the main content of a typical text follows the life-line of Western civilization.

There is nothing wrong with stories of the development of Western civilization. But when a text claims—as most do—to be "the story of mankind," such a strong Western orientation is misleading. The problem arises, just whose world is being described? When an area is discussed in a world history textbook only at the point that it comes in contact with Western civilization, the impression is inevitable that this area is important only because of Western contact. Well over half-way through a very well-written text, this statement occurs:

> Earlier parts of this book concentrated on certain areas on the globe. Even the great empire of Rome covered only a section of the earth. In modern times, history is in the fullest sense *world* history and Part Eight covers events that affected all lands and peoples. (*Emphasis the text's.*)

Part Eight is entitled "Great Power Rivalries," and imperialism is the context in which India, China, Japan, and Africa are considered. India, China, and Japan receive backward glances, but Africa is apparently born with the partition of that continent.

Publishers and textbook writers have not ignored the pleas for history in a wider context. The book quoted above has a great deal of material on modern world problems. The most recent edition of a widely used twenty-five-year-old textbook is a compromise between the old book and new demands: as in previous editions, there is a chapter each for Great Britain, France, and other European countries or blocks of countries, but an earlier chapter on Latin America is much expanded and three new parts have been added in a bow to the modern world—the Far East, Africa, and India and Southeast Asia. However, these new parts do little to change the main emphasis of the text, which is on what Western civilization "owes" to ancient civilizations, and on the development of nationalism along with Western civilization.

Efforts to keep up to date with the importance of non-Western areas are obvious in several volumes. Last chapters are expanded to take into account each new nation or event. These efforts sometimes founder as when last-minute assessments conflict with even later news reports. Only two of the books reviewed make a sharp break with the typical Western-oriented tradition and use an area approach.

In summary, the farsightedness and clearsightedness of historians and educators about the need for a wider view of the world has resulted in a patching operation on Western civilization histories in order to bring in the rest of the world, and in two new approaches to world history in which area organization is important. The trend is clear, but it is far from complete, and there is still need to emphasize that world history is not Western history.

THE CONCEPT OF CULTURE

The transformation of "our world" into "the world" brings with it increased use of anthropological materials. There is some evidence, however, that in the adoption of anthropological concepts in support of world history teaching, there is not always a clear understanding of those concepts. As the use of anthropology becomes more common, this lack of understanding becomes more serious.

Anthropology is the comparative study of all mankind. It is not restricted to early man and the American Indians, or to exotic peoples. Except for physical anthropology, all branches of the study center on culture. Culture is the total way of life of a people, the content and pattern of their learned behavior and beliefs. How cultures form and how they change is a major part of history. More than that, the idea of culture is itself a useful tool in understanding world history because it explains how peoples act and are likely to act, what values and judgments they employ and are likely to employ. It helps to explain or point out what is universally human about mankind in its response to basic needs, and to indicate why differences have come about. These explanations all lead toward a greater understanding of other peoples, and of ourselves.

Many other ideas flow from this fundamental notion of culture. Some of them are: the way cultures are integrated and their underlying value systems, ethnocentrism and cultural relativism, the distribution of common cultural elements, and the ways culture spreads and the nature of culture change.

The Other Culture

The concept of culture seems simple, but it is apparently deceptively simple, from the evidence of the world history textbooks. The fault lies in the etymology of the word itself, which has accustomed us to think automatically of the artistic or the intellectual life as the "cultured" one. Culture derives from "cultivate," meaning "create." Most people when they think of culture think of those things or ideas consciously created by artistic or intellectual effort. But anthropologists use the term to mean the whole body of institutions, customs, beliefs, and artifacts developing therefrom that have been created by man. The culture of anthropology includes the other "culture," but it also includes all those ways of everyday living that each person acquires from the society into which he is born.

The other "culture" is a significant concept and deserves the attention it receives in the history books. However, it is important not to confuse the two aspects of the word because of the implications of such confusion. When we speak of the other "culture," we are likely to have a ranking of societies against a very specific yardstick, one perhaps marked off in our own aesthetic values. This is a legitimate measurement against which to judge societies, if one cares to use it, and many do. It is not, however, the whole story, and as a descriptive device it omits much that would make the ways of the peoples of the world understandable to us.

What is the evidence from the textbooks about their use of the concept of culture? None makes an attempt, beyond a quick definition, to explore culture as an idea. Most of the definitions are anthropological, but actual use of the word thereafter often does not correspond with the definition. In one text there is a fundamental misunderstanding; the whole brunt of the word's use, in spite of sporadic corrective gestures, is that the economic and political history of a nation is not discussed in terms of culture, and that a nation's "contributions to" or "achievements in" the fields of literature, music, art, philosophy, and science are so discussed. The practical effect of this is evident. We are not asked to admire the first category, whole culture and its history; we *are* asked to admire the "culture" as fine arts. So the gulf between peoples is to be bridged by selective "understanding:"

> Many Americans have difficulty finding anything to admire in the political and economic institutions of Communist Russia. But we must not forget that Russian authors, musicians, and scientists have given the world fine books, important ideas, and beautiful music.

This is a good bridge, but not adequate to the traffic.

Of the textbooks studied, the one which does most in the direction of widening the scope of world history and presenting the cultural background of societies uses the term culture prolifically but inconsistently. Culture is defined as "the way of life of a society—the habits, ideas, and practices of its members," and the observation is made that this definition is broad enough to cover any form of human organization. This good definition is marred by the following statement that "a culture, however, ceases to be such and becomes a civilization when it reaches a further state of development." This assumption that culture excludes civilization is not borne out by the texts's own further usage.

Moreover, throughout this book the use of culture veers back and forth from the anthropological to the other meaning. At the two extremes are the section on Africa, which is definitely written from an anthropological point of view, and the section on the United States, where the phenomenon termed "mass culture" adds still another meaning. The authors at a few points indicate an awareness that there is a problem of usage, but this never jells into a real understanding, partly prevented by the practice in book organization of treating culture in chapters separate from those on economy and politics. Quite near the end of the volume, cultural differences are discussed:

> The term "culture" as used here does not refer to the arts, such as painting, sculpture, or poetry. Rather, it refers to a people's total way of life—to the way in which they think and believe and act.

Had the text followed this definition throughout, this remarkably successful volume would have been much improved.

Culture patterns and values

The pattern of a culture is the way in which cultural elements are integrated—their relationship to each other and to the underlying values or goals of a culture. The texts vary to the extent that they attempt to describe a way of life in terms of that culture's own values. All of them recognize integrating principles in the development of Western civilization, but only some of them discuss the difference between culture as it really is lived and culture as it is supposed to be lived—that is, between real and ideal culture.

One text tends to regard the motivations of African and Asians as replicas of our own, but historically more recent. We are told that ". . . all peoples want a good life," but there is no indication that definitions of the good life may vary. Another text also looks at other cultures with our own values in mind, but occasionally tries to describe the assumptions and values of others' ways. The books organized by area fully appreciate that peoples have developed different ways in response to common needs. One discusses pattern in terms of "style" of civilization and effectively portrays certain societies from the point of view of what those societies consider important.

The old province of anthropologists, the American Indian, does not fare well in any of the texts. In one book with a special Latin American section, Indians are consistently referred to as "poor and barefoot" or living in "ignorance and poverty." The absence of further portrayal gives the impression that poverty and ignorance (of the kind of things that Westerners know) create a vacuum that cannot or need not be described until the things our culture deems important begin to fill it. In other places in all the texts the term "different traditions and customs," without further specifications, is used liberally either because of space or data limitations.

Ethnocentrism and Cultural Relativism

Enthnocentrism means the tendency for a people to take for granted that their way is the human or right way. Cultural relativism is the other side of the coin, and means that the "right way" depends on the culture in which one is brought up, and that peoples should be considered in that light.

No text can or should escape being ethnocentric. Nevertheless, it is desirable that the texts be understanding enough of other cultures and critical enough of our own to provide a basis for some objectivity in facing world problems. As discussed above, all the texts but two exhibit ethnocentrism in their answer to the question, whose world? It is also ethnocentric to be overprotective of our own history, and two of the books seem to err in this direction. Such assessments are a matter of judgment, however, and are bound to vary. The problem of ethnocentrism can be attacked directly by discussion of the idea itself, but none of the texts does this, although all contain illustrations of it, as below:

> ... through the centuries, the Chinese people were taught that China was literally the central country of the universe, and all other lands were merely outlying regions. Hand in hand with this idea went the firm belief that Chinese society was the only good way to live. All other peoples were considered barbarians.

This important concept of ethnocentrism is rarely recognized in connection with other countries, and is particularly missing where needed most—for our own. At best, there are references to the Chinese view of Europeans as "long-nosed barbarians" and this thought-provoking passage in one text:

> Not understanding the native traditions, [the Europeans] felt that the "savage" needed to learn European ways, to become Christian, and to experience the blessings of European medical knowledge and higher standards of living. . . . Each of the European nations believed its culture was the most advanced, and each therefore felt it was best fitted to help the natives.

The two volumes that deal with non-Western cultures extensively are both very good in pointing out that these cultures must be regarded from the viewpoint of their own value systems, that behavior is relative to culture.

Culture Areas

The idea of culture area refers to a geographic area—transcending political boundaries—whose populations exhibit in common a number of culture traits. The idea can be used in different ways, depending on how many cultural elements are shared and which of them are considered meaningful. That is, culture areas are not rigid, mutually exclusive divisions of the same degree of commonality. They are useful ways of looking at the world and their extent depends on who has decided what elements or group of elements are important for what particular purpose.

Most of the texts do not use the idea, although history is inevitably discussed in terms of distinct civilizations and the areas encompassed by them. One text pioneers in organization and approach based on large culture areas, but assimilates land mass, regardless of related cultures, to the idea. This volume selects seven "great societies" and then attempts to discuss each one in terms of its roots, a traditional period, and the impact of Western civilization or modern technology. This is an effective scheme, except that current culture areas or societies do not necessarily correspond with pre-historic ones. Fossil man and the American Indians are fitted into niches defensible on the basis of geography, not culture. Another text, partly organized by culture area, solves this problem of "roots" by prefacing the area approach with a chronological exposition.

Culture Change

All histories are a documentation of cultural change, but they vary in their recognition of the processes involved and in the assumptions made about the nature of those processes. In all of the texts, culture change is considered against a background of "progress" or "advancement." Progress must be toward something, but the texts usually assume that we know what that something is. In general, one text uses scientific and technological knowhow as a yardstick for progress, another uses achievement of a "better life," and another emphasizes nationalism. In all three, progress and the development of Western civilization are virtually synonymous. Two of the more recent texts have a wider context in keeping with their wider worlds, and it is simply civilization and progress that go hand in hand.

All of these texts recognize in final chapters that, from the point of view of modern war and peace, progress and civilization have somehow parted company. This recognition seems to open no doors to doubt about the suitability of coupling the two ideas throughout the rest of history. In other words, all of the texts tend to overuse evaluating words as opposed to descriptive words in recounting the development of cultures. If one part of a culture (technology) is valued highly (for efficiency), the assumption is often made that the rest of the culture should be equally rated, although the reason for this is not made clear. While it is important to understand that a culture tends to be integrated, such integration does not mean that the same standards can be applied meaningfully throughout the culture. A list of overt and covert culture traits does not readily fit onto an "advancement" continuum with its assumption of superiority. If it is forced to fit, mistaken connotations occur, understanding is hindered instead of helped, and critical thinking about ourselves and others is hampered. Criteria that are uncertain and descriptive terms that are value-laden reduce the usefulness that generalized comments about progress might otherwise have.

It is no belittlement of our own advanced technology and democratic values to realize that if all history is written with progress understood in terms of the values of one culture, naturally other cultures won't be "advanced" until they conform. Pointing this out should not discourage one from making evaluations, since these are necessary as a basis for action, when the standards used are made clear. The fact remains that culture change is not comparable to climbing a ladder, and history can better be understood in terms of the substance of changes than in terms of progress toward unstated goals. It is more important to be clear about the denotations of civilization (urbanization, specialization, and so on) than to assume its connotations (generalized advancement or progress).

The actual processes of culture change—innovation, internal growth, diffusion, the recasting and integration of borrowed elements—are not discussed as such in most of the texts, but there are many good descriptions of particular changes and the factors involved. Occasionally culture change is described so as to indicate planned change or stubborn resistance to change which may not have been the case. This is undoubtedly merely a matter of writing style, but the result is not a sense of the processes involved, but a sense of unreasoning perversity on the part of the people. Two examples are:

> Yet the Chinese peasant could not be easily persuaded to change the honored ways of his forefathers. Nor would he organize with hundreds of other farmers to meet new conditions with new methods.
> ... The American Indians did not want to adapt themselves.

Related inversely to these examples are the following:

> [The peoples of Eastern Europe] have often tried to become part of Western European society.
> But Asoka tried a different way of uniting his great empire. He tried the Buddhist religion.

In conclusion about the use of concepts, it is clear that an alert student may very well wring a knowledge of the nature of culture from these books— more easily from some than from others—but the books are not planned to facilitate it, with the exception of some sections of the most recent. A systematic explanation of the concepts themselves is missing.

ANTHROPOLOGICAL DATA

In addition to clarifying the nature of culture so that it can be a useful tool in understanding world history, anthropologists can supply data that illuminate particular areas. The extent to which the texts deal with the wider world has increased their dependence on the kinds of data anthropologists in particular are likely to compile—that is, information about peoples whose cultures vary a great deal from our own.

It is evident from reading through the texts that anthropologists should be more forward in making available their data and that authors and publishers should be more aware of the need for checking data. Errors occur in particular about early man, evolution and race, and linguistics.

Some descriptions of early man are fanciful instead of accurate. One intimates that large-brained Neanderthal man had a small brain-case. Another makes the statement about Heidelberg man, who has been represented since 1907 by a solitary jawbone, that he is "presumed to be the oldest *complete* skeleton yet unearthed." (Emphasis the text's.) And there is little reason to resort to dinosaurs to pique students' interest. Decorating the beginning page of a section entitled "Old Stone Age Men Were Hunters" in one text are two pictures of dinosaurs. This juxtaposition would fool no high-school student in this dinosaur-aware age, but the review question, "What is historically wrong with the comic strip that shows a cave man riding a dinosaur?" might better have been asked about the text's own layout.

Brief explanations of evolution and race are always well-intentioned, always inadequate, and usually inaccurate. One text asks a review question, "Why is there no such thing as a pure or superior race?" when the body of the text has given the student no basis at all for thinking about such a question.

Much more care should be taken in the way that identifying labels are applied to groups. Linguistic, physical, national, and cultural names are mixed with abandon, even though—and sometimes immediately after—most texts state very clearly that these are separate categories and not to be confused. For example, after one text has stated that race must not be confused with language, religion, and nation, and that there can be one race and many languages and vice versa, these passages occur:

> It is true that the Jews of Biblical times resided in Palestine and belonged either to the Semitic or Armenoid branches of the Mediterranean Caucasoids.
> England . . . was occupied in very early times by Nordics, Mediterraneans, and Alpines. Later it was invaded by Saxons, Norwegians, Danes, and Normans. Thus instead of one physical type in England, we see there an excellent mosaic of Caucasoid subraces.

In another text, Slavs are variously referred to as being so identified because of race, language, background, or nationality.

One text mistakenly refers to the Ainus of Japan as Indo-European, apparently under the impression that this purely linguistic term means Caucasoid, a physically-descriptive term. This error is illustrative of the less obvious kind of misuse of labels that occurs constantly. When the linguistic term Dravidian, for example, is used to apply to "dark-skinned peoples of India," which is a physical description, that is not accurate. It really means that most Dravidian-speaking people in India also have dark skins. The fact that there may be a near coincidence of the linguistic and the physical groups does not diminish the need for distinguishing between the two categories. Racial, cultural, and linguistic relationships have a history too burdened by misunderstanding to add to the confusion in any way.

The examples given above are important only in that they illustrate the kinds of things an anthropological editing might catch. More important.

anthropological data on particular cultures can fill in outlines necessarily only sketched in the textbooks.

CONCLUSIONS

In teaching social studies, including world history, the schools wish not only to inform and instruct but to promote good intentions and good works in the world community. To do this, attitudes that question, consider alternatives, and seek information instead of make assumptions are to be encouraged. In the context of world history, a comparative look at world cultures—at the various solutions man has made to the same problems—is essential to the stimulation of critical thinking.

Anthropologists can join historians and social studies teachers in impressing on writers and publishers the need for widening their concept of world history to include the non-Western world. And anthropologists must share the task of providing data on those cultures. As more and more people are won over to this point of view, however—and the trend is evident—anthropologists have a special responsibility. This responsibility is to head off confusion about the nature of culture, and to prepare material that will add to our understanding of other peoples and ourselves. The Anthropology Curriculum Study Project of the American Anthropological Association is engaged in this work at present. As material pointed specifically toward social studies in the secondary schools is developed, teachers will be appraised of it.

References

[1] The five texts analyzed are: Boak, Slosson, Anderson and Bartlett, *The History of Our World,* 1959; Mazour and Peoples, *Men and Nations,* 1961; Rogers, Adams, and Brown, *Story of Nations,* 1960; Ewing, *Our Widening World,* 1960; and Stravrianos, Andrews, Blanksten, Hackett, Leppert, Murphy, and Smith, *A Global History of Man,* 1962. The eight other texts were published between 1940 and 1962.

In order to save space, documentation, even in the case or direct quotations, is omitted. This was done so that examples can be cited without concern for the balanced judgment of the books that only complete documentation could give. Complete documentation is available to those interested from the Anthropology Curriculum Study Project, 5632 Kimbark Avenue, Chicago, Illinois 60637.

REFLECTIVE THINKING, VALUES, AND SOCIAL STUDIES TEXTBOOKS

James P. Shaver
Utah State University

Intelligent debate over public policy in a democratic society should take into account the full scope and complexity of societal evaluative commitments. It is important, therefore, not only that citizens be able to relate specific decisions to their own value positions but that they have some understanding of the nature of the "American Creed," that is, the general values of our society, to which each of us has some commitment. Yet the relationships of these values to each other, and to policy stands, are frequently misunderstood. For example, on the campus of a western state university during the 1962–63 academic year, a well-known educator—former professor of philosophy and college president—stated during an address that southern leaders opposing racial integration in southern colleges were acting outside the ethical framework of this society. That is, their positions and acts in this opposition were absolutely wrong and could not be justified by any general values of the American society. Such a statement, although perhaps more upsetting from the lips of a person with a rich educational background, could have been heard in any number of discussions of this country's racial problems.

To see questions of public policy as having absolute right or wrong answers vis-a-vis general American values is to ignore the fundamental operational basis of our democratic, pluralistic society. The conflict of values engendered as individuals or groups with different backgrounds (i.e., coming from different subcultures) differ in their interpretations of central values, such as freedom or equality, or argue in a particular situation that one value is more important than another, is inevitable.[1] In the dispute over racial segregation, the Negro's claims for integration are supported by our commitment to brotherhood, to equality of opportunity, and to equal protection of the law. By the same token, however, the segregationist's position has been defended in terms of freedom of association, of property rights, and even of the right to local control in such matters. Each of these is also an important American value.

Reprinted with permission of the author and the publisher, from *The School Review*, 73 (Autumn, 1965): 226-236, 250-253.

Gunnar Myrdal, in *An American Dilemma*[2] has posed clearly the apparent conflicts between our general values and our actions in specific situations. It is clear as well, however, that the general values themselves conflict when applied to specific situations, and that in many situations the enhancement of one is to the detriment of another.[3] For example, Robinson, Morton, and Calderwood in their *An Introduction to Economic Reasoning*[4] continually stress the conflicting objectives of society that must be considered in making public policy decisions of an economic nature. McCloskey notes lack of consensus among Americans on the fundamental values of the society, as well as the logical inconsistency among the components making up what democratic ideology does exist in the minds of individual leaders of society.[5] William J. Brennan, Jr., associate justice of the U.S. Supreme Court, has emphasized the balancing of societal goals that must take place in arriving at judicial decisions involving civil rights.[6]

In general, then, debate over public issues in this society takes place between opposing subgroups, each of which sees its position as contributing most to the central long-range goal of a democratic society—the dignity and worth of the individual. This very disagreement, so crucial to the free expression of a wide range of possible solutions and so typical of the pluralistic society, is supported by our commitment as a society to personal freedom. Rarely can one subgroup of the antagonists on a particular public issue be judged *absolutely* wrong if the total array of this society's values are taken into account. To state this another way, most positions can be reasonably defended within the context of the "American Creed." There may well be a little disagreement on some issues. Criminal action destroying the peace and order of the society requires the restriction of individual freedom; censorship is imposed with little contest in time of war. The basic context of value conflict is there, however, even though most men may agree clearly as to the appropriate choice at one point in time.

SOCIAL STUDIES TEXTBOOKS

In the light of the expectation, and even nourishment, of value conflict in our pluralistic society, what reasonable expectations might one have about social studies textbooks prepared for secondary-school use? A commonly stated objective of instruction in the social studies is to teach students to think "reflectively" or "critically" so that they will be better able as adult citizens to make intelligent decisions about the crucial problems facing society. If a framework of reflective thinking is to serve validly as a basis for instruction in the social studies, it must include a consideration of choices between values. Determining matters of fact and carefully defining terms to enhance communication and avoid the pitfalls of propaganda are important, but not sufficient, elements in the decision-making process. Learning to deal with the value questions central to public decision-making must involve learning to recognize and clarify value conflicts—as the former college president failed or was unable to do—as well as learning an intellectual process that will allow one to arrive at a rationally sound and personally satisfactory choice between or among the values conflicting in a particular situation.

It is not the purpose of this article to develop a conceptual strategy for handling value conflict[7] or to debate alternative strategies. To the extent that the authors and publishers of textbooks take heed of statements of objectives for social studies instruction, however, an important element in many secondary-school social studies textbooks should be the presentation of a conceptual framework for reflective thinking about societal issues, including alternatives for dealing with value conflicts. This article is a report of a review aimed at determining whether social studies textbooks adequately fulfil this mandate.

The textbook is the teaching tool most commonly available to teachers, and tends to be relied upon heavily.[8] Thus, the treatment accorded reflective thinking, and in particular, value conflicts, in the majority of social studies classrooms is likely to reflect that of the textbooks. It is possible that the social studies teacher might have learned a conceptual framework for instruction in reflective thinking as part of the social studies methods course taken in the teacher-preparation program. If one is to judge by the social studies methods textbooks available, however, this is not likely to be the case. My own conclusions in this regard were confirmed by Ballinger.[9] The authors of only two of the methods textbooks seem aware of the value conflicts involved in controversial issues, and only one of these textbooks provides the prospective teacher with an extensive treatment of intellectual strategies for dealing with evaluative decisions in the context of societal controversy.[10] It seems likely, then, that the emphasis given reflective thinking by the secondary-school textbooks is a generally valid index of the emphasis in social studies classrooms across the country.

THE STUDY

In order to determine the treatment of reflective thinking, especially its evaluative elements, in current secondary-school social studies textbooks, I reviewed the ninety-three textbooks available in the Utah State University Curriculum Library. As these included up-to-date copies of the best-known textbooks, the sample was very satisfactory. The Curriculum Library groups its social studies textbooks under several classifications. The following categories were particularly relevant to this study: American government, American problems, and citizenship (civics). A cursory inspection of U.S. and world-history textbooks was also made.

No quantitative content-analysis technique was used for the study. Each of the books in the three categories, excluding for the moment the history books, was looked through to determine its general treatment of reflective thinking, its treatment of values in this society, and any presentation of a conceptual approach to value conflict in making public policy decisions. Obviously, there are certain dangers to a procedure of this sort. The reviewer may, for example, place emphasis on part of a book out of proportion to the actual space it is accorded, or remember especially those statements that support his previous biases. On the other hand, the task did not seem to call for more systematic counting techniques. For one thing, the purpose of the investigation was to determine if certain ideas were presented or treated and not to obtain sentence or word counts to estimate extent of treatment. Careful note-taking and an awareness of one's own biases for the purpose of controlling them seem the best antidotes to the dangers of selective perception in reviewing. Both were utilized in this case.

AMERICAN GOVERNMENT TEXTBOOKS

Probably few people conversant with traditional approaches to the study of government would expect secondary textbooks in American government to provide instruction in reflective decision-making. Political scientists have tended to regard the intellectual processes for making political decisions as an area of study distinct from their own concern for the governmental framework within which decisions are made and enforced. While the importance to a democracy of an informed, intelligent electorate has been stressed by the political scientists, they have provided little by way of analysis of political intelligence. The authors of this group of textbooks[11] are by no means all political scientists, but each is committed to the need for political intelligence. As Posey and Huegli put it: "Democracy is a system of government which demands mature thinking."[12] One set of authors even presents the view that "democratic process . . . resembles the methods used by the scientist in his work."[13]

As I looked through the books, however, I was struck by the emphasis on one facet of "mature thinking" that characterized the approach of each of the texts, namely, the need for the citizen "to increase his understanding of political issues through intelligent use of existing sources of information."[14] In a word, "mature" thinking becomes in these texts awareness of the media utilized by groups competing for the citizen's attention and vote *and* propaganda analysis. Almost without exception the books fail to deal with methods for substantiating factual claims,[15] as, for example, would be essential to determining the effects of alternative policy decisions. They do not deal with the problems of making political-ethical judgments. Each, however, makes at least cursory mention of public opinion, the sources of information upon which it is based, and the propaganda techniques for influencing it. The treatment of propaganda is, however, usually brief—limited to a page or two or to a table of various techniques.

If the general approach to reflective thinking in these textbooks were to be summarized by one word, that word would be "exhortive." Students are exhorted to "think critically," to "weigh and sift the facts,"[16] but they are given little in the way of a conceptual framework from which to meet the summons. It should not be inferred that the textbooks are being criticized for including sections on public opinion and propaganda. But, why limit the treatment of "mature" or critical thinking to dealing with sources of information? And, why not treat this one aspect of reflectiveness with depth and rigor?

What of the treatment of values and value conflict in public controversy? Unfortunately, this aspect of reflective thinking suffers, not only from omission as does the factual element, but from inadequate conceptualization as well. In defining democracy and discussing the basis upon which public policy decisions are made in this society, each book presents and discusses, at least briefly, the basic values of the society. Some of the statements about democracy seem incredibly naive. Although one who quotes material out of its context always risks misrepresenting his sources, some examples follow: "It [our concern for the individual spirit of man] means that each man's place is the one he earns."[17] (Some people in our society might question whether a man has earned a classification when it is based on his race or religion.) "Democracy protects the rights of all people."[18] "The people determine the government's policies."[19] "Americans readily recognize the right of all men to freedom from discrimination, freedom to live where they wish, freedom from persecution, the right to have rest and leisure, the right to have an education, and the right to have an adequate standard of living."[20]

(Recent events raise obvious doubts as to what Americans "readily recognize" about, for example, discrimination and housing, and, during the recent presidential election, the right to education was questioned.) In reading such statements, the student must either be deceived into an unrealistically optimistic view of this society, or he must wonder about the obvious discrepancies between what he reads in the text and what he reads in his newspaper.

Certainly, as one text puts it, "agreement has to be on fundamentals,"[21] and it makes a great deal of sense to present students with the funadmental ideals of our society. They should be presented as ideals, however, or the likely result is pessimism and even rejection of the values as, especially in our high-communication era, the student becomes aware that the ideals are not consonant with reality. Experiences in Korea, where many American prisoners-of-war were first dramatically made aware of this country's shortcomings, seem to justify this concern. The emphasis present in a statement by Allen and Wirth that democratic ideals "are goals toward which we as citizens must strive, rather than situations that mankind has already developed to a stage of perfection,"[22] needs to be more systematically woven into the treatment of American national values in the government textbooks.

Of course, the problem that results from possible dissonance between values expressed as reality and contact with reality is not the only one. There is also the general problem that behavior in our society cannot always exemplify perfectly the values, because in most public policy decisions a choice between values must be made. The classical dilemma, of course, is between freedom and equality. If men are completely free, then there are going to be inequalities; but as we try to insure equality for all we will impinge on the freedoms of some. It is unfortunate that the textbooks on government refer to our commitment to freedom and to equality a number of times in the same sentence or paragraph without noting the inevitable dilemmas in carrying out what must often be conflicting goals.[23]

This is not to say that the texts do not recognize that the exercise of rights in this society cannot be unlimited. Restrictions are often noted. Free speech and press are restricted by slander and libel laws and by the Supreme Court's "clear and present danger" doctrine.[24] They must be restricted because "advocating an idea through speech and action may affect other people's liberty and property."[25] Censorship in the interests of the society may conflict with rights to freedom of expression.[26] Even though it may make law enforcement more difficult, we restrict search and seizure "to avoid the risk of having officials bully innocent people."[27] Freedom of religion may be limited in the case of polygamists and conscientious objectors.[28] Restrictions are necessary when religious practices "conflict with public order."[29] It is necessary to balance the desire for economic freedom against the need for government control to correct abuses, [30] and ownership of private property may be interfered with in the interests of the public welfare.[31] The right of assembly must be limited in the interests of safety.[32] The majority has the power to make decisions, but the minority also has rights to be protected.[33] Liberty is limited by concern for the general welfare, [34] and the two must be balanced.[35]

On the other hand, it is not difficult to find instances where the need to restrict or "balance" rights seems to slip from the conscious frame of reference of those writing the texts. For example, Brown and Peltier conclude a statement about the value foundation of American government in the following way: "People who believe in our system of government believe that every individual has worth and dignity precisely because *he is human;* they believe that all human beings are equal and that they have certain inalienable rights. So fundamental are these principles that to change or deny any one of them is to invite tyranny."[36] The basic commitment of the society is well put. But if the "principles" that are not to be changed or denied include the "inalienable rights"—which we take to be rights such as "the freedom to choose"[37]—then their denial is inevitable. This is the point of the many quotes in the paragraph preceding this one. In a similar vein, Paquin and Irish proclaim that Americans "recognize that ideas such as freedom, justice, and respect for the individual are matters on which there is no compromise."[38] Again overlooked is the basic point that making important societal decisions involves just such compromise.[39] The need is not to avoid such compromise, but to consider carefully what compromises are in the long run most likely to contribute to the type of society desired. One more example: "Only as local citizens see that free assemblies are part of the grand scheme of democracy will this right be fully respected."[40] But can the right ever be "fully respected" in the face, for example, of threatened mob violence and breakdown of law and order in the community?

Generally, the textbooks examined fail to treat systematically the problem of handling the inevitable clash of values as decisions are made in this society.[41] When the necessity of restricting rights is recognized, it tends to be considered in a limited way as involving restrictions in rather individual, isolated instances. The restriction of rights is not construed as a crucial element in a pluralistic society that has differing commitments from group to group and individual to individual, nor as the result of a general characteristic of our American creed of which we need to be cognizant as we attempt to translate general values to explicit policies. There is, then, no attempt to provide the student with a general framework that takes into account the pluralistic quality of our multigroup society[42] and the nature of the American creed and relates these to the difficulties of dealing rationally with the evaluative aspects of policy decisions. And, of course, no rationale is provided for resolving value clashes into policy decisions. Speech can be curbed when "society's interest in preventing panic in a theater clearly outweighs the individual's right to express himself irresponsibly,"[43] and "drawing the line between unlimited expression of ideas by free individuals and government control of speech is an important current problem."[44] But when is speech "irresponsible"? How is the student to decide the crucial point at which violation of one value is so extreme that it is justifiable for the government to violate another?

Magruder comments, "Drawing the line between these expressions of opinion that are protected by the First and Fourteenth Amendments and those which are not is an extraordinarily difficult task. Putting the problem another way, where is the reasonable line between the power of the government to protect the public safety and the right of the individual to express himself?"[45] How is the student to determine for himself where that line should be? The problem is also posed well by White and Imel in a supplementary "Increase Your Understanding" section following a chapter entitled, "Definition of the Government of the United States":

> Is a certain action democratic or not? Often democracy means different things to different people. Often, too, one has to select from considerations which seem to oppose one another. For example, is it democratic to have separate classes in schools for pupils of different abilities? Those who would say "yes" probably are influenced by a belief that democracy includes the opportunity for each person to develop to the fullest on the basis of ability and merit. On the other hand, some opposing the special classes might emphasize their belief that democracy means equality and that these special classes produce inequality.[46]

How does one clarify his own position and determine the stand he shall take? Unfortunately, the texts in American government avoid any attempt to answer this crucial question. At the same time, their treatment of values and value conflicts in this society, as they relate to governmental decisions, is at best haphazard and lacking in order, and at worst inaccurate and misleading. To the extent that the other authors of government textbooks shared the view of Dimond and Pflieger that one purpose of their text was "to promote careful thinking about governmental problems,"[47] an important aspect of the task has been overlooked or mishandled. . . .

The results of a review such as reported in this article must be sorely disappointing to social studies educators committed to the idea that the citizenship-education function of the social studies should include as an essential ingredient teaching students to think reflectively about important societal issues. The disappointment in textbooks will be especially great for educators who believe that an adequately comprehensive framework of reflective thinking must embody consideration of the value conflicts inherent in our pluralistic society. Some textbooks do treat propaganda techniques; others present steps in problem-solving schemata related to factual problems, although history texts ignore historical methods; none treats adequately the evaluative aspects of societal issues. There is no *systematic* conceptualization of the pluralistic society with its inevitable variation in emphasis and interpretation of the general values of our society which are logically contradictory of themselves, or of the relationship of these features to the inter- and intrapersonal evaluative conflicts that arise when societal issues are considered. Intellectual strategies for handling these clashes of values are not presented. Whatever other strengths the textbooks reviewed might have, it must be concluded that to the extent they serve as the basis for instruction in social studies classrooms across the nation (and little else is available to most teachers), social studies programs must give students only minimal conceptual preparation for dealing with the basic issues that face our nation. What intellectual competencies adult citizens have for making decisions about controversial problems must be attributed to social studies teachers' efforts to go beyond the textbooks and to natural abilities and learning in incidental experiences outside the social studies classroom.

References

[1] See Donald W. Oliver, "The Selection of Content in the Social Sciences," *Harvard Educational Review,* XXVII (Fall, 1957), 271-300; and James P. Shaver, "Americanism: A Definition for Educators," *Utah Educational Review,* LVII (January-February, 1964), 8-9, 38-40.

[2] New York: Harper & Bros., 1944.

[3] See Donald W. Oliver and James P. Shaver, *The Analysis of Political Controversy: An Approach to Citizenship Education* (A Report to the U.S. Office of Education [Cambridge, Mass.: Laboratory for Research in Instruction, Harvard Graduate School of Education, 1963]), chaps. ii, iii.

[4] Marshall A. Robinson, Herbert C. Morton, and James D. Calderwood, *An Introduction to Economic Reasoning* (3d ed.; Washington, D.C.: Brookings Institution, 1962).

[5] Robert G. McCloskey, "The American Ideology," in *Continuing Crisis in American Politics,* ed. Marian D. Irish (Englewood Cliffs, N.J.: Prentice-Hall, Inc., 1963), pp. 10-25.

[6] "Teaching the Bill of Rights," *Social Education,* XXVII (May, 1963), 238-43, 256.

Also see C. Peter Magrath, "Nine Deliberative Bodies," *Commentary,* XXXII (November, 1961), 399-407.

[7] For alternative approaches to such a strategy, see Oliver and Shaver, *op. cit.,* chaps. v, vi, and vii; and Maurice P. Hunt and Lawrence E. Metcalf, *Teaching High School Social Studies* (New York: Harper & Bros., 1955).

[8] See, for example, Richard E. Gross, "American History Teachers Look at the Book," *Phi Delta Kappan,* XXXIII (January, 1952), 290-91.

[9] Stanley E. Ballinger, "The Social Studies and Social Controversy," *School Review,* LXXI (Spring, 1963), 97-111.

[10] Hunt and Metcalf, *op. cit.,* Earl S. Johnson, *Theory and Practice of the Social Studies* (New York: Macmillan Co., 1956). Hunt and Metcalf present the more extensive treatment.

[11] Jack Allen and Fremont P. Wirth, *This Government of Ours* (New York: American Book Co., 1955); Stuart G. Brown and Charles L. Peltier, *Government in Our Republic* (New York: Macmillan Co., 1964); George G. Bruntz, *Understanding Our Government* (Boston: Ginn & Co., 1961); Stanley E. Dimond and Elmer F. Pflieger, *Our American Government* (Chicago: J. B. Lippincott Co., 1961); Oka S. Flick and Henry L. Smith, *Government in the United States* (River Forest, Ill.: Laidlaw Bros., 1956); John H. Haefner, Harold R. Bruce, and Robert K. Carr, *Our Living Government* (Chicago: Scott, Foresman & Co., 1962); Frank A. Magruder, *Magruder's American Government,* revised by William A. McClenaghan (Boston: Allyn & Bacon, Inc., 1962); Laurence G. Paquin and Marian D. Irish, *The People Govern* (New York: Charles Scribner's Sons, 1958); Rollin B. Posey and Albert G. Huegli, *Government for Americans* (Evanston, Ill.: Row, Peterson & Co., 1959); Robert Rienow, *American Government in Today's World* (Boston: D. C. Heath & Co., 1962); Edith C. Starratt and Morris Lewenstein, *Our American Government Today* (Englewood Cliffs, N.J.: Prentice-Hall, Inc., 1958); Robert White and H. L. Imel, *American Government: Democracy at Work* (Princeton, N.J.: D. Van Nostrand Co., 1961).

[12] *Op. cit.,* p. 464.

[13] Allen and Wirth, *op. cit.,* p. 7.

[14] *Ibid.,* p. 3.

[15] One text, Bruntz, *op. cit.,* does have a section at the end of each chapter called "Using Your Skills To Understand Government." This section emphasizes understanding quotations and word usage, as well as how to find facts, analyze them, and come to conclusions. The treatment is brief and not systematic.

[16] Brown and Peltier, *op. cit.,* p. 410.

[17] Rienow, *op. cit.,* p. 3.

[18] White and Imel, *op. cit.,* p. 37.

[19] White and Imel, *op. cit.,* p. 4. See Fred M. Newmann, "Consent of the Governed and Citizenship Education in Modern America." *School Review,* LXXI (Winter, 1963), 404-24.

[20] Paquin and Irish, *op. cit.,* p. 22.

[21] Haefner *et al., op. cit.,* p. 35.

[22] *Op. cit.,* p. 8.

[23] E.G., *ibid.,* p. 64; Haefner *et al., op. cit.,* p. 28; Magruder, *op. cit.,* pp. 5, 11; Starratt and Lewenstein, *op. cit.,* pp. 24-25.

[24] E.G., Posey and Huegli, *op. cit.,* p. 418; Rienow, *op. cit.,* p. 82; White and Imel, *op. cit.,* pp. 482-85.

[25] Starratt and Lewenstein, *op. cit.*, pp. 86-87.

[26] Magruder, *op. cit.*, p. 115.

[27] Rienow, *op. cit.*, pp. 464-65.

[28] *Ibid.*, p. 82; Haefner *et al.*, *op. cit.*, p. 151.

[29] Magruder, *op. cit.*, pp. 110-11.

[30] Posey and Huegli, *op. cit.*, pp. 464-65.

[31] Allen and Wirth, *op. cit.*, pp. 66-67.

[32] Magruder, *op. cit.*, p. 115.

[33] Haefner *et al.*, *op. cit.*, pp. 26-27.

[34] Dimond and Pflieger, *op. cit.*, p. 8.

[35] *Ibid.*, p. 10.

[36] *Op. cit.*, p. 34.

[37] *Ibid.*, pp. 33-34.

[38] *Op. cit.*, p. 22.

[39] While compromise is traditionally an element in any treatment of democracy, e.g., Brown and Peltier (*op. cit.*, 35-39) include a section on "Democracy—the Compromise of Differences," the texts tend to look at compromise from a limited point of view. They see it as a matter of groups competing for their own interests (see, e.g., Starratt and Lewenstein, *op. cit.*, p. 475) rather than in terms of the diversity of interpretations of our basic values as individuals and groups construe the goals of society in pushing for policy decisions.

[40] Rienow, *op. cit.*, p. 84.

[41] Looked at in its entirety, *Our Living Government* by Haefner, Bruce, and Carr comes closer to this sort of systematic treatment than do any of the other government textbooks.

[42] Although two books—Brown and Peltier, *op. cit.*, pp. 395-98, 416, and Starratt and Lewenstein, *op. cit.*, pp. 5-6—treat the diversity of people in this society, there is little attempt to tie this diversity systematically to the problems involved in thinking reflectively about policy decisions. Starratt and Lewenstein do note the different viewpoints that result (*op. cit.*, p. 23) and that "the government must protect a variety of interests" because of the idea "that all persons have value and are entitled to respect" (*ibid.*, p. 25). Brown and Peltier note that "our very belief in the dignity of the individual creates endless conflict. Since each individual is as good as every other, there are endless differences in thinking, speaking, and acting" (*op. cit.*, p. 34).

[43] Haefner *et al.*, *op. cit.*, p. 47.

[44] *Ibid.*, pp. 148-49.

[45] *Op. cit.*, p. 112.

[46] *Op. cit.*, p. 46.

[47] *Op. cit.*, p. v.

THE NEGRO IN AMERICA
A Legacy Unrecognized

Thomas L. Millard
Montclair State College
Montclair, New Jersey

The Supreme Court's decision in Brown v. Board of Education, May 17, 1954, was an important and historic reaffirmation of America's commitment to equal education for all. Yet today, more than a decade later, equal education remains a goal, not an achievement.

But tragic as is this denial of equality in educational opportunities, still more deplorable is the marked inequality in textbook and curriculum treatment of the Negro's achievements and contributions to the growth of American society. That this obvious form of discrimination in educational practice has existed to the present day is lamentable, for better racial understanding is possible only as the whole truth of our cultural development is revealed and acknowledged.

It cannot be denied that the most profound bond that links us in all of our cultural, political, and racial diversity is our shared relationship to and identification with the retelling of America's growth and development. But except in vague and sketchy references the Negro, according to history, does not really exist. This omission of the Negro's contributions to America's greatness is a major factor in the continued unsettled status he experiences in American society. Furthermore, living in a hostile society which has gone to such extraordinary lengths to negate that which is black and champion that which is white has dealt deep wounds to the Negro psyche. Their external manifestations are found in unsatisfactory human relationships in American life, and also in an uncomfortable and uncertain identification with American social institutions and the democratic process.

Indeed, the absence from textbooks of historical truths about Negro accomplishment and contributions, with nonstereotypic descriptions, suggests an irrational and deep-seated fixation which clearly demonstrates the extent to which racism is institutionalized in American culture.

This kind of social practice and racist attitude, the persistent attempt at "disassociating" the Negro from all aspects of American life, is the source of frustration for the Negro youngster in his attempt at finding meaning behind

Reprinted with permission of the publisher, from *The Clearing House,* 40 (September, 1965): 38-41.

the inconsistency between democratic beliefs and social practices. And this inconsistency is manifesting itself in the steadily rising number of Negro school dropouts and underachievers. In a study of a slum area of 125,000 people, mostly nonwhites, a sampling of the youth population showed that roughly 70 per cent of the boys and girls aged 16 to 21 were out of school and unemployed.[1]

Against the backdrop of automation and rapidly advancing technology, uneducated, unskilled, and unprepared Negroes are at best recipients of limited and diminishing social and economic opportunities. The end results are usually seen in untold adult problems—unstable families, crime, illegitimacy, desertions, slum living, and all the other social and cultural deprivations visited upon the low wage earner unable to better his environmental conditions.

The strain on existing private and public agencies in relief services, family counselling, unemployment, health care, and crime prevention can only be surmised. Obviously, reforms are necessary in the inconsistency between our cultural goals and social practices, if we are to deal with this problem more effectively.

But problems that are deeply rooted in a society can only be solved by changes in the institutions and practices which generate them.[2]

Thus the continued denial of the Negro's place in American history has the gravest implications not only for the Negro but for all Americans.

This denial of the Negro's role in history and indeed the rejection of him as a person is parallel to the case of the American Indian. Both are denied a place in American history. But the remarkable phenomenon about the Negro, unlike the American Indian, is that he has managed to survive and endure and in spite of social, cultural, and psychological barriers is increasingly moving towards the mainstream of American society.

American society is a unique socio-political experiment in its makeup of diverse racial and cultural minorities. As such, we are proud to export the fact that from this nation's beginning every man, no matter what his origin, has had the right to his individuality—to think and believe as he sees fit, to develop what talents he may possess, and to worship the Almighty as he may choose. To us, the right to be different, to be an individual of our own making, has been our most precious heritage. But, again, this heritage is denied the Negro. He alone is the "unpossessed."

The fact that education has been unfair in the things that it has not told about the Negro is an indictment of our culture. It has been unfair also in the things that it has let people think about the Negro, and herein lies the educational dilemma—the commingling of virtuous pretension and outright indifference.

In this sense, America's cultural life is the poorer, for culture in America cannot rise to the heroic heights of its potentialities until all groups, be they black or white, are fully accorded historical credit, thus enabling all Americans to take pride in their historic past and develop what talents they possess, thereby further contributing to a rich heritage that is truly democratic and pluralistically American.

When one considers that it was a Negro, Crispus Attucks, who was the first to die in the American Revolution and that it was a Negro, Benjamin Bannaker,[3] mathematician, astronomer, surveyor, whose advocacy of a world peace plan in 1793 later formed the basis for President Woodrow Wilson's League of Nations proposal, it is enough to suggest that the continued exclusion of factual reporting in textbooks of Negro accomplishments and contributions is morally and democratically indefensible.

We are living in unsettled times in which there is increasing need for understanding in developing a broad, cosmopolitan cultural awareness, skills, and rational, non-stereotyped ways of thinking. Education must therefore begin to provide meaningful social information and valid concepts about the nature and diversity of our group life, to the end that social inequities may be adjusted.

In this context, education must be both a challenge and an opportunity, and must be all things to all people. It must be fashioned on unreserved acceptance of the concept of education as the basic instrumentality through which the young child is prepared for lifetime tasks as a useful citizen.

Children in a minority group, be they Negro, Mexican, Puerto Rican, American Indian, or Oriental, have a right to be proud of what they are and to have the same ambition as anyone else and a fair chance at success.

Viewed in these terms, emotional security and the feeling of identity with the cultural heritage are fundamental needs, and they must be met if education is to be intellectually satisfying for the Negro child in his efforts to adapt himself to his socio-physical environment, and to utilize the opportunities it presents. In short, the Negro wants and deserves his cultural heritage as well as his constitutional rights.

As a basic social institution, a guardian of our values, the school influences and shapes our ideas, habits, ambitions, and life-value-orientation to such an extent that it is almost unbelievable to find any person or group having to readjust his mental makeup so as to compensate for the shortcomings of his educational experience.

Yet this is precisely the situation in which the Negro child finds himself.

In the final analysis, the question of the cultural heritage is essentially a question of distributive acknowledgment of all of the varied culture-contributing groups that comprise the general culture. Herein must lie the fundamental institutional characteristic of education in a multiracial society.

The most urgent task in education regarding Negro aspirations in this immediate period and in the decades that lie ahead will be bringing the Negro into the main current of social and economic opportunities with meaningful and equitable educational experiences, so as to foster goals and incentives for closing the enormous educational and cultural gap that exists.

A nationwide ferment is going on in all of our cultural and social institutions, and the school's readiness to subject its shortcomings to frank examination must be demonstrated in mutual concern with other institutions in process of change to cultural commonality.

But there are hopeful signs emerging from current institutional practices that we are beginning to concede to these realities, and this may indicate, even though slightly, a beginning acceptance of Negroes into mainstream America with a growing consciousness of the part Negro achievements and contributions have played in past and contemporary history.[4]

From this we see that if this reality is to have meaning and evolve into the kind of heterogeneous society we profess to be, education must abandon those timeworn textbook practices of depicting the Negro in menial and low-status positions in American society.

In these present times, the "Negro revolt" has provided the dramatic impetus in reminding us of what we do not know about the Negro and—even more, perhaps—what we do not want to know about the Negro. And this unwillingness is largely the result of our inability to shake off the influence of a bygone era.

Considering the present social unrest, there is a great deal to be said for the notion that what we are really witnessing in society's response to Negro demands for equality is a struggle within our national conscience over our "moral inertia," symptomatic of a painful awareness of the moral questions posed by a society pregnant with social tension and needed changes. This "agonizing reappraisal" is symbolic of the ever-growing recognition of the naïveté of our present conception of the larger human family and our value relationship to it.

This brings us directly to the principle on which a new understanding of our pluralistic and multi-value society must be based. For each of us—our personal needs, values, and beliefs notwithstanding—our cultural image as a nation of free men can never be a finished and completed product until there is acceptance of and action upon the fact that others in the world are as real as ourselves, and possess the same wants, values, and cultural ambitions.

References

[1] J. B. Conant, *Slums and Suburbs*. New York: McGraw-Hill Book Co., Inc., 1961, p. 34.

[2] Responding to this requirement, the New York City Board of Education, in a statement of policy last year to all textbook publishers, served notice that it would no longer purchase textbooks that contained discriminatory treatment of minority groups.

To insure that all future textbooks would deal honestly with minorities, social studies textbook appraisal committees have adopted criteria for determining adequate treatment of all minority groups.

Also, in a report to the California State Department of Education, seven history texts widely used in that state were strongly criticized by University of California (Berkeley) historians who prepared the report.

Among other things, the report stated that the greatest defect in these textbooks is the virtual omission of the Negro, that "it is the kind of bad history that reenforces notions among whites of their superiority and among Negroes of their inferiority," that they "reflect views on racial and sectional themes that have been rejected or drastically modified by the best of current historical scholarship."

Books criticized were *Trail Blazers of American History,* Mason and Cartwright (Ginn, 1961); *The Story of American Freedom,* McGuire (Macmillan, 1961); *America is My Country,* Brown and Guadagnolo (Houghton Mifflin, 1961); *The Growth of America,* Liebman and Young (Prentice-Hall, 1959); *Story of the American Nation,* Casner, Gabriel, Biller, and Hartley (Harcourt, Brace and World, 1962); *The Story of American Democracy,* Casner and Gabriel (Harcourt, Brace, 1955); *Story of America,* Harlow and Miller (Henry Holt, 1957).

[3] Among his other accomplishments, Benjamin Bannaker made what was said to be one of the first clocks manufactured in America, and he also published one of the first series of almanacs brought out in the United States. Because of these meritorious achievements, Bannaker was sought by prominent men like James McHenry, once Vice-President of the United States, and Thomas Jefferson, as Secretary of State and later as President. The latter was so impressed with Bannaker's genius that he secured for him an appointment to the L'Enfant Commission which laid out Washington in the District of Columbia. For more on this and other examples of Negro contributions, see Carter Godwin Woodson, *The Story of the Negro Retold* (Washington, D.C.: The Associated Publishers, Inc., 1942).

[4] But the "separate but equal" solution in "Negro History Week" held annually in many school districts is neither the answer nor desirable. What the Negro requires and what he wants is full integration of his role in the story of America and its development.

The elementary schools of Detroit, Michigan, which is 47 per cent Negro, have made a start in this direction by supplementing courses with a 52-page paperback on Negro history that ranges from ancient times to the Reverend Dr. Martin Luther King.

· Also last year in Washington, D.C., public schools (86 per cent nonwhite), *The Negro in American History,* a 130-page teacher's guide, was introduced for use by all teachers in the system and to be read by eleventh graders as part of their regular assignment.

Sample information in this guide:

George Washington barred Negroes from the Continental Army until the British began recruiting slaves. Alarmed, the Americans then enlisted more than 5,000 Negro soldiers, and used them in integrated units.

Contrary to folklore, the United States had 488,000 free Negroes by 1860, almost half of them in the South.

The first successful suit in the United States against school segregation occurred not in the South in the 1950's but in Boston in 1849.

American G.I.'s of World War II and later can be grateful for their recovery to Dr. Charles Drew, a Negro physician who developed the theory of blood plasma and pioneered the blood bank program.

In the Civil War, more than 210,000 Negroes fought in the Union army and navy, and won twenty Congressional Medals of Honor. More than 38,000 were killed in battle.

CURRENT CONTROVERSY:
MINORITIES IN AMERICAN HISTORY TEXTBOOKS

Lucian Davis
San Jose, California, Public Schools

There is an aspect of the Civil Rights Movement in the United States practically buried in the avalanche of picketing, protests, and complaints; the treatment of Negroes in American history textbooks.

A chronic complaint of minority groups is that schools and textbooks ignore the minorities' own distinctive past and contributions to the majority culture. The image of the Negro projected by some textbooks is being criticized with increasing frequency by representatives of the Negro community. This criticism is having an impact on all texts that touch upon the subject. In fact, responses to protest thus far portend extensive changes in the treatment of all minority groups in school textbooks.[1]

In theory, the American public schools take pride in their "melting pot" function. In practice, it is often charged, the stirring of the pot's mixture aims at eliminating the minorities' cultural flavor in order to produce a homogenized blend. Inevitably, too, the minorities are sensitive about any aspect of literature used in the classroom that presents them in an unfavorable light.[2] Pressures created by some Negro action groups have played a role in influencing publishers to revise their textbooks. A major aim of these groups is to rid the textbooks of myths and stereotypes that do America no good.[3] The current controversy of minorities in history textbooks in American education

Reprinted with permission of the author and the publisher, from *Journal of Secondary Educatic*, 41, no. 7 (November, 1966): 291-94.

has reached monumental proportions in some of the nation's leading metropolitan areas.

It is worthwhile to consider the experience of the Detroit Board of Education. The object of controversy was an American history text adopted in 1961 for use in the 7th and 8th grades. In the fall of 1962, the local branch of the National Association for the Advancement of Colored People asked the Detroit Board of Education to withdraw immediately *Our United States* as a required text. The NAACP alleged that the book "was an insult to every Negro in Detroit and promotes an image of the Negro in the remainder of the community that is not only false, but helps to lay the foundation for future community problems."[4]

A committee of school personnel was set up to review the problem and to make recommendations for a solution. *SEVEN CATEGORIES OF OBJECTION.* The critique cited seven major categories of objections to the treatment of the Negro in the American history textbook. Most relate to the period from the beginning of the North-South dispute to the Reconstruction Period following the Civil War: (1) the book's casual approach to the introduction of slavery in colonial America, (2) the presumed lack of interest of the Negro in freeing himself from slavery, (3) the thesis of the positive, paternalistic slave owner, (4) a biased description and discussion of the Reconstruction Period, (5) a distorted image of the Negro, (6) failure to discuss the historic and current struggle of the Negro to achieve equitable civil rights, (7) failure to mention the emergence of a single black African nation.[5]

The NAACP critique contended that:

> This book gives little justification to the Negro child to consider himself or his heritage as worthy and significant. Rather, he is forced by this book to look to other sources to refute the negative image of himself as presented by this alleged history of his native land. Unfortunately, such material is not always made easily available to him and he is forced to adjust to a self-image which he instinctively rejects but cannot easily invalidate.
>
> Despite the consequences of this negative self image of the Negro child, the result of its impact on the white child is even more alarming. All too frequently, there is no opportunity to expose the white child to information which might effectively correct or condition the impressions that result from a description of the Negro as presented in this book.[6]

The decision of the review committee of the Detroit schools was that the complaints by the Negro community were justified and that corrective steps should be taken. The board issued a statement reaffirming its commitment "to a policy of having the schools contribute in maximum degree to understanding and good will among different racial, religious, and nationality groups."[7]

In November, 1963, the Detroit Board of Education voted to discontinue use of *Our United States,* and the process of selection of a replacement text was set in motion. Meanwhile, a revised edition of the same book was issued and was considered together with competing texts. It was this new edition of the rejected book that was adopted for use in September, 1964. The revised edition omits the objectionable features of the earlier one. An additional feature that was the result of the Detroit controversy was a well-written supplement on Negro history, prepared by the teachers of the Detroit School System.

The Detroit controversy, however, has ramifications that extend beyond a particular book and a particular school system. The Detroit experience has initiated in earnest the search for solutions. New and wiser approaches will surely evolve as the problem is recognized and honestly wrestled with in countless communities across the land.

The State of California is the second major scene of minority controversy to consider. The dispute in California centers around a recent American history text for junior high school titled, *Land of the Free.* The book was one of two considered under State Board of Education order that the selected text portray "fully, fairly and factually the role of the Negro in American history."[8]

Since its release, the book has been the target of conservative attack on grounds that it is too favorable to minority groups. State Superintendent of Public Instruction, Max Rafferty, said the controversial history text, *"Land of the Free,* needs a major salvage effort."[9] He went on to say:

> Because of deadline pressure, the book is a work of haste. Its spelling is often shaky and that more seriously it uses some howlingly non-historical terminology, for instance, "Senator McCarthy . . . declared war on the Army." McCarthy may have annoyed, attacked or even harassed the Department of the Army, but he certainly did not declare war on it. Only a sovereign state can declare war. The authors of the book showed obvious bias and they should write of historical fact and not opinion.[10]

The State Superintendent of Public Instruction has little jurisdiction over the Curriculum Committee and Board of Education in California because both are independent of the other. He does, however, sit in on the hearings. A review panel was selected to review the book and accept suggestions from educators and State legislators for possible changes in the text. Its report will go to the curriculum commission and will be made available to the public. The recommendations will then be sent to the publisher, who will deliver final proofs to the State Board of Education for approval in December of this year.[11]

The controversies in Michigan and California clearly indicate the beginning of widespread departure from the traditional treatment of minority groups, particularly Negroes in American history textbooks. Regardless of the nature of the controversy in the matter, change is imminent. Omission has long been a favored device by which the textbook publishers seek to avoid controversy. Wholesale omission has the more serious effect of distorting history, that distortion builds up an unfavorable and untrue image of America's minorities. This in turn creates serious psychological effects upon Negro and White children alike.

The self image of Negro youngsters, already distorted if they attend schools in economically and educationally deprived areas, suffers even more if their own ethnic group is overlooked in a study of the country's and mankind's past. More emphasis on Negro history may be effective in helping the student acquire a historical frame of reference.[12]

Obviously, what holds true for the Negro student must be equally valid for the children of all minority groups. The need for a historical frame of reference then, includes all of America's minorities. In California, Dr. Myron Schussman, Assistant Superintendent of Instruction of Education of Santa Clara County, said:

> The real conscience historians have always recognized the role of Chinese and Spanish contributions in California's history.[13]

The controversy will continue. The end result will inevitably mean a wider area of historical research for historians, increased course offerings in colleges and universities, and a new frontier for the publishing industry. It is indispensable that the publishers accent factual historial information and develop readable and dramatic stories, while scrupulously preserving historical accuracy and perspective in their treatment of America's minorities.

References

[1]Sol M. Elkin, "Minorities in Textbooks," *Teachers College Record,* LXVI (March, 1965), p. 502.

[2]Fred M. Hechinger, "For Minorities: A Place in History," *New York Times,* October 25, 1964, p. 9.

[3] Robert H. Terte, "Historians Find Negro Role Gains," *New York Times,* August 1, 1963, p. 16.

[4] Elkin, *loc. cit.*

[5] Elkin, *op. cit.,* p. 503.

[6] *Ibid.*

[7] *Ibid.,* p. 504.

[8] *San Francisco Chronicle,* August 20, 1966, p. 2.

[9] *Ibid.*

[10] *Ibid.*

[11] *San Francisco Chronicle,* August 17, 1966, p. 3. Authors of *Land of the Free* are Ernest May, professor of history at Harvard, John Caughey, California historian at University of California at Los Angeles and John Hope Franklin, Negro historian at the University of Chicago. The publisher is Franklin Publications of Pasadena, California The review panel consists of two prominent historians: Allan Nevins and Charles G. Sellers, Jr. and State College Chancellor Glen Dumke.

[12] Clement E. Vontress, "Our Demoralizing Slum Schools," *Phi Delta Kappan,* XLV (November, 1963), p.77.

[13] Interview with Dr. Myron Schussman, Assistant Superintendent of Instruction of Education of Santa Clara County, August 26, 1966.

SECTION B   Other Learning Resources

BEYOND THE TEXT
Paperbacks Vitalize Social Studies

Willis J. Larkin
Stanford University

At one time there was some justification for social studies teachers' using the textbook as the sole or principal source of instruction, but this is no longer true. With the resurgence of paperback books a whole new world of reading material is available to students.[1] The teachers and administrators who continue to perpetuate the textbook tyranny are doing a great disservice to students and school alike.

Much has been written about the textbook—both pro and con—and its influence on the social studies.[2] Few would question the value of a textbook's providing a general survey of material to be covered and serving as a bibliographical source. This the text can do, if it is thoughtfully selected.[3] However, when a social studies course is centered around a textbook, both creative teaching and maximum student learning become much more difficult.[4]

Modern high school textbooks are at best a limited secondary source, and most of them do not even meet this criterion, as they are usually written from secondary source material. The result is "deadly" reading for the students.[5] This is not to argue that texts should be abandoned; rather it is to urge that they be used as the foundation upon which the course is built—the text never becoming an end in itself. Who should receive the blame for the perpetuation of the textbook course of instruction? It must be placed at the door of teachers and school officials who permit convenience and economics to take precedence over a better social studies program. The advent of paperback books cancels these excuses.[6] Their relatively inexpensive prices, in comparison with those of hard cover books, and the new plastic covers which

Reprinted with permission of the publisher, from *The Clearing House,* 40 (September, 1965): 47-49.

provide durability, make it economically possible for school districts to provide a great number and variety of these books for students and classroom libraries.[7]

Of what advantage are these paperback books to the teacher of social studies? For the first time students can possess and use many books to aid in expanding their knowledge of the topics under discussion. At the same time the motivation problem will diminish because the great variety of materials at the disposal of the classes makes it possible to meet more individual needs in subject matter and reading ability.[8] However, it is not enough just to provide supplemental paperback textbooks. Instead, texts should be the springboard into a variety of works. Many good secondary works, monographs, biographies, collections of documents, novels,[9] travelogues, and anthologies are available in paperback and should be used so that students can more ably formulate insights and conclusions based on a wide range of material.[10]

In the history-centered courses especially students study about important documents, but they seldom study the document itself. The Magna Charta is a standard document studied in world history courses, but few students ever read it. Students of American history can speak of Washington's Farewell Address, but few have studied it. Most students erroneously believe that it was a statement devoted to foreign policy, though one reading of the document would correct this misconception. With the availability of paperback document collections, the study of important primary source materials is now possible.[11]

There are many other areas in which the teacher can make wide use of paperback materials. In studying river boat travel, what better source can be used than Mark Twain's *Life on the Mississippi? Gone With the Wind* by Margaret Mitchell will enliven and stimulate any study of the Civil War era, as will Mrs. Stowe's *Uncle Tom's Cabin.* Any study of the westward movement and settlement of the West should include such works as Parkman's *The Oregon Trail, Old Jules* by Mari Sandoz, Willa Cather's *O Pioneers* or *My Antonia,* or the works of A. B. Guthrie, Jr. These and many other titles would give students a better insight into a period of history, as well as an increase in desire to study more about topics under discussion. The wide variety of biographies and works of fiction and poetry available in paperback editions surely lead to clearer understanding of the times.[12]

Extensive use of the many works now available in paperback will have a great impact on the development of topical units and the problems approach in the social studies. This is particularly encouraged by the appearance of the flexible multi-text and uni-text paperbacks. The new world of books will enable and encourage students to go beyond the text, seeking many points of view before drawing conclusions on the topics studied.[13] The break with social studies textbook courses is possible with paperback books, and it will come when teachers and school officials decide to put the needs of students at the top of their "must do" list.

References

[1] See John Tebbel, "The Paperback Textbook Revolution," *Saturday Review* (March 11, 1961), pp. 81 and 90.

[2] See Fred P. Barnes, "The Textbook Dilemma," *Teachers College Record* (April, 1954), pp. 369-83, for a general survey of textbooks and their use. In defense of textbooks see Kenneth S. Cooper, "How Good Are American History Textbooks?" *Social Education* (December, 1950), pp. 341-43; Morris G. Sica, "Do You Understand Your Social Studies Textbook?" *The Social Studies* (April, 1959), pp. 148-50; and Nicholas C. Polos, "Textbooks–What's Wrong With Them?" *The Clearing House* (April, 1964), pp. 451-56. The opposite view is presented by John F. Ohles, "The Curse of the Textbook," *The Social Studies* (February, 1953), pp. 64-66, and George Rudisill, Jr., "Homogenized History," *The Nation* (May 9, 1959), pp. 430-33.

[3] Guides for selecting texts are presented in Dorothy McClure Fraser, "Improving Social Studies Textbooks," *Journal of Education* (March, 1955), pp. 16-18, and Morris G. Sica, *op. cit.*

[4] The entire issue of *Phi Delta Kappan,* November, 1952, is devoted to the study of textbooks and their place in the school.

[5] See John F. Ohles, "Needed: Living Texts," *The Social Studies* (November, 1957), pp. 235-37, for one view on the subject.

[6] The following sources present a strong case for the use of paperback books in the school: Stanley L. Clement, "Why Paperbound Textbooks Are Worth Considering," *Nation's Schools* (July, 1962), p. 68; S. Alan Cohen, "Using Paperbacks in the Secondary School," *Journal of Education* (April, 1964), pp. 19-26; James F. Francis, "Preferences and Readability of Paperback Books," *Journal of Education* (April, 1964), pp. 16-18; Dora M. Perks, "Paperbacks Preferred," *High Points* (December, 1961), pp. 40-42; and William J. Rioux, "Nine Tested Reasons for Using Paperback Books," *Nation's Schools* (November, 1962), pp. 74-76.

[7] See William D. Litzinger, "Paperback Usage in Schools," *The Clearing House* (April, 1964), pp. 474-77, for a report on the use of paperbacks in schools and some of the problems encountered.

[8] David H. Moscow, "Individualizing Instruction with Paperbacks," *NEA Journal* (April, 1964), pp. 21-22.

[9] For one use of novels in the study of American history, see George G. Dawson, "The American Labor Novel," *Social Education* (May, 1961), pp. 233-36.

[10] For a list of some 19,500 titles of all American paperback books in print–listed by subject, author, and title, with publisher and price–see *Paperback Books in Print,* published by R. R. Bowker Co.

[11] See John S. Bowes, "Using Documentary Material in the American History Courses," *Social Education* (February, 1964), pp. 88-90.

[12] See Morris Gall, "Using Paperback Classics in the Social Studies," *Social Education* (March, 1963), pp. 141-44.

[13] In Morris Gall, *op. cit.,* p. 144, is one view of the use of paperbacks in the schools: "The school board, which normally *lends* a textbook to a student, would be expected to *give* the book to the student. The advantages of this procedure are obvious. Children would own their books, take better care of them, use them more effectively, treat the books as tools for learning, and retain them as sources of reference and as a nucleus for a personal library, thus developing the habit of building a personal collection of books. Giving an unmarked, attractive, new book to a student is in itself an invitation to learning."

CASE STUDY APPROACHES IN SOCIAL STUDIES

Fred M. Newmann   and   **Donald W. Oliver**
University of Wisconsin   *Harvard University*

The "case study" approach is one of the most applauded and least analyzed methods in social studies instruction. Along with programed instruction and team teaching, the mention of "case studies" signifies innovation in the language of educational magic. Just as administrators and teachers ask for comparative evaluations of team teaching versus conventional teaching, they also ask, "Which is better, case study or conventional teaching?" It is the purpose of this article to demonstrate that queries into the effectiveness of *the* case-study approach are misconceived and inappropriate—mainly because there is no single method that can rightfully be identified as *the* case-study method.

The use of "cases" for instructional purposes is nothing new. For years they have been standard equipment at the professional, graduate level, most traditionally in the fields of medicine, law, and business, and more recently in certain approaches to political science and international affairs. The attempt to broaden the application of cases to various aspects of social studies at lower levels has accentuated the need for clarification and differentiation among varied approaches. One of the major sources of confusion and ambiguity is the tendency to construe case study approaches under a single

Reprinted with permission of the authors and the National Council for the Social Studies, from *Social Education,* 31 (February, 1967): 108-113.

umbrella or unitary concept, depending upon objectives of instruction, styles of materials and their uses. We believe that the variety of approaches occurring within the general label will result in differences in learning. Moreover, these differences may be greater than those variations in learning accounted for by a comparison between "the" case-study technique and some other general method such as programed instruction.

This is not to suggest that case studies as a class of materials cannot be differentiated from other approaches; they do have something in common which sets them apart as distinguishable approaches to instruction. In general, case studies are investigations of *single* institutions, decisions, situations, or individuals. The object is to gather detailed information about a relatively small class of phenomena, such as the growth of a corporation, the decision to enter World War I, the living conditions of a Negro family in an urban slum, or the behavior of a politician in an election. Although case studies focus extensively on discrete instances, rather than on sweeping sets of events, the implicit assumption is that examination of a limited incident will yield conclusions that may be validly applied to a more general class of such incidents.[1]

The Harvard Social Studies Project operates on this assumption; that is, intensive study of detailed situations will lead the student toward valid generalizations. The Project, therefore, has been considered an exponent of the case-study approach.[2] In perusing its material and materials from other curricula, we notice considerable variety in both the *style* of materials and the *uses* of pedagogical application of them. Because of a general failure in the field to distinguish between varieties of *style* and *use,* case-study approaches are lumped together as a single method—an oversimplification that has beclouded curriculum theory. As one attempt to resolve this problem, we shall describe below different styles and uses of case studies.[3] The illustrations quoted below are all selected from a unit on Labor in the Harvard Project.

STYLE OF CASE STUDY MATERIALS

Story

The story, written in the style of a novel, portrays concrete events, human action, dialogue and feelings. It tells of an episode, having characters and a plot. The story may represent authentic events, as in historical novels, or it may be totally fictitious.

Illustration:

YELLOW-DOG AND BLACKLIST

The bell rang. Immediately the men in the pressroom turned off the machines and began preparing to go home. After the continuous throb and roar since morning, the silence was shocking.

Jeff Sargent was trying to wash away the black web of ink which clung to the seams of his palms. "The mark of the printer's trade," he thought to himself. He was proud of his hands—supple, calloused, ink-webbed, they were like tools which he had molded during thirteen years as a press feeder. But today he wanted to get them cleaner than usual. It was his tenth wedding anniversary, and he was going to surprise Sally by taking her out dancing like old times. He had secretly arranged with the landlady to take care of the kids for the evening.

Whistling loudly over the clatter of the water drumming against the wooden sink, Jeff didn't hear Lou Silver whispering at his side until the small, balding compositor nudged Sargent's elbow. "Oh hi, Lou." He turned off the water. "Now I can hear you better. What's up?"

Silver looked carefully behind him, toward the printing machines which stood in grey afternoon shadows like a herd of stolid, silent animals. "Heard about Price and Williamson?"

"What do you mean?" Sargent's thick eyebrows pulled together in a frown as he looked down at Silver, whose head barely reached his shoulder. "What about them?"

"They got the heave-ho today."

"Fired? But why? They're the best typesetters in the plant."

"Sure, but they're loudmouths. Remember last week when they were bitchin' to the foreman about the paycut? And last month when Price said the lead fumes were gettin' so bad someone ought to tell the board of health to fix the air ducts? And when Williamson said he thought we should have more than ten minutes for lunch?" . . .

The meeting had already begun when Sargent arrived. About 25 men were sitting in Silver's living room—on chairs, on tables, on the floor—smoking cigars or pipes, drinking beer, and listening attentively. Silver's small hands were slicing and shaping and pounding the air as he spoke in his clipped, nasal manner. ". . . and how long are we going to take it? Don't we have rights, too? Aren't we the men who do the work while Harper is the one who sits back and gets the profits? Is our only right to work ten hours a day, six days a week, until Harper decides to fire us?"[4]

[As the story continues, the men begin to organize workers in the plant. Finally, during a confrontation with the boss, both men are fired. Jeff Sargent decides to change his name when he learns that he has been black-listed.]

Stories seem to be one of the rarer forms of case studies in social studies; the style is more conventionally found in English courses. We find the story especially effective for the purpose of involving students emotionally in a situation. The suspense of a plot and a high level of concreteness focusing on "real" human beings tends to capture student attention.

Vignette

Written generally in the same style as the story, the vignette is a short excerpt or slice of experience. It has no completed plot.

Illustration:

CARRIE MEEBER

The pieces of leather came from the girl at the machine to her right and were passed on to the girl at her left. Carrie saw at once that an average speed was necessary or the work would pile up on her and all those below would be held up. She had no time to look around, so she bent anxiously to her work.

She worked continually at this job for some time. She felt strange as the minutes passed, for the room was not very light, and it had a thick smell of fresh leather. She felt the eyes of the other people upon her, and she worried for fear she was not working fast enough.

Once, when she was fumbling at the little clamp, having made a small mistake in setting in the leather, a great hand appeared before her eyes and fastened the clamp for her. It was the foreman. Her heart thumped so that she could hardly see to go on.

"Start your machine," he ordered, "start your machine! Don't keep the line waiting."

As the morning wore on, the room became hotter. She felt the need of a breath of fresh air and a drink of water, but she did not dare move. The stool she sat on was without a back or foot-rest, and she began to feel uncomfortable. She found, after a while, that her back was beginning to ache. She twisted and turned from one position to another, but it did not help her for long. She was beginning to get very tired. . . .

Her hands began to ache at the wrists and then in the fingers, and towards the last she seemed one mass of dull, complaining muscles, fixed in an unchanging position and performing a single mechanical movement which became more and more unpleasant until at last it was absolutely sickening. . . .

For this hard, tiring, disagreeable work, Carrie was paid $4.50 a week. After she had paid $4.00 for room and board, this left her with 50 cents a week with which to buy clothes and entertainment and to ride on the street-car on days when it rained or snowed.[5]

Journalistic Historical Narrative

This is told as a news story—a narrative of concrete events, with no conscious attempt to create a plot or characterization. It could be an hour-by-hour, day-by-day description, or it might be an eye-witness account of static conditions. The historical narrative often describes the actions of institutions as well as individual people.

Illustration:

THE MINE

Now you go up the chamber, taking care not to stumble over the high caps, into the notches of which the wooden rails of the track are laid. On one side of you is a wall, built up with pieces of slate and bony coal and the refuse of the mine, on the other you can reach out your hand and touch the heavy wooden props that support the roof, and beyond the props there is darkness, or if the rib of coal is visible it is barely distinct. Up at the face there is a scene of great activity. Bare-armed men, without coat or vest, are working with bar and pick and shovel, moving the fallen coal from the face, breaking it, loading it into the mine car which stands near by. The miners are at the face prying down loose pieces of coal. One takes his lamp in his hand and flashes its light along the black, broken, shiny surface, deciding upon the best point to begin the next drill hole, discussing the matter with his companion, giving quick orders to the laborers, acting with energy and a will. He takes up his drill, runs his fingers across the edge of it professionally, balances it in his hands, and strikes a certain point on the face with it, turning it slightly at each stroke. He has taken his position, lying on his side perhaps, and then begins the regular tap, tap of the drill into the coal. The laborers have loaded the mine car, removed the block from the wheel, and now, grasping the end of it firmly, hold back on it as it moves by gravity down the chamber to the gangway. You may follow it out, watch the driver boy as he attaches it to his trip, and go with him back to the foot of the shaft . . . .[6]

THE HAYMARKET RIOT

People in Chicago had feared violence, bloodshed, full-scale revolution on Saturday, May 1. That is what they had been told to expect by alarmed newspapers, apprehensive employers and a few radical labor leaders. Chicago, the site of numerous strikes already in progress, was to be the spearhead of the eight-hour movement's general strike. When both Saturday and Sunday passed peacefully, however, the citizens, the police and the newspaper editorials relaxed. But it was an uneasy peace, one which smoldered with passions. . . .

On May 3, two days after the demonstration by the eight-hour movement, the Lumber Shovers' Union held a mass meeting of about 6,000 people at the corner of Wood Street and Blue Island to demand shorter hours from their various employers. A half-mile away, across a stretch of open field, was the McCormick factory, many of whose striking workers attended the Lumber Shover's meeting. As August Spies, one of Chicago's most outspoken leaders of social protest, was addressing the crowd, the bell of the McCormick plant rang to signal the end of a shift. Against the warning of Spies, about 500 of the McCormick strikers advanced toward the factory and began to attack the "scabs" who were leaving for home. As the "scabs" retreated back into the plant, a few guns blazed between the aroused strikers and the police guards. Soon about 200 additional policemen arrived, charged the strikers with clubs and revolvers and drove them away after killing at least one striker (exact fatalities are unknown) and seriously wounding several others. Some police were injured, but none was killed.

The incident outside the McCormick factory snapped the patience of August Spies, who had hurried to the scene after finishing his speech. Low wages and "scabs" were one thing; killing was quite another. Within a few hours he published the following handbill and distributed about 1300 copies among the workers:

REVENGE! WORKINGMEN! TO ARMS!

Your masters sent out their bloodhounds—the police—they killed six of your brothers at McCormick's this afternoon. They killed the poor wretches, because they, like you, had courage to disobey the supreme will of your bosses. They killed them because they dared ask for the shortening of the hours of toil. They killed them to show you "free American citizens" that you must be satisfied and contented with what ever your bosses condescend to allow you, or you will get killed! . . .[7]

"The Mine" is an eye witness description of conditions, while "The Haymarket Riot" narrates action of people and institutions. Eye-witness accounts are often included as "source" materials in books of readings designed for history courses. Narratives (written long after the events take place) begin to appear more frequently in instruction in history, political science (accounts of the making of political decisions, the paths of legislation, election campaigns, etc.), business and economics (tales of the growth and problems of particular enterprises and companies).

Documents

These include court opinions, speeches, letters, diaries, transcripts of trials and hearings, laws, charters, contracts, commission reports. Public documents have the status of formal and legally valid records.

Illustration:

AN UNEMPLOYED TEXTILE WORKER

Q. What is your business? A. I am a mule-skinner by trade. I have worked at it since I have been in this country—eleven years.

Q. Are you a married man? A. Yes, sir; I am a married man; have a wife and two children. I am not very well educated. I went to work when I was about eight or nine years old. I was going to state how I live. My children get along very well in summertime, on account of not having to buy fuel or shoes or one thing and another. I earn $1.50 a day and can't afford to pay a very big house rent. I pay $1.50 a week for rent, which comes to about $6 a month.

Q. That is, you pay this where you are at Fall River? A. Yes, sir.

Q. Do you have work right along? A. No, sir, since that strike we had down in Fall River about three years ago I have not worked much more than half the time, and that has brought my circumstances down very much...And another thing that helped to keep me down: A year ago this month I buried the oldest boy we had, and that brings things very expensive on a poor man. For instance, it will cost there, to bury a body, about $100 ... Doctor's bills are very heavy—about $2 a visit; and if a doctor comes once a day for two or three weeks it is quite a pile for a poor man to pay.[8]

MULLER V. OREGON

Excerpts from Supreme Court Opinion

... The single question is the constitutionality of the statute under which the defendant was convicted, so far as affects the work of a female in a laundry....

It is the law of Oregon that women, whether married or single, have equal contractual and personal rights with men....

That woman's physical structure and the performance of maternal functions place her at a disadvantage in the struggle for subsistence is obvious. This is especially true when the burdens of motherhood are upon her. Even when they are not, by abundant testimony of the medical fraternity continuance for a long time on her feet at work, repeating this from day to day, tends to injurious effects upon the body, and, as healthy mothers are essential to vigorous offspring, the physical well-being of woman becomes an object of public interest and care in order to preserve the strength and vigor of the race....[9]

Court opinion, briefs, and official testimony are most typically used in the teaching of law, the area which provides, perhaps, the most widely understood referent for the term "case."

Research data

Reports of experimental and survey studies, with statistical data that can be used as empirical evidence in the testing of factual claims.

Illustration:

THE ECONOMIC SCENE, 1890

The Census of 1890 revealed a total population in the United States of just under 63 million people, of whom 23 million belonged to the labor force. The distribution of these workers among the sectors of the economy was (in round figures) as follows:

Agriculture   10,000,000 (until recently farm workers had constituted over
                    50 percent of the labor force.)
Manufacturing 5,000,000
Trade and finance 2,000,000
Transportation 1,500,000
Construction 1,500,000
Domestic Service 1,500,000
Professional and governmental service 1,000,000
Mines, forestry, fishing 700,000
Miscellaneous 700,000

The labor force can also be divided by sex and age. Of the 23 million workers, roughly 83 percent were males, 17 percent females. About 1.5 million of all the workers were between the ages of 10 and 15 (although these figures do not count many children working part-time on farms or in tenements). Approximately one out of every 16 workers was a child, and about one out of every six persons between the ages of 10 and 15 was working.[10]

Such data can be used to train for skills in the analysis of statistics in tabular and graph form for reaching generalizations "inductively" from raw data rather than secondary sources.

Text

The text decribes general phenomena and institutional trends; detail and specifics about individual humans are included mainly to illustrate generalizations. The text also *explains,* by giving definitions, casual theories and explicit "reasons" for the occurrence of the events it describes. It presumably offers objective knowledge—information which the reader accepts at face value, because he assumes it to be unbiased truth.

Illustration:

KNIGHTS OF LABOR

In seeking better wages and hours, the American worker depended upon the willingness of his employer to grant them. Clearly the employer had the advantage in this relationship, for he was under little direct pressure to improve his employees' economic conditions. If a worker threatened to quit the job, the employer probably would have little trouble finding a new man to take his place. This was especially true at a time when jobs were scarce.

A worker alone dealing with an employer was at a disadvantage; but many workers acting together could exert greater pressure. If all the employees of a factory joined together (formed a *union*) and demanded more pay or less hours, their employer would hesitate to ignore them. For they might simultaneously stop work *(strike)*, thus halting all production and attempting (by a *picket line* in front of the factory) to prevent other workers from taking the jobs just vacated. An employer could try to hire a whole new work force despite the pickets, but that would take time, and meanwhile his factory would be idle, producing nothing and therefore earning nothing for him. So rather than ignore the workers or fire them, he probably would negotiate with them as a group (engage in *collective bargaining*).

During the first three-quarters of the 19th century, American workers tried in various ways and at various times to form labor unions, usually on a local level and occasionally on a national level. By the year 1877, most of these efforts had collapsed. One of them had not, however. The Order of the Knights of Labor had been formed in 1869 by nine inconspicuous tailors meeting in the hall of the American Hose Company in Philadelphia. Their leader was Uriah S. Stephens, who had become a tailor after the Panic of 1837 had forced him to abandon his studies for the Baptist ministry. Stephens gave to the Order of the Knights its essential principles and character. It was a secret society (to be referred to in public documents only as "*****") in order to protect it from retaliation by employers. Moreover, its activities centered around elaborate rituals of almost religious character. In the initiation vow, for example, a new member had to declare:

I . . . do truly and solemnly swear that I will never reveal by word, act, art or implication, positive or negative, to any person or persons whatsoever, the name or object of this Order, the name or person of any one a member thereof, its signs, mysteries, arts, privileges or benefits, now or thereafter given to or conferred on me, any words spoken, acts done or objects intended; except in a legal and authorized manner or by special permission of the Order granted to me . . . . [11]

Although this selection relates to a single organization, and in that sense may be considered a "case," it is written in the style of a text and differs from a conventional textbook for a course only in the sense that it focuses on a narrower range of events. We have noticed a number of published "cases" written at a highly abstract level, providing not just description, but explicit explanation.

Interpretive Essay

Clearly intended as explanation and *evaluation,* the essay reaches interpretive conclusions on abstract issues such as "What were the causes of the Civil War?" "Was Rockefeller a responsible businessman?" or "Is the welfare state inevitable?" As opposed to the text, the essay attempts to construe objective reality, rather than simply report it. The essay attempts to *persuade* the reader to accept its evaluation or explanation; that is, the reader is assumed to be critical. Essays attempt to judge the present and past in terms of ethics, aesthetics and prudence; they offer definitions of concepts; they attempt to predict the future.

Illustration:

DOLDRUMS DECADE

In June, 1927, *The New Republic* published an editorial entitled "A Motionless Labor Movement?":

More and more observers of the American trade-union movement, both without and within, are asking the question, Why does not the movement get ahead? In numbers it is almost stationary. In ability to organize the basic, heavily capitalized industries such as steel, automobiles, electrical equipment and power, it shows little progress. In other industries hitherto strongly organized, such as bituminous coal, it is fast losing ground. In ideas it often appears to be sterile. Against the vivid background of hope for social regeneration from labor, which prevailed during the War and after, the existing prospect seems especially stale.

An observer noting these facts must admit as a preliminary to any further discussion that the unions have been beset with unprecedented obstacles. Their war increase in membership, gained through temporary and superficial pressures, represented in large part a hot-house growth which could not withstand the chill winds of deflation. Labor is traditionally slow-moving and is stirred by confused, deep currents; its process of reaction and of recovery is necessarily longer than that of a trim, executive-driven capitalist organization. In addition, it has to face the determined hostility of employing and financial groups who have laid aside none of their ancient hatred for the unions, and have gained immensely both in power and in wile. . . .

Pending the germination of leadership, labor marks time. Perhaps it is fallacious at present to speak of a labor movement in this country. A real movement would attempt not merely to get more of the same things which owners and investors already possess, it would tend to transform industry and in doing so would create important issues for public life. At present, the economic drift of the profitmaker dictates the sanctions of civilization within and without our borders; we are overborne by the brute power of accumulated things. Many are capable of seeing the danger; labor has a peculiar opportunity of doing something to avert it. Alone, it cannot save us, but it stands at the intersection of the conflict and occupies a position where strategy might count for something. Yet it finds necessary merely a defensive battle, because it is incapable of giving an aggressive lead. Its old men have apparently ceased dreaming fine dreams, and its young men are discouraged from testing their visions.

Some of the most famous "source materials" included in "readings books" are essays by political philosophers (Locke, Rousseau, the Federalist papers), economic thinkers (Marx, Keynes), or behavioral scientists (Weber, Freud).

The above categories of style represent in a sense a continuum from specific concrete portrayals of individual human action to general, abstract interpretation of institutional trends. The categories are obviously not mutually exclusive; that is, any given message may contain within itself *several* levels of style. Gathering information about the style or format of materials, however, is only a first step in the assessment of any set of "cases." In addition, one must deliberate about how the materials may be used.

USES OF CASE-STUDY MATERIALS

Case studies are employed for at least two general purposes, either: (A) to illustrate foregone conclusions, or (B) to provoke controversy and debate on issues for which "true" conclusions do not yet exist. The distinction between A and B is merely the extent to which the issue at hand has been previously decided or remains open-ended. Both categories allow for the study of descriptive issues (what the world was, is, and will be like) *and* prescriptive issues (what people should have done or ought to do). Let us consider each use separately.

Illustrating Foregone Conclusions

It is often argued that the most effective way to teach important factual information is to embed the facts in an exciting or dramatic narrative. Using the suspense or value-conflict of a well-told story tends to involve students emotionally, which renders facts intrinsically relevant, resulting in more permanent retention of the lesson to be learned. Cases quoted above contain extensive background material about the problems and institutions related to the growth of organized labor in the United States. In addition to specific facts, the teacher may wish to convey definitions of key concepts or technical terms such as boycott, public hearings, supply and demand, self-interest or free enterprise. Historical narratives, stories and hearings provide concrete examples of behavior illustrating such concepts. Similarly, the teacher may wish the students to "discover" a set of basic generalizations; for example, "employers used tactics that discouraged workers from organizing"; "wage level is partly a function of the available labor supply"; "rulings of the Supreme Court have an important effect on labor's relations to management." Cases may be used to illustrate and verify the validity of such generalizations. Finally, the cases can be used to support certain prescriptive conclusions or moral lessons: "Businessmen wrongfully exploited innocent women and children"; "Workers should use only peaceful protest and should be harshly punished for violence against the state." From these examples, it should be clear that the use of case materials does not necessarily protect the student from didactic teaching. One may use cases to support predetermined "answers," dogmatic positions, and rigid indoctrination. However, one may also use them to foster intellectual autonomy, as in the following category.

Provoking Thought on Unresolved Issues

Cases may be used in an open-ended fashion to stimulate inquiry and debate on unresolved questions of fact, definition, and policy judgments. The cases provide data relevant to controversial historical and factual issues: Did nineteenth century workers have reasonably decent standards of living compared to what they left in the old country? What was the major cause of labor riots? Answering these questions raises thorny definitional issues: the meaning of "reasonably decent," or "major cause." The cases also raise important *policy* issues on both the general and specific levels: What responsibility should an employer bear for the welfare of his employees? Should workers use violence as a threat? Should Jeff Sargent have joined the strike? Should August Spies be hanged?

The object of inquiry into issues of this kind is not to have the student learn or discover the correct answer. Rather it is to have the student analyze various positions or take a position and justify it rationally. Performance is evaluated, not on the basis of the student's mastery of substantive truth, but on the student's performance in constructing reasonable justifications of whatever position he reaches. Using cases in this way requires that the teacher be willing to accept from students conclusions that may be contrary to the teacher's beliefs; conversely it implies that students should not accept a teacher's opinion at face value, but only if supported by rational justification.

Having outlined alternative styles and uses of case materials, what can we say about the relationship between style and use. Intuitively, we might feel that some styles lend themselves more appropriately to certain uses; for example, texts usually convey unquestioned conclusions, thus they would be conducive to less provocative discussion perhaps than short stories. Comparison of sharply opposing interpretive essays would probably lead to open-ended debate, whereas a single research report or a single historical narrative may tend to answer more questions than it raises. In the final analysis, however, the teacher's objectives and attitudes toward inquiry are the most crucial determinants of how cases will be used. Nevertheless, a taxonomy on style and uses, such as the one offered above, may help to initiate greater clarification of the all-too-ambiguous notion, "case study."

References

[1] B. Berelson and G. A. Steiner. *Human Behavior: An Inventory of Scientific Findings.* New York: Harcourt, Brace and World, 1964. An instructive contrast between the *survey* and the *case-study* methods in social science research. The former, in gathering small bits of evidence from large numbers of individuals, aims to make general or nomothetic statements about groups; while the latter attempts to make individual or idiographic statements about discrete subjects. The survey technique looks for what large classes of phenomena have in common, while the case study tries to locate idiosyncratic differences among members of a general class. This attempt at definition is not adequate to allow one to differentiate clearly all materials into two mutually exclusive categories; case studies vs. something else. It is offered only as a general description of characteristics which many case studies have in common.

[2] Donald Oliver and Susan Baker. "The Case Method." *Social Education* 23:25-28; January 1959.

[3] For an alternative scheme for categorizing curriculum materials, see Donald W. Oliver and James P. Shaver. *Teaching Public Issues in the High School.* Boston: Houghton Mifflin, 1966. p. 143-146.

[4] Harvard Social Studies. Project *Transition and Conflict in American Society: 1865-1930.* Part IV, "Labor," p. 101.

[5] *Ibid.,* Case based on *Sister Carrie* by Theodore Dreiser.

[6] *Ibid.,* Taken from Homer Greene. *Coal and the Coal Mines.* Boston: Houghton Mifflin, 1894.

[7] *Ibid.,* p. 115. Based on Henry David. *The History of the Haymarket Affair.* New York: Russell and Russell, 1958.

[8]*Ibid.,* p. 91. Testimony before the Senate Committee on Education and Labor, October 18, 1883.
[9]*Ibid.,* p. 183.
[10]*Ibid.,* p. 99. Statistics taken from several sources.
[11]*Ibid.,* p. 107.

SOCIAL SCIENCE TEACHING WITH INTER-NATION SIMULATION: A REVIEW

R. Roger Majak
The Ohio State University

Crude simulation exercises have long been used in social science teaching at the secondary school level. "Thought-study" questions urging students to "Imagine you are . . . " have become standard fare at the conclusions of chapters in many civics, history, current problems, and economics texts. In effect, these questions ask the student to simulate a situation in his imagination. Similarly, mock political conventions, legislatures, and model United Nations are becoming increasingly common as annual social studies exercises in secondary schools. Local governments in many cities and towns cooperate with school officials by allowing students to assume the roles of local government officials for one day each year.

A more sophisticated simulation, designed for use in the classroom at the advanced high school level, now promises to reduce dependence upon students' imaginations and on local officials to devise simulated environments. A conceptual and mathematical model of the international system has been developed that can be taught to students, and that works much like the international system, with students participating as national and international decision makers. The simulation "game" is contained in a pair of manuals (a classroom instructor's manual and a student participant's manual) written by Northwestern University Professors Harold Guetzkow and Cleo H. Cherryholmes, principal developers of the model. These short (41 and 56 pages, respectively) handbooks, along with several tablets of forms needed for the simulation exercise, comprise a newly published *Inter-Nation Simulation Kit* (Science Research Associates, Chicago, Ill., 1966).

Reprinted with permission of publisher, from *The Social Studies,* 59, no. 3 (March, 1968): 116-119.

The Inter-Nation Simulation is one of several models of the international system (ranging from relatively simple war games to complex computer-operated simulations) originally developed by international relations scholars and various government agencies for international politics research. The Inter-Nation Simulation combines mathematical indicators and formulae with the behavior of human participants, thereby offering educational as well as research possibilities. The interaction of human participants with an international relations model produces a "simplified representation of a system of nations and international organizations" that "gives the participants the experience of making decisions in a miniature prototype of the complicated international world" (Participant's Manual, p. 2). While the temptation is great to call the simulation a "game," developers of the model and those who use it in research reject the use of that word. Unlike a game, no winner or loser emerges in the Inter-Nation Simulation—just as the ongoing process of international politics produces no winners or losers. Furthermore, unlike most games, one nation's gains in the Inter-Nation Simulation are not necessarily another nation's losses—that is to say, there is no fixed amount of resources or "chips" for which participants compete in an attempt to win everything and thus put the other participants out of the game. Rather, nations prosper, stagnate, or decline according to the skill and cleverness with which they allocate resources and conduct relations with one another.

The simulation is conducted in periods of from forty-five to ninety minutes. For classroom use, each period can be the length of a class period. As many periods may be conducted as the instructor and the class desire, either in immediate succession, or with as long as several days between periods. To begin, the classroom instructor (acting as simulation director) assigns from two to five students to each of from five to eight nations (depending upon the number of available students). Following directions in the Instructor's Manual, the instructor gives each nation information about its wealth, form of government, defense position, population, and basic resources—most of this information in the form of numerical indicators (suggested figures are provided, or the instructor may construct his own sets of national indicators). Students acting as national decision-makers communicate largely by written message, except in conferences or international meetings arranged through the simulation director. Following the procedural rules of the model, students allocate resources, produce goods, make decisions for their nations, devise national strategies, hold national meetings, and interact with other nations. All decisions and allocations are recorded on special forms. At the end of each period these allocations and decisions are calculated for each nation (in part by the students themselves, and partly by the instructor), again following manual directions. On the basis of the newly calculated figures for each nation, the simulation continues into the next period.

As presented in the S.R.A. kit, the Inter-Nation Simulation seems both deceptively easy and deceptively difficult to use in the classroom. Experimental use of the model with high school students showed that they learn the seemingly complex sets of names, concepts, relationships, and procedures with surprising ease. Mathematical equations are used, but these are no more difficult than the student would encounter in an introductory algebra course. The Instructor's manual suggests that one class period of discussion after the students have had one week to read and master the Participant's Manual constitutes a sufficient orientation and instruction period prior to simulating. This writer's experience suggests, however, that except for all but the most capable and motivated students at least three class periods of lecture, explanation, and discussion of the model are needed to prepare students for simulation participation.

As with any complex laboratory teaching technique, the Inter-Nation Simulation requires considerable time and effort in teacher preparation. The model provides its own rules and procedures, and once the game is in progress the instructor is not called upon to act as a judge of the quality of the students' performance. The instructor may be called upon, however, to remind students of the rules dictated by the model, making it important that he be fully familiar with it in order to be accurate and consistent in his enforcement of simulation procedures. This requires a thorough knowledge of the working details of the model best attained through simulation experience.

While the simulation can be conducted with minimum facilities, a flexible room in which furnishings and materials can be rearranged is necessary. Each simulation nation requires a reasonably private office consisting, at minimum, of an area separated from other national offices by a temporary screen. A critical part of the simulation is the "World Newspaper" which can be edited by a participating student (or students) or by an assistant to the simulation director. The newspaper gleans news of happenings in the simulation world from messages exchanged among decision-makers, from conferences, and from decision forms, and publishes several brief editions each period. Ditto or mimeograph facilities and an editor proficient in typing are necessary. In short, the physical logistics, planning, and personnel required to run a classroom simulation, while not extensive, demand considerable time and effort by both instructor and students.

Finally, no matter how good the training of participants and the planning on the part of the instructor, errors, confusion, and misunderstanding occur in the first several simulation periods until students get the feel of the system. Thus, it is often not until the third, fourth, or even fifth period that the full impact of the simulation experience can be obtained as it begins to run smoothly. Adding orientation time and the time devoted to actual simulating, therefore, the simulation requires a minimum of six to seven class periods. To obtain best results from classroom use of the model, from six to about twelve class periods, or an equivalent amount of time, should be allocated for it.

The educational benefits of the simulation technique as compared to more conventional teaching methods are not yet certain. The impressions of teachers who have used the Inter-Nation Simulation as a teaching device are the students who have participated gain a more "empathetic understanding of foreign-policy decision-making than when they are exposed only to textbook materials," that students' "attitudes about international affairs . . .tend to be more explicit . . . ." and that student motivation and enthusiasm increase (Instructor's Manual, pp. 29-30). Careful research on the impact of simulation teaching, however, has only begun. One recent study concludes that the simulation is no more effective than classroom study of published case materials in promoting fact mastery in the study of international relations. But considerable additional research is needed to reconfirm this finding and to test the effects of simulation techniques on other types of learning.

Despite this lack of hard research, some informed speculation about the effects of simulation teaching is possible based on the nature of the stimulation experience and the kinds of teaching environments educators suggest promote learning. The environment created by the Inter-Nation Simulation, for example, removes the teacher from the role of judge—a condition which many educators suggest improves the learning environment. The success of the student's nation in attaining its goals (which the students themselves establish) is the only indicator of student performance in the simulation. Similarly, the simulation permits the student to confront a responsive, manipulable environment in which errors, while they produce consequences in terms of the success or failure of the simulation nation in attaining its goals, do not impose the kinds of penalties that often follow errors in dealing with the real-world environment. Thus, the simulation provides an apparent "psychosocial moratorium" in which the student can experiment with the environment without fear of real-world sanctions. Finally, the Inter-Nation Simulation permits the student to deal with a simplified, understandable model of a complex environment—an environment that is remote to his adolescent experience and with which he would ordinarily have no direct experience until adulthood. Indeed, much teaching in the social sciences involves teaching about activities and environments that students have not yet experienced. This problem is partially overcome in the physical sciences by permitting students to perform experiments in the biology, chemistry, or physics laboratory. Simulation exercises offer a possible laboratory solution for the social sciences.

In more concrete terms, the Inter-Nation Simulation contains working examples of basic concepts and processes taught not only in high school civics and current problems courses, but also in World and American history, sociology, and economics. Simulation nations, for example, differ in their production efficiencies for consumer goods, capital goods, armaments, basic resources, and so forth. Students engaged in arranging trades for their respective nations, therefore, experience the possibilities and constraints imposed by the "law of comparative advantage." At the same time, the model imposes upon the student other "endogenous constraints" typical of political processes at the national and international level, forcing him to "grapple with 'realities' rather than bend the game to his wishes" (Instructor's Manual, p. 4).

Whether the Inter-Nation Simulation model is a valid representation of the real world of international relations is still being tested by political scientists and others interested in simulation validity problems. One indication that it does recreate many of the essential elements of international political interaction is that real-world diplomats from a large sample of foreign embassies in Washington who have participated in simulation exercises report that the constraints imposed and the atmosphere created by the Inter-Nation Simulation model feel very much like real-world diplomatic situations and activities.

The authors are commendably restrained in their claims for the simulation as a teaching technique—if anything, too restrained. The Inter-Nation Simulation is exceedingly rich in detail. Considerable effort has been made to explain the model with care and precision, justifying its assumptions whenever possible with available data about real-world nations and international relationships. The classroom teacher first approaching Inter-Nation Simulation might wish for a more thorough background explanation of the derivation of the model and the rationale behind some of its component indexes and relationships. The concepts of "validators" seems particularly ill-defined in terms of the kinds of values to be used when the instructor or groups of students act as decision "validators." For the most part, however, the authors have skillfully rendered a sophisticated model into understandable concepts. The result is a simulation teaching device that seems eminently operational for use in high school classrooms, that is rich in learning possibilities, and that promises—among the flood of simulations and games likely to appear for secondary school use in the foreseeable future—to retain a commanding position.

EVALUATION OF PROGRAMED INSTRUCTION IN THE SOCIAL STUDIES

Fred M. Newmann
University of Wisconsin

The enthusiasm with which programing is received in some circles has been matched by vehement opposition in others. Both the welcome and the reaction have tended to obstruct systematic evaluation of programing in general and social studies programs in particular.[1] This discussion will consider some of the obstacles to systematic evaluation and will suggest some alternative lines along which evaluation should proceed.

OBSTACLES TO EVALUATION

General Resistance to Programed Instruction

Most obvious of the stumbling blocks is a resistance to examine and to use programing at all. Rejection of the technique can be explained in many ways, but the negative reactions might be boiled down to two broad elements.

First, we find a "fear-of-robot" anxiety. Naive observers frequently equate programing with "machines," and they visualize a mechanical learning environment, devoid of human teachers. This arouses a certain horror that the human encounter might vanish from the educational process; thus, the refusal to experiment with and to consider programing seriously. Such a vision is exceptionally threatening to social studies teachers, for they are fundamentally committed (so they say) not to the mechanical learning of facts, but

Reprinted with permission of the author and the National Council for the Social Studies, from *Social Education,* 29 (May, 1965): 291-295.

to the development of attitudes, the ability to think critically and to engage productively in verbal interaction with human beings, not machines.

The second common element of opposition to programed instruction has roots in a fear of intellectual tyranny. Teachers dedicated to intellectual flexibility—taking the position that there may be several "correct" answers to certain kinds of questions—fear that programing, because it has been advertised as being so educationally effective, will dogmatically indoctrinate students with irrevocable and unrevisable bits of knowledge. Carried to its extreme, this would render students incapable of exercising intellectual autonomy. Social studies teachers operate in a field notorious for its ambiguities and diverse explanations. Committed to vigilance against intellectual tyranny, many tend to oppose programing, for it suggests to them the conditioning of rigid sets of responses in a field where so little absolute truth can be found.

Both the "fear-of-robot" and "fear-of-intellectual-tyranny" reactions are, to a great extent, wrongheaded. Competent advocates of programed instruction point out quite honestly limitations of the technique. They are known to agree that programing cannot replace aspects of the learning process that depend uniquely upon human interaction (the basic question is *which* aspects of learning do depend on spontaneous human interaction). Furthermore, competent programing specialists would not recommend the teaching of knowledge as absolute where no such knowledge exists (if there can be many correct responses to a frame, they should be so recognized). These counter arguments, however, usually fail to overcome emotional resistance to programed instruction, and the affective rejection blocks careful trial and evaluation.

Construing Programed Instruction As A Categorical, Even Unidimensional, Variable.

Enthusiasts in the programing movement (e.g., programers, publishers, and psychologists-turned-capitalists) have promoted their product as a unitary technique, a categorical device claimed to be more effective than other devices such as talking, reading, or viewing films. Over-simplifying programed instruction in this manner clouds over the significant degree of variation *within* programing and within other media of instruction. Making claims in terms of unidimensional conceptions encourages insensitivity to problems of evaluating the effect of the many variables, *within* a given program, that may account for its success or failure. Would it be sound to advise teachers to use films, simply because films may be considered "better" than books? Would we advise teachers to use tape recordings because they might be considered "better" than reading aloud in class? It is more useful, I submit, to evaluate materials on their own merits, giving greatest attention to the multitude of variables *within* the media that might be related to learning. Evaluation on the basis of categorical class seems foolish to me because I hypothesize (and trust I am not alone) that the broad categorical labels given to various techniques and media account for only insignificant amounts of the total variation in learning.

Evaluation Via Truth Tests

In their zeal to demonstrate the effectiveness of programed instruction, promoters have tended to use as criterion measures conventional tests of academic achievement. These "short-answer," "objective" tests measure the extent to which the learner can recognize, recall, discriminate, and reproduce information that has previously been transmitted to him. Favorable results on such tests can be conveniently used to show that particular programs accomplish educational objectives related to the acquisition of information in various degrees of concreteness or abstraction. The preponderance of truth tests in social studies indicates that the transmission of information is a primary target for evaluation. These tests may adequately measure the degree to which programed instruction accomplishes this facet of learning. However, heavy reliance on such tests forces evaluation down a narrow and limited path. I suggest that in completing programs, students perform and learn a variety of behavior other than that measured by the conventional tests. Systematic evaluation of programed instruction should also concern itself with those dimensions of learning not assessed by the familiar truth tests. We will deal later with more specific suggestions on this matter.

Premature Development of Lists of Criteria

There exists in the literature a certain emphasis on the need to specify criteria upon which programs should be evaluated prior to their purchase or use.[2] We applaud the concern for rigor in the selection of materials, especially to keep publishers honest as they ride the wave of educational innovation. However, it makes no sense to check programs against long lists of criteria when the reliability of the criteria have not been established, and, more important, when the relationship of the criteria on the list to various

measures of success has not been demonstrated. Detailed check lists constitute a presumptuous attempt to identify the *predictors* of success before the
success measures themselves have been developed. It is interesting to me that
for other instructional tools (films, books, teachers, etc.) we tend comfort-
ably to accept the fact that we lack valid measures of success, thus we
realistically rely on general intuitive hunches in the selection of media.
Perhaps programed instruction is considered so effective in some circles that
it is seen as virtually "dangerous" and must, therefore, be subjected to much
harsher scrutiny than the other relatively "harmless" media. I suggest that
first priority should be given to the establishment of instruments that validly
assess the learning outcomes of programs in terms of a variety of "terminal"
behaviors.

After such measures have been developed, then it becomes feasible to
examine programs internally, searching for those variables that constitute the
predictors of different dimensions of "success." This later stage of research
may yield a set of criteria that could be used as a checklist in the selection of
materials, but until that stage is reached, our unsystematic intuitions must
continue to provide the only basis for evaluation.

The four developments mentioned above have tended to obstruct systematic evaluation of programed instruction in the social studies. Evaluation
would be more systematic if there were (1) greater sensitivity to variables that
affect learning *within* programs, and (2) greater emphasis on the diagnosis of
behaviors performed and learned as the student works through a program. As
I address myself to this latter consideration, it should be clear that I am
concerned with learning outcomes not currently specified or measured.

THE NEED TO FOCUS ON INTELLECTUAL PROCESS: THE PERFORMANCE AND TEACHING OF DISTINGUISHABLE INTELLECTUAL OPERATIONS

What has a student done and learned to do in completing a program? The
pure behaviorist would answer this complicated question very simply by
referring to the frames and the list of correct responses and then asserting
that the student has emitted the given set of responses in the presence of the
given set of stimuli (frames). I would suggest that in emitting the "terminal"
behaviors, the student performs and possibly learns a variety of distinct cognitive operations: (a) many of which were unconsciously assumed by the
programer in the construction of the frames; (b) some of which were
consciously assumed; (c) some of which may have been taught, but
intentionally programed as such; and (d) perhaps some that were intention-

ally taught. Systematic evaluation, especially in social studies, should attend to aspects of intellectual process, even though behaviorist-programers often choose to ignore what they call the "inside" of the "black box." This is not to suggest that every program evaluator be a specialist in cognitive psychology, but only that he have some scheme or system of categories that aids him in describing the intellectual operations rewarded by a given program. The work of Bruner, Goodnow, and Austin (1956)[3] on the nature of categorizing, Bloom's taxonomy of educational objectives (1956), and Ennis' categories of critical thinking (1962) provide at least some clues from which to build alternative schemes for describing intellectual process. Presumably our commitment to "critical thinking" in social studies carries with it an obligation to be concerned with the nature of thought processes cultivated by the instructional materials we use. Outlines of the schemes of Bloom and Ennis are here presented as different ways of construing the cognitive operations that any particular frame or set of frames might represent.

OUTLINE OF BLOOM'S TAXONOMY OF EDUCATIONAL OBJECTIVES: COGNITIVE DOMAIN[4]

Knowledge

1.00 Knowledge
    1.10 Knowledge of specifics
    1.11 Knowledge of terminology
    1.12 Knowledge of specific facts

1.20 Knowledge of ways and means of dealing with specifics
    1.21 Knowledge of conventions
    1.22 Knowledge of trends and sequences
    1.23 Knowledge of classifications and categories
    1.24 Knowledge of criteria
    1.25 Knowledge of methodology

1.30 Knowledge of the universals and abstraction in a field
    1.31 Knowledge of principles and generalizations
    1.32 Knowledge of theories and structures

Intellectual Abilities and Skills

2.00 Comprehension
    2.10 Translations
    2.20 Interpretation
    2.30 Extrapolation

3.00 Application

4.00 Analysis
   4.10 Analysis of elements
   4.20 Analysis of relationships
   4.30 Analysis of organizational principles

5.00 Synthesis
   5.10 Production of a unique communication
   5.20 Production of a plan, or proposed set of operations
   5.30 Derivation of a set of abstract relations

6.00 Evaluation
   6.10 Judgments in terms of internal evidence
   6.20 Judgments in terms of external criteria

TWELVE ASPECTS OF CRITICAL THINKING
PROPOSED BY ENNIS [5]

1. Grasping the meaning of a statement
2. Judging whether there is ambiguity in a line of reasoning
3. Judging whether certain statements contradict each other
4. Judging whether a conclusion follows necessarily
5. Judging whether a statement is specific enough
6. Judging whether a statement is actually the application of a certain principle
7. Judging whether an observation statement is reliable
8. Judging whether an inductive conclusion is warranted
9. Judging whether the problem has been identified
10. Judging whether something is an assumption
11. Judging whether a definition is adequate
12. Judging whether a statement made by an alleged authority is acceptable

I would predict that most of the responses in currently available social studies programs reflect Bloom's category of "knowledge." Examples of programs dealing with "intellectual abilities and skills" can be found in a discussion by Lauren B. Resnick (1963).[6]

In evaluating current programs in terms of Ennis' categories, I predict that only operation No. 1 (grasping the meaning of a statement), No. 6 (judging whether a statement is actually the application of a certain principle), and No. 11 (judging whether a statement made by an alleged authority is acceptable) are typically performed. No. 6 and No. 11 appear only rarely.

At the risk of taking material out of context and with due apologies to the authors, I have included below three examples of programed instruction in social studies. In almost all programs we might generally characterize the student's cognitive operation as a search for clues that will lead him to write words, or to make choices between phrases consisting of a few words. To provoke discussion, let us consider the following interpretations of these three examples.

THE BILL OF RIGHTS
SET I
THE DEVELOPMENT OF THE BILL OF RIGHTS[7]

1-1 Immediately after the Revolutionary War, the 13 states set up a government without any important central power. During the next five years they became dissatisfied and decided to adopt a *new* form of government. A Constitutional Convention was called in order to draw up a *new* document providing for a ——(?)—— form of government.

new (better)

1-2 Each of the 13 states was like a separate country. But many problems arose between the 13 states—problems of trade, boundary disputes, non-payment of war debts—because the government was not satisfactory. So the people decided that they needed a new form of *federal*—— (?)——.

government

1-3 The Constitutional Convention was held in Philadelphia where leaders from 12 states wrote the Constitution, a document providing for a new form of ____(?)____ government.

federal

1-4 People did not feel that the reform of government was satisfactory, so the leaders wrote the C--st-t-t--n.

Constitution

1-5 The Constitution went into effect in 1789. Leaders from 12 states signed the Constitution and it was adopted by 11 states before it went into effect in the year, ——(?)——.

1789

In this introduction to the Bill of Rights, the significant cues consist of underlined words (*new, federal*) and some letters of words to be filled in the blanks (*f*_____ , *C--st-t-t--n*). Assuming that the student can identify these cues, he could probably make the correct responses *without* reading much of the verbal material. Looking only at the list of responses, one might assume that the objective is to have the student use the words, *new, government, federal, Constitution,* and *1789* as he begins to learn about the Bill of Rights. The responses give no evidence that the student comprehends the verbal material dealing with why the people wanted a new federal government, when the Constitution was written in relation to other events, how many states were involved, etc.

HOW A BILL BECOMES A LAW[5]

146. Before a bill ever reaches the President, it is voted on by *(both)* houses of Congress. The President vetoes a bill, and returns it to the *(house)* where the bill was first introduced. Now Congress has a chance to *(vote)* on the bill again. If two-thirds of the voters in EACH *(house)* are for the bill, it will become a law in spite of the President's *(veto)*.

147. Suppose, as President, you send the bill prohibiting teenage driving back to the Senate. The bill will become *(law)* in spite of your veto, if at least two-thirds of the votes in the Senate are (for/against) *(for)* the bill, and at least (what proportion) *(two-thirds)* of those voting in each house. If each house gives this required number of votes for the teenage driving bill, then your attempt to veto will have (failed/succeeded) *(failed)*.

The cues in the above frames are less obvious than those in the previous example. Many of the responses depend upon earlier frames in the program, and many depend upon assumptions that the student will use subtle logical operations (either consciously or unconsciously) in emitting his response. The logical operations are more evident in those frames containing "if . . . then" statements. Frame No. 147 gives a fairly clear structure; that is, discrete alternatives (for/against, failed/succeeded) within which the student is asked to make choices. As we glance at the responses (inserted in parentheses in the above examples), we see no reason why they should be grouped together, but we might conclude that if this series of responses has been made, the student will have performed the intellectual operations that, in this context, lead to the general fact that a two-thirds vote of each house can override a Presidential veto—perhaps a somewhat indirect way of teaching such a fact.

THE SUPREME COURT AND SCHOOL DESEGREGATION[9]

1-2 Homer Plessy was going by railroad from New Orleans to Covington, Louisiana. The coach in which Plessy sat had a sign, "For Whites Only." Although all but one of Plessy's great-grandparents were white, Louisiana law considered him a Negro; he was ordered out of the "White" car. When he refused, a policeman removed him from the car. The next day, Plessy was tried before Judge Ferguson for breaking the Louisiana law which required special railroad coaches for Negroes and whites.

According to Louisiana law, Negroes and whites were required to sit in *separate)* railroad coaches.

1-3 When Plessy sat in the coach marked "For Whites Only," he was *(breaking) (violating)* Louisiana law.

1-4 Plessy was tried before judge *(Ferguson)*.

1-5 The Fourteenth Amendment, passed after the Civil War, guaranteed all citizens equality before the law. Homer Plessy argued that the Louisiana law which required separate railroad coaches for Negroes and whites was unconstitutional because it deprived him of equal treatment granted by the Fourteenth Amendment.

The purpose of the Fourteenth Amendment was to *(guarantee equality before the law)*.

1-6 Plessy believed that the Louisiana law which required separate railroad coaches was *(unconstitutional)*.

1-7 Plessy said that the Louisiana law was unconstitutional because it *(violated)* the Fourteenth Amendment.

1-8 The Fourteenth Amendment required (1) *(equal treatment before the law)*, while the Louisiana law required (2) *(separate coaches for Negroes and whites)*.

The school desegregation program uses a different format—paragraphs in regular prose, each followed by test items, essentially in reading comprehension. We note here instances of greater flexibility, compared to the first two examples. That is, various combinations of words are correct for some items (1-3, 1-5, 1-8). This loosening of the structure could be advantageous, but it creates some problems of evaluation. What are the cues? Does the program *teach* the student to make correct answers? Or does it simply assume that if the student can read and if he "pays attention," he will acquire a growing fund of information that he may be able to use in later frames?

These examples raise several questions and issues for the evaluator. Perhaps he can offer nothing in the way of analysis but the simple statement that the frames are leading the student to attend to his reading, to pay attention. Can he identify the particular stimuli in a frame that trigger the correct response? Can he identify the combination of stimuli and responses that signify the performance of various intellectual operations as categorized by Bloom, Ennis, or others? How often does the programer expect the students to perform complicated cognitive operations without having consciously taught them to do so? To the extent that a program changes the conventional prose of social science instruction by merely inserting blanks, the program fails to meet psychologically sophisticated standards.

THE ACQUISITION OF BELIEFS REGARDING THE NATURE OF LEARNING AND KNOWLEDGE

We can hypothesize that, as a student performs different intellectual operations and is rewarded and punished for his behavior, he begins to acquire a set of beliefs about the nature of learning and knowledge. The methodology of learning (in this case programing) that might reinforce these beliefs should be carefully scrutinized, especially in fields and disciplines faced with epistemological issues as they themselves try to create viable bodies of knowledge. May I suggest that most of the programs I have seen (including the above examples) tend to cultivate the following kinds of beliefs:

1. Questions have clearly correct and incorrect answers.
2. Knowledge consists in the accumulation of a fund of correct responses.
3. Learning occurs while attending to relatively small amounts of material.
4. Learning occurs when one makes responses that consist of only a few words at a time.
5. Whenever you make a response, you will receive information about the correctness of your answer.
6. Learning is easy; i.e., without much mental effort one can almost always make correct responses.
7. The most efficient way to gain knowledge is through interaction with controlled and constant stimuli like the printed word, pre-recorded material, etc.

To the extent that these beliefs are considered educationally undesirable, one should evaluate programs and all instructional materials with an eye to preventing them and encouraging those considered more desirable. These observations are not intended as an indictment of programed instruction as such (that would violate my recommendation not to judge things categorically), but only to direct the attention of evaluators to the materials' possible influence on student conceptions of the learning process.

CONCLUSION

In response to the plea that evaluation take account of distinct intellectual operations and beliefs about learning and knowledge, I find two general arguments. First, there is a contention that programing as a technique can perform only a limited function—information giving. Therefore, the responsibility for attaining other education objectives (e.g., critical thinking, creative research, aesthetic appreciation, civic participation, etc.) rests uniquely with more spontaneous, less controlled activities such as interaction with dynamic teachers, independent student research, travel, etc. I oppose the contention that programed instruction should be construed categorically and that it is by its nature limited to information giving. There is no reason why programing, systematically and imaginatively developed, using a variety of visual (not only verbal) materials cannot teach more complicated intellectual, perhaps even affective, processes.

Second, the orthodox behaviorist would envision a much broader role for programed instruction, arguing that once we are able to specify the behavioral indexes of various intellectual operations and affective dispositions, then even programing will be able to accomplish educational experiences previously thought to be reserved to the exclusive domain of the human teacher. For the moment I find it less useful to argue over what programing in general can or cannot do than to concern ourselves with the systematic description of what any given program does, or at least seems to do. To perform this sort of analysis, we need to transcend some of the criteria of evaluation currently used by programers and publishers in their effort to implement quickly and distribute their products. Our knowledge of the learning process and our ability to affect it cannot be improved without more concern for subtleties easily obscured by the many passages of prose, interrupted by blanks, now sold as scientific learning devices. Programing in the form now commonly developed also raises the additional, perhaps more philosophical, question regarding the concepts of learning and knowledge that educators intend students to have. To cope with this issue, the evaluator should be on the lookout for those dimensions of learning outcomes that the programers have not consciously intended to shape.

References

[1] The most current and complete bibliography of programs available is compiled by Carl H. Hendershot, *Programmed Learning: A Bibliography of Programs and Presentation Devices,* published by the National Society for Programmed Instruction, Trinity University, 175 Stadium Drive, San Antonio 12, Texas. Current bibliography, through October 30, 1964, priced at $5.00; looseleaf, $8.00; supplements, $1.00.

[2] Leonard W. Ingraham: "Programed Instructional Materials in Social Studies: 1963." *Social Education* 28:15-17, 26; January 1964.

[3] Jerome S. Bruner, Jacqueline J. Goodnow, and G. A. Austin. *A Study of Thinking.* New York: John Wiley and Sons, 1956.

[4] Benjamin S. Bloom et al. *Taxonomy of Educational Objectives, The Classification of Educational Goals. Handbook I: Cognitive Domain.* New York: Longmans, Green, 1956. p. 201-07.

[5] R. H. Ennis. "A Concept of Critical Thinking." *Harvard Educational Review.* Winter 1962.

[6] Lauren B. Resnick. "Programed Instruction and the Teaching of Social Studies Skills." Helen McCracken Carpenter, editor. *Skill Development in Social Studies.* Thirty-Third Yearbook. Washington, D.C.: National Council for the Social Studies, 1963.

[7]*The Bill of Rights.* Tempe, Arizona: Programed by Learning Incorporated for Coronet Instructional Films, 1963. p. 1.

[8]Fred M. Newmann. *How A Bill Becomes a Law.* New York: Macmillan Company, 1963. p. 65.

[9]Alan Gartner. *The Supreme Court and School Desegregation.* Cambridge, Mass.: Harvard University Committee on Programmed Instruction, 1964.

PART FIVE

Research and Evaluation

Fred A. Johnson

"For truth is this to me and that to thee." H. H. Remmers has stated that these words of Alfred Lord Tennyson are too often an apt characterization of the dialogue in education,[1] and this observation seems to have singular relevance to the social studies. As numerous efforts are being made to revise the teaching of social studies, examination of its professional literature seems to reveal diverse assumptions, conflicting opinions, but relatively little empirical knowledge. The need for more reliable knowledge about such topics as inductive learning, the relationship of knowledge and behavior, and the process of curriculum change has been recognized by many social studies educators, who have taken action to stress the importance of research. In 1963, the National Council for the Social Studies published its first research bulletin, a year later its official journal, *Social Education,* began presenting an annual review of the research and in 1965 the Thirty-Fifth Yearbook of the Council was devoted to evaluation, a topic closely related to research. Recent publications by individual social studies educators also have been devoted to or given great emphasis to research.[2]

Despite the obvious need for reliable knowledge, several factors make it difficult to assess the influence of research upon the teaching of social studies. First, it must be acknowledged that what constitutes valuable, reliable knowledge in this field is controversial. Roy A. Price has reported that social studies educators at a recent conference experienced considerable difficulty in reaching a common understanding concerning the character, scope, and methods of research.[3] This controversy is not new, in fact, some educators believe it has contributed to the development of a schism between theory and empirical research. Lawrence E. Metcalf has cogently described this development as follows:

> One group of investigators has worked on building a comprehensive theory of social studies education. This group has pretty much rejected controlled experimentation. It claims, however, that its theory is not in conflict with well established facts. Another group has gathered and counted facts with-

out weighing their significance for basic theoretical problems. There has been notably little interaction or communication between the two groups. Each has worked independently of the other. Each probably always will be unappreciative of each other's conception of research.[4]

Whether the division described by Metcalf is real or assumed, until it is bridged, the value of research remains somewhat impaired.

The impact of research upon social studies education has been further reduced by the inadequate dissemination and in some cases improper use of research findings. Most of the research in the social studies has been conducted by doctoral students, and this research more often than not is never published. Though the review of research now presented annually in *Social Education* has done much to alleviate this problem, it still appears that much research may not be reported in the professional literature.[5] Even if research is published, it is doubtful that it will reach and influence teachers. For example, a recent study by C. A. Weber casts doubt upon the assumption that teachers have working knowledge of learning theory.[6] The findings and opinions of other educators also support the contention that research has not significantly affected educational practice.[7] Although none of these studies were specifically concerned with the social studies, there is little reason to believe that their findings do not apply with equal force to our field. Indeed, it seems reasonable to assume that existence of a controversy concerning research may have compounded our dissemination problem.

Educators aware of the dissemination problem have offered several remedies. For example, professors of education have been asked to stress research findings in their courses, professional journals have been urged to print more research, and teachers are challenged to engage in purposeful research projects. As of yet, it is difficult to assess the effect of these general suggestions. However, the most promising specific innovation has been the establishment of several regional educational laboratories to test, demonstrate, and publicize research findings. The basic purpose of these research oriented institutions is to provide a means for more rapid dissemination and implementation of proven educational practices.

If the social studies field is to derive full benefit from the newly created educational laboratories, we must as a profession end our ambivalence regarding research and seek its improvement. A detailed discussion of how this goal might be achieved is beyond the scope of this introduction, but certain basic propositions need to be stated. First, all research should be directly related to a comprehensive teaching theory. This procedure should enable researchers and research consumers alike to distinguish between significant research and that which is trivial in nature. Second, the concept *research* should be defined broadly to include studies which are philosophical and historical in nature as well as those which employ empirical methods. Only the nature of the question studied should determine the research methods used. However, if an empirical study is undertaken, care should be exercised so that appropriate statistical procedures are employed. Also to aid in the assessment of findings, all studies should include a description of how the data was acquired and analyzed. Finally, it must be recognized that quality research demands that we extend and improve our procedures of evaluation.

Evaluation is a comprehensive educational concept in and of itself. It is a broader, more inclusive term than measurement, for it includes not only the collection and analysis of data but also the placing of value upon it or reaching of some conclusion regarding its worth. Therefore, all evaluation as contrasted with mere measurement must be made with reference to values or educational objectives. In fact, evaluation is such a vital, inclusive concept that many educators believe it should be an integral part of all aspects of the educational process.

Evaluation and research are closely related concepts. Two conceptions of this relationship are common in the literature of the social studies. Traditionally, evaluation has been regarded as a tool of research. In this construct, evaluation is the process by which data are gathered, measured, and appraised. More recently, particularly in the literature of curriculum development, evaluation and research have been conceived of as a similar process lying along a confidence continuum. Studies may be labeled as evaluation or as research. Description of a study as an "evaluation" usually implies the use of techniques and methods of measurement which are less reliable and/or valid than normally found in studies characterized as "research." Readers should become familiar with these conceptualizations of research and evaluation because both are found in the readings of this chapter.

In the past, evaluation in the social studies has been hampered by a controversy concerning tests and measurement. First, there has been a general controversy between the advocates of essay type questions and the advocates of objective type questions. This disagreement seems now to be alleviated. A more serious problem has been the tendency to limit measurement and evaluation to factual cognitive objectives. This has meant that the development of many of the important skill and affective goals of the social studies have not been appraised. This gap between objectives and evaluation may be due to a value in our culture that maintains that a person's beliefs are private and privileged information, but it appears that the lack of adequate tests also has contributed most to the creation of this problem. However, recent developments seem to indicate that efforts to create the needed devices are succeeding. Let us hope that this assessment is correct for this attainment seems so vital to the future development of empirical research which in turn seems a necessary prerequisite to improving the teaching of social studies.

The readings in this section are organized into groups. The first group deals with problems of evaluation. Teachers concerned with the evaluation of effective thinking and the construction of objective and essay test items should find the three articles by Kurfman, Berg, and Solomon very helpful.

The five readings in Section B were selected to illustrate recent research and curriculum evaluation procedures in the social studies. Obviously, no attempt has been made to present an exhaustive review of the research or an inclusive discussion of curriculum evaluation.

The first four articles present completed research dealing with political socialization, critical thinking and values, simulation and a report of the Harvard Curriculum Project. Then, Dana Kurfman describes the evaluation procedures used to improve materials developed by the High School Geography Project. This article provides a model that could be used by any group interested in the evaluation of curricular innovations.

Today, nearly everyone concerned with the social studies seems convinced that change is necessary, but "change to what" and the "how" of change remains unresolved. However, it is clear to all, that change in the social studies should be accompanied by evaluation and research.

References

[1] H. H. Remmers, "Editors Introduction." In M. J. Francis Runnel, *An Introduction to Research Procedures in Education* (New York: Harper and Brothers, 1958), p. xiii.

[2] For examples, see Bryon G. Massialas and Frederick R. Smith, eds., *New Challenges in the Social Studies,* (Belmont, California: Wadsworth Publishing Company, Inc., 1965); C. Benjamin Cox and Bryon Massialas eds., *Social Studies in the United States,* (New York: Harcourt, Brace and World, Inc., 1967), or Donald W. Oliver and James P. Shaver, *Teaching Public Issues in the High School* (Boston: Houghton Mifflin Company, 1966).

[3] Roy A. Price, "The Major Issues and Recommendations of Conference Presentations and Discussion." In Roy A. Price, ed., *Needed Research in the Teaching of the Social Studies* (Washington, D.C.: National Council for the Social Studies, 1964), p. 1.

[4] Lawrence E. Metcalf, "Research on the Teaching of the Social Studies," N. L. Gage ed., *Handbook on Research on Teaching* (Chicago: Rand, McNally and Co., 1963), p. 962.

[5] Emily S. Girault and Benjamin C. Cox, "Review of Research in Social Studies: 1966," *Social Education* (31) May, 1967, p. 388.

[6] C. A. Weber, "Do Teachers Understand Learning Theory," *Phi Delta Kappan* (46), May, 1965, p. 433.

[7] Samuel S. Brodbelt, "Research—Unknown, Ignored and Misused," *Educational Forum* (31), January, 1967, p. 151-157, cites many examples supporting this opinion.

SECTION A   Evaluation

THE EVALUATION OF EFFECTIVE THINKING

Dana Kurfman
Director, High School Geography Project
Boulder, Colorado

The evaluation of effective thinking is a complex procedure but no more so than the development of effective thinkers. In fact, the evaluation of effective thinking is directly related to its development. Teachers and schools need to see whether their curricular plans and the everyday instructional processes of the classroom are actually productive of thought. And this is the function of evaluation. Close analysis of actual classroom experiences and their outcomes suggests the curricular features that have been valuable and those that should be improved.

Moreover, as any teacher knows, what is evaluated exerts great influence on what students see as important to learn. The first part of this chapter will include a discussion of the evaluation process in relation to testing and grading. In the second part two aspects of effective thinking, the creative and the critical, are identified and described. Each aspect is considered with respect to relevant student behaviors and the teacher behaviors which establish classroom conditions conducive to student thought.

The major purpose of the chapter is to describe various ways of obtaining information about the thinking effectiveness of students. Related to this are ways by which teachers can become better informed about their own classroom behavior as it affects student thought processes. A final section suggests some directions that evaluation of effective thinking may take in the future.

EVALUATION, TESTING, AND GRADING

Evaluating, testing, and grading are inseparable in the minds of most teachers. Sometimes evaluation and testing are even thought to be synony-

Reprinted with permission of the author and the National Council for the Social Studies, from Jean Fair and Fannie R. Shaftel, eds., *Effective Thinking in the Social Studies* (Washington: National Council for the Social Studies, 1967), pp. 231-253.

mous and, in a certain sense, they can be. Many teachers build into their examinations the whole process of evaluation in a beautifully over-simplified fashion. Any test which has a pre-arranged grading schedule associated with it does just that. When a teacher gives a test with the understanding that anyone who gets between 90% and 100% on it will receive an "A," the testing process and evaluating process are, in that case, synonymous. The evaluation criteria are very clear: 60-70 is low and is graded "D;" 90-100 is the highest category and is graded "A." Student performance is judged in terms of the percentage of questions answered correctly. When nine out of 10 questions are answered correctly, this information is placed against the evaluative criteria and the student is given an "A."

Of course, some major assumptions are built into this testing-evaluating procedure. One of these is that the test deals with the objectives of the teacher; in other words, with what the teacher is trying to see that students learn. A second assumption is that the test actually measures these ideas, attitudes, or abilities accurately. A third assumption follows from the previous two; that higher performance on the test is an indication of greater achievement of the objectives. When all these assumptions are met, it is clear that a test is truly an evaluation instrument. In this context, a letter grade is merely the outcome of the evaluation process. It is simply the symbol used to distinguish better from poorer performance.

In most discussions of testing and evaluation it is assumed that students are the subjects to be evaluated. However, it is just as easy to think of evaluating teaching procedures or curriculum materials. In these instances educators define the objectives they want to accomplish; devise a way to determine whether the procedures or materials measure up; and finally grade them by using such terminology as "adequate" or "inadequate," "acceptable" or "unacceptable."

Whether evaluation is focused on students, instructional procedures, or instructional materials, there are three aspects to the process:

1. A clear formulation of the objectives in terms of anticipated student behaviors in identified content areas.
2. The process of obtaining information about the achievement of the objectives.
3. A "grading" system, a way of delineating adequacy, so that the information obtained can be classified or "graded" along a continuum of acceptability.

For some educational objectives, it is easy to define what is intended, and it is also easy to measure the behavior. Finally, teachers have devised relatively acceptable ways of classifying behavior in terms of the traditional "A," "B," "C," or "D" grades. For example, such is the case when the objective is knowing the capitols of 50 states or the presidents of the United States. What these objectives mean is clear. A way of obtaining information about student knowledge of state capitals or presidents is easily devised in the form of a simple test. And the teacher has little difficulty in establishing standards. He may, for example, require that students know all 50 states for an "A," possibly 45 states for a "B," 40 states for a "C," and so on. For other types of objectives—those involving understandings, abilities, or attitudes—each of these tasks can become complex.

Effective thinking is one of the most difficult educational objectives to evaluate. In the first place, educators are usually not quite sure what is meant by effective thinking. In the second place, there are very few instruments for finding evidence of it. And finally, it is difficult to establish clear-cut grades along a continuum from "ineffective" to "effective" thinking. This is the case whether evaluation is of student performance, materials, or teaching procedures.

If tests are thought of as a means of obtaining information about behavior as a basis for evaluation, then clearly most objective tests used in classrooms do not provide much information about the behavior called thought. Most of the objective questions in teacher tests require primarily the recall of knowledge. Even in carefully prepared standardized tests it is unusual to find that more than one in three questions require some thought. The questions that do so often call for interpretation of passages, graphs, and cartoons. Others require the application of a generalization in a somewhat unusual context or the recognition of common characteristics in two seemingly unrelated phenomena.

However, more than these relatively conventional types of questions are needed to assess the complex variety of abilities and processes that go into effective thinking. Objective questions that directly measure identified thinking abilities offer some prospect of success, as do essay questions which are carefully formulated to require thought. Even more promising is the analysis of classroom interaction processes to identify evidence of effective thinking on the part of students, as well as evidence of teaching behavior that stimulates thought in the classroom. These three sources should yield the sort of information needed to make judgments about the effectiveness of thinking.

Information-gathering methods, such as these, need to be used in evaluation or students are not likely to pay much attention to improving their thought processes. Whether or not teachers place their emphasis on intrinsic rather than extrinsic rewards, it is an established feature of our school culture that grades symbolize reward and to a certain degree punishment for the students receiving them. If evaluation and the grades that ensue continue to be based primarily on tests of specific knowledge, evaluation is likely to reward primarily the temporary attainment of such knowledge. As a result students, as well as teachers, are not likely to take the objective of effective thinking seriously. As long as teachers judge the effectiveness of classroom procedures in terms of acquiring knowledge, productive procedures for promoting thought are likely to be ignored or confused.

DISTINGUISHING TWO ASPECTS OF EFFECTIVE THINKING

Throughout the educational literature from Dewey to Bruner, two aspects of effective thinking are identifiable, a creative component and a critical component. The creative aspect includes curiosity and hypothesis formation. It is the stage where inquiry and ideas originate. The critical aspect includes the rigorous analysis of questions and ideas. It is the stage where questions are clarified and ideas are tested. In effective thinking the two aspects interact continuously, but for the purpose of describing teacher and student behaviors the creative-critical distinction is useful.

Without curiosity or a disposition to inquiry, thinking rarely gets started. Unless students are curious, unless they ask questions of life around them, there is little chance that thinking will proceed. To this end several of the chapters in this yearbook have encouraged a teaching climate and teaching processes that will facilitate asking and seeking answers to questions. The climate in a classroom must be open to student question, opinions, and points of view. What is needed is the classroom in which the teacher asks open-ended questions and encourages students to do the same. It stands in contrast to a classroom oriented to the reward of right answers and the punishment of wrong ones.

Teacher behavior in classrooms oriented to thinking is different in important respects from teacher behavior in classes where thinking is not a major objective. In inquiry-centered classrooms the teacher stimulates question-asking by providing data and opinions in a variety of forms designed to arouse the curiosity of students. The stimulus might be a series of pictures of some phenomena which do not appear at first glance to be similar. When a student or a teacher asks "What can be seen here?" and then "What do these things have in common," the process of conceptualizing begins. Pictures, also, can be used to show apparent anomalies, discrepancies, departures from students' expectations, which may provoke students to ask why an unaccounted-for occurrence is taking place or what could explain it. Such questions are the beginning of the process of explanation. Another type of question asks what can be concluded from data. This is the process of interpretation. Still another thoughtful type of question can be stimulated by presenting apparently casual conditions and noting the results. Students can be led to ask what will happen if the conditions are varied. Responses to such questions are predictive in their import. In addition, questions of meaning or definition can be raised, as well as questions of value.

What distinguishes such questions from the ones commonly asked by many teachers is their open-endedness. Questions of the sort mentioned are likely to lead to hypothesizing on the part of students because no "right" answer is readily evident. Students are not merely recalling an answer developed by someone else. Teacher behavior that encourages students to propose generalizations, reasons, tentative conclusions, or predictions maximizes the prospect of creative hypothesis formation.

On the other hand, the "right-answer" classroom tends to focus on the sort of question to which there is some clear-cut, definite, and known answer. This sort of teaching behavior, with its emphasis on factual questions and pre-established answers, tends to have a deadening effect on curiosity and the disposition to inquire. Of course, some factual questions can stimulate effective thinking, but these must be questions that inspire students to seek an answer. Generally speaking, questions of established fact have a negative influence on thinking in the classroom.

In describing question-asking and hypothesis-formulating behaviors, the emphasis has been upon identifying conditions in the classroom that encourage such behavior. When the focus is on individual students, the basic behavior to be identified is simply whether a student raises questions and suggests possible answers. The behaviors that distinguish more effective from less effective questions and hypotheses are less readily identifiable, primarily because their effectiveness depends on what follows. Does the question stimulate and clearly direct inquiry? Is a student able to support his hunch with plausible reasons so that its examination seems worth the effort? Does the hypothesis clearly direct the search for data? Since evidence of thoughtful behavior is likely to come in the classroom, the importance of a classroom climate that will encourage such behavior is evident.

The second major aspect of effective thinking is distinguishable from the creativity involved in raising questions and suggesting answers. The critical-analytic feature of the total process focuses on the questions that have been raised and the answers that have been suggested. Students are asked to test the soundness of their generalizations, explanations, and predictions. Involved here are such student behaviors as checking the reliability and adequacy of information, identifying unstated assumptions, and following logically valid lines of reasoning. It is with critical thinking skills that most success has been achieved thus far in distinguishing effective from ineffective student thinking. In order to apply these skills there are rules to be learned and applied. There are criteria for determining the reliability of sources and for judging the logical validity of an argument. Students are called effective thinkers in the critical-analytic sense when they can demonstrate the ability to apply the relevant criteria in testing hypotheses.

This is not to suggest, however, that the critical aspect of thinking should be or is restricted to the stage of testing of hypotheses. Students also need to raise issues of clarity and relevance at the question-asking and hypothesis-formulating stage. This critical approach to the way in which questions are stated and hypotheses formulated is primarily an attitudinal matter; it is a tendency to probe questions and statements in order to clarify their meaning and their relevance. The introduction of a critical attitude needs to be handled very delicately by the teacher, however, because inappropriate teacher behavior may discourage the disposition to inquire. If the teacher emphasizes a critical attitude too soon, students who are not accustomed to laying themselves open to criticism may respond with silence.

It is clear that teachers can discourage curiosity and the formulation of hypotheses. But it is also clear that teacher behavior and other characteristics of a classroom determine whether concepts, generalizations, explanations, and predictions are treated as hypotheses and receive the critical examination they warrant. It is possible that a teacher might establish an environment where curiosity and hypothesis-formulation are encouraged, but at the same time, never help students develop criteria for more effective questions, never insist that the hypotheses receive a rigorous analysis. Often, in such situations, one opinion is considered to be as good as another, with no attempt to establish ground rules by which to make distinctions. In these circumstances students are not much more likely to become effective thinkers than they are in atmospheres where inquiry, curiosity, and free expression of ideas are discouraged.

EVALUATING BEHAVIOR RELATED TO QUESTIONING
AND HYPOTHESIZING

Little has been done in the evaluation of questioning-hypothesizing behaviors that is of much direct use to teachers and curriculum workers. No paper-and-pencil tests are available, largely because they are so inappropriate with respect to questioning-hypothesizing abilities. The use of paper-and-pencil instruments, in fact, is largely a denial of the dynamics involved in these aspects of the thinking process. Therefore, it is not surprising that much of the research in this area has utilized recordings of classroom interaction. The attempt to obtain information about a number of teaching variables and especially about thought processes in the classroom by recording teacher-student dialogues is certainly one of the significant and unique features of recent educational research.[1]

Keeping records of classroom interactions can be a useful way of obtaining information about thought processes. For high school teachers with 150 students such record keeping is useful primarily in evaluating their own teaching procedures; teachers may record samples of classroom dialogue for examination. Since few examples of any one student's thinking behavior will be evident in records of classroom interactions, high school teachers will find this technique less useful in the evaluation of student thought processes. Of course, this need not be the case in elementary school classrooms where teachers with from twenty to thirty students will be able to obtain information about many individual children as well as about their own teaching procedures. Over the course of a number of recordings of elementary school classroom dialogues, it should be possible to identify a sufficient number of instances of individual student behaviors to make evaluative judgments about the quality of at least some individual students' thinking.

It is feasible for many teachers to utilize tape recorders as a means of obtaining information about thought processes in their classrooms. Lacking such facilities, a teaching assistant or a student teacher can record significant points as the discussion progresses in the classroom. It might even be possible to train students as recorders. Some teachers have found it useful to keep logs of significant points in discussion.

The critical matter, of course, is what to look for in the classroom dialogue. Questions such as the following are needed to identify the significant points in the discussion.

1. What is it that evokes thoughtful student response? What are the problems, the areas of concern? What focuses dialogue upon the things that matter?
2. What kinds of questions are asked or raised? Are they definitional, factual, or value questions? Are questions soliciting conceptualizing, interpretation, analysis, prediction, evaluation?
3. What additional questions come up? Do they help clarify the major questions or do they lead thinking astray?
4. What proposals, suggestions, explanations, and predictions are made relevant to the question? Which receive attention and which do not? What happens to fresh or unusual ideas?
5. By what means are certain questions and ideas dropped from further consideration?
6. How are ideas which are suggested as hypotheses treated in the classroom? What kinds of questions and evidence are proposed to test these hypotheses?
7. Is an inquiry that is considered important by a number of students or by the teacher carried to a satisfactory conclusion? Or is it dropped before any closure is reached? That is to say, is there a conclusion to the process of testing the hypothesis?

As is suggested above one of the high points in a classroom dialogue is the question or statement that prompts subsequent thinking on the part of the students. Another critical point in such discussions is the occasion when the student proposes an opinion, a solution, or hypothesis. What the teacher does and what other students do when a particular question or proposal appears to be quite irrelevant to the pattern of previous conversation is significant. Clearly, effective teacher behavior in instances when irrelevancies are introduced must neither squelch the sincere student nor permit the irrelevancy to distract the group from the development of a particular line of thought. How the teacher and other students handle such situations so as not to discourage proposals, but at the same time keep the inquiry process moving along relevant channels is of major importance in evaluating the conditions conducive to effective thinking.

There are also occasions in the dialogue where students provide evidence of effective and ineffective thinking. For example, the failure to distinguish a factual question from a value issue, or to note that a particular term is being used in two different ways, are instances of ineffective thinking. Another type of ineffective thinking is that of mistaking a definitional problem for a factual problem and using an incorrect strategy to try and resolve it.

Using students to record significant points in the classroom dialogue could easily lead to their involvement in a self-conscious appraisal of the quality of thought in classroom discussions. Such appraisal would help both students and teachers identify examples of effective thinking and examples of ineffective thinking. Then both students and teachers are participating in the evaluation process. As a result they are likely to increase their insight into the attitudes and abilities involved in effective thinking.

Since so much of the creative aspect of effective thinking is attitudinal, the systematic assessment of relevant student attitudes should be considered. The attitude scales developed by Rokeach and others[2] suggest a promising way of measuring whether student attitudes toward the free and open consideration of questions change in the process of the systematic attention to effective thinking in the classroom.

Another fruitful possibility may lie in the preparation of cognitive preference instruments, one of which was developed to measure cognitive-attitudinal outcomes of the PSSC physics program.[3] This instrument contained a number of questions for which students were assured there were no right answers. Students were asked to indicate their preference for (1) specific facts or terms, (2) practical applications, (3) questioning the information given, or (4) fundamental principles. It would be helpful if comparable instruments were available in social studies to provide some insight into student preferences for open-ended or closed types of questions, determinant or indeterminant situations, and certain or probable conclusions. Such devices would be useful additions in evaluating questioning-hypothesizing behaviors.

EVALUATING CRITICAL THINKING BEHAVIORS

Far more progress has been made with the critical thinking aspect of thought than with the creative aspect. A few tests are available which are particularly useful in suggesting types of questions teachers can develop themselves. In addition a number of publications identify behaviors and provide useful examples of questions which might be used to tap critical thinking skills. Two taxonomies of educational objectives, though not limited to aspects of critical thinking, are valuable.[4] The NCSS Bulletin, *Selected Items for the Testing of Study Skills and Critical Thinking* includes several hundred items measuring several types of skills.[5] Also useful are two NCSS yearbooks dealing with skill development and evaluation.[6]

The evaluation of information-gathering skills, even though important, is not a concern of this chapter. These skills center on knowing where to go for information and how to obtain information from a variety of sources, such as the library, books, maps, and graphs. Some of the tests devised to help evaluate such objectives often include a critical thinking component, usually identifiable by such questions as "Which source is the most reliable?" and "What is a sound interpretation of the information found in the graph or map?" Clearly, reliability and interpretation are within the province of effective thinking as the term is used in this Yearbook.

Reference has been made above to a few useful tests: the Watson-Glaser Critical Thinking Appraisal,[7] the Social Issues Analysis Tests developed by Oliver and Shaver,[8] and the Social Studies Inference Test developed by Taba, Levine, and Elzey.[9] Together they include most of the types of critical thinking questions developed in recent years. They will be considered briefly to indicate what abilities appear to be measured. Teachers may find certain types of questions upon which they can model their own tests. Of course, it is possible that the tests themselves may measure the kinds of skills a teacher considers important, and therefore be useful instruments for teachers in their present form.

One part of the Watson-Glaser Critical Thinking Appraisal[10] deals with inference. Inference is here defined as a conclusion a person draws from certain observed or supposed facts. After a brief passage is read, students are asked to mark "true," "probably true," "insufficient data," "probably false," or "false" with respect to several statements. A sample exercise follows.

"Two hundred eighth graders voluntarily attended the recent weekend student forum conference in a Midwestern city. At this conference the topics of race relations and means of achieving lasting world peace were discussed, since these were the problems that students selected as being most vital in today's world.

1. "As a group the students who attended this conference showed a keener interest in humanitarian or broad social problems than have most eighth grade students." (Answer: probably true.)

2. "The students came from all sections of the country." (Answer: insufficient data.)

3. "The students discussed only labor relations problems." (Answer: false.)

Ability in drawing inferences is, thus, very similar to the ability to determine whether existing data are sufficient for making conclusions of one sort or another.

The questions in an interpretation section require students to judge whether or not each of the proposed conclusions logically follows beyond a reasonable doubt from the information given in a brief preceding paragraph. As can be seen by the following example, questions in the interpretation part of the Appraisal are very similar in appearance to the questions in the inference part of the Appraisal.

"A study of vocabulary growth in children from 8 months to 6 years shows that the size of spoken vocabulary increases from zero words at 8 months to 2,562 words at age 6 years. Therefore . . ."
1. "None of the children in this study had learned to talk by the age of 6 months." (Answer: conclusion follows.)
2. "Vocabulary growth is lowest during the period when children are learning to walk." (Answer: conclusion does not follow.)

Another part of the Appraisal is called "Recognition of Assumptions." An assumption is defined as something presupposed or taken for granted. In the sort of question used to determine skill in recognizing assumptions, a statement is given and followed by several other statements which may or may not be assumptions underlying the original statement. The student is to indicate whether each potential assumption is really an assumption underlying the preceding statement or is not. The following is an example of such an exercise.

Statement: "We need to save time in getting there, so we'd better go by plane."
1. "There is a plane service available to us for at least part of the distance to the destination." (Answer: assumption made.)
2. "Travel by plane is more convenient than travel by train." (Answer: assumption not made.)

The next part of the Appraisal deals with deductions. In the questions requiring the process of deduction, the student is to determine whether a given conclusion necessarily follows from two given statements, assumed to be true. Deduction questions appear to require an understanding of the rules of formal logic.
An example of deduction is the following:

"Some holidays are rainy; all rainy days are boring; therefore . . . "
1. "Some holidays are boring." (Answer: conclusion follows.)
2. "Some holidays are not boring." (Answer: conclusion does not follow.)

A fifth section of the Appraisal is called "Evaluation of Arguments." The questions in this section follow the pattern of a debate proposition. Each group of questions is preceded by an issue: "Should the government do thus and so?" Judgments are to be made with respect to several statements. Each statement includes a "yes" or a "no," followed by a reason. Students are to distinguish between strong arguments and weak arguments by designating each one as strong or weak. Information in the arguments is assumed to be true enough. Students are told that a strong argument is one which is important and directly related to the question; an argument is said to be weak if it does not directly relate to the question, even though it may be of considerable general importance. A sample exercise is the following:

> "Should all young men in the United States go to college?"
> A weak argument is said to be: "Yes; college provides an opportunity for them to learn school songs and cheers."
> A strong argument is said to be: "No; a large percent of young men do not have enough ability or interest to derive any benefit from college training."
> Another weak argument is considered weak because of its irrelevance: "No; excessive studying permanently warps an individual's personality."

Clearly, many of the questions in the Watson-Glaser Critical Thinking Appraisal suggest useful ways of measuring certain identifiable critical thinking abilities. All parts of the Appraisal appear to draw upon abilities involving the relationship between two statements. One statement takes the form of a conclusion and the other takes the form of supporting evidence. The student is called upon to demonstrate his ability to see acceptable relationships between the two types of statements. High school teachers who see a similarity between these critical thinking abilities and ones they are trying to develop are likely to find the Appraisal useful.

Social studies teachers often need to find out the extent to which students can see relationships between supporting evidence and conclusions in some particular problem area under study, such as school segregation, causes of World War I, the shifting social roles of men and women, or causes of the Depression. For such problems an understanding of terms, facts, and ideas in the social sciences or history is needed. The Appraisal does not attempt to measure ability to use such knowledge.

In *Teaching Public Issues in the High School,* Oliver and Shaver describe four tests they developed for use with junior high school students. These tests focus upon the abilities involved in oral argument about public policy decisions. The first two Social Issues Analysis Tests are paper-and-pencil tests. The purpose of the first (Social Issues Analysis Test No. 1) is to assess how well students can identify selected intellectual operations occurring in an argumentative dialogue.[11] Students are provided with a dialogue between two persons about some such controversial subject as labor unions. At several points during the dialogue, students are referred to a question, such as the following:

> What does Joe's statement (i) do in the discussion?
> a. Gives examples to support a factual claim.
> b. Gives examples to suggest that a definition is not adequate.
> c. Suggests that Mike's position in the argument needs qualifying.
> d. Gives examples to support or illustrate a definition.
> e. Clarifies a word or phrase in the argument.

It would appear that Social Issues Analysis Test No. 2 may have wider applicability than the preceding test for classrooms in which intellectual operations have not been spelled out in the framework used by Oliver and Shaver. The purpose of Social Issues Analysis Test No. 2 is "to assess both how well the student can identify the substance of an argumentative dialogue (in contrast to the intellectual operations occurring in it) and the student's ability to select the best rebuttals which might be used to counter arguments in the dialogues."[12]

Each set of questions is based upon a dialogue between two persons on a controversial subject. (a) The first thing students are asked to do is to determine which of several statements best summarizes the argument. (b) Next, students are asked to select the one question out of the several listed, which best expresses the issue at a general value level. Both of these test questions depend on ability to comprehend what was read about labor unions. (c) The next two groups of questions deal more directly with reading comprehension. In this set of questions, the student is to identify statements that either one or the other discussant might have made. Students are instructed to say "can't tell" if neither or both persons in the argument may have made the statement. Then students are asked to identify the relevance of several statements of new information to the two positions presented in the dialogue. For example, students are asked to indicate whether the following statement would have supported the position of one person or the other in the argument: "Workers who belong to powerful unions are generally paid better than workers who belong to no union at all." Students also have the option of indicating "can't tell."

(d) In the final section of SIAT No. 2, students are given a series of tasks based on statements made during the dialogue. The procedure is to quote a statement from the dialogue and follow it with five questions. The student is to pick the two which to him constitute the best replies that might have been made to the statement quoted from the dialogue. Students are told that "best" means those statements which clarify the disagreement or move the argument forward toward some agreement. In other words, students must analyze the argument to choose as "best" replies those which are "important" and "relevant." This section of SIAT No. 2 is similar to the part of the Watson-Glaser Critical Thinking Appraisal which deals with the evaluation of arguments; however, SIAT No. 2 relies more heavily upon understanding of the substance of a problem area, in this case issues about labor unions. It seems to be a very useful model for the evaluation of critical thinking skills.[13]

Oliver and Shaver are realistically aware of the inadequacy of paper-and-pencil tests to provide information on the thinking performance of students in classroom discussion situations. Therefore, their efforts in SIAT No. 3 and 4 center upon interview techniques and a systematic content analysis of "free" discussion. SIAT No. 4 involves an evaluation process which appears far too complex for teacher use. However, SIAT No. 3 suggests a way of evaluating thinking processes that many teachers might like to try out. In this test, the interviewer reads the dialogue aloud. The student is asked to indicate how he would go about settling or clarifying the points of disagreement which have been described. He is first allowed to proceed at his own pace and in his own way in analyzing the dialogue without specific promptings from the interviewer. Next, the student is asked a series of questions centering on the type of disagreement involved in each phase of the dialogue and how he, the student, would go about clarifying or resolving each controversy. If the student has difficulty in identifying the type of disagreement as definitional, factual, or evaluative, he is told what it is and asked again for an appropriate way to deal with it.

It is very possible that this type of interview test might be conducted by several small groups in the classroom after some practice in the process under the leadership of the teacher. It is easy to imagine, at least in some classes, five or six groups of students, each one of which includes an interviewer, the student to be evaluated, and two or three judges or evaluators. The model of SIAT No. 3 and its analysis can serve as a guideline by which teachers might prepare their own dialogue tests to evaluate critical-analytic skills.

For students in grades three through six one of the few tests of thinking abilities is the Social Studies Inference Test developed by Taba and her associates.[14] It consists of a number of situations described in terms appropriate for the age group. A descriptive passage is followed by several statements,

each of which is to be designated as "probably true," "probably false," or
"can't tell." Some of these statements are simply translations of what appears
in the description. Some of them are inferences going beyond the data provided in the description. The statements which are merely a translation of the
information provided test "the ability to discriminate." This appears to be
simply the ability to recognize and translate what is presented to the students
and therefore constitutes a form of reading comprehension. A discrimination
score for the test as a whole is the sum of the correct responses to these
reading comprehension items. An inference score is obtained for the test as a
whole and is based on the sum of all of the correctly identified inferences.
Two other scores are derived. One of these is a caution score which is
obtained when the nature of the data is such that the most plausible answer is
either "probably true" or "probably false" and yet the student selects "can't
tell." A fourth score is the overgeneralization score. Some of the items in the
test are overgeneralizations that is, they go too far beyond the data; when the
student selects "probably true" or "probably false" as the answer to these
items, he adds to his overgeneralization score.

An example of a passage and a set of questions is called "Pambo and
Tom."

Pambo is twelve years old. There are no schools where Pambo lives. He
does not read or write. He fishes with his father every day. Pambo is
starting to cut bark from trees in order to make a canoe. His father teaches
him many things and is proud of how well Pambo can do them."

Tom is also twelve years old. He works hard at school and gets good
grades. When he comes home from school he reads his books so that he
will learn things that will help him.

Item 1. "Tom is smarter than Pambo." Since this is an overgeneralization, the student should answer, "Can't tell."

Item 2. "Pambo's father can read and write." The answer is "probably
false." This is an inference rather than a discrimination or comprehension
statement.

Item 3. "Tom reads every day because he is behind in his school work."
This is a discrimination item which should be answered "probably false."

The types of questions that make up the Social Studies Inference Test are
primarily discrimination in reading comprehension and data sufficiency items.
Since there has been little test development dealing with these abilities for
middle grade students, teachers of these grades particularly will find some of
the sets of questions most useful as models for making up their own test
items.

Two features that stand out in the critical thinking tests which have been examined are their emphasis on comprehension and on abilities involved in establishing proper relationships between conclusions and supporting statements. Several different types of stimulus material can be used for such reading comprehension, interpretation and inference questions. In addition to verbal passages such as those cited above, maps, graphs, tables, charts, and cartoons are possibilities. The argumentative dialogue as a stimulus can provide the basis for an even wider variety of critical thinking questions, questions which require identification of issues, selection of relevant supporting statements, and selection of good affirmative or negative arguments. Dialogues are possible on virtually any controversial subject. History teachers can devise dialogues based on the major positions taken with respect to controversial issues of the past. Such issues as constitutional ratification, the tariff, slavery, imperialism, the economic role of government, and involvement in wars all provide the occasion for dialogues upon which to base critical thinking questions. Such contemporary issues as poverty or taxation, the role of power in international affairs, ways of resolving interpersonal conflicts at school or at home can also be cast into the form of dialogue.

Although objective questions can be used to measure several of the critical thinking skills, their inadequacy lies in a failure to provide opportunity for the student to indicate why he takes the position that he does. In other words, they give the student no opportunity to explain himself. One way to permit a student to exhibit this explanatory skill is to provide him with questions that have several options from which one is to be chosen. He can then be asked to indicate briefly why he chose the option that he did. This kind of question works when the required response is predictive or explanatory in nature. For example, the student can be given certain conditions and asked to indicate which of several possibilities is most likely to occur. When he also is given the opportunity to explain his answer, he must clarify his thinking more so than he would in a question which does not include this explanation possibility.

More informal ways of evaluating the effectiveness of student thinking have always been employed by some teachers. These usually involve some form of essay writing. The evaluation of essay responses involves considerable difficulty, but ways of obtaining more reliable information from such responses are available.[15] Certainly the use of essay questions does not, in itself, assure that student thought processes will be exposed for examination. Most essay questions are of the factual type, even those couched in explanatory terms. "Describe two military campaigns in the Civil War" and

"Indicate the causes of the Civil War" are both factual, textbook oriented, and unlikely to produce evidence of student thought.

A number of suggestions have already been made about the type of questions likely to stimulate thoughtful answers. Their common element is the existence of an issue, either historical or contemporary. The issue can be based on the subject matter of a discipline or it can be a citizenship problem. In any case, the student is asked to take a position and support it. Students can write in a classroom testing situation or outside of class. It is probably more realistic to ask students to write a paper supporting a position without the ordinary time limits or pressures of a testing situation and with ample opportunity to use data without having to recall it. Moreover, students are often involved in controversial discussions and debates. An informal evaluation of their effectiveness in oral controversy can be obtained, particularly when students and the teacher have identified clearly some criteria for effectiveness in argument.

FUTURE EVALUATION PROSPECTS

Unquestionably, a major impetus to effective thinking as an educational objective has come from recent curriculum research and development projects. Research has centered on obtaining information about what actually happens in classrooms. The practice of recording classroom behavior should lead increasingly to clearer conceptions of effective thinking and better means of developing the abilities and processes involved. Moreover, at least two projects, those discussed above, have contributed promising instruments and suggestions for evaluating the effectiveness of thinking.

In other social studies projects, the emphasis has been more on the development of curriculum materials than on research. Most of these projects include effective thinking or inquiry as a major objective of their materials. However, little appears to have been done as yet to clarify precisely what is meant by the process of thinking, and correspondingly little attention has been given so far to evaluating thinking abilities and attitudes. Nevertheless, these materials provide excellent prospects for improving the evaluation of effective thinking. They promise to do this by increasing our insight into what effective thinking involves. Subjecting the materials to analysis can identify the thinking behaviors or thought processes the materials are likely to elicit. Although this can begin with the materials themselves, it should also include observations of students and teachers as they interact with the materials. As the anticipated thinking behaviors are identified, the means by which they can be measured and evaluated are also likely to be forthcoming.

Similarly, little has been done to evaluate the impact of educational games and decision-making activities on the development of thinking skills. Such simulation exercises represent another type of educational innovation with great promise for the development of thinking. But, in this case also, the thought processes presumably being called forth have not received an appropriate degree of analysis. This analysis is needed to provide a sound foundation for evaluation.

The exploration of the use of computers as teaching devices is just beginning. Computers also may provide an opportunity for evaluating the full complexity of thinking. An instrument that records verbal behavior while it prompts further behavior makes possible a dynamic rather than a static assessment of thought processes.

The use of a computer as an evaluator might begin with the presentation of a film describing a situation likely to arouse student curiosity. Attention could be directed to several types of problem situations, some of which might evoke explanatory questions such as "Why do the Eskimos behave like that?" Other situations might be set up to stimulate inquiry into moral and policy issues.

The computer would be stored with information relevant to the problem. The student would be urged to ask for whatever information he considered necessary to solve the problem. When the student felt able to propose a solution, he could again ask for the sort of information that would permit him to test the effectiveness of his solution.

The use of a properly programmed computer to interact with the student would permit an analysis of thought processes previously not accessible to description and evaluation. In using a computer this way the variable of the behavior of others would be excluded. As a counterpart to the highly promising classroom interaction procedures for evaluating productive thinking in a group context, there would then be available a student-computer interaction model with which to evaluate student thought processes in a non-social context.

With the recent and growing emphasis on effective thinking as an educational objective, school systems are likely to incorporate relevant materials and procedures in all grades. If these are to be effective, tests and other evaluation devices also will have to be developed and utilized.

What is needed is systematic study of the kinds of curricular patterns discussed in this yearbook—and others—as they function in actual classrooms and schools. Such study leads to whatever adaptations and revisions may be needed and to new and perhaps more productive patterns. What is more, students need real opportunities to see their own progress. Then they, as well as their teachers, will know that the improvement of thought processes is truly an objective of their schools.

References

[1] Several promising research studies are discussed in one volume. Bellack, Arno, editor *Theory and Research in Teaching*. New York: Teachers College, Columbia University, 1963. See also Taba, Hilda, and others. *Thinking in Elementary School Children*. San Francisco State College, U.S.O.E. Cooperative Research Project No. 1574, 1964. Oliver, Donald, and Shaver, James. *Teaching Public Issues in the High School*. Boston: Houghton Mifflin Company, 1966. Particularly p. 286-304. Massialas, Byron. "The Indiana Experiments in Inquiry." *Bulletin of the School of Education, Indiana University* 39: No. 3. May 1963. Massialas, Byron, and Zevin, Jack. "Teaching Social Studies through Discovery." *Social Education* 28: 384-87. November 1964.

[2] Rokeach, Milton. *The Open and Closed Mind*. New York: Basic Books, Inc., 1960.

[3] Heath, Robert W. "Curriculum, Cognition, and Educational Measurement." *Educational and Psychological Measurement* 24: 239-53; No. 2, Summer 1965.

[4] Bloom, Benjamin S., and others. *Taxonomy of Educational Objectives: Cognitive Domain*. New York: Longmans, Green, and Co., 1956. Krathwohl, David R., and others. *Taxonomy of Educational Objectives: Affective Domain*. New York: David McKay Company, 1964. Also helpful as a translation of the *Cognitive Domain* for social studies teachers is Sanders, Norris M. *Classroom Questions*. New York: Harper and Row, 1966.

[5] Morse, Horace T., and McCune, George H. *Selected Items for the Testing of Study Skills and Critical Thinking*. Bulletin Number 15. Washington, D.C.: National Council for the Social Studies, a department of the National Education Association, 1964.

[6] Carpenter, Helen McC., editor. *Skill Development in Social Studies*. Thirty-Third Yearbook. Berg, Harry D., editor. *Evaluation in Social Studies*. Thirty-Fifth Yearbook. Washington, D.C.: National Council for the Social Studies, a department of the National Education Association, 1963 and 1965.

[7] Watson, Goodwin, and Glaser, Edward M. *Watson-Glaser Critical Thinking Appraisal*. New York: Harcourt, Brace, and World, 1961.

[8] Oliver and Shaver. *Op. cit.*, Chapters 10 and 11.

[9] Taba. *Op. cit.*, p. 187-92.

[10] Watson and Glaser. *Op. cit.*

[11] Oliver and Shaver. *Op. cit.*, Chapters 10 and 11. See also Chapter VI of this Yearbook.

[12] Oliver and Shaver. *Op. cit.*, p. 194.

[13] The model itself is included in Oliver and Shaver. *Op. cit.*, p. 194-99.

[14] Taba. *Op. cit.*, p. 77-94 and 187-92.

[15] Solomon, Robert J. "Improving the Essay Test in Social Studies." Berg, *Evaluation. Op. cit.*, Chapter 7.

THE OBJECTIVE TEST ITEM

Harry D. Berg
Michigan State University
East Lansing

An objective test is made up of a series of scoring units selected in such a manner and of such a number that a valid sample of the trait to be measured is provided. The objective test item is the term applied to one of these scoring units. Its distinguishing characteristic is that it poses a task with a solution that is pre-determined by the item writer. This quality is incorporated in the testing situation by asking a question and then providing the student with two or more alternative answers, only one of which is correct.[1]

For written testing purposes, the objective item is commonly contrasted with the free response, or essay question, in which the student has considerable latitude in composing his answer, with the adequacy of this answer to be subjectively evaluated by an expert reader.[2] In comparison with the essay question, the objective item can be scored rapidly in a completely uniform and impersonal fashion; the trait tested for can be widely sampled; and the tasks presented can be made identical for all students. Also, when well conceived and written, the objective item can oblige the student to recall information and follow a built-in line of reasoning, with no chance of evading the item writer's intent. On the other hand, it cannot provide a direct measure of writing ability, and it is not well adapted to measuring the capacity to organize material and to demonstrate knowledge in depth. To fully exploit the possibilities of written testing the two kinds of questions, essay and objective, should be regarded as complementing one another, since the limitations of one are matched by corresponding strengths in the other. However, inherent limitations in either type should not be confused with those which merely are the result of continued poor practice. The products of hurried and unthinking item building have led to the mistaken belief that objective items are useful only for measuring the retention of factual information, and that essay questions must always be used to evaluate more sophisticated outcomes. It is the purpose of this chapter to offer some suggestions for improving and expanding the uses of the objective type test question.

Reprinted with permission of the author and the publisher, from Harry Berg, ed., *Evaluation in Social Studies,* Thirty-Fifth Yearbook of the National Council for the Social Studies (Washington: National Council for the Social Studies, 1965).

CLASSIFICATIONS OF OBJECTIVE ITEMS

Items can be classified according to form or according to function (what they require of students). The major forms of the objective item are the true-false, matching, completion, and multiple-choice. Each of these has uses to which it is best adapted. The true-false is particularly useful in testing situations in which there are only two good available responses—for example, those involving common misconceptions. The matching exercise can economize on space and time in testing for a knowledge of terms, names and places. The completion type is useful for drill exercises. But although the various item forms have their specialized uses, what is accomplished *within* any particular type is far more important than the differences among them.

A more difficult but more pertinent problem develops when an attempt is made to classify items, regardless of form, according to what they actually measure. Objectives in the social studies are commonly listed under such headings as "an appreciation of," "an understanding of," "an ability to apply," "a desirable attitude towards" and the like. In most cases little attention is given to thinking through such objectives in behavioral terms, and even less to determining whether test items truly require the student to demonstrate the desired behavior. The items may have a superficial validity in that one may contain the word "understanding" and another the word "appreciation," but all may measure only the recall of memorized, factual information.[3] It is possible that we have been oversanguine in our selection of objectives and the testing situations in which their achievement is to be demonstrated. Assuming this to be true, a classification is about to be offered which attempts to divide objective items according to what can be done rather than what we would like to be able to do. The classification is not pure in the sense that any item can be neatly fitted into only one of the categories. But it does take into consideration the fact that every item has a content and a mental process aspect; that items differ chiefly in the kind and significance of the knowledge they demand of students and in what the student is required to do with his knowledge. The major distinction is between those items which require only recognition, and those which are based on thought and understanding.[4]

Items based on the recognition of
　　1. memorized content details
　　2. specific factual information
　　3. concepts

Items which require thought and understanding through
　　1. the translation of knowledge into other terms

2. the use of knowledge in problem-solving situations
3. the ability to interpret social studies data

Items Which Require the Recognition of Memorized Content Detail

Ease of construction is the only quality which recommends the content detail item so frequently found in classroom tests. Items of this kind are objectionable in that they place a premium on rote learning and are unrelated to any major objective. These are the type of items which a high school student may get right, because he has been drilled upon the point involved, but an expert in the field may answer incorrectly. Content detail items should be used much less often not only because their continued use tends to keep students from working toward more important goals, but because they give a false notion of what is ultimately useful in a given course. The two following items belong in this category:

1. The clause "the powers not delegated to the United States by the Constitution, nor prohibited to it by the states, are reserved to the states, respectively, or to the people" is to be found in
   1. the Fifth Amendment
   2. the Eighth Amendment.
   *3. the Tenth Amendment.
   4. the Fourteenth Amendment.

It is likely that the ability to answer this item correctly involves for most students only the memorizing of what is to them a bit of meaningless information. The particular amendment in which a clause is to be found is much less important as a subject for teaching and testing than the meaning of that clause or why it was included in the Constitution.

2. The "necessary and proper" or "elastic" clause in the Constitution is the basis for
   1. delegated powers.
   2. reserved powers.
   *3. implied powers.
   4. concurrent powers.

The subject of this item can be justified if one is testing for meanings and implications. However, the item as it is written requires only that the pupil recall the invariably taught and memorized association of the two terms in the stem with "implied powers."

Items Which Require the Recall or Recognition of Specific Factual Information

The point made in the foregoing section is that items which reward rote learning, and which are included in examinations merely because their content appears in required reading, should be avoided. This statement should not be construed to mean that there is no place in a test for questions dealing with specific facts. "Having the facts" is essential to accurate thinking about social problems. The real point is that the test maker must make a distinction between facts that are useful and those likely to be sterile. An achievement test in the social studies should include a number of items that test directly for factual information about events, persons, places, etc. It may not be important to know in which Amendment to the Constitution a certain clause is to be found, but it is useful to know that the Declaration of Independence was signed in 1776 and not 1876, and that India is in Asia and not South America. Factual knowledge about the nature of an index and a scale of miles, and about various standard reference works is also important. The chief caution to be offered is not to overload the test with items of this kind merely because they are easy to construct. The following test item is representative of this class:

3. Qualifications for voting in the U.S. are primarily established by
   1. local government units.
   *2. state legislation.
   3. the Fourteenth Amendment.
   4. state conventions held by each political party.

Items Which Require the Recognition of Concepts

The term "concept" includes interpretations that have been given to specific facts, and to "big" ideas developed by scholars to make the social world more meaningful. More specifically, the classification, "recognition of concepts," includes items which test for terminology, principles, theories, cause-and-effect relationships, trends, generalizations, and values. Most of the knowledge which we seek to impart in the social studies lies in this broad area.[5] Items dealing with concepts are always to be preferred to those dealing with content detail. However, the basic point to be made in this discussion is that significant concepts may be tested for (1) at the level of recognition, or (2) at the level of demonstrated understanding.

In one of the articles of the required readings in the Michigan State University social science course the following statement appears, "government tax revenue should be higher relative to government expenditures in periods of high employment than in periods of substantial unemployment." A related test item in the category under discussion would be the following:

4. Which of these would be appropriate government policy during a period of full employment?
   1. Money spent on public works projects should be increased.
   *2. Taxes should be kept relative to government spending.
   3. Taxes should be lowered to increase consumer purchasing power.
   4. New government spending should be financed by borrowing rather than taxes.

Although the concept dealt with is significant, inspection of the above item in relation to the material from which it was drawn makes apparent that no great amount of thought or understanding is needed to arrive at the correct answer. The item, as stated, does not provide proof that the student knows the reasons for, or sees the implications of, the statement.

Items Which Require Thought and Understanding Through the Translation of Knowledge into Other Terms

Whatever the merits of the subject matter tested for, test items that belong in the three categories just discussed require the same mental process—straight recall or recognition. The student responding correctly to such test items uses his knowledge in almost the same context in which it was learned. In translation items, on the other hand, the student must re-orient himself by translating the specific knowledge he possesses into more general and non-directive terms. In doing this he cannot take an immediate "know-don't know" approach, but must exercise some judgment in deciding just what information from his store of knowledge is relevant. A step which requires the student to show that he has learned some of the properties of his knowledge is, in effect, interposed between the question and the correct answer. Translation, used either alone or as an element in problem-solving items, is one of the most useful techniques in the field of testing. The stems of such items often end with the words "which concerned" or "in regard to." The following two items are examples:

5. The provisions of the Compromise of 1850 which were most favorable to the South were those which concerned

1. the admission of a state.
2. slavery in the District of Columbia.
3. runaway slaves.
4. slavery in newly acquired territories.

6. What important change took place in the line-up of the nations fighting each other in 1917?
1. One of the Central Powers switched to the Allies.
2. The Allies lost one member but gained another.
3. An Ally of Germany dropped out of the war.
4. One of the Allies switched to the Central Powers.

In the first item the student must translate the broadly stated responses into more specific information. For example, "the admission of a state" becomes "the admission of California as a free state." The second item involves a similar process.

Items Which Require Thought and Understanding Through the Use of Knowledge in Problem-Solving Situations

At the opposite end of the testing spectrum from items placing a premium on rote learning of trivial information are those which require the student to use his knowledge in new contexts. In the problem-solving type of item the stem presents a new situation which must be analyzed and defined; and the responses become possible solutions which must be weighed against one another. The purpose of items of this kind is to discriminate among students on a basis of whether or not their knowledge has become functional and meaningful. A major concern is to identify and reward the imaginative but disciplined thinker. In the best problem-solving items, the information or previous learning needed to determine the answer can be assumed to be in the possession of most students. But the fuzzy thinker and the rote learner will be unable to see its applicability in making new comparisons, arriving at new generalizations, or drawing inferences. (An item of this kind may be difficult, but not because the needed information is obscure.) More items which require such abilities of students must be included in classroom tests if we believe that an objective of instruction is to develop genuine understanding of subject matter content and the ability to use it in thinking about important problems and issues. Items which require only the recognition of past thinking, no matter how socially significant, do not meet this standard. Two characteristics of problem-solving items should be noted in the examples that follow: (1) The question posed has not been asked in that particular form before. Therefore it requires the student to give careful thought to its inherent requirements. There may be a critical clause to be evaluated; definition of terms may be involved; some translation may be needed.[6] (2) The responses are so selected that the entire stem must be carefully assessed and kept in mind. The correct response is often of the best answer variety. (An absolutely correct answer, which can be selected without reference to the other responses, is more likely to be found in highly factual items.)

7. The difference in the approaches taken by the Interstate Commerce Act and the Sherman Act was to a large extent due to recognition of the fact that
    *1. competition is not feasible as a public safeguard in some industries.
    2. competition will invariably result in maximum production at lowest cost.
    3. size alone does not make an industry a combination in restraint of trade.
    4. the power to regulate interstate commerce is vested in the national government by the Constitution.

The above item poses a problem in which a comparison must be made. The Sherman and Interstate Commerce Acts must be compared, keeping in mind the critical elements of the problem. These are suggested by the phrases "difference in the approaches" and "due to recognition of the fact." Since both acts placed restrictions on business activity in the public interest, this concept should be seen as the referent of "approaches." The problem then becomes one of accounting for the differences in approaches to this end, and the selection of the response must be made in terms of a fact or principle to be recalled. Hence the further knowledge is needed that railroads and other utilities ("some industries") operate under peculiar economic conditions which makes competition infeasible as a public safeguard.

8. One factor which greatly influenced the selection of the specific organizational device used for the operation of nationalized industries in Great Britain was a desire to
    1. give the rank and file of workers a voice in policy-making.
    *2. prevent political considerations from unduly influencing economic decisions.
    3. keep these industries under the immediate supervision of Parliament.
    4. produce a truly socialized economy.

This item is intended to test the student's understanding of the organizational device known as the public corporation. The discerning student will note that the problem is not concerned with the reasons for nationalization, but with the reasons for selecting a particular means of operating nationalized industries. He will also find it necessary to translate "the specific organizational device" into "public corporation" in order to establish connections with his previous learning.

9. Assume that over a 10-year period consumer purchases had dropped from 75 percent to 65 percent of GNP, and that investment and net exports had remained the same, proportionately. On a basis of this information alone, we can *be certain that*
   1. total expenditures had declined, percentagewise.
   2. the size of GNP had declined.
   *3. government spending had increased, percentagewise.
   4. the size of disposable income had declined.

To correctly appraise this item the student must selectively recall and apply the knowledge that the purchase of the gross national product is always accounted for by four sectors of the economy, and that a decline in purchases in one sector must be accounted for by an increase in one of the others.

Items Which Require the Ability to Interpret Social Science Data

The items in this classification are not self-contained, but call for the ability to interpret an accompanying reading selection, graph, chart, cartoon or map. With test exercises of this type it is possible to measure a wide variety of concepts and mental skills. This approach has particular value in assessing the ability to think critically. An additional advantage derives from the fact that the interpretive exercise can closely approximate previous learning experience and the situations in which the skills and information involved ultimately will be used.

Whatever the nature of the reference material used (reading selection, graph, map, chart), the dependent items may be divided into three broad categories based on their relationship to the reference material. In the first category are items which are essential to a full understanding of the reference material, but could be answered without it. Items which require the definition of terms in their commonly used sense and items which are derived from the answers to previous items belong in this group. Such items should be held to a minimum since their content could be as effectively measured in discrete multiple-choice form.

The second category includes items which require both an understanding of the reference material and the selective recall and application of social science content not included in the test exercise. Although difficult to construct, items of this type should be used rather than those in the previous category.[7] The following exercise should be studied so that the reader will understand how these items differ from those in the previous category.

"... the Republicans had not reckoned with destiny. In a few short years that lay ahead it was their fate (1) to double the territory of the country, making inevitable a continental nation; (2) to give the Constitution a generous interpretation that shocked many a Federalist; (3) to wage war on behalf of American commerce; (4) to re-establish the hated United States Bank; (5) to enact a high protective tariff; (6) to see their Federalist opponents in their turn discredited as nullifiers and provincials; (7) to announce high national doctrines in foreign affairs; (8) and to behold the Constitution exalted and defended against the pretensions of states by a son of old Virginia. ..."

10. The point of time from which the author views coming events lies somewhere between
   *1. 1800 and 1805.
   2. 1805 and 1810.
   3. 1810 and 1815.
   4. 1815 and 1820.   (Category 2)

11. Which of these might the author have added to the measures listed?
   1. To adopt the Virginia and Kentucky Resolutions
   2. To protest against the Alien and Sedition Act
   3. To fight a war with France
   *4. To increase the national debt   (Category 2)

12. Which of these is being referred to in line six?
   *1. The Hartford Convention
   2. The Virginia and Kentucky Resolutions
   3. The Missouri Compromise
   4. The South Carolina Ordinance of Nullification   (Category 2)

13. The development in the previous item resulted in the
   1. election of Thomas Jefferson.
   *2. proposal of Constitutional amendments.
   3. refusal to enforce a tariff law.
   4. secession of a state.   (Category 1)

14. A protective tariff is one which is enacted to
   1. raise revenue.
   *2. aid domestic industry
   3. protect shipping interests.
   4. support a foreign policy.   (Category 1)

15. It is the intent of the author that the measures listed should represent

1. sources of partisan conflict.
2. Republican mistakes.
3. a growing spirit of isolationism.
*4. reversals of former policies.   (Category 2)

The third category is comprised of items which can be answered after a critical analysis of the reference material alone, i.e., the student need not recall social science content not included in the test exercise to answer the given item. Test items of this kind are useful in measuring critical thinking objectives such as the ability to make generalizations, to distinguish fact from opinion, to recognize assumptions, to detect biases, and others of a similar nature. Some examples are given in the exercise which follows:[8]

Read the following statement about education in the United States.

Financial support for public education in the United States comes almost entirely from local and state tax revenues. States of low financial ability, with few exceptions, rank at the top in the percentage of their income devoted to schools. Nevertheless, these states rank at the bottom with respect to the quality of schooling provided. It has now become evident that no plan of local or state taxation can be devised and put into operation that will support in every local community a school which meets minimum acceptable standards.

16. The central thought of the statement above is that
1. the poorer states devote a greater part of their income to education than do the richer states.
2. the richer states have better schools than the poorer states.
*3. education will be inadequate in many areas as long as it depends on local or state revenues.
4. no fair system of state or local taxation can be developed.
(Category 3)

17. The author of the statement apparently assumes that
*1. minimum educational standards should be higher than the levels now maintained by some schools.
2. there is no way to achieve greater educational equality in the United States.
3. people in the United States are taxed too heavily.
4. there is a direct ratio between the percentage of state income devoted to education and the quality of the schools.   (Category 3)

18. Which of the sentences in the statement deals most nearly with a matter of belief or opinion rather than of fact? The sentence beginning with
1. Financial support . . .
2. States of low . . .

    3. Nevertheless, they rank . . .
  *4. It has now become evident . . .   (Category 3)

19. In order to weigh the validity of the author's argument in his final sentence, one would need to have information about
  *1. what is meant by minimum acceptable standards and what it would cost to achieve them.
  2. how the various states actually rank in terms of percentage of income devoted to schools and in quality of schooling provided.
  3. the taxing capacity of the various local and state units of government.
  4. all of the above.   (Category 3)

Suggestions and cautions. The following suggestions and cautions are especially applicable to constructing and using exercises of the interpretive type.

1. Select reference materials which do not duplicate in point of view or content those commonly used in the classroom. Avoid items which can be answered on a basis of commonly possessed social science knowledge. A good check is to administer the items without the reference material to determine whether they can be answered correctly.
2. Avoid items which are merely variations of the same concept. Avoid items which are, in turn, derived from information needed to answer a previous item correctly.
3. Construct enough items to justify the inclusion of a selection of given length. One of the length of this page should yield six to ten items.
4. Avoid items which can be answered merely by glancing at a sentence in the selection. Such items may merely repeat word for word something stated in the selection.
5. A good idea for an item should not be discarded merely because it does not fit neatly into a predetermined skills category.
6. Edit the reference material to eliminate needless words and to make the material appropriate for the reading level of the group. Sometimes, as a result of careful editing, a student can be asked to infer what previously was specifically stated. Otherwise excellent reference material may also require editing so that the inferences called for are not too difficult.
7. Use a variety of reference materials if several exercises are to be made, including materials representative of such different classifications as the analytical, the descriptive and the opinionated.[9]
8. Observe the suggestions given in this chapter for making good self-contained multiple choice items.

Qualifications and Limitations on Items Measuring Thought and Understanding

1. What a particular item will measure cannot be predicted with absolute certainty. The validity of any item is affected by previous learning experiences of the student, and it can vary even within the same classroom. Any item may function at the rote learning level if the concept involved has been taught in the same way that it is used in the testing situation. In view of this, we must do our utmost to increase the likelihood that an item requires reasoning and understanding. Some items, by their nature, cannot function above the factual recognition level; others have potentialities for measuring higher levels of ability. This observation is illustrated by the following two items. The first merely repeats a piece of standard textbook information, the second is more likely to require thought.

20. Which of these was a President during the Reconstruction Period?
    1. Andrew Jackson
    2. James Polk
    *3. Andrew Johnson
    4. Theodore Roosevelt
21. Which of these Presidential powers did Andrew Johnson feel no need to use?
    1. To veto legislation
    *2. To call special sessions of Congress
    3. To pardon
    4. To act as Commander-in-Chief

2. Statistical data on item discrimination and difficulty are generally unrelated to the thought content of an item. A factual item measuring an obscure bit of information may yield a very satisfactory index of discrimination and also be quite difficult.[10] The real justification for the inclusion of thought items is their effect on the student's learning. Because tests are used as a basis for assigning grades, they assume great importance to most students. If tests emphasize facts, then the memorization of facts will become the goal of study, and not the development of a reasoned understanding of significant concepts. In other words, what the teacher attempts to teach and what the students try to learn may not be the same.

3. In the sample items which follow students are asked to make comparisons and inferences, to draw conclusions from data and to generalize, and to demonstrate other similar abilities. In making a subject matter achievement test, however, it is best not to regard these abilities as the primary objects of

item writing. They should be regarded rather, as useful techniques for the development of good items which measure an understanding of important concepts. For example, an item based on generalizing should not be included for the purpose of testing the ability to generalize but to determine whether, through the use of generalizing, the student shows understanding of an important content objective. There are several reasons for this qualification. The specialized abilities have not been sufficiently distinguished from one another; other factors than the specified ability may affect item difficulty; and sub-scores based on only a few items are likely to be unreliable.[11]

Item Ideas

Items which measure thought and understanding can be described and illustrated, but no simple formula can be offered for facilitating their construction. Experienced item writers with an extensive knowledge of content and of the principles of testing find that each succeeding item is as difficult to write as each of the preceding ones. One or two good test items an hour is usually maximum productivity. Often the idea for an item proves unworkable and must be discarded, and another approach has to be adopted. A good deal of editing to insure clarity, accuracy, and conciseness is usually needed. The following item ideas are offered as an aid rather than a solution to the development of good items. They do have the merit of illustrating procedures which may be used in testing a variety of concepts.[12]

Ask for a common factor.

22. Both the Wagner and Taft-Hartley Acts
   *1. increased the role of government in labor-management relations.
    2. definitely favored labor.
    3. definitely favored management.
    4. sought to eliminate communists from labor leadership.
Make certain that the incorrect responses apply to one or the other of the key elements in the stem.

Ask to have a development placed in a broader context.

23. With regard to which of these were Western European nations *least* in support of contemplated United States policy?
   *1. Conquest of North Korea
    2. Maintaining the independence of West Berlin
    3. Aiding the Hungarian revolutionists

4. The quarantine of Cuba

Requiring students to place a development in a broader context than that in which it was originally studied has possibilities (also item 56).

Ask for that which does or does not belong in a classification.

24. Which of these would come under a different basic classification than the other three when computing national income?
    1. The salary of the President of the United States
    *2. The interest received by a bondholder
    3. The fees received by a doctor
    4. The wage received by a factory worker

The student must first determine the nature of the classification and then find the item which does or does not belong in it.

Ask for the effect or result of a development.

25. One direct effect of the widespread use of the injunction in labor disputes in the United States was to
    1. protect workers against arbitrary discharge from their jobs.
    2. strengthen national labor unions.
    3. make the courts impartial arbiters in labor-management disputes.
    *4. strengthen the employer's position in dealing with labor.

Ask for a comparison, contrast, or an analogy.

26. The Point Four Program and the Alliance for Progress are similar in that both
    1. are chiefly recovery rather than development programs.
    2. are limited to the Latin American nations.
    3. require the gradual outlay of huge sums of money.
    *4. are intended to assist underdeveloped countries.

Ask to have a conclusion drawn from data.

27. In country A, 50 percent of national income is spent on food, while in country B only 25 percent is so spent. Which of these is a reasonable conclusion to draw from these figures?
    1. A smaller percentage of the population is engaged in agriculture in A than in B.
    *2. Per capita income is higher in B than in A.
    3. A is considerably better fed than B.
    4. B is less highly industrialized than A.

Ask for the analysis of a quotation.

28. "Happily formulated, favored by the times, and backed in effect by the British navy, it at once gained a potency in world affairs that went far beyond the military strength of the rising American republic." What is being referred to in this quotation?
   1. The Declaration of Independence
   *2. The Monroe Doctrine
   3. The Emancipation Proclamation
   4. The Fourteen Points of Woodrow Wilson

The quotation item is highly useful, but two precautions should be taken. The quotation should be drawn from some source other than the required readings, and non-functioning content should be deleted. (See item 58.)

Ask for an illustration or example given in the stem or the responses.

29. Of the following, which would furnish the best example to support the statement that property rights are not absolute in the United States?
   1. Factory workers in most cases legally do not own the machines with which they work.
   *2. Railroads may not increase their rates without the permission of the Interstate Commerce Commission.
   3. The consumer demand for a product contributes to determining the price at which it can be sold.
   4. Hired managers rather than stockholders are increasingly determining the policies of corporations.

30. Which of the following is representative of the goods which are subject to the most extreme fluctuations in production during the course of the business cycle?
   1. Wheat
   *2. Machine tools
   3. Electricity
   4. Clothing

Ask for comparisons within the responses.

31. Each of the following responses contains a pair of economic stabilization measures. Which pair is contradictory or self-cancelling?
   1. Increasing transfer payments, increasing deficit financing
   *2. Increasing personal income taxes, decreasing the interest rate
   3. Increasing bank reserve requirements, increasing the interest rate
   4. Increasing transfer payments, decreasing bank reserve requirements

Ask for what is essential, basic, ultimate or necessary as contrasted with what may be incidental or intermediate.

32. Which of these is *essential* to the "welfare state" as practiced in Great Britain?
    1. Public ownership of basic industries
    *2. Transfer payments to maintain minimum standards
    3. Fixing of prices and wages
    4. Lessened government regulation of the economy

33. Which of these is the *ultimate* source of funds for investment?
    *1. Income not spent for consumer goods
    2. Sale of stocks and bonds
    3. Personal savings
    4. Retained earnings of corporations

Ask for the consequences of a possible change.

34. At present Presidential electors are chosen at large rather than from single member districts within a state. What would be a likely development if the latter became the case?
    1. Only a candidate with a majority of the popular votes could win an election.
    2. Campaigns would be concentrated within the most populous states.
    3. The two-party system would be strengthened.
    *4. The electoral votes of a state would be split among rival candidates.

Ask for the explanation of a sequence.

35. The open shop, the closed shop, and the union shop have been prominent, in that order, since the 1920's. This succession can be accounted for chiefly by changes in the
    1. objectives of national unions.
    2. methods of organizing for production.
    3. attitudes of workers towards their jobs.
    *4. laws affecting labor-management relations.

Ask for a trend.

36. All but one of the following have been trends in the American labor force. *Select the exception.*
    1. To increase in productivity per man hour.
    2. To contain an increasing percentage of women.
    *3. To have an increasing percentage of union members.
    4. To expand at a faster rate than the general population.

Ask for the application of a principle or technique.

37. In a notable experiment in industry it was discovered that giving workers a sense of belonging and importance was more effective in increasing productivity than improvements in wages, hours, or physical conditions of work. It is likely that this study made use of
   1. content analysis.
   2. random sampling.
   3. the structured questionnaire.
   *4. the control of variables.

Ask for the implications of a policy, point of view or principle.

38. Those who believe that increasing consumer expenditures would be the best way to stimulate the economy would advocate
   1. an increase in interest rates.
   2. an increase in depreciation allowances.
   *3. tax concessions in the lower income brackets.
   4. a reduction in government expenditures.

The Responses

The careful selection of responses is as important in item construction as the wording of the question. The two major parts of the item, stem and responses, should be made to relate to one another in such a manner that the item will achieve its intended purpose. To accomplish this, the responses must be such that the student is obliged to consider all of the elements in the stem, and should be as nearly parallel in phrasing and length as possible. The following item fulfills the requirements of carefully phrased responses:

39. In contrast with the earlier technological developments which made mass production possible, automation is likely to lead to
   *1. an emphasis on skilled, rather than semi-skilled, labor
   2. a change in the geographical location of important industries.
   3. an increase in the productivity of workers.
   4. a substitution of capital for labor.

Note that all of the developments listed are likely outcomes of automation, but that all but one characterize mass production as well. In this item, the critical element "in contrast with" must be considered. Thought items are often those in which selection of the correct answer hinges on such phrases as "in contrast with," "is essential to," "shares in common with" and "may be concluded from." But the responses must be of such a nature that they make these phrases functional.

In contrast with the preceding item, the next one is characterized by defective responses. The correct answer applies conceptually to the total stem, but it could have been chosen even if the stem had read "which of these has been a result of the rise of modern industry?" Unless the responses are carefully checked, a key part of the question may be ignored in answering.

40. The rise of modern industry increased family problems because
   1. the proportion of women gainfully employed outside the home increased rapidly.
   2. the workers gained control of the tools of production.
   3. after the Industrial Revolution, the family became a relatively self-sufficient economic group.
   4. the center of industrial activity moved from the factory to the home.

Desirable incorrect responses are often those which are true statements in themselves, but are not appropriate in relationship to the stem. The following item is illustrative.

41. The Alliance for Progress, to a greater extent than earlier American aid programs, embodies the belief that
   1. a country with a rising standard of living is unlikely to go communist.
   2. repayment cannot always be expected in convertible currencies.
   *3. loans may be of little permanent value unless they are accompanied by reforms.
   4. attaching strings to loans tends to build anti-American sentiment in the borrowing nations.

Items with lengthy responses are not, *per se,* more thought-provoking than those with brief responses. Either may be factual or require insight. Generally speaking, the responses should not be more detailed than needed for the student to make essential distinctions among them. Highly detailed responses increase reading time and may cause the item builder to believe that he is testing for more profound insights than he actually is. The first of the following items has unnecessarily long responses. The much briefer second item serves the same purpose.

42. The most significant difference between the British and American political party systems is that
   1. the policy platforms of American national party conventions are not binding on the parties but the policy resolutions of British national party conventions are binding.

2. the American parties are less concerned with local issues than the British parties.

*3. the American parties do not regularly discipline their legislative members to maintain a unified party position on legislation, while British parties generally do.

4. the American party system has always been a two-party system while the British have always had several major national parties.

43. A major difference between the British and American political party systems is concerned with
   1. the number of major parties.
   2. eligibility for party membership.
   *3. party discipline in the national legislature.
   4. the existence of single member districts.

In most items, the student is provided with four or five positively stated, substantive responses. He is told, in effect, that the answer must be one of these. When "none of the above" is used as a last response the question asked is left open-ended, and the student must consider whether or not any of the substantive answers apply. Certain precautions should be observed in the use of "none of the above." (1) It should never be used in a best-answer type item (one in which the correct answer is only relatively correct). (2) The test builder should avoid consistently making it the correct or incorrect response, lest the student become aware of a pattern. (3) It should not be used unthinkingly as a desperation response. If it is, an absurd item such as one following may result.

44. A considerable increase in the income of an individual would probably result in
   *1. an increase in his personal savings.
   2. a decrease in his personal savings.
   3. leaving his personal savings unchanged.
   4. none of the above.

"None of the above" is most effectively used when it, in itself, makes a pertinent point in the concept being tested for, as in the following example.

45. Which of these operates outside of supply and demand to determine price?
   1. An increase in wages won by a labor union
   2. A general increase in prices
   3. A buyers' strike on the part of consumers
   *4. None of the above.

It should be added, parenthetically, that the use of "none of the above" or "more than one of the above" takes care of the weighting and scoring difficulties encountered in the use of items in which the student may check more than one answer as being correct.

"All of the above" is sometimes used as the final response, or in conjunction with "none of the above." "All of the above" has a weakness in that the student will have a clue if he finds that two of the substantive content responses apply. There is also the possibility that the first substantive response will be selected as being the right one without further reading of the responses.

All possible correct answers should not be covered in two or three of the responses. Note that the student does not need to consider responses four and five in the next item:

46. The maldistribution of income in the United States
    1. results in a generally higher standard of living.
    *2. results in a generally lower standard of living
    3. sustains a single, uniform level of living for all.
    4. is the result of a large public debt, in that poor people become poorer in paying their share of the debt.
    5. is, without question, desirable for the country as a whole.

Desirable correct answers are often those which are correct only in degree and in relationship to the other responses. The next item illustrates this point.

47. Which of these probably has been the basic factor which has produced changes in the other three in American society? Changes in
    1. the structure and functions of the family
    *2. economic production techniques
    3. rural-urban population balances
    4. the organization of labor

Items containing the words "most" and "least" are also of this nature.

48. Which is *least* likely to be a function of a trade association?
    *1. Encouraging competition
    2. Standardizing types of products
    3. Influencing government policy
    4. Protecting the reputation of the industry

The correct response need not always be of significance in itself. The concern should be that the student recalls and relates important knowledge in arriving at it. The following item is an example, as are those items based on illustrations (see items 29 and 30).

49. The part of the Compromise of 1850 which most nearly constituted a compromise in itself was that concerning
    1. the admission of a state.
    2. fugitive slaves.
   *3. slavery in the District of Columbia.
    4. the creation of territories.

A number of factors may contribute to a given development, or an institution may have several qualities. In either of these cases, testing possibilities can be increased through the use of the negative item; the one in which the response which does not apply is to be selected. The following manner of phrasing negative items is preferable to the use of the word "not" in the stem since it is more likely to call the student's attention to the nature of the item. (Double negatives are confusing and should be avoided.)

50. According to Marxian socialist theory, all but one of these would increase in a mature, capitalistic economy. *Select the exception.*
    1. The severity of depressions
    2. Class conflict
   *3. Wages as a percentage of the national income
    4. The percentage of unemployed in the population

The responses, as well as the stem, should be stated as concisely as is compatible with clarity. Avoid including in the responses introductory words which could as well be at the end of the stem, as in this item.

51. The geographical theory of cultural change maintains that
    1. geographic factors determine race.
   *2. geographic factors set limits on the cultures of people.
    3. geographic factors alone determine economic activities.
    4. geographic factors directly determine almost the whole culture of a people.

Four effective responses can sometimes be secured by varying the quantitative relationships between two elements of two basic alternatives.

52. In assessing the legislative infringements on private rights, the Warren Court, in contrast with the Hughes Court, has been
   *1. more concerned with personal and less with property rights.
    2. more concerned with property and less with personal rights.

3. less concerned with both personal and property rights.
4. more concerned with both personal and property rights.

It is permissible, but not desirable, to make what might be a good correct response incorrect through verbal tricks, such as reversing key words or inserting a negative. The reversal of "Protestant" and "Catholic" in response 4 of item 55 is an example, as is response 1 in the following item.

53. Horace Greeley is known for his
   1. advice to young men not to go west.
   2. discovery of anesthetics.
 *3. editorship of the *New York Tribune.*
   4. humorous anecdotes.

Professional test builders consistently use either four or five responses. This number usually exhausts all plausible responses while reducing guessing to a practical minimum. It should be added that the number of responses need not be kept constant throughout the test unless there is to be correction for guessing.

Finally, the responses should be examined to determine whether more than one can qualify as a correct answer. This may seem like a needless caution but dual answers are one of the more common defects in test items. Preoccupation with the correct answer or a concern for making the other responses plausible may be explanations why test authors make this mistake. It is desirable to have a colleague check test items to guard against this and other weaknesses in test construction.

Clues and Non-Functioning Content

One of the major advantages of the objective item lies in its potentialities for controlling quite precisely the knowledge and skills needed by a student to respond correctly. In practice this advantage is often lost through weaknesses in phrasing. Every item measures something, but what an item appears to measure and what it actually measures can be two different things. Effective item construction requires that the "something" corresponds with the intended purpose of the item writer. Difficulty factors that are extraneous to what an item purports to measure may unfairly handicap the students tested; for example, needlessly difficult vocabulary. On the other hand, students who would be unable to deal with an item as it is intended to function, may answer it correctly because of unintended clues or non-functioning content. The term "clues" refers to elements in an item which enable the student to select the correct response on some irrelevant basis such as common sense, simple logic or peculiarities in the vocabulary. An item has non-functioning content when only a part of the stem or part of a response are needed to respond to the item correctly. The existence of clues negates the apparent purpose of an item. Items with non-functioning content are objectionable in that they may give the student credit for knowing more than he really knows.[13] Some illustrations with comments will make these observations more concrete.

Clue—Interlocking Items

54. Which of the following nations was the dominant power in Europe in the sixteenth century?
    1. France   2. Italy   *3. Spain   4. Sweden

55. Which of the following best explains why Spain enjoyed a dominant position in Europe during the sixteenth century?
    1. She had extended her authority beyond the Pyrenees into northern Europe.
    *2. She led the other European nations in the discovery and conquest of the new world.
    3. She had extensive possessions and trading posts in the Far East.
    4. She assumed the leadership of the Protestant countries against the Catholics.

Neither of the above items contains a clue in itself. However, if the two are used in the same test the stem of the second will give away the answer to the first. It is tempting, of course, to wish to determine whether the student first has the basic fact and then whether he has the explanation of it. But for the reason given, interlocking items should not be used. Apart from this caution, the two items are instructive in pointing out how a concept may be tested for at different levels. The second item assumes that the student has the information being tested for in the first.

Clue—Items in Context

56. "Two apparently conflicting groups are able to establish a set of rules by which they agree to govern themselves in their relations toward one another for a period of time." This quotation has reference to the
    1. Fair Trade laws.
    2. loan and storage agreement in agriculture.

    *3. collective bargaining contract.
    4. two houses of Congress.

The above item draws its responses from widely separated areas. If it were included with items dealing with labor relations, the student would have a lead towards assuming that three is the correct answer. Such items should be separated in the test from others dealing with the same subject.

Non-functioning Content

57. The modern state system with the nation as a sovereign, independent unit goes back to the treaty of
    *1. Westphalia, 1648, which terminated the Thirty Year War.
    2. Utrecht, 1713, which brought to a close the War of the Spanish Succession.
    3. Vienna, 1815, which ended the Napoleonic Wars.
    4. Versailles, 1919, which brought World War I to a close.

Test makers sometimes seek to accomplish the purpose of interlocking items by including both specific facts and elaborations of those facts in a single item. Non-functioning content is usually the result, since the student is provided with more than one basis for answering correctly.

58. "In many respects he was the most wonderful man of the age; certainly the greatest in the United States. As a statesman, he was pure and incorruptible, but too irascible to lead men's judgments. He was the oracle of the House, of which he was, at the time of his decease, a member." This quotation describes
    1. George Washington.
    2. Thomas Jefferson.
    *3. John Quincy Adams.
    4. Daniel Webster.

It was indicated earlier that quotations to be analyzed may make excellent items. There is the chance, however, that only a small portion of the quotation may be the functioning part. When the preceding quotation was used in a test, it was discovered that the stem might as well have read, "Which of these was a member of the House of Representatives when he died?"

Clue—Position of the Correct Answer

59. What was the approximate population of the United States in 1790?
    1. 1,000,000   *3. 4,000,000
    2. 2,000,000   4. 5,000,000

In items dealing with quantities, there is an understandable tendency to wish to determine whether the student underestimates or overestimates the correct amount. If this procedure is consistently followed, it may become apparent to students that one of the mean amounts is likely to be the best bet as the correct answer.

Clue—Specific Determiners

   60. The Supreme Court
      1. always follows its own precedents.
      2. never follows its own precedents.
   *3. overrules its previous decisions only after careful consideration when they seem unsound.
      4. does not have precedents.

The words "always" and "never" seldom apply to human affairs, and the student learns that responses containing these words can usually be rejected as incorrect. Response 3 is also attractive because it is the longest and sounds appealing.

The following item eliminates these defects and is also more thought-provoking. (Note that all of the responses are facts about the Supreme Court.)

   61. Which of these facts about the Supreme Court was made evident by its decision that segregated schools violate the "equal protection of the laws" clause in the Fourteenth Amendment. That it
      1. has the power to declare a law of Congress unconstitutional
   *2. sometimes in effect reverses its previous interpretation of the Constitution
      3. often upholds laws under the "implied powers" clause
      4. has generally been the most conservative of the three branches of the national government

Non-functioning Content

   62. The average consumer today is usually
      1. a member of a consumer cooperative.
      2. well informed about the quality of the goods he purchases.
   *3. not well informed about the quality of the goods he purchases.
      4. consulted by the retailer before the retailer buys a stock of goods.

The alert student can almost immediately reduce his choices to 2 and 3 because between them all possibilities pertaining to a characteristic of the average consumer are accounted for.

Clue—General Vocabulary

63. When we say that an industry is *vertically organized,* we mean that it
    1. controls distribution and ultimate consumption.
    2. controls international trade and similar products.
    3. has no labor unions.
    *4. owns all the means of production upwards from mine to factory.

This item can be answered by merely associating the general vocabulary word "vertically" with "upwards" in response 4.

Clue—Verbal Consistency

64. Railroad companies and other companies carrying on interstate commerce are now regulated by a commission appointed by the President of the United States. This commission is called
    1. the Civil Service Commission.
    2. the National Chamber of Commerce.
    *3. the Interstate Commerce Commission.
    4. the Federal Trade Commission.

Key terms appearing in the stem should not be repeated in the correct response. However, when such terms are used in an incorrect response the item may be strengthened. This is the case in the use of "interstate commerce" in response 4 of item 7.

Non-functioning Content in the Stem

65. Government is the continuation, by the whole society, of a process of regulation already highly developed in the family. The family was created by the necessity to regulate
    1. sex.
    2. property.
    *3. the young.
    4. none of the above.

Only the second sentence is functional in this item; but the first is at least as important as a social studies concept. The item appears to be measuring for much more than it actually is. However, it is legitimate to use an introductory sentence to set up a testing situation, as in the next item.

66. Mass society is described as being composed of anonymous individuals. The word "anonymous" is used to convey the idea that the individuals involved
   1. are unaware that there are mass audiences.
   2. have little influence on decision making since they are unorganized.
   3. are known only to those who control the mass media of communication.
   *4. are unaware of other individuals exposed to the same stimuli.

Clue—Common Sense

67. In World War II, the U.S. Air Force devised tests to select in advance those men who stood a good chance of getting through pilot training. Even after all of the elaborate tests had been used it was found that four percent of the group that had scored highest on the tests failed to get through pilot training. The best statement we can make about this is that
   1. man is too unpredictable to study objectively.
   2. any experiment that is not perfect is not scientific.
   3. because of the amount of error, it is probable that the experiment should have been discontinued.
   *4. a small error in prediction does not make an experiment useless.

Some significant concepts may become obvious when used in a multiple-choice item. Another aspect of this experiment should have been tested for, or it should have been left to essay testing.

Clue—Inclusive Correct Response

68. The United States has essentially a two-party system because
   1. the Constitution of the United States discourages third parties.
   2. the Founding Fathers decided that a two-party system works better than a multi-party system such as is found in France.
   3. third parties tend to be absorbed into one of the larger parties when they seem to have extensive support.
   *4. this pattern of political activity developed due to factors in this country's history.

Response 4 is so inclusive and broadly true that anyone with good judgment would be likely to take it as the correct answer.

Clue—Overly Specific and Lengthy Correct Response.

69. The Protestant Reformation came largely because
   1. the "cycle of history" turned that way and the Protestantism of the ancient world repeated itself.
   2. of the great leadership of Luther, Calvin, Knox and Zwingli.
   3. of the corruption in the Catholic Church.
   *4. of a combination of causes long in the making—the rise of nationalism, the rise of strong monarchs jealous of the Pope's authority, the rise of a middle class which wanted to keep its gold from going to Rome, the Renaissance—converged in the fifteenth century to produce a religious revolution.

A clue may be provided when item writers consistently make the correct response longer and more detailed than the other responses. The phrase "of a combination of causes long in the making" also gives this item the defect of the previous one.

Clue—Incorrect Responses that are Variations of a Single Idea

70. The social scientists' explanation of the relationship of the leader to history is that
   1. every great movement is the lengthened shadow of a great man.
   *2. leaders are a product of their times.
   3. had any great leader been different than he was, the course of history would have been different.
   4. history is a reflection of great leaders.

The discerning student will note that incorrect responses 1 and 3 are variations of 4. Incorrect responses should not be more like one another than they are like the correct response. The particular item should either be reconstructed or put in true-false form.[14]

Clues—Verbal Associations and Grammatical Consistencies

71.	1803	(74)	First National Bank
72.	"War Hawks"	(78)	French Minister to the U.S. (only
73.	Alien and Sedition Acts		French name)
74.	1791	(85)	Negotiated a treaty with England,
75.	Napoleonic Decrees and		1795
	Orders in Council	(80)	Defeated by Indians in the North-
76.	Lewis and Clark		west
77.	Alexander Hamilton	(89)	French attempt to bribe envoys

78.	Genet	(86)	Party opposed to the Republics (only party listed)
79.	Virginia and Kentucky Resolutions	(76)	Explorers of the Louisiana Territory (only plural names)
80.	Anthony Wayne		
81.	Hartford Convention	(91)	Seizure of American seamen
82.	Thomas Pinckney	(88)	Prohibited American vessels from sailing to foreign ports (embargo means prohibit)
83.	Assumption Policy		
84.	1812		
85.	John Jay	(87)	Leader of an Indian uprising (only Indian name)
86.	Federalists		
87.	Tecumseh	(72)	Those who demanded war with England (pat verbal association)
88.	Embargo Act		
89.	XYZ Affair	(81)	Protest against the War of 1812
90.	1815	(83)	Making the national government responsible for state debts
91.	Impressment		
		(73)	Gave the President power to deport aliens (repetition of the word "aliens")
		(79)	Declared nullification the rightful remedy for unconstitutional acts
		(75)	French and English decrees against neutral carrying trade (repetition of the word "decrees")

The preceding matching exercise contains a variety of clues which could also appear in multiple-choice items. A number of them are indicated by the words in parentheses which accompany the righthand entries. Furthermore, the entire exercise rewards persistence and searching ability more than it does a knowledge of history.

If a test is to serve its intended purpose the items should be carefully scrutinized for the presence of clues and non-functioning content. Three general questions should be borne in mind when doing so.[15]

1. Is there any basis, other than that intended, on which the pupil can respond correctly to the item?
2. What is the minimum amount of information, skill, or understanding that the pupil must possess in order to respond correctly? How does this minimum amount compare with the intended purpose of the item?
3. Is there any element in the item that the pupil may disregard entirely and yet respond correctly? Are these any elements that need not necessarily function in determining the pupil's response?

The Key-List Exercise

Next to the multiple-choice item, the key-list or grouped identification exercise is most useful in objective testing. This exercise is essentially a series of multiple-choice items in which the responses are given in a key and remain the same for all of the items. The key may be made up of substantive entries as in the following exercise.

Key: 1. Applies to consumer expenditures
2. Applies to private investment expenditures
3. Applies to government expenditures
4. Applies to all of the above
5. Applies to none of the above

92. Likely to be the least stable of the three   (2)
93. Equal in amount to disposable income   (5)
94. Helps to account for buying the gross national product   (4)
95. Accounts for the largest portion of total demand   (1)
96. Most closely related to fiscal policy   (3)

Or the key may indicate the kind of answer to be looked for. Four exercises of this type in which the keys have wide application are given below.

Key: 1. A wished to preserve B
2. A wished to bring about B
3. A wished to get rid of B

Column A	*Column B*	
97. The New Deal in 1933	Loose construction of the Constitution with reference to the regulation of industry	(2)
98. Andrew Jackson	The United States Bank	(3)
99. Labor Unions	Use of the injunction in labor disputes	(3)

Key: 1. The statement is true, and the reason for it is also true.
2. The statement is true, but the reason for it is false.
3. The statement, itself, is false.

100. Civilization declined in the countries conquered by the Arabs—because the Arabs had little use for learning.   (3)
101. Moslem sculptors and artists produced few statues of persons—because such works were forbidden by their religion.   (1)
102. Islam is similar in many ways to Christianity—because Mohammed was originally a Christian.   (2)

Key 1. The entry in column A is an example of the opposite entry in column B.
2. The entry in Column A is synonymous with the opposite entry in column B.
3. The entry in column A and its opposite entry in column B are parallel (terms which are subpoints under the same topic).

Column A	*Column B*	
103. Villein	Serf	(3)
104. Baptism	Sacrament	(2)
105. Middle Ages	Medieval period	(1)

Key: 1. If "a" and "a" make a true and complete statement
2. If "a" and "b" make a true and complete statement
3. If "b" and "a" make a true and complete statement
4. If "b" and "b" make a true and complete statement

106. (a. Like, b, unlike) a political party, a pressure group is likely to (a. have a poorly defined and changing membership, b. consistently advocate a specific legislative program.)   (4)
107. (a. Like, b. unlike) political parties, pressure groups have tended to have (a. centralized, b. decentralized) organizations.   (3)
108. (a. Like, b. unlike) the political party, a major activity of pressure groups is (a. lobbying, b. harmonizing numerous diverse interests).
(2)

The suggestions made for writing multiple-choice items apply for the most part to the key-list exercise. A few additional comments are needed, however.

1. There is often a tendency to use a greater number of items than can be justified by the key. Do not have more than you would discrete multiple-choice items dealing with approximately the same material.
2. The entries in the key should be so broad and significant that they can reasonably be expected to be familiar to nearly all students. A student should not miss several items just because a part of the key is a highly specialized bit of knowledge.
3. The items can be made so that some of the entries in the key apply to more than one of them; and some to none at all. This possibility should be indicated in the accompanying directions.

SUMMARY

An objective test is more than a collection of individually good items. To develop an effective measuring instrument, considerations of difficulty, length and sampling must be taken into account. These will be discussed in Chapter 9. However, a test can be no better than its component items. It has been the purpose of this chapter to point out some ways in which item construction can be improved. How to increase the thought content of multiple-choice items has been a special concern. In attempting to make items more thought-provoking there is the danger, however, that appearances will depart from actual substance. For this reason considerable attention has been given to the nature of clues and non-functioning content. Numerous item examples to support and clarify the suggestions and cautions have been offered. These should be studied carefully.

The objective test has inherent limitations, but it also has advantages which other forms of measurement do not have. A problem in test construction is to secure the maximum benefit from these advantages through improved item construction.

References

[1] In the supply or completion type item the alternatives are not stated, but the correct answer is still pre-determined.

[2] The essay examination is discussed in detail in Chapter 7.

[3] Objectives and test items bear a reciprocal relationship to one another in the sense that the test items are useful for determining whether objectives are being achieved, but the possibilities of making truly relevant test items may, in turn, cast light on the attainability of objectives.

[4] For illustrative purpose, the multiple-choice form will be used since in it the maximum potential of the objective item can be realized. This form can require the student to make subtle, yet significant, distinctions, and it is the only one which can ask for the selection of a relatively best answer. Suggestions for the construction of other forms of the objective item are to be found in most standard texts on educational measurement. One of the very best discussions is "Writing the Test Item" by Robert Ebel in E. F. Lindquist, (ed.), *Educational Measurement*. Washington, D.C.: American Council on Education, 1951, pp. 185-249.

[5] An extensive compilation of major concepts in the social studies may be found in *A Guide to Contents In The Social Studies*. Washington, D.C.: National Council for the Social Studies, 1958.

[6] This is the most that can be tested for in a single item. Additional material will result in the forms of non-functioning content discussed later in this chapter.

[7] If the potential of the interpretive exercise is to be realized, the reference material must be truly functional. Merely having satisfactory data with respect to difficulty and discrimination are not sufficient to justify the inclusion of items.

[8] Additional examples are to be found in Chapter 4.

[9] Taken from Harry D. Berg, "Evaluation in Social Science," in Paul L. Dressel, (ed.), *Evaluation In Higher Education*. Boston: Houghton Mifflin Co. 1961, pp. 102-104.

[10] This observation has been confirmed by research. See D. L. Cook, "Relevance Categories and Item Statistics" in *The Sixteenth Yearbook of the National Council on Measurements Used in Education,* 1959, pp. 86-94. The nature and uses of the index of discrimination are dealt with in Chapters 9 and 10.

[11] This is the problem of construct validity discussed in Chapter 2.

[12] The sample items in this chapter follow the format used in most published tests. The stem may be either a question or an incomplete statement; or a sentence followed by a question or incomplete statement. Clarity and economy of words should be the determinants. If an incomplete sentence is used, the first words of the responses should be in lower case, unless such words are proper nouns, and the responses should end with periods. Upper case should be used with questions. The spacing and indentations should be as it is in the sample items. Key words or phrases may be underscored.

[13]Non-functioning content has sometimes been justified on the grounds that tests should be teaching as well as testing instruments. Admittedly, the ultimate purpose of a test is to promote learning. But its teaching and learning value comes from the use made of it after administration. The sole function of a test, when it is being given, is to secure information from the student in as exact a manner as possible.

[14]This item represents a special case. It is not a general weakness of the multiple-choice type item that the correct answer may be arrived at through eliminating the incorrect responses. In fact this procedure is necessary in "best answer" testing situations. However, items should be inspected to determine whether the same type of understanding is needed in eliminating incorrect responses as when the correct answer is arrived at directly.

[15]Hawkes, Lindquist and Mann, *The Construction and Use of Achievement Examinations,* Boston: Houghton Mifflin Co., 1936, p. 80.

IMPROVING THE ESSAY TEST IN THE SOCIAL STUDIES

Robert J. Solomon
*Vice-President, Educational Testing Service
Princeton, New Jersey*

In the classroom teacher's repertory of evaluation techniques, none is more highly valued than the essay test. Its reputed versatility and scope and its apparent ease of construction make it an attractive instrument for measuring student achievement. To the social studies teacher particularly, the value of the essay test lies in its potential to call forth from students the skills that are necessary tools of the historian and the social scientist.

That the essay test often fails to fulfill the promise that it seems to hold is well known to all teachers. The familiar comment that essay tests are easy to construct but difficult to grade is a clue to one important source of this failure. But this cliché is also misleading because essay tests only seem to be easy to construct. Paradoxically, it may be that the only way to make essay tests easier to grade is to give more care and attention to their construction.

Although tests can be used for instruction—and they inevitably have instructional implications—the main purpose of a test is to obtain information. The information is usually about somebody in relation to something.

Reprinted with permission of the author and the publisher, from Harry Berg, ed., *Evaluation in Social Studies,* Thirty-Fifth Yearbook of the National Council for the Social Studies (Washington: National Council for the Social Studies, 1965), pp. 137-153.

For example, does John (somebody) understand the United States Constitution (something)? As with any other system for obtaining information, we hope that the information obtained from the test will be dependable and relevant. If the information is dependable, it means that if we again sought the same information about somebody in relation to something, we would get similar results. If the information is relevant, it means that the assumed or apparent relationship of the somebody to the something is a genuine relationship.

Common sense tells us that information that is undependable is useless or, if used, possibly harmful. Moreover, information that is undependable can never be relevant; if the results are markedly different each time we gather them, the genuine relationship of the somebody to the something can never be established. But, it is also true that information that is dependable may not necessarily be relevant. For although dependability is essential, it is not sufficient in itself to establish the relevancy of information. As a means of obtaining information, an essay test must be both dependable and relevant.

In the terminology of testing, reliability and validity are the technical terms given to what has here been described as dependability and relevance. The intention is not to substitute a new terminology, but to dramatize by the use of less technical words the importance of these concepts for teacher-developed tests and particularly for the classroom teacher's development and use of essay tests. Throughout the discussion that follows the objective will be to emphasize those techniques of test construction and grading that contribute to the dependability and relevancy of essay tests.

The basic characteristic of the essay test that leads teachers to value it as an evaluation instrument is that it elicits a "free" response. In the freedom of the student to decide the what and how of his answer and to present it in his own words, lies the potential power of the essay test to provide unusual insight into the student's ability to generalize, to interpret, to analyze, and to evaluate—in short, to display the qualities of thought that are among the most important goals of education. By permitting the student great latitude in his answer, the essay test gives him an opportunity to demonstrate his learning, his intellect, and his imagination—or his lack of these qualities.

Nevertheless, the essay test does not allow complete freedom of response. It establishes a framework and a setting within which the student responds. It provides a basis for making comparisons among students by requiring the same tasks of all students or, if there is choice, limiting the choice of tasks to a few that are assumed to be relatively equal in difficulty. Thus the freedom given the student to display his talents is not intended to be license to use the test to conceal his ignorance. Ironically, the unintended happens more often than we like. The gamesmanship of essay testing is celebrated in the humor and folklore of education.

> Every student should train himself to be like the conjurer Houdini. Tie him as you would, lock him in as you might, he got loose. A student should acquire this looseness. . . . there are a great number of methods of evasion. Much can always be done by sheer illegibility of handwriting and by smearing ink all over the exam paper and then crumpling it up into a ball.
>
> But apart from this, each academic subject can be fought on its own ground. . . . I remember in my fourth year in Toronto (1891) going into the exam room and picking up a paper which I carelessly took for English philology; I wrote on it, passed on it and was pleasantly surprised two weeks later when they gave me a degree in Ethnology. I had answered the wrong paper. This story, oddly enough, is true.[1]
>
> "But sir, I don't think I really deserve it, it was mostly bull, really." This disclaimer from a student whose examination we have awarded a straight "A" is wondrously depressing. Alfred North Whitehead invented its only possible rejoinder: "Yes sir, what you wrote is nonsense, utter nonsense. But ah! Sir! It's the right *kind* of nonsense!"[2]

Like much humor, these stories have the ring of truth. The dilemma of the essay test is how to achieve the advantages of the free response with none of the disadvantages. How this is accomplished depends on the extent to which consideration is given to the fundamentals of validity (Is the test relevant?) and reliability (Is the test dependable?) in both construction and grading of the tests.

Although it is probably self-evident, it is worth noting that there are two critical stages in an essay test that bear on its validity and reliability. The first is concerned with the construction of the test; the second is concerned with its scoring. Both stages require adherence to certain measurement principles. At either stage the usefulness of the test as an evaluation instrument can be impaired. How well the test is constructed has a bearing on how well it can be graded. How well it is graded will enhance or diminish the test construction effort.

The first steps in constructing an essay test are the same as those in the construction of any other type of test. Before writing a single question—or thinking about one—major attention should be given to the reasons for the test and the ends to be served by it. At the same time, or prior to such considerations, the nature of the group to be tested must be considered. The classroom teacher making a test usually has the advantage of having taught each of the classes to be tested. By and large, he knows what they are like and what they can do. This is an advantage that should be maximized. The more familiar one is with the background and ability of the group to be tested, the less reason there is for him to present students with a test that ignores these factors. Unless there is a valid reason for not doing so, such as the desire to make comparisons among classes, the test should be geared closely to the abilities of the students taking it. The same test given to two groups that are quite different will not be equally useful in both situations in giving the teacher insight into the students' achievements. For example, a test for an honors class in American history composed entirely of college-bound students is not equally appropriate for a below-average, noncollege-bound group. (Nor should the course necessarily be the same.) A test that is too easy for an honors class or too difficult for a below-average class tells you a great deal less about each of these groups of students than one that gives each student in each of the groups a full opportunity to show what he can do.

However, the entire question of gearing a test to the group for which it is intended and in terms of the objectives to be served has important educational implications for classroom tests that should be considered in a larger context than test construction. All tests, but particularly teacher-made classroom tests, have an obvious and overt relation to the purposes and content of instruction. They also bear a subtle and covert relation to the students' perceptions of the purposes and content of instruction; and, to the extent that teachers' actions and decisions are based on tests, they may tell more about the real purposes and content of instruction than anything else.

A classroom test can be more than a means of measurement and evaluation. It can motivate and it can teach. By challenging the student's intellect or by stimulating his imagination a test can make a subject more meaningful or more interesting. By requiring that he think about things in a new way or use his knowledge to solve unfamiliar problems, a test can leave a student with a new appreciation for and understanding of his subject. Unfortunately, the reverse is not only possible, but easier to achieve. Because a test is often the capstone for all or part of the course work, it can assume an intellectual and emotional significance for the student that may be far greater than the teacher intends. Because the test is the criterion (or an important part of it) for assessing a student's achievement, it represents to him direct, material evidence of what has been defined as achievement. And, consciously or subconsciously, the student may perceive this evidence as representing not only the goals of learning in a particular course but also the modes of thought in the scholarly discipline that the course represents.

A social studies essay test that uniformly requires only the memorization of facts, or that pretends to require generalization and interpretation but in actuality requires only the memorization of *ex cathedra* generalizations and interpretations, fails in several respects. It neglects the potential that exists in the essay test form to measure higher levels of achievement. It corrupts the goals of instruction. It distorts the intrinsic meaning and worth of the discipline. And it risks alienating curious, inquiring students from developing an interest in and intellectual commitment to the social studies.

Therefore, because classroom tests have an impact on instruction and learning and because a test is likely to measure only what it is constructed to measure, the time devoted to planning a test is essential. In thinking about the test, there are a host of questions that need answers.

Why is the test being given? What will be learned from it? What will be learned about each student? About the students as a class? About the course, or the curriculum? How is this test a part of the total evaluation program for this course?

How does the test relate to the goals of instruction? Which objectives will be measured by this test? Will certain ones be excluded? How much weight will be given in the test to each of the objectives to be measured? How will these weights correspond to the relative importance of these objectives in the course? Which questions will be concerned with which objectives?

What level of performance will be expected of the students? Is this test a mastery test; will all students, or almost all, be expected to answer all the questions? Will all questions be of equal difficulty, or will some be intended to differentiate the more able students from the less able? What kind of response to each question will be expected of the typical student? How are these responses related to what the students have been expected to learn?

The answers to the foregoing questions will determine, in large measure, the character of the test to be developed. Ultimately, they will have an important bearing on the validity and reliability of the test results—particularly on the validity. Since the main purpose of a test is to obtain information, it is at this planning stage of test construction that many of the crucial decisions are made that will determine the nature and the worth of the information that is eventually obtained. Of course, a poorly executed plan may still thwart the collection of useful and meaningful information, but testing in the absence of planning begs the question as to the meaning and usefulness of the information collected. The schools are full of tests that in format and other outward appearances suggest that they meet the criteria of sound essay test construction. But in too many cases, because the fundamental issue of "Why test?" has not been considered in any depth, the tests do not ask the right questions and, therefore, do not provide the right information.

CONSTRUCTING THE ESSAY TEST

Having identified the objectives to be measured, there still remains the need to translate objectives into test questions. In doing so, there are two characteristics of each question to consider. The first is the content of the question; the second is its structure. The consideration of content is related to the need to develop valid questions. The consideration of structure is related to the need to develop reliable questions.

In thinking about the writing of essay questions for classroom tests, one should first of all put aside any preconceptions as to format. There is no standard model that is superior to all others. There is an almost infinite variety of ways in which to present a question. Initially, we should concern ourselves with its content—with what it asks the student to do.

The best procedure for writing a test question is to consider first what is to be measured—without regard to how the question will eventually appear. What do we wish to learn about the student from this question? If, for example, we wish to assay his powers of historical analysis, what kind of intellectual behavior (in the classroom or outside of it) would be evidence of his having developed such skills? Finally, what kind of test question could elicit a response that would most closely parallel the desired behavior?

Approaching the writing of questions in this way means that the format of the question is determined by what is to be measured. It offers the teacher an opportunity to let his imagination and ingenuity operate freely. It implies correctly that he can probably invent the form of the question once he has a clear conception of the behavior to be measured.

Essay questions need not always follow the classic formula of "Give the main causes of . . . ." or "Describe the principal events that led to . . . ." If the purpose of the question is to determine whether the student has learned certain important facts, such questions may be useful. However, they would be just as effective and less time-consuming if they asked the student simply to "list" the causes, the events, etc.

For example, an essay question can require the student to read and to analyze one or more documents, graphs, or maps and to use these as the basis for his answer. If testing time is short, the stimulus material can be distributed the day before the test. If the questions are not known in advance and if the documents may be used during the test, this procedure may not only provide an opportunity for an unusual kind of question, it may also help to standardize the basis for each student's answer and thereby make the grading more reliable.

Or, in this era of paperbacks, students may be asked to use several references to answer a question that requires them to analyze dissimilar data and to synthesize generalizations that can be drawn from the data.

In a simpler vein, a question may test whether a student understands relationships by presenting a pair of events and asking that he explain in one or two sentences the relationship between the events. Or, if the purpose of the question is to learn whether the student can perceive new relationships, the paired events may be the ones that, for him, are not obviously related.

Although the preceding examples—representing questions that experienced classroom teachers have used at one time or another—are not unique, they serve to illustrate three principles to be observed in writing essay questions. First, essay questions should be constructed with the purpose of the question clearly in mind. Second, the content of the question should be related to an important objective of instruction, an objective that can be defined in terms of expected student behavior. Third, the format of the question should vary with the purpose and content of the question.

These three principles, particularly the first two, suggest a fourth which has been implied but which deserves special attention. Namely, the desired student response to each essay question should be anticipated at the time that the purpose and content of each question is decided. The best procedure is to outline or summarize what is expected in an acceptable answer. This procedure has several merits. It provides insight into the complexity and level of thought required to answer a question satisfactorily. It introduces a note of reality by placing the teacher in the role of the student to test the feasibility of expecting students to respond satisfactorily to a question. It provides a check on such practical matters as whether the question is clear and unambiguous and whether it can be answered in the time allotted. Also, it will later provide an excellent initial basis for grading the students' papers. If a teacher has only modest difficulty in delineating the expected response to one of his questions, it can be predicted that the students will have a great deal more difficulty. In the final analysis, it is the teacher who must decide if a question is an appropriate one for his class. But, answering one's own question (or asking a colleague to do so) is one of the most useful techniques for reviewing an essay test and anticipating problems in it.

After the content of the question has been determined, the structure of the question needs attention. The most ingenious question can sometimes produce the most disappointing results because, for one of several reasons, the structure of the question may defeat the purpose that the questioner intended.

One of the paradoxes of the essay test is that the student's freedom of response, the main attraction of this evaluation instrument, must be channeled and restricted in order for the essay test to be most effective. The reason for this is that a fair (and useful) evaluation of a student's response depends on obtaining from the student a relatively reliable sample of his competence in the area being tested. If the student's response is not a reliable sample, the evaluation that follows from it has no relevance, no validity. Therefore, to insure that a valid evaluation can be made of the student's response, it is necessary to control any elements in the structure of the test that have no relevant bearing on his performance. To do so implies restricting the completely free response and channeling the way in which a student answers the questions.

There appear to be two major elements in the structure of the essay test that require deliberate care in test construction. The first is primarily a problem of test communication. It concerns such matters as the wording of questions and their internal directions and timing. The second is a problem of test strategy. It has to do with how many questions each student answers and whether or not the student may choose the questions that he will answer.

The problems of test communication are obvious yet subtle. Everyone recognizes that the student needs to understand a question in order to answer it properly. Yet, one of the ticklish characteristics of essay tests is that even bright students will fail to respond to a question in the way that the teacher expects. One possible cause of this is the loose or ambiguous wording of questions. A question such as "Discuss the events leading up to the second World War" can be answered in a variety of ways. Some students will start with Munich; others will dwell on Danzig and the Polish Corridor; still others may start with Versailles. Some will catalogue Hitler's territorial expansion; others may discuss the social and economic malaise that beset the West between the two World Wars. Who is right; which is best?

It is perhaps unfair to use so poor an example as the foregoing, yet key words such as *discuss* have prompted many students to respond in an inappropriate way and have given others the opportunity to hide what they do not know. In this example, the use of *discuss* has two limitations. First, its meaning is not clear. It can be defined as a sifting of considerations for and against, but the dictionary and popular usage define it as also meaning to discourse about or to talk over. Second, in the example, *discuss* is the only instruction given the student as to how he should organize and present his response. The example points up the need for giving special attention to words in questions that give the student directions or instructions for formulating his response. Also, it calls attention to the importance of being as explicit as possible in letting the student know what is expected of him in his response. The vocabulary of the question should be as precise as possible. Words such as *list, define, illustrate, explain, defend, compare, differentiate, outline* and *summarize* are relatively unambiguous. The use of each, of course, would depend on the purpose of each question.

In addition, the question should be precise about other desired characteristics of the student's answer, such as the types or number of factors to be considered or the period of time to be covered. If analysis or evaluation is desired, the question should specify this. However, a question such as "Analyze the events leading up to the second World War" is no better than "Discuss . . . ." Most questions can be improved by qualifying terms and by providing referents. The question "Show how the international political events of 1933-1939 leading up to the second World War were influenced by the international political decisions made by the Allied powers in 1919" is one example (only one and not necessarily the best) of how the original question may be revised. It also illustrates how providing the student with more information in the question does not necessarily make the question easier. However, structuring the question and then allowing the student to respond freely within the limits imposed does make it easier for the abler student to demonstrate his competence and for the teacher grading the student's response to evaluate his competence.

The evaluation of the student's competence may depend, too, on the test strategy on which the test is structured. Given the need to obtain information about a student's achievement, what is the best way to obtain information from an essay test? Within a limited amount of time, how can the essay test yield the most reliable and valid sample of the student's achievement? Putting aside other factors that will have a bearing on test design, the best strategy is to obtain from each student in the time allotted as many *different* samples of his achievement as possible and to obtain the *same* samples for all the students in a class. More, shorter questions are better than fewer, longer questions. And, having all students answer the same questions is better than allowing students a choice of questions.

The argument for such procedures is based on what we know about sampling. Given the need to appraise a student's achievement in a course, we know that any one sample of his work may not be representative of his competence. He may not know the answer to one question, but he may know the answer to many others. Or, he may fortuitously know the answer to the one question he happens to have been asked. The more samples of a student's performance, the less likelihood that some chance element will deny him the opportunity to demonstrate his ability. Also, any one sample of a student's work is not representative of the content or the objectives of a course. To be able to make a fair evaluation of a student's achievement in a course, we need as many samples of his performance for as many different expected course outcomes as possible.

An essay test cannot always provide the extensive sampling that valid and reliable measurement prescribe. To have a student demonstrate the depth of his understanding, the richness of his thought, or the power of his analytic abilities may require devoting large portions of time to a very few questions. While this may often be true, a useful criterion to apply to each essay question is to weigh the time the student will devote to thinking in relation to the time he will devote to writing. The ratio of thinking to writing is probably impossible to determine precisely because they more or less occur simultaneously. But it is a useful theoretical model to use as a basis for judging whether the time devoted to a question is an efficient and effective use of that time or whether some of that time might be better used for another question that would yield another sample of the student's ability.

The need for extensive sampling has another important implication for the classroom teacher's use of essay tests. If it is desirable in a test to have a student answer several questions rather than one, it follows that it is also desirable to give students several tests rather than one. The same principles apply. Several tests given at intervals during a course are likely to yield a more valid and reliable estimate of the student's achievement than one or two tests. One of the major criticisms of the essay test is its unreliability. Unfortunately, much of the criticism is well founded. But the classroom teacher has the opportunity to obtain during the school year many samples of a student's performance, thereby overcoming one source of essay test unreliability. A judgment of a student's ability that is based on a single essay test may be inaccurate and unjust. A judgment based on a great many essays written on different subjects and at different points in time is almost certainly to be significantly more accurate and just than a judgment based on a single essay.

In the name of justice, too, classroom teachers have often given students a choice of questions. In part, this has probably stemmed from the recognition by teachers that an essay test is not likely to provide the extensive sampling of a domain needed to insure a reliable and valid measure of each student's achievement. If, as is frequently the case, the grade on an essay test is to be based on a student's responses to a relatively small number of questions, the teacher is aware that when all students are required to answer the same questions there will be a few students who will be "unlucky." Although these students are able and conscientious, it is their misfortune that one of the questions, perhaps counting for as much as one-third or one-half of the test grade, deals with an area in which their preparation is poorest. Other equally able and conscientious students, who are more fortunate, will receive higher grades because the match between their preparation and the test questions is a better one. To avoid this inequity, the teacher gives students a choice of questions so that each student will have an equal opportunity to demonstrate his competence.

Ironically, letting students choose questions is an effort to give each an equal opportunity often has the opposite effect. A freedom of choice introduces additional subtle variables into the test situation that probably increase the possibility that able and conscientious students will be "unlucky" in the evaluation that the test grade represents. The freedom to choose which test question to answer implies that the student can decide which question presents him with the best opportunity to demonstrate his competence. It assumes that he will understand equally well the task that each question presents and that he will know his own strengths and weaknesses well enough to select the question that will enable him to show to best advantage. In addition, and perhaps most crucial, it assumes that the student can anticipate the criteria for grading each question so that he can select the question that will give him the best opportunity to score high. In short, in a test where a choice of questions is offered, although he may not realize it, the student may be faced with decisions of strategy and gamesmanship that are not entirely relevant to the measurement of his achievement.

Giving students a freedom of choice may be justifiable if the difficulty of the questions gives students of equal ability about an equal opportunity to do well on the questions each selects. There is considerable evidence, however, to show that it is very difficult to construct essay questions of equal difficulty. Furthermore, there is evidence to show that students, even good ones, cannot consistently judge the questions on which they will perform best. Also, good students often select the more challenging and demanding questions thereby making it more difficult for them to show themselves to best advantage in comparison to other students who select easier questions. Who is the better student, the one who selects a difficult question and does moderately well or the one who selects a less difficult question and does very well? How do you compare students who, in effect, have taken different tests?

One technique to mitigate the potentially distorted and unjust results of tests in which a choice of questions is permitted is to adjust students' test grades to account for the differences in the difficulties of the questions they selected. There are statistical methods for doing this, but the classroom teacher may have neither the time nor the training to use them. In a less precise way, however, the teacher (after having made every effort to write questions of equal difficulty and to grade them with equal severity) can compare the results for groups of students who have chosen different questions. Since the choice of questions should not prevent students of equal ability from doing equally well on the test, the teacher should expect that every question has produced about the same proportions of high, middle, and low grades and that no group of students has been penalized because the questions they selected were significantly more or less difficult than the questions chosen by other groups of students of about equal ability. If this is not the case, the teacher should consider some adjustment in the grading of the exceptionally difficult or easy questions. Of course, differences in grades for different groups of students who choose different questions may be the result of differences in ability or preparation. If the test contains some questions which all students answer, then these questions may serve as a basis for making comparisons among the groups of students choosing different questions. But, at best, the teacher who permits students to choose which questions they will answer on an essay test is introducing a factor the effects of which are not only difficult to control but also capable of frustrating the reliable and valid measurement that is the reason for the test.

Since the preceding discussion may leave the impression that essay tests are unfair if they permit no choice and are unfair if they do, it warrants repeating here that the solution for the classroom teacher is to obtain many different samples of the achievement of each student in the class and to obtain the same samples for all students. The dilemma can be solved by more frequent essay tests in which all students answer the same questions.

A final consideration in the preparation of essay tests concerns letting the students know the "ground rules" for the test so that each has the same opportunity to plan and organize his effort. The ground rules include such obvious matters as the total time for the test, and, often, the suggested time for each question. Also, if questions are to be weighted so that answers to certain questions or certain parts of questions are to receive greater weight in the grade than other questions or parts, the students should have this information. In the same vein, the directions for the test should include information as to the general criteria on which all papers will be judged. If, for example, the quality of English will be considered in the grading, students should be so advised. The following, taken from an examination in history, is an example of such directions.

> These questions are a test of your judgment, knowledge, and ability to present such knowledge in an appropriate manner. Cite specific facts to substantiate your generalizations. Be as specific as possible in illustrating your answers. Do not neglect to give dates where they are necessary for a fuller understanding of your response. Clearness of organization as well as the quality of your English will be factors considered in scoring your answers. Remember that you have forty-five minutes to plan, write, and review each question. Be sure to number your answers as the questions are numbered in the test.

GRADING THE ESSAY TEST

The student taking an essay test has not completed his examination until it has been graded. The actual process of measuring the student's ability begins with the student's responding to a question, but it does not end until someone has assigned a value to his response. Therefore, the effectiveness of the essay test depends on how well it is graded. A poorly planned and poorly constructed test cannot be redeemed by the most sophisticated and careful grading, but the most thoughtful efforts in planning and construction can be thwarted by improper grading standards or procedures.

The most crucial problem in grading essay tests is probably the need to maintain the same standards for all students. If the standards vary for each student, there is no way to make valid comparisons among students. Moreover, if standards vary, there is no reason to be confident that the evaluation of any student is valid, since any student's grade may be different if his paper is graded again.

The most effective way to insure that the same standards underlie the grading of each student is to spell out the criteria for scoring each question. What is the definition of a very good response, an average response, and a poor response? What interpretations, generalizations, or facts should be included in each answer? How much credit will be given for each part of an answer? Although it is not too late to prepare these standards immediately before the essays are graded, the best time to do so, as has been pointed out earlier, is when the questions are written.

The following is an example of grading standards, in this case from the College Entrance Examination Board's 1964 Advanced Placement Examination in American History, a test for academically talented students in senior high schools.

Question: The Civil War left the South with a heritage of intense regional self-consciousness. In what respects and to what extent was this feeling weakened during the next half-century, and in what respects and to what extent was it intensified?

Grading Standards:

General Criteria:

1. Does the student state clearly the forces a) weakening southern regional self-consciousness and b) intensifying southern regional self-consciousness? (See Checklist.)

2. Does he develop his statement by showing how these forces actually operated to weaken or strengthen southern self-consciousness?

3. Does he draw an over-all conclusion as to the condition of southern self-consciousness at the turn of the century?

High Honors: Summarizes clearly the forces weakening and strengthening southern self-consciousness and develops them fully by showing explicitly how they operated. Draws an explicit over-all conclusion.

Honors: Summarizes the forces clearly, but develops them less effectively, OR treats one side of the question well and the other less well. Draws an over-all conclusion, but does so more implicitly or more generally.

Satisfactory: Discusses the forces weakening or strengthening southern self-consciousness, but develops them rather thinly, OR shows noticeable imbalance in treating the two sides of the question. May draw an over-all conclusion in a few general remarks.

Passing: Discusses only one side of the question, but does so with some thoroughness, OR discusses, with some development, a few forces on each side, OR merely catalogues forces on both sides without developing them.

Fail: Merely talks about the South in general.

Checklist:

Forces weakening southern regional self-consciousness:
Growth of railroads and desire for federal subsidies
Old Whigs join northern businessmen in Compromise of 1877
Desire for northern capital to industrialize the South
Efforts of magazines and writers to interpret the South
The vision of the New South
Aid to Negro education by northern philanthropists

New state constitutions stressing public education
Supreme Court decisions affecting Negro rights
Tom Watson's early Populist efforts
Booker T. Washington's "submissiveness"
The Spanish-American War. The white man's burden
After 1890, new issues did not conform to a North-South political
  alignment
First World War

Forces strengthening southern regional self-consciousness:
Destruction caused by the war and its long-range effects
Reconstruction policy of Congress
One-crop economy, crop-lien system, and sharecropping
Carpetbaggers, Ku Klux Klan, Red Shirts
Waving the bloody shirt
Memories of the lost cause
Glorifying the prewar tradition
Continuing weakness of southern education compared with rest of
  Union
Populism
Jim Crow laws after 1890
Solid South

How the grading standards are used is also important. Since the standards must be realistic to be useful, they should first be tried out. This can be accomplished more easily by using the standards experimentally to score a sample of student papers. No grades are actually assigned to these papers; the purpose is to see if the grading standards have correctly anticipated the content and level of the students' responses. If the standards have not, if the students appear to have interpreted the questions differently or to have uniformly responded at a different level of understanding, there is an opportunity to revise the standards before the actual grading begins. Once the grading has begun, the standards should not vary.

However, there is considerable evidence indicating that it is not easy to grade a group of essay tests uniformly. The quality of earlier papers can easily influence a teacher's judgment. For these reasons, as the reading of the papers progresses, the papers graded later should occasionally be compared with those that were graded earlier to check whether the standards are being applied consistently.

An effective technique that helps to maintain consistency of grading is reading the answers to the same question in all of the papers before moving on to another question. This accomplishes two things. It enables the teacher to concentrate on the standards for each question by avoiding the distraction of moving from one question to another. Also, it permits the teacher to judge a student's response to each question independently of his responses to other questions. This reduces the "halo effect" that the quality of a student's response to one question may have on the teacher's evaluation of his response to another question. In using this technique, it is also helpful to read the papers in a different order for each question so that the possible disadvantage to some students of having their papers among the first or the last to be graded is dissipated.

A teacher's general impression of a student, based on his previous class-work, can also have a "halo effect" on the evaluation of that student's test paper. Although it is difficult for a classroom teacher not to recognize each student's paper by its handwriting, it is recommended that, if possible, the teacher avoid learning the name of the student whose paper he is grading. One easy way of preserving the anonymity of the student is to have him write his name on the back of the test paper instead of on the front. A somewhat more complicated method is to assign a number to each student so that his name does not appear anywhere on the paper. Perhaps the simplest method is for the teacher to fold out of sight the part of the paper bearing the student's name before he grades the paper.

Factors such as handwriting and the use of English also have a bearing on grading. Although they should not be ignored—effectiveness of expression and neatness of handwriting are legitimate instructional concerns—the weight that each receives in the grading should be a conscious decision. Students who write illegibly may be hoping that no one will read too closely; conversely, students who write in a beautiful script and punctuate and spell correctly may also be hoping that no one will read too closely. The standards for each question should make provision for criteria such as the student's ability to write, but such criteria should be considered separately from other criteria. And, it should be tempered by the recognition that an essay test, with all its special purposes and pressures, is not necessarily the best way to measure the elegance of student prose.

After grading has been completed, one further step remains. It is one of analysis and reflection. Although it can have no influence on the quality of the test just completed, it may help the teacher to improve future tests. Also, it is likely to contribute to the improvement of instruction.

From the results of a test, a great deal may be learned about the group tested as well as the test itself. An analysis of the answers to the questions in the test may help to determine those areas in which instruction has been effective and those in which it has not. Also, by re-examining the objectives and the standards for each question in relation to students' responses, the teacher may be able to identify certain sources of students' deficiencies. For example, an analysis of the papers may show that students have a grasp of the facts, but do not perceive the significant relationships among them. Or, it may indicate that students are able to generalize, but unable to support generalizations with data. This kind of diagnosis is most useful for the class as a whole because an individual's paper may not contain enough consistent evidence to be a dependable indicator of his strengths or weaknesses. However, an analysis of a student's paper can often serve as a useful point of departure for teacher-student conferences.

In planning for future tests, the results of a completed test can be extremely helpful. To a large extent, once test questions have been prepared, it is difficult to remedy any limitations they may contain. But the study of how those questions worked in terms of the criteria for valid and reliable measurement is one of the best ways of beginning to plan for the next essay test.

References

[1] Stephen Leacock, letter to the Editor, *The Daily Princetonian,* January 26, 1938.

[2] "Examsmanship and the Liberal Arts" by William G. Perry, Jr., in *Examining in Harvard College,* 1963.

Suggested Readings

BLOOM, BENJAMIN S., (ed.), *Taxonomy of Educational Objectives: Cognitive Domain.* New York: Longmans, Green and Company, 1956.

STALNAKER, JOHN M. "The Essay Type of Examination," *Educational Measurement,* edited by E. F. Lindquist. Washington: American Council on Education, 1951. pp. 495-530.

SECTION B   Current and Needed Research

ASSUMPTIONS ABOUT THE LEARNING OF POLITICAL VALUES

Roberta Sigel
State University of New York, Buffalo

ABSTRACT: Political socialization refers to the learning process by which the political norms and behaviors acceptable to an ongoing political system are transmitted from generation to generation. The goal of political socialization is so to train or develop individuals that they become well-functioning members of political society. Such learning begins very early in the person's life and need not be acquired solely through deliberate indoctrination. In fact, most of this norm-internalization goes on casually and imperceptibly—most of the time without our ever being aware that it is going on. It proceeds so smoothly precisely because we are unaware of it. We take the norms for granted, and it does not occur to us to question them. The stability of a political system depends in no small measure on the political socialization of its members. A well-functioning citizen is one who accepts (internalizes) society's political norms and who will then transmit them to future generations. Without a body politic so in harmony with the on-going political values, a political system would have trouble functioning smoothly and perpetuating itself safely. And survival, after all, is a prime goal of the political organism just as it is of the individual organism.—Ed.

... Political socialization is the gradual learning of the norms, attitudes, and behavior accepted and practiced by the ongoing political system. For example, members of a stable democratic system are expected to learn to effect change through elections, through the application of group practice, rather than through street riots or revolutions.

Viewed this way political socialization would encompass *all* political learning, formal and informal, deliberate and unplanned, at every stage of

Reprinted with permission of the author and the publisher, from *The Annals of the American Academy of Political and Social Science*, 361 (September, 1965): 1-9.

the life cycle, including not only explicitly political learning but also normally not political learning which affects political behavior, such as the learning of politically irrelevant social attitudes and the acquisition of political relevant personality characteristics.[1]

The goal of political socialization is to so train or develop individuals that they become well-functioning members of the political society. While the definition of a well-functioning member will vary with the political system— from obedient passive subject in one system to active participating citizen in another—well-functioning citizen is one who accepts (internalizes) society's political norms and who will then transmit them to future generations. For without a body politic so in harmony with the ongoing political values the political system would have trouble functioning smoothly and perpetuating itself safely. And survival, after all, it a prime goal of the political organism just as it is of the individual organism.

At no time in history has the importance of successful political socialization been demonstrated more dramatically than today. Old and new nations today are faced with the problem of rapid political change. This change has brought about disruption of the old familial social patterns, ideological orientations, and economic conditions, to name but a few. Such change—like change in general—is always fraught with tension, discomfort, and disequilibrium. If it proceeds with a minimum of these, all is well for the political system. But the danger always exists that the tensions are more than the system can endure. Chances are that one of the factors which contribute to relatively tension-free change—and hence to system stability—is the successful political socialization of its members. One of the many difficulties besetting the newly developed nations is precisely this one: how to quickly train or socialize young and old alike so that they will internalize the norms of the new nation and thus assure its survival. And even for the older, stabler nations this is an important task, for they are confronted with the problem of how to insure the loyalty and engagement of their members in the face of rapid political, technological, and social changes and in the presence of governments ever growing in complexity, geographical distance, and general impersonality. To the extent, for example, that in a modern industrialized nation the citizen finds political decisions to have become increasingly complex, technical, and difficult to understand, the danger exists that the citizen will lose his touch with the political system, and he will become disengaged, apathetic, or even alienated. An apathetic citizen in times of crisis, even in times of hardship and political or economic setbacks, forms a very shaky foundation for any political system. The system cannot count on his active support or loyalty. An alienated citizen is an even greater threat to the system, since he can become its active foe. Tanks and bayonets can and do keep disloyal citizens subdued but they can at best maintain an uneasy peace. It is perhaps no exaggeration to say that a nation's stability and survival depends in large measure on the engagement of its members.

No wonder that both philosopher and practicing politician as long ago as Plato—and probably long before that— have devoted thought and effort to the question of how to bring about such engagement. Such practitioners and philosophers, however, did not call the training process political socialization; rather they called it civic education, lessons in patriotism, training for citizenship, or character-training. Every one of these terms indicates that political values and attitudes are acquired, not inborn—that they are the result of a learning process. The reason we today prefer to call this learning process political socialization rather than civic education is that the latter has too deliberate a connotation. It presumes that system-appropriate political values are acquired as a result of deliberate indoctrination, textbook learning, conscious and rational weighing of political alternatives, and the like. It seems to assume that there is a definite point in time—a certain grade in school—when such learning can profitably start and a certain point when it is completed. This view is far too naïve and narrow; it completely ignores what we know about the way in which people go about "learning" society's norms. For instance, it ignores the fact that much of this norm-internalization goes on casually and imperceptibly—most of the time in fact without our ever being aware that it is going on. It proceeds so smoothly precisely because we are unaware of it. We take the norms for granted, and it does not occur to us to question them. What Cantril has to say about the learning of religious norms would probably apply with equal force to the learning of political norms.

> The relative uniformity of a culture from one generation to another, the usual slow rate of change, is clear indication that many norms of the culture are uncritically accepted by a large majority of the people. . . .For the norms of society are by no means always merely neutral stimuli from which the individual may pick and choose as he pleases, which he may regard as good or bad, as right or wrong when the spirit moves him. Most of them have already been judged by society, by the individual's predecessors, when he first experiences them. When people learn about a specific religion they generally learn at the same time that it is the "best" or that it is the "true" religion.[2]

Easton and Dennis graphically describe the uncritical way in which norms are accepted:

In many ways a child born into a system is like an immigrant into it. But where he differs is in the fact that he has never been socialized to any other kind of system. . . .He learns to like the government before he really knows what it is.[3]

No doubt this is the reason why for young boys in an American summer camp a word like *freedom* was not a neutral stimulus but one evoking positive feelings while the word *power* brought mixed reactions.[4] American society had prejudged for them and told them that freedom is a good thing. It had told them that when they had been much younger than they were then, when they had had no basis—or desire—to question the accuracy of such information.

And if such learning takes place at "every life cycle," then obviously we cannot be content with studying adults only, but we must look at adolescents and even children to see what values and norms they acquire which may have a bearing on later adult political behavior. . . .

. . . political socialization is a learning process which begins very early and is most influenced by the same agents or forces which influence all social behavior: first and foremost, the family; then socially relevant groups or institutions, such as school, church, and social class; and finally—last but not least—society at large and the political culture it fosters. Another thread which seems to run through this volume is that much of this learning is incidental to other experiences (Marvick points out. . .the political consequences of Negro youth's self image): it is acquired in a subtle, nondeliberate way, often in a context which seems totally void of political stimuli yet is often rife with political consequences.

Because the consequences are political, political scientists recently have begun to ask questions such as: How and when is such learning acquired? Who most influences the young? What is the content of political socialization across cultures and subcultures? What are the consequences for the political system of different socialization processes and contents? Probably the least researched of all these questions is the one concerning the acquisition of learning. Unfortunately, political socialization studies are not yet sufficiently plentiful—nor sufficiently learning-oriented—to chart for us a detailed, empirically derived map which illustrates just how the above agents and institutions go about "socializing" the young. In the absence of such a map it seems safe to proceed from the assumption that political learning, like other social learning, falls into two broad categories: learning which is the result of deliberate conscious teaching and learning which is acquired incidentally and almost unbeknown to the learner himself (or even unbeknown to the teacher).

Deliberate teaching may be further subdivided into formalized and informal teaching. Civic education in public schools would be an example of formal teaching while a father's talk to his son about the merits or demerits of trade unions would be an example of informal deliberate teaching.

Important though deliberate indoctrination is, it is probable that incidental learning—precisely because it is incidental—has a more lasting effect on the acquisition of political values and behavior. Incidental learning can perhaps also be further subdivided into the learning of politically relevant "lessons" and into the learning of social values which in and of themselves are not political but which carry in themselves the potentials for later political orientation. Incidental political learning can be acquired in a variety of ways. At times it may be the by-product of observation—watching a public official accept a bribe affords a youngster a certain view of the rectitude of government officials. Observations such as these can lead to political cynicism which in turn seems to be closely tied to political apathy, alienation, and the like. Incidental learning can also be acquired in the course of overhearing adult conversations. Wylie observed that French children in the Vaucluse constantly hear

> ... adults referring to government as a source of evil and to the men who run it as instruments of evil. There is nothing personal in this belief. It does not concern one particular government ... it concerns government everywhere and at all times.[5]

Little wonder that Pinner found that French (as well as Belgian) youths had rather cynical attitudes toward politics and public officials. He attributes these attitudes, among other things, to parental child-rearing practices and makes a persuasive case demonstrating this. Perhaps another explanation for children adopting parental political views can be found in the nature of the parent-child relationship. The child trusts his parents' judgements. As a rule, the young child who hears his parents voice political opinions has no personal information from which to judge the wisdom of parental opinions. In the South, for instance, he may never have asked a Negro if, indeed, he is as happy with segregation as his parents claim him to be. But the child sees no reason to doubt his parents' claim. He has accepted their standards on all other matters, why not on politics as well? Another important incidental way in which young people become politically socialized is, of course, life itself and the experience it brings to bear on youths. No Negro youth needs social studies classes to tell him that discrimination is condoned in wide sectors of American life. If, in addition, some close friends or relatives had in vain tried to fight such discrimination and perhaps had lost their livelihood or even lives in the process, it is quite possible that the political lessons learned from life experience for such a youngster will be that the safest way to get along is to be politically nonengaged, passive, and indifferent.

The second type of incidental political learning to which we referred involves social values, notions of morality, and the like, which are not *per se* political but which may well influence how political stimuli are perceived and internalized. For example, a child is taught to save part of his allowance for a weekly donation to the foreign missions of his church. If he is told it is his Christian duty to help those less fortunate than himself and that their misfortune is not of their own making, he has received some deliberate indoctrination into the norms governing charity. On the surface, such deliberate indoctrination on the part of his family has no political implications. But it is not hard to see how such attitudes can later on predispose a person to develop attitudes with respect to governmental welfare measures, social security, and taxation. Similarly, what a family teaches its young about the evil of or the justification for violence and aggression carries in it the seeds for later views on capital punishment, war and peace, and a host of other political issues.

Nor must we overlook that the *manner* in which a child becomes socialized is as important as the content itself. Adorno *et al.*[6] found that American college youth with pronounced Fascist tendencies almost invariably came from homes where they had been treated harshly and with little respect, where they had been given little opportunity to express themselves, to make their own decisions, and the like. The homes did not espouse fascism; they merely failed to provide the youth with the atmosphere and opportunity to develop democratic, co-operative skills. Thus *the how as well as the what* of the familial socialization process contributes to political socialization in that it may or may not teach the child the skills which will facilitate adult political effectiveness. Lucian Pye in his study of Burma illustrates the all-pervasive political consequences of political socialization. Referring to general methods of socializing, he relates that the very young Burmese child is treated most indulgently. The school-age child is treated inconsistently but is expected to be totally submissive, passive, and yielding.

He is not, however, given a clear set of standards of performance, the achievement of which might yield predictable rewards. The parents make few demands for achievement; indeed, there appears to be very little in the Burmese that would produce. . .a high sense of the need for achievement. . . .He learns only that he should avoid as best he can becoming in any sense a nuisance. He thus tends to expect security from being sub-servient and yielding to all who are his superiors.[7]

In a childhood setting like the Burmese the child never learns to express his own ideas, to participate in decision-making. Nor does he gain any confidence in himself. Yet self-confidence and some such skills as experience in partici-pation, discussion, or decision-making are skills which are essential for people who wish to become actively involved in politics.[8]

The general *Weltanschauung* which the Burmese child learns during child-hood further adds to his liabilities when it comes to the task of nation-building. For example, he is taught that only members of the family can be trusted and to have "unrestrained suspicion of strangers."[9] Consequently, he finds it difficult to work together with others and "to perform effectively in any organizational context."[10] Pye, in fact, bases many of his gloomy prog-noses for Burma's chance for nation-building on the political effects of the nonpolitical aspects of childhood socialization. The Almond-Verba five-nations study[11]...has offered clear evidence that home atmosphere and adult political competence are closely interwoven. By and large, those people in the five nations became active, participating citizens who at home had been given the opportunity to express their opinion, make their own decisions, and the like. Litt comments on the fact that immigrant children and lower-class children are often given fewer opportunities in school to learn political skills, such as debating and running student governments, than are upper-class children in more exclusive schools.[12] This may, in part, explain why mem-bers of the working class are significantly less active in the United States adult political life than are those of the upper middle class.

In summary, then, we can say that the child learns from adults the philoso-phical, social, and political values (not to mention outright political opinions) and the social and political skills with which to act upon these values. He acquires most of these without being aware that he is learning or that there may be other lessons with other morals to be learned. More of the learning probably proceeds in a casual, non-politically charged setting than does in a deliberately political one.

There is, however, also an *essentially personal basis* for political behavior. This basis is furnished by personality. The authors of the *The Authoritarian Personality* found that Americans with marked Fascist and ethnocentric political views have certain personality characteristics in common which are not as commonly found among people of more democratic persuasions. The origin for personality development is no doubt to be found in the socializa-tion experience, but, once developed, personality does make a contribution all of its own to the articulation of political attitudes and behaviors. Historians have frequently commented on the extent to which Woodrow Wilson's stern idealism and uncompromising internationalism were rooted in his personality problems.[13]...The authors of *The American Voter* pointed out that people who are well adjusted and feel effective tend to differ significantly in political orientation from people who are not so adjusted.[14] Studying the views of ten men on the subject of Soviet Russia leads Smith, Bruner, and White to conclude:

> The Russias to which our ten men were reacting were different objects, differently composed. That these objects of opinion shared common features reflecting world events and constancies in the information environment is evident. But the first and most striking impression...was that the Russia to which each referred was a conception selectively fashioned, a reflection of individuality.[15]

In short, people with different personality structures simply perceive the political world differently; their perceptions (opinions) are to some extent a reflection or extension of their personality. Thus, although political values are learned by the child at a very early age and tend to be in harmony with his important reference groups (notably the family), personality accounts for some of the variation in political beliefs. However, in a stable political system—personality differences notwithstanding—great numbers of people seem to be in consensual agreement on political norms, and these norms tend to be designed to perpetuate existing arrangements. Political socialization, in other words, is essentially a conservative process facilitating the maintenance of the *status quo* by making people love the system under which they are born.

The above discussion concentrated on the influence of adult institutions or adults over youth. It is, of course, patently clear that adults in turn are not independent agents who choose and pick what values they wish to transmit to the young; rather, adults have themselves been influenced—if not actually molded—by the political system and what it rewards and supports: or, as Greenstein points out..."The political and social systems...provide the socializing environment."

The essentially conservative effect of political socialization should not lead one, however, to equate it with complete or nearly complete changelessness. In none but the most static systems is the political value system transmitted completely intact from generation to generation. As generational and group needs change, values, too, do change. It must always be borne in mind that the political world of one generation differs from that of the next. The external and technological changes of modern society, for example, bring with them gradual or sudden changes in political values which then get transmitted as part of the socialization process. During the war many mothers went to work in defense plants. Today the acute need for women workers has passed, but working mothers have become part of the American scene. Consequently, young people are beginning to accept women as part of the working force to an extent their fathers never did—so much so that in 1964 a woman unsuccessfully competed for the Presidential candidacy without many protests that politics was strictly man's business. The gradual abandonment (or dilution) of the American ideal of rugged individualism seems to have come about in response to the Great Depression and the altered economy of the twentieth century. Values thus respond to changes in the environments.

Not only are there differences in the political worlds of different generations; there are also differences within the same generation. Different social, ethnic, and religious groups perceive the political world differently. Lipset has demonstrated that members of the working class seem less attached to values centering around individual liberty and civil rights than do members of the middle class.[16] In the 1920's Merriman and Gosnell pointed out that immigrants did not condone active political participation (such as voting) on the part of their women while immigrant men often exceeded natives in such participation.[17] The immigrants' view of appropriate political behavior was thus at variance with that of the rest of the nation (or at least with wide segments thereof). Conflict is apt to occur when the value variance between generations or between groups is large. Conflict is also apt to crop up when different agents try to socialize the same person toward different, mutually exclusive norms. Such conflict at times can amount to individual or group trauma. Witness, for example, the agony experienced by some Southern Roman Catholics when the diocese decreed the integration of the parochial schools while public schools remained segregated. Wishing to be faithful to region and religion, some Catholics found themselves in the predicament of having to choose between excommunication and social ostracism. Another type of conflict situation occurs when political reality clearly contradicts political norms taught. The child who experiences police brutality, sees school doors closed to him because of race, or observes his father pay protection money to the police (and grow prosperous) cannot easily internalize the norms taught by society at large but rather will experience culture conflict or will develop attitudes learned from his personal experience. Marvick illustrates this for the case of the Negro who is taught to believe in the

American norms but not to practice them. Conflict is an all too frequent experience during the socialization process. The political socialization literature, in its heavy emphasis on culture learning and consensus, so far has paid far too scant attention to the role of conflict and tension. Yet conflict and tension play crucial roles in the political socialization process—at times creative ones and at times disruptive ones. In the future we would do well to try to establish both their empirical and their conceptual linkage. For when we speak of socialization as a process by which political values are transmitted from generation to generation, we must always be mindful of the fact that some values change in the process of transmission and that not all segments of society share all the values of the larger society. Conflict engenders tension among generations and among political groups and such tension in turn can lead to change. The nature of the political system (police state or democracy) and the power or strategic position of the groups in conflict will determine what forms such conflict is apt to take; whether it will lead to withdrawal from public life or to attempts to effect change. It seems reasonable to assume that for a political society to flourish in the twentieth century, political socialization must teach the young to accept conflict as a natural ingredient of the political process and to consider change as inevitable. In other words, the socialization process must be congenial to change and not just to continuity . . . Suffice it here to say that different systems vary in the ways in which they prepare their citizens for the acceptance of political change; some resist it more and others less. It is possible to speculate that a culture based on notions such as progress and the perfectibility of life by human efforts could accept change much more readily. This would be so most particularly where the process of political socialization also equips people with the tools by which to assert themselves in demands for change. Almond and Verba elaborate on this point when they talk about the multidirectional flow of influence in socializing experiences. They contend that, due to the practice of political democracy in the United States, citizens subsequently demand the practice of democracy in school, shop, and church. Since the demand is often met, school children, workers, and others acquire practice in articulation, debate, and decision-making. These experiences in turn help them towards developing the skills with which to participate[18] in political life and either to help bring about or to accept political change. Thus the socialization process contributes not only to a society's political stability but also to change and to the strain or ease with which change takes place.

Nonetheless, the net over-all effect of political socialization is in the direction of supporting the *status quo* or at least the major aspects of the existing political regime. "Political socialization in both stable and unstable societies is likely to maintain existing patterns."[19] And therein lies its significance for political-system survival and stability.

References

[1] Fred I. Greenstein, "Political Socialization," article prepared for *International Encyclopedia of the Social Sciences* (in preparation), offprint p. 1.

[2] Hadley Cantril, *The Psychology of Social Movements* (New York: John Wiley & Sons, 1963), p. 6.

[3] Cited from their article in this volume, pp. 57, 56. *The Annals,* 361, September, 1965.

[4] These observations are drawn from lengthy, unstructured interviews conducted at a Young Men's Christian Organization camp by Eugene B. Johnson and Roberta S. Sigel (Report to be published later).

[5] Lawrence Wylie, *Village in the Vaucluse* (Cambridge, Mass.: Harvard University Press, 1951), p. 208.

[6] T. W. Adorno, Else Frenkel-Brunswik, D. J. Levinson, and R. N. Sanford, *The Authoritarian Personality* (New York: Harper, 1950).

[7] Lucian W. Pye, *Politics, Personality, and Nation-Building* (New Haven: Yale University Press, 1962), pp. 182-183.

[8] Angus Campbell, Philip Converse, Warren E. Miller, and Donald Stokes, *The American Voter* (New York: John Wiley & Sons, 1960), pp. 326–328, have shown that a sense of efficacy correlates highly with political participation.

[9] Pye, *op. cit.,* p. 205.

[10] *Ibid.,* p. 186.

[11] Gabriel Almond and Sidney Verba, *The Civic Culture* (Princeton, N.J.: Princeton University Press, 1963), chap. xi.

[12] In addition to his paper in this volume, see also his "Civic Education, Community Norms, and Political Indoctrination," *American Sociological Review* 28 (1963), pp. 69–75.

[13] This interpretation is most fully developed by Alexander L. and Juliette L. George, *Woodrow Wilson and Colonel House: A Personality Study* (New York: Dover, 1956).

[14] Campbell *et al., op. cit.,* pp. 326–328.

[15] M. Brewster Smith, Jerome S. Bruner, and Robert W. White, *Opinions and Personality* (New York: John Wiley and Sons, 1964), p. 244.

[16] Martin S. Lipset, *Political Man* (Garden City, N.Y.: Doubleday, 1959), pp. 231–232.

[17] Charles E. Merriam and Harold F. Gosnell, *Non-Voting: Causes and Methods of Control* (Chicago: University of Chicago Press, 1924), pp. 110–122.

[18] Almond and Verba, *op. cit.,* chap. xi.

[19] Greenstein, *op. cit.,* p. 8

CRITICAL THINKING:
Open and Closed Minds

C. Gratton Kemp
Ohio State University

A significant turning in the path of research into the popular "authorization character" theme is reported. The links of dogmatism, authority, and experimental thinking are ingeniously delineated by the author . . . . Important practical applications are now within reach.

Research in the psychology of thinking confronts two problems. The first is to build an acceptable theory of the phenomena of thought. The second is to witness the impact of the theory on perceived reality.

Association theory supplied the first need for intelligible theory. The illumination of thinking in this regard descended in a long line of brilliant theorists from Hobbes, Locke and the Mills to Wundt and Titchener, and later in a closely related line Thorndike, Watson, Holt, and Hull. To make thought intelligible by the mechanisms of association, each made it a relatively simple matter of learning.

Associationism failed on the second problem. It was too simple to explain the many complexities of thinking and when held up to the mirror of reality it appeared somewhat foolish to other schools of thought.

The Gestalt psychologists viewed thinking differently. Wertheimer who was a student of Kulpe disagreed with Wundt's theory that complex perceptions are built by the synthesis of elementary sensations and insisted that the perceptual pattern is primary.

Although early Gestalt experiments dealt chiefly with perception and depended on subjective data, Kohler in 1917 applied the approach to the behavior of apes in solving problems. Wertheimer in 1945 viewed thinking as the reorganization of patterns rather than a piecemeal attack on the problem. Both considered good thinking a matter of seeing the problem clearly and restructuring it as necessary.

Koffka, through expanding the concept of figure and ground, focused attention on the structure of cognitive and social, as well as perceptual fields. Tolman, using objective procedures, attempted to infer the cognitive maps of rats and thus the term cognition received respectable attention.

"Critical Thinking: Open and Closed Minds" by C. Gratton Kemp is reprinted from the *American Behavioral Scientist*, Volume V, Number 5 (January, 1962), pp. 10-15, by permission of the Publisher, Sage Publications, Inc.

Lewin's topological theory of personality has dealt with regions of the ego and life space, with their differentiation and their overlapping. His insights have provided the meanings which have been expanded, leading to another significant approach to thinking, the Open and Closed Belief System. This new approach studies thinking indirectly. It assumes a dynamic relationship between the personality and the way the person thinks. He thinks as he does because of the kind of person he has become. Thinking *per se* is not the focus but a means of studying the whole person in action.

OPEN-CLOSED SYSTEMS

The author[1] considers the theory of the Open and Closed Belief Systems more comprehensive than previous formulations. He believes Gestalt theory contributes to psychological understanding to the extent that man has open belief systems; psychoanalysis and behaviorism do so to the extent that man's belief systems are closed. Neither contributes directly to the understanding of the many persons who have systems that are relatively open or relatively closed.

The approach known as the Open-Closed Belief Systems includes both viewpoints in its theoretical framework. It was developed on the premise that each individual is motivated "by both rational and rationalizing forces." It is assumed that *"all belief-disbelief systems serve two powerful and conflicting sets of motives at the same time; the need for a cognitive framework to know and to understand and the need to ward off the threatening aspects of reality."*[2]

THE FACTORS IN THOUGHT

In any situation that requires a decision there are both relevant and irrelevant factors. The kind of decision reached depends upon their use. To use only relevant factors requires evaluation and action based on the intrinsic elements in relation to the requirements of the situation. Irrelevant factors in many forms, such as anxiety and the need to be accepted, are heightened by the external pressures of reward and punishment that may be exerted by parents, peers, other authority figures, cultural, and institutional norms. The extent to which a person's system is open is "the extent to which the person can receive, evaluate, and act on relevant information received from the outside on its own intrinsic merits unencumbered by irrelevant factors in the situation, arising from within the person or from the outside."[3]

Postman and his associates[4] concluded from their research that irrelevant factors function as a perceptual defense against inimical stimuli. Anderson[5] from experience in working with the Stanford Binet Intelligence Test has provided examples of this perceptual defense. Allport[6] observed in his study of rumor that what leads to obliteration of some details and falsification of others is that the force of the intellectual and emotional context existing in the individual's mind leads to the assimilation of ideas in accordance with the values resident within the individual. This, Maslow[7] concludes, wards off threatening aspects of reality, while at the same time providing the individual with a compensatory feeling that he understands reality.

These behaviors indicate the influence of emotional factors on critical thinking. The relationship between personality and cognitive variables was established by the research of Else Frenkel-Brunswik[8] who found that as a result of the early parent-child relationships there emerge degrees of variance in the ability of the youth to tolerate ambiguity and that such emotional and social ambivalence manifests itself in the cognitive spheres (thinking, perception, and memory).

DOGMATISM AND CRITICAL THINKING

The interaction between emotional and cognitive variables suggests a difference in performance in critical thinking between those with relatively closed and those with relatively open belief systems. A comparison of those who were low with those who were high in dogmatism with reference to their ability in critical thinking, as indicated by problem-solving, was made by Kemp.[9] The sample was a total of 500 male and female freshmen students from Olivet College, Alma College, Michigan State University, and Salem College, West Virginia.

Of these the 150 who were highest (more closed belief system) and 150 who were lowest (more open belief system) were selected through the use of the Dogmatism Scale, Form E.[10] By means of a pilot study 50 discriminating items were selected as a test of critical thinking and it was discovered that *those who had relatively open belief systems were superior (.01 per cent level) in critical thinking to those with closed belief systems.*

It was concluded that those with closed belief systems have a higher percentage of errors in problems which require the study of several factors of criteria for decision and the deferment of a conclusion until judicious consideration has been given to each factor. Apparently the high dogmatic has difficulty in tolerating ambiguities and is thus impelled toward a "closure" before full consideration is given to each piece of contributing evidence. This sometimes results in the perceptual distortion of facts and in a conclusion that does not encompass all elements of the problem.

THE EHRLICH STUDIES

Ehrlich[11] hypothesized in his two studies that (1) dogmatism was inversely related to the degree of learning in an introductory sociology course, and (2) that dogmatism and learning were independent of academic aptitude.

The original sample consisted of 100 students enrolled in four introductory sociology sections, who were present for both the first and second administration of the test battery, and for whom Ohio State Psychological Examination (OSPE) scores were available from the University. For the second, a follow-up by mail, only 90 of the 100 respondents could be contacted; and from these 65 completed returns.

During the first week of the academic quarter the subjects were given the Dogmatism Scale (Form E) and a 40 item true-false test of sociological knowledge. Half the test items were statements of empirical generalizations and the other half, statements of definition. The sociology test was readministered during the last week of the quarter, an approximate time lag of 10 weeks. Five years later the Dogmatism Scale and Sociology Test were mailed to the original subjects.[12]

The findings confirmed the hypotheses that *dogmatism is independent of academic aptitude,* (intercorrelation with OSPE −.001) and that *it is inversely related to the degree of learning in a classroom situation,* (intercorrelation with results on sociology tests ranged from −.29 to −.043).

THE ROKEACH STUDIES

Rokeach and his associates[13] developed several ingenious tasks as a means of comparing the operation of analysis and synthesis among those with relatively open and relatively closed belief systems. These four related tasks were named in order of their development and use, the Doodlebug Problem, or the No Canopy Problem; the Canopy Problem; the Impossible Problem; and the Chessboard Problem.

Through these tasks a "miniature cosmology" was presented whose operational principles were basically different from the conditioned expectancies of the subjects. In order to correctly solve the problems using analysis and synthesis it was necessary for the subjects to overcome their customary mental sets.

The first problem in this hypothetical world was that connected with the little creature Joe Doodlebug. Joe, the subjects were told is a strange sort of bug; he can jump in only four directions, north, south, east or west, not diagonally. Once he starts in any direction, he must jump four times in that direction before he can switch directions. He cannot crawl, fly or walk; he can only jump. He can jump very long distances and very short distances. He cannot turn around.

Joe's master, the story continues, places some food, larger in diameter than Joe, three feet directly west of him. Joe stops dead in his tracks, facing north. After surveying the situation, Joe concludes that he will have to jump four times to get to the food. We impress upon the subject that Joe is dead right in his conclusion. He is given anywhere from 30 to 45 minutes, in different experiments, to tell us why Joe reaches this conclusion. Like the detective in a murder story, the subject is confronted with the end result and is asked to reconstruct the circumstances that led up to it.

This problem requires the subject to make an analysis and then a synthesis. In the analytic phase he overcomes three currently held beliefs (1) the facing belief; in everyday life we have to face the food we eat, (2) the direction belief; usually we can change direction at will, but Joe can change direction only by jumping sideways and backwards; (3) the movement belief; usually we can change direction when we desire in any direction; Joe could move only in a particular direction and has to continue four times before he can stop. In the synthesizing phase the subject organizes and integrates his conclusions into a new system.

The same two thought processes are tested in the remaining three problems under varying conditions for different purposes. In the Canopy Problem the canopy prevents Joe from landing on the food to eat it. After taking three more jumps to the west and landing on the canopy, he must jump once backwards and is now in a position to eat the food.

In the Impossible Problem the situation is the same except for one change. The subject is told that Joe had been jumping east, when his master placed the food down. The problem is that Joe had jumped once to the west. How then could Joe have been jumping east? To get to the food Joe would have to change directions twice from east to west, and from west to south. This will take at least five jumps not four. The problem then is impossible to solve. However, Rokeach reports that some subjects creatively decide Joe's world is really round. This makes it possible for Joe to jump three more times to the east, land on the canopy, jump once backwards to the south off the canopy and be in a position ready to eat.

The Chessboard Problem is identical with the No Canopy except that it has been reformulated into a game to be played between two opposing players on a chessboard. Joe Doodlebug's stand-in is now a piece of wood painted red on one side, black on top, and black on the three remaining sides. It moves according to certain rules, which are of course identical with Joe's rules. Its job is to capture the opponent's piece. Our purpose in introducing this variation is to make the Doodlebug system psychologically more familiar to some—those who play chess; and psychologically new to others—those who do not play chess, without in any way affecting the internal structure of the problem. Exactly the same thought processes are involved, but now we can study the effects of past experience and basic attitude toward newness on the ability to synthesize new beliefs into new systems.

DOGMATISM AND RIGIDITY CONTRASTED

We turn now to consider the methods and results in the use of these devices, to analyze critical thinking. It was theorized that although rigid and dogmatic thinking appeared to be synonymous, there was a plausible distinction which could be tested. Although both refer to resistance to change of single beliefs, sets or habits, dogmatism also is the resistance to the change of systems of beliefs. It is said that a person performs a task rigidly, not dogmatically.

If then the referent of dogmatic thinking is the total configuration of ideas and beliefs organized into a relatively closed system, and rigidity is the difficulty experienced in overcoming single sets or beliefs encountered in attacking, solving or learning something specific, certain differences in their thinking might be distinguished.

Since the rigid thinker could be expected to experience difficulties in breaking down or overcoming beliefs when they are no longer appropriate, his analytic thinking should suffer. On the other hand the dogmatic thinker is concerned to keep intact his total ideological system, rather than with a particular belief in his system. He then is not threatened by analysis but could be expected to experience difficulty in making a synthesis if he perceives that the synthesis to which he is inclined will necessitate a change in his total belief system.

One hundred and nine students in introductory psychology in Michigan State University participated in this experiment. They were administered the Gough-Sanford Rigidity Scale and Form C of the Dogmatism Scale. From the results a group of 60 were chosen, 30 with open and 30 with closed belief systems (highly dogmatic), 15 of each group of 30 were nonrigid and 15 were rigid.

They were presented the Doodlebug Problem by experimenters who were uninformed regarding classification of the subjects. After 15 minutes those who had not overcome the "facing belief" were given hints and again at the end of 20 and 25 minutes. They were encouraged to talk as they worked and their comments were recorded.

To ensure that whatever differences came to light were not the result of differences in intelligence, correlations were made between the American Council on Education Test scores and Dogmatism scores. These correlations were $-.02$ and correspondingly low for correlations between rigidity and intelligence.

The results give empirical support to the theoretical distinctions between rigid and dogmatic thinking. *Those who were low in rigidity differed significantly from those who were high on measures of analysis but not on synthesis. Highly dogmatic or closed subjects experienced to a significant degree greater difficulty in synthesizing or integrating beliefs but did not differ from the open subjects in analysis.* Dogmatic and rigid thinking are discriminable but not necessarily independent processes.

Rokeach and Vidulich probed more deeply into the synthesizing process. They hypothesized that synthesizing is in part dependent upon memory. If so, making the new beliefs available in the person's visual field, so that the memory of them is unnecessary, should facilitate the synthesis of new beliefs into a new system.

From a group of 249 sophomores, 30 with relatively closed and 30 with relatively open systems were selected. The Doodlebug Experiment was used in the same manner as previously described except that the Experimental Group was allowed to keep the cards on which hints concerning the three beliefs were given, while the Control Group was allowed only to read them and then they were withdrawn.

Following an interlude of 10 minutes after the completion of the test or the 40 minute time limit, each subject was given 3 minutes within which to recall and express the three hints which had been given. He then filled out a short 5-item questionnaire to assess his rejection or acceptance of the problem situation. A week later he returned and again was asked to recall the 3 hints within the three minute interval

The closed group synthesized more slowly than the open, taking longer to solve the problem after the new beliefs had been overcome. The time required for the visual group to synthesize is much less than that required by the memory group. Those with closed belief systems take longer to synthesize since they more frequently reject situations requiring new modes of thought. The greater rejection of the problem by the closed group is evidenced in the spontaneous comments made by the subjects during the test situation. The number of statements classified by three judges as indicating rejection are significantly greater for those with closed belief systems.

We come now to the fourth in the series of tasks designed by Rokeach and his associates. This task, names the Chessboard Problem, is identical in principle with the Doodlebug Problem except that Joe the Doodlebug is replaced by the chessmen. For those who play chess the resemblance between the tasks demanded by this problem and those encountered in a chess game are identical in principle. Joe's movements in sequence of four jumps in one direction (the movement belief) are similar to the movements of the knight in chess; many of the chessmen "face" in the direction of the opponent, but can nevertheless move backwards and sideways (the direction belief); and the chessmen capture their opponent's pieces by landing on top of them (facing belief).

The purpose of the task was to explore the rate of synthesis of those who played chess and therefore were familiar with the principles and those who did not. It was hypothesized that there would be no difference in the speed of synthesis between those who had an open and those who had a closed system and played chess, but for those who were not chess players there would be a difference between the open and the closed. The experiment gave no significant difference for chess players between those with relatively closed and those with relatively open minds, but for those who do not play chess the open-minded synthesize more rapidly (.01 per cent level) than those with closed minds. *When the task is familiar those with open and closed minds synthesize equally well, but when it is unfamiliar those with closed minds apparently resist the formation of new systems.*

PARTY-LINE THINKING

Exploration of the synthesizing process of the open-minded and closed-minded was further investigated by an ingenious use of the Doodlebug Experiment and the presentation of hints regarding the beliefs to be overcome. This experiment provides insights concerning what is commonly known as party-line thinking. Rokeach describes the party-line thinker as a person "who not only resists change but can also change only too easily.

What he does, depends on what his authorities do, and his changes and refusals to change, conform with authority."

Before examining the experiments let us consider the theory of party-line thinking. The cognitive system is conceived to have three regions: the central region which contains the earliest formed beliefs; the intermediate region, the beliefs concerning authority and authority figures; and the peripheral region. In the open systems the peripheral beliefs are intrinsically related to each other as well as to beliefs about authority. In closed systems, the peripheral beliefs are isolated or segregated from each other but are interconnected via the authority region; that is, they arbitrarily seem to be interrelated because they are all seen to emanate together from the same authority. Party-line thinking is the thought-process wherein each peripheral belief is isolated from every other, but is in communication with the others through the intermediate region. The party-liner's closed system has its common origin in authority rather than in intrinsic logical connections.

We recall that the Doodlebug Experiment required the overcoming of three beliefs (direction, movement and facing) for its successful solution. The same two experiments were repeated, the No Canopy Problem, in which Joe could land on top of the food and proceed to eat, followed by the Canopy Problem, in which due to a canopy over the food, he had to jump backwards in order to eat the food from the edge. That is, the Canopy Problem required the overcoming of a belief which had been used in the No Canopy Problem.

One change was introduced; necessary hints for the working of each problem were provided on 3" x 5" cards in advance. This was for the purpose of making analysis unnecessary and to focus upon the problem of the synthesis of the hints given to find the solutions.

Twenty extremely closed and 20 extremely open subjects chosen from a pool of 600 participated in these experiments. Using the hints presented on the cards for the No Canopy Problem it was found that the Open and Closed completed the task in approximately the same length of time.

Then they were presented the hints for the Canopy Problem. Once again each group took about the same length of time. When all the hints were presented at the commencement of the problem the rate of solution was approximately the same for each group. This result was puzzling to those conducting the experiments until they realized that the close-minded subjects accepted the hints, whereas the open-minded subjects worked them through before they accepted them.

To check on this conclusion, the hints were supplied one at a time instead of all at once. This of course required a synthesis and procedure based on it before a second hint was given. The results now were different. The closed-minded group took longer to do the problem when the hints were presented one at a time, approximately 65 minutes as compared with 45 minutes for the open-minded group. When presented all together the closed-minded took approximately 42 minutes compared with 45 minutes for the open-minded group. With reference to the time required for synthesis alone, the closed-minded required 41 minutes compared with 24 minutes for the open-minded. *These experiments demonstrate the inefficiency which results from the dynamic resistance due to isolation among beliefs and uncritical acceptance of authority. These are indicative of party-line thinking.*

IMPROVING CRITICAL THINKING

Experimentation has concentrated upon the analysis of critical thinking in relation to open and closed belief systems. Little has been done to understand the conditions which engender closed-mindedness, or to see what can be done to improve the critical thinking of those with closed belief systems.

Conditions conducive to open and closed mindedness were explored by Kemp[14] and reported in the Open and Closed Mind. He also[15] engaged in research in the improvement of critical thinking. The purpose of the study was to compare the improvement in critical thinking of those with open belief systems and those with closed belief systems. A total of 80 college freshmen, 40 in the Control Group and 40 in the Experimental Group participated in the study. The two groups were matched in intelligence and in degree of open and closed mindedness using the Dogmatism Scale (Form E) and the Otis Test of Mental Ability. Each group took the Glaser-Watson Test of Critical Thinking Appraisal, at the beginning and conclusion of the experiment.

Both groups were taught by the same instructor but the Control Group received no special help in solving critical thinking problems.

The Experimental Group was divided into 5 subgroups, of 8 each, 4 with closed and 4 with open systems. Each of these subgroups participated in 10 one-hour meetings. Each meeting was used in solving critical thinking problems. Reasons for correct and incorrect conclusions were discussed.

At the commencement of the study the open-minded subjects in both groups performed significantly better (.05 level) than those with closed belief systems. At the completion of the study there was no significant improvement in either the open or closed subgroups of the Control Group. In the Experimental Group those with closed belief systems improved but the improvement was not significant. Those with open belief systems had improved significantly (.01 level).

This research suggests that *conditions conducive to improvement in critical thinking may be permissive (safe) small group situations in which the usual threats are minimized and in which intensive attention given to the factors in critical thinking is accompanied by extensive practice.*

THE STATE KNOWLEDGE SUMMARIZED

Pure thought is an illusion. Emotion is an integral constituent of thought and emotional components influence the process and condition the outcomes. Those with closed belief systems are hindered by the pervasive feeling of threat and dependence upon an authority. These experience great difficulty in the examination of ideas on the basis of intrinsic worth and in the integration of ideas into a new system.

Those with open belief systems confront new experience very differently. They perceptively examine different aspects of the experience, try to clarify the ambiguity, and to see the relationship among parts. Little threat is experienced in integration of ideas into a new system.

In the thought processes which do not involve the total belief system of the individual, those with closed minds are not threatened. In the problems demanding only analysis they perform efficiently, but their performance is impaired if they are required to pursue the outcomes of the analysis into a new synthesis.

If however the closed-minded are provided with hints by an authority, thus eliminating much of the need for consideration and pointing clearly to the outcomes which follow, they are no longer impeded in the process of synthesis since they rely implicitly on the authority and directions given and do not feel the need to test them as do the open-minded, who are not inclined to accept the suggestions of authority but prefer to check on the information themselves.

Research is essential to discover those experiences which are conducive to closed-mindedness. Indications are that the character of parent-child relations may be of large importance. Of equal or greater need is research to increase and improve understanding of the conditions which could be expected to help the closed-minded. If indications are correct these would be conditions of safety, and those encouraging the individual to become more self-directive.

References

[1] In Milton Rokeach, *The Open and Closed Mind.* New York; Basic Books, 1960, 66.

[2] *Ibid.,* 67.

[3] *Ibid.,* 57.

[4] L. Postman, J. Bruner, and E. McGinis, "Personal Values as Selective Factors in Perception." *Journal of Abnormal and Social Psychology,* 1948, 43, 142-154.

[5] Gladys L. Anderson, "Qualitative Aspects of the Stanford-Binet" in *An Introduction to Projective Techniques* Harold H. and Gladys L. Anderson, Editors, New York, Prentice-Hall, Inc., 1951, 581-605.

[6] Gordon L. Allport, and Leo Postman, *The Psychology of Rumor,* New York, Henry Holt and Company, 1947, Chapter 6.

[7] A. H. Maslow, *Motivation and Personality.* New York: Harper and Bros., 1954.

[8] Else Frenkel-Brunswik, "Intolerance of Ambiguity as an Emotional Perceptual Personality Variable," *Journal of Personality,* 1949, 18, 108-143.

[9] C. Gratton Kemp, "Effect of Dogmatism on Critical Thinking" *School Science and Mathematics.* April, 1960.

[10] *Ibid.,* Rokeach, 73-80.

[11] Howard J. Ehrlich, "Dogmatism and Learning," *Journal of Abnormal and Social Psychology,* 1961, Vol. 69, No. 1, 148, 149.

[12] *Ibid.*

[13] *Ibid.,* Rokeach, Chapters 8-12.

[14] C. Gratton Kemp in *The Open and Closed Mind,* by Milton Rokeach, New York: Basic Books. 1960, Chapter 19.

[15] C. Gratton Kemp, "Improvement of Critical Thinking in Relation to Open-Closed Belief Systems," *Journal of Experimental Education,* (in print).

SIMULATIONS AND CHANGES IN RACIAL ATTITUDES

Paul DeKock
History Instructor, El Capitan High School
Lakeside, California

Social Studies teachers have been hiding too long behind that old cliché, "Sure, you can teach knowledge and skills, but you can't teach attitudes."

Reprinted with the permission of the author and the National Council for the Social Studies, from *Social Education*, (February, 1969): 181-183.

True, teachers can't *teach* students to change their attitudes, but teachers can establish an environment where students *learn* to change their own attitudes. The secret lies in approach.

A new approach found in the work of David R. Krathwohl and his associates recommends that teachers help students change their attitudes by organizing five levels of learning:

1. *Receiving* (Attending)
   Students read, listen, observe, intuit.
2. *Responding*
   Students question, discuss, introspect, write, respond emotionally.
3. *Valuing*
   Students examine, evaluate, commit themselves, argue, act upon conviction, join a group, try to convince others.
4. *Organizing*
   Students face situations calling for value judgments, make decisions, solve problems.
5. *Being characterized by*
   Students regularly reveal commitment on the issue and are considered predictable on certain values.

Krathwohl's work makes obvious that teachers who want student attitudes to change must stop talking so much, hoping that *receiving* (attending) is taking place on level one. Instead, they must permit students to interact with one another through *responding, valuing, organizing,* and *being characterized by* —levels two to five.

THE GAME OF SUNSHINE

A learning environment suited to Krathwohl's five levels is simulation—the use of game theory in the classroom. The following paragraphs illustrate how my colleague Dave Yount and I organized these levels of learning into *Sunshine,* our educational simulation of current racial problems in a typical American city. We developed *Sunshine* during the last four years in our American Studies classes at El Capitan High School, a suburban San Diego high school of 1600 students who represent a relatively typical cross section of Caucasian American youth. Statistical evidence based upon pre- and post-attitudes tests demonstrates that this simulation changes students' racial attitudes. (See chart.)

Before the simulation formally begins, students anonymously take a thirty-item racial attitudes test written by Thomas Gillette, a sociologist with San Diego State College and the Western Behavioral Sciences Institute, La Jolla, California. Then comes the first exciting moment of the simulation: "rebirth" as a white or black. All students draw colored I.D. tags (white, tan, brown, black) whose color signifies ethnic background. On the tags are other portions of their identities: yearly income, vocation, education, street address, neighborhood. The students then pin their tags and move to chairs grouped into various streets and neighborhoods with varying degrees of segregation. For example, one of the six neighborhoods is Dead End, a black ghetto with tenements, rental housing, homes under $10,000; another is Mt. Olympus, a white ghetto with individually designed homes from $35,000 to $50,000.

During the next three weeks students work with the history and literature of the American Negro, all the time simulating their identities. As they study and interact, their self-images increase in proportion to the IMPS (image points) they earn. However, pressure cards introduced to the simulation by the teachers move the community into racial crisis, for these chance cards arbitrarily take away citizens' IMPS—particularly Negroes' IMPS. And since IMPS are students' grade points for the unit of study, students begin reacting to the pinch of prejudice. Eventually these pressures cause factions to arise in *Sunshine,* and the factions present proposals for their seven member city council to vote upon (one member elected from each neighborhood and a mayor elected at large).

The First Simulation

In the beginning
God created Man
And instructed him
To play the role of
Human Being

Book of Dan

The simulation ends with the administering of various tests: knowledge of nineteen key generalizations about the history of the Negro; a second anonymous attitudes test about racial relations in America (designed to measure any change in attitude brought about by *Sunshine*); and an essay test evaluating the simulation experience itself. Finally, the test results are tabulated by all who have participated, and then discussed for validity.

FIVE LEVELS OF LEARNING

Obviously, a simulation forces students to experience all five levels of Krathwohl's taxonomy. Students still *receive* teachers and movies talking (level one), but they soon find themselves interacting at the four levels where attitude change really takes place. The next paragraphs present a few examples of our students' experiences on all five levels.

Level One: *Receiving* (Attending)

Taking lecture notes on the slave trade, plantation origins of myths about the American Negro, the scar of Reconstruction, the Negro during the Great Depression;

viewing movies and debates on Washington v. DuBois, San Diego Negroes arguing regarding the leadership Negroes should locally follow;

attending Hollywood films in class: "Raisin in the Sun" and "Nothing But a Man."

Level Two: *Responding*

Feeling irritation, shame, relief when pulling a Negro or white I.D. tag;

finding key points and attitudes of Negro and white authors when reading magazine articles and listening to taped speeches;

analyzing Negro poetry, art, and magazines;

asking questions of Negro speakers;

feeling irritation due to consequences of fate (the loss of IMPS when pressure cards take away grade points).

Level Three: *Valuing*

Feeling glee or shame when students jeer and hoot at those who by chance pull Negro I.D. tags (the darker the tag the louder the jeering);

feeling revulsion for slave ships and by the parallel showing how both slavery and concentration camps changed human personality;

choosing Negro poems and cuttings from "In White America" to present to the class;

finding a problem in *Sunshine* to research in depth because of concern (social relations, crime, education, jobs—e.g. the blatant *de facto* segregation in *Sunshine's* two high schools).

Level Four: *Organizing*

Arguing with other students about *Sunshine's* problems both inside and *outside* the classroom;

backing a candidate for *Sunshine's* mayor because he/she represents "correct" solutions to the city's racial crises;

forming a faction to pressure the city council to act (e.g. abolishing the *de facto* segregation by redrawing the school attendance boundaries; or keeping *de facto* segregation by retaining existing school attendance boundaries);

planning a speech or dramatization for the city council (carefully utilizing materials studied during Valuing stage).

Level Five, *Being Characterized by*

Being sought out to speak for or against a proposal in front of the city council;

hearing groans or cheers when standing to speak on an issue because *Sunshine* citizens recognize the racial attitude about to be presented;

recognizing, when taking a second racial attitudes test, that a change has taken place due to experience of living in the simulated community.

INFLUENCE OF GAME ON STUDENTS

The following chart shows that participating in *Sunshine* does change students. Their attitudes are affected. Thus, simulations are more than fun and games. They change attitudes. And very likely teachers will be utilizing educational simulations increasingly to get their students involved in social studies subjects. The resulting involvement and interaction *will* result in attitude change.

The chart shows results of pre- and post-tests on racial attitudes administered to 398 high school juniors, El Capitan High School, Lakeside, California, 1965-1968. Between tests students participated in *Sunshine* an educational simulation. Potential intolerance scores are from -1 to -60; potential tolerance scores are from $+1$ to $+60$.

SCORES	PRE-TEST	POST-TEST
+40 or higher	13	46
+30 to 39	40	55
+20 to 29	63	76
+10 to 19	91	84
+0 to 9	84	66
−1 to 9	56	32
−10 to 19	44	20
−20 to 29	13	9
−30 to 39	3	8
−40 or higher	1	2
Total	398	398

	PRE-TEST	POST-TEST
High Tolerance Scores:		
+20 or higher	116	177
Intolerance Scores:		
Any Minus Score	117	71

TEACHING STUDENTS TO ANALYZE PUBLIC CONTROVERSY: A CURRICULUM PROJECT REPORT

James P. Shaver and Donald W. Oliver
Utah State University   *Harvard University*

Research investigating the teaching of "critical" or "reflective" thinking within the context of the social studies curriculum has been relatively scarce and unproductive,[1] as have been reported attempts to develop comprehensive approaches to teaching for this end.[2] The final report[3] of a curriculum development and research project attempting to fill these gaps was recently submitted to the U.S. Office of Education, which provided a major portion of the project's financial support. Presented here is a brief summary of the major facets of that project. More detailed information and more comprehensive discussion are available in the two-volume report.[4]

BACKGROUND

The Harvard Social Studies Project, directed by Donald W. Oliver, grew out of concern with several long-standing problems in the social studies. One such problem is the often noted discrepancies between lists of objectives for the social studies and actual classroom instruction, especially with regard to the frequently reiterated importance of education for reflective thinking in preparation for adult citizenship. Often social studies curricula provide the students no conceptual model for handling the important issues facing society. Even when some such conceptual framework is part of the curriculum, the schemes of reflective thinking available to teachers, e.g., in secondary social

Reprinted with permission of the author and the National Council for the Social Studies, from *Social Education,* 28 (April, 1964): 191-194, 248.

studies texts and college methods texts, are based almost exclusively on scientific method, especially as expounded by John Dewey,[5] and/or propaganda analysis.[6]

Scientific method and propaganda analysis speak well to the problems of proof process (e.g., establishing matters of fact) and clarity of language, both of which are important in dealing effectively with societal issues. But neither is concerned directly with the value conflicts—such as that between equality and property rights in the current racial segregation controversy—which are at the heart of political controversy.[7] Propaganda analysis warns us to watch for the value loadings of words and their emotional impact. Scientific method becomes relevant when we have decided what ends are desirable and want to draw conclusions as to the possible outcomes of alternative courses of action. But neither will tell us what values we ought to choose as ends.[8]

Another problem giving root to the Project was the fragmented nature of the social studies curriculum. The frequently noted lack of relationship between social studies courses, and even between parts of individual courses, pointed to the need for further consideration of organizational structure for the social studies. Structure has become of particular concern in the social studies as the central position of history has been challenged; and the present trend is toward trying to derive structure from the social sciences. The Harvard Project was concerned with selecting and organizing materials and methods of instruction on the basis of the objectives of the social studies as a curriculum area which depends upon the social sciences for content and process.

Other factors adding impetus to the attempts of the Project to build a curriculum consonant with the objectives of citizenship education were the commonly reported dissatisfaction of students with social studies courses and the lack of observable effects on citizenship behavior of the present curriculum.

The result of concern with such problems was an attempt by the staff of the Harvard Project to develop a curriculum for seventh and eighth grade social studies, to be taught within the context of the common two-year geography and U.S. history sequence, but logically based upon a consideration of the citizen as a political being involved in the analysis of public controversy in exercising his decision-making role. Relying on two sources— the philosophical literature dealing with logic, scientific method, and reflective thinking[9] and the introspection of the Project members about strategies they found productive in clarifying political controversy—a tentative set of rather specific concepts and operations was developed to be taught to students.[10] This scheme for handling public controversy focused on three kinds of problems: (1) Settling factual issues; (2) Handling problems of word usage and meaning; (3) Dealing with value conflicts.

The crucial research question was, of course: Could curricular materials and instructional methods be developed to teach this framework of critical thinking—its concepts, their interrelations, and their applications—to secondary school students? Also, recognizing that attempting to teach students such a scheme and its applications to societal problems would take a great deal of time, we wanted to investigate the effect of this "time loss" upon the learning of "traditional" social studies content. And, we wanted to explore the relative effectiveness of different teaching styles that might be used in teaching the students to apply the scheme to problems such as those posed by racial segregation.

PROJECT SETTING

In order to be able to work within a school setting while developing and evaluating curriculum materials, the Project director established a cooperative relationship with a school district in a suburban Boston community. The Project staff spent two years in developing the framework for dealing with public issues, developing curricular materials, and carrying out some pilot studies. This was followed by two years of further curriculum development and more extensive and careful research sponsored by the U.S. Office of Education.[11] During this time, the four Project teachers (one of whom had previously been regularly employed by the district) had the responsibility for the social studies curriculum of five classes of students as they moved through the seventh and eighth grades of one junior high school.

The usual social studies program in the school was U. S. history from the explorations to the Civil War, plus placement geography, in the seventh grade; U.S. history from the Civil War to the present, with a unit on vocational choice, in the eighth grade. The Project developed a set of experimental units focusing on the historical development (within the last 100 years) and contemporary status of a number of national problems (e.g., school desegregation and the power and responsibility of the labor movement). These units were inserted at appropriate points in the chronological history courses e.g., a unit on school desegregation was studied after the Civil War. Other materials were developed to teach ethical and Constitutional principles underlying decisions in our society, as well as the strategies for handling the controversies presented in the problem units.

During the two years, the Project's students spend approximately one-third of their class time on what was considered a "conventional" approach to U.S. history. This involved reading and discussion based on the texts used in the school.[12] Slightly more than one-half of the experimental groups' class time was spent with the curriculum materials developed by the Project staff. Also, about eight weeks were taken up by the Project testing, including both learning outcomes measures and an extensive battery of personality tests.[13]

EVALUATION

It should be noted that a major thrust of the Project was in the area of curriculum evaluation. We found the available tests of "critical thinking" inadequate for a number of reasons: (1) The tests were too unlike the situations in which it was hoped the students would be able to apply the conceptual framework to be taught. The available tests tend to measure fragments of critical thinking (e.g., an item might attempt to determine if a student can see the relevance of a particular statement to an argument presented in a paragraph), but in actual discussions of societal problems the various aspects of critical thinking are interrelated; no one will tell the student when it is appropriate to decide if a statement is relevant. The structured nature of the multiple-choice tests usually used is also unrealistic. In an argument, or in making a decision alone, one does not just choose the correct response; he must structure his own response. It is also fairly obvious that in real life we don't sit at a desk checking or writing responses, but are often engaged, as part of the political process, in dialogue with others. Also, items too often ask students to deal with trivia, such as advertisements for storm windows, rather than being set in the context of significant public policy questions. (2) The models used to determine what to include in the tests of critical thinking are based on logic and on scientific method. This means that while such matters as evaluating evidence and testing the relevance of statements tend to be covered, the recognition and handling of value conflicts are ignored. (3) On the basis of factor analyses[14] there is some indication that the existing tests are measuring a general reasoning factor which may be as stable as general intelligence. Such an attribute would not likely be affected by classroom instruction.

Actually, these points are a reiteration of common complaints by teachers and researchers about the lack of validity of available tests. In an attempt to develop more valid estimates of student growth in the type of critical analysis and decision-making in which the Project was interested, testing situations were set in the context of dialogues involving important societal problems. Some paper-and-pencil tests were used which asked the students, for example, to analyze the functions played by statements in a written dialogue, or to choose the best responses to statements in such a dialogue. But the students were also called upon to discuss, either in an interview situation or with a group of fellow students, issues presented by case materials. Their task was to come to a decision about the best policy to be followed. These discussions were recorded, and the content analyzed to evaluate the ability of students to use the concepts of the project's critical-thinking scheme in such a setting.[15] This type of situational evaluation holds great promise, although the problems—including its time-consuming nature—are also great. Work on developing more adequate scoring categories to be used in analyzing discussions is continuing at the Harvard Social Studies Curriculum Center.[16]

RESULTS

In order to determine whether the gains of our students were greater than those which would have occurred without the experimental instruction, students from two similarly suburban junior high schools, one outside of Boston and the other on Long Island, were used as control groups against which to compare the progress of our students. For some comparisons, students taking the conventional curriculum in the same junior high school as the experimental students were used as controls.

Four types of tests were used in the Project's evaluation program: standardized tests of critical thinking or reasoning; the tests developed by the Project staff as more valid measures of the desired outcomes; standardized tests of conventional social studies content; and, a measure of interest in social issues. The results[17] will be reported below in the order in which the types of tests are listed.

Two standardized tests of critical thinking were administered at the beginning and end of the two-year period. Items that seemed most relevant to the Project's teaching objectives were selected from the Watson-Glaser Critical Thinking Appraisal and the Michigan Test of Problem Solving, and, with the permission of the publishers, combined into one test for purposes of administration. The Iowa Test of Educational Development No. 5, Interpretation, was also administered. The students in the experimental class showed as much gain on these measures as did the students in the two control schools. It was not surprising that the Project students did not exceed the others. The experimental curriculum placed little emphasis on the particular types of intellectual operations required by these tests. Also, the results lend credence to the idea that these tests are measuring general reasoning, likely a very stable attribute not apt to be affected by changes in curricular patterns.

Consistently significant differences favoring the experimental groups were obtained on the tests developed by the Project staff, including both paper-and-pencil tests and situational tests in which the students' oral discussions of societal issues were analyzed. The differences with the latter type tests were not as striking nor clear cut as might have been expected. This is probably due in part to the difficulty of devising adequate categories for quantifying the more complex intellectual operations performed in the oral discussion of complicated issues; the tests did not always reflect the level of competence which the teachers had expected on the basis of their experience with the groups. This experience reinforced our belief that the development of adequate evaluative instruments is one of the major problems facing those in social studies curriculum development and research.

Despite such difficulties, the measures developed by the Project were more directly related to its curricular objectives than those otherwise available. On the basis of the comparisons using those measures, it was concluded that students of junior high age can be taught to: (1) think in the abstract conceptual terms of the Project's framework for analyzing political controversy; (2) evaluate the statements of others on the basis of this conceptual framework; and, (3) use these concepts in a fruitful and meaningful way when involved in dialogues dealing with important political issues. As would be expected, students of low intellectual ability did not learn to apply the concepts to complex issues as well as did more capable students; but the level of intelligence below which such a curriculum is unproductive needs to be explored further.

In order to determine whether spending large portions of time on an analytical experimental curriculum penalized the experimental students in their knowledge of the usual social studies content, the following tests were administered; The Iowa Test of Educational Development No. 1, Understanding Basic Social Concepts; the California Tests in Social and Related Sciences, Part I and II (an American history test); and, the Principles of American Citizenship Test (developed by the Columbia University Citizenship Education Project). On each of these tests, the gain of the experimental group over the two-year period was as great as the gains of the control groups. Moreover, the analysis of some item breakdowns on the California Test (U.S. history) indicated that on items based on information the experimental students had studied within both the context of the conventional coverage of history and a problem unit, they scored higher than students in the regular history course in the same school. These results held up when the California Test was administered again a year after the Project ended.[18]

To get an indication of the effect of the experimental curriculum on the students' interest in societal issues, a measure similar to one developed by the Columbia Citizenship Education Project was used. This test asked students to rank newspaper article headings in sets of three according to how interested they would be in reading the three articles. Two types of sets of items were used: those with a heading related to national issues studied as a part of the Project; and those with a heading based on other societal issues of national concern. The results were interesting, and somewhat perplexing. On the "project" items, the control students showed greater gain in interest than did the experimental students. It is possible that this result reflects a general tendency during this stage of adolescence to become more interested in broad ideological issues as presented, for example, by racial segregation. At the same time, the experimental students were possibly perplexed by the complexities of the issues or had their interest satiated by the intensive treatment of them. The soundness of this interpretation is supported by the finding that the experimental students showed significantly greater gain on the items dealing with the issues not studied as Project units. General interest in important national problems, as measured by this test, was enhanced rather than suppressed by the experimental curriculum.

Two "styles" of teaching were used with the experimental students when discussing some fifty controversial cases and the application of the conceptual framework to the problems presented in the cases. For this instruction, each regular class was split into two groups matched on sex, intelligence test scores available in the school records, the Iowa Test of Educational Development No. 5, Interpretation, the test made up of items from the Watson-Glaser and Michigan tests, and ratings by the experimental teachers as to amount of participation in class discussions. With one of each pair of matched groups a "Socratic" style was used, and with the other group of each pair a "recitation" style was used. As implied by the labels, the first was a probing style, in which the teacher expected the student to take a personal stand on the societal issue under discussion and defend it. In using the recitation style, the teacher dispersed among the group questions about the background of the problem and possible solutions to it, not forcing any student to defend a personal decision about policy.[19]

No over-all differences on any of the measures were found between students taught by the two styles.[20] This result, coupled with the significant gains over the control students on the reflective thinking tests developed by the Project staff, indicates that having an explicit conceptual framework to teach students may well be more important than the particular "style" used by the teacher when discussing controversial issues.

Several personality measures were administered to the experimental students. There were few consistent significant correlations between the personality measures and the measures of learning. But in some instances students high on a personality measure showed greater improvement on a measure of learning if the teacher had used one of the styles, while those low on the personality measure gained more with a teacher using the other style. That is, the statistical analysis revealed interactions between teacher style and student personality in terms of student gains on learning measures.[21] This finding suggests some interesting avenues for further research, as well as providing some provocative suggestions for the grouping of students on criteria other than scores on tests of intellectual ability.

CONCLUSIONS

This discussion of the Harvard Social Studies Project has necessarily been brief. Those interested in a more comprehensive treatment of the Project's philosophy, curriculum, experimental design, or findings are urged to turn to the more complete report.

For at least two reasons, readers will want to be cautious in generalizing from this article. First, the difficulties of adequately treating all of the facets of an extensive curriculum project within the space limitations of an article are obvious. We have only hoped to lay out the outlines of the Project and indicate the types of results obtained. Secondly, it must be remembered that the Project tried out its curriculum in a particular setting: the experimental school was located in a suburban community in which nearly 45 percent of the breadwinners hold "managerial, professional, and technical" positions; the teachers were selected for their teaching skill and their interest in curriculum development and research; the teachers and students were aware that they were part of an experimental program (the time span of the Project should have helped to mitigate this effect); the classes were often split into groups of ten to thirteen students for instructional purposes (a practice more common now with "team teaching").

Nevertheless, the experimental curriculum did produce positive results. The Project's research findings indicate that students learned to apply a complex framework of analysis to the discussion of public issues, and that their gains in knowledge of traditional social studies content and in interest in societal issues compared favorably with those of control students exposed to more conventional curricula. The results might well warrant the substitution of the experimental curriculum—set in the context of the U.S. history course as it is—for more conventional curricula in schools where this is possible. As noted, however, cautious generalizing is called for. As teachers and supervisors interested in teaching students to analyze controversial issues reflect upon the applicability of the Project's curricular approach to the specific situations of their schools and classrooms, conclusions will be drawn in proper perspective. The challenge, then, is to explore the range of conditions under which the same results can be expected.

It should also be re-emphasized that the Project had both a developmental and a research orientation, and that it is in effect continuing in existence through the activities of the Harvard Social Studies Curriculum Center. The Center will be concerned, among other things, with extending the curricular framework of the Harvard Project into the high school social studies program, and with continuing the task of developing more valid measures of learning to be used in evaluating curricula that deal with the analysis of contemporary societal issues. This continuing curriculum effort, and others like it, will continue to develop structure for the social studies from the analysis of the function of the social studies in a democracy. This approach, which views the social sciences as sources of knowledge (including knowledge about scientific method) to be used in accomplishing social studies objectives, is likely to be more fruitful for citizenship education than looking to the disciplinary structure of the social sciences for the structure of the social studies. In that sense, the Harvard Social Studies Project has been a major step in establishing the social studies as a discipline[2] intellectually autonomous from the social sciences, though related to them as sources of instructional materials and methods.

References

[1] James P. Shaver. "Educational Research and Instruction for Critical Thinking." *Social Education* 26:13; January 1962.

[2] Kenneth B. Henderson. "The Teaching of Critical Thinking." *Phi Delta Kappan* 39:280, 1958.

[3] Donald W. Oliver and James P. Shaver. *The Analysis of Public Controversy: A Study in Citizenship Education.* A report to the U. S. Office of Education. Cambridge, Mass.: The Laboratory for Research in Instruction, Harvard Graduate School of Education, 1963.

[4] The U. S. Office of Education distributes final reports to repository libraries. A list of these libraries is available from the Office. Microfilms of final reports can also be obtained from the Photoduplication Service of the Library of Congress at a very low cost. Major portions of the report will be published by Houghton Mifflin Company in a volume probably to be entitled, *The Analysis and Teaching of Controversial Problems in High School.*

[5] John Dewey. *How We Think.* Revised edition. Boston: D. C. Heath. 1933.

[6] A notable exception is the text, *Teaching High School Social Studies* by Maurice P. Hunt and Lawrence E. Metcalf. New York: Harpers, 1955.

[7] Oliver and Shaver, *op. cit.,* Part I. Also see: Shirley H. Engle. "Decision Making: The Heart of Social Studies Instruction." *Social Education* 24:301; November 1960; William J. Brennan, Jr. "Teaching the Bill of Rights. "*Social Education* 27:256; May 1963; Hunt and Metcalf, *op. cit.* Chapter 5.

[8] See, for example, Charles A. Beard. *The Nature of the Social Sciences.* New York: Scribners, 1934. Chapters 7 and 8.

[9] E. g., M. R. Cohen and Ernest Nagel. *An Introduction to Logic and Scientific Method.* New York: Harcourt, Brace, 1934; Max Black. *Critical Thinking: An Introduction to Logic and Scientific Method.* New York: Prentice-Hall, 1952; John Dewey, *op. cit.;* John Haspers. *An Introduction to Philosophical Analysis.* New York: Prentice-Hall, 1953; C. L. Stevenson. *Ethics and Language.* New Haven: Yale University Press, 1944.

[10] Oliver and Shaver, *op. cit.,* Chapters 5, 6 and 7. Also, *Learning to Think Critically,* a booklet developed by the Project for teaching purposes was published by the Utah State Department of Public Instruction for the use of Utah teachers, 1963.

[11] Cooperative Research Project Number 551.

[12] The basic text used was: H. B. Wilder, R. P. Ludlum, and H. M. Brown. *This is America's Story.* Boston: Houghton-Mifflin.

[13] For a more detailed description of the Project's setting and materials, see Oliver and Shaver, *op. cit.,* Chapters 8, 9 and 11 and Appendixes A and B.

[14] See, Velma Rust, R. S. Jones, and H. F. Kaiser. "A Factor Analytic Study of Critical Thinking." *Journal of Educational Research* 55:258; March 1962.

[15] Oliver and Shaver, *op. cit.,* Chapter 10. Also see, Donald W. Oliver and James P. Shaver, "Evaluating the Jurisprudential Approach to the Social Studies." *The High School Journal* 46:53; November 1963.

[16] Gerald R. Smith. "Project Social Studies—A Report." *Social Education* 27:357; November 1963.

[17] Oliver and Shaver. *The Analysis of Public Controversy, op. cit.,* Chapter 11. Analysis of covariance was the statistical technique use; for evaluating most differences. Covariance provides a method for statistically controlling differences between groups on measures such as intelligence tests while making comparisons between gains in scores.

[18] James P. Shaver and Donald W. Oliver. "The Effect of an Experimental Junior High School Social Studies Curriculum upon the Students' Knowledge of American History." *Utah Academy of Sciences, Arts, and Letters Proceedings* 40:225-232; Part II, 1963. For corroborating results, see Arnold Rothstein. "An Experiment in Developing Critical Thinking Through the Teaching of History." *Dissertation Abstracts* 21; 1960.

[19] Oliver and Shaver, *op. cit.,* Chapter 12. Also see, James P. Shaver. "The Ability of Teachers to Conform to Two Styles of Teaching." *Journal of Experimental Education,* in press.

[20] Oliver and Shaver, *op. cit.,* Chapter 12.

[21] *Ibid.*, Chapter 13.

[22] See Samuel P. McCutchen. "A Discipline for the Social Studies." *Social Education* 27:61-65; February 1963; and, Stanley P. Wronski. *A Philosophy of the Social Studies.* Address delivered at a section meeting of the 1963 annual meeting of the National Council for the Social Studies in Los Angeles. Page 1 of a mimeographed copy.

IMPROVING THE NEW GEOGRAPHY THROUGH EVALUATION

Dana Kurfman
Director, High School Geography Project
Boulder, Colorado

From the beginning of the High School Geography Project, evaluation has been an integral feature of its work. Evaluation specialists from the Educational Testing Service in Princeton, New Jersey, have assisted HSGP geographers in preparing each unit of the Settlement Theme course currently being developed.

Evaluators serve three major functions in the Project's curriculum development process. (1) At a very early point in the development of each unit they ask the geographer responsible for that unit what specific concepts and skills he wishes to convey, and what he hopes the students will be able to do as a result of their work on the unit. (2) They obtain information from the teachers and students about the effectiveness of each unit. (3) They help establish comparison groups of teachers and students to determine, for example, the effectiveness of the training given teachers for the Project's curriculum materials, and appropriateness of materials for students with different verbal aptitudes and socio-economic backgrounds.

In assigning these varied functions to evaluate specialists, the HSGP conception contrasts sharply with the traditional view of evaluators as concentrating on ways to compare new and old sets of materials. Although it is important to compare the effectiveness of one set of course materials with another, our primary objective has been improvement of the new materials.

Reprinted with permission of the author and the publisher, from *The Bulletin of the National Association of Secondary School Principles,* 50 (February, 1967): 37-43, Copyright National Association of Secondary School Principals, Washington, D.C.

For this reason evaluators must be actively involved throughout the development of curriculum materials.

Emphasis on immediate "feedback" of information for revision purposes does not preclude evaluation of long-range outcomes sought by the Project, such as the student's ability to use the concepts and skills conveyed in the material at some later date. We will also be interested in students' attitudes toward geography sometime after taking the course and in their choice of college courses in this field.

THE DEVELOPMENT-EVALUATION-REVISION CYCLE

Each unit in the HSGP urban-age geography course follows a cycle of development, evaluation, and revision, which is sometimes repeated two or three times. A unit begins with an idea or theme in the mind of the geographer. As the idea evolves, a unit of study begins to take shape. The author of the unit and his fellow geographers make judgments about the relative importance of relevant concepts and about the interpretations which are legitimate from their geographic perspective.

The geographers who have planned the new HSGP course are not interested only in concepts and subject matter, however; they also seek to convey something of the spirit of geography, of the skills and attitudes that characterize geographic investigation. They are interested in planning course materials that encourage students to seek similar learning experiences in the future. They are interested, in other words, in student attitudes as well as the development of skills and concepts.

In this initial development stage, evaluation specialists can help the unit author focus attention on his more important objectives rather than simply on the flow of subject matter. The evaluator raises such questions as "What is it you really want to get across to the students?" or, stated in another way, "How do you expect or hope the students who study this unit will change as a result of the experience?" The answers to such questions determine the content of the tests and evaluation questionnaires, as well as the character of teaching procedures and student activities.

After the responsible geographer has identified his major objectives and has developed procedures for teaching them, he discusses with high school teachers the way these concepts and skills have been organized and presented. He relies on their perspective to indicate how teachable the new materials are, how well organized they are for student learning, how well adapted they are for both slow learners and more able students.

When the initial version of the unit has been developed, the unit materials are subjected to their first tryout. These informal school trials, as we call them, usually involve about five teachers and 300 students. They are held in schools easily accessible to the unit author, so that he can observe classes and sometimes teach the unit himself. An effort is made to have the five teachers represent a wide variety of students and schools. However, since teachers in academically-oriented schools tend to volunteer for the tryout of new curriculum materials, it is very easy to obtain a biased sample of better-than-average students. By administering an aptitude test to the students, we can more accurately judge the academic ability that they represent.

A unit test is also administered, both before and after the unit is taught, to find out how well young people are learning the concepts and skills of the unit. Since we are interested also in student attitudes, we use questionnaires to determine the degree of student interest in various parts of the unit.

"FEEDBACK" DURING TRIALS

Authors of some units have found it valuable to meet with the teachers during these informal trials. Critical appraisals coming directly from teachers and students help in visualizing needed changes and also provide new ideas of ways to utilize the materials. At the conclusion of the three- or four-week trial of the unit, teachers are brought together with members of the unit-development team and an evaluator for an extended discussion designed to improve the unit. The evaluator follows this with interviews with certain of the teachers in which he seeks elaboration of teachers' comments during the group discussion and on their questionnaires.

The evaluator thus has information from many sources, ranging from the subjective judgments of teachers to data from student tests and questionnaires. This prevents undue reliance on opinions of the more articulate teachers and on the sometimes misleading characteristics of objective data. Within one week after the end of the informal school trials the evaluator can recommend modification of certain points in the unit. Armed with these recommendations and his own impressions, the unit author can now begin revisions.

After the unit has been revised, the next stage in the development-evaluation-revision cycle is an expanded school tryout. In the two such limited trials carried out so far with the help of the Educational Testing Service, from three to six units and from 45 to 75 teachers have been involved. In these trials a more systematic analysis of the results is possible than in the informal school trials. The 1965-66 limited school trials provided information about the relative effectiveness of different parts of the units for students with high and low academic aptitudes, for students from cities, suburbs, and rural areas, and for boys and girls. The limited school trials being carried out this year continue our investigation of the relative effectiveness of different types of unit organization and activities.

An additional purpose of the limited school trials is the investigation of teacher training methods. This year we divided 50 of our teachers into two matched groups. One group was given an intensive short course in the geographic concepts and teaching procedures underlying the new materials, and the control group was not. To assess the effectiveness of this training period we will compare test scores and questionnaire responses for teachers in both groups and for the students they taught. Assessment of different types of teacher training in the use of the new materials will probably be emphasized even more in the national school trials planned for the 1967-68 school year. Because the success of new curriculum materials depends on the teachers who use them, teacher training procedures promise to become a significant focus for this and other course improvement projects.

USE OF TESTS TO IMPROVE COURSE MATERIALS

What may be of particular value to principals and teachers interested in improving their present course materials is the experience we have had in using tests to improve our materials. The tests we develop with the help of the Educational Testing Service are designed primarily to test the effectiveness of our curriculum materials. In other words, we have little interest in the accurate ranking of students through their test performance. Instead, our attending is directed toward the identification of the weak and strong features of our curriculum materials.

The process of test development to evaluate curriculum materials is somewhat different from that involved in preparing tests to grade students. In the former, questions must quite accurately test achievement of the specific concepts and skills considered important in the unit. In writing questions for most classroom tests, however, it is usually sufficient for questions to be identified roughly with the major topics covered in the subject matter to be tested.

When course materials are designed to communicate understanding of a particular concept and test questions measure an understanding of that concept, we can use test results to identify weaknesses in teaching procedures and student activities. Thus, if a group of three or four questions indicates that a concept is little understood by students, we can conclude with considerable confidence that the relevant teaching procedure or student activity failed to accomplish the purpose for which it was designed.

It is important that test questions be tried out on students prior to their exposure to the curriculum material. The same test questions are administered after study of the material. Comparison of the percentage of right answers on the pre-test with the percentage of right answers on the post-test provides a basis for judgment of the effectiveness of the teaching procedure or student activity involved.

Determining what constitutes adequate improvement in student pre-test to post-test performance is a major problem. The kinds of questions in which we are most interested are those which measure understanding of a concept rather than the mastery of some bit of factual knowledge. Such questions seldom reach the point where most students get the right answer, even on the post-test. We find that on the pre-test between 30 percent and 45 percent of the students recognize correct answers to questions requiring the understanding of a concept or generalization. On the post-test between 50 percent and 75 percent of the students recognize the right answer. Our experience suggests that an increase of approximately 20 percent from pre-test to post-test means that the teaching procedure or student activity related to these questions is successful.

VARIETY OF FACTS OBTAINED

The data we obtain on each question yields considerably more information than simply the percentage of students getting a question right at the pre-test and at the post-test stage. Analysis of each question also enables us to determine the proportion of able students (that is, high achievers on the total test) who get this particular question right, as well as the proportion of poor students who succeed on the question. From this, we are able to make inferences about the relative success of a teaching procedure with high-aptitude students and low-aptitude students.

Our analysis of each question also tells us something about the types of students who choose the correct answer at the pre-test stage and then shift to an incorrect option in the post-test administration. From this we can sometimes infer how the materials are misleading, and the unit author can correct the misleading feature.

To prepare more useful tests for evaluating curriculum materials, we need (1) to take even greater care to develop questions closely relevant to the concepts and skills the unit author intends to communicate, (2) to write more questions which require the application of new geographic concepts and skills in a context different from the learning situation, and (3) to use more effectively the data we now obtain from each question. Only with more experience will we achieve greater insight into what constitutes satisfactory improvement in student understanding of a concept or generalization. It may be that 20 percent improvement between pre-test and post-test will be adequate for certain types of concepts but inadequate for others. It may be that questions dealing with certain kinds of elementary skills should show a 30 percent or 40 percent improvement from pre-test to post-test.

We know already that when a unit explicitly presents information that students had little possibility of learning prior to the unit, the result is a great increase from pre-test to post-test performance, often as much as 60 percent. While this might be expected for new information, it is a level of increase that probably will never be attained for questions requiring an understanding of a rather complex concept. At any rate, the ways by which test questions may become more effective in improving curriculum materials are clear. Additional experience with school trials should result in a sharpening of our test questions as tools for curriculum improvement.

USE OF QUESTIONNAIRES

Questionnaires have been a second important source of information for curriculum evaluation. Teacher questionnaires provide a wider base of teacher opinion than that obtained by discussions with a group of teachers. In such discussions, the impressions of the more articulate teachers dominate, while the views of more reticent teachers are lost to the evaluator.

All of our questionnaires include yes-no questions and questions to which teachers may respond very positively, somewhat positively, somewhat negatively, or very negatively. For example, with respect to reading materials we ask teachers to answer "yes" or "no" to the following: "Do you believe that the reading materials are clearly written and understandable for the average student?" and "Should there be more student reading in the unit?" With these and other brief-response questions, space is included for teachers to indicate their reasons or to make suggestions. We also ask teachers about the subject matter in the unit; we ask them, for example, to rate the manner in which it is organized as "excellent," "generally good," "somewhat poor," or "definitely poor." We ask them about the teacher's guidelines, which describe student activities and indicate various ways of teaching given parts of the unit; for example, we ask them how helpful these guidelines are in suggesting a variety of learning activities or in suggesting supplementary reading materials for students.

The tabulation of responses clearly indicates which aspects of the teachers' guides or of the reading materials are considered effective and the ways in which they may be somewhat defective. By asking teachers about the greatest single strength and greatest single weakness of the unit, we are able to identify features to be modified or discarded in revising it.

Such questions are asked upon completion of the unit. While the unit is in progress, however, we obtain teacher ratings of specific features of the unit, such as map activity or a student exercise. We also find out which parts of the unit teachers find most difficult to teach, and which parts the teacher thinks should be retained, revised, or deleted.

Student questionnaires are also an integral feature of our evaluation procedures. We are interested not only in how students perform on tests but also in their attitudes toward the materials with which they are working. If students learn a great deal but dislike the experiences they are having, this is likely to be a deterrent to future learning. At the end of each unit we ask students which of its activities and exercises were most interesting and least interesting. We obtain separate tabulations for students with high and low academic aptitudes, and thereby determine which parts of the unit have particular appeal for above-average and for below-average students. We also ask students which activity or procedure in the unit was most difficult for them and why. Finally, we ask them to note their suggestions for improving the unit.

Thus, from a variety of sources—tests, teachers, the opinions of students themselves—we formulate specific recommendations for the improvement of HSGP teaching materials. In this way, after each tryout of the materials, we are able to revise them intelligently into more effective instruments for teaching the ideas, skills, and attitudes of the new geography.

Index